Fodor's 2009

ALASKA

W9-AGQ-439

Fodor's Travel Publications New York, Toronto, London, Sydney, Auckland

www.fodors.com

Share your trip with Fodor's

Alaska 2009, one of Fodor's first full-color guides, owes much of its success to travelers like you whose contributions appear within its pages. We've included several of our favorite submissions to our Show Us Your Alaska photo contest in this special edition. We were neither prepared for the quantity of images entered in the contest, nor were we expecting to be so inspired by the quality and range of experiences represented. We feel that these candid shots, like the one opposite taken by grand prize winner Laura Plaks in Prince William Sound, represent the wonder, excitement, and beauty inherent in any trip to the Last Frontier.

Sharing your trip with us and other travelers is easy. Look for "Word of Mouth," excerpts of your unvarnished feedback, throughout this guide. From tips to funny anecdotes, the experiences of the Fodor's community have been included for their fresh and unique perspectives. To connect with other travelers like you, join us online at Fodors.com. Our members are as diverse as the destinations they visit, but they all share one thing in common—a passion for travel. Review a hotel, restaurant, or sight. Write a report of your trip or answer questions from other travelers about your trip on our Forums. Our editors are members of this community too and relish both answering questions and asking their own.

Pair this guide with the guidance shared on Fodors.com to dream, craft, and plan the Alaska trip that you've always imagined taking. On your return, give us your opinion instantly by posting on the Forums, writing a review, leaving feedback at www.fodors.com/feedback, or writing to us at editors@fodors.com with "Alaska Editor" in the subject line. Or send your suggestions and comments by mail to Alaska Editor, Fodor's, 1745 Broadway, New York, NY 10019. Your feedback goes a long way in helping us to make our books better.

You and travelers like you are the heart of the Fodor's community. Make our community richer by sharing your experiences. No two trips are ever the same—that's why we all want to hear about yours.

Happy Traveling!

Tim Jarrell, Publisher

FODOR'S ALASKA 2009

Editors: Stephanie E. Butler, Kelly Kealy

Editorial Contributors: Teeka Ballas, Catherine Bodry, Jessica Bowman, E. Readicker-Henderson, Tom Reale, Laurel Schoenbohm, Sarah Wyatt

Editorial Production: Tom Holton
Maps & Illustrations: David Lindroth, Mark Stroud, *cartographers*; Bob Blake, Rebecca Baer, *map editors;* William Wu, *information graphics*
Design: Fabrizio LaRocca, *creative director*; Guido Caroti, Siobhan O'Hare, *art directors*; Tina Malaney, Chie Ushio, Ann McBride, Jessice Walsh, *designers*; Melanie Marin, *senior picture editor;* Moon Sun Kim, *cover designer*
Cover Photo: (Bald eagle, Homer): Don Pitcher
Production/Manufacturing: Matthew Struble

ISBN 978–1–4000–0706–6

ISSN 0271–2776

SPECIAL SALES

This book is available at special discounts for bulk purchases for sales promotions or premiums. Special editions, including personalized covers, excerpts of existing books, and corporate imprints, can be created in large quantities for special needs. For more information, write to Special Markets/Premium Sales, 1745 Broadway, MD 6-2, New York, New York 10019, or e-mail specialmarkets@randomhouse.com.

AN IMPORTANT TIP & AN INVITATION

Although all prices, opening times, and other details in this book are based on information supplied to us at press time, changes occur all the time in the travel world, and Fodor's cannot accept responsibility for facts that become outdated or for inadvertent errors or omissions. So **always confirm information when it matters**, especially if you're making a detour to visit a specific place. Your experiences—positive and negative—matter to us. If we have missed or misstated something, **please write to us.** We follow up on all suggestions. Contact the Alaska editor at editors@fodors.com or c/o Fodor's at 1745 Broadway, New York, NY 10019.

PRINTED IN SINGAPORE

10 9 8 7 6 5 4 3 2 1

CONTENTS

ALASKA IN FOCUS

CONTENTS

ABOUT THIS BOOK

Our Ratings

Sometimes you find terrific travel experiences and sometimes they just find you. But usually the burden is on you to select the right combination of experiences. That's where our ratings come in.

As travelers we've all discovered a place so wonderful that its worthiness is obvious. And sometimes that place is so unique that superlatives don't do it justice: you just have to be there to know. These sights, properties, and experiences get our highest rating, **Fodors Choice**, indicated by orange stars throughout this book.

Black stars highlight sights and properties we deem **Highly Recommended**, places that our writers, editors, and readers praise again and again for consistency and excellence.

By default, there's another category: any place we include in this book is by definition worth your time, unless we say otherwise. And we will.

Disagree with any of our choices? Care to nominate a place or suggest that we rate one more highly? Visit our feedback center at www.fodors.com/feedback.

Budget Well

Hotel and restaurant price categories from ¢ to $$$$ are defined in the opening pages of each chapter. For attractions, we always give standard adult admission fees; reductions are usually available for children, students, and senior citizens. Want to pay with plastic? **AE, D, DC, MC, V** following restaurant and hotel listings indicate whether American Express, Discover, Diners Club, MasterCard, and Visa are accepted.

Restaurants

Unless we state otherwise, restaurants are open for lunch and dinner daily. We mention dress only when there's a specific requirement and reservations only when they're essential or not accepted—it's always best to book ahead.

Hotels

Hotels have private bath, phone, and TV and operate on the European Plan (aka EP, meaning without meals), unless we specify that they use the Continental Plan (CP, with a Continental breakfast), Breakfast Plan (BP, with a full breakfast), or Modified American Plan (MAP, with breakfast and dinner) or are all-inclusive (AI, including all meals and most activi-

ties). We always list facilities but not whether you'll be charged an extra fee to use them, so when pricing accommodations, find out what's included.

Many Listings
★	Fodor's Choice
★	Highly recommended
⊠	Physical address
✚	Directions
⌂	Mailing address
☎	Telephone
🖷	Fax
⊕	On the Web
✉	E-mail
🎟	Admission fee
☉	Open/closed times
Ⓜ	Metro stations
▭	Credit cards

Hotels & Restaurants
🏨	Hotel
⇥	Number of rooms
⚤	Facilities
❍	Meal plans
✕	Restaurant
⚲	Reservations
⚐	Smoking
♗	BYOB
✕🏨	Hotel with restaurant that warrants a visit

Outdoors
🏌	Golf
⛺	Camping

Other
☺	Family-friendly
⇨	See also
⊠	Branch address
☞	Take note

Experience
Alaska

WHAT'S WHERE

The following numbers refer to chapters in the book.

4 **Southeast Alaska.** Southeast Alaska ("the Panhandle" or "Southeast") encompasses the Inside Passage. Only Haines and Skagway have roads to "the Outside." Juneau, the state capital, and Sitka, the former Russian hub, are here. In Southeast long fjords snake between the mountains, timbered slopes plunge to the rocky shores, and marine life abounds.

5 **Anchorage.** With nearly half the state's population, Anchorage is Alaska's biggest city and a common jumping-off point for visitors. Alaskans often deride the place as "Los Anchorage." But the occasional moose ambling down a bike trail hints at the wilderness just beyond the borders.

6 **South Central Alaska.** South Central offers great fishing, hiking, rafting, and wildlife viewing. Seek out the towns of Seward and Homer on the Kenai Peninsula. Kodiak, in the Gulf of Alaska, is known for its green-carpeted mountains and Kodiak brown bears. Charter outfits can get you to remote wilderness spots.

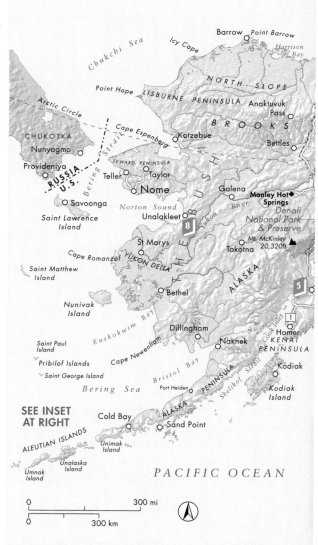

7 **The Interior.** Bounded by the Brooks Range to the north and the Alaska Range to the south, the Interior is home to Mt. McKinley and Denali National Park & Preserve. The weather can be extreme. Fairbanks is the gateway to the towns of the Arctic, the Bering Coast, and Canada's Yukon Territory.

8 **The Bush.** Many call the Bush the "real" Alaska. Inupiaq people share permanently frozen land with the Prudhoe Bay oil fields. Brown bears roam Katmai National Park. Volcanoes shake up the Alaska Peninsula. Minus the Dalton Highway and a handful of short roads near Nome, the region is essentially roadless. Traveling here requires research and planning; the reward is true adventure.

ALASKA PLANNER

What to Wear

When preparing for your trip, it is imperative that you learn the first rule of Alaskan thumb: be an onion. Always pack layers, and never leave your hotel without wearing them. This basically requires your first layer to be thin and airy so that if it gets warm your skin can breathe. Every layer over that, however, should aim to keep you warm and dry. In Alaska it is quite common for a hot and sunny day to abruptly change.

What to Pack

Don't forget your valid passport. In 2009 the U.S. will begin requiring tourists crossing over the Canadian border, which you're likely to do if traveling by ferry, cruise, or car, to show a passport. ⇨ *See Travel Smart Alaska for more information.* While disposable and small digital cameras are very handy for candid shots, they are not much good for catching wildlife from afar. A good zoom lens can be heavy, but can make all the difference. If you don't have a quality camera, pack binoculars. Be sure to take bug spray during the summer months, as the mosquitoes are large, plentiful, and fierce.

When to Go

Due to the sheer size of the state, Alaska's climates and seasons vary dramatically from region to region. The Arctic Circle, the northernmost part of the state, is also known as The Land of the Midnight Sun. In summer this region experiences 82 consecutive days of sunlight, and in the winter it's dark for 60 days straight. In contrast, on the longest day of the year Southeast Alaska gets 18 hours of daylight; on the winter solstice it experiences 6 hours of daylight. Skies that are often overcast, however, cut dramatically into Southeast Alaska's hours of sunlight.

May through September is the easiest time to navigate the state. Summer marks not only the arrival of tourists but also the return of the humpback, gray, and orca whales; it's also when the bears come out of hibernation, geese and terns migrate north, and salmon spawn.

Peak season is from mid-June to mid-August. This is of course when you will experience higher rates for cruises, airfare, and gasoline. To avoid crowds and costs, go during the spring or fall.

Winter Travel

Don't let winter's endless days of darkness deter you. It is the season for skiing, sledding, iceskating, dog mushing, ice fishing, and at least a dozen other sports. The urban parks in Anchorage and Fairbanks light up their ski trails for good visibility 24 hours a day. The long winter nights are also ideal for viewing the northern lights (the aurora borealis). To see the stunning multifarious colors drape and shoot across the sky, you need a dark, clear night, distance from city lights, and sufficient solar activity. The best viewing with accommodations nearby is outside of Fairbanks; Chena Hot Springs Resort is our top recommendation.

Be Bear (and Moose) Aware

Ego and arrogance are two of the greatest dangers in Alaska. Being prepared and taking educated precautions does not mean you're faint of heart. Bears pose a serious threat. Don't mistake them for cute and cuddly creatures. When hiking, carry bear mace and wear a bear bell. They are less likely to attack when they can hear you coming. If you forget your bear bell, feel free to occasionally call out, "Hey Bear!" Don't worry, you won't be the only one doing it; Alaskans do it too.

Campers: remember to keep your food out of bears' reach. Everything has a smell, even propane, so you must keep it far from your tent and off the ground. Most campgrounds in Alaska are equipped with bear poles, but you must bring your own rope and bags. Use bear-proof containers (bear barrels) if you're planning to camp in flat, treeless areas.

Moose are also a hazard in Alaska, particularly in the early fall when they are breeding and in May or June when they give birth. Cows and calves need extra room. Biologists call this "personal space." If you get in their personal space they are likely to charge. Moose are also a hazard on the roadway. Motorists kill hundreds of moose every year. Keep alert and don't drive tired.

It's always a good idea to register with Parks Services before taking off on your own. If you decide to take an impromptu hike, leave a note on your windshield stating when you left and what direction you were heading. That way, if park rangers notice your car has been parked for longer than a day or two, they will know if there is reason to sound the alarm and organize a search party.

⇨ *For more safety tips, see Chapter 2.*

Getting Around

About half of Alaska's visitors experience the state by cruise, but ferries, trains, and scenic roadways allow do-it-yourself travelers the flexibility to linger in towns or regions. The **Alas-kaPass** (☏ 206/463–6550 or 800/248–7598 ⊕ *www.alas-kapass.com*) allows unlimited travel on ferry and rail lines, with access to British Columbia and the Yukon. Options include 15 consecutive days of travel ($929); eight days of travel in 12 days ($799); or 12 days of travel in 21 days ($979). There is an $85 booking fee (per itinerary). Most travelers book their entire itinerary in advance.

Mark Your Calendar

During the winter months Alaskans amuse themselves with concerts and celebrations to counteract the long darkness. In the summer they do the same, but outside, as Alaskans like to make the most of the daylight hours.

Notable events include the Anchorage Fur Rendezvous in February, the Iditarod Trail Sled Dog Race in March, Juneau's Alaska Folk Festival in April, the World Eskimo-Indian Olympics held in Fairbanks in July, and Sitka's Alaska Day festival in October.

ALASKA TODAY

Politics

Alaska's politics and policies seem as wild as its hundreds of thousands of untamed acres. This is partly due to the fact that the largest state in the nation comes with a seemingly limitless amount of natural resources, and with them come conflict and controversy. Alaska's politics are thus saddled with a vast array of fiscal and environmental responsibilities, none of which are easily governed.

Gas and mining corporations have enormous influence on public policy in Alaska, but not without rivalry from environmentalists and subsistence advocates. An ongoing and highly publicized battle is over the proposed Pebble Mine project in Bristol Bay in Southeast Alaska. It will be the largest gold and copper mine in the world. Supporters of the mine claim it will bring much-needed jobs to the local native population. Opponents say it will irrevocably pollute the lakes, rivers, and bay, destroying the large fishing industry on which the local population relies.

Gaining national attention is the Arctic National Wildlife Refuge (ANWR), 19.2 million roadless acres supporting 45 species of land and marine mammals, 36 species of fish, and 180 species of birds. ANWR is in the northeast corner of the state and has been dubbed the Last Great Wilderness. The only way to get there is by small bush plane. Area 1002, 1.5 million acres along the refuge's coastal plain, has long been a subject of controversy, as it is thought to contain a large supply of oil.

From the Iditarod to cabin building, everything in Alaska is steeped in politics. This is inevitable, as there are more politicians per capita than police officers.

Economy

More than 75% of Alaska's revenue is derived from oil extraction. The state is also the nation's leader in commercial fishing, but ranks dead last in number of farms and farm products. There is very little manufacturing in the state. Thus, the cost of manufactured goods, produce, and other food goods is considerably higher than in other states.

Because Alaska is predominantly comprised of rural villages, thousands of miles from any origin of distribution, the cost of living in Alaska is relatively high. In Barrow, for instance, one can expect to pay $10 for a gallon of milk.

The Personal Fund Dividend (PFD) is a sacred check that Alaskans receive once a year, and for many in the bush it is quite literally a lifesaver. In 1977 the fund was created to receive 25% of Alaska's oil royalty income. It was designed to maintain a state income even after the reserves had been tapped out. Residents receive a check every October in amounts that vary from year to year but are in the ballpark of $1,200. For many who live in the Bush, this annual check provides the funds they need to heat their homes in the winter.

Global Warming

Political discourse is heating up, as global warming is becoming a frontline issue in Alaskan politics. Fewer and fewer people disagree that the glaciers and permafrost are melting; to Alaskans it's just a fact. It is what to do about it that has politicians and constituents bickering.

Regardless of anyone's political persuasion, however, things are undeniably changing in Alaska. Icebergs are melting, and unfortunately for polar bears, that's where they live. In 2008 the Inte-

rior Department put polar bears on the protected species list; some environmentalists, however, believe that without addressing the causes of global warming, the designation will do little to help the bears.

As oceanic temperatures rise, new migrations are starting to take affect. One unfortunate one, however, is the steady migration north of the Humboldt giant squid. It is a voracious predator that travels in packs and is starting to be found as far north as Sitka. This is posing a serious threat to the salmon population and the fishing industry in general.

Warmer temperatures also mean new economic opportunities. As the Arctic ice melts, the region is becoming more accessible, which means there is greater possibility for more oil and gas exploration.

Many of the indigenous tribes in the Arctic region have already begun to adapt to the changes. Their hunting patterns have adjusted to the new migration times and routes of their game. Unfortunately permafrost, the frozen ground they live upon, is also melting. Centuries-old towns and villages are sinking, and the cost of possible relocation is rising into the billions of dollars.

The Arts

Visitors are often surprised to find Alaska is filled with talented contemporary artists. For many Alaskans though, the long, dark winter is a great time to hunker down, season their craft, and prepare to sell their wares in the summer. Galleries, museums, and theaters all over the state feature local talent. During the summer months, weekend outdoor markets are also a great place to find local and native talent.

Sports

In a state of renegades, thrill seekers, and aficionados of extreme forms of entertainment, it is no wonder that the biggest sporting event occasionally requires a racer to permanently relinquish the feeling in a finger or a foot. The Iditarod Great Sled Race, a 1,150-mile long sled dog race, is by far the most popular sporting event in Alaska. It began in 1973 as an homage to the brave souls who ventured to Nome in 1925 to take medicine to villagers struck with one of the worst outbreaks of diphtheria ever recorded. Now more than 100 racers and their packs of canines converge on the ice and snow every year on the first Saturday in March. The sport is not without controversy though; mushers have come under scrutiny since several groups have made allegations of animal cruelty.

Although Alaskans from all over the state are passionate about their dog mushers, the most popular team sport is hockey. College hockey all over the state is big news, as are the Alaska Aces, the state minor-league team that feeds into the NHL's St. Louis Blues.

TOP ALASKA ATTRACTIONS

Katmai National Park

(A) When people come to Alaska they want to see bears. Yet most visitors never get a glimpse, because bears prefer their privacy. But at Katmai National Park, which boasts the largest brown bear population in the world, you're almost guaranteed a photograph of bears doing bear things. Remember, though they look cute, their teeth and claws are still mighty big.

Alaska Native Heritage Center

(B) There are over 200 Native tribal entities in Alaska. At the Heritage Center, experience the lifestyles and traditions of these Native cultures through art and artifact displays and activities like blanket tossing, parka sewing, and drumming.

Mt. McKinley

(C) There are a dozen places between Anchorage and Fairbanks that boast the best viewing of Mt. McKinley. At 20,320 feet, McKinley is the highest peak in North America, and just about any place within 100 miles can be deemed a good viewing area. The crowning jewel of Alaska is often shrouded in clouds, but even a glimpse will reveal the sheer size of the snow-covered giantess.

Denali State Park

(D) Denali State Park is one of the most popular destinations in the state for tourists. It is a spectacular region that can be experienced by saddle safari, bus trip, or flightseeing tour. Hike, bike, stroll, or raft through it. Camp out, or bundle up in a cabin. The first 15 mi of the park road is paved, but after that there's just gravel. Visitors must ride on a bus or get off and see Denali on foot. No matter how you get there or which adventure you choose, Denali is truly a wonderful experience.

The Aurora Borealis

(E) The most popular attraction in the wintertime doesn't charge admission or have set viewing times. The northern lights seem to appear without rhyme or reason. Seeing the northern lights requires that there be no nearby city light, very little moonlight, the cold fall and winter months, and a lot of luck. Hot springs outside Fairbanks keep the hopeful warm while they watch the skies.

Mendenhall Glacier

(F) Alaska's capital, Juneau, is surrounded by ice and water and can only be reached by boat or plane. The best way to understand this is to visit the Mendenhall Glacier. Only 13 mi from downtown Juneau, this gargantuan glacier is right outside the city in plain view. It's 12 mi long—nearly the same distance as between it and downtown Juneau.

The Inside Passage

(G) If you don't arrive in Alaska by cruise ship, make a point of taking a ferry trip along the longest, deepest fjord in North America. Depending on which ferry you take, the trip from Juneau to Skagway can be 2 or 6 hours long. We recommend taking your time. In the summer, the tall peaks surrounding the boats release hundreds of waterfalls from snow and glacial melt. If you're lucky you'll see pods of orcas, humpbacks, and dolphins.

Celebrate Independence with a Race

(H) On the 4th of July, the scenic small town of Seward hosts the Mt. Marathon Race. This race is 1½ mi straight up and 1½ mi straight down. It began with a bet between two sourdoughs in 1915, and now the celebration turns a town of 2,000 into a city of 40,000 overnight. It's a great way to participate in Alaskan life, and you don't even have to race.

TOP EXPERIENCES

Drive the Alcan

When driving the Alaska Highway, or Alcan, you quickly realize that "rural" means something entirely different in Alaska. You will drive through regions, villages, and towns that are nearly 1,000 mi from the nearest city. Inhabitants have never seen anything that even slightly resembles a shopping mall or fast-food stand. Gas stations can be 75 to 150 miles apart, and mechanics rarer than a wolverine sighting. The Alcan is the true Alaskan experience. Driving 1,000 mi on a long, potholed stretch of highway can put things into perspective. It is also a great way to be guaranteed wildlife sightings.

Sleep on a Deserted Island

Gustavus is the gateway to Glacier Bay, the place that the father of the national parks system, John Muir, called "unspeakably pure and sublime" in 1879. It is considered by many to be 70 mi of the finest sea kayaking in the world. The first 24 square miles comprise the Beardslee Islands, a complex system for kayakers who glide atop flat water between tides, enveloped in silence except for the sound of water slapping paddles, the soft spray from a nearby porpoise, and the howl of a wolf in the distance. And you'll likely be enjoying these sights with no other travelers nearby. Still, kayaking in this region presents challenges. There is a lively population of moose and bears on the islands, so it is imperative to choose wisely when setting up camp. Most visitors only kayak to the top of the Beardslees, which can take between 3 and 5 days round-trip.

Safari through the Last Great Wilderness

The Arctic National Wildlife Refuge (ANWR) is 19.2 million acres of untamed land in the northeastern corner of Alaska. This is where there is still a sense of the unknown, where mountain peaks are still unnamed, and valleys are yet to be explored. There are no shops and no roads. The only way to get to ANWR is by small bush plane. You can be dropped off by air taxi, or you can arrange a guided group tour. The refuge is a great place to hunt, hike, camp, paddle, or climb in solitude. Less than 1,000 people visit this region every year, but tours must be booked months if not a year in advance. Even Alaskans dream of getting to this place someday.

Bed, Breakfast, and Snowmachine

Everywhere there is snow there seems to be a bitter rivalry between snowmachiners (a.k.a. snowmobilers) and skiers. If you're looking to have the perfect snowmachine experience without enmity or opposition, the best way to do it is to find one of the many rural wilderness lodges around Alaska that offer snowmachine rentals and tours. Yentna Station Roadhouse and Kenny Creek Lodge are just two of the many stellar rural establishments that are a day's drive or a short bush flight away. It's a great adrenaline rush to speed over frozen lakes and untouched powder with a motorized sled beneath you and wind in your face.

Ski Under the Stars

There is something about the incongruous number of hours of sunlight and darkness Alaska gets that makes Alaskans yearn to break the rules of time. When you arrive in Alaska you may feel inclined to do the same. In many parts of the state bars still

stay open all night long, fishermen can be sitting on the ice all hours of the night, and some people ski best when the witching hour strikes. At Alyeska Ski Resort in Girdwood, skiers can take the lift and bite the powder under the stars. On weekends this popular ski resort offers night skiing, and afterwards, in the bar, rewards its visitors with live, high-energy, danceable music. This provides a good look at local Alaskan culture, as it caters to tourists and residents alike.

The Longest Museum in the World

In the 1890s, during the gold rush, more than 20,000 stampeders disembarked from their steamships in Skagway, Alaska, and hiked the 35 mi of the Chilkoot Trail, just to get back into a boat and travel the remaining 600 miles to Dawson City (where the gold was). It took approximately three months to hike that trail back then. Their packs were heavy, their shoes were hard, and they had to hike the trail several times in order to get all of their possessions over the pass. These days, hiking history buffs can retrace the stampeders' steps in three to five days, with the help of lighter gear and equipment.

Drink Like an Alaskan

Every state in the nation has a list of attributed symbols: the state bird, flag, flower, song—and in Alaska there is the state drink. It's called the Duck Fart. It is quintessentially Alaskan, as it manages to weed out the meek and shy just by its name alone. It is comprised of Kahlua, Bailey's Irish Cream, and Crown Royal. No need to be timid when it comes to ordering this drink; locals drink it too. Once you've had a Duck Fart, you can honestly say you've experienced Alaska like an Alaskan.

Ski Like it's Halloween

Many Alaskans like to embrace their eccentricities, and a popular way to do it is to get dressed up in costume and ski. One such event is called the Ski Train. Every year in March, since 1972, approximately 1,000 people from all over the country come to Anchorage to get on a train. They come dressed up in a mad array of homemade costumes and bring liquid libations, food, and skis. It's a hilarious event that entails a long, scenic train ride that eventually dumps you off in the middle of nowhere to cross-country ski for an afternoon. After a couple of hours, it's back on board to dance in the back cabin where a live polka band plays in rhythm with the sway of the train.

Halibut Cove

Sometimes the best thing to do is nothing at all. Halibut Cove is a gorgeous little piece of euphoria-inducing land tucked into a corner of Kachemak Bay State Park, Alaska's first state park. It is a town of only 22 year-round residents, but there are two fantastic lodges and several across the bay that offer the same thing: a peaceful look at the gorgeous scenery. Halibut Cove has no stores but does offer a handful of art galleries, a post office (only open on mail-boat days), a high-end restaurant, and a floating espresso bar. There are plenty of outdoor activities, but there's not much else to do there, which is a good thing.

QUINTESSENTIAL ALASKA

Seafood & Sourdough

Alaska's primary claim to gastronomic fame is seafood. The rich coastal waters produce prodigious quantities of halibut, salmon, crab, and shrimp, along with such specialties as abalone, sea urchin, herring roe, and sea cucumbers. If you haven't yet tasted fresh Alaska salmon, do so here—there's nothing quite like a barbecued Copper River king salmon.

Sourdough bread, pastries, and pancakes are a local tradition, dating back to the gold-rush days. Prospectors and pioneers carried a stash of sourdough starter so that they could always whip up a batch of dough in short order. The old-timers became known as sourdoughs, a title that latter-day Alaskans earn by living here for 20 years. Newcomers and those still working to earn the title are referred to as Cheechakos.

After you return from your outdoor adventure, indulge your cravings with the best of Alaskan culinary delights. Start with sourdough pancakes for breakfast; for lunch go for smoked salmon spread on sourdough bread; top it off with a dinner of fresh halibut and wild-berry cobbler. Then you can consider yourself an honorary Alaskan sourdough.

Kayaking

Sea kayaking is big among Alaskans. It was the Aleuts who invented the kayak (or *bidarka*) to fish and hunt sea mammals. When early explorers encountered the Aleuts, they compared them to sea creatures, so at home did they appear on their small ocean craft. Kayaks have the great advantage of portability. More stable than canoes, they also give you a feel for the water and a view from water level. Oceangoing kayakers will find plenty of offshore Alaska adventures, especially in

the protected waters of the Southeast, Prince William Sound, and Kenai Fjords National Park.

The variety of Alaska marine life that you can view from a sea kayak is astonishing. It's possible to see whales, seals, sea lions, and sea otters, as well as bird species too numerous to list. Although caution is required when dealing with large stretches of open water, the truly Alaskan experience of self-propelled boating in a pristine ocean environment can be a life-changing thrill. ⇨ *Find more information about kayaking in Chapter 2.*

Native Crafts

Alaska's rich native culture is reflected in its abundance of craft traditions, from totem poles to intricate baskets and detailed carvings. Many of the native crafts you'll see across the state are results of generations of traditions passed down among tribes; the craft process is usually labor-intensive, using local resources such as rye grasses or fragrant cedar trees.

Each of Alaska's native groups is noted for particular skills. Inuit art includes ivory carvings, spirit masks, dance fans, baleen baskets, and jewelry. Also be on the lookout for mukluks (seal- or reindeer-skin boots). The Tlingit peoples of Southeast Alaska are known for their totem poles, as well as for baskets and hats woven from spruce root and cedar bark. Tsimshian Indians also work with spruce root and cedar bark, and Haida Indians are noted basket makers and carvers. Athabascans specialize in birch-bark creations, decorated fur garments, and beadwork. The Aleut, a maritime people dwelling in the southwest reaches of the state, make grass basketry that is considered among the best in the world. ⇨ *For tips about buying an authentic item, check out Made in Alaska, in Chapter 4.*

IF YOU LIKE

Mountains & Glaciers

Alaska has roughly 100,000 glaciers and ice fields covering more than 29,000 square mi, and 17 of the 20 highest mountains in the United States. Most of these awe-inspiring sights are in remote and inaccessible regions. However, with time, effort and, on occasion, a few bucks, these scenic wonders can be yours.

- **Mendenhall Glacier, Juneau.** This drive-up glacier comes complete with visitor center, educational exhibits, nature trails, and, when the cruise ships are in town, lots of bused-in tourists. Don't let the crush of visitors dissuade you from stopping by, though—it's a great resource for learning about glacier dynamics and the natural forces that have shaped Alaska.

- **Mt. Roberts, Juneau.** The tram takes you up the mountain and, if the weather cooperates, offers great views of the area. It's another cruise ship favorite, but at least you can have a quick beer as you soak in the scenery.

- **Glacier Bay National Park, Gustavus.** Whether you view this natural wonder by air, boat, or on foot, Glacier Bay is well worth the effort and expense it takes to get there.

- **Portage Glacier, Anchorage.** This glacier has been receding rapidly, but you can ride the tour boat Ptarmigan across the lake to view the face of the glacier. Keep an eye out for office building–size chunks of ice falling into the water.

- **Exit Glacier, Seward.** You can take a short, easy walk to view this glacier, or if you're in the mood for a challenge, hike the steep trail onto the enormous Harding Icefield. Scan the nearby cliffs for mountain goats and watch for bears.

- **Flattop Mountain, Anchorage.** Drive to the Glen Alps parking lot in Chugach State Park, and take the short walk west to a scenic overlook—on a clear day the view sweeps from Denali south along the Alaska Range past several active volcanoes on the other side of Cook Inlet. Or follow the hikers to the top of the mountain for even more stunning scenery.

- **Mt. McKinley, Talkeetna.** For the ultimate mountain sightseeing adventure, take a flight from Talkeetna and land on a glacier—if you're early enough in the summer, you can fly onto the Kahiltna Glacier, where the teams attempting to summit the mountain gather.

Bicycling

The paved-road system is straightforward, and traffic is usually light. However, the road shoulders can be narrow, and people drive fast in rural areas. Unpaved highways are bikable but tougher going.

- **Anchorage, Alaska.** Anchorage has an excellent bike-trail system. Biking this city is a good way to appreciate its setting as a metropolis perched on the edge of vast wilderness—but beware the occasional furry creature sharing the bike trail with you!

- **Denali National Park & Preserve.** Take your mountain bike on the Alaska Railroad and bike Denali. Although the park road is largely unpaved, it has a good dirt surface and only light traffic.

- **The Interior.** Fairbanks has miles of scenic bike paths along the Chena River. Most roads have wide shoulders and those

incredible Alaska views. Trails used in winter by mushers, snowmobilers, and cross-country skiers are taken over by bikers when the snow melts.

■ **Southeast Alaska and the Ferry System.** You can bring your bike on Alaska's ferry system at an extra charge. Use it to explore the Southeast's charming communities and surrounding forests, but come prepared for heavy rain.

Creature Comforts

Alaska isn't only tundra hiking, grizzly bear watching, and salmon fishing. It's possible to spend your vacation pampering yourself, enjoying a nice glass of wine and excellent food, and still experience outdoor adventures.

Lodging properties can be divided into those on the road system, and those that require a boat or air journey. In Southeast Alaska many lodges can be reached by boat from a nearby town or village, while properties elsewhere in the state usually require a flight in a small plane.

■ **Alaska's Capital Inn, Juneau.** Luxury meets history in this gracious hilltop bed-and-breakfast with upscale services, delicious breakfasts, and period furnishings from the early 1900s.

■ **Alyeska Prince Hotel, Girdwood.** An hour south of Anchorage, this luxurious hotel offers plenty of opportunities for spoiling yourself silly. The crown jewel of the resort is the Seven Glaciers Restaurant, a 7-minute tram ride up Mt. Alyeska. There you can enjoy the stunning view of the valley and the namesake glaciers; knowledgeable diners consider the restaurant to be Alaska's finest.

■ **Chena Hot Springs Resort, Chena Hot Springs.** If you are in or near Fairbanks, some thermal soaking is a must. Here you can spend the day enjoying a wide range of outdoor activities, followed by a long soak in the hot springs–warmed hot tubs, topped off by an exceptional dinner.

■ **Kachemak Bay Wilderness Lodge, Homer.** Across Kachemak Bay from Homer, and accessible by boat or floatplane, you can fill your days hiking, fishing, boating, and sightseeing, followed by delicious seafood dinners. The owners are longtime Alaskans who cater to nature lovers.

■ **Kenai Princess Wilderness Lodge, Cooper Landing.** Charming bungalows with fireplaces and vaulted ceilings of natural-finish wood make up this sprawling complex on a bluff overlooking the Kenai River. Try flightseeing, fishing, and hiking, or just read a good book and enjoy the view.

■ **Pearson's Pond Luxury Inn and Adventure Spa, Juneau.** Yoga in the morning; wine and cheese in the evening; whirlpool tubs with rain showers; private balconies; and a well-stocked breakfast nook—luxurious amenities define this B&B on a small pond near Mendenhall Glacier.

■ **Seven Seas *Mariner*, Seven Seas Cruises.** Cordon Bleu cuisine, a luxurious spa, and impeccable service make this all-suites, all-balcony ship a top choice for high-end relaxing while cruising amid dramatic Alaska scenery.

GREAT ITINERARIES

ANCHORAGE TO THE KENAI

2 Days: Hello Anchorage!

Explore the fun and somewhat kitschy downtown shops, head to the outdoor markets on the weekend, take in the sights at Ship Creek, and visit the city's museums. **Logistics:** Getting to town is a snap (buses, reasonable taxis, and hotel shuttles make the short ride). Car-rental offices are in the South Terminal of the airport.

1 Day: Chugach State Park

Anchorage's ½-million-acre backyard wilderness has glaciers, tundra meadows, forested valleys, and wildlife. In September, this is one of the best places to see moose. **Logistics:** This is a do-it-yourself park: the only facilities are trailheads, a few basic campgrounds, and picnic areas. A good place to start is 3,350-foot Flattop Mountain, Alaska's most-climbed peak. There's a fantastic viewpoint near the parking lot ($5 parking fee).

2 Days: Seward

Surrounded by lush mountains at the head of Resurrection Bay, Seward is the primary gateway to Kenai Fjords National Park. You can join a coastal wildlife tour, explore the Alaska SeaLife Center, and take a stroll along the waterfront trail. **Logistics:** The spectacular drive south from Anchorage takes about two hours on the Seward Highway. An alternative is to take the Alaska Railroad.

2–4 Days: The Kenai's Wild Country

Option #1: Kenai Fjords National Park. Tidewater glaciers, rugged fjords, Exit Glacier, and ocean life are highlights of this spectacular coastal parkland. **Logistics:** Take a tour from Seward to spot whales. You can also stay in public-use cabins, hike up to the Harding Icefield from Exit Gla-

cier, and travel by kayak out of Miller's Landing.

Option #2: Chugach National Forest. Sprawling across much of the Kenai Peninsula and Prince William Sound, this 6-million-acre area is the country's second-largest national forest. Girdwood, Seward, Cooper Landing, and Cordova offer convenient access points to trailheads and campgrounds as well as visitor services and outfitters. **Logistics:** Stop in the **Seward Ranger District Headquarters** (⊠*334 4th Ave.* ☎*907/224–3374*) for trail and hiking info—they've got plenty.

Option #3: Kenai National Wildlife Refuge. Covering nearly 2 million acres, the Kenai refuge encompasses part of the vast Harding Icefield as well as rugged peaks and forested lowlands inhabited by moose, black bears, and grizzlies. **Logistics:** The Kenai refuge is enormous, but road access is limited to a few trailheads and campgrounds. The Skilak Loop Road between Cooper Landing and Sterling is a gravel road that offers a chance to escape traffic. In Soldotna, the visitor center on Ski Hill Road has maps and updates on wildlife and park conditions.

1–2 Days: Kenai & Soldotna

The sportfishing hubs of South Central, these sister cities lie along the world-famous Kenai River. Pacific salmon spawn here each summer, including the mighty king salmon. Be sure to take a stroll through Kenai's old town to see the Russian Orthodox Church.

1–2 Days: Homer

This end-of-the-road coastal town calls itself the halibut capital of the world, but it also has a thriving community of artists and writers. Take a water taxi to nearby Kachemak Bay State Park and visit the Pratt Museum. **Logistics:** The Sterling

Highway ends in Homer; it's a four hour drive from Anchorage. Take the scenic Kalifornsky Beach Road loop from Soldotna, which loops back to the Sterling Highway and offers great views of volcanoes in the Alaska Range.

ANCHORAGE TO THE INTERIOR

1 day: Talkeetna

Mountaineers congregate at this rural community before flying into the Alaska Range. Denali National Park's entrance area is another 140 mi up the highway; if you can't get a bus reservation in the park, you can book a flightseeing trip here and land on a glacier. ■TIP➜Talkeetna is a two-hour drive north on the Parks Highway from Anchorage. Even if you don't stay at the Talkeetna Alaskan Lodge, stop by to take in the view from the patio. Try your fishing luck on one of the three rivers that converge here.

1–2 Days: "Little Denali"

Denali State Park has some of South Central's best tundra hikes, along the Curry-Kesugi Ridge. The park's spectacular views of Mt. McKinley are among the finest anywhere. **Logistics:** At Byers Lake you can camp or stay in public-use cabins. For more details, go to ⊕*www.dnr. state.ak.us/parks/units/denali1.htm.*

2–5 Days: Denali National Park & Preserve

Larger than the state of Massachusetts, Alaska's most famous parkland is a wilderness of high mountains, glacial rivers, forest, and tundra plains. Mt. McKinley rises 20,320 feet into the heavens, while grizzly bears roam alpine meadows and wolves hunt caribou, moose, and Dall sheep. **Logistics:** We highly recommend making shuttle-bus reservations in advance, getting out on the first bus in the morning, and going as far as Fish Creek for the best wildlife viewing. Check out ⊕*www.nps.gov/dena.*

1–2 Days: Fairbanks

Born as a gold-mining camp, the Golden Heart of Alaska is the starting point for trips into much of northern Bush Alaska. Near town, you can hike the trails in Creamer's Field Migratory Waterfowl Refuge; enjoy exhibits at the Museum of the North; visit Pioneer Park, a theme park with native and gold-rush exhibits; and take a riverboat tour. **Logistics:** Consider taking the scenic Alaska Railroad ride back to Anchorage to catch your flight home. For more information check out ⊕*www.akrr.com.*

ALASKA'S HISTORY

The First People

No one knows when humans first began living in the northwest corner of the North American continent, and it is still a subject of great controversy and debate. One popular theory is that 12,000 years ago humans followed the eastern migration of Ice Age mammals over the Bering Land Bridge, a 1,000 mi wide stretch of land that connected present-day Alaska to Siberia. To date, however, the oldest human remains found in Alaska are 10,300 years old, believed to be an ancestor of the Tlingit tribe.

No matter when humans first arrived, by 1750 there were 57,300 native peoples living in Russian Alaska, including Aleuts, Alutiiqs, Yup'iks, Inupiats, Athabascan, Tlingit, and Haida. Today, there are more than 100,000 American Indian and Alaska Native persons living in Alaska.

Russians in Alaska

Alaska was a late bloomer on the world scene. It wasn't until 1741, when Danish navigator Vitus Bering, under Russian rule, made the Alaska region known to the world. Bering died before he could ever explore the continent or return to Russia.

Politically speaking, Russia imposed itself on Alaska in varying degrees. It was the arrival of the *promyshlenniki,* or fur hunters, that had the biggest impact on the native cultures. By most accounts, the hunters were illiterate, quarrelsome, hard-drinking, and virtually out of control. They penetrated the Aleutian Chain and made themselves masters of the islands and their inhabitants, the Aleuts. Several times the natives revolted; their attempts were squelched, and they were brutalized.

By 1790 the small fur traders were replaced by large Russian companies. Siberian fur trader Aleksandr Andreyevich Baranov became manager of a fur-trading company and director of a settlement in Kodiak Island in 1791. He essentially governed all Russian activities in North America until 1818, when he was ordered back to Russia. Word was spreading to the Russian government that foreigners, particularly Americans, were gaining a disproportionate share of the Alaskan market. The Russian Navy was ordered to assume control of Alaska, and by 1821 they had barred all foreign ships from entering Alaskan waters. Russia created new policies forbidding any trade with non-Russians and requiring that the colonies only be supplied by Russian ships.

The 1853 Crimean War between Imperial Russia and Britain and France put a great financial burden on Russia. It fiscally behooved the country to sell Russian Alaska. In 1867, under decree of a treaty signed by U.S. Secretary of State William H. Seward, Alaska was sold to the United States for $7.2 million. On October 18, 1867, the territory officially changed hands. Newspapers around the nation hailed the purchase of Alaska as "Seward's Folly." Within 30 years, however, one of the biggest gold strikes in the world would bring hundreds of thousands of people to this U.S. territory.

The Gold Rush

The great Klondike gold discoveries of 1896 gained the attention of men around the nation. Due to the Depression of 1893, the need for food, money, and hope sparked a gold fever unmatched in history. Men and women alike clamored for information about Alaska, not realizing

that the Klondike was in the Yukon Territory of Canada. Perhaps if they'd known their geography Alaska would never have become the state that it is now.

The most popular route for the gold stampeders was to go entirely by water. It wasn't cheaper, but it was by far easier than going the inland route. They would start in either San Francisco or Seattle, buy passage on a steamship, and disembark more than 1,000 nautical mi later in Skagway, Alaska. No gold was in Skagway, but overnight it became a city of 20,000 miners. Gold-seekers used it as a place to negotiate and get ready for the only part of their journey that would be traversed on foot. The Chilkoot Trail was 35 challenging miles that were too rugged for pack horses. The hardest part of the journey was the climb to the summit, Chilkoot Pass. This climb was known as the Golden Staircase, a 45-degree angled hike of nearly 3/4 of a mile. Chilkoot Pass was the gateway to Canada and the point at which the Canadian government required each person entering the territory to have at least a year's supply, approximately one ton of food. This is partially why it took most stampeders one to three months to complete this 35-mile stretch. Once into Canada, they built boats and floated the remaining 600 miles to Dawson City, where the gold rush was taking place. By 1899 the Yukon Gold Rush was over, however, and the population of Skagway shrank dramatically.

Alaska experienced its own gold strike in Nome, on the Seward Peninsula, in 1898. The fever didn't actually hit until 1900, but because it did, gold mining all over Alaska began to get national attention.

World War II

In 1942, after the U.S. entered the war, the War Production Board deemed gold mining nonessential to the war effort and forced gold mining all over the country to come to a halt. Despite the closing of mines, World War II was still financially beneficial to parts of Alaska. Numerous bases and ports were strategically built around the state, and to supply them, the Alaska Highway was created.

The only time Alaska had any direct involvement with the war was in June 1942, when the Japanese attacked Attu and Kiska Islands in the Aleutian Chain. The attack has been recorded in history as an "incident," but it had a great impact on many lives; a few hundred casualties occurred due to friendly fire and nearly one thousand inhabitants of the area were relocated.

Statehood

On January 3, 1959, "Seward's Folly" became the 49th state in the nation—more than 100 years after Seward first visited. Statehood gave Alaska national appeal. A mass of investors, bold entrepreneurs, tourists, and land grabbers began to arrive. It is still a new state, far from direct scrutiny by the rest of the nation. With a constantly growing, competitive industry of oil and other natural resources, Alaska has made an identity for itself that resembles no other state in the nation. It boasts the second-highest production of gas and oil in the country, is twice the size of the second-largest state, and has millions of lakes, minimal pollution, and endless possibilities.

FLORA & FAUNA OF ALASKA

FAUNA

Arctic Ground Squirrel (C) (*Spermophilus parryii*): These yellowish brown, gray-flecked rodents are among Alaska's most common and widespread mammals. Ground squirrels are known for their loud, persistent chatter. They may often be seen standing above their tundra den sites, watching for grizzlies, golden eagles, and weasels.

Arctic Tern (F) (*Sterna paradisaea*): These are the world's long-distance flying champs; some members of their species make annual migratory flights between the high Arctic and the Antarctic. Sleekly beautiful, the bird has a black cap and striking blood-red bill and feet. They often can be seen looking for small fish in ponds and coastal marshes.

Bald Eagle (A) (*Haliaeetus leucocephalus*): With a wingspan of 6 to 8 feet, these grand Alaska residents are primarily fish

eaters, but they will also take birds or small mammals when the opportunity presents itself. The world's largest gathering of bald eagles occurs in Southeast Alaska each winter, along the Chilkat River near Haines.

Beluga Whale (B) (*Dephinapterus leucas*): Belugas are gray at birth, bluish gray as adolescents, and white as adults (the word *byelukha* is Russian for "white"). Though they seem to favor fish, belugas' diet includes more than 100 different species, from crabs to squid. They live along much of the coast, from the Beaufort Sea to the Gulf of Alaska.

Black-capped Chickadee (D) (*Parus atricapillus*): This songbird is one of Alaska's most common residents. As with two close relatives, the chestnut-backed and boreal chickadees, the black-cap gets through the winters by lowering its body temper-

ature at night and shivering through the long hours of darkness.

Caribou (G) (*Rangifer tarandus*): Sometimes called the "nomads of the north," caribou are long-distance wandering mammals. They are also the most abundant of the state's large mammals; in fact, there are more caribou in Alaska than people! The Western Arctic Caribou Herd numbers more than 400,00, while the Porcupine Caribou Herd has ranged between 120,000 and 180,000 over the past decades. Another bit of caribou trivia: they are the only members of the deer family in which both sexes grow antlers. Those of bulls may grow up to 5½ feet long with a span of up to 3 feet.

Common Loon (E) (*Gavia immer*): Some sounds seem to be the essence of wilderness: the howl of the wolf, the hooting of the owl, and the cry of the loon. The common loon is one of five *Gavia* species to

inhabit Alaska (the others are the Arctic, Pacific, red-throated, and yellow-billed). Common loons are primarily fish eaters. Excellent swimmers, they are able to stay submerged for up to three minutes.

Common Raven (*Corvus corax*): A popular character in Alaska native stories, the raven in indigenous culture is both creator and trickster. Entirely black, with a wedge-shape tail and a heavy bill that helps distinguish it from crows, the raven is Alaska's most widespread avian resident.

Common Redpoll (*Carduelis flammea*): Even tinier than the chickadee, the common redpoll and its close cousin, the hoary redpoll (*Carduelis hornemanni*), are among the few birds to inhabit Alaska's Interior year-round. Though it looks a bit like a sparrow, this red-capped, black-bibbed songbird is a member of the finch family.

FLORA & FAUNA OF ALASKA

Dall Sheep (*Ovis dalli dalli*): One of four wild sheep to inhabit North America, the white Dall is the only one to reside within Alaska. Residents of high alpine areas, the sheep live in mountain chains from the St. Elias Range to the Brooks Range. Though both sexes grow horns, those of females are short spikes, while males grow grand curls that are "status symbols" displayed during mating season.

Dolly Varden (*Salvelinus malma*): This sleek, flashy fish inhabits lakes and streams throughout Alaska's coastal regions. A member of the char family, it was named after a character in Charles Dickens' novel *Barnaby Rudge* because the brightly colored spots on its sides resemble Miss Dolly Varden's pink-spotted dress and hat. Some members of the species remain in freshwater all their life, while sea-run dollies may live in the ocean for two to five years before returning to spawn.

Golden Eagle (*Aquila chrysaetos*): With a wingspan of up to 7½ feet, this inland bird can often be spotted spiraling high in the sky, riding thermals. The bird usually nests on cliff faces and feeds upon small mammals and ptarmigan. The plumage of adult birds is entirely dark, except for a golden head. These migratory eagles spend their winters as far away as Kansas and New Mexico.

Great Horned Owl (*Bubo virginianus*): The best known of Alaska's several species of owls, and one whose call is a familiar one here. It is a large owl with prominent ear tufts and a white throat with barred markings. Residing in forests from Southeast Alaska to the Interior, it preys on squirrels, hares, grouse, and other birds.

Harbor Seal (*Phoca vitulina*): Inhabiting shallow marine waters and estuaries along much of Alaska's southern coast, harbor seals may survive up to 30 years in the wild, on a diet of fish, squid, octopus, and shrimp. They, in turn, may be eaten or killed by orcas, sea lions, or humans. Solitary in the water, harbor seals love company on land, and will gather in large colonies. They weigh up to 250 pounds and range in color from black to white.

Hermit Thrush (*Catharus guttatus*): Some Alaskans argue that there is no northern song more beautiful than the flutelike warbling of the hermit thrush and its close relative, the Swainson's thrush (*Catharus ustulatus*). The two birds are difficult to tell apart, except for their songs, the hermit's reddish brown tail, and the color of their eye rings. Among the many songbird migrants to visit Alaska each spring, they begin singing in May while seeking mates and defending territories in forested regions of southern and central Alaska.

Horned Puffin (H) (*Fratercula corniculata*): Named for the black, fleshy projections above each eye, horned puffins are favorites among birders. Included in the group of diving seabirds known as alcids, puffins spend most of their life on water, coming to land only for nesting. They are expert swimmers, using their wings to "fly" underwater and their webbed feet as rudders. Horned puffins have large orange-red and yellow bills. A close relative, the tufted puffin (*Fratercula cirrhata*), is named for its yellow ear tufts.

Lynx (*Lynx canadensis*): The lynx is the only wild cat to inhabit Alaska. It's a secretive animal that depends on stealth and quick-

Top: Dall Sheep

ness. It may kill birds, squirrels, and mice, but the cat's primary prey is the snowshoe hare (*Lepus americanus*), particularly in winter; its population numbers closely follow those of the hare's boom-bust cycles. Large feet and a light body help the lynx run through deep snowpack.

Moose (*Alces alces gigas*): The moose is the largest member of the deer family, the largest bulls standing 7 feet tall at the shoulders and weighing up to 1,600 pounds. The peak of breeding occurs in late September. Females give birth to calves in late May and early June; twins are the norm. Bulls enter the rut in September, the most dominant engaging in brutal fights. Though most commonly residents of woodlands, some moose live in or just outside Alaska's cities.

Mountain Goat (*Oreamnos americanus*): Sometimes confused with Dall sheep, mountain goats inhabit Alaska's coastal mountains. As adults, both males and females have sharp-pointed horns that are short and black (sheep have buff-colored horns). They also have massive chests and comparatively small hindquarters, plus bearded chins.

Musk Ox (*Ovibos moschatus*): The musk ox is considered an Ice Age relic that survived into the present at least partly because of a defensive tactic: they stand side by side and form rings to fend off predators such as grizzlies and wolves. Unfortunately for the species, that tactic didn't work very well against humans armed with guns. Alaska's last native musk oxen were killed in 1865. Musk oxen from Greenland were reintroduced here in 1930; they now reside on Nunivak Island. The animal's most notable physical feature is its long guard hairs, which form "skirts" that nearly reach the ground. Inupiats called the musk ox *oomingmak*, meaning "bearded one." Beneath those coarser hairs is fine underfur called qiviut, which can be woven into warm clothing.

Pacific Halibut (*Hippoglossus stenolepis*): The halibut is the largest of the flatfish to inhabit Alaska's coastal waters, with females weighing up to 500 pounds. Long-lived "grandmother" halibut may survive 40 years or more, producing millions of eggs each year. Bottom dwellers that feed on fish, crabs, clams, and squid, they range from the Panhandle to Norton Sound. Young halibut generally stay near shore, but older fish have been found at depths of 3,600 feet.

Pacific Salmon (I) (*Oncorhynchus*): Five species of Pacific salmon spawn in Alaska's waters, including the king, silver, sockeye, pink, and chum. Hundreds of millions of salmon return to the state's streams and lakes each summer and fall, after spending much of their lives in saltwater. They form the backbone of Alaska's fishing industry and draw sportfishers from around the world.

Rainbow Trout (*Salmo gairdneri*): A favorite of anglers, the rainbow trout inhabits streams and lakes in Alaska's coastal regions. The Bristol Bay region is best known for large 'bows, perhaps because of its huge returns of salmon. Rainbows feed heavily on salmon eggs as well as the deteriorating flesh of spawned-out salmon. Sea-run rainbows, or steelhead, grow even larger after years spent feeding in ocean waters. The state record for steelhead/rainbow trout is 42 pounds, 3 ounces.

Top left: Lynx
Top right: Moose

FLORA & FAUNA OF ALASKA

Red Fox (*Vulpes vulpes*): Though it's called the red fox, this species actually has four color phases: red, silver, black, and cross (with a cross pattern on the back and shoulders). An able hunter, the red fox preys primarily on voles and mice, but will also eat hares, squirrels, birds, insects, and berries.

Sandhill Crane (*Grus canadensis*): The sandhill's call has been described as "something between a French horn and a squeaky barn door." Though others may dispute that description, few would disagree that the crane's calls have a prehistoric sound. And, in fact, scientists say the species has changed little in the 9 million years since its earliest recorded fossils. Sandhills are the tallest birds to inhabit Alaska; their wingspan reaches up to 7 feet. The gray plumage of adults is set off by a bright red crown. Like geese, they fly in Vs during migratory journeys.

Sea Otter (K) (*Enhydra lutris*): Sea otters don't depend on blubber to stay warm. Instead, hair trapped in their dense fur keeps their skin dry. Beneath their outer hairs, the underfur ranges in density from 170,000 to one million hairs per square inch. Not surprisingly, the otter takes good care of its coat, spending much of every day grooming. Otters also spend a lot of time eating. In one study, researchers found that adult otters consumed 14 crabs a day, equaling about one-fourth of their body weight.

Sitka Blacktailed Deer (*Odocoileus hemionus sitkensis*): The Panhandle's rain forest is the primary home of this deer, though it has been transplanted to Prince William Sound and Kodiak. Dark gray in winter and reddish brown in summer, it's stockier than the whitetails found in the Lower 48. The deer stay at lower elevations during the snowy months of win-

ter, then move up to alpine meadows in summer.

Snowy Owl (L) (*Nyctea scandiaca*): Inhabiting the open coastal tundra, the snowy owl is found from the western Aleutian Islands to the Arctic. Adults are largely white (though females have scattered light brown spots) though immature birds are heavily marked with brown. Their numbers rise and fall with swings in the population of lemmings, their primary prey. Rather than hoots, the snowy emits loud croaks and whistles.

Steller's Sea Lion (Q) (*Eumetopias jubatus*): Its ability—and tendency—to roar is what gives the sea lion its name. Because they can rotate their rear flippers and lift their bellies off the ground, sea lions can get around on land much more easily than seals can. They are also much larger, the males reaching up to 9 feet and weighing up to 1,500 pounds. They feed pri-

marily on fish, but will also eat sea otters and seals. They have been designated an endangered species because their populations north of the Panhandle have suffered huge declines.

Walrus (P) (*Odobenus rosmarus*): The walrus's ivory tusks can be dangerous weapons; there are stories of walruses killing polar bears when attacked. Weighing up to 2 tons, the walrus's primary food includes clams, mussels, snails, crabs, and shrimp.

Willow Ptarmigan (O) (*Lagopus lagopus*): One of three species of ptarmigan (the others are the rock and the white-tailed), the willow is the most widespread. It is also Alaska's state bird. It tends to live in willow thickets, where it feeds and hides from predators. Aggressively protective parents, willow ptarmigan have been known to attack humans to defend their young.

FLORA & FAUNA OF ALASKA

Wolf (*Canis lupus*): The largest and most majestic of the Far North's wild canines, wolves roam throughout all of mainland Alaska. They form close-knit family packs, which may range from a few animals to more than 30. Packs hunt a variety of prey, from small mammals and birds to caribou, moose, and Dall sheep. They communicate with each other through body language, barks, and howls.

Wolverine (*Gulo gulo*): Consider yourself lucky if you see a wolverine, because they are among the most secretive animals of the North. They are also fierce predators, with enormous strength and endurance. Denali biologists once reported seeing a wolverine drag a Dall sheep carcass more than 2 mi; an impressive feat, since the sheep likely weighed four times what the wolverine did. They have been known to run 40 mph through snow when chased by hunters. Though they look a lot like bears and have the ferocity of a grizzly, wolverines are in fact the largest members of the weasel family.

Wood Frog (*Rana sylvatica*): One of the few amphibians to inhabit Alaska, and the only one to live north of the Panhandle, these frogs range as far north as the Arctic, surviving winters through the help of a biochemical change that keeps them in a suspended state while frozen. Come spring, the bodies revive after thawing. Though they mate and lay eggs in water, wood frogs spend most of their lives on land.

FLORA

Balsam Poplar and Black Cottonwood (*Populus balsamifera* and *Populus trichocarpa*): These two closely related species sometimes interbreed and are difficult, if not impossible, to tell apart. Mature trees of both species have gray bark that is rough and deeply furrowed. In midsummer they produce cottony seed pods. They also have large, shiny, arrowhead-shaped leaves.

Birch (*Betula*): Ranging from Kodiak Island to the Brooks Range, birch trees are important members of Alaska's boreal forests. Deciduous trees that prefer well-drained soils, they have white bark and green heart-to-diamond-shape leaves with sharp points and toothed edges. One species, the paper birch (*Betula papyrifera*), is easily distinguished by its peeling, paperlike bark.

Blueberry (J) (*Vaccinium*): A favorite of berry pickers, blueberries are found throughout Alaska, except for the farthest northern reaches of the Arctic. They come in a variety of forms, including head-high forest bushes and sprawling tundra mats. Pink, bell-shape flowers bloom in spring and dark blue to almost black fruits begin to ripen in July or August, depending on the locale.

Cow Parsnip (R) (*Heracleum lanatum*): Also known to some as Indian celery, cow parsnip resides in open forests and meadows. The plant may grow several feet high, with dull green leaves the size of dinner plates; thick, hairy, hollow stalks; and clusters of white flowers. Anyone who harvests—or walks among—this species must take great care. Oils on the stalks, in combination with sunlight, can produce severe skin blistering.

Top: Wood frogs

Devil's Club (N) (*Echinopanax horridum*): This is a prickly shrub that may grow 4 to 8 feet high and forms dense, spiny thickets in forests ranging from the Panhandle to South Central. Hikers need to be wary of this plant: its large, maple-like leaves (which can be a foot or more across) have spines, and needles cover its pale brown trunk. In late summer, black bears enjoy its bright red berries.

Salmonberry (M) (*Rubus spectabilis*): The salmonberry canes, on which the leaves and fruits grow, may reach 7 feet tall; they grow in dense thickets. The juicy raspberry-like fruits may be either orange or red at maturity; the time of ripening is late June through August.

Spruce (*Picea*): Three species of spruce grow in Alaska. Sitka spruce (*Picea sitchensis*) is an important member of coastal rain-forest communities; white spruce (*Picea glauca*) prefers dry, well-drained soils in boreal forests that stretch from South Central to the Arctic; black spruce (*Picea mariana*) thrives in wet, boggy areas.

Tall Fireweed (*Epilobium angustifolium*): The fireweed is among the first plants to reinhabit burn areas and, in the proper conditions, it grows well. Found throughout much of Alaska, it's a beautiful plant, with fuchsia flowers that bloom from the bottom to the top of stalks; it's said that the final opening of flowers is a sign that winter is only weeks away. Spring fireweed shoots can be eaten raw or steamed and its blossoms can be added to salads. A related species is dwarf fireweed (*Epilobium latifolium*); also known as "river beauty," it is shorter and bushier.

> **IN THE WILD**
>
> For our suggestions for best wildlife experiences, see Enjoying Alaska's Wildlife in Chapter 2.

Wild Prickly Rose (S) (*Rosa acicularis*): Serrated leaves grow on prickly spines, and fragrant five-petal flowers begin blooming in late spring. The flowers vary from light pink to dark red. Appearing in late summer and fall, bright red rose hips rich in vitamin C can be harvested for jellies, soups, or pie.

Willow (*Salix*): An estimated three dozen species of willow grow in Alaska. Some, like the felt-leaf willow (*Salix alaxensis*), may reach tree size; others form thickets; still others, like the Arctic willow (*Salix arctica*), hug the ground in alpine terrain. They often grow thickest in the subalpine zone between forest and tundra. Whatever the size, willows produce soft "catkins" (pussy willows), which are actually columns of densely packed flowers without petals.

—*By Bill Sherwonit*

Top left: Wolf
Top center: Wolverin
Top right: Sitka spruce

LET THE JOURNEY BEGIN

Getting to your destination is as much a part of the Last Frontier experience as being there. Whether traveling by sea, air, or land, keep your eyes open in Alaska: the only thing you can expect is the unexpected. Whales suddenly breach beside ferries; Mt. McKinley peeks through train windows; moose amble along scenic roadways; and the tundra spreads out beneath bush planes.

ON THE WATER

About 50% of visitors choose to cruise Alaska, but for a real adventure, travel Alaska Marine Highway System ferries. Either way, you'll see glaciers, forests, and maybe a whale or two.

The ferry system operates year-round and has two different routes: Bellingham, Washington to Skagway mimics the most popular cruise ship itinerary; the second route runs from Homer to the Aleutian Chain and Dutch Harbor.

Unlike cruise ships, which follow set itineraries, ferries come and go frequently for added flexibility. Consider, though, that they can arrive at inconvenient times whereas cruises dock for daytrips.

At first glance, the $363 one-way ticket to Skagway is a dream compared to the bare minimum $700 for a cruise ship berth. Add a cabin or bring a vehicle and the price can double or triple—and food isn't included. If you go without amenities, need to bring a car, or want flexibility, the ferry price is right; for those on a budget, an all-inclusive cruise may work better. The AlaskaPass

can mitigate ferry costs if adding rail or car travel to a trip. (⇨ *Travel Smart Alaska*)

Ferries might not be as luxurious as cruise ships, but they're comfortable. Each has an observation lounge, and cafeterias serve inexpensive meals. Most cabins have private washrooms. Daring passengers sleep outside on cots beneath the heat lamps free of charge. ■ **TIP**➔ The schedule comes out in January or February, and cabins fill up almost instantly for summer trips; advance booking is essential.

Ferry travel is generally slow: maximum speed is 16.5 knots, compared with 21 knots or better for a cruise ship. Taking your time has its advantages, though; you'll take in the scenery with the locals who add their own color to the mix.

CONTACTS Alaska Marine Highway (☎ *907/465–3941* or *800/642–0066* ⊕ *www. dot.state.ak.us/amhs*). Pick up tickets at your starting point or have them mailed to you. **AlaskaPass** (☎*206/463–6550* or *800/248– 7598* ⊕ *www.alaskapass.com*).

ON THE PATH,
OR OFF

Dalton Highway

These maps illustrate major ferry landings, scenic roads, and main rail lines. Beyond Southeast, South Central, and Interior Alaska, you're in the Bush—remote and accessible largely by small plane.

ROADS

With mountains, marine vistas, and miles of open tundra you'll be hard-pressed to find a drive in Alaska that isn't scenic, and not just because there are so few to find. There's always the potential for wildlife encounters, so be alert to something furry darting—or strolling, in the case of moose—out of the roadside brush.

Every year, tourists bring home on the road in RVs. Campgrounds can accommodate trailers, but only private RV parks have hookups. Most drives connect South Central and the Interior, but the Dalton takes adventurers to the Arctic Ocean.

RAILROADS

On Alaska's rails you'll ride history. Relive the Gold Rush on Southeast's only railroad, the cliff-hugging White Pass & Yukon Route, the same trail followed by prospectors.

In South Central, one of the best ways to see Alaska's myriad landscapes is to take the Alaska Railroad from Anchorage to Denali National Park. Don't forget to look for Mt. McKinley; while it's the highest peak in North America, it's frequently hidden in clouds.

PLANES

Bush planes are inextricably part of the Alaskan landscape. To get to that remote wilderness lodge or fly-fishing location, there's often no other choice. The flight you take to a native village off the road system is also a trip on that community's lifeline to the rest of the world.

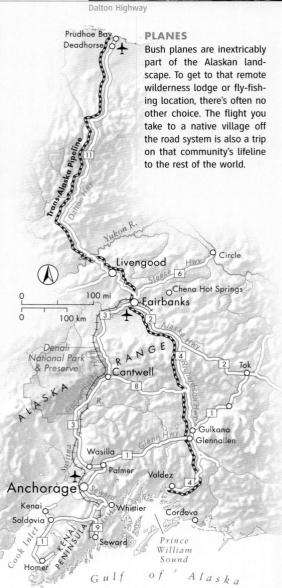

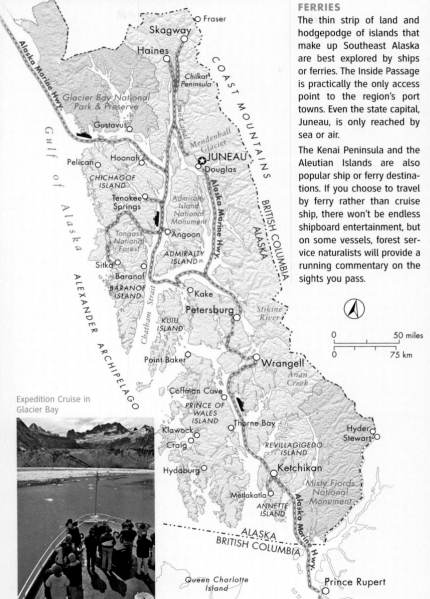

FERRIES

The thin strip of land and hodgepodge of islands that make up Southeast Alaska are best explored by ships or ferries. The Inside Passage is practically the only access point to the region's port towns. Even the state capital, Juneau, is only reached by sea or air.

The Kenai Peninsula and the Aleutian Islands are also popular ship or ferry destinations. If you choose to travel by ferry rather than cruise ship, there won't be endless shipboard entertainment, but on some vessels, forest service naturalists will provide a running commentary on the sights you pass.

0   50 miles

0   75 km

IN FOCUS LET THE JOURNEY BEGIN

1

Expedition Cruise in Glacier Bay

Fraser

Skagway

Haines

Chilkat Peninsula

COAST MOUNTAINS

Alaska Marine Hwy

Glacier Bay National Park & Preserve

Gustavus

Mendenhall Glacier

JUNEAU

Douglas

Pelican

Hoonah

CHICHAGOF ISLAND

Gulf of Alaska

Tenakee Springs

Admiralty Island National Monument

BRITISH COLUMBIA

ALASKA

Alaska Marine Hwy

Angoon

ADMIRALTY ISLAND

Tongass National Forest

Sitka

Baranof

BARANOF ISLAND

Chatham Strait

Kake

Petersburg

Stikine River

KUIU ISLAND

ALEXANDER ARCHIPELAGO

Point Baker

Wrangell

Anan Creek

Coffman Cove

PRINCE OF WALES ISLAND

Thorne Bay

Klawock

Craig

REVILLAGIGEDO ISLAND

Hyder

Stewart

Hydaburg

Ketchikan

Misty Fiords National Monument

Metlakatla

ANNETTE ISLAND

Alaska Marine Hwy

ALASKA

BRITISH COLUMBIA

Queen Charlotte Island

Prince Rupert

IN THE SKIES

No roads, rails, or even airstrips? No problem. Bush planes are meant to go where the trappings of civilization aren't, and pilots deftly land on riverbanks, fields, even water. Lake Hood, outside of Anchorage, is the world's busiest port for seaplanes (and a great place from which to charter a direct flight to remote wilderness spots). One in 78 residents here is a pilot—the most per capita in the U.S.

Bush planes aren't for everyone, though. Extremely nervous fliers should consider how to cope with the effects of updrafts, downdrafts, and even breezes—not to mention the sharp, steeply banked turns pilots make to view wildlife or scenery.

GETTING THERE. Because of the Alaska bypass-mail program (rural towns receive mail and goods at parcel-post rates through regional air carriers), there are more pre-scheduled flights to hidden-away villages than you might think. Flights travel from Anchorage and Fairbanks to regional hubs like Bethel, Nome, Kotzebue, Dillingham,

and Kodiak; you'll transfer at least once (sometimes the following day) to get elsewhere.

If you're on a tight schedule or headed to a location without mail service, charter an air taxi. When arranging a flight, ask for and check references, and inquire about insurance coverage and safety records—any hesitation to fully address your concerns is a sign to move on.

PACK RIGHT. As for what to wear, *always* carry rain gear. If traveling by floatplane, you can buy, borrow, or rent hip waders. Pack in small, soft-sided bags; gear gets stashed in a plane's nooks and crannies. Finally, don't schedule a small-plane pickup for the same day you're flying out of Alaska—weather can delay flights for days.

CONTACTS Commuter lines include **Arctic Circle Air** (⊕ *www.arcticcircleair.com*) and **Frontier Flying Service** (⊕ *www.frontier-flying.com*). For a list if Alaska air taxis, see ⊕ *www.flyalaska.com*. The **National Transportation Safety Board** keeps a database (⊕ *www.ntsb.gov/ntsb/query.asp*) of air taxi safety records.

(top) de Havilland Turbine Otter on skis near Alaska Range

ALONG THE RAILS

Sit back and relax as the train chugs along and the panorama of alpine meadows, snowcapped peaks, and taiga forests unfolds. There's not a bad seat in the house!

Alaska Railroad trains run between Seward and Fairbanks via Anchorage. The *Coastal Classic* goes from Seward to Anchorage in about 4 hours. The *Denali Star* makes the Anchorage to Fairbanks trip in 12 hours. Standard railroad-coach passengers have access to dining cars, lounges, and dome cars (with windows to the ceiling). One-way, peak-season tickets range from $70 to $265, depending on the route and seat-

ing class. Service is less expensive but limited off-season.

Princess Tours and Gray Line of Alaska run luxury class service in cars connected to Alaska Railroad trains between Anchorage and Fairbanks. Day- and multiday trips are available.

MOOSE SPOTTING. Conductors may encourage you to give a "moose salute" to passing trains (see photo.) Hold your hands up as though you're being held at gunpoint, and touch your thumbs to your temples to create moose antlers. It's a fun way to say hi to your fellow travelers.

RIDE HISTORY. Since 1923, Alaskans have been flagging down the *Hurricane Turn* much like you'd hail a taxi. One of the last flag-stop trains in America, it still makes unscheduled stops to transport locals to remote cabins in the Interior.

HOW TO HAIL A TRAIN

■ Stand 25 feet from the tracks and wave a large, white cloth above your head.
■ The conductor will acknowledge you by blowing the train whistle.
■ When the train stops and the conductor opens the door (and not before), proceed toward the train.
■ Hop aboard with fellow homesteaders, hikers, and anglers.

CONTACTS Alaska Railroad Corporation (☎ *907/265-2494* or *800/544-0552* ⊕ *www. akrr.com*). **Gray Line of Alaska** (☎ *206/281-3535* or *888/452-737* ⊕ *www.graylinealaska. com*). **Princess Tours** (☎ 800/774-6237 ⊕ www.princess.com).

(top) Friendly moosing—Seymour Levy, Fodors.com photo-contest winner

ON THE ROAD

SEWARD HIGHWAY
(127 mi, Anchorage to Seward)
Region: South Central (⇨ Ch. 6)
Points of Interest: This All-American Highway (the highest designation for a National Scenic Byway) shoulders Turnagain Arm and Chugach National Forest. Dall sheep roam the mountainsides, and beluga whales swim Cook Inlet. Just north of Seward is the easily accessible Exit Glacier.

GLENN HIGHWAY
(328 mi, Anchorage to Glennallen, Gakona Junction to Tok)
Region: South Central (⇨ Ch. 6)
Points of Interest: Chugach and Talkeetna mountains, Matanuska-Susitna Valley. At Mile 50, stop at the Musk Ox Farm to learn about the animal's rare underwool (*qiviut*); head to Matanuska Glacier at Mile 101.

GEORGE PARKS HIGHWAY
(358 mi, Wasilla to Fairbanks)
Regions: South Central and Interior (⇨ Chs. 6 & 7)
Points of Interest: Enter Denali National Park & Preserve at Mile 237. At the Mile 135 turnout get an exceptional view of Mt. McKinley and access Denali State Park.

RICHARDSON HIGHWAY
(364 mi, Fairbanks to Valdez)
Regions: South Central and Interior (⇨ Chs. 6 & 7)
Points of Interest: Wrangell–St. Elias National Park and Preserve. Mile 28 provides an eyeful of Worthington Glacier near Thompson Pass. See the tumbling waterfalls and rock walls of Keystone Canyon, 15 mi north of Valdez.

DALTON HIGHWAY
(414 mi, starting 84 miles north of Fairbanks near Livengood to Deadhorse)
Regions: Interior and the Bush (⇨ Chs. 7 & 8)
Points of Interest: Watch for caribou ducking under the above-ground portion of the Trans-Alaska Pipeline. Don't get so distracted you that miss Coldfoot—your last chance to get supplies before trekking the last 234 mi to Deadhorse.

FOR MORE INFO

The Milepost (⊕ *http://milepost.com*), an extensive guide to Alaska's roadways, is an absolute must. At the end of this book, you'll find safety tips and road rules in *Travel Smart Alaska*.

(top) Taylor Highway—Som Vembar, Fodors.com photo-contest participant

Sports & Wilderness Adventures

WORD OF MOUTH

"I saw this particular bear around the camp . . . On this particular evening I took a boat ride and saw him fighting with another bear. I stopped the boat to take some photos of them, and he stood up and stared us down, then gave us a slight bluff charge. We were safe because we were in a boat, but it was still exciting."   —Brian Embacher, Photo Contest Winner

Updated
by Jessica
Bowman

Interspersed among Alaska's great mountain ranges are canyons and waterfalls, alpine valleys, salmon-rich rivers, clear lakes, blue glaciers, temperate rain forests, and sweeping, spongy tundra plains. Adding to this wealth are thousands of miles of spectacular tidal coastline. Prepare for some unforgettable outdoor adventuring!

Flip through this chapter to find tips on how best to plan your adventure in Alaska; in-depth descriptions of sports, from kayaking to skiing to biking; our favorite regions and guides for each sport; and, finally, our best wildlife-viewing advice and experiences. In regional chapters, we recommend more local outfitters and guides.

Alaska has more land in parks, wilderness areas, and wildlife refuges than all the other states combined. About one-third of Alaska's 375 million acres is set aside in protected public lands, and they are as varied as they are magnificent; recreational activities include wildlife-viewing, hiking, mountain biking, kayaking, rafting, canoeing, fishing, hunting, mountaineering, skiing, and snowboarding. Limited road access (Alaska averages only 1 mi of road for every 42 square mi of land; the U.S. average ratio is 1 to 1) means that many destinations can only be reached via airplane, boat, or all-terrain vehicle.

Even the most-visited parks—Denali National Park & Preserve, Glacier Bay National Park & Preserve, Kenai Fjords National Park, and Chugach State Park—allow backpackers and kayakers abundant opportunities for remote wilderness experiences. Parks closer to roads, and to cities like Anchorage and Fairbanks, draw more visitors. Particularly remote and solitary experiences await in the state's least-visited places, such as Wood-Tikchik State Park, where only two rangers patrol 1.6 million acres, or Aniakchak National Monument & Preserve, south of Katmai, where trekkers can go days or weeks without seeing another human.

BEST WILDLIFE VIEWING		Bears	Birds	Caribou	Dall Sheep	Whales or Marine Animals
SOUTHEAST	Alaska Chilkat Bald Eagle Preserve & Chilkat River	◑	●	○	○	○
	Alaska Marine Highway	◑	●	○	○	●
	Glacier Bay National Park & Preserve	◑	●	○	○	●
	Mendenhall Wetlands State Game Refuge	◑	●	○	○	◑
	Pack Creek	●	●	○	○	●
SOUTH CENTRAL	Chugach State Park	●	●	○	●	●
	Kenai Fjords National Park	◑	●	○	○	●
INTERIOR	Creamer's Field Migratory Waterfowl Refuge	◑	●	○	○	○
	Denali National Park & Preserve	●	●	◑	●	○
BUSH	Arctic National Wildlife Refuge	◑	●	●	○	○
	Katmai National Park	●	●	◑	○	◑
	Kodiak National Wildlife Refuge	●	●	○	○	○
	Pribilof Islands	○	●	○	○	●
	Round Island (Walrus Islands State Game Sanctuary)	○	●	○	○	●

KEY: ● = likely ◑ = somewhat ○ = not likely

PLANNING YOUR ADVENTURE

Trips to Alaska are best planned months, or even a year, in advance, particularly to the most-popular destinations, such as Denali and Glacier Bay national parks. Prime time for summer backcountry sports is June through early September. Winter sports are better enjoyed later in the season, in late February and March, when longer daylight hours return, temperatures start to rise a little, and snow conditions are unsurpassed for snowshoeing, skiing, and mushing.

Alaska's wilderness is enormous almost beyond comprehension. Visitors to the farther-flung reaches should come prepared for constantly changing and often harsh weather, difficult or impassable terrains, mosquitoes and gnats, bear or moose encounters, and other backcountry challenges. A keen knowledge of the country, proper clothing, quality camping gear, good physical condition, and excellent navigation skills are vital to suc-

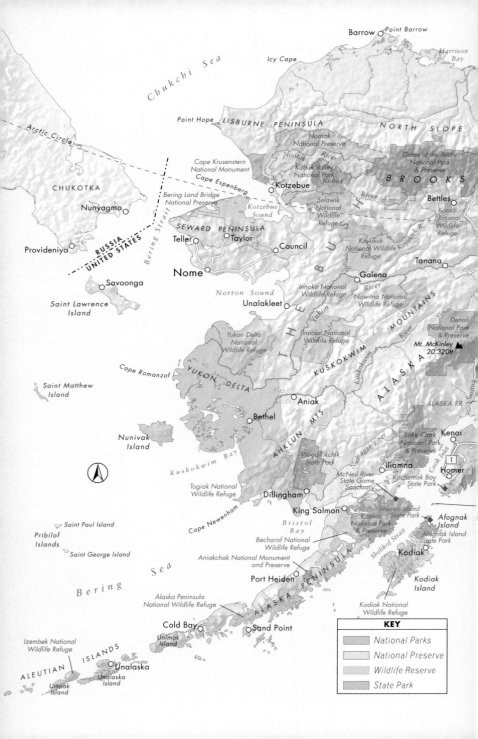

Alaska Parks & Wildlife Refuges

Beaufort   Sea

rison Bay

Prudhoe Bay
Deadhorse
Kaktovik
Mackenzie Bay
Arctic National Wildlife Refuge
Trans-Alaska Pipeline
[11]

Dalton Hwy.

PE

RANGE

Yukon Flats National Wildlife Refuge

White Mountains National Recreation Area

Fort Yukon
Steese Hwy.
Circle
Yukon-Charley Rivers National Preserve

Livengood [6]
Creamer's Field Migratory Waterfowl Refuge
Eagle

Minto Flats State Game Refuge
Fairbanks [3]

INTERIOR

Dawson

Arctic Circle

NORTHWEST TERRITORIES

0   200 miles
0   200 kilometers

Denali al Park eserve ft

RANGE [2]
Cantwell [4] [8]
Tanana River
Alaska Hwy.
[5]
Tok [2]

YUKON TERRITORY

George Parks Hwy.
[3]
Richardson Hwy.
Slana [1]
Gulkana
Nabesna
[2]

Denali State Park
Talkeetna
Wasilla
SOUTH CENTRAL
Glennallen
Chitina
McCarthy
Wrangell-Saint Elias National Park & Preserve
Alaska Hwy.
[1]

Palmer [4]
Chugach State Park

Anchorage
Girdwood
Valdez
Columbia Glacier
Copper River
Haines Junction
Hwy.
[2]
Whitehorse

Whittier [9]
Prince William Sound
Cordova
Mt. St. Elias 18,008ft
[3]

Seward
Kenai National Wildlife Refuge

BRITISH COLUMBIA

Skagway
[7]
Haines
Chilkat State Park
[1]

Kenai Fjords National Park
Yakutat
Coast Mountains

Ushagat Island/Alaska Maritime National Wildlife Refuge– Gulf of Alaska Unit

Glacier Bay National Park & Preserve
Gustavus
Juneau

gnak nd Island
Hoonah
Chichagof Island
Admiralty Island National Monument
CANADA UNITED STATES

Gulf   of   Alaska
Sitka
Baranof Island
Petersburg
Wrangell

SOUTHEAST

Alaska Marine Highway
Ketchikan

PACIFIC OCEAN
Misty Fiords National Monument
Dixon Entrance

Queen Charlotte Islands

Not all public and state lands are shown.
Less than 1% of land in Alaska is privately owned.

cessful and safe trips. Visitors without extensive wilderness experience can avoid logistical headaches and hazards by hiring local tour guides to provide equipment, direction, and necessary expertise.

CHOOSING A TRIP

Opportunities for outdoor adventures sit beyond the edge of every Alaska village, port, and city. A day—or a week—of sea-kayaking in Prince William Sound may begin a stone's throw from the streets of Whittier, which is a scenic hour's drive south of Anchorage. A much more complex trip, such as a 10-day navigation of the North Fork Koyukuk River, may require a commuter flight from Fairbanks to the remote community of Bettles, and from there a prearranged flight into the headwaters high in the Brooks Range. So the first question is whether an organized tour or a do-it-yourself trip is most appropriate for you.

The answer depends upon how much wilderness experience you have, what kind of physical condition you are in, how much time you have, and how much money you can afford to spend on gear and logistics. ■TIP→ The Alaska wilderness can be as difficult to navigate as it is beautiful; do not step into "the last frontier" poorly prepared. Plan ahead. Know when to enlist the services of local guides or outfitters; allowing these professionals to provide vital gear, expertise, and direction can make your adventure safer, more comfortable, and more fulfilling.

RESOURCES

With proper planning and the help of local professionals, there's an Alaska trip to be had—and likely many trips—just for you, no matter your age, physical ability, or level of wilderness savvy. The first step is to obtain a list of outfitters and guides who are permitted to operate in the regions you plan to visit. Such a list is available from the staff of the refuge, forest, or park you want to visit. When contacting businesses, learn about the guides, the nature of the activities they offer, and the area you want to explore. Also be sure to determine how well the guides know the area and how long they've been in operation. Make it a point to ask for references. Throughout this book you'll find in-depth information about all of Alaska's regions; contact information and insider tips are provided for every park, refuge, and wildland that we deem worthy of a visit.

Here are some top organizations to help you get started:

A state-produced *Alaska Vacation Planner* (which also contains information on ecotourism) can be obtained from the **Alaska Travel Industry Association** (☎907/929–

MOUNTAINS' MAJESTY

Four great mountain ranges—the St. Elias, Alaska, Brooks, and Chugach—and more than 30 lesser chains sweep through the state. The St. Elias Mountains form the highest coastal range in the world; the Alaska Range contains North America's highest peak (Mt. McKinley, 20,320 feet); the Brooks Range roughly follows the Arctic Circle; and the Chugach arcs through Alaska's most populous region.

2200, 800/862–5275 to order vacation planners ⊕www.travelalaska.
com).

The **Alaska Wilderness Recreation and Tourism Association** (☎907/258–3171 ⊕www.awrta.org) can provide information on many businesses and activities across the state.

Recreational Equipment Inc. (☎907/272–4565 ⊕www.rei.com) is a great resource for equipment needs.

Larger tour companies will take care of everything if you want to just sit back and be guided through a specific part of the state doing a variety of activities. In some cases they offer shorter tours and activities for independent travelers. Ask about timing and pricing.

Gray Line of Alaska (☎206/281–3535 or 800/542–1737 ⊕www.graylinealaska.com).

Princess Cruises and Tours (☎800/426–0500 ⊕www.princesslodges.com).

Smaller, independent tour companies and agencies offer, you guessed it, smaller-scale tours and packages; they are good resources for tailor-made Alaska journeys. See individual sports listed in this chapter for specialized Alaska-based companies.

Alaska Bound (☎231/439–3000 or 888/252–7527 ⊕www.alaskabound.com).

Alaska Tour & Travel (☎907/245–0200 or 800/208–0200 ⊕www.alaskatravel.com).

Alaska Tours (☎907/277–3000 or 866/317–3325 ⊕www.alaskatours.com).

Viking Travel, Inc. (☎907/772–3818 or 800/327–2571 ⊕www.alaskaferry.com).

MONEY MATTERS

To reserve a spot, most tour operators require a deposit, with the balance due before your start date. In most cases, if you cancel your reservation you get at least a partial refund, but policies vary widely. ■TIP→ Find out how far in advance you must cancel to get a full refund, and ask whether any allowances are made for cancellations due to medical emergencies. If cancellation insurance is available, you may want to take it. You'll receive a full refund regardless of the reason for your cancellation.

Taxes are generally not included in the quoted price and can add substantially to the cost of your trip. Depending on the program, you should inquire about which members of the tour personnel customarily get tipped and what the going rate is.

SAFETY FIRST

In choosing a guide, a primary concern should be safety. A guide should be equipped with proper technical and first-aid gear and should know how to use it.

If you have no experience in the activity, ask what sort of training you'll receive. Explain your own goals and abilities, and ask about the difficulty of the terrain; 1 mi across hilly, trail-less tundra may demand the same energy as 2 or 3 mi on a flat, maintained trail. Most guides plan trips so that you'll have time to relax, enjoy the landscape, and look for wildlife, but it's a good idea to ask about the travel schedule and number of miles to be covered daily. As a general rule, hikers in good physical condition should be able to travel 2 mi an hour on maintained trails and about 1 mi per hour or less across trail-less terrain. Traveling 6 or 7 mi per day, even on trails, is likely to be tiring for a novice. Be honest with the guide regarding your level of expertise.

The amount of weight carried on your back will also influence your traveling ability, especially if you haven't carried a heavy pack before, so determine the amount of gear you'll be required to carry, particularly if you'll be hiking, backpacking, or glacier trekking.

GEAR & WEATHER

Ask what gear the company will provide. Guides normally provide group gear, such as tents and tarps, and expect you to provide your own personal equipment, such as boots, rain gear, a pack, and a sleeping bag. Some guides rent gear such as sleeping bags and packs.

Ask about the weather. From the temperate rain forests of the Tongass National Forest in Alaska's Southeast to the inland deserts of the Northwest, climates vary greatly. No matter what region you visit, always come prepared for cool, wet weather, even in midsummer. Insect repellent (and sometimes head nets) may be required to ward off mosquitoes, flies, and no-see-ums during all snow-free months.

LODGING

From beautiful wilderness lodges to remote campsites to spongy tundra, your lodging options are immensely varied. Where will you be happiest settling in to sleep after a day of adventuring?

PUBLIC-USE CABINS

Not all Alaska wilderness trips require the expense of luxury lodges or the sacrifices of tent camping. For between $15 and $65 per night, backcountry travelers can have a million-dollar view and a roof over their heads at one of more than 250 public-use cabins available across the state. Cabin costs and locations depend upon which of five land-management agencies they fall under—the U.S. Forest Service, National Wildlife Refuges, National Park Service, Bureau of Land Management, or Alaska State Parks. Most cabins are remote or semiremote and must be reached by plane, boat, or trail. ■TIP➜ Almost all must be reserved in advance, either

EVERYBODY LOVES THE SUNSHINE

In most parts of the state, June through August are considered prime months for summer backcountry trips. July is usually the warmest month. Hope for sunshine, but come prepared for rain, especially in August.

in person, by mail, or online; in some cases nominal service fees may be charged for cancellations.

Accommodations are rustic; most cabins have bunks or wooden sleeping platforms, tables, heating stoves, outdoor fire pits, outhouses, and, sometimes, skiffs. Agency Web sites offer descriptions of individual cabins, including the number of bunks, types of stoves, and other amenities visitors can expect. Visitors who fly to cabins located on lakes or in coastal areas where skiffs are provided can usually rent outboards and gasoline tanks in the closest town and bring them along.

STEP LIGHTLY

Ecotourists aim to travel responsibly. Typically, ecotourism is on a smaller scale and involves more education than traditional tourism; often, you are led by guides who know the local natural history and cultures. Itineraries allow you a closer connection to the areas explored. As one Alaska guide says, "Slow down, take a deep breath, feel where you are." The **International Ecotourism Society** (⊕ *www.ecotourism.org*) is a great resource.

The most convenient way to shop for public-use cabins is to visit the listings posted online by the agencies that oversee them. Listings for individual cabins include notes on accessibility (you may need to charter a floatplane from the nearest community, paddle a sea kayak, hike, mountain-bike, or travel in on horseback). Logbooks are provided at most cabins; check out entries from previous guests about area hikes, wildlife sightings, and fishing opportunities.

For the central **National Park Service** (⊕*www.nps.gov/aplic/cabins*) information listing about the cabins, visit their Web site.

In order to reserve any public-use cabin, log on to ⊕*www.recreation. gov* or call ☎*877/444–6777, 518/885–3639 international.*

Alaska State Parks. More than 50 cabins are maintained over a huge area between Ketchikan and Fairbanks. Some are road accessible; reservations can be made up to six months in advance. Cabins vary in size, with sleeping capacity ranging from 3 to 10 people. For more information or to reserve a cabin online, contact the Department of Natural Resources Public Information Center in Anchorage. ☎*907/269–8400* ⊕*www.dnr.state.ak.us/parks/cabins/index.htm.*

Bureau of Land Management. Several public-use cabins are in the White Mountains National Recreation Area near Fairbanks. Cabins can be booked up to 30 days in advance by mail or phone or in person. Contact the Bureau of Land Management Land Information Center. ☖*1150 University Ave., Fairbanks, 99709-3844* ☎*907/474–2200 or 800/437–7021* ⊕*www.blm.gov/ak/st/en.html.*

National Park Service. Cabins are available in Kenai Fjords National Park, Wrangell–St. Elias National Park, and Yukon–Charley Rivers National Park. ☎*907/224–2132 in Kenai Fjords, 907/822–5234 in Wrangell–St. Elias, 907/547–2233 in Yukon–Charley* ⊕*www.nps. gov/akso*

National Wildlife Refuges. Kodiak National Wildlife Refuge on Kodiak Island has eight public-use cabins. They can only be reached by floatplane or boat. Reservations are scheduled by a lottery. Applications, which may be mailed or delivered in person, are accepted until the last business day before the drawing date. ⌂*1390 Buskin River Rd.,,Kodiak 99615* ☎*907/487–2600 or 888/408–3514* ⊕*kodiak.fws.gov.*

U.S. Forest Service. The agency maintains more than 150 cabins in the Southeast's Tongass National Forest, and more than 40 in the Chugach National Forest in South Central. Most cabins can be reached only by boat or plane; those accessible by trails are very popular and frequently booked months in advance. Maximum stays range from three to seven nights in summer. Cabin reservations may be made up to six months ahead. ☎*877/444–6777, 518/885–3639 international* ⊕*www.fs.fed. us/r10.*

WILDERNESS LODGES

If your goal is to really get away from it all, consider booking a remote Alaska wilderness lodge. Some of the most popular are in the river drainages of Bristol Bay, in the secluded bays of Southeast Alaska, along the western edge of Cook Inlet, around Katmai and Lake Clark national parks, and in the Susitna Valley north of Anchorage. Most of these lodges specialize in fishing and/or bear-viewing. Lodges in and near Denali emphasize opportunities to explore the wilderness as well as natural-history programs. Activities can also include dog-mushing, hiking, rafting, flightseeing, horseback riding, and gold panning.

Lodge stays generally include daily guided trips and all meals. Fees can be expensive (daily rates of $300–$900 per person). Study their Web sites and list your favorites. E-mail or phone (many lodge operators provide toll-free numbers) with questions regarding activities offered, prices, gratuities, and what you should expect. ■TIP➔ Some of the more popular lodges need to be booked at least a year in advance, though last-minute cancellations can create openings even late in the season.

For listings of wilderness lodges throughout Alaska, including individual Web sites, phone numbers, and general information, visit ⊕*www.travelalaska.com* or ⊕*www.alaska.com.* As you read through this book, you'll find plenty of recommendations for great wilderness lodges. Below we've listed three options.

Afognak Wilderness Lodge. This rustic log lodge is set amid the coastal wilderness of Afognak State Park on Afognak Island north of Kodiak. Featured activities include fishing, photography, and guided wildlife-viewing—including brown bear, deer, whales, and other marine wildlife. Guests stay in private, two-bedroom cabins with hot running water and other creature comforts. ☎*907/486–6442 or 800/478–6442* ⊕*www.afognaklodge.com.*

Denali Backcountry Lodge. It's in the very heart of Denali National Park & Preserve. Activities for overnight guests include naturalist programs; hiking; fishing; gold panning; mountain biking; and, for an extra fee, flightseeing when weather permits. Family-style meals emphasizing

Alaska fare are included in the room rate. ☎*907/376–1992 or 877/233–6254* ⊕*www.denalilodge.com.*

Tutka Bay Wilderness Lodge. Perched among spruces and coastal western hemlocks overlooking Kachemak Bay, the lodge is reached via plane or boat. You can spend your time sea-kayaking, sportfishing, birding, bear and marine wildlife-viewing, and relaxing in the open-air hot tub. ☎*907/235–3905 or 800/606–3909* ⊕*www.tutkabaylodge.com.*

CAMPING

There are hundreds of campgrounds, public and private, along Alaska's roads. They typically include sites for tent and RV camping, with fire pits, latrines, running potable water, and picnic benches. Most campsites are on a first-come, first-served basis.

BACKCOUNTRY & PARKLAND CAMPING

If you wish to explore Alaska's vast wilderness, you will almost certainly have to establish your own campsites (though some parks do have remote tent sites). Before heading into the backcountry, contact the appropriate management agency, such as the state or national park that you'll be visiting for advice and/or restrictions.

Whenever camping in the wilderness, be on the lookout for water sources, effective drainage, protection from high winds, and game trails (which in bear country should be avoided—and nearly all of Alaska is bear country). Campers should practice low-impact camping techniques to minimize environmental damage. For example carry out *all* garbage; avoid camping on fragile vegetation; if possible, camp on already-established sites; never cut standing trees; wash yourself, your clothes, and your dishes at least 100 feet from water sources; bring a trowel and dig "cat-hole" latrines for human waste at least 100 feet from your camp, water sources, and trails; and burn or carry out toilet paper. When traveling in trail-less, particularly tundra, areas fan out instead of walking single file to avoid trampling vegetation.

RESOURCES   Information on roadside camping can be obtained at **Alaska Public Land Information Centers** (⊕ *www.nps.gov/aplic/center)* in Tok, Fairbanks, and Anchorage, and at park, refuge, and national-forest headquarters across the state.

CAR & RV CAMPING

RV camping is popular along Alaska's road systems because it allows visitors the freedom to create their own itineraries while traveling in relative comfort. Although many drive their own vehicles up the Alaska Highway from Canada and the Lower 48, others choose to fly or cruise to Alaska and rent SUVs or motor homes once they arrive. Between

June and August—peak summer season—motor-home rentals range from $125 to $200 per day, depending upon size and model. To save money, opt for weeklong packages and off-season prices offered by most rental companies.

Campgrounds and dump stations—including state, federal, and privately owned operations—as well as propane services are in or near almost all communities along Alaska's highway system. State campgrounds provide overnight camping for $10 to $15 per night, depending upon the facility; dump-station use fees are $5. On public lands along remote stretches of highway, pleasant, free camping can sometimes be found in clearings, pulloffs, and old gravel pits.

RESOURCES   *The Milepost* (⊕ *www.themilepost.com*) offers mile-by-mile information on all of Alaska's main highways.

The state of Alaska publishes a free informative guide called *RV Tips: Trip Information Planning Booklet: A practical guide to campgrounds, dump stations, and propane services along Alaska's highways.* To view the guide online, go to ⊕ *www.dced.state.ak.us/ oed/student_info/pub/rvtips.pdf.*

For more information about individual state campgrounds, locations, fees, and services, visit the **Alaska Department of Natural Resources** (⊕ *www.dnr.state.ak.us/parks/asp/fees.htm)* Web site.

EQUIPMENT

Get the best equipment you can afford; it's an absolute must in Alaska. Quality gear is a good investment, and it can make your trip to Alaska safer and that much more comfortable and enjoyable. ■TIP→ Before you go on an organized trip, ask your guide what gear will be supplied, and what won't.

THE ESSENTIAL ITEMS

When setting out for a day hike from base camp, it's wise to carry a first-aid kit, including bandages and moleskin; bear spray; a plastic bottle of drinking water; high-energy snacks; a warm sweater or jacket; windproof rain gear, in case the weather suddenly changes (avoid cotton clothing as it does not retain body warmth when wet); a disposable lighter; fire starters, such as a candle or heat tab; a flare or flashlight; a knife (preferably a multifunctional pocketknife); a topographical map; toilet paper; sunglasses and sunblock; bug repellent; duct tape, for all kinds of emergencies; and a compass or a handheld global-positioning device. This list

COMPASS NOTE

The farther north you travel, the more the compass needle will be skewed upward and to the east of north by several degrees. U.S. Geological Survey maps show this difference between magnetic and true north, called magnetic declination, at the bottom of maps. With these maps you can use your compass accordingly; otherwise, allow for this deviation as you do your compass reading. Or, better yet, get a handheld global-positioning system.

Alaska offers plenty of adventure for travelers on two wheels.

may seem long, but these items should combine to weigh less than 10 pounds and fit easily into a day pack. If you somehow get lost, hurt, or caught in a sudden weather event, these things could save your life.

BACKPACKS First decide whether to get a pack with an internal or external frame. If you choose the latter, pick one that balances the pack upright when you set it on the ground; this is a great help in the areas of Alaska that don't have trees. Internal frames are an advantage when going through brush, which is common in Alaska. A rainproof cover for your pack is a good idea, even if it's just a heavy plastic garbage bag.

TENTS Because winterlike storms can occur almost anytime, a freestanding four-season tent is recommended, one that can withstand strong winds and persistent rainfall (or even snow squalls). Tie-down ropes and tent flies are essential items, and mosquito netting is another must.

SLEEPING GEAR For sleeping comfort, bring a sleeping pad to add cushioning and insulation beneath your sleeping bag. Be sure your bag is warm enough for the changing conditions; even in midsummer, nighttime temperatures may fall to the freezing mark, especially in the mountains.

COOKING GEAR Bring a lightweight camping stove with fuel. Firewood may be scarce and what there is may be wet. Burning wood in many parklands is frowned upon or prohibited in order to protect the surroundings.

Besides a stove, fuel, and matches or a butane lighter, necessary cooking items include light but sturdy utensils; a bowl and mug (drinking hot beverages is a great way to stay both warm and hydrated); a pot or two for heating water and cooking; a potholder; and a dependable—because everything can depend on it—pocketknife.

After an uphill climb, a hiker enjoys the view of a massive glacier.

SPORTS, TOP REGIONS & TOURS

Alaska! It's a gigantic, vibrant state teeming with fish-packed rivers, snow-dusted mountaintops, and massive glaciers. Who has a travel wish list that *doesn't* include this enormous frontier? Thrill-seekers might check out helicopter skiing in the Chugach Mountains out of Girdwood, Valdez, or Cordova, or rafting in Denali National Park and Preserve. Sea kayakers will find solitude and abundant marine wildlife in the Southeast's Glacier Bay or South Central's Kenai Fjords.

Backcountry adventurers can escape civilization with a sled-dog team in Gates of the Arctic National Park far above the Arctic Circle, or in the Susitna Valley less than a two-hour drive north of Anchorage. The Aleutian and Pribilof islands are bird-watching meccas, while Katmai National Park and Kodiak National Wildlife Refuge are hot spots for bear viewing. An increasing number of trips and tours now make it possible to spend a week or two (or more) learning—and performing—feats from horse packing within sight of Mt. McKinley to hiking or mountain biking through some of the state's most challenging landscapes. Below you'll find our favorite sports, along with recommended trips and experiences, questions to consider, and suggestions to help you choose the right program. Check out the "Sports, the Outdoors & Guided Tours" sections in our regional chapters, from Anchorage to South Central to Southeast, for more details and additional rental and tour options.

BIKING

There's just nothing like pedaling through weaving stalks of fireweed and feeling a light breeze on your face as you take in the lush, intimidating, and all-encompassing landscape of Alaska. Biking is an excellent way to see the state, whether it's on a prearranged tour or an afternoon jaunt on some rented wheels. There are bike-rental shops in larger communities such as Anchorage and Fairbanks; they frequently offer street maps and can tell you their favorite routes. Alaska's dirt trails, including many within city parks, promise biking opportunities for cyclists of all abilities, while hundreds of miles of paved trails and highways provide choice touring routes. Whether you plan to grind your way up a dusty mountain path or cruise swiftly along a well-traveled highway, come prepared to handle emergencies. Always carry a basic bicycle repair kit including chain tool, Allen wrenches, spare inner tubes, and tube-repair materials, along with a compact bicycle-tire pump. Bring plenty of fluids (either in water bottles or camel packs), enough food to sustain your energy, and a light jacket or rain shell.

TOP REGIONS & EXPERIENCES

Biking is especially popular within the larger cities and along the road systems of South Central and the Interior. Favored touring routes include the unpaved Denali and Taylor highways and McCarthy Road. The Copper River Highway outside Cordova and some of the less-traveled roads north of Fairbanks also beckon cyclists seeking several-speed adventures. Biking is a fantastic way to explore the Southeast's coastal towns via the Alaska Marine Highway System.

UNDERSTATEMENT OF THE YEAR

Calling Alaska "gigantic" is a serious understatement: if you place a map of Alaska on top of a map of the Lower 48 states, its boundaries would extend from the Canadian border to the Mexican border and from the Atlantic to the Pacific.

SOUTHEAST Biking Southeast Alaska can be an exhilarating if sometimes wet experience. The **Alaska Marine Highway System** (⊕*www.dot.state.ak.us/ amhs*) charges a fee ($15–$50, depending on your route) if you bring your bike aboard. It's well worth it. While aboard the ferry, watch for breaching whales, then stop in small towns to check out gold-rush history, salmon bakes, and cute boardwalks and bed-and-breakfasts.

ANCHORAGE & ENVIRONS Alaska's largest city is laced with excellent biking opportunities—some challenging, others easy, all scenic—within and just outside city limits. For a comprehensive guide to mountain biking in the Anchorage area, pick up a copy of *Mountain Bike Anchorage* by Rosemary Austin. The **Tony Knowles Coastal Trail** is 11 glorious mi of paved trail following the coastline from downtown past Westchester Lagoon. Check out the spectacular views of Mt. Susitna (locally called Sleeping Lady), Cook Inlet, and the Chugach Range. Ride the trail all the way to **Kincaid Park** to enjoy its 40 mi of dirt trails through acres of spruce and birch forest. Keep an eye out for moose! Our favorite trails include those along Anchorage's eastern edge in **Far North Bicentennial Park** and around **Eklutna Lake,** located a short drive northeast of the city.

KENAI PENINSULA & PRINCE WILLIAM SOUND A relatively short drive from Anchorage, the Kenai Peninsula offers outstanding opportunities for mountain bikers seeking thigh-busting challenges amid extraordinary scenery. **Crescent Creek Trail** (at Mile 44.9 of Sterling Highway; drive 3 mi to the trailhead at end of gravel road); **Devil's Pass** (at Mile 39.5 of Seward Highway); **Johnson Pass** (at Miles 32.6 and 63.7 of Seward Highway); and the **Resurrection trail systems** offer miles of riding for a wide range of expertise. Cyclists here are subject to highly fickle mountain weather patterns. But remember that you're never really alone in wild Alaska: be sure to bring along bear spray and bug dope (repellent). For maps and descriptions of trails, visit the state Department of Natural Resources Web site at ⊕*www.dnr.state.ak.us/parks/aktrails/ats/ken-ats.htm.*

FAIRBANKS   Visitors to Alaska's Golden Heart City will find plenty of biking opportunities around town. People in these parts are becoming big biking fans—it's a trend that keeps lots of the trails well maintained. The **Back Door Trail** is part of the **Ester Dome Trails system**, which has miles of mountain-biking trails ranging from single tracks to fire roads. Back Door Trail stretches over 8 mi with an 800-foot elevation gain; it's rated by the Fairbanks Cycle Club as easy. To get started, drive west of Fairbanks on Parks Highway; turn right on Old Nenana Highway. Park at Ester Community Park near the firehouse just before the Ester turnoff.

BIKING TO CRESCENT

The ascent is gradual, but the trek over Crescent Creek Trail, 100 highway mi south of Anchorage, can feel steeper and longer under a hot July sun. In places, the trail goes almost vertical, and hairpin switchbacks broken by spruce roots require caution. None of that seems to matter, though, once Crescent Lake appears through the cottonwoods. On a windless afternoon the lake resembles an ice-blue gem surrounded by rocky ridgelines and an endless sky.

One of our favorite rides, the paved multiuse **Farmers Loop Bike Path** winds through suburbs and farmlands, passing by Creamer's Field Migratory Waterfowl Refuge. The path starts on the University of Alaska campus (at the corner of University and College) and takes you on a loop to the Steese Highway and back to town. The **University Ski Trails** on the University of Alaska Fairbanks campus (look for the well-marked trailhead and parking lot off Tanana Loop Road) are pretty good stuff with 15 mi of dirt trails and a 1,500-foot elevation gain.

RESOURCES & GUIDES

★ **Alaska Backcountry Bike Tours.** Based in Palmer, north of Anchorage, this company offers guided day and multiday trips; rental options include hard-tail and full-suspension bikes. ☎866/354–2453 ⊕*www.mountainbikealaska.com.*

★ **Alaska Bicycle Tours/Sockeye Cycle Company.** Based in Haines, and in summertime in Skagway, these folks specialize in guided bike tours of the Southeast and remote sections of Canada's Northwest and Yukon. They also recently celebrated 20 years of business in Alaska. ☎907/766–2869 or 877/292–4154 ⊕*www.cyclealaska.com.*

Alaskabike. Starting in Anchorage, these multiday touring packages explore South Central and nearby scenic highways. ☎907/245–2175 ⊕*www.alaskabike.com.*

★ **Alaska Outdoor Rentals & Guides.** This family-operated Fairbanks business provides bicycle rentals and guided tours of the area, as well as information on touring and routes. ☎907/457–2453 ⊕*www.akbike.com.*

Backroads. Offering a challenging eight-day trip through South Central, this tried-and-true tour company is worth the investment. ☎*510/527– 1555 or 800/462–2848* ⊕*www.backroads.com.*

Denali Outdoor Center. This operator in Denali National Park & Preserve offers bicycle rentals and guided tours into the park. ☎*907/683–1925 or 888/303–1925* ⊕*www.denalioutdoorcenter.com.*

Downtown Bicycle Rental, Inc. Located in downtown Anchorage near the head of the popular Tony Knowles Coastal Trail, this rental shop has a large selection of quality bikes and accessories. ☎*907/279–5293* ⊕*www.alaska-bike-rentals.com.*

Fairbanks Cycle Club. Find information on touring and mountain-biking routes around Fairbanks. ☎*907/459–8008* ⊕*www.fairbankscycle-club.org.*

Lifetime Adventures. Operating out of the state parks campground at Eklutna Lake, about 26 mi northeast of Anchorage, Lifetime rents bikes and trailers. They also have a popular Paddle & Pedal package in which you paddle in one direction and pedal your way back. ☎*800/952–8624* ⊕*www.lifetimeadventures.net.*

CANOEING

The art of canoeing is peaceful, invigorating, and unsurpassed in Alaska, as the state boasts 3 million lakes and 3,000 rivers. Although it's possible to launch at any of hundreds of lakes and streams crossing Alaska's road system, the most easily accessed canoe trail systems with well-marked, maintained portages are found in South Central. Canoes, paddles, and life vests can be rented for $20 to $30 a day from area rental outfits.

Lakes and rivers around sea level in South Central are usually ice-free from mid-May through September, while those at higher elevations and in the Interior and northern regions are more likely ice-free from early June to mid-September. Many paddlers find the first couple of weeks after breakup and the final two weeks before freeze-up the most pleasant, for their cool temperatures and absence of mosquitoes and black flies.

TOP REGIONS & EXPERIENCES

Three spectacular canoe trail systems are located in South Central, including the **Swan Lake Canoe Trail** and **Swanson River Canoe Trail,** both set in the 1.3-million-acre Kenai

PEACEFUL PADDLING

From your canoe seat the world seems a simpler place. The air is still, the lake reflects autumn colors and blue sky. A trout rises for a midge, skims gracefully on the water's skin, and leaves behind a silver wake that brightens as it spreads. The full moon peeks over the mountains to the east—there will be frost in the morning—and you wonder as you paddle quietly back to camp if tonight you'll hear wolves howling.

National Wildlife Refuge on the Kenai Peninsula, and the **Nancy Lake Canoe Trail** in the Susitna Valley.

The **Nancy Lake Canoe Trail** system is off the Parks Highway about a 90-minute drive north of Anchorage. The system is managed by Alaska State Parks and features an 8-mi-long chain of lakes. Portages are well marked with orange, diamond-shape signs marked with a "P." Wet sections are covered with boardwalk.

Experienced wilderness paddlers seeking some truly far-flung waters should explore systems like the Interior's Fortymile River Trail, Innoko River Trail, or Lower Beaver Creek Water Trails.

The **Swan Lake Canoe Trail** system includes a 60-mi-long series of lakes and small streams connected by overland portages ranging from a few hundred feet to more than a mile. The system can be entered through any of three trailhead entrances off Swanson River Road outside Sterling (head out of town on the Sterling Highway and turn off at Milepost 83.4). Trails are managed by the Kenai National Wildlife Refuge, which accurately describes the landscape as rolling hill country. There are plenty of spruce and birch forests here, plus amazing views of the Kenai Mountains to the east. Portages vary in condition.

The popular **Swanson River Canoe Trail** system, also set within the Kenai National Wildlife Refuge, is 50 mi long. The landscape is as wonderful as that of Swan Lake, with maintained portages ranging from a few hundred feet to more than a mile long. Follow the same driving directions as for Swan Lake out of Sterling.

RESOURCES & GUIDES

Alaska Canoe & Campground. This outfit rents within Kenai National Wildlife Refuge. ☎*907/262–2331* ⊕*www.alaskacanoetrips.com.*

Alaska Department of Natural Resources. Check out the listings of canoe trails throughout the state, along with maps. ⊕*www.dnr.state.ak.us/ parks/aktrails/atstrans.htm*

★ **Alaska Discovery.** One of the oldest outfits in the state and part of the Mountain Travel Sobek Company, these folks are based in the Southeast and organize trips in the region and beyond, including a river trip on the Noatak River in the Brooks Range. ☎*800/586–1911* ⊕*www. akdiscovery.com.*

Backcountry Safaris. This Anchorage outfit, with 20 years of experience, has reasonable canoe-rental rates. ☎*907/222–1632 or 877/812–2159* ⊕*www.backcountrysafaris.com.*

Recreational Equipment Inc. The Anchorage outpost rents canoes and accessories. ☎*907/272–4565* ⊕*www.rei.com.*

DOGSLEDDING

Decades ago, before snowmobiles and airplanes became mainstays of winter travel, dog teams provided transportation for rural Alaskans. Some of the finest dog teams in the state hailed from remote native villages. Today mushing is widely considered Alaska's state sport. That said, it's definitely not for everyone. For one thing, you have to like the cold. You also have to like roughing it. Even the nicest accommodations are only a step or two removed from camping. You also have to like dogs—a lot. Contrary to the romantic image you may have of sled dogs, they're not all cuddly, clean Siberian huskies. Most mushers, including the people who run dogsled tours, take very good care of their dogs, but the dogs are working animals, not show dogs; they're not, in the general sense of the word, pets.

Here are some facts to consider: on some mushing trips, participants travel by cross-country skiing or snowshoeing, rather than actually mushing, for at least part of the trip; some introduction to these sports is usually included in your orientation. ■ **TIP→ If you're not interested in skiing or snowshoeing, make sure you'll be given a sled. It's always a good idea to ask the outfitter how strenuous the pace is.** If you're expecting a relaxing vacation, don't pick an outfitter who will have you doing everything from hitching up the dogs to pitching tents.

TOP REGIONS & EXPERIENCES

ANCHORAGE & SOUTH CENTRAL
There are notable mushing communities in South Central, especially the Mat-Su Valley and Kenai Peninsula, and in the Interior around Fairbanks. Every year mushers traverse the wilderness between Anchorage and Nome in the famous **Iditarod Trail Sled Dog Race**. Other sprint and long-distance races in the area draw competitors and fans. Among the best are the **World Championship Sled Dog Race** held each February in Anchorage during the Fur Rendezvous celebration. On the Kenai Peninsula, Kasilof (off the Sterling Highway) is home to many notable mushers.

FAIRBANKS & THE INTERIOR
The **Open North American Championships** are held every March in Fairbanks. The 1,000-mi-long **Yukon Quest** between Fairbanks and Whitehorse, Yukon, also lures mushers from around the globe. Local outfitters can set you up for a daylong sled ride, complete with a visit to the kennels.

RESOURCES & GUIDES

Chugach Express Dog Sled Tours. Year-round mushing tours pass through a valley surrounded by the Chugach Mountains, about an hour's drive south of Anchorage. The one-hour tours include a visit to the kennel of the owner, a former Iditarod musher. ☎*907/783–2266 for reservations ⊕www.chugach-express.com.*

WOOF

"Hike!" yells a musher as she releases the brake. On command, a team of surprisingly small but amazingly strong huskies charges off, howling with excitement. Of all the wild sporting adventures out there, dogsledding may be the wildest. There's usually enough snow for dogsled runs from late October or November through March or early April.

Cotter Kennels. Operating outside Fairbanks, at the Chena Hot Springs Resort, these Yukon Quest winner and Iditarod top-three finishers offer dogsled rides in winter and dog-cart rides in summer. ☎907/451–8104 or 800/478–4681 ⊕www.chenahotsprings.com.

IdidaRide Sled Dog Tours. This family outfit out of Seward—including Mitch Seavey, winner of the 2004 Iditarod and the 2008 Alaska Sweepstakes—on the Kenai Peninsula runs wintertime tours out of Anchorage, Seward, and Sterling with their Iditarod dogs. ☎907/224–8607 or 800/478–3139 ⊕www.ididaride.com.

Plettner Sled Dog Kennels. Lynda Plettner, Iditarod veteran, offers mushing tours through the Mat-Su Valley, with prices starting at $100; reservations are required. Summer kennel tours are offered as well. The kennels are located a 90-minute drive north of Anchorage off the Parks Highway. ☎877/892–6944 ⊕www.plettner-kennels.com.

FLIGHTSEEING

Amelia Earhart said, "You haven't seen a tree until you've seen its shadow from the sky." Alaska is full of trees, and luckily, full of flightseeing opportunities as well. Air-taxi services in all major cities and many smaller communities offer flightseeing tours. Most offer a variety of packages, allowing clients to design their own tours if discussed in advance. The smaller companies are often more flexible, while the multiplane companies can better match plane size to your needs. Prices usually depend on the size of the plane, number of clients, and length of the tour. As with taxicabs, passengers can often split costs. Generally, a half-hour flightseeing trip runs each person between $65 and $85, with a two- or three-person minimum, depending on aircraft size. Hourly rates, depending on the plane's size and the competition, can run from $85 to more than $300. If there's a drop-off and pick-up involved, you pay for all the time the plane is operating, in both directions. ■TIP→ Shop around before committing to any one service; some very good flightseeing bargains are available.

Flights in smaller planes and helicopters are particularly dependent upon weather. In some cases, clouds may simply obscure certain sites, while bad weather often grounds pilots altogether, forcing tours to be canceled. Ask about cancellation policies if you've paid in advance, and never push a pilot do something he or she is reluctant to do; rearranging your schedule is a much better option than flying into a mountain.

TOP REGIONS & EXPERIENCES

SOUTHEAST   In the Southeast, flightseeing services based in communities surrounding **Misty Fiords National Monument, the Tongass National Forest, Mendenhall Glacier,** and **Glacier Bay National Park & Preserve** offer aerial views of coastal mountain ranges, remote shorelines, glaciers, ice fields, and wildlife. Some even include opportunities to land and fish, or view local wildlife, such as brown bears, black bears, sea otters, seals, and whales. Visitors passing through the Southeast on cruise lines or via the Alaska Marine Highway System will find flightseeing options in all ports.

Flightseeing over Mt. McKinley may be one of the most awesome experiences the state has to offer.

ANCHORAGE & SOUTH CENTRAL

This area is the state's air-travel hub. Plenty of flightseeing services operating out of city airports and floatplane bases can take you on spectacular tours of **Mt. McKinley, the Chugach Range, Prince William Sound, Kenai Fjords National Park,** and the **Harding Icefield.** Flightseeing services are available in Seward, Homer, Talkeetna, and other South Central communities. Anchorage hosts the greatest number and variety of services, including those operating fixed-wing aircraft, floatplanes, and helicopters.

THE BUSH

Why not head to the state's most remote parts in a small plane? Check out scenic **Katmai National Park & Preserve** and the **Valley of 10,000 Smokes,** a volcanic region of steaming calderas and hardened lava moonscapes. Most services are based in the communities of King Salmon or Naknek, which are served by a common airport with jet service from Anchorage.

RESOURCES & GUIDES

★ **Emerald Air Service.** A company that gets great reviews on Fodors.com, Emerald is based in Homer; they'll take you to remote southwestern bear country. All-day trips run $550 per person. ☎907/235–6993 ⊕www.emeraldairservice.com.

Frontier Flying Service Inc. This Fairbanks-based operation serves Interior Alaska's isolated towns and villages. ☎907/450–7200 or 800/478–6779 ⊕www.frontierflying.com/index.shtml.

Katmailand. This outfit has concessions at Brooks and Grosvenor lodges in Katmai National Park. ☎800/544–0551 ⊕www.katmailand.com.

★ **Rust's Flying Service.** An Anchorage company in business since 1963, Rust's will take you on narrated flightseeing tours of Mt. McKinley and Denali, Columbia Glacier, and Prince William Sound. ☎907/243–1595 or 800/544–2299 ⊕www.flyrusts.com.

Southeast Aviation. This Ketchikan-based operation offers floatplane tours of the glaciers and mountains of Misty Fiords National Monument. Wildlife sightings are quite common. ☎907/225–2900 or 888/359–6478 ⊕www.southeastaviation.com.

Talkeetna Aero Services. These folks are located a two-hour drive north of Anchorage, in the shadow of McKinley; take a twin-engine aerial tour of the mountain. ☎*907/733–2899, 907/683–2899, or 888/733–2899* ⊕*www.talkeetna-aero.com.*

Talkeetna Air Taxi. Check out McKinley and environs, then swoop down to a glacier to test your boots. ☎*907/733–2218 or 800/533–2219* ⊕*www.talkeetnaair.com.*

★ **Wings Airways and Taku Glacier Lodge.** This Juneau-based company specializes in tours of the surrounding ice fields and the Taku Flight & Feast ride on which a salmon feast awaits you. ☎*907/586–6275* ⊕*www.wingsairways.com.*

GLACIER TREKKING

Roughly 100,000 glaciers flow out of Alaska's mountains, covering 5% of the state. These slow-moving "rivers of ice" concentrate in the Alaska Range, Wrangell Mountains, and the state's major coastal mountain chains: the Chugach, St. Elias, Coast, and Kenai ranges. Alaska's largest glacier, the Bering, covers 2,250 square mi. If you're an adventurous backcountry traveler, glaciers present icy avenues into the remote corners of premier mountain wilderness areas. And every traveler enjoys the opportunity to walk on water. ■TIP→ **For information about glaciers, flip to** *Glaciers: Notorious Landscape Architects* **in Chapter 6.**

Glacier terrain includes a mix of ice, rock debris, and often-deep surface snow; sometimes frigid pools of meltwater collect on the surface. Watch out for glacier crevasses. Sometimes hidden by snow, especially in spring and early summer (a popular time for glacier trekking), these cracks in the ice may present life-threatening traps. Though some are only inches wide, others may be several yards across and hundreds of feet deep. ■TIP→ **Glacier travel should be attempted only after you've been properly trained. If you haven't been taught proper glacial travel and crevasse-rescue techniques, hire a backcountry guide to provide the necessary gear and expertise.** Some companies offer day or half-day hikes onto glaciers that don't have the same physical demands as longer treks but that still require proper equipment and training. For instance, St. Elias Alpine Guides takes hikers of all ages and abilities on one of its glacier walks.

TOP REGIONS & EXPERIENCES

SOUTHEAST In the Southeast, visitors to the capital city of Juneau can drive or take the bus to **Mendenhall Glacier,** located on the outskirts of town. This 85-mi-long, 45-mi-wide sheet of ice provides awesome glacier trekking opportunities. Guided tour packages are a very good idea for beginners.

SOUTH CENTRAL & THE INTERIOR The mountains outside the state's largest city have their share of glaciers. Among the most popular for trekkers of all abilities is **Matanuska Glacier,** located at Mile 103 off the Glenn Highway (about a 90-minute drive northeast of Anchorage). Anchorage-based guides often use the Matanuska as a training ground for those new to navigating glaciers.

Crampon-clad feet meet Alaskan ice— unforgettable.

Talkeetna, a two-hour drive north of Anchorage, is a small community famous as the jump-off point to some of the world's greatest and most-challenging glacier treks. The town rests a short bush-plane hop from the foot of the Alaska Range and the base of Mt. McKinley. Miles of ice await the most-intrepid and experienced trekkers. Local and Anchorage-based guide services offer training and tours into the region.

Far to the east, off McCarthy Road between Valdez and Glennallen, are the great ice fields of the Wrangell Mountains. Experienced outfitters based in the town of McCarthy get newcomers in touch with awesome ice where few outsiders dare visit.

RESOURCES & GUIDES

Above & Beyond Alaska, LLC. If you're in the Juneau area and want to get your glacier fix, these folks offer treks to the popular Mendenhall Glacier. ☎ *907/364–2333* ⊕ *www.beyondak.com.*

Adventure Bound. Based in Juneau, these guides offer all-day summertime trips to Sawyer Glacier within Tracy Arm. ☎ *907/463–2509 or 800/228–3875* ⊕ *www.adventureboundalaska.com.*

Alaska Mountaineering School. Whether it's on mountaineering expeditions to McKinley or less extreme treks into the Alaska Range, this Talkeetna company takes the time to train you before heading out to pristine backcountry. ☎ *907/733–1016* ⊕ *www.climbalaska.org.*

Exposure Alaska. A variety of small-group options, from ice climbing and short treks on the blue ice of the Matanuska Glacier, to more intense multiday outings from Prince William Sound to Denali, are offered through this Anchorage company. ☎ *907/761–3761 or 800/956–6422* ⊕ *www.exposurealaska.com.*

NorthStar Trekking. A Juneau-based operation specializing in helicopter glacier trekking on the Juneau Icefield, these folks accommodate a broad range of physical abilities. All trips are conducted in small groups, and gear is provided. Flightseeing tours are also offered.

HELPFUL WEB SITES

List of Alaska air taxis: ⊕ www. flyalaska.com/directoryp.html.

National Transportation Safety Board database to check air-taxi safety records: ⊕ www.ntsb.gov/ NTSB/query.asp.

DID YOU KNOW?

Denali National Park's six million acres of land are home to moose, caribou, Dall sheep, wolves, grizzly bears, and one road. The 91 mi, mostly-gravel road terminates at Kantishna, an old mining town.

☎*907/790–4530 or 866/590–4530*
⊕*www.northstartrekking.com.*

FodorśChoice ★ **St. Elias Alpine Guides.** Based in the town of McCarthy, within Wrangell–St. Elias National Park, these über-experienced guides conduct day hikes to nearby glaciers and extended glacier treks well beyond. ☎*907/345–9048 or 888/933–5427* ⊕*www.steliasguides.com.*

★ **Ultima Thule Outfitters.** Based at a fly-in-only lodge on the Chitina River within Wrangell–St. Elias National Park, Ultima Thule leads guided activities in the surrounding mountains, including alpine and glacier treks. A longtime presence in these parts, they're known for family-style hospitality. ☎*907/258–0636* ⊕*www.ultimathulelodge.com.*

BLISS IN BOOTS

In late June and early July, when the sun barely sets in much of Alaska, it's tempting to shoulder your pack and keep on hiking. Around 10 PM the light grows mellow and golden. The birds seem prepared to call all night long. Your boots crunch softly over gravel bars and hillocks. During this time of year Alaska rarely sleeps; there will be time for rest when summer is over.

HIKING & BACKPACKING

From the Southeast's coastal rain forests and the Interior's historic Yukon River country to the high Arctic tundra, Alaska presents some of the continent's finest landscape for wilderness hiking and backpacking. Or, if remote backcountry is not your preference, it's possible to travel well-maintained and well-marked trails on the edges of Alaska's largest cities and still get a taste of the wild—in some places just a few steps take you into the heart of a forest or to the base of a mountain pass. Many of the trails in road-accessible parklands, refuges, and forests are well maintained and cross terrain that is easy for novice hikers, seniors, and families.

TOP REGIONS & EXPERIENCES
Most of Alaska is pristine wilderness, with few or no trails. In such areas it's best to be accompanied by an experienced backcountry traveler who understands the challenges of trail-less wilderness: how to behave in bear country, how to navigate using map and compass techniques, and how to cross glacial streams. Below we've listed some notable exceptions—trails where you can experience Alaska's wilderness on slightly beaten paths. ■TIP➜ For information about hiking Southeast's Chilkoot Trail, flip to *Gold! Gold! Gold!* in Chapter 4.

SOUTHEAST Virtually all Southeast hiking is in the 17-million-acre Tongass National Forest, administered by the U.S. Forest Service. It can be wet and steep here, but you also will be walking through temperate rain forest—lush and gorgeous!

FROM ANCHORAGE TO DENALI **Chugach State Park,** along Anchorage's eastern edge, has dozens of trails, many of them suited for day hikes or overnight camping. Across Turnagain Arm, near Hope, hikers can step onto the **Resurrection Pass Trail** which traverses the forests, streams, and mountains of the Chugach

HIKING TERRAINS

RIVERS

Crossing Alaska's rivers requires care. Many are hard-to-read, swift, silty streams. They often flow over impermeable bottoms (either rock or permafrost), which means a good rain can raise water levels a matter of feet, not inches, in a surprisingly short time. For this very reason, avoid pitching tents near streams, particularly on gravel or sandbars. Warm days can also dramatically increase the meltwater from glaciers. Be aware of weather changes that might affect river crossings. Look for the widest, shallowest place you can find, with many channels. This may entail traveling up- or downstream. A guide who knows the region is invaluable at such times.

A sturdy staff, your own or made from a handy branch, is useful to help you keep your balance and measure the depths of silty water. You should unbuckle your pack when crossing a swift stream. Avoid wearing a long rain poncho; it can catch the water and tip you over. For added stability it helps for two or more people to link arms when crossing.

Hikers debate the best footwear for crossing Alaska's rivers. Some take along sneakers and wear them through the water; others take off their socks so they will remain dry and can comfort cold feet on the opposite shore. But bear in mind that Alaska waters are generally frigid, and the bottom is often rocky and rough; bare feet are not advised.

TUNDRA

Tundra hiking, especially in higher alpine country, can be a great pleasure. In places, the ground is so springy you feel like you're walking on a trampoline. In the Arctic, however, where the ground is underlaid with permafrost, you will probably find the going as wet as it is in the Southeast forests. Summer sunshine melts the top, leaving puddles and marshy spots behind. Comfortable waterproof footgear can help when traversing such landscapes. Tundra travel can require the skill and stamina of a ballet dancer if the ground is tufted with tussocks.

FORESTS

Forest trails are hard to maintain and often wet, especially in coastal lowlands, and they may be potholed or blocked with beaver dams. The ground stays soggy much of the time, and brush grows back quickly after it is cut. Especially nasty is devil's club, a large, broad-leaved plant with greenish flowers that eventually become clusters of bright red berries; it's also thickly armored with stinging, needle-sharp thorns.

National Forest. And though it is best known for its trail-less wilderness, **Denali National Park & Preserve** has some easy-to-hike trails near the park entrance, not to mention miles of taiga and tundra waiting to be explored. Nearby "Little Denali"—**Denali State Park**—has the 36-mi-long Kesugi Ridge Trail, within easy reach of the Parks Highway.

FAIRBANKS &
THE INTERIOR
If you're in the Interior's main hub, definitely check out **Creamer's Field Migratory Waterfowl Refuge** for easy trails and great birding. Some 100 mi east of Fairbanks, the **Pinnell Mountain National Recreation Trail** offers a great three-day hike above the tree line.

Alaska's wide-open tundra and fantastic scenery draw hikers from around the globe.

2

RESOURCES & GUIDES

Alaska Mountaineering School. Best known for its McKinley expeditions, this Talkeetna-based company also leads custom-designed backcountry expeditions in the Alaska Range. ☎907/733–1016 ⊕*www.climbalaska.org.*

Fodor'sChoice
★ **Alaska Nature Tours.** This company in Southeast Alaska leads summer hiking trips into the Alaska Chilkat Bald Eagle Preserve near Haines. Other trips include beach walks and rain-forest hikes. ☎907/766–2876 ⊕*www.alaskanaturetours.net.*

★ **Arctic Treks.** These wilderness hiking and backpacking trips, sometimes combined with river floats, explore areas throughout the Arctic region's Brooks Range, including Gates of the Arctic and the Arctic National Wildlife Refuge. ☎907/455–6502 ⊕*www.arctictreksadventures.com.*

Go North Alaska Adventure Travel Center. Since 1991, this Fairbanks business has been organizing Brooks Range tours. ☎907/479–7272 *or* 866/236–7272 ⊕*www.paratours.net.*

Great Alaska Gourmet Adventures. This Anchorage-based operator offers fun hiking trips with great guides. ☎907/346–1087 ⊕*www.hikealaska.com.*

Fodor'sChoice
★ **St. Elias Alpine Guides.** For more than a quarter-century, this outfitter has been leading mountain hikes, nature tours, and extended backpacking expeditions in the St. Elias and Wrangell mountain ranges. ☎888/345–9048 *or* 907/554–4445 ⊕*www.steliasguides.com.*

HORSE PACKING

Horseback riding can be a rustic, elemental experience. Horseback riding in Alaska can be the experience of a lifetime. To minimize a horse-packing group's impact on the environment, most are limited to 12 riders, and some to just 3 or 4. Most outfits post at least two wranglers for 12 guests, and some bring along another person who serves as cook and/or assistant wrangler. Outfitters who operate on federal lands must have a permit.

■TIP→ It's a good idea to find out how difficult the riding is and how much time is spent in the saddle each day. Six hours is a long day in the saddle, and although some outfitters schedule that much, most keep the riding time to about four hours. Most trips move at a walk, but some trot, lope, and even gallop. As with many other guided adventures, special expertise is not required for horse packing, and guides will train you in the basics before setting out.

SADDLE UP!

There are no traffic jams or overcrowded campgrounds on horse-packing vacations. The farther into the wilderness you go, the more untouched and spectacular the landscape will be. You can also cover a lot more ground with less effort than you can backpacking. Before you book, ask your outfitter for suggestions on appropriate clothing, footwear, and gear.

On trips into the wilderness, expect the food to be straightforward cowboy fare, cooked over a campfire or cookstove. Guides often pull double duty in the kitchen, and often a little help from group members is appreciated. If you have dietary restrictions, make arrangements beforehand. For lodging, don't allow yourself to be surprised: find out what the rooms are like if you're going to be staying in motels or cabins, and if the trip involves camping, ask about the campsites and the shower and latrine arrangements.

TOP REGIONS & EXPERIENCES

SOUTH CENTRAL

Encompassing more than 13 million acres of mountains, glaciers, and remote river valleys, **Wrangell–St. Elias National Park & Preserve** is wild and raw. There's no better way to absorb the enormity and natural beauty of this region than on horseback. Centuries-old game trails and networks blazed and maintained by contemporary outfitters wind through lowland spruce forests and into wide-open high-country tundra. From there, horses can take you almost anywhere, over treeless ridgelines and to sheltered campsites on the shores of scenic tarns.

Closer to the state's population center in South Central, yet no less magnificent for horse packing, is the Kenai Peninsula. Outfitters frequently travel the well-groomed mountain trails of the **Chugach National Forest** and **Kenai Mountains.** In both regions, wildlife is abundant: moose, bear, Dall sheep, mountain goats, and wolves are frequently seen. Although overnight cabins are occasionally available, guests should come prepared to camp outdoors.

RESOURCES & GUIDES

Alaska Horsemen Trail Adventures. This Cooper Landing–based company offers multiday pack trips into the Kenai Mountains via Crescent Lake, Resurrection, and other area trail systems. ☎*907/595–1806 or 800/595–1806 ⊕www.alaskahorsemen.com.*

Castle Mountain Outfitters. Based in Chickaloon, north of Anchorage in Matanuska Valley, this outfitter conducts a variety of trips ranging from guided hour-long horseback rides to one-week expeditions. ☎*907/745–6427 ⊕www.mtaonline.net/~cmoride/index.html.*

D & S Alaskan Trail Rides, Inc. Specializing in short rides in Denali State Park, these outfitters are right off the Parks Highway, north of Anchorage. ☎*907/733–2207, 907/733–2205, 907/745–2208 winter months* ⊕*www.alaskantrailrides.com.*

Wrangell Outfitters. This husband-and-wife team from Fairbanks takes visitors on horse-packing trips into the heart of Wrangell–St. Elias National Park & Preserve. ☎*907/479–5343* ⊕*www.wrangelloutfitters. com.*

RIVER RAFTING

So much of Alaska is roadless wilderness that rivers often serve as the best avenues to explore the landscape. This is especially true in several of Alaska's premier parklands and refuges. Here, as elsewhere, rivers are ranked according to their degrees of difficulty. ■TIP➜ Class I rivers are considered easy floats with minimal rapids; at the other extreme, Class VI rivers are extremely dangerous and nearly impossible to navigate. Generally, only very experienced river runners should attempt anything above Class II on their own. Also be aware that river conditions change considerably from season to season and sometimes from day to day, so always check on a river's current condition. The National Weather Service Alaska–Pacific River Forecast Center keeps tabs on Alaska's most popular streams. The center's Web site (⊕*aprfc.arh.noaa.gov/ ak_ahps2.php*) provides the latest data on water levels and flow rates, including important flood-stage alerts.

Do-it-yourselfers would be wise to consult two books on Alaska's rivers: *Fast & Cold: A Guide to Alaska Whitewater* (Skyhouse), by Andrew Embick (though intended primarily for white-water kayakers, it has good information for rafters as well), and *The Alaska River Guide: Canoeing, Kayaking, and Rafting in the Last Frontier* (Alaska Northwest Books), by Karen Jettmar.

Fortunately you don't have to be an expert river runner to explore many of Alaska's premier waterways. Experienced rafting companies operate throughout the state. Some outfits emphasize extended wilderness trips and natural-history observations, whereas others specialize in thrilling one-day (or shorter) runs down Class III and IV white-water rapids that will get your adrenaline—and possibly your arms—pumping. And some combine a little of both.

TOP REGIONS & EXPERIENCES

Never has the term "it's all good" been truer than in the context of river rafting in Alaska—be it a Class I or Class VI, it's an experience that, with the right preparation and safety considerations, can make you feel like a class-act adventurer. With thousands of rivers to choose from, virtually every region of the state promises prime rafting. Which region and river you float depends largely upon the impetus of your trip. White-water thrill-seekers will find challenging streams tumbling from the mountainous areas of South Central, while rafters interested in sportfishing may choose extended float trips on the gentler salmon- and trout-rich rivers of the Southwest. Birders and campers may consider the pristine rivers draining the North Slope of the Brooks Range or Northwest Alaska. Beyond your agenda, though, which river you choose to float should depend upon your rafting and backcountry skills. If there's any question at all, go with an experienced river guide.

RIOTOUS RIVERS

From the Southeast Panhandle to the far reaches of the Arctic, Alaska is blessed with an abundance of wild, pristine rivers. The federal government has officially designated more than two dozen Alaska streams as "wild and scenic rivers," but hundreds more would easily qualify. Some meander gently through forests or tundra. Others, fed by glacier run-off, rush wildly through mountains and canyons.

SOUTH CENTRAL For those seeking the adrenaline surge of white-water rafting, South Central offers many accessible and affordable options. **Chugach National Forest's Six-Mile River,** about a 90-minute drive south of Anchorage on the Seward Highway, is relished for its Class V and VI white water and spectacular canyon scenery. Options available off the highway system north of Anchorage include the glacial **Eagle** and **Matanuska** rivers, each known for varying degrees of white water.

THE INTERIOR & THE BUSH North of Anchorage via the Parks Highway, the **Nenana River** flows along the eastern side of Denali National Park & Preserve, offering a variety of conditions ranging from calm to Class III and IV.

Flowing north out of the eastern Brooks Range to the Arctic Ocean, the **Kongakut** and **Hulahula** rivers promise far-flung wilderness adventures. Trips here are as much about seeing the high Arctic tundra landscape and wildlife such as caribou, grizzly bears, musk ox, and thousands of nesting birds as they are about the water.

RESOURCES & GUIDES

Be certain that the guide gives you a safety talk before going on the water. It's important to know what you should do if you do get flipped out of the raft or if the boat overturns. Also, when arranging your trip well in advance, find out what gear and clothing are required. Ask if you'll be paddling or simply riding as a passenger. Reputable rafting companies will discuss all of this, but it never hurts to ask.

★ **Alaska Discovery.** This Juneau-based outfitter leads 9- to 12-day trips down two of North America's wildest rivers, the Tatshenshini and Alsek. The trips begin in Canada and end in Glacier Bay. Also check out the rafting/hiking trips in the Arctic National Wildlife Refuge and Gates of the Arctic. ☎*800/586–1911* ⊕*www.akdiscovery.com.*

Alaska Outdoor Adventures. South Central's Six-Mile River and Turnagain Pass are two trips offered by this Whittier-based company. ☎*907/472–2534 or 877/472–2534* ⊕*www.akadventures.com.*

Alaska Wildland Adventures. Head down the Kenai River and learn about the surroundings and wildlife with these guides. ☎*800/478–4100* ⊕*www.alaskarivertrips.com.*

Chugach Adventure Guides. Right outside Anchorage, this company has plenty of trips on offer, from Six-Mile River to a Talkeetna four-day float. ☎*907/783–4354* ⊕*www.alaskanrafting.com.*

Chugach Outdoor Center. Head to Hope, about a 90-minute drive south of Anchorage, for a broad regional menu ranging from nearby **Six-Mile River's** Class IV and V white water to the Talkeetna River north of Anchorage and Denali's **Nenana River.** Van shuttles from Anchorage are available with advance reservations. ☎*907/277–7238 or 866/277–7238* ⊕*www.chugachoutdoorcenter.com.*

Denali Raft Adventures, Inc. River trips are conducted on the glacially fed, white-water Nenana River, which skirts the eastern boundary of Denali National Park & Preserve. Trips vary from two-hour scenic floats to all-day white-water canyon trips. ☎*907/683–2234 or 888/683–2234* ⊕*www.denaliraft.com.*

Fodor'sChoice
★

Nova. These superexperienced guides offer white-water trips down the Matanuska, Chickaloon, and Talkeetna rivers in South Central Alaska; multiday float trips through Wrangell–St. Elias, and part-day trips on the Kenai Peninsula's Six-Mile River. White-water ratings range from Class I to Class V. ☎*800/746–5753* ⊕*www.novaalaska.com.*

SEA KAYAKING

Fodor'sChoice
★

Sea kayaking can be as thrilling or as peaceful as you want. More stable than a white-water kayak and more comfortable than a canoe, a sea kayak, even one loaded with a week's worth of gear, is maneuverable enough to poke into hidden crevices, explore side bays, and beach on deserted spits of sand. Don't assume, though, that if you've kayaked 10 minutes without tipping over you'll be adequately prepared to circumnavigate Glacier Bay National Park & Preserve. There's a lot to learn, and until you know your way around tides, currents, and nautical charts, you should go with an experienced guide who also knows what and how to pack and where to pitch a tent.

It's important to honestly evaluate your tolerance for cold, dampness, and high winds. Nothing can ruin a trip faster than pervasive discomfort, and it's worse once you're out on the water with no choice but to keep going. ■**TIP➔ Ask whether the outfitter stocks a variety of boats, so you can experiment until you find the kayak that best fits your weight, strength, ability, and paddling style.**

TOP REGIONS & EXPERIENCES

SOUTHEAST This largely roadless coastal region is the setting of North America's last great temperate wilderness. Sometimes called Alaska's Panhandle, this appendage of islands, mainland, and fjords is a sparsely populated, scenic paradise for sea kayaking. In the deep Southeast, Ketchikan is a popular starting point for many sea kayakers. Set in the heart of the **Tongass National Forest** and well within paddling range of the **Misty Fiords National Monument,** this former logging town is home to several sea kayaking guides and rental businesses. Ketchikan is also a stop on the Alaska Marine Highway, making it convenient for travelers to simply

Never fear: It doesn't take long to get the hang of paddling a sea kayak.

drive or walk off the state ferry and spend a couple of days exploring local bays and fjords before boarding another ferry.

An equally popular destination for Southeast saltwater paddlers is **Glacier Bay National Park & Preserve.** The hub for this region is Juneau, where kayakers can hop a plane or ferry to the small community of Gustavus, located within the park.

SOUTH
CENTRAL

Prince William Sound, with its miles of bays, islands, forests, and glaciers, is a big draw for sea kayakers. Popular ports include Whittier, Cordova, and Valdez. Of the three, Whittier and Valdez are on the state highway system, making them most accessible (Whittier is a one-hour drive south from Anchorage). Guides catering to ocean paddlers are found in all three ports.

Two Kenai Peninsula venues also lure sea kayakers. About a two-hour drive south of Anchorage, at the terminus of the Seward Highway, **Resurrection Bay** serves up awesome scenery and marine wildlife. Homer, perched over **Kachemak Bay,** at the terminus of the Sterling Highway (a five-hour drive south of Anchorage), is also an excellent spot.

RESOURCES & GUIDES

Fodor'sChoice
★

Alaska Discovery. These experienced guides know Southeast Alaska intimately, and they emphasize skills and safety. Destinations include Tracy Arm, Glacier Bay, Icy Bay, Point Adolphus (for whale-watching), and Admiralty Island (with bear viewing at Pack Creek). Also check out the inn-to-inn paddling trip through the Kenai Peninsula's Kachemak Bay. ☎*800/586–1911* ⊕*www.akdiscovery.com.*

Anadyr Adventures. Prince William Sound comes alive from a sea kayak. See for yourself with Anadyr, based in Valdez. ☎*907/835–2814 or 800/865–2925* ⊕*www.anadyradventures.com.*

Prince William Sound Kayak Center. Operating out of Whittier since 1981, this center provides kayak rentals, introductory classes, guided day tours, and escorted trips in Prince William Sound. ☎*907/276–7235 in winter, 877/472–2452* in summer ⊕*www.pwskayakcenter.com.*

Southeast Exposure. More than twenty years in the business translates into great trips with this Ketchikan outfit. Its most popular paddle is through Misty Fiords National Monument. ☎*907/225–8829* ⊕*www. southeastexposure.com.*

Spirit Walker Expeditions. This veteran Southeast company (based in Gustavus) gives guided wilderness sea kayaking trips that combine scenery, wildlife, solitude, and paddling within the Inside Passage. Guides prepare meals, offer instruction, and provide all gear. Beginners are welcome. ☎907/697–2266 or 800/529–2537 ⊕ *www.seakayak alaska.com.*

Sunny Cove Sea Kayaking. Extended trips in and around Kenai Fjords National Park involve paddling among icebergs, seals, and seabirds as tidewater glaciers calve in the distance. Day and overnight trips explore Resurrection Bay, near Seward. Tours include equipment, instruction, and meals. ☎907/224–8810, 800/770–9119 *reservations* ⊕*www.sunnycove.com.*

> **THE STROKES**
>
> Anyone who doesn't mind getting a little wet and has an average degree of fitness can be a sea kayaker. The basic stroke is performed in a circular motion with a double-bladed paddle: you pull one blade through the water while pushing forward with the other through the air. Most people pick it up with a minimal amount of instruction.

2

SKIING & SNOWBOARDING

Yes, Alaska has a lot of snow. It's not surprising then, that the state is also a great destination for Nordic, downhill, and extreme downhill skiing. Three of the state's largest cities—Anchorage, Fairbanks, and Juneau—have nearby ski areas, complete with equipment rentals and ski schools. Anchorage's trail system ranks among the nation's finest and hosts world-class races.

For those who are more ambitious, Alaska's wilderness areas present plenty of opportunities and a variety of challenges. Unless you are knowledgeable in winter backcountry travel, camping techniques, and avalanche dangers, the best strategy is to hire a guide when exploring Alaska's backcountry on skis. ■TIP➔ Given the extremes of Alaska's winters, your primary concern should be safety: be sure your guide has had avalanche-awareness and winter-survival training.

TOP REGIONS & EXPERIENCES

SOUTHEAST **Eaglecrest** gets high marks for excellent spring skiing. 12 mi outside Juneau, ski season runs December through mid-April. This hill is rarely crowded, and the views on a bright day are remarkable. ⊕*www.ski juneau.com.*

SOUTH CENTRAL & THE INTERIOR **Alyeska Resort,** located 40 mi south of Anchorage in Girdwood, is Alaska's largest and best-known downhill ski resort. It encompasses 1,000 acres of terrain for all skill levels. Ski rentals are available at the resort. Local ski and snowboard guides teach classes on the mountain and offer helicopter ski and snowboard treks into more remote sites in the nearby Chugach and Kenai ranges. ⊕*www.alyeskaresort.com.*

Closer to Anchorage, two much smaller ski-hill operations, **Alpenglow** and **Hilltop,** offer great runs for beginners. Both are also good options when the weather occasionally rules out Alyeska. ⊕*www.skialpenglow.com.* ⊕*www.hilltopskiarea.org.*

Moose Mountain, outside Fairbanks, is the ski and snowboard draw for visitors to the Interior. More than 1,250 feet of terrain includes everything from bunny slopes to vertical. Best of all, while the city is known for frigid winters, the mountain enjoys warmer temperatures. ⊕*fairbanks-alaska.com/moose-mountain-ski-resort.htm.*

RESOURCES & GUIDES

Alaska Mountaineering School. Custom cross-country ski trips of varying lengths and degrees of difficulty can be arranged, primarily through Denali National and state parks, with an emphasis on natural history. ☎*907/733–1016* ⊕*www.climbalaska.org.*

Fodor'sChoice **Alaska Nature Tours.** This company in Southeast rents ski and snowboard
★ gear and conducts trips into the amazing Alaska Chilkat Bald Eagle Preserve near Haines. ☎*907/766–2876* ⊕*www.alaskanaturetours.net.*

Chugach Powder Guides. This decade-old helicopter-ski and Sno-Cat operation focuses on backcountry skiing and snowboarding in the Chugach Range out of Girdwood and Seward; Alaska Range adventures are also featured. ☎*907/783–4354* ⊕*www.chugachpowderguides.com.*

SPORTFISHING

Fodor'sChoice Alaska's biggest hobby in the warmer months is sportfishing; the
★ Anchorage Daily News even has a "fishing dude" who posts inside tips and videos online for those seeking the perfect catch (w *http://www.adn.com/outdoors/fishing*). Five species of Pacific salmon (king, silver, sockeye, pink, and chum) spawn in Alaska's innumerable rivers and creeks, alongside rainbow trout, cutthroat trout, steelhead, arctic char, sheefish, Dolly Varden char, arctic grayling, northern pike, and lake trout, among other freshwater species. Salmon are also caught in saltwater, along with halibut, lingcod, many varieties of rockfish (locally called snapper or sea bass), and salmon sharks that can weigh more than 800 pounds.

Even though the world-record king salmon, weighing 97¼ pounds, was caught in the Kenai River, and halibut exceeding 300 pounds are caught annually, some anglers will tell you that bigger isn't necessarily better. Sockeyes, salmon averaging 6 to 8 pounds, are considered by many to be the best tasting and best fighting of any fish. And though the sail-finned arctic grayling commonly weighs a pound or less, its willingness to rise for dry flies makes it a favorite among fly fishermen.

■TIP➔ Sportfishing regulations vary widely from area to area. Licenses are required for both fresh- and saltwater fishing. To learn more about regulations, contact the **Alaska Department of Fish and Game** (☎*907/465–4180 sportfishing seasons and regulations, 907/465–2376 licenses* ⊕*www.adfg.state.ak.us*). To purchase a fishing license online, visit the State of Alaska Web site (⊕*www.admin.adfg.state.ak.us/license*).

TOP REGIONS & EXPERIENCES

Roadside fishing for salmon, trout, char, pike, and grayling is best cast in **South Central** and **Interior Alaska.** In fact, Alaska's best-known salmon stream, the **Kenai River,** parallels the Sterling Highway. But in most of the state, prime fishing waters can be reached only by boat or air. Not

Utter bliss: fishing pole, rubber boots, and a quiet morning.

2

surprisingly, hundreds of fishing charters and dozens of sportfishing lodges operate statewide, attracting anglers from around the world. **Southwest Alaska,** in particular, is known for its fine salmon, trout, and char fishing; many of its best spots are remote and expensive to reach, but fishing opportunities here are unparalleled.

SOUTHEAST   This huge coastal region is renowned for its outstanding sportfishing for salmon, rockfish, and halibut. Charters operate out of all main ports, and the action is frequently so good that catching your limit is almost a given. Splendid scenery is guaranteed—even when shrouded in misty rains, which are common. Streams offer fine angling for steelhead, cutthroat, rainbow, and Dolly Varden trout. The waters of **Prince of Wales Island** are especially popular among steelhead, salmon, and trout anglers, with the Karta and Thorne rivers among the favorites.

SOUTH CENTRAL & THE INTERIOR   Alaska lives up to its reputation for angling excellence in South Central. From the hub of Anchorage, the Seward and Sterling highways provide access to the world-famous spots on the Kenai Peninsula. Anglers seeking rainbow trout, Dolly Varden, and salmon will do no better than the **Kenai River.** This dream stream—tinted an opaque emerald from glacial runoff—serves up fine fishing from ice-out in spring to freeze-up in late fall. The **Russian River,** a tributary that joins the upper Kenai River near Cooper Landing, is a dashing mountain stream that runs crystal clear—except when it's chock-full of red salmon from mid-June through August. Other fine Kenai Peninsula streams include **Quartz Creek, Deep Creek,** and **Anchor River.** Many excellent trout and salmon guides are based in the Kenai River towns of Cooper Landing, Sterling, Soldotna, and Kenai.

Saltwater angling out of the ports of **Whittier, Seward,** and **Homer** is legendary for king, pink, and silver salmon as well as for rockfish, lingcod, and huge halibut. Charter operators are in all three ports, offering half-day and full-day fishing trips.

North of Anchorage, the Parks Highway courses through the **Mat-Su Valley,** a scenic piece of wilderness backed by Mt. McKinley and veined with fine streams. Five species of salmon, rainbow trout, Dolly Varden, grayling, northern pike, and lake trout are among the draws here. Some of the most popular Parks Highway streams include **Willow, Sheep, Montana,** and **Clear** creeks. Fishing guides based in Wasilla, Houston, Willow, and Talkeetna offer riverboat and fly-in trips. Remember that salmon runs are seasonal. Kings run late May through mid-July, and silvers run from mid-July through August. And don't forget the lakes; scores of them brim with trout, landlocked salmon, arctic char, and grayling. Cast for them from canoes or float tubes on calm summer afternoons.

The most popular bush sportfishing region is the roadless **Southwest,** home of the richest salmon runs in the world. Along with huge schools of red salmon, kings, silvers, chums, and pinks, anglers will find trophy rainbow trout, Dolly Varden, arctic grayling, and arctic char. Many anglers fish with guides based out of remote fishing lodges located on rivers and lakes. Others do it themselves, arranging for bush planes to drop them off in headwater streams, then floating the river in rafts, fishing along the way until reaching a prearranged pickup point.

RESOURCES, GUIDES & CHARTERS

When hiring a guide, ask about species likely to be caught when you'll be visiting, catch limits, and any special equipment or clothing needs. Normally, all necessary fishing gear is provided, and the guides will teach you the appropriate fishing techniques. In some cases, catch-and-release may be emphasized. Prime time for saltwater fishing is July through mid-August; for river trips, mid-June through September.

Alaskan Fishing Adventures, Inc. Anglers are guided in several areas of the Kenai Peninsula, including Resurrection Bay, Cook Inlet, and the Kenai River, home of the famous Kenai king salmon that may weigh 90 pounds. Among the other species they catch are halibut, sockeye and silver salmon, and rainbow trout. Boats have a four-person limit on rivers, a six-person limit on saltwater. ☎ *800/548–3474* ⊕ *www. alaskanfishing.com.*

Alaska Fishing Online. This Web resource provides listings of fishing charter services, air-taxi operators, and angling lodges around the state. Browse listings by region, and shop around for the best price. Also, ask plenty of questions to ensure you find the outfit best suited to your needs. ⊕ *www.alaskafishing.com.*

Alaska River Adventures. These Cooper Landing–based guides take small groups fishing throughout the region, with self-professed "well-seasoned old pros." ☎ *907/595–2000 or 888/836–9027* ⊕ *www.alaskariveradventures.com.*

Alaska Wildland Adventures. From their lodge in Cooper Landing south of Anchorage, these folks provide fishing adventures on the upper and lower Kenai River. ☎ *907/783–2928 or 800/334–8730* ⊕ *www.alaskawildland.com.*

Central Charter Booking Agency. In Homer, this company can arrange fishing trips in outer Kachemak Bay and Lower Cook Inlet——areas known for excellent halibut fishing. Boat sizes vary considerably; some have a 6-person limit, whereas others can take up to 16 passengers. ☎ *907/235–7847 or 800/478–7847* ⊕ *www.centralcharter.com.*

The Fish House. Operating out of Seward since 1974, this booking agency represents dozens of Resurrection Bay and Kenai Peninsula

ALASKA'S TOP FISH & THEIR SOURCES

SPECIES	COMMON NAME	WHERE FOUND
Arctic Char (F, S)	Char	SC, SW, NW, I, A
Arctic Grayling (F)	Grayling	SE, SC, SW, NW, I, A
Brook Trout (F)	Brookie	SE
Burbot (F)	Lingcod	SC, I, SW, NW, A
Chinook Salmon (F, S)	King	SE, SC, SW, I
Chum Salmon (F, S)	Dog	SE, SC, SW, NW, I
Coho Salmon (F, S)	Silver	SE, SC, SW, NW, I
Cutthroat Trout (F, S)	Cutt	SE, SC
Dolly Varden (F, S)	Dolly	SE, SC, SW, NW, I, A
Lake Trout (F)	Laker	SC, SW, NW, I, A
Northern Pike (F)	Northern	SC, SW, NW, I
Pacific Halibut (S)	'But	SE, SC, SW, NW
Pink Salmon (F, S)	Humpy	SE, SC, SW, NW
Rainbow Trout (F)	'Bow	SE, SC, SW, I
Sheefish (F)	Shee, Inconnu	NW, I
Smelt (F, S)	Hooligan	SE, SC, SW, NW, I, A
Sockeye Salmon (F, S)	Red	SE, SC, SW, NW, I
Steelhead (F, S)	Steelie	SE, SC, SW

(F) = Freshwater, (S) = Saltwater, (F, S) = Freshwater and Saltwater, A = Arctic,
SC = South Central, I = Interior, SE = Southeast, NW = Northwest, SW = Southwest

fishing charters and can hook you up for half-day or full-day charters. ☎ *907/224–3674 or 800/257–7760* ⊕ *www.thefishhouse.net.*

Great Alaska Adventure Lodge. Fishing packages are run out of this Kenai River lodge. Trips with expert guides include fly-in fish camps, river floats, and saltwater charters. Stories and tall fishing tales are traded at happy hour in the lodge. ☎ *907/262–4515 in summer, 360/697–6454 in winter, 800/544–2261 year-round* ⊕ *www.greatalaska.com.*

ENJOYING ALASKA'S WILDLIFE

Imagine a calm hike on a dewy morning—to the right, a fox shyly observes your progress through the trees with a mute, curious greeting. Alaska's 375 million acres support more than 800 species of mammals, birds, and fish. The 105 different mammals range from whales to shrews (Alaska's shrews are the smallest of North America's land mammals, weighing 1/10 ounce). Some 478 species of birds range from hummingbirds to bald eagles, including species found nowhere else in North America. Migrant birds come here annually from every continent and many islands to take advantage of Alaska's rich breeding and rearing grounds in its wetlands, rivers, shores, and tundra. Among the 430 different kinds of fish—including five kinds of salmon—some weigh more than 400 pounds (halibut) whereas others more commonly weigh less than a pound (arctic grayling).

The largest numbers of animals are seen during migration periods. The state is strategically positioned for creatures that migrate vast distances. Some birds fly from the southern tip of South America to nest and rear their young on sandbars in Alaska's wild rivers. Others travel from parts of Asia to thrive in Alaska's summers. The arctic tern comes all the way from Antarctica. Sea mammals congregate in great numbers in the waters of Prince William Sound, the Panhandle, the Gulf of Alaska, and the Bering, Beaufort, and Chukchi seas. Hundreds of thousands of caribou move across the Arctic, including the Porcupine Herd (named after the Porcupine River), which travels between Canada and Alaska. Anadromous fish (or "fish that run upward") by the millions swim up Alaska's rivers, returning unerringly to the waters where they were born.

Bears live in virtually every part of the state, and though they are often solitary, it is not unusual to see a sow with cubs. In some areas bears gather in large numbers to feed upon rich runs of salmon. Several world-class bear-viewing areas from Southeast to Southwest Alaska attract visitors. Moose abound in the wetter country of the Southeast, as well as in forested portions of South Central and Interior Alaska. Caribou wander over the tundra country of the Arctic, sub-Arctic, and South Central. The coastal mountains of the Southeast and South Central harbor mountain goats, and the mountains of the South Central, Interior, and Arctic regions are home to white Dall sheep. Wolves and lynx, though more rarely seen, live in many parts of the Southeast, South Central, Interior, and Arctic regions, and, if you're lucky, a wolf may dash across the road in front of you, or a smaller mammal, such as a red fox or snowshoe hare, may watch you when you're rafting or even when you're traveling on wheels.

STRATEGIES FOR SPOTTING WILDLIFE

Know what you're looking for. Season and time of day are critical. Many animals are nocturnal and best viewed during twilight, which in summer in Alaska's northern regions can last all night. In winter, large creatures such as moose and caribou can be spotted from far away, as their dark bodies stand out against the snow. It is also possible to track animals after a fresh snowfall. You have only a few hours of sunlight each day during which you can look for wildlife in winter, and in northern Alaska there won't be any direct sunlight at all in winter months.

Be careful. Keep a good distance, especially with animals that can be dangerous. Whether you're on foot or in a vehicle, don't get too close. A pair of good binoculars or a spotting scope is well worth the expense and extra weight. Don't get too close to or touch wildlife (and, if you're traveling with pets, keep them leashed). **Move slowly,** stop often, look, and listen. The exception is when you see a bear; let the animal know you're there by making noise. Avoid startling an animal and risking a dangerous confrontation, especially with a mama bear with cubs or a cow moose with a calf.

Keep your hat on if you are in territory where arctic terns, gulls, or pomarine jaegers nest, often around open alpine or tundra lakes and tarns. These species are highly protective of their nests and young and are skillful dive-bombers. Occasionally, they connect with human heads, and the results can be painful.

Be prepared to wait; patience often pays off. And if you're an enthusiastic birder or animal watcher, **be prepared to hike over some rough terrain** to reach the best viewing vantage. **Respect and protect** the animal you're watching and its habitat—you, after all, are a visitor in its territory. Don't chase or harass the animals. The willful act of harassing an animal is punishable in Alaska by a $1,000 fine. This includes flushing birds from their nests and purposely frightening animals with loud noises.

Don't disturb or surprise the animals, which also applies to birds' eggs, the young, the nests, and such habitats as beaver dams. It's best to let the animal discover your presence quietly, if at all, by keeping still or moving slowly (except when viewing bears or moose). If you accidentally disturb an animal, limit your viewing time and leave as quietly as possible. **Don't use a tape recorder or any device** to call a bird or to attract other animals if you're in bear country, as you might call a hungry bear. And **don't feed animals**, as any creature that comes to depend on humans for food almost always comes to a sorry end. Both state and federal laws prohibit the feeding of wild animals.

Even those traveling by car in Alaska have abundant opportunity to spot wildlife. For those traveling by boat, the **Alaska Marine Highway**, the route plied by Alaska's state ferries, passes through waters rich with fish, sea mammals, and birds. Throughout the Southeast, ferries often provide sightings of whales, porpoises, and sea otters, and virtually always of bald eagles. In **Kenai Fjords National Park**, tour boats enable you to view sea mammals and seabirds. Smaller boats and touring vessels are found in such places as **Glacier Bay National Park & Preserve**, an especially good place to spot humpback whales, puffins, seals, shorebirds, and perhaps a black or brown bear. **Denali National Park & Preserve** is known worldwide for its wildlife; you are likely to see grizzlies, moose, Dall sheep, caribou, foxes, golden eagles, and wolves. The **Alaska Chilkat Bald Eagle Preserve** hosts the world's largest gathering of bald eagles each fall and winter. And Dall sheep that inhabit **Chugach State Park** can often be seen along the Seward Highway south of Anchorage.

BEARS You can't be absolutely sure you'll spot a grizzly bear in **Denali National Park & Preserve** (☎ *907/683–2294* ⊕ *www.nps.gov/dena*), but chances are better than 50–50, especially in the early morning, that you'll see grizzlies digging in the tundra or eating berries. Sometimes females even nurse their cubs within sight of the park road. Talk with the staff at the visitor center near the park entrance when you arrive.

TOP REGIONS & EXPERIENCES

Katmai National Park (☎907/246–3305 ⊕*www.nps.gov/katm*), on the Alaska Peninsula, has an abundance of bears, on average more than one brown bear per square mile, among the highest densities of any region in North America. In July, when the salmon are running up Brooks River, bears concentrate around Brooks River falls, resulting in a great view of these animals as they fish, and the spectacle of hundreds of salmon leaping the falls.

Kodiak National Wildlife Refuge (☎907/487–2600 or 888/408–3514 ⊕*kodiak.fws.gov*), on Kodiak Island, is an excellent place to see brown bears, particularly along salmon-spawning streams.

The **McNeil River State Game Sanctuary,** on the Alaska Peninsula, hosts the world's largest gathering of brown bears. As many as 70 have been counted at one time at McNeil Falls and thus affords unsurpassed photographic opportunities. Peak season, when the local salmon are running, is early June through mid-August. Much-sought-after reservations are by a lottery conducted in March by the **Alaska Department of Fish and Game** (☎907/267–2182 ⊕*www.wildlife.alaska.gov*).

At **Pack Creek,** on Admiralty Island in Southeast, brown bears fish for spawning salmon—pink, chum, and silver. To get here, you can fly by air charter or take a boat from Juneau. If you time your visit to coincide with the salmon runs in July and August, you will almost surely see bald eagles. Permits are required to visit during the peak bear-viewing period; contact **Admiralty Island National Monument** (☎907/586–8800 ⊕*www.fs.fed.us/r10/tongass/districts/admiralty/packcreek/index.shtml*).

The **Silver Salmon Creek Lodge** (☎888/872–5666 ⊕*www.silversalmoncreek.com*) conducts a bear-viewing program along the shores of western Cook Inlet, near Lake Clark National Park, with lodging, meals, and guide services for both bear viewing and sportfishing.

For a more in-depth look at bears, head to ⇨ Welcome to Bear Country in Chapter 8.

BIRDS If you come on your own, try the following sure and easily accessed bets for bird spotting. In **Anchorage,** walk around Potter Marsh or Westchester Lagoon or along the Tony Knowles Coastal Trail and keep your eye out for shorebirds, waterfowl, and the occasional bald eagle. Songbird enthusiasts are likely to see many species in town or neighboring Chugach State Park. The **Anchorage Audubon Society** (☎907/338–2473 ⊕*www.anchorageaudubon.org*) has a bird-report recording and offers various trips, such as the Owl Prowl and Hawk Watch.

In **Juneau,** visit the Mendenhall Wetlands State Game Refuge, next to the airport, for ducks, geese, and swans. There are trails and interpretive signs. In **Fairbanks,** head for the Creamer's Field Migratory Waterfowl Refuge on College Road. If you're lucky, you'll see sandhill cranes in summer and spectacular shows of ducks and geese in spring.

Wilderness Safety Tips

PREPARATION & ORGANIZATION
You need to be in good physical shape to venture into the backcountry. Avoid traveling alone. If your outdoor experience is limited, travel with a guide. If you are traveling by boat along the coast, bring a tide book. If backpacking overland, know in advance whether you'll have to cross large glacial rivers. Always pay attention to the weather. When you're hiking in any protected land, check in and out with a ranger. Leave an itinerary and the names of people to call in case of an emergency with at least one person. Be specific about your destination and estimated date of return.

MAPS
Use maps (preferably 1 inch: 1 mi maps published by the U.S. Geological Survey) and a compass at the very minimum. Cell phones usually don't work in remote wilderness areas. Other options for emergency use are electronic locator devices, global positioning systems, and handheld aviation radios.

WEATHER
Always be prepared for storms and wintry conditions. Also be prepared for unexpected delays. One of the most common phrases used by pilots in Alaska is "weather permitting." Never "push" the weather; every year people die in aviation, boating, and overland accidents because they want to get home on schedule despite dangerously stormy conditions.

STAY FOUND
Plan your hiking routes carefully, carry detailed maps, and know how to operate your compass or handheld GPS unit. Other precautions include

leaving a detailed itinerary with family or park rangers. If you do get lost, those you've notified in town will know when and where to start looking. It's also smart to carry a whistle.

HYPOTHERMIA
Hypothermia, the lowering of the body's core temperature, is an ever-present threat in Alaska's wilderness. Wear warm clothing (in layers) when the weather is cool and/or wet; this includes a good wind- and waterproof parka or shell, warm head- and hand gear, and waterproof or water-resistant boots. Eat regularly to maintain energy and drink enough liquids to stay properly hydrated.

The onset of hypothermia can be recognized by the following symptoms: shivering, accelerated heartbeat, and goose bumps; this may be followed by clumsiness, slurred speech, disorientation, and unconsciousness. In the extreme, it can result in death. If you notice any of these symptoms in yourself or your traveling companion, stop, add layers of clothing, light a fire or camp stove, and warm yourself; a cup of tea or any hot fluid also helps. Avoid alcohol, which only speeds hypothermia and impairs judgment. If your clothes are wet, change immediately. Be sure to put on a warm hat (most of the body's heat is lost through the head) and gloves. If there are only two of you, stay together: a person with hypothermia should never be left alone.

WATER SAFETY
Alaska's waters, even its wildest rivers and lakes, often carry *Giardia*, locally called beaver fever, a parasite that can cause diarrhea and sap your strength. In the backcountry, boil water or treat it with iodine tablets.

Great crowds of bald eagles visit the Chilkat River, near **Haines** in Southeast Alaska, each November and December. In summer, rafting on almost any Alaska river brings the near certainty of sighting nesting shorebirds, arctic terns, and merganser mothers trailed by chicks. Approximately 200 species of birds have been sighted on the **Pribilof Islands**, but you will almost certainly need to be part of a guided tour to get there.

The folks at **Alaska Birding & Wildlife** (☎ *877/424–5637* ⊕ *www.alaskabirding.com*) can take you to St. Paul Island to see the huge range of birds and get to know local Aleut culture and customs.

Alaska Discovery (☎ *907/780–6226 or 800/586–1911* ⊕ *www.akdiscovery.com*) offers trips to Pack Creek, including a floatplane trip, sea kayaking, and bear viewing.

With **Mariah Tours** (☎ *877/777–2805* ⊕ *www.alaskaheritagetours.com*) the Kenai Fjords National Park comes to life on tailor-made birding and photography boat tours.

Ouzel Expeditions (☎ *800/825–8196* ⊕ *www.ouzel.com*), appropriately named after a type of bird, offers seven-day birding float trips in Southwest Alaska and the Arctic National Wildlife Refuge. Trips are in remote fly-in locations; camping and floating quietly along rivers provides wonderful birding opportunities. Southwest birding trips begin in Anchorage; trips in Arctic National Wildlife Refuge begin in Fairbanks.

The Web site of the **University of Alaska Fairbanks** (⊕ *www.uaf.edu/museum/bird/products/checklist.pdf*) has a checklist of Alaska's 485 bird species.

★   The owners of **Wilderness Birding Adventures** (☎ *907/694–7442* ⊕ *www.wildernessbirding.com*) are both experienced river runners and expert birders. Among their trips is a rafting, hiking, and birding expedition through one of the world's last great wilderness areas, the Arctic National Wildlife Refuge.

CARIBOU   The migrations of caribou across Alaska's Arctic regions are wonderful to watch, but they are not always easy to time because of annual variations in weather and routes that the herds follow. The U.S. Fish and Wildlife Service and Alaska Department of Fish and Game will have the best guess as to where you should be and when. Or you can settle for seeing a few caribou in places such as Denali National Park & Preserve.

MARINE ANIMALS   Skip ahead to the next section in this chapter for in-depth information about whale-watching cruises. For more on whales, go to ⇨ *Keepers of the Deep* in the next section.

At **Round Island,** outside Dillingham in the Southwest, bull walruses by the thousands haul out in summer. Part of the Walrus Islands State Game Sanctuary, Round Island can be visited by permit only. For details, contact the **Alaska Department of Fish and Game** (☎ *907/842–2334* ⊕ *www.wildlife.alaska.gov/index.cfm?adfg=refuge.rnd_is*). Access is by floatplane or, more commonly, by boat. Expect rain, winds, and the possibility of being weathered in. Rubber boots are essential, as are a four-season tent, high-quality rain gear, and plenty of food.

It's easier, but expensive (more than $1,000 for travel and tour), to visit the remote **Pribilof Islands**, where about 80% of the world's northern fur seals and 200 species of birds can be seen, but you may also encounter fog and Bering Sea storms. Tours to the Pribilofs leave from Anchorage. Contact the **Alaska Maritime National Wildlife Refuge** (☎ *907/235–6546 ⊕ www.r7.fws.gov/nwr/akmar/index.htm*) for information about wildlife viewing.

WHALE-WATCHING CRUISES

Fodor's Choice
★
A close encounter with whales in their natural environment can be a thrilling experience—the term "world's largest mammal" is hard to understand until you witness their graceful largesse as they glide through the water. Hearing the resonant whoosh of a whale exhaling and witnessing such acrobatics as "spy-hopping" (a whale poking its head straight out of the water for a look around), breaching, and skimming, you can't help but feel amazed and humbled by the awesome presence of these majestic creatures.

Whales migrate along much of Alaska's coast from March through September: from the Southeast region's Inside Passage to South Central's Prince William Sound, Kodiak Archipelago, and Kenai Fjords National Park, and then north through the Bering, Chukchi, and Beaufort seas in Arctic waters. The whales most commonly seen on whale-watching trips are orcas (or killer whales) and humpbacks.

Whale-watching is not the average spectator sport. It's more like a sea-going game of hide-and-seek. Whales are unpredictable, so be prepared to wait patiently, scanning the water for signs. Sometimes the whales can seem elusive; other times they might rub up against the boat. Also unpredictable are the weather and sea conditions. Bring along a jacket or fleece outerwear and rain gear to keep from getting wet and chilled, and consider using Dramamine or scopolamine patches if you're prone to seasickness.

Most cruises travel in or through waters that attract several species, although some focus on a particular type of whale. ■ TIP➔ Ask when the best time to take a specific trip is; the whale-sighting record is likely better during some months than others. You have to weigh the pros and cons of traveling on small versus large boats. A trip with 15 people will be quite different from one with 150. Larger boats can handle stormy seas much better than smaller boats and offer much better indoor accommodations when the weather turns nasty. Smaller boats will appeal to those who want to steer clear of crowds and those who like to feel closer to the surrounding seascape. More flexible itineraries are another benefit of small boats.

RESOURCES & GUIDES

Hop aboard the **Alaska Marine Highway** (☎ *800/642–0066* ⊕ *www.ferryalaska.com*) and enjoy one of Alaska's greatest means of travel: its ferry system plies the waters of the Inside Passage and South Central all the way to the far reaches of the southwestern chain.

Fodor'sChoice ★ Part of the native-owned Alaska Heritage Tours, **Kenai Fjords Tours** (☎ *907/265–4501 or 877/777–2805* ⊕ *www.kenaifjords.com*) will take you to explore Resurrection Bay and Kenai Fjords National Park. They range from three-hour natural-history tours to five-hour gray whale–watching tours out of Seward.

Mariah Tours (☎ *907/265–4501 or 877/777–2805* ⊕ *www.alaskaheritagetours.com*), also part of Alaska Heritage Tours, offers small-boat trips out of Seward for summertime whale-watching and glacier tours in Kenai Fjords National Park. Besides orcas and humpback whales, you're likely to see bald eagles, sea otters, sea lions, seals, and birds.

Step aboard the **M/V TAZ** (☎ *907/766–3000 or 888/698–2726* ⊕ *www.gustavus.com/taz/tours.html*) and check out Glacier Bay, Icy Straits, and Point Adolphus for awesome views of humpback whales and many other marine mammals. All tours out of Gustavus include binoculars, snacks, and hot beverages. Half-day tours and custom charters accommodating up to 23 passengers are offered.

Juneau-based **Orca Enterprises (with Captain Larry)** (☎ *907/789–6801 or 888/733–6722* ⊕ *www.orcaenterprises.com*) offers whale-watching tours via jet boats designed for comfort and speed. The operator boasts a whale-sighting success rate of 99.9% between May 1 and October 15. Humpbacks and orcas are most frequently seen.

Sailing out of Whittier into Prince William Sound since 1989, **Sound Eco Adventures** (☎ *888/471–2312* ⊕ *www.soundecoadventure.com*) takes only six guests at a time aboard 30-foot boats. It's a convenient hour-long drive south of Anchorage; expect to see everything from harbor seals to humpbacks.

KEEPERS OF THE DEEP:
A LOOK AT ALASKA'S WHALES

(top) A breaching humpback (left) An Orca whale

It's unforgettable: a massive, barnacle-encrusted humpback breaches skyward from the placid waters of an Alaskan inlet, shattering the silence with a thundering display of grace, power, and beauty. Welcome to Alaska's coastline.

Alaska's cold, nutrient-rich waters offer a bounty of marine life that's matched by few regions on earth. Eight species of whales frequent the state's near-shore waters, some migrating thousands of miles each year to partake of Alaska's marine buffet. The state's most famous cetaceans (the scientific classification of marine mammals that includes whales, dolphins, and porpoises) are the humpback whale, the gray whale, and the Orca (a.k.a. the killer whale).

BEST REGIONS TO VIEW WHALES

Whales can be viewed throughout the world; after all, they are migratory animals. But thanks to its pristine environment, diversity of cetacean species, and jaw-dropping beauty, Alaska is perhaps the planet's best whale-watching locale.

From April through October, humpbacks visit many of Alaska's coastal regions, including the Bering Sea, the Aleutian Islands, and Prince William Sound. The **Inside Passage,** though, is the best place to see them: it's home to a migratory population of up to 600 humpbacks. Good bets for whale-viewing include taking a trip on the **Alaska Marine Highway,** spending time in **Glacier Bay National Park,** or taking a day cruise out of any of Southeast's main towns. While most humpbacks return to

Mutually curious!

Hawaiian waters in the winter, some spend the whole year in Southeast Alaska.

Gray whales favor the coastal waters of the Pacific, which terminate in the Bering Sea. Their healthy population—some studies estimate that 30,000 gray whales populate the west coast of North America—make

THE HUMPBACK: Musical, Breaching Giant

Humpbacks' flukes allow them to breach so effectively that they can propel two-thirds of their massive bodies out of the water.

Known for their spectacular breaching and unique whale songs, humpbacks are captivating. Most spend their winters in the balmy waters off the Hawaiian Islands, where females, or sows, give birth. Come springtime, humpbacks set off on a 3,000-mile swim to their Alaskan feeding grounds.

Southeast Alaska is home to one of the world's only groups of bubble-net feeding humpbacks. Bubble-netting is a cooperative hunting technique in which one humpback circles below a school of baitfish while exhaling a "net" of bubbles, causing the fish to gather. Other humpbacks then feed at will from the deliciously dense group of fish.

The Song of the Humpback

All whale species communicate sonically, but the humpback is the most musical. During mating season, males emit haunting, songlike calls that can last for up to 30 minutes at a time. Most scientists attribute the songs to flirtatious, territorial, or competitive behaviors.

QUICK FACTS:

Scientific name: *Megaptera novaeangliae*

Length: Up to 50 ft.

Weight: Up to 90,000 pounds (45 tons)

Coloring: Dark blue to black, with barnacles and knobby, lighter-colored flippers

Life span: 30 to 40 years

Reproduction: One calf every 2 to 3 years; calves are generally 12 feet long at birth, weighing up to 2,000 pounds (1 ton)

them relatively easy to spot in the spring and early summer months, especially around **Sitka** and **Kodiak Island** and south of the **Kenai Peninsula,** where numerous whale-watching cruises depart from Seward into **Resurrection Bay.**

Orcas populate nearly all of Alaska's coastal regions. They're most commonly viewed in the **Inside Passage** and **Prince William Sound,** where they reside year-round. A jaunt on the Alaska Marine Highway is one option, but so is a kayaking or day-cruising trip out of **Whittier** to Prince William Sound.

When embarking on a whale-watching excursion, don't forget rain gear, a camera, and binoculars!

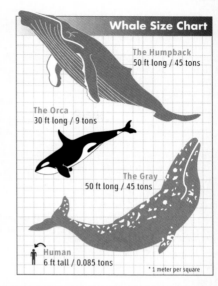

Whale Size Chart

The Humpback
50 ft long / 45 tons

The Orca
30 ft long / 9 tons

The Gray
50 ft long / 45 tons

Human
6 ft tall / 0.085 tons

* 1 meter per square

2

IN FOCUS KEEPERS OF THE DEEP

THE GRAY WHALE: Migrating Leviathan

Though the average lifespan of a gray whale is 50 years, one individual was reported to reach 77 years of age—a real old-timer.

While frequenting Alaska during the long days of summer, gray whales tend stay close to the coastline. They endure the longest migration of any mammal on earth—some travel 14,000 mi each way between Alaska's Bering Sea and their mating grounds in sunny Baja California.

Gray whales are bottom-feeders that stir up sediment on sea floor, then use their baleen—a comb-like collection of long, stiff hairs inside their mouths—to filter out sediment and trap small crustaceans and tube worms.

Their predilection for near-shore regions, coupled with their easygoing demeanor—some "friendly" gray whales have even been known to approach small tour boats—cements their spot on the short list of Alaska's favorite cetacean celebrities. (Gray whales aren't always in such amicable spirits: whalers dubbed mother gray whales "devilfish" for the fierce manner in which they protected their young.)

QUICK FACTS:

Scientific name:
Eschrichtius robustus

Length: Up to 50 ft.

Weight: Up to 90,000 pounds (45 tons)

Coloring: Gray and white, usually splotched with lighter growths and barnacles

Life span: 50 years

Reproduction: One calf every 2 years; calves are generally 15 feet long at birth, weighing up to 1,500 pounds (3/4 ton)

AN AGE-OLD CONNECTION

Nearly every major native group in Alaska has relied on whales for some portion of its diet. The Inupiaq and Yup'ik counted on whales for blubber, oil, meat, and intestines to survive. Aleuts used whale bones to build their semisubterranean homes. Even the Tlingit, for whom food was perennially abundant, considered a beached whale a bounty.

Subsistence whaling lives on in Alaska: although gray-whale hunting was banned in 1996, the Eskimo Whaling Commission permits the state's native populations to harvest 50 bowhead whales every year.

Other Alaskan whale species:
Bowhead, northern right, minke, fin, and beluga whales also inhabit Alaskan waters.

barnacles

BARNACLES These ragged squatters of the sea live on several species of whales, including humpbacks and gray whales. They're conspicuously absent from smaller marine mammals, such as Orcas, dolphins, and porpoises. The reason? Speed. Scientists theorize that barnacles are only able to colonize the slowest-swimming cetacean species, leaving the faster swimmers free from their unwanted drag.

THE ORCA: Conspicuous, Curious Cetacean

Why the name killer whale? Perhaps for this animal's skilled and fearsome hunting techniques, which are sometimes used on other, often larger, cetaceans.

Perhaps the most recognizable of all the region's marine mammals, Orcas (also called killer whales) are playful, inquisitive, and intelligent whales that reside in Alaskan waters year-round. Orcas travel in multigenerational family groups known as pods, which practice cooperative hunting techniques.

Orcas are smaller than grays and humpbacks, and their 17-month gestation period is the longest of any cetacean. They are identified by their white-and-black markings, as well as by the knifelike shape of their dorsal fins, which, in the case of mature males, can reach 6 feet in height.

Pods generally adhere to one of three common classifications: **residents,** which occupy inshore waters and feed primarily on fish; **transients,** which occupy larger ranges and hunt sea lions, squid, sharks, fish, and whales; and **offshores,** about which little is known.

QUICK FACTS:

Scientific name:
Orcinus orca

Length: Up to 30 ft.

Weight: Up to 18,000 pounds (9 tons)

Coloring: Smooth, shiny black skin with white eye patches and chin and white belly markings

Life span: 30 to 50 years

Reproduction: One calf every 3 to 5 years; calves are generally 6 feet long at birth, weighing up to 400 pounds (0.2 ton)

Cruising in Alaska

WORD OF MOUTH

"My husband and I went on a Princess cruise, Whittier to Vancouver, and although the balcony was a major splurge, I didn't regret it for a moment. Is it overpriced? Sure. But how often do you do an Alaskan cruise?"

—susieQ122

Alaska, it would seem, was made for cruising. Alaska is one of cruising's showcase destinations, and there are a wide variety of options available.

The traditional route to the state is by sea, through a 1,000-mi-long protected waterway known as the Inside Passage. From Vancouver, B.C., in the south to Skagway in the north, it winds around islands large and small, past glacier-carved fjords and hemlock-blanketed mountains. This great land is home to breaching whales, nesting eagles, spawning salmon, and calving glaciers. The towns here can be reached only by air or sea; there are no roads between them. Juneau, in fact, is the only water-locked state capital in the United States. Beyond the Inside Passage, the Gulf of Alaska leads to Prince William Sound—famous for its marine life and more fjords and glaciers—and Anchorage, Alaska's largest city.

Itineraries give passengers more choices than ever before—from traditional loop cruises of the Inside Passage, round-trips from Vancouver or Seattle, to one-way Inside Passage–Gulf of Alaska cruises. A number of smaller boats sail only in the Inside Passage and Prince William Sound, away from big-ship traffic.

For more detailed information on cruising in Alaska, see *Fodor's Alaska Ports of Call 2009.*

CHOOSING YOUR CRUISE

TYPES OF SHIPS

The type of ship you choose is the most important factor in your Alaska cruise vacation, because it will determine how you see Alaska. Large cruise ships sail farther from land and visit major ports of call such as Juneau, Skagway, and Ketchikan. Small ships spend much of their time hugging the coastline, looking for wildlife, waterfalls, and other natural and scenic attractions. For more independent types, there's no better way to see Alaska than aboard the ferries of the Alaska Marine

Highway System, which allow you to travel with your car or RV and explore at your own pace.

CRUISE SHIPS

Alaska's cruise-ship fleet represents the very best that today's cruise industry has to offer. Nearly all the ships were built within the last two decades and have atrium lobbies, state-of-the-art health spas, high-tech show lounges, elaborate dining rooms, and a variety of alternative restaurants. By night they come alive with Vegas-style revues, pulsating discos, and somewhat more sedate cabaret or comedy acts. Most of the latest liners have cabins with verandas—a great bonus in Alaska for watching the scenery go by from the privacy of your own stateroom. The newest cruise ships are lined with glass throughout their corridors and public rooms, so you're never far from the sea or a great view.

GO TO THE EXPERTS

Although most other kinds of travel are booked over the Internet nowadays, for cruises, booking with a travel agent who specializes in cruises to Alaska is still your best bet. Agents have built strong relationships with the lines, and have a much better chance of getting you the cabin you want, and possibly even a free upgrade.

SMALL SHIPS

Unlike larger cruise ships, the smaller vessels cruising in Alaska are designed to reach into the most remote corners of the world. Shallow drafts allow them to navigate up rivers, close to coastlines, and into shallow coves. Motorized rubber landing craft, known as Zodiacs, are usually kept on board, making it possible for passengers to go ashore almost anywhere. Alaska, not casinos or spa treatments, is the focus of these cruises. Lectures and talks—conducted daily by naturalists, Native Alaskans, and other experts in the Great Land's natural history and native cultures—are the norm. But in comparison with those on cruise ships, cabins on expedition ships can be quite small and are often less luxurious. Small ships usually have just one dining option, and entertainment is usually limited to lectures and videos, but passengers enjoy greater opportunities to see scenery and wildlife, and a better chance to get to know their fellow passengers.

FERRIES

The state ferry system is known as the Alaska Marine Highway, because its vessels carry vehicles as well as passengers. Each ferry has a car deck that can accommodate every size vehicle—from the family car to a Winnebago. You can take your vehicle ashore, drive around, even live in it, and then transport it with you to the next port of call. From Skagway or Haines (the only Inside Passage towns connected to a road system), you can drive farther north to Fairbanks and Anchorage by way of the Alaska Highway. Each ferry also has a main, or "weather," deck to accommodate passengers, and onboard camping is allowed year-round.

ITINERARIES

You'll want to give some consideration to your ship's Alaskan itinerary when choosing your cruise. The length of the cruise will determine the variety and number of ports you visit, but so will the type of itinerary and the point of departure. **Loop cruises** start and end at the same point and usually explore ports close to one another; **one-way cruises** start at one point and end at another and range farther afield.

SEASONAL CHANGES

The landcape along the Inside Passage changes dramatically over the course of the summer. You'll see snowcapped mountains and dramatic waterfalls that are made by the melting process cascading down the cliff faces in May and June, but by July and August, most of the snow and waterfalls will be gone.

Cruise ships typically follow one of two itineraries: round-trip Inside Passage loops starting and finishing in Vancouver, B.C., or Seattle, and one-way Inside Passage–Gulf of Alaska cruises sailing between Vancouver or Seattle and Anchorage. Both itineraries are usually seven days, though some lines offer longer trips. A few lines also schedule one-way or round-trip sailings from San Francisco or Los Angeles. Small ships typically sail within Alaska, setting out from Juneau, Sitka, or other Alaskan ports.

Whether you sail through the Inside Passage or along it will depend on the size of your vessel. Smaller ships can navigate narrow channels, straits, and fjords. Larger vessels must sail farther from land, so don't expect to see much wildlife from the deck of a megaship.

CRUISE TOURS

Most cruise lines give you the option of an independent, hosted, or fully escorted land tour before or after your cruise. Independent tours allow maximum flexibility; you have a preplanned itinerary with confirmed hotel reservations and transportation arrangements, but you're free to follow your interests and whims in each town. A hosted tour is similar, but tour-company representatives are available along the route to help out should you need assistance. On fully escorted tours, you travel with a group, led by a tour director. Activities are preplanned (and typically prepaid), so you have a good idea of how much your trip will cost (not counting incidentals) before you depart. Most cruise-tour itineraries include a ride aboard the Alaska Railroad in a glass-dome railcar.

Independent travel by rental car or RV before or after the cruise segment is another popular option. Generally passengers will plan to begin or end their cruise in Anchorage, the most practical port city to use as a base for exploring the state. Almost any type of car or recreational vehicle, from a small, two-person RV to a large, luxurious motor home, can be rented.

SHORE EXCURSIONS

Shore excursions arranged by the cruise line are a convenient way to see the sights, although you pay extra for this convenience. Before your cruise, you'll receive a booklet describing the shore excursions your cruise line offers. A few lines let you book excursions in advance; all sell them on board during the cruise. If you cancel your excursion, you may incur penalties, the amount varying with the number of days remaining until the tour. Because these trips are specialized, many have limited capacity and are sold on a first-come, first-served basis.

Among the many options available, some are "musts." At least once during your cruise, try flightseeing—it's a sure-fire way to grasp just how huge and wild the state is. Go to an evening salmon feast, where you can savor freshly caught fish cooked over an open fire. And experience an outdoor adventure—you don't have to be an athlete to raft down a river or paddle a sea kayak along the coastline.

WHEN TO GO

Cruise season runs from mid-May to late September; the most popular sailing dates are from late June through August. May and June are the driest months to cruise. Daytime temperatures along the cruise routes in May, June, and September are in the 50s and 60s. July and August averages are in the 60s and 70s, with occasional days in the 80s. Bargains can be found both early and late in the season. Cruising in the low seasons provides plenty of advantages besides discounted fares. Availability of ships and particular cabins is greater in the low and shoulder seasons, and the ports are almost completely free of tourists.

November is the best month for off-season ferry travel, after stormy October and while it's still relatively warm on the Inside Passage (temperatures will average about 40°F). It's a good month for wildlife-watching as well. Some animals show themselves in greater numbers during November. In particular, humpback whales are abundant off Sitka, and bald eagles congregate by the thousands near Haines.

CRUISE COSTS

Cruise costs can vary enormously. If you shop around and book early, you'll undoubtedly pay less. Your cruise fare typically includes accommodation and all onboard meals, snacks, and activities. It does not normally include airfare to the port city, shore excursions, tips, alcoholic drinks, or spa treatments. Only the most expensive Alaska cruises include airfare. Virtually all lines offer air add-ons, which may be less expensive than the latest discounted fare from the airlines.

Shore excursions can be a substantial expense; the best in Alaska are not cheap. But if you skimp too much on your excursion budget, you may deprive yourself of an important part of the Alaska experience.

Tipping is another extra. At the end of the cruise, it's customary to tip your room steward, server, and the person who buses your table, though some lines include the tips in the fare. If tips are not included, expect to pay an average of $10 to $12 per day in tips. For more, *see* Tipping, *in* On Board, *below*; each ship also provides guidelines in its literature.

There are few single cabins on most ships; taking a double cabin for yourself can cost as much as twice the advertised per-person rates (which are based on two people sharing a room). Some cruise lines will find roommates of the same sex for singles so that each can travel at the regular per-person, double-occupancy rate.

BEFORE YOU GO

Once you've chosen your cruise and signed on to go, it's time to get ready. Preparations for a cruise may involve many distinct tasks, but none of them are difficult, especially if broken down into manageable steps. Most important, allow plenty of time to get ready, so you don't get harried in the last couple of weeks.

TICKETS & VOUCHERS

After you make the final payment to your travel agent, the cruise line will issue your cruise tickets and vouchers for airport–ship transfers. Depending on the airline, and whether you have purchased an air-sea package, you may receive your plane tickets or charter-flight vouchers at the same time; you may also receive vouchers for any shore excursions, although most cruise lines issue these aboard ship. Should your travel documents not arrive when promised, contact your travel agent or cruise line. If you book late, tickets may be delivered directly to the ship.

PASSPORTS & VISAS

For Alaska cruises, whether they begin in the United States or in Canada, American and Canadian citizens require proof of citizenship. As a result of laws enacted in 2007, all American citizens must have a passport for travel by air or sea to or from Canada. Permanent residents of the United States and Canada who are not citizens should also carry proof of permanent residence (their Green Card or Permanent Resident Card).

If you are a citizen of another country, you may be required to obtain visas in advance. Check with your travel agent or cruise line about specific requirements. If you do need a visa for your cruise, your travel agent should be able to help you obtain it, but there may be a charge for this service, in addition to the visa charge. Read your cruise documents carefully to see what documents you'll need for embarkation. You don't want to be turned away at the pier.

Immigration regulations require every passenger boarding a cruise ship from a U.S. port to provide additional personal data, such as your current mailing address and telephone number, to the cruise operator in advance of embarkation. Failure to provide this information required by the U.S. government may result in denial of boarding.

ACCESSIBILITY ISSUES

More than the usual amount of preplanning is necessary for smooth sailing if you have special needs. All major cruise lines offer a limited number of wheelchair- and scooter-accessible staterooms. Booking a newer vessel will gener-

PRE-BOARDING TIP

To expedite pre-boarding paperwork, most cruise lines have convenient forms on their Web sites. As long as you have your reservation number, you can provide the required immigration information, pre-reserve shore excursions, and even indicate any creature-comfort special requests. Be sure to print copies of any forms you fill out and bring them with you to the pier.

ally assure more choices. On newer ships, public rooms are generally accessible, and more facilities have been planned with wheelchair users in mind. Auxiliary aids, such as flashers for the hearing impaired and buzzers for visually impaired passengers, as well as lifts for pools and hot tubs, are available upon request.

The best cruise ship for passengers who use wheelchairs is one that ties up right at the dock at every port, at which time a ramp or even an elevator is always made available. Unfortunately, it's hard to ascertain this in advance, since a ship may tie up at the dock at one port on one voyage and, on the next, anchor in the harbor and have passengers transported to shore via tender. Ask your travel agent to find out which ships are capable of docking. If a tender is used, some ships will have crew members carry the wheelchair and passenger from the ship to the tender. Unfortunately, other ships will refuse to take wheelchairs on tenders, especially if the water is choppy.

Passengers who require continuous oxygen or have service animals can bring both aboard a cruise ship; be sure to bring proof of your animal's vaccinations for entry into Canada.

WHAT TO PACK

Certain packing rules apply to all cruises. Always take along a sweater to counter cool evening ocean breezes or overactive air-conditioning. Rain gear is essential—many travelers who plan on indulging in some of the more active shore excursions pack a complete rain suit. Be prepared to dress in layers, since temperatures can vary considerably during the day. Make sure you take at least one pair of comfortable walking shoes for exploring port towns, and waterproof footwear will be useful as well. Ankle-high rubber boots are ideal for many shore trips.

Generally speaking, plan on one outfit for every two days of cruising, especially if your wardrobe contains many interchangeable pieces. Ships often have laundry facilities. Don't forget your toiletries and sundry items, but if you do, these are readily available in port shops or

DON'T FORGET THE BASICS

Getting ready for an Alaska cruise can be very exciting—so much so that sometimes it's tough to peel yourself from the Inuit phrasebook or photoblog of ice formations and tend to less exotic preparations. Here's a quick list of things you'll be glad you did when, say, you're flightseeing at 20,000 ft. and realize you left your bag with the traveler's checks in the taxi you took from the port.

■ Pack a list of the offices that supply refunds for lost or stolen traveler's checks.

■ Take an extra pair of eyeglasses or contact lenses in your carry-on luggage.

■ If you use a prescription drug, pack enough to last the duration of the trip or have your doctor write a prescription using the drug's generic name, because brand names vary from country to country.

■ Always carry medications in their original packaging to avoid problems with customs officials. Don't pack medications in luggage that you plan to check, in case your bags go astray.

■ Make a copy of your passport and keep it separate from your actual passport. If the original gets lost or stolen, having a copy can make replacement much less of a headache.

■ Make copies, or write down the numbers, of your credit cards in case those should be lost or stolen.

the ship's gift shop (though usually at a premium price). Cabin amenities typically include soap and often shampoo, conditioner, and other lotions and potions.

Outlets in cabin bathrooms are usually compatible with U.S.–purchased appliances. This may not be the case on older ships or those with European registries; call ahead if this is a concern for you. Most cabin bathrooms are equipped with low-voltage outlets for electric shavers, and most newer ships have built-in hair dryers.

FORMAL/INFORMAL/CASUAL

Although no two cruises are quite the same, evening dress tends to fall into three categories.

Formal cruises celebrate the ceremony of cruising. Jackets and ties for men are the rule for dinner, tuxedos are not uncommon, and the dress code is observed faithfully throughout the evening.

Informal cruises are a bit more relaxed than their formal counterparts. Men almost always wear a sport coat and tie; women might wear a dressier dress, pants outfit, or a nice skirt and top. Check your documents carefully for a specific definition.

Casual cruises are the most popular. Shipboard dress and lifestyle are always relaxed. An evening might call for no jeans or shorts in the dining room, but otherwise anything goes. Smart Casual, increasingly popular with a corresponding decline in the dressier Informal category, is defined as slacks and sports shirt or sweater for men and skirt of trousers and sweater or blouse for women.

Most cruise lines have reduced the focus on formal and informal dining and offer multiple dining options, including room service. However, it would be wise to ask the cruise line about its dining dress code so you know what to expect and what to pack.

ARRIVING & DEPARTING

If you have purchased an air-sea package, you will be met by a cruise-company representative when your plane lands at the port city and then shuttled directly to the ship in a bus or minivan. Some cruise lines arrange to transport luggage between airport and ship so passengers don't have to deal with baggage claim at the start of the cruise or with baggage check-in at the end. If you decide not to buy the air-sea package but still plan to fly, ask your travel agent if you can use the ship's transfer bus. Otherwise, you will have to take a taxi to the ship.

If you live close to the port of embarkation, bus transportation may be available. If you are part of a group that has booked a cruise together, this transportation may be part of your package. Another option for those who live close to their point of departure is to drive to the ship, an increasingly popular option. Major U.S. and Canadian cruise ports all have parking facilities.

EMBARKATION

CHECK-IN

On arrival at the dock, you must check in before boarding your ship. An officer will collect or stamp your ticket, inspect or even retain your passport or other official identification, ask you to fill out a tourist card, check that you have the correct visas, and collect any unpaid port or departure tax.

Seating assignments for the dining room are often handed out at this time, too, although most cruise ships are now offering you the opportunity to dine when and with whom you like in any of several restaurants aboard. You may also register your credit card to open a shipboard account, or that may be done later at the purser's office. After this, you will be required to go through a security check and to pass your hand baggage through an X-ray inspection similar to those found at airports.

Although it takes only 5 or 10 minutes per family to check in, lines are often long, so aim for off-peak hours. The worst time tends to be immediately after the ship begins boarding; the later it is, the less crowded. For example, if boarding is from 2 to 4:30, lines are shorter after 3:30.

BOARDING THE SHIP

Before you walk up the gangway, the ship's photographer will probably take your picture; there's no charge unless you buy the picture (usually $7 to $8). On board, stewards may serve welcome drinks in souvenir glasses—for which you're usually charged between $3 and $5.

You'll either be escorted to your cabin by a steward or, on a smaller ship, given your key—now usually a plastic card—by a ship's officer and directed to your cabin. Some elevators are unavailable to passengers during boarding, since they are used to transport luggage. You may arrive to find your luggage outside your cabin or just inside the door; if it hasn't arrived a half hour before sailing, contact the purser. If your luggage doesn't make it to the ship in time, the purser will have it flown to the next port.

DISEMBARKATION

The last night of your cruise is full of business. On most ships you must place everything except your hand luggage outside your door, ready to be picked up by midnight or early in the morning. Color-coded tags, distributed to your cabin in a debarkation packet, should be placed on your luggage before the crew collects it. The color of your tag will determine when you leave the ship and help you retrieve your luggage on the pier.

Your shipboard bill is left in your room during the last day of a cruise or on the morning of your departure from the ship; to pay the bill (if you haven't already put it on your credit card) or to settle any questions, you must stand in line at the purser's office. Tips to the cabin steward and dining staff are distributed on the last night of the cruise or are automatically added to your onboard account. If you haven't already paid it by credit card or wish to dispute any charges on it, go to the purser immediately to settle or discuss your account. Some lines close down their computer files for the cruise by 9 AM or 10 AM to prepare for the next cruise, and may be unable to credit your account with any disputed charges, requiring you to contact your credit-card company or the cruise line later for a refund.

On the morning the cruise ends, in-room breakfast service may not be available because stewards are too busy, but you'll usually find breakfast being served in both the formal dining room and at the ship's buffet dining area. Most passengers clear out of their cabins as soon as possible, gather their hand luggage, and stake out a chair in one of the public lounges to await the ship's clearance through customs. Be patient—it takes a long time to unload and sort thousands of pieces of luggage.

Passengers are disembarked in groups according to color-coded luggage tags; those with the earliest flights get off first. If you have a tight connection, notify the purser before the last day, and he or she may be able to arrange faster pre-clearing and debarkation.

ON BOARD

SHIPBOARD ACCOUNTS

Because a cashless society prevails on cruise ships, during booking or check-in an imprint is made of your credit card or you place a cash deposit for use against your onboard charges. Then you're issued a charge card that usually doubles as your stateroom "key." Most onboard expenditures are charged to your shipboard account with your signature as verification, with the exception of casino gaming— even so, you can often get "cash advances" against your account from the casino cashier.

An itemized bill listing your purchases is provided at the end of the voyage. In order to avoid surprises, it's a good idea to set aside your charge slips and request an interim printout of your bill from the purser to ensure accuracy. Any discrepancies in your account should be taken care of before leaving the ship, usually at the Purser's Desk. Should you change your mind about charging onboard purchases, you can always inform the purser and pay in cash or traveler's checks instead and get a refund for the difference, if any.

TIPPING

For better or worse, tipping is an integral part of the cruise experience. Like their land contemporaries, cruise-ship service personnel depend on gratuities for a major portion of their compensation. Educate yourself about gratuities by reading your cruise-line brochure, where suggested tipping levels are usually listed in the back with the rest of the fine print or the small booklet that comes with your cruise documents for up-to-the-minute information.

During your cruise, room-service waiters generally receive a cash tip of $1 to $3 per delivery. A 15% gratuity will automatically be added to each bar bill during the cruise. If you use salon and spa services, a similar percentage is generally added to the bills there. If you dine in a specialty restaurant, you will usually be asked to provide a onetime gratuity for the service staff.

There will be a "Disembarkation Talk" on the last day of the cruise that explains tipping procedures. If you're expected to tip in cash, small white "tip" envelopes will appear in your stateroom that day. If you tip in cash, you usually give the tip envelope directly to each person on the last night of the cruise. Tips generally add up to about $10 to $12 per person per day. You tip the same amount for each person who shares the cabin, including children, unless otherwise indicated.

DINING

Cruise ships serve food nearly around the clock. There may be as many as four breakfast options: early-morning coffee and pastries on deck, breakfast in bed through room service, buffet-style dining in the cafeteria, and a more formal breakfast in the dining room. There may also be several lunch choices, mid-afternoon hors d'oeuvres, teatime, and late-night buffets. You may eat whatever is on the menu, in any quantity, at any meal. Room service is traditionally, but not always, free.

RESTAURANTS

Every large ship has at least one main restaurant and a casual, buffet alternative. Increasingly important are specialty restaurants. Meals in the primary and buffet restaurants are included in the cruise fare, as are round-the-clock room service, midday tea and snacks, and late-night buffets. Most mainstream cruise lines levy a surcharge for dining in alternative restaurants that may, or may not, also include a gratuity, although there generally is no additional charge on luxury cruise lines.

You may also find a pizzeria or a specialty coffee bar on your ship—increasingly popular favorites cropping up on ships old and new. Although pizza is complimentary, expect an additional charge for specialty coffees at the coffee bar and, quite likely, in the dining room as well. You will also likely be charged for any drinks during meals other than iced tea, regular coffee, tap water, and fruit juice; this includes soft drinks.

There is often a direct relationship between the cost of a cruise and the quality of its cuisine. The food is very sophisticated on some (mostly expensive) lines, but on most mainstream cruise lines the food is the quality that you would find in any good hotel dining room—perfectly acceptable but certainly not great.

SMALL SHIPS

Food on small ships is often less ubiquitous, but also very good. The food tends to be fresh and wholesome, but not elaborate, with a home-cooking, rather than restaurant-style presentation. There's usually just one dining room with set dining times, but drinks and snacks are generally available, such as during cocktail hour, or if the chef decides to whip up some freshly baked cookies. On very small ships, passengers eat together family-style at one table, though many meals are served as picnics on shore excursions.

SEATINGS

If your cruise ship has traditional seatings for dinner, your seating choices may set the tone for your entire trip. Which is best? Early dinner seating is generally scheduled between 6 and 6:30 PM, while late seating can begin from 8:15 to 8:45 PM. So the "best" seating depends on you, your lifestyle, and your personal preference.

Families with young children and older passengers often choose an early seating. Early-seating diners are encouraged not to linger too long over dessert and coffee because the dining room has to be readied for late seating. Late seating is viewed by some passengers as more romantic and less rushed.

Open seating is primarily associated with more upscale lines; it allows you the flexibility to dine any time during restaurant hours and be seated with whomever you please. Led by Norwegian Cruise Line and Princess Cruises, more contemporary and premium cruise lines are exploring open seating options to offer variety and a more personalized experience for their passengers.

Cruise lines understand that strict schedules no longer satisfy the desires of all modern cruise passengers. Many cruise lines now include alternatives to the set schedules in the dining room, including à la carte restaurants and casual dinner menus in their buffet facilities where more flexibility is allowed in dress and mealtimes.

THE CAPTAIN'S TABLE

You'll know if you have been included in this exclusive coterie when an embossed invitation arrives in your stateroom on the day of a formal dinner. RSVP as soon as possible; many people covet this special experience, and if you're unable to attend, someone else will be invited in your place. Who is invited to the captain's table? If you're a frequent repeat cruiser, the occupant of an Owner's Suite, or hail from the captain's hometown, you may be considered. Honeymoon couples are sometimes selected at random, as are couples celebrating a golden wedding anniversary. Attractive, unattached female passengers often round out an uneven number of guests. Requests made by travel agents on behalf of their clients sometimes do the trick.

SPECIAL DIETS

Cruise lines make every possible attempt to ensure dining satisfaction. If you have special dietary considerations—such as low-salt, kosher, or food allergies—be sure to indicate them well ahead of time and check to be certain your needs are known by your waiter once on board. In addition to the usual menu items, "spa," low-calorie, low-carbohydrate, or low-fat selections, as well as children's menus are usually available. Requests for dishes not featured on the menu can often be granted if you ask in advance.

WINE

Wine by the bottle is a more economical choice at dinner than ordering it by the glass. Any wine you don't finish will be kept for you and served the next night. Gifts of wine or champagne ordered from the cruise line (either by you, a friend, or your travel agent) can be taken to the dining room. Wine from any other source will incur a corkage fee of approximately $10 to $25 per bottle.

GOING ASHORE

Traveling by cruise ship presents an opportunity to visit many places in a short time. The flip side is that your stay in each port of call will be brief. For this reason cruise lines offer shore excursions, which maximize passengers' time. There are a number of advantages to shore excursions arranged by your ship: in some destinations, transportation may be unreliable, and a ship-packaged tour is the best way to see distant sights. Also, you don't have to worry about missing the ship. The disadvantage of a shore excursion is the cost—you pay more for the convenience of having the ship do the legwork for you. Of course, you can always book a tour independently, hire a taxi, or use foot power to explore on your own. Most of the towns have hiking trails easily accessible to port areas, and a stop at the local visitor center can help you plan a walking tour within your time limit. However, be sure to carry along rain gear and drinking water, even for the most leisurely stroll. The weather in Alaska is very fickle and subject to rapid changes.

> **GOING SOLO**
>
> Craving some alone time? If there's a port call that doesn't particularly interest you, you may choose to spend some time on the ship while almost everyone else is in town. Although the number of activities is somewhat curtailed, onboard programs don't cease entirely. There are still exercise classes, the spa and fitness center remain open, and games and movies are sometimes planned.

Many of the busier port cities tend to have several ships in port at a time, and the more popular shore trips can fill up quickly. If your heart is set on a particular experience, book it before your cruise or on board as soon as you can. Some excursions, such as flightseeing trips and the Skagway narrow-gauge rail trip, are in very high demand. Information on local tours is available at the visitor-information counter usually close to the pier in each port.

PORTS OF CALL

Alaska cruise itineraries usually explore either the Inside Passage, or the Gulf of Alaska. Possible ports of call along the Inside Passage are: Haines, Juneau, Ketchikan, Metlakatla, Misty Fjords National Monument, Petersburg, Sitka, Skagway, and Wrangell. Ports of call on Gulf of Alaska cruises include: Anchorage, Cordova, Homer, Kodiak, Seward, Tracy Arm, and Valdez. Other ships sometimes sail to more out-of-the-way ports, such as Nome, or places on the way to Alaska from the lower 48, such as Prince Rupert, B.C., and Victoria, B.C. For more information about these ports, *see* Ch. 4, Southeast, *and* Ch. 6, South Central.

ARRIVING IN PORT

When your ship arrives in a port, it will either tie up alongside a dock or anchor out in a harbor. If the ship is docked, passengers walk down the gangway to go ashore. Docking makes it easy to go back and forth between the shore and the ship.

TENDERING

If your ship anchors in the harbor, you will have to take a small boat—called a launch or tender—to get ashore. Tendering is a nuisance. Passengers wishing to disembark may be required to gather in a public room, get sequenced boarding passes, and wait until their numbers are called. The ride to shore may take as long as 20 minutes. If you don't like waiting, plan to go ashore an hour or so after the ship drops its anchor.

MISSING THE BOAT

If the ship sails without you, immediately contact the cruise line's port representative, whose phone number is often listed on the daily schedule of activities. You may be able to hitch a ride on a pilot boat, although that is unlikely. Passengers who miss the boat must pay their own way to the next port.

Because tenders can be difficult to board, passengers with mobility problems may not be able to visit certain ports. The larger ships are more likely to use tenders. It is usually possible to learn before booking a cruise whether the ship will dock or anchor at its ports of call.

Before anyone is allowed to walk down the gangway or board a tender, the ship must be cleared for landing. Immigration and customs officials board the vessel to examine passports and sort through red tape. It may be more than an hour before you're allowed ashore. You will be issued a boarding pass, which you'll need to get back on board.

RETURNING TO THE SHIP

Cruise lines are strict about sailing times, which are posted at the gangway and elsewhere and announced in the daily schedule of activities. Be sure to be back on board at least a half hour before the announced sailing time or you may be stranded. If you are on a shore excursion that was sold by the cruise line, however, the captain will wait for your group before casting off. That is one reason many passengers prefer ship-packaged tours.

THE CRUISE FLEET

In this chapter, large and luxury cruise lines and their ships are presented first, in alphabetical order, followed by small-ship cruise lines, also in alphabetical order. Ships for each cruise line are listed individually or by "class." When ships belong to the same class—or are basically similar—they're listed together with their names separated by commas. Some ships owned by the cruise lines listed do not include regularly scheduled Alaska cruises on their published itineraries as of this writing and thus aren't included here. For a complete description of the ships that are scheduled to sail in the 2009 cruising season, *see* Fodor's Alaska Ports of Call 2009.

CRUISE SHIPS

CARNIVAL CRUISES

The world's largest cruise line originated the "Fun Ship" concept in 1972 with the relaunch of an aging ocean liner that got stuck on a sandbar during its maiden voyage. In true entrepreneurial spirit, founder Ted Arison shrugged off an inauspicious beginning and introduced "superliners" a decade later. Sporting red-white-and-blue flared funnels, which are easily recognized from afar, new ships are continuously added to the fleet and rarely deviate from a successful pattern.

3

Your Shipmates. Carnival's passengers are mostly American couples in their mid-30s to mid-50s. During holidays and school vacation periods you'll see many families with kids on board. "Camp Carnival" offers year-round programs for children and teens from age 2 to 17. Daytime group babysitting is offered for infants two and under until noon on all port days, as well as from 10 PM to 3 AM, when slumber party–style group babysitting is available for ages 4 months to 11 years. As long as diapers and supplies are provided, toddlers do not have to be toilet trained to participate.

Food. Carnival ships have flexible dining options, with four seatings for dinner, casual alternative restaurants, and upscale supper clubs on the newest ships that serve cuisine comparable to high-end steak houses and seafood restaurants ashore. "Georges Blanc Signature Selections" expand main dining room, Lido restaurant, and Supper Club menus with a variety of gourmet-quality choices. In addition to the regular menu, vegetarian, low-calorie, low-carbohydrate, low-salt, no-sugar, and children's selections are available. If you don't feel like dressing up for dinner, the Lido buffet serves full meals and excellent pizza.

Fitness & Recreation. Carnival's trademark spas and fitness centers are some of the largest and best equipped at sea. State-of-the-art cardiovascular and strength-training equipment, a jogging track, and basic exercise classes are available at no charge in the fitness centers. There's a fee for personal training and specialized classes such as yoga and Pilates.

Service & Tipping. Service on Carnival ships is friendly but not polished. Stateroom attendants are not only recognized for their attention to cleanliness, but also for their expertise in creating "towel animals"—cute critters fashioned from bath towels that appear most nights during turn-down service. Gratuities of $10 per passenger, per day, are automatically added to onboard accounts. A 15% gratuity is automatically added to bar and beverage tabs.

Carnival Cruise Lines, ☎305/599–2600 or 800/227–6482 ⊕*www.carnival.com.*

THE SHIP *Carnival Spirit.* In 2009 Carnival will offer seven-day, one-way cruises between Vancouver and Whittier, which call at Ketchikan, Juneau Skagway, and Sitka, and cruise through College Fjord and Lynn Canal; and round-trip loop cruises from Vancouver that stop at Juneau, Skagway, and Ketchikan, and cruise through Glacier Bay.

CELEBRITY CRUISES

Founded in 1989, Celebrity has gained and retained a reputation for fine food and professional service. The cruise line has built premium, sophisticated ships and developed signature amenities, including a specialty coffee shop, martini bar, large standard staterooms with generous storage, spas, and butler service for passengers booking the top suites. ConciergeClass makes certain premium ocean-view and balcony staterooms almost the equivalent of suites in terms of amenities and service.

Entertainment choices range from Broadway-style productions, captivating shows, and lively discos to Monte Carlo–style casinos and specialty lounges. Multimillion-dollar art collections grace the entire fleet, which merged with Royal Caribbean International in 1997.

Your Shipmates. Celebrity caters to Americans, primarily couples from their mid-30s to mid-50s. During summer months and holiday periods you'll see many families with kids aboard. Each vessel has a dedicated playroom and offers planned activities for children and teens aged 3 to 17, plus Toddler Time for parents and their children under age 3. Some activities have additional fees; evening in-cabin babysitting can also be arranged for a fee.

Food. In early 2007, Celebrity announced plans to advance its already distinguished fleetwide culinary program to the next level. Las Vegas-based Blau & Associates, a strategic restaurant planning and development firm, now consults on shipboard cuisine on all ships. Alternative restaurants on some ships offer fine dining in classic ocean-liner splendor.

Fitness and Recreation. Celebrity's fitness centers and AquaSpa by Elemis are some of the most tranquil and nicely equipped at sea. State-of-the-art exercise equipment, a jogging track, and some fitness classes are available at no charge. Spa treatments include a variety of massages, body wraps, and facials. Each ship has an Acupuncture at Sea program administered by a specialist in Oriental medicine. Hair and nail services are offered in the salons.

Service & Tipping. Service on Celebrity ships is unobtrusive and polished. ConciergeClass adds an unexpected level of service and amenities that are usually reserved for passengers in top-category suites on other premium cruise lines. Gratuities can be added to shipboard accounts or personally distributed in cash by passengers on the last night of the cruise. Suggested guidelines are per person, per day: each waiter and cabin steward $3.50 ($4 in Concierge class); butler: $3.50 (suites only); assistant waiter $2; assistant chief housekeeper 50¢; maitre d' $1 (half these totals for children under 12 who share their parents' cabin). An automatic gratuity of 15% is added to all beverage tabs.

Celebrity Cruises, ☎*305/539–6000 or 800/437–3111* ⊕*www.celebritycruises.com.*

THE SHIPS   *Celebrity Infinity, Celebrity Millennium.* In 2009 *Celebrity Millennium*
★   will make seven-day, one-way Gulf of Alaska cruises between Vancou-

ver and Seward calling at Ketchikan, Juneau, Skagway, and Icy
Strait Point and cruising Hubbard
Glacier, as well as round-trip cruises
from Vancouver for either seven
days, calling at Juneau, Skagway,
and Ketchikan, and cruising Hubbard Glacier, or adding port calls in
Icy Strait Point and Sitka for a ten-

day sailing; Celebrity *Infinity* will sail the Inside Passage round-trip
from Seattle with stops at Ketchikan, Juneau, Icy Strait Point, Victoria,
BC, and cruising Hubbard Glacier.

Celebrity Mercury. Celebrity Mercury will cruise the Inside Passage
from Vancouver in 2009, with stops at Juneau, Ketchikan, and Sitka,
as well as cruising Hubbard Glacier.

HOLLAND AMERICA LINE
Founded in 1873, Holland America Line (HAL) is one of the oldest
names in cruising. Its cruises are classic, conservative affairs renowned
for their grace and gentility. As its ships attract a more youthful clientele, Holland America has taken steps to shed its "old folks" image,
now offering stops at a private island in the Bahamas, trendier cuisine,
a culinary arts center, and an expanded children's program. Still, these
are not party cruises, and Holland America has managed to preserve
the refined and relaxing qualities that have always been its hallmark,
even on sailings that cater more to younger passengers and families.

Luxury bedding, magnifying makeup mirrors, robes, fresh fruit baskets, flat-screen TVs, and DVD players are found in all cabins. In addition, suites have duvets, fully stocked minibars, personalized stationery,
and access to the exclusive Neptune Lounge. Explorations Café, powered by *The New York Times,* combines a coffee bar, computer center,
and cozy library-reading room complete with tabletop versions of the
Times' crossword puzzles.

Your Shipmates. No longer your grandparents' cruise line, today's Holland America also attracts families and discerning couples, mostly from
their late 30s and up. Retirees are often still in the majority; however,
during holidays and summer months you'll find more families with
kids. Group activities are planned for children ages 3 to 7 and 8 to 12
in Club HAL. Club HAL After Hours offers late-night activities from
10 PM until midnight for an hourly fee. Teens aged 13 to 17 have their
own lounge with activities.

Food. You have your choice of two assigned seatings or open seating for
evening meals in the formal dining room. In the reservations-required,
Pinnacle Grill alternative restaurant ($30), fresh seafood and premium
cuts of beef are used to prepare creative specialty dishes. Delicious
onboard traditions are afternoon tea, a Dutch Chocolate Extrava-
ganza, and Holland America Line's signature bread pudding. Casual
evening dining in the Lido restaurants offers a combination of buffet
and waiter service.

Fitness and Recreation. Well-equipped and fully staffed fitness facilities contain state-of-the-art exercise equipment; basic fitness classes are available at no charge, though you pay for personal training, yoga, and Pilates. You'll also find a jogging track, multiple swimming pools, and sports courts. Promenade decks encircle each ship and are popular for walking. The Greenhouse Spa offers a variety of treatments and salon services.

Service & Tipping. Professional, unobtrusive service by the Indonesian and Filipino staff is a fleetwide standard on Holland America Line. A standard gratuity of $10 per passenger per day is automatically added to shipboard accounts and distributed to stewards and wait staff. Room-service tips are offered in cash. An automatic 15% gratuity is added to bar-service tabs.

Holland America Line, ☎*206/281–3535 or 800/577–1728* ⊕*www.hollandamerica.com.*

THE SHIPS   *Amsterdam.* Round-trips from Seattle stopping in Juneau, Sitka, Ketchikan, and Victoria, BC, and scenic cruising at Hubbard Glacier.

☾ *Zuiderdam, Westerdam. Zuiderdam*: Round-trips from Vancouver stop at Juneau, Skagway, Ketchikan, and cruise Tracy Arm and Glacier Bay; *Westerdam*: Round-trips from Seattle stop at Juneau, Sitka, Ketchikan, and Victoria, BC, and cruise through Glacier Bay.

☾ *Volendam, Zaandam. Volendam*: Round-trip from Vancouver stopping at Skagway, Juneau, and Ketchikan, with scenic cruising through Tracy Arm and Glacier Bay; *Zaandam*: round-trip from Seattle with stops in Juneau, Sitka, Ketchikan, and Victoria, BC, and scenic cruising in Glacier Bay.

Ryndam, Statendam, Veendam. Statendam: One-way from Anchorage or Vancouver stopping at Skagway or Haines, Juneau, and Ketchikan, with cruising through College Fjord and Glacier Bay; *Ryndam*: one-way from Anchorage or Vancouver with stops at Juneau, Skagway or Haines, Sitka, and Ketchikan, and cruising at Hubbard Glacier; *Veendam*: one-way from Anchorage or Vancouver with stops at Juneau, Skagway or Haines, and Ketchikan, and cruising through Glacier Bay and College Fjord.

NORWEGIAN CRUISE LINE

Norwegian Cruise Line (NCL) was established in 1966, when one of Norway's oldest and most respected shipping companies, Oslo-based Klosters Rederi A/S, acquired the *Sunward* and repositioned the ship from Europe to the then-obscure Port of Miami. With the formation of a company called Norwegian Caribbean Lines, the cruise industry as we know it today was born. NCL launched an entirely new concept with its regularly scheduled cruises to the Caribbean on a single-class ship. No longer simply a means of transportation, the ship became a destination unto itself, offering guests an affordable alternative to land-based resorts.

Always a cruise industry innovator, Norwegian Cruise Line's "Freestyle" cruising introduced a wider variety of dining options in a casual, free-flowing atmosphere. Noted for top-quality, high-energy entertainment and emphasis on fitness facilities and programs, NCL combines action, activities, and a resort-casual atmosphere.

Your Shipmates. NCL's mostly American cruise passengers are active couples ranging from their mid-30s to mid-50s; some passengers may be in the over-55 age group. Many families enjoy cruising on NCL ships during summer months on Alaska itineraries. Each NCL vessel offers the "Kid's Crew" program of supervised entertainment for young cruisers ages 2 to 17. For 13- to 17-year-olds there are clubs where they can hang out in adult-free zones.

Food. Main dining rooms serve what is traditionally deemed continental fare, although it's about what you would expect at a really good hotel banquet. Where NCL stands above the ordinary is in their specialty restaurants, especially the French-Mediterranean Le Bistro (on all ships), the Pan-Asian restaurants, and steak houses (on the newer ships). In addition, you may find a Spanish tapas bar and an Italian trattoria. Most, but not all, specialty restaurants carry a cover charge and require reservations. An NCL staple, the late-night Chocoholic Buffet continues to be a favorite event.

Fitness and Recreation. Mandara Spa offers a long list of unique and exotic spa treatments fleet-wide on NCL. State-of-the-art exercise equipment, jogging tracks, and basic fitness classes are available at no charge. There's a fee for personal training and specialized classes such as yoga and Pilates.

Service & Tipping. Although somewhat inconsistent, service is nonetheless congenial. A fixed service charge of $10 per person, per day, is added to shipboard accounts (half that for kids 3 to 12). An automatic 15% gratuity is added to bar tabs and 18% for spa services. Staff members are permitted to accept cash gratuities. Passengers in suites are asked to offer a cash gratuity to their concierge and butlers.

Norwegian Cruise Line, ☎ *305/436–4000 or 800/327–7030* ⊕ *www. ncl.com.*

THE SHIPS *Norwegian Pearl.* In 2009 *Norwegian Pearl* offers round-trip cruises from Seattle that stop in Juneau, Skagway, Ketchikan, and Victoria, BC, as well as scenic cruising through Glacier Bay.

Fodor'sChoice *Norwegian Star.* In 2009 *Norwegian Star* offers round-trip cruises from Seattle that stop in Ketchikan, Juneau, Skagway, and Prince Rupert, ★ BC, with scenic cruising at Sawyer Glacier.

Norwegian Sun. In 2009 *Norwegian Sun* sails round-trip from Vancouver with stops in Ketchikan, Juneau, and Skagway, and scenic cruising at Sawyer Glacier.

PRINCESS CRUISES

Rising from modest beginnings in 1965, when it began offering cruises to Mexico with a single ship, Princess has become one of the world's best known cruise lines. Catapulted to stardom in 1977, when its flagship became the setting for *The Love Boat* television series, Princess introduced millions of viewers to the still-new concept of a seagoing vacation. While the line does have some medium-size vessels, Princess more often follows the "big is better" trend. Its fleet sails to more destinations each year than any other major line, though many cruises depart from the West Coast.

All Princess ships feature the line's innovative "Personal Choice Cruising" program that gives passengers choice and flexibility in customizing their cruise experience—multiple dining locations, flexible entertainment, and affordable private balconies are all highlights. Enrichment programs featuring guest lecturers and opportunities to learn new skills or crafts, but you'll still find staples such as bingo and art auctions.

Your Shipmates. Princess Cruises attract mostly American passengers ranging from their mid-30s to mid-50s. Longer cruises appeal to well-traveled retirees. Families can be found cruising together on the Princess fleet, particularly during summer months, when many children are on board. For young passengers aged 3 to 17, each Princess vessel, except *Pacific Princess,* allows parents independent time ashore; youth centers operate as usual during port days.

Food. Personal choices regarding where and what to eat abound, but unless you opt for traditional assigned seating, you might have to wait for a table in one of the open-seating dining rooms. Menus are varied and extensive, and the results are good to excellent. A special menu is designed especially for children. Alternative restaurants are a staple throughout the fleet, but vary by ship class. Lido buffets on all ships are almost always open, and a pizzeria and grill offer casual daytime snack choices. The fleet's patisseries and ice-cream bars charge for specialty coffee, pastries, and ice-cream treats. With balcony accommodations, you can enjoy a private Champagne Breakfast or Ultimate Balcony Dinner.

Fitness and Recreation. Spa and salon rituals include massages, body wraps, facials, and numerous hair and nail services, including treatments designed specifically for men, teens, and couples. Modern exercise equipment, a jogging track, and basic fitness classes are available at no charge. Grand-class ships have a resistance pool for lap swimming.

Service & Tipping. Professional service by an international staff is efficient and friendly. Princess suggests tipping $11 per person per day for passengers in suites and mini-suites and $10 per person, per day for all other passengers (including children). Gratuities are automatically added to onboard accounts; spa personnel are tipped at your discretion; 15% is added to bar bills.

Princess Cruises, ☎661/753–0000 or 800/774–6237 ⊕*www.princess. com.*

THE SHIPS *Coral Princess, Island Princess.* In 2009 *Coral Princess* and *Island Princess* sail one-way cruises from Vancouver or Anchorage, stopping at Ketchikan, Juneau, and Skagway, and cruising Glacier Bay and College Fjord.

Diamond Princess, Sapphire Princess. In 2009 *Diamond Princess* and *Sapphire Princess* offer one-way cruises from Vancouver or Anchorage and stop at Ketchikan, Juneau, and Skagway, with scenic cruising at Glacier Bay and College Fjord.

Golden Princess, Star Princess. For 2009 *Golden Princess* and *Star Princess* offer round-trip cruises from Seattle with stops at Juneau, Skagway, Ketchikan, and Victoria, BC, and scenic cruising through Tracy Arm Fjord.

Pacific Princess. In 2009 *Pacific Princess* will offer 14-night round-trip sailings from Seattle with calls at Ketchikan, Skagway, Valdez, Seward, Kodiak, Juneau, Icy Strait Point, and Victoria, BC, and scenic cruising of Glacier Bay.

☾ *Sea Princess.* In 2009 Sea *Princess* offers round-trip 10-night cruises from San Francisco stopping at Icy Strait Point or Skagway, plus Juneau, Ketchikan, and Victoria, BC, and scenic cruising in Tracy Arm Fjord.

REGENT SEVEN SEAS CRUISES

Regent Seven Seas Cruises sails an elegant fleet of vessels that offer a nearly all-inclusive cruise experience in sumptuous, contemporary surroundings. The line's spacious ocean-view staterooms have the industry's highest percentage of private balconies, and almost all drinks (except some wines) are now included.

Subtle improvements throughout the fleet are ongoing, such as computer service with Wi-Fi capability for your own laptop and cell phone access. New luxury bedding, Regent-branded bath amenities, flat-screen TVs, DVD players, and new clocks have been added to all cabins. Top suites also feature iPods and Bose speakers. Ships feature exquisite service, generous staterooms with abundant amenities, a variety of dining options, and superior enrichment programs. Cruises are destination focused, and most sailings host guest lecturers—historians, anthropologists, naturalists, and diplomats.

Your Shipmates. Regent Seven Seas Cruises are inviting to active, affluent, well-traveled couples ranging from their late 30s to retirees who enjoy the ships' elegance and destination-rich itineraries. Longer cruises attract passengers in the over-60 age group. Regent vessels are adult oriented and do not have dedicated children's facilities; however youth programs are offered on some sailings. Selected Alaska departures feature the Ambassadors of the Environment Youth program created by Jean-Michel Cousteau, son of the famous oceanographer, which introduces children, teens, and their families to natural wonders while demonstrating ways to build environmental sustainability into their everyday lives at home.

Food. Menus may appear to include the usual cruise-ship staples, but the results are some of the most-outstanding meals at sea. Specialty dining varies within the fleet; when available, the sophisticated Signatures features the cuisine of Le Cordon Bleu of Paris; Latitudes offers menus either inspired by regional American favorites or nouveau international cuisine. In addition, Mediterranean-inspired bistro dinners are served in the venues that are the daytime casual Lido buffet restaurants. Wines chosen to complement dinner menus are freely poured each evening.

Fitness and Recreation. Although gyms and exercise areas are well equipped, these are not large ships, so the facilities tend to be on the small side. Each ship has a jogging track, and the larger ones feature a variety of sports courts. Exclusive to Regent Seven Seas, the spa and salon are operated by high-end Carita of Paris.

Service & Tipping. The efforts of a polished European staff go almost unnoticed, yet special requests are handled with ease. Butlers provide an additional layer of personal service to guests in the top-category suites. Gratuities are included in the fare, and none are expected. Passengers are allowed to contribute to a crew welfare fund that benefits the ship's staff.

Regent Seven Seas Cruises, ☎954/776–6123 or 877/505–5370 ⊕www.rssc.com.

THE SHIP
Fodor'sChoice
★

Seven Seas Mariner. For 2009 *Mariner* will sail one-way from Vancouver or Seward, including stops at Sitka, Juneau, Skagway, and Ketchikan, and scenic cruising at Hubbard Glacier and Tracy Arm Fjord.

ROYAL CARIBBEAN INTERNATIONAL

Big, bigger, biggest! More than a decade ago, Royal Caribbean launched the first of the modern megacruise liners for passengers who enjoy traditional cruising with a touch of daring and whimsy tossed in. All Royal Caribbean ships are topped by the company's distinctive signature Viking Crown Lounge, and expansive multideck atriums and the generous use of floor-to-ceiling glass windows give each vessel a sense of spaciousness and style.

A variety of lounges and high-energy stage shows draws passengers of all ages out to mingle and dance the night away. Comedians, acrobats, magicians, jugglers, and solo entertainers fill show lounges on nights when the ships' singing and dancing companies aren't performing. The action is nonstop in casinos and dance clubs after dark, although daytime hours are filled with games and traditional cruise activities. Port

Cruise ships offer passengers panoramic views of Inside Passage glaciers.

"talks" tend to lean heavily on shopping recommendations and the sale of shore excursions.

Your Shipmates. Royal Caribbean cruises have a broad appeal for active couples and singles, mostly in their 30s to 50s. Families are partial to the newer vessels that have larger staterooms, excellent kids' facilities, and seemingly endless choices of activities and dining options. Supervised age-appropriate activities are designed for children ages 3 through 17. For infants and toddlers 6 to 36 months of age, interactive playgroup sessions are planned, while a teen center with a disco is an adult-free gathering spot. "Family-size" staterooms are available on most newer ships, but there are no self-service laundry facilities.

Food. Dining is an international experience with nightly changing themes and cuisines from around the world. Windjammer Café and, on certain ships, the sunny Seaview Café are casual dining options. Each ship has a pizzeria, coffee bar, and ice-cream parlor, and Johnny Rockets 1950s-style diners (extra fee) can be found on most ships. Royal Caribbean doesn't place emphasis on celebrity chefs or specialty alternative restaurants, although the line has introduced a more upscale and intimate dinner experience in the form of an Italian-specialty restaurant and a steak house on some ships.

Fitness and Recreation. Fabled for its range of top-of-the-line recreation, Royal Caribbean also delivers on the basics: most exercise classes, aimed at sweating off those extra calories, are included in the fare (although there's a fee for spinning, yoga, and Pilates classes, as well as personal training). Each ship has multiple swimming pools and a rock-climbing wall. Spas feature extensive treatment menus and full services for pampering for adults and teens.

Service & Tipping. Service on Royal Caribbean ships is friendly but not consistent. Assigned meal seatings assure that most passengers get to know the waiters and their assistants, who in turn get to know the passengers' likes and dislikes; however, that can lead to a level of familiarity that some find uncomfortable. Tips can be prepaid when the cruise is booked, added onto shipboard accounts, or given in cash on the last night of the cruise. Suggested gratuities per passenger, per day, are: $3.50 for the cabin steward (or $5.75 for suite attendant); $3.50 for the waiter; $2 for the assistant waiter; and $0.75 for the head waiter. A 15% gratuity is automatically added to all bar tabs.

Royal Caribbean International, ☎305/539–6000 or 800/327–6700 ⊕ *www.royalcaribbean.com.*

THE SHIPS
Ⓒ
★ *Radiance of the Seas, Serenade of the Seas.* In 2009 *Radiance of the Seas* will sail one-way from either Anchorage or Vancouver and stop at Ketchikan, Juneau, Skagway, and Icy Strait Point and cruise Hubbard Glacier; *Serenade of the Seas* will sail round-trip from Vancouver, stopping at Juneau, Skagway, and Icy Strait Point and cruising Hubbard Glacier.

Ⓒ *Rhapsody of the Seas.* In 2009 *Rhapsody of the Seas* will sail one-way cruises from either Vancouver or Anchorage with stops at Juneau, Skagway, Ketchikan, and Icy Strait Point and cruising Tracy Arm Fjord/ Sawyer Glacier.

SILVERSEA CRUISES

Intimate ships, paired with exclusive amenities and unparalleled hospitality, are the hallmarks of Silversea luxury cruises. Personalization is a Silversea maxim. Ships offer more activities than other comparably sized luxury vessels, with guest lecturers on nearly every cruise. A multitiered show lounge is the setting for classical concerts, big-screen movies, and folkloric entertainers from ashore. All accommodations are spacious outside suites, most with private verandas. Silversea ships have large swimming pools in expansive Lidos.

Although these ships schedule more activities than other comparably sized luxury vessels, you can either take part or opt instead for a good book and any number of quiet spots to read or snooze in the shade. Silversea is so all-inclusive that you'll find your room key/charge card is seldom used for anything but opening your suite door.

Your Shipmates. Silversea Cruises appeal to sophisticated, affluent couples who enjoy the country club-like atmosphere, exquisite cuisine, and polished service. You might see the occasional child, but children less than one year of age are not permitted.

Food. Dishes from the galleys of Silversea's master chefs are complemented by those of La Collection du Monde, created by Silversea's culinary partner, the world-class chefs of Relais & Châteaux. Perhaps more compelling is the line's flair for originality. The pasta chef's daily special is a passenger favorite, as is the galley brunch, held just once each cruise, when the galley is transformed into a buffet restaurant. Special off-menu orders are prepared whenever possible. Nightly alternative theme dinners in La Terrazza (by day, the Terrace Café) feature regional specialties from the Mediterranean.

Fitness & Recreation. The rather small gyms are well equipped with cardiovascular and weight-training equipment, and fitness classes are held in the mirror-lined, but somewhat confining, exercise room. South Pacific–inspired Mandara Spa offers numerous treatments, including exotic-sounding massages, facials, and body wraps.

3

Service & Tipping. Personalized service is exacting and hospitable, yet discreet; staff members strive for perfection and often achieve it. Personal preferences are remembered and satisfied. Tipping is neither required nor expected.

Silversea Cruises, ☎*954/522–4477 or 800/722–9955* ⊕*www.silversea.com.*

THE SHIPS *Silver Shadow.* In 2009 *Silver Shadow* will make 9-day round-trip voyages from Vancouver, 7-day cruises between Anchorage and Vancouver, and 12-day San Francisco round-trip sailings. Port calls vary by sailing and include Ketchikan, Juneau, Skagway, Wrangell, Sitka, Haines, Valdez, Prince Rupert, BC, or Victoria, BC, and scenic cruising in College Fjord, Hubbard Glacier, or Sawyer Glacier.

SMALL SHIPS

AMERICAN SAFARI CRUISES

"Luxury in pursuit of adventure" is the tagline for this high-end yacht-cruise line, which operates some of the smallest vessels in Alaska. With just 12 to 21 passengers and such decadent amenities as ocean-view hot tubs, American Safari's yachts are among the most comfortable small ships cruising Alaska.

Shallow drafts mean these little ships and their landing craft can reach hidden inlets and remote beaches and slip in for close-up looks at glaciers and wildlife. Itineraries are usually flexible; there's no rush to move on if the group spots a pod of whales or a family of bears. All sailing is in daylight, with nights spent at anchor in secluded coves, and the yachts stop daily to let you kayak, hike, or beachcomb. An onboard naturalist offers informal lectures and guides you on shore expeditions. Guests on all ships have access to the bridge, so they can sip coffee and chat with the captain during the day. All three ships carry exercise equipment, kayaks, mountain bikes, Zodiac landing craft, and insulated Mustang suits for Zodiac excursions. All shore excursions and activities are included in the price.

Your Shipmates. Unlike most other yachts, which have to be chartered, American Safari's vessels sail on a regular schedule and sell tickets to individuals: there's no need to charter the whole ship, though that is an

CLOSE UP

Health & Safety at Sea

FIRE SAFETY

The greatest danger facing cruise-ship passengers is fire. All cruise lines must meet international standards for fire safety, which require sprinkler systems, smoke detectors, and other safety features.

Once settled into your cabin, locate life vests and review posted emergency instructions. Make certain the ship's purser knows of any physical infirmities that may hamper a speedy exit from your cabin. If you're traveling with children, be sure that child-size life jackets are placed in your cabin. Within 24 hours of embarkation, you will be asked to attend a mandatory lifeboat drill. Only in the most extreme circumstances will you need to abandon ship—but it has happened.

HEALTH CARE

All large ships have an infirmary to deal with minor medical emergencies. For complicated medical conditions, the ship's medical team evacuates passengers to the nearest hospital ashore. You'll need supplementary insurance to cover these costs.

SEASICKNESS

Many first-time passengers are anxious about whether they'll be stricken by seasickness, but there is no way to tell until you actually sail. Modern vessels are equipped with stabilizers that eliminate much of the motion responsible for seasickness. On an Alaska cruise you will spend most of your time in very calm, sheltered waters, so, unless your cruise includes time in the open sea (say, between San Francisco and Vancouver), you may not even feel the ship's movement—particularly if your ship is a megaliner.

If you have a history of motion sickness, don't book an inside cabin. For the terminally seasick, it will begin to resemble a movable coffin in short order. If you do become seasick, you can use common drugs such as Dramamine and Bonine. Some people find anti-seasickness wristbands and the Transderm Scop patch helpful. You'll need a prescription from your physician for the patch and, while wearing it, be vigilant for possible side effects including blurred vision, dry mouth, and drowsiness.

NOROVIRUSES

Noroviruses are a group of related viruses that cause acute gastroenteritis in humans. Low-grade fever also occasionally occurs and vomiting is more common in children. Dehydration is the most common complication, especially among the young and elderly, and may require medical attention. Symptoms generally last 24 to 60 hours. To avoid illness, wash your hands thoroughly and often. The Centers for Disease Control (CDC) also advise the use of an alcohol-based hand sanitizer along with hand washing.

option. Many people charter the entire ship for family reunions and other group events.

Food. The chefs serve nicely presented dinner entrées, featuring fresh local ingredients and plenty of seafood. All cruises are all-inclusive, so premium wines and liquors are available at every meal.

Tipping. All shore excursions and alcoholic drinks are included in the fare. Tips are discretionary, but 5% to 10% of the fare is suggested. A lump sum is pooled among the crew at the end of the cruise.

American Safari Cruises, ☎*206/284–0300 or 888/862–8881* ⊕*www.amsafari.com.*

THE SHIPS ★

Safari Quest. Quest will make weeklong, one-way Inside Passage sailings between Juneau and Sitka. There are two two-week repositioning cruises between Seattle and Juneau.

> **WORD OF MOUTH**
>
> "I just want you to know that I went on the *Safari Quest* through American Safaris, 10 cabins, Sitka to Juneau. And it was one of the best trips of my life!" –mbt127

Safari Escape. Escape offers eight-night cruises, May through August, one-way between Juneau and Prince Rupert, BC. There are two two-week repositioning cruises between Seattle and Juneau.

Safari Spirit. Spirit makes weeklong, one-way Inside Passage cruises between May and August. There are two two-week repositioning cruises between Seattle and Juneau.

Safari Explorer. Explorer makes weeklong, round-trip cruises from Juneau calling at Admiralty Island and Ford's Terror and cruising Glacier Bay, Icy Strait, and Frederick Sound.

MAJESTIC AMERICA LINE

In the 19th century, paddle wheelers were a key part of Alaska's coastal transport, taking adventurers and gold seekers north. In 2003 *Empress of the North* became the first overnight stern-wheeler to ply these waters in 100 years. This faithful re-creation recalls the grand coastal paddle wheelers of the past, from the lavish interior to the paddle wheel powering the ship. A naturalist and historian give lectures on local history and culture. Gold-rush follies, Russian-American dances, and Native American songs and dances bring the region's past to life. Variety shows, ranging from golden oldies and big bands to country-and-western, play nightly. A shore excursion is included at each port of call, including a trip on the White Pass and Yukon Railroad, and all 2008 itineraries included scenic cruising in Glacier Bay National Park. Because the ship is highly maneuverable with a shallow draft, it is able to explore intriguing places larger ships are unable to reach. In Alaska, that makes small inlets and narrow fjords open to access. Additionally, the captain has latitude when it comes to the day's itinerary, and depending on weather conditions, can take the vessel to the day's best viewing options.

Your Shipmates. This novel small ship attracts passengers from all over the world—Italy, Spain, Australia—with an average age of about sixty-plus, and includes a few families.

Food. A gourmet chef prepares five-star cuisine, featuring Pacific Northwest beef and fish, although the staff easily caters to vegetarians and special diets, too. The captain's farewell dinner is a special—and informal—occasion to savor truly exceptional food.

Tipping. As with most small ships, tips are pooled by the crew at the end of the cruise. A tip of $12 to $14 per person per night is suggested.

Majestic America Line, ☎206/292–9606 or 800/434–1232 ⊕*www.majesticamericaline.com.*

THE SHIP   *Empress of the North.* Pending the sale of Majestic America Line at the time of this writing, no 2009 itineraries were available.

CRUISE WEST

The yachtlike vessels that make up Cruise West's Caribbean fleet are small, American-built and U.S.-registered coastal cruisers. With their shallow drafts and inflatable, motorized landing craft, they are well suited to exploring remote and otherwise inaccessible tropical waters. Cruises are billed as soft adventure and educational, and every sailing features at least one Cruise West Exploration Leader, who leads lectures and field trips. Schedules are flexible enough that captains can stop or make course changes for unexpected encounters with wildlife. Itineraries include a full range of organized shore excursions, one of which is complimentary in each port of call.

There are no discos, casinos, or musical reviews aboard these diminutive vessels, and reading, socializing, and board games are the most popular activities. Sometimes local entertainers perform on board, and there may be movies in the dining room after dinner.

Your Shipmates. The passengers, who inevitably get to know one another during the cruise, are typically active, well-traveled over-fifties. There are no organized activities for children or teens.

Food. These cruises don't sacrifice aesthetics, and such shipboard refinements as fine dining in a single open seating are emphasized. The dress requirements are as relaxed and casual as the onboard ambience—there is no need to pack dress-up finery.

Fitness & Recreation. Serious exercise sessions are limited to long walks on the beach, swimming, and exploring ports of call. There are no gyms aboard Cruise West ships.

Service & Tipping. Service by the American staff is friendly, but not the white-glove variety. Gratuities are included in the cruise fare, and additional tipping is not required or expected. However, you are welcome to tip individuals directly to recognize exceptional service. No service charges are added to wine or bar bills.

Cruise West, ☎206/441–8687 or 888/851–8133 ⊕*www.cruisewest.com.*

THE SHIPS *Spirit of Glacier Bay.* From May through August *Glacier Bay* offers three- and four-night getaway cruises from Juneau featuring two nights in Glacier Bay; in May and September, 10-night sailings between Juneau and Seattle.

Spirit of Yorktown. The *Yorktown* makes eight-night round-trip Inside Passage trips between Juneau and Ketchikan that include Skagway, Haines, Glacier Bay, Sitka, Tracy Arm, Frederick Sound, Petersburg, Metlakatla, and Misty Fjords. Ten-night repositioning cruises between Juneau and Seattle are scheduled for May and September.

Fodor'sChoice *Spirit of Oceanus.* The *Oceanus* sails one-way cruises between Vancou-
★ ver and Whittier for 12 nights via Metlakatla, Misty Fjords, Petersburg, Skagway, Glacier Bay, Sitka, Tracy Arm, and Prince William Sound. Also available in July is a 13-night voyage to the Bering Sea, from Whittier to Nome via Kodiak, Katmai National Park, Shumagin Islands, Dutch Harbor, Pribilof Islands, remote islands in the Yukon Delta National Wildlife Refuge and Russia's Chukotka Peninsula, Arctic Circle, Bering Sea. The Bering Sea cruise can be combined with a 12-night cruise for a 24-night sailing called In Harriman's Wake.

Spirit of Endeavour. The *Spirit of Endeavour* sails Inside Passage cruises for eight nights between Juneau and Ketchikan via Misty Fjords, Metlakatla, Petersburg, Frederick Sound, Tracy Arm, Sitka, Glacier Bay, Skagway, and Haines, and 10-night Inside Passage cruises between Juneau and Seattle.

Spirit of '98. This ship offers one-way Inside Passage cruises between Juneau and Ketchikan that include Misty Fjords, Metlakatla, Petersburg, Frederick Sound, Tracy Arm, Sitka, Glacier Bay, Skagway, and Haines. There are also repositioning cruises between Juneau and Seattle.

Spirit of Discovery. The *Spirit of Discovery* sails an eight-night Inside Passage route round-trip from Juneau to Gastineau Channel, Tracy Arm, Sitka, Frederick Sound, Icy Strait, Elfin Cove, Glacier Bay National Park, and a port call at a remote Alaskan Village. Ten-night repositioning cruises are scheduled between Juneau and Seattle in May and September.

Spirit of Alaska. Spirit of Alaska sails eight-night Inside Passage journeys round-trip from Juneau to Gastineau Channel, Tracy Arm, Sitka, Frederick Sound, Icy Strait, Elfin Cove, Glacier Bay National Park, and a port call at a remote Alaskan Village. Ten-night repositioning cruises are scheduled between Juneau and Seattle in May and September.

Spirit of Columbia. Spirit of Columbia will sail three- and four-night round-trip cruises from Anchorage/Whittier to College Fjord and Esther Passage, Icy Strait, Cordova (on four-night only), Change Glacier, and Knight Island. Ten-night repositioning cruises are scheduled between Juneau and Seattle in May and September.

LINDBLAD EXPEDITIONS

The ships of Lindblad Expeditions spend time looking for wildlife, exploring out-of-the-way inlets, and making Zodiac landings (on inflatable boats) at isolated beaches. Each ship has a fleet of kayaks as well as a video-microphone: a hydrophone (an underwater microphone that picks up whale calls) is combined with an underwater camera so passengers can listen to whale songs and watch live video of what's going on beneath the waves. In the evening, the ships' naturalists recap the day's sights and adventures over cocktails in the lounge. A video chronicler makes a DVD of the entire cruise that you may purchase. An "open bridge" policy provides passengers the opportunity to meet the captain and his officers and learn the intricacies of navigation.

In July and August some family expeditions are offered, which follow the same itinerary as Lindblad's other trips, but include a crew member dedicated to running educational programs for school-age kids. All Lindblad cruises offer substantial discounts for young people up to 21 traveling with their parents.

Food. Lindblad prides itself on serving fresh Alaska seafood, including Dungeness crab, halibut, and Alaska King salmon, but there are also plenty of meat and vegetarian options. Breakfast is buffet-style; lunch is family-style. The recently launched "Seafood for Thought" program is meant to ensure that sustainable seafood is being served.

Tipping. All shore excursions except flightseeing are included. While gratuities are at your discretion, tips of $12–$15 per person per day are suggested; these are pooled among the crew at journey's end. Tip the massage therapist individually following a treatment.

Your Shipmates. Lindblad attracts active, adventurous, well-traveled over-forties, and quite a few singles, as the line charges one of the industry's lowest single supplements. They are making a push, however, to be more family-friendly, and staff members have undergone extensive training to tailor activities toward children. Smoking is not permitted on board.

Lindblad Expeditions, ☎*212/765–7740 or 800/397–3348* ⊕*www.expeditions.com.*

THE SHIPS *National Geographic Sea Bird, National Geographic Sea Lion.* These ships sail eight-day one-way cruises from Juneau to Seattle, stopping in Tracy Arm, Petersburg, Frederick Sound, Glacier Bay, and Sitka (passengers disembark and fly together from Sitka to Seattle).

Southeast Alaska

INCLUDING KETCHIKAN, JUNEAU, HAINES, SITKA & SKAGWAY

WORD OF MOUTH

"We hiked to the tongue of the Mendenhall Glacier to find this roaring waterfall crashing into the bay. It gave us a perspective on man's insignificance next to Mother Nature."

–Chris Marlow, Photo Contest Winner

WELCOME TO SOUTHEAST ALASKA

TOP REASONS TO GO

★ **Native art and culture:** Ancestral home of the Tlingit, Haida, and Tsimshian, the Southeast is dedicated to preserving native heritage. Native crafts include totem poles and masks.

★ **Rivers of ice:** Visitors relish the opportunity to walk on the Southeast's accessible glaciers or to admire them from flight-seeing or kayak trips.

★ **Tongass National Forest:** America's largest national forest, the Tongass is home to old-growth forests, bears, bald eagles, Sitka black-tailed deer, wolves, and marine mammals.

★ **Fishing for nirvana:** The Southeast is an angler's paradise. The region's healthy populations of salmon and halibut—as well as the wealth of charter boats and fishing lodges—make this a premier fishing destination.

★ **Taking the ferry:** The Alaska Marine Highway is the primary means of transportation here, providing scenic voyages to many communities. It's a low-cost, high-adventure alternative to cruise-ship travel.

1 Ketchikan & Vicinity. The self-proclaimed "Salmon Capital of the World," Ketchikan is a welcoming doorway to the Southeast. The town retains its surly but amiable frontier spirit. Be sure to check out the area's charter-fishing opportunities and wealth of local art. Ketchikan is a jumping-off point for Misty Fiords National Monument and Metlakatla.

2 Wrangell & Petersburg. These towns provide access to the magnificent Stikine River. Wrangell, dependent on the dwindling timber trade, is learning to adapt to the cruise-ship industry; it's the primary hub for travel to bear viewing at Anan Creek. Petersburg (aka "Little Norway") has a vibrant fishing community and stellar access to fishing and hiking.

3 Sitka. With its mixed history of Tlingit, Russian, and American rule, Sitka is home to a lively community, impressive architecture, an excellent park system (including Sitka National Historical Park), and outdoor activities galore. Sitka is a must-see for anyone traveling in the Southeast.

4 Juneau & Vicinity. Cruise passengers flock by the hundreds of thousands to take in the state capital's historic charm, artsy community, and natural beauty, including world-famous Mendenhall Glacier. Juneau is also the access point for many surrounding attractions, including Admiralty Island National Monument, home to the Southeast's largest population of brown bears.

5 Glacier Bay National Park & Preserve. The Southeast's signature attraction, Glacier Bay is home to the continent's largest collection of tidewater glaciers, which make for incredible viewing. The park's remote, undeveloped location—Gustavus, the closest town, isn't really a town at all—ensures that travelers in search of quiet repose will not be disappointed.

6 Haines & Skagway. The northern outposts of the Inside Passage, these two towns seem to have it all. Haines, on stunning Chilkat Peninsula, is home to fishermen, helicopter-skiing guides, and eagle aficionados who flock to the nearby Chilkat Bald Eagle Preserve. Skagway has gorgeous scenery, an incredible railway, and a boisterous gold-rush history.

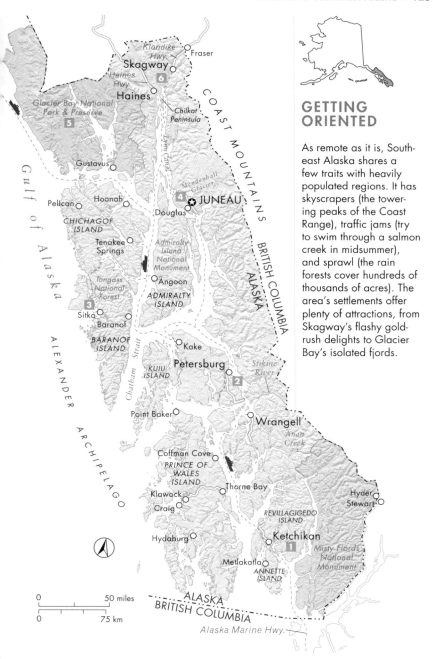

GETTING ORIENTED

As remote as it is, Southeast Alaska shares a few traits with heavily populated regions. It has skyscrapers (the towering peaks of the Coast Range), traffic jams (try to swim through a salmon creek in midsummer), and sprawl (the rain forests cover hundreds of thousands of acres). The area's settlements offer plenty of attractions, from Skagway's flashy gold-rush delights to Glacier Bay's isolated fjords.

SOUTHEAST ALASKA PLANNER

Getting Here & Around

Southeast Alaska is best explored by ship or plane. **Alaska Airlines** (☎800/252–7522 ⊕www.alaskaair.com) operates several flights daily from Seattle and other Pacific Coast and southwestern cities to Ketchikan, Wrangell, Petersburg, Sitka, Glacier Bay, and Juneau. The carrier also connects Juneau to the northern Alaska cities of Yakutat, Cordova, Anchorage, Fairbanks, Nome, Kotzebue, and Prudhoe Bay. Unless your destination is Haines, Skagway, or Hyder, forget about driving to the Southeast. Cars don't do much for travelers, as roads typically run just a few miles out from towns and villages, then they dead-end. Many people elect to transport their vehicles (and themselves) via the ferries of the Alaska Marine Highway system. Serious cyclists bring their bikes along. Visitor information centers are generally open mid-May through August, daily 8 to 5, with additional hours when cruise ships are in port; between September and mid-May, they're typically open weekdays 8 to 5.

Seeing the Southeast from On High

There's no better way to view the Southeast's twisting channels, towering mountains, and gleaming glaciers than from one of the region's many small-aircraft flights.

There are at least four services offering daily flights between the Southeast's larger towns—Juneau, Haines, Skagway, Ketchikan, Sitka, Petersburg, and Wrangell—as well as bevy of helicopter flightseeing services that specialize in short, scenic flights. Tops among the fixed-wing carriers are **L.A.B. Flying Service** (☎907/789–9160 ⊕www.labflying.com) and **Wings of Alaska** (☎907/789–0790 ⊕www.wingsofalaska.com), both of which offer connecting flights and scenic air tours of Southeast landmarks.

Flying between destinations in the Southeast—while significantly more expensive—is an experience you won't forget. If your itinerary includes an extra day or two in the Southeast (particularly in Juneau), consider spending a day flying to and from a neighboring community. Round-trip tickets from Juneau to Skagway, for instance, start at $350, as compared to approximately $170 for a one-hour flightseeing trip in and around Juneau.

A host of floatplane services offer access to remote cabins and remote freshwater fishing destinations. Check out **Southeast Aviation** (☎888/359–6478 ⊕www.flymisty.com) for flight details.

Southeast by Sea

Southeast Alaska includes a number of popular ports of call for cruise ships (⇨ Chapter 3, Cruising Alaska). For those looking to avoid cruise travel or for more flexibility, the **Alaska Marine Highway** (☎907/465–3941 or 800/642–0066 ⊕www.dot.state.ak.us/amhs) allows you to construct an itinerary that is all your own; it's quite popular with budget-conscious, adventurous visitors.

Major Ports of Call: Ketchikan, Metlakatla, Wrangell, Petersburg, Sitka, Juneau, Glacier Bay National Park & Reserve, Haines, Skagway

Major Ferry Landings: Ketchikan, Wrangell, Petersburg, Sitka, Juneau, Haines, Skagway

Cabins Galore

☂**U.S. Forest Service Cabins** are scattered throughout Tongass National Forest; these rustic sites offer a charming and cheap escape (up to $45/night per cabin). Most are fly-in units, accessible by floatplanes from virtually any community in the Southeast. They offer bunks for six to eight occupants, tables, stoves, and outdoor privies—but no electricity or running water. You provide your own sleeping bag, food, and cooking utensils. Bedside reading in most cabins includes a diary kept by visitors—add your own adventure. (☎907/586–8800, 877/444–6777 reservations ⊕www.recreation.gov).

About the Hotels & Restaurants

From scallops to king salmon, fresh seafood dominates menus in the Southeast. Juneau, Sitka, and Ketchikan all have a variety of ethnic eateries, along with notable gourmet restaurants.

Lodging choices along the Inside Passage range from remote Forest Service cabins to top-end hotels. In general, the latter are a pricey option, but rates drop substantially in the off-season (mid-September to mid-May).

Budget travelers will find hostels in many of the larger towns. Fine hotels are found in Ketchikan and Juneau, and luxurious fishing lodges attract anglers on Prince of Wales Island and other places in the Southeast. Bed-and-breakfasts are also popular in the Inside Passage.

WHAT IT COSTS				
¢	$	$$	$$$	$$$$
RESTAURANTS				
under $10	$10–$15	$15–$20	$20–$25	over $25
HOTELS				
under $75	$75–$125	$125–$175	$175–$225	over $225

Restaurant prices are per person for a main course at dinner. Hotel prices are for two people in a standard double room in high season.

Timing & Weather

The best time to visit is from May through September, when weather is mildest, rain is less frequent, daylight hours are longest, wildlife is most abundant, and festivals and tourist-oriented activities are in full swing. Summertime high temperatures hover around the low to mid-60s, with far warmer days interspersed throughout. Shoulder-season temperatures are cooler, and the region is less crowded. Bring rain gear, layered clothing, sturdy footwear, a hat, and binoculars.

How Much Time?

Allow yourself at least a week here. Plenty of adventures await ambitious independent travelers who plan ahead and ride state ferries.

If strolling through downtown shopping districts and museum-hopping is your idea of a perfect afternoon, journey to Haines, Skagway, Sitka, or Petersburg. For a wilderness experience in a peaceful, remote location, consider booking a multiple-night stay at one of Southeast's remote fly-in lodges.

Updated by
Sarah Wyatt

Southeast Alaska stretches below the state like the tail of a kite. It is a world of massive glaciers, steep-shouldered islands, cliff-rimmed fjords, and snowcapped peaks. Glacier Bay National Park and Preserve, one of the region's most prized attractions, is home to the largest concentration of coastal glaciers on Earth.

Lush stands of spruce, hemlock, and cedar blanket thousands of islands. The region's myriad bays, coves, lakes, and swift, icy rivers provide some of the continent's best fishing grounds. Many of Southeast Alaska's wildest and most pristine landscapes are within Tongass National Forest, comprised of nearly 17 million acres—almost three-quarters of the Panhandle's land.

The Southeast lacks only one thing: pavement. The near-total lack of connecting roads between the area's communities presents obvious challenges to four-wheeled transport. The isolation and the wet weather keep people from moving in; otherwise Southeast Alaska would probably be as densely populated as Seattle. To help remedy the transportation question, Alaskans created the Alaska Marine Highway System, a network of passenger and vehicle ferries, some of which have staterooms, observation decks, video theaters, arcades, cafeterias, cocktail lounges, and heated, glass-enclosed solariums.

The Southeast's natural beauty and abundance of wildlife have made it one of the world's fastest-growing cruise destinations. About 20 big cruise ships ply the Inside Passage—once the traditional route to the Klondike goldfields and today the centerpiece of many Alaska cruises—during the height of summer. Regular air service to the Southeast is available from the Lower 48 states and other parts of Alaska.

Three groups of native peoples inhabit the Southeast coastal region: the Tlingit, Haida, and Tsimshian (*sim*-shee-ann). These peoples, like their coastal neighbors in British Columbia, preserve a culture rich in totemic art, including carved poles, masks, baskets, and ceremonial objects. Many live among nonnatives in modern towns and continue their cultural traditions.

Residents—some from other states, some who can trace their ancestors back to the gold-rush days, and some whose ancestors came over the Bering Land Bridge from Asia thousands of years ago—are an adventurous bunch. The rough-and-tumble spirit of the Southeast often combines with a worldly sophistication: those who fish might also be artists, Forest Service workers may run a bed-and-breakfast on the side, and homemakers may be native-dance performers.

WET YET WONDERFUL

The Southeast has its drawbacks. For one thing, it rains a lot. If you plan to spend a week or more, be prepared for showers during at least a few of those days. Hard-core Southeast residents just throw on slickers and rubber boots and shrug it off. Their attitude is philosophical: without the rain, there would be no forests; no lakes; no streams running with salmon and trout; and no healthy populations of brown and black bears, moose, deer, mountain goats, and wolves.

EXPLORING SOUTHEAST ALASKA

The Southeast Panhandle stretches some 500 mi from Yakutat at its northernmost point to Ketchikan and Metlakatla at its southern end. At its widest point, the region measures only 140 mi, and in the upper Panhandle just south of Yakutat, at 30 mi across, it's downright skinny by Alaska standards. Most of the Panhandle consists of a sliver of mainland buffered on the west by islands and on the east by the imposing peaks of the Coast Mountains.

Those numerous coastal islands—more than 1,000 throughout the Inside Passage—collectively constitute the Alexander Archipelago. Most of them present mountainous terrain with lush covers of timber, though large clear-cuts are also common. Most communities are on islands rather than on the mainland. The principal exceptions are Juneau, Haines, and Skagway, plus the hamlets of Gustavus and Hyder. Island outposts include Ketchikan, Wrangell, Petersburg, Sitka, and the villages of Craig, Pelican, Metlakatla, Kake, Angoon, and Hoonah. Bordering Alaska just east of the Panhandle lies the Canadian province of British Columbia.

KETCHIKAN

Ketchikan is famous for its colorful totem poles, rainy skies, steep–as–San Francisco streets, and lush island setting. Some 14,000 people call the town home, and, in summer, cruise ships crowd the shoreline, floatplanes depart noisily for Misty Fiords National Monument, and salmon-laden commercial fishing boats motor through Tongass Narrows. In the last decade, Ketchikan's rowdy, blue-collar heritage of logging and fishing has been softened by the loss of many timber-industry jobs and the dramatic rise of cruise-ship tourism. With some effort,

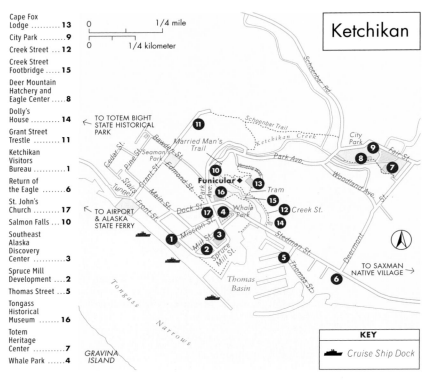

though, visitors can still glimpse the rugged frontier spirit that once permeated this hardscrabble cannery town.

The town is situated at the foot of 3,000-foot Deer Mountain, near the southeast corner of Revillagigedo (locals shorten it to Revilla) Island. Prior to the arrival of white miners and fishermen in 1885, the Tlingit used the site, located at the mouth of Ketchikan Creek, as a summer fish camp. Gold discoveries just before the turn of the 20th century brought more immigrants, and valuable timber and commercial fishing resources spurred new industries. By the 1930s the town bragged it was the "salmon-canning capital of the world." You will still find some of the Southeast's best salmon fishing around here.

EXPLORING KETCHIKAN

This town is the first bite of Alaska that many travelers taste. Despite its imposing backdrop, hillside homes, and many staircases, Ketchikan is relatively easy to walk through. Downtown's favorite stops include the Spruce Mill Development shops and Creek Street. A bit farther away you'll find the Totem Heritage Center and Deer Mountain Hatchery. Out of town (but included on most bus tours) are two longtime favorites: Totem Bight State Historical Park and Saxman Native Village.

TAKE THE FERRY

The **Alaska Marine Highway System** operates stateroom-equipped vehicle and passenger ferries from Bellingham, Washington, and from Prince Rupert, British Columbia. Popular among budget-minded travelers, and those seeking an alternative to cruise-ship travel, the Alaska Marine Highway allows passengers to create their own itineraries. In Southeast Alaska, the vessels call at Metlakatla, Ketchikan, Wrangell, Petersburg, Kake, Sitka, Angoon, Tenakee Springs, Hoonah, Juneau, Haines, and Skagway—though it's possible to take the ferry all the way to South Central and southwestern Alaska.

■TIP→ In summer, staterooms on the ferries are sold out before sailing time; reserve months in advance. There are common areas on the ferries where you can throw a sleeping bag or sit in a recliner seat. If you are planning to take a car on the ferry, early reservations for vehicle space are also highly recommended. This is particularly true for recreational vehicles.

A separate ferry, operated by the Inter-Island Ferry Authority, runs between Ketchikan and Hollis (on Prince of Wales Island) and from Coffman Cove (also on Prince of Wales Island) to Wrangell and Petersburg.

Information **Alaska Marine Highway** (⊠ *6858 Glacier Hwy., Juneau* ☎ *907/465–3941 or 800/642–0066* ⎙ *907/277–4829* ⊕ *www.dot.state. ak.us/amhs*) **B.C. Ferries** (⊠ *1112 Fort St., Victoria, BC, Canada* ☎ *250/386–3431 or 888/223–3779* ⊕ *www.bcferries.com*). **Inter-Island Ferry Authority** (⌂ *Box 495, Craig 99921* ☎ *907/826–4848 or 866/308–4848* ⎙ *907/826–4849* ⊕ *www.interislandferry.com*).

GETTING HERE & AROUND

Ketchikan is a regular stop on cruise ship and ferry routes, but Alaska Airlines also flies in from Seattle and other Pacific Northwest locations. If you're traveling out of the town on the highway in either direction, you won't go far before you run out of road. The North Tongass Highway ends about 18 mi from downtown, at Settler's Cove Campground. The South Tongass Highway terminates at a power plant about 8 mi from town. Side roads soon end at campgrounds and at trailheads, viewing points, lakes, boat-launching ramps, and private property.

ESSENTIALS

Medical Assistance **Ketchikan General Hospital** (⊠ *3100 Tongass Ave.* ☎ *907/225–5171* ⊕ *www.peacehealth.org*).

Pharmacies **Downtown Drugstore** (⊠ *300 Front St.* ☎ *907/225–3144*). **Island Pharmacy** (⊠ *3526 Tongass Ave.* ☎ *907/225–6186*).

Visitor Info **Ketchikan Visitors Bureau** (⊠ *131 Front St.* ☎ *907/225–6166 or 800/770–3300* ⊕ *www.visit-ketchikan.com*). **U.S. Forest Service** (⊠ *648 Mission St.* ☎ *907/225–3101* ⊕ *www.fs.fed.us/r10/tongass*).

WHAT TO SEE

⑬ Cape Fox Lodge. For the town's best harbor views and one of Southeast Alaska's most luxurious lobbies, walk to the top of steep Venetia Avenue or take the funicular ($2) up from Creek Street. ⊠ *800 Venetia Way* ☎ *907/225–8001 or 800/225–8001* ⊕ *www.capefoxlodge.com.*

⑨ City Park. The Deer Mountain Hatchery and Eagle Center lead into this small but charming park, which has picnic tables, a fountain, and paved paths. Ketchikan Creek runs through it. ⊠ *Park and Fair Sts.*

⑫ **Creek Street.** This was once Ketchikan's infamous red-light district. During Prohibition, Creek Street was home to numerous speakeasies, and, in the early 1900s, more than 30 houses of prostitution operated here. Today the small, colorful houses, built on stilts over the creek waters, have been restored as trendy shops. Sea kayakers often paddle up the creek at high tide.
★

⑮ Creek Street Footbridge. Stand over Ketchikan Creek for good salmon-viewing when the fish are running. In summer you can see impressive runs of coho, king, pink, and chum salmon, along with smaller numbers of steelhead and rainbow trout heading upstream to spawn. ■TIP→ Keep your eyes peeled for sea lions snacking on the incoming fish.

⑧ **Deer Mountain Hatchery and Eagle Center.** Tens of thousands of king and coho salmon are raised at this hatchery on Ketchikan Creek. Midsummer visitors can view natural spawning in the creek by pink, chum, and coho salmon and steelhead trout as well as workers collecting and fertilizing the salmon eggs for the hatchery. Owned by the Ketchikan Indian Corporation, the hatchery has exhibits on traditional native fishing. Also here is a nesting pair of injured bald eagles. Although unable to fly, they will catch salmon that swim into their enclosure. ⊠ *1158 Salmon Rd.* ☎ *907/228–5537 or 800/252–5158* ⊕ *www. kictribe.org/hatchery/hatchery.htm* ⊠ *$12* ☉ *Early May–Sept., daily 8–4:30.*

⑭ Dolly's House. Formerly owned by the inimitable Dolly Arthur, this steep-roofed home once housed Creek Street's most famous brothel. The house has been preserved as a museum, complete with furnishings, beds, and a short history of the life and times of Ketchikan's best-known madam. ⊠ *Creek St.* ☎ *907/225–6329 (summer only)* ⊠ *$5* ☉ *Daily 8–4, when cruise ships are in port.*

⑪ Grant Street Trestle. At one time virtually all of Ketchikan's walkways and streets were made from wooden trestles, but now only one of these handsome wooden streets remains, constructed in 1908.

❶ Ketchikan Visitors Bureau. This helpful visitors bureau is on Front Street, next to the cruise-ship docks. ■TIP→ Half the space is occupied by day-tour, flightseeing, and boat-tour operators offering a range of nearby adventures. ⊠ *131 Front St.* ☎ *907/225–6166 or 800/770–3300* ⊕ *www.visit-ketchikan.com* ☉ *Weekdays 8–5 and when cruise ships are in port.*

CLOSE UP

Alaska's Wild Salmon & the Aquaculture Debate

Five species of wild Pacific salmon are found in Alaska waters. All are anadromous (they go from the sea and up rivers), and all five species have at least two common names: pink (humpback) salmon, chum (dog) salmon, coho (silver) salmon, sockeye (red) salmon, and Chinook (king) salmon. The smallest of these five, the pink salmon, has an average weight of only about 3 or 4 pounds, while king salmon can often tip the scales at more than 25 pounds. King salmon is generally considered the most flavorful, but sockeye and coho are also very highly regarded. Pinks and chum salmon are the mainstay of canneries.

After spending a year or more in the ocean (the length of time varies among the species), Pacific salmon return to their native streams to spawn and die. The annual summertime return of adult salmon is a major event in Alaska, both for the animals (including bears) that depend upon this bounty, and for thousands of commercial fishers and sport anglers.

Alaska has long been famous for its seafood, and one of the first acts following statehood in 1959 was to protect fisheries from overharvesting. Today the stocks of salmon and other fish remain healthy, and careful management ensures that they will be there in the future. In the 1980s and 1990s, aquaculture, or fish-farming, grew into an enormous international business, particularly in Norway, Chile, the United Kingdom, and British Columbia. Leery of the consequences to wild salmon, Alaska has never allowed any salmon aquaculture.

Pen-raised fish are affordable, available year-round, and of a consistent quality, but controversy surrounds the practice of fish-farming. Many people believe it has a disastrous impact on the environment, citing such examples as disease; pollution from the waste of huge concentrations of fish; and fish farms harvesting nonnative species, such as Atlantic salmon.

On the other side of the debate, there are those who believe that fish-farming is helping to protect Earth's valuable—and decreasing—populations of salmon. Proponents of fish farms point out that the practice also offers revenue and more jobs. Offshore fish-farming in the United States is a hugely incendiary topic of current debate; those supporting it believe that if the farms are placed in deep ocean pockets, the pollution from and medication given to the pen-raised fish will be scattered better by strong currents. Many environmentalists beg to differ, hoping to establish stringent guidelines before opening the ocean to fish-farming corporations.

One Alaska bumper sticker says: "Friends don't let friends eat farmed salmon." Just across the border, in British Columbia, many people find employment as fish-farm workers. No matter which side you agree with in the aquaculture debate, be sure to enjoy a plate of delicious wild salmon during your visit to Alaska—with luck, it could be a fish you've hooked yourself!

—Don Pitcher

4

Ketchikan's Totem Pole Parks

There are 14 poles in Ketchikan's two most famous totem pole parks. For the most part, they're 60-year-old replicas of older totem poles brought in from outlying villages as part of a federal works–cultural project during the late 1930s.

Totem Bight (⊠ *N. Tongass Hwy. 10 mi north of town* ☎ *907/247–8574* ☏ *Free* ◷ *Dawn–dusk* ⊕ *www. alaskastateparks.org*) has many totem poles and a hand-hewn native tribal house; it sits on a scenic spit of land facing the waters of Tongass Narrows. The clan house is open daily in summer. About a quarter of the bus tours of Ketchikan include Totem Bight.

A 2.5-mi paved walking path–bike trail parallels the road from Ketchikan to **Saxman Native Village** (⊠ *S. Tongass Hwy., 2 mi south of town* ☎ *907/225–4846* ⊕ *www. capefoxtours.com*), named for a missionary who helped native Alaskans settle here before 1900. A totem park dominates the center of Saxman, with poles that represent a wide range of human and animal-inspired figures, including bears, ravens, whales, and eagles.

Saxman's Beaver Clan tribal house is said to be the largest in the world. Carvers create totem poles and totemic art objects in the adjacent carver's shed (free and open whenever the carvers are working). You can get to the park on foot, by taxi, or by city bus, and you can visit the totem park on your own, but to visit the tribal house and theater you must take a tour. Tickets are sold at the gift shop across from the totems. Call ahead for tour schedules.

6 Return of the Eagle. Twenty-one native students created this colorful mural on a wall of the Robertson Building on the Ketchikan campus of the University of Alaska–Southeast. ⊠ *Stedman St.*

17 St. John's Church. Built in 1903, this church is the oldest remaining house of worship in Ketchikan. Its interior is formed from red cedar cut in the native-operated sawmill in nearby Saxman. ⊠ *Mission St.* ☎ *907/225–3680* ⊕ *www.stjohnsketchikan.com.*

10 Salmon Falls. Get out your camera and set it for high speed at the fish ladder, a series of pools arranged like steps that allow fish to travel upstream around a dam or falls. When the salmon start running from June onward, thousands of fish leap the falls (or take the easier fish-ladder route). They spawn in Ketchikan Creek's waters farther upstream. Many can also be seen in the creek's eddies above and below the falls. The falls, fish ladder, and a large carving of a jumping salmon are just off Park Avenue on Married Man's Trail. (The trail was once used by married men for discreet access to the red-light district on Creek Street.) ⊠ *Married Man's Trail off Park Ave.*

3 Southeast Alaska Discovery Center. This impressive information center features exhibits—including one on the rain forest—that focus on the resources, native cultures, and ecosystems of Southeast Alaska. The U.S. Forest Service and other federal agencies provide information on Alaska's public lands, and a large gift shop sells natural-history books, maps, and videos about the sights in Ketchikan and the Southeast. America the Beautiful–National Park and Federal Recreational Land Passes are accepted and sold. ✉ *50 Main St.* ☎ *907/228–6220* ⊕ *www. fs.fed.us/r10/tongass/districts/discoverycenter* 🎫 *$5 May–Sept., free Oct.–Apr.* ☉ *May–Sept., weekdays 8–5, weekends 8-4; Oct.–Apr., Thurs.–Sun. 10–4.*

② **Spruce Mill Development.** This complex is modeled after 1920s-style cannery architecture. Spread over 6.5 acres along the waterfront—much of it built out over the waters of Tongass Narrows—five buildings contain a mix of retail stores, souvenir shops, galleries, and restaurants. Cruise ships moor just a few steps away, filling the shops with tourists all summer long. ✉ *Mill and Front Sts.*

⑤ **Thomas Street.** From this street you can see Thomas Basin, the most accessible of Ketchikan's four harbors and home port to pleasure and commercial fishing boats. Old buildings, including the maroon-fronted Potlatch Bar, sit atop pilings, and you can walk out to the breakwater for a better view of busy Tongass Narrows.

⑯ **Tongass Historical Museum.** Native artifacts and pioneer relics revisit the mining and fishing eras at this somewhat ho-hum museum in the same building as the library. Exhibits include a big, brilliantly polished lens from Tree Point Lighthouse, well-presented native tools and artwork, and photograph collections. Other exhibits rotate, but always include Tlingit items. ✉ *629 Dock St.* ☎ *907/225–5600* 🎫 *$2* ☉ *May–Sept., daily 8–5; Oct.–Apr., Wed.–Fri. 1–5, Sat. 10–4, Sun. 1–4.*

⑦ **★** **Totem Heritage Center.** Gathered from uninhabited Tlingit and Haida village sites, many of the authentic native totems in this rare collection are well over a century old—a rare age for cedar carvings, which are frequently lost to decay in the Southeast's exceedingly wet climate. The center also features guided tours and displays crafts of the Tlingit, Haida, and Tsimshian cultures. Outside are several more poles carved in the three decades since this center opened. ✉ *601 Deermount St.* ☎ *907/225–5900* 🎫 *$5* ☉ *May–Sept., daily 8–5; Oct.–Apr., weekdays 1–5.*

④ **Whale Park.** This small park, on a traffic island across from St. John's Church, is the site of the **Chief Kyan Totem Pole,** now in its third incarnation. The original was carved in the 1890s, but over the decades it deteriorated and was replaced in the 1960s. The current replica was erected in 1993, and the 1960s version is now housed in the Totem Heritage Center.

OUTDOOR ACTIVITIES & GUIDED TOURS

CANOPY TOURS

Often associated with rain forests of the tropical sort, canopy tours are Ketchikan's fastest-growing outdoor activity. Featuring a series of zip lines, aerial boardwalks, and suspension bridges, canopy tours provide an up-close view of the coastal forests. Granted, you won't spend the whole tour admiring the foliage: at **Alaska Canopy Adventures**

(⊕*www.alaskacanopyadventures.com*)—a course at the Alaska Rainforest Sanctuary, 16 mi south of town—the longest of the tour's eight zip lines stretches more than 800 feet, and whisks you along some 130 feet off the ground. Book online or with your cruise line. A 60-foot-high rain-forest zip-line course is offered through **Southeast Exposure** (☎*907/225–8829* ⊕*www.southeastexposure.com*), a well-known kayaking outfit in the area.

FISHING

Sportfishing for salmon and trout is excellent in the Ketchikan area, in both saltwater and freshwater lakes and streams. As a result, a plethora of local boat owners offer charter and guide services. A good one is Ketchikan Outdoors (✉*1251 Millar St.* ☎*907/617–2716* ⊕*www. ketchfish.com*), operated by local guides who combine sightseeing with fishing. Contact the **Ketchikan Visitors Bureau** (☎*907/225–6166 or 800/770–3300* ⊕*www.visit-ketchikan.com*) for information on guide services and locations.

HARBOR & AIR TOURS

Alaska Travel Adventures (☎*800/323–5757, 907/247–5295 outside Alaska* ⊕*www.bestofalaskatravel.com*) runs paddle-wheel boat tours of the Ketchikan waterfront, during which you'll learn local history and get a sea-level view of this bustling town. The company also provides speedy catamaran and catamaran-floatplane combo excursions to Misty Fiords National Monument.

If you want to head out on a floatplane to see the environs, contact **Southeast Aviation** (☎*907/225–2900 or 888/359–6478* ⊕*www.flymisty. com*). They offer tours of the glaciers and mountains of Misty Fiords National Monument, bear viewing, and charters.

HIKING

Get details on hiking around Ketchikan from the Southeast Alaska Discovery Center *(⇨ What to See, above)*. The 3-mi trail from downtown to the 3,000-foot summit of **Deer Mountain** will repay your efforts with a spectacular panorama of the city below and the wilderness behind. The trail begins at the corner of Fair and Deermount streets, and passes through dense forests before emerging into the alpine country. A shelter cabin near the summit provides a place to warm up.

Ward Lake Recreation Area, about 6 mi north of town, has hikes next to lakes and streams and beneath towering spruce and hemlock trees; it also has several covered picnic spots and a pleasant campground. An easy 1.3-mi nature trail circles the lake, which is popular for steelhead and salmon fishing. **Ward Creek Trail** begins from the lake and follows the creek 2.5 mi, with shoreside paths to creek-side platforms. The trail is hard-packed gravel, and is wide and gentle enough for wheelchairs. More ambitious hikers head up the 2-mi **Perseverance Trail,** a challenging set of steps and boardwalk that take hikers through the open muskeg (peat bog) to a small lake.

LOCAL INTEREST

A native-owned company, **Cape Fox Tours** (☎907/225–4846 ⊕*www.capefoxtours.com*) leads tours of Saxman Native Village and the historic George Inlet Cannery. You can book most of these tours aboard the cruise ships or at the Ketchikan Visitors Bureau.

SEA KAYAKING

Southeast Exposure (☎907/225–8829 ⊕*www.southeastexposure.com*) offers waterfront paddles to Eagle Islands in Clover Pass. **Southeast Sea Kayaks** (☎907/225–1258 or 800/287–1607 ⊕*www.kayak-ketchikan.com*) leads kayak tours of Ketchikan's historic waterfront and offers kayak lessons and rentals. They specialize in remote day trips and guided multinight trips to Misty Fiords.

LUMBERJACKS LIVE!

The **Great Alaskan Lumberjack Show** is a 60-minute lumberjack contest providing a Disney-esque taste of old-time woodsman skills, including ax throwing, bucksawing, springboard chopping, log-rolling duels, and a 50-foot tree climb. Shows take place in a covered, heated grandstand directly behind the Spruce Mill Development and go on rain or shine all summer. ✉ *420 Spruce Mill Way* ☎ *907/225–9050 or 888/320–9049* ⊕ *www.lumberjackshows.com* ⊛ *$34* ☼ *May–Sept., 2–5 times daily; hrs vary.*

4

WHERE TO EAT

$$–$$$$
AMERICAN
✕**Annabelle's Famous Keg and Chowder House.** Nestled into the ground floor of the historic Gilmore Hotel, this unpretentious Victorian-style restaurant serves a hearty array of seafood and pastas, including several kinds of chowder and steamer clams. Prime rib on Friday and Saturday evenings is a favorite, and the lounge with a jukebox adds a friendly vibe. ✉*326 Front St.* ☎*907/225–6009* ⊕*www.gilmorehotel.com* ⊟*AE, D, MC, V.*

¢–$$
MEXICAN
✕**Ocean View Restaurant.** This locals' favorite eatery has burgers, steaks, pasta, pizzas, and seafood. They're all fine, but the main draws are authentic and very filling south-of-the-border dishes prepared under the direction of the Mexican-American owners. Three tables in the back have nice views of the Tongass Narrows. The kitchen is open until 11 PM nightly, after which the restaurant morphs into a noisy nightclub until 2 AM. ✉*1831 Tongass Ave.* ☎*907/225–7566* ⊕*www.oceanviewmex.com* ⊟*MC, V.*

$–$$$$
AMERICAN
✕**Steamers.** Anchoring Ketchikan's Spruce Mill Mall, this lively, noisy, and spacious restaurant is popular with cruise passengers, and features an extensive menu of fresh seafood (including king crab and steamer clams), pasta, and steaks. Vegetarian choices are available, and the servings fill you up. Tall windows face Ketchikan's busy waterfront, where cruise ships and floatplanes vie for your attention. ✉*76 Front St.* ☎*907/225–1600* ⊟*AE, D, MC, V* ☼*Closed Oct.–Apr.*

WHERE TO STAY

$$$–$$$$ 🚹 **Cape Fox Lodge.** Ketchikan's most distinctive property offers scenic views of the town and Thomas Basin from 135 feet above the village. The setting is cozy yet luxurious. A towering, log-framed lobby has Tlingit and Haida artwork, an interesting collection of museum-quality artifacts, and a roaring fire. An exhibit on native history on the second floor is worth a visit. The spacious rooms are attractively decorated with traditional tribal colors and watercolors of Alaska birds. All have views of either Tongass Narrows or Deer Mountain. Numshee Jitters (that's "Crazy" Jitters in Tlingit) is the lobby's coffee shop, and the busy Heen Kahidi Dining Room serves three meals a day, with seafood, pasta, chicken, and steaks highlighting the dinner menu. Be sure to reserve one of the window tables that overlook Ketchikan. **Pro:** Excellent views from every room. **Con:** Rooms are rather plain. ✉ *800 Venetia Way* 🕿 *907/225–8001, 866/225–8001 reservations* ⊕ *www. capefoxlodge.com* 🛏 *72 rooms, 2 suites* 🛗 *In-room: refrigerator, Wi-Fi. In-hotel: 2 restaurants, room service, bar, laundry facilities, laundry service, public Internet, public Wi-Fi, some pets allowed, no-smoking rooms* 🚭 *AE, D, DC, MC, V.*

$–$$ 🚹 **Gilmore Hotel.** Crammed between the large buildings along Front Street, the Gilmore is a boutique hotel with slightly less-than-boutique prices. Thanks to its small dimensions, the late 1920s-era lobby has a European feel. Rooms and bathrooms, though not large, blend old-fashioned comfort with modern furnishings. All rooms are on the second or third floors, with no elevator. Downstairs, Annabelle's Famous Keg and Chowder House serves seafood, pasta, and prime rib. ■ TIP➔ **Upgrade to one of the marina-view rooms, otherwise you will be facing the wall of the building next door. Traffic and bar noise make earplugs a handy item for guests in street-side rooms.** **Pros:** Marina views are nice, if you can get one. **Cons:** Not handicapped accessible, lots of stairs, lobby could use renovation. ✉ *326 Front St.* 🕿 *907/225–9423 or 800/275–9423* ⊕ *www.gilmore-hotel.com* 🛏 *34 rooms, 5 suites* 🛗 *In-room: refrigerator (some), Wi-Fi. In-hotel: restaurant, room service, bar, no elevator, laundry service, public Internet, public Wi-Fi, airport shuttle, no-smoking rooms* 🚭 *AE, D, MC, V* 🍽 *CP.*

$–$$$ 🚹 **Inn at Creek Street & New York Hotel.** More than a century old, this quaint hotel has one of the nicest eateries in Ketchikan. It's open for breakfast and lunch and offers fabulous specialty coffees. The delightfully old-school hotel rooms are on the small side, but they have character in spades: one-of-a-kind antique

B&B RESERVATIONS

Bed-and-breakfasts are exceedingly popular in the Inside Passage, and for good reason. Dozens of regional B&Bs are excellent alternatives to local hotels; they also provide the opportunity to meet fellow travelers, dig into a homemade breakfast (such as smoked salmon omelets or authentic sourdough pancakes), and learn about the area from local business owners.

Local Agents Alaska Travelers Accommodations (⊕ *www.alaska-travelers.com*).

furnishings, handmade quilts on the queen beds, and tile floors with pedestal sinks in the bathrooms. The three luxury suites along Creek Street include kitchenettes, jetted tubs, loft bedrooms with spiral staircases, and decks overlooking the water. Suite amenities at other locations vary, so check with the hotel. **Pro:** Hotel has added two new rooms. **Con:** The outdoor kiosk that served crab and shrimp is no longer open. ✉ *207 Stedman St.* ☎ *907/225–0246, 866/225–0246 outside Alaska* ⊕ *www.thenewyorkhotel.com* ⤶ *8 rooms, 6 suites* ♿ *In-room: kitchen (some), refrigerator, DVD (some), VCR (some), Wi-Fi. In-hotel: restaurant, room service, bar, no elevator, public Internet, public Wi-Fi, airport shuttle, no-smoking rooms* ⊟ *D, MC, V.*

$$$ **The Landing.** Located near the airport, this Best Western property is named for the state ferry landing directly across the road. The Landing has large, comfortable rooms decorated with Mission-style furniture, professional service, and a 25-spot underground parking garage. Although the hotel is more than a mile from downtown, there's no need for a car; the free shuttle provides transport around town. The Landing Restaurant is usually packed with families and a colorful breakfast clientele of locals and ferry passengers. Upstairs, Jeremiah's Fine Food and Spirits offers upscale dining in cozy digs and a relaxing no-smoking lounge built around a stone fireplace. **Pro:** Recently renovated. **Con:** Somewhat overpriced given its location and amenities. ✉ *3434 Tongass Ave.* ☎ *907/225–5166 or 800/428–8304* ⊕ *www.landinghotel.com* ⤶ *107 rooms, 21 suites* ♿ *In-room: Wi-Fi. In-hotel: 2 restaurants, room service, bar, gym, laundry facilities, laundry service, public Internet, public Wi-Fi, airport shuttle, parking (no fee), some pets allowed, no-smoking rooms* ⊟ *AE, D, DC, MC, V.*

$$–$$$$ **The Narrows Inn.** Three miles from the center of town and 0.25 mile north of the airport parking lot, the Narrows is a modern lodge where rustic wood trim enlivens the small rooms with simple furniture. Waterside rooms, including three spacious suites, have balconies overlooking Tongass Narrows—a good place to watch seals, otters, and eagles. Ask for a room with a view unobstructed by the restaurant. The inn offers a courtesy van to anywhere within the city limits, but if you don't feel like riding into town for dinner, the property has a delicious steak-and-seafood restaurant with limited hours. Thornlow's Waterfront bar offers free use of binoculars for patrons. **Pro:** Great views of Tongass in selected rooms. **Con:** Inconvenient location. ✉ *Box 8296, 99901* ☎ *907/247–2600 or 888/686–2600* ⊕ *www.narrowsinn.com* ⤶ *47 rooms, 3 suites* ♿ *In-room: refrigerator, DVD (some), Wi-Fi. In-hotel: restaurant, room service, bar, no elevator, laundry service, public Internet, public Wi-Fi, airport shuttle, some pets allowed, no-smoking rooms* ⊟ *AE, D, DC, MC, V* ⃟*CP.*

$$$$ **Salmon Falls Resort.** Perched along Clover Passage next to a beautiful waterfall, this high-end resort is near the end of the road, 17 mi north of Ketchikan. Guests tend to appreciate the variety of deals, starting with a three-night package that includes two days of fishing, a guide, a cabin cruiser, and all meals for $1,860 per person. ■TIP➜ The huge, octagonal restaurant is worth the half-hour drive from town. Specialties

include steaks and Alaska seafood, including blackened salmon or halibut. The restaurant is built of pine logs and, in the center, a 40-foot section of pipe—originally manufactured for the Alaska pipeline—rises to support the roof. Big windows overlook the waters of Clover Passage. **Pros:** Outstanding restaurant, interesting architecture. **Con:** Property is not disability-friendly. ⊠ *16707 N. Tongass Hwy.* ☎ *907/225–2752, 800/247–9059 outside Alaska* ⊕ *www. salmonfallsresort.com* ↩ *52 rooms*

> **SEAFOOD STOP**
>
> For some of the Southeast's best canned, smoked, or frozen salmon and halibut, along with crab and clams, try **Salmon Etc.** on Mission Street. **Simply Salmon**, its sister store, is on Creek Street. ⊠ *322 Mission St., Ketchikan* ☎ *907/225–6008 or 800/354–7256* ⊠ *10 Creek St.* ☎ *907/225–1616* ⊕ *www. salmonetc.com.*

⚒ *In-hotel: restaurant, bar, water sports, no elevator, airport shuttle, no-smoking rooms* ⊟ *AE, MC, V* ⊗ *Closed Oct.–May.*

¢ ⚑ **Ward Lake Campgrounds.** Two rain-forest campgrounds are located 8 mi north of Ketchikan; turn right onto Revilla Road and follow it to the exceptionally scenic Ward Lake area, popular for fishing, hiking, and picnicking. Both are managed by the Forest Service, with sites reservable ($9 extra) through the **National Recreation Reservation Service** (☎ *518/885–3639 or 877/444–6777* ⊕ *www.recreation.gov*). Signal Creek Campground is adjacent to Ward Lake, and Last Chance Campground is a mile farther up Revilla Road. ☎ *907/225–2148* ⊕ *www. fs.fed.us/r10/tongass* ↩ *Signal Creek: 24 sites. Last Chance: 19 sites.* ⚒ *Restrooms, running water, no showers.* ⊟ *AE, D, MC, V.*

$ ▦ **Wild Huckleberry Bed and Breakfast.** Half–vacation rental, half–B&B, the Wild Huckleberry is tucked away in a quiet, creek-side, rain-forest neighborhood north of town. Groups of fishermen enjoy the Salmonberry apartment for its size, autonomy, and proximity to Knudson Cove Marina and Clover Pass Resort. Guests staying in the smaller Huckleberry room (inside the B&B proper) get treated to better-than-average continental breakfasts, complete with fresh fruit, homemade baked goods, and yogurt parfaits. **Pros:** Excellent continental breakfasts, quiet location. **Cons:** Somewhat remote location, guests need a car. ⊠ *14142 Riddle Rd.* ☎ *907/225–1060* ⊕ *www.wildhuckleberrybnb.com* ↩ *1 room, 1 apartment* ⚒ *In-room: kitchen (some), refrigerator (some), DVD (some), no TV (some). In-hotel: no elevator, laundry facilities, public Internet, no-smoking rooms* ⊟ *No credit cards* ⛛ *CP.*

NIGHTLIFE

BARS

Ketchikan has quieted down in recent years as the economy shifted from logging to tourism, but it remains something of a party town, especially when crews stumble off fishing boats with cash in hand. You won't have any trouble finding something going on at several

Ketchikan. "On a cool spring day, after walking on glaciers and seeing so much wildlife in the Tundra and sea coast, Ketchikan is comfortable and warm." —*Sandy Cook, Fodors.com photo contest participant*

downtown bars. **First City Saloon** (⊠*830 Water St.* ☎*907/225–1494*) is the main dance spot, with live music throughout summer. The **Potlatch Bar** (⊠*126 Thomas Basin* ☎*907/225–4855*) delivers up music on weekends as well.

SHOPPING

ART GALLERIES

In business since 1972, **Scanlon Gallery** (⊠*318 Mission St.* ☎*907/247–4730 or 888/228–4730* ⊕*www.scanlongallery.com*) carries prints from a number of well-known Alaska artists, including Byron Birdsall, Rie Muñoz, John Fehringer, Barbara Lavallee, and Jon Van Zyle.

Design, art, clothing, and collectibles converge in the stylish **Soho Coho Contemporary Art and Craft Gallery** (⊠*5 Creek St.* ☎*907/225–5954 or 800/888–4070* ⊕*www.trollart.com*), where you'll find an eclectic collection of art and T-shirts featuring the work of owner Ray Troll—best known for his wacky fish art—and other Southeast Alaska artists.

BOOKS

Upstairs from the Soho Coho Gallery, **Parnassus Books** (⊠*5 Creek St.* ☎*907/225–7690* ⊕*www.ketchikanbooks.com*) is a book lover's bookstore, with creaky floors, cozy quarters, many Alaskan titles, and a knowledgeable staff.

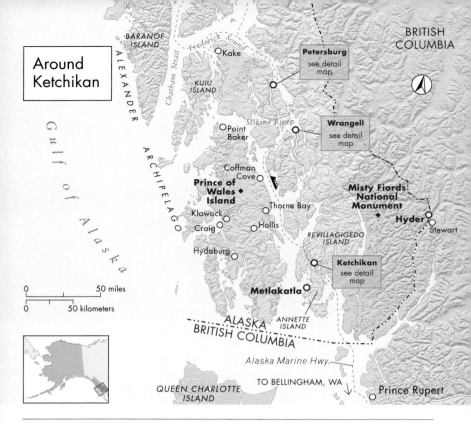

BRITISH
COLUMBIA

BARANOF
ISLAND

Frederick Sound

Kake

KUIU
ISLAND

Petersburg
see detail
map

Chatham Strait

ALEXANDER

Point
Baker

Stikine River

Wrangell
see detail
map

Gulf of Alaska

ARCHIPELAGO

Coffman
Cove

**Prince of
Wales ◆
Island**

Thorne Bay

Klawock

Craig

Hollis

**Misty Fiords
National
Monument**

◆ **Hyder**

Stewart

REVILLAGIGEDO
ISLAND

Hydaburg

0   50 miles
0   50 kilometers

Metlakatla

ANNETTE
ISLAND

Ketchikan
see detail
map

ALASKA
BRITISH COLUMBIA

Alaska Marine Hwy.

TO BELLINGHAM, WA

QUEEN CHARLOTTE
ISLAND

Prince Rupert

AROUND KETCHIKAN

MISTY FIORDS NATIONAL MONUMENT

40 mi east of Ketchikan by air.

Just east of Ketchikan, Misty Fiords National Monument is a wilderness of cliff-faced fjords (or fiords, if you follow the monument's spelling), mountains, and islands with spectacular coastal scenery, wildlife, and recreation. Small boats enable close-up views of breathtaking vistas. Travel on these waters can be an almost mystical experience, with the green forests reflected in the waters of the monument's many fjords. You may find yourself in the company of a whale, see a bear fishing for salmon along the shore, or even pull in your own salmon for an evening meal. ■TIP→ Note that the name Misty refers to the weather you're likely to encounter.

Fodor'sChoice   Most visitors to Misty Fiords arrive on day trips via floatplane from
★   Ketchikan or on board a catamaran run by **Alaska Travel Adventures**
(☎800/478–0052, 800/791–2673 outside Alaska ⊕*www.bestofalaskatravel.com*).

METLAKATLA

12 mi south of Ketchikan.

The village of Metlakatla—whose name translates roughly to "salt water passage"—is on Annette Island, just a dozen miles by sea from busy Ketchikan but a world away culturally. A visit to this quiet community offers visitors a chance to learn about life in a small Inside Passage native community.

In most Southeast native villages, the people are Tlingit or Haida in heritage. Metlakatla is the exception, as most folks are Tsimshian (*sim-shee-ann*). They moved to the island from British Columbia in 1887, led by William Duncan, an Anglican missionary from England. The town grew rapidly and soon contained dozens of buildings on a grid of streets, including a cannery, a sawmill, and a church that could seat 1,000 people. Congress declared Annette Island a federal Indian reservation in 1891, and it remains the only reservation in Alaska today. Father Duncan continued to control life in Metlakatla for decades, until the government finally stepped in shortly before his death in 1918.

During World War II the U.S. Army built a major air base 7 mi from Metlakatla that included observation towers for Japanese subs, airplane hangars, gun emplacements, and housing for 10,000 soldiers. After the war it served as Ketchikan's airport for many years, but today the long runways are virtually abandoned save for a few private flights.

GETTING HERE & AROUND

The **Alaska Marine Highway System** offers daily ferry service from Ketchikan to Metlakatla and back. If you prefer to arrive from above, **ProMech Air** has scheduled floatplane flights between Ketchikan and Metlakatla. Run by the Metlakatla community, **Metlakatla Tours** leads local tours that include visits to Duncan Cottage, the cannery, and the longhouse, along with a Tsimshian dance performance. Local taxis can take you to other sights around the island, including Yellow Hill and the old Air Force base.

ESSENTIALS

Airplane Contact **ProMech Air** (☎ *907/225–3845 or 800/860–3845* ⊕ *www. promechair.com*).

Ferry Contact The **Alaska Marine Highway System** (☎ *907/465–3941 or 800/642–0066* ⊕ *www.dot.state.ak.us/amhs*).

Tour Info **Metlakatla Tours** (☎ *907/886–4441* ⊕ *www.metlakatlatours.com*).

EXPLORING METLAKATLA

Metlakatla's religious heritage still shows today. The clapboard **William Duncan Memorial Church**, topped with two steeples, burned in 1948 but was rebuilt several years later. It is one of nine churches in tiny Metlakatla. **Father Duncan's Cottage** is maintained to appear exactly as it would have in 1891, and includes original furnishings, personal items, and a collection of turn-of-the-20th-century music boxes. ⊠ *Corner of 4th Ave. and Church St.* ☎ *907/886–8687* ⊕ *www.metlakatlatours. com* ☎ *$2* ☉ *Weekdays 8:30–12:30, or when cruise ships are in port.*

Father Duncan worked hard to eliminate traditional Tsimshian beliefs and dances, but today the people of Metlakatla have resurrected their past; they perform old dances in traditional regalia. The best place to catch these performances is at the traditional **longhouse** (known as *Le Sha'as* in the Tsimshian dialect), which faces Metlakatla's boat harbor. Three totem poles stand on the back side of the building, and the front is covered with a Tsimshian design. Inside are displays of native crafts and a model of the fish traps that were once common throughout the Inside Passage. Native dance groups perform here on Wednesday and Friday in summer. Just next to the longhouse is an **Artists' Village** where booths display locally made arts and crafts. The village and longhouse open when groups and tours are present.

Two miles from town is a boardwalk path that leads up the 540-foot **Yellow Hill.** Distinctive yellow sandstone rocks and panoramic vistas make this a worthwhile detour on clear days.

WHERE TO STAY

$ 　Metlakatla Inn. This two-story building, decorated with native art, offers standard motel accommodations with private decks off the upstairs rooms. All rooms share the same phone line. The restaurant is no longer open to the public, but inn guests can still get three meals a day from the kitchen. Vehicle and truck rentals are available for guests. **Pro:** Property has recently been renovated. **Con:** Guests share the same phone line. ✉*3rd Ave. and Lower Milton St.* ☎*907/886–3456* ⊕*www.metlakatlainn.com* ➪*9 rooms, 2 apartments* ᕼ*In-room: kitchen (some), refrigerator, DVD. In-hotel: no elevator, public Internet, airport shuttle, some pets allowed, no-smoking rooms* ▭*MC, V.*

$ 　Tuck'em Inn Bed & Breakfast. This family-run lodging is located in two separate downtown houses. Rooms are functional, with down comforters, quilts, private and shared baths, and access to a kitchen and sitting room. A make-it-yourself continental breakfast is included. Be sure to ask about bedding arrangements, as some rooms feature twin beds. **Pro:** Convenient location. **Con:** Some rooms share bathrooms. ✉*Hillcrest and Western Aves.* ☎*907/886–6611* ⊕*www.alaskanow.com/tuckem-inn* ➪*6 rooms* ᕼ*In-room: no phone (some), kitchen (some), refrigerator (some), VCR. In-hotel: no elevator, laundry facilities, public Internet, no-smoking rooms* ▭*AE, MC, V* ⧉*CP.*

HYDER

90 mi northeast of Ketchikan.

The tiny town of Hyder sits at the head of narrow Portland Canal, a 70-mi-long fjord northeast of Ketchikan. The fjord marks the border between Canada and the United States, and Hyder sits just 2 mi from the larger town of Stewart, British Columbia. ■TIP→ **It's also one of the few Southeast settlements that is accessible by paved road.**

The 1898 discovery of gold and silver in the surrounding mountains brought a flood of miners to the Hyder area, and the town eventually became a major shipping port. Mining remained important for decades, but a devastating 1948 fire destroyed much of the town, which had been built on pilings over the water. A small amount of mining still takes place here, but the beauty of the area now attracts increasing numbers of tourists. Today Hyder calls itself "the friendliest ghost town in Alaska."

GETTING HERE & AROUND
From Stewart, in Canada, Highway 37A continues over spectacular Bear Pass to Hyder and connects the town with the rest of Canada. **Taquan Air** has year-round service between Ketchikan and Hyder every Monday and Thursday. **Seaport Limousine** leads guided tours of the Hyder area, including Fish Creek and Salmon Glacier. (Don't expect any stretch Hummers here, though—Seaport uses vans and SUVs for its tours.)

ESSENTIALS
Airplane Contact **Taquan Air** (☎ *907/225–8800 or 800/770–8800* ⊕ *www.taquanair.com*).

Visitor & Tour Info **Seaport Limousine** (☎ *250/636–2622* ⊕ *www.seaportnorthwest.com*). **Stewart-Hyder Chamber of Commerce** (✉ *Box 306, Stewart, BC VOT 1WO* ☎ *250/636–9224* ⊕ *www.stewart-hyder.com*).

EXPLORING HYDER
The **Stewart Historical Society Museum,** housed in the town's former fire hall, contains wildlife displays and exhibits on the region's mining history. ✉ *6th and Columbia Sts.* ☎ *250/636–2568* ⊕ *www.stewartmuseum.homestead.com* 🖃 *$5* ⊙ *May, June, and Sept., weekends 1–4; July and Aug., daily 1–4.*

NOW YOU KNOW

A small, empty stone storehouse stands along the road as you enter Hyder. Built in 1896, this is the oldest masonry building in Alaska.

Six miles north of Hyder on Salmon River Road is the **Fish Creek Wildlife Observation Site.** From late July to early September, a large run of salmon attracts black and brown bears, which, in turn, attract more than a few photographers. The creek produces some of the largest chum salmon anywhere.

Twenty-five miles east of Stewart on Highway 37A is the imposing **Bear Glacier.** The glacier sits across a small lake that is often crowded with icebergs.

A dirt road from Hyder into Canada leads 17 mi to remote **Salmon Glacier,** one of few glaciers accessible by road in Southeast Alaska.

Getting "Hyderized" (which involves drinking and drinking-related silliness) is a term that you will hear upon arrival in the area. You can get Hyderized at **Glacier Inn** (✉ *Main St.* ☎ *250/636–9243*), where the walls are papered with thousands of signed bills. The tradition supposedly began when prospectors would tack a dollar bill on the wall in case they were broke when they returned.

WHERE TO STAY & EAT

$–$$$$
CAFÉ

✕ **Bitter Creek Café.** This bustling Stewart café serves a variety of cuisines, including gourmet steaks, pizzas, lasagna, burgers, seafood, and even Mexican dishes. It's all made in-house, including the freshly baked breads. The quirky interior is adorned with a fun collection of antiques as well as a 1930 Pontiac. Relax on the outside deck on a summer afternoon. ⊠ *5th Ave., Stewart* ☎ *250/636–2166* ⊕ *bittercreek.homestead.com* ☐ *AE, MC, V* ⊙ *Closed Oct.–Apr. No lunch.*

¢–$

🏠 **Ripley Creek Inn.** Stewart's best lodging option covers five historic downtown buildings. All rooms are bright, with Mission-style and antique furnishings; some also include sofa beds, decks, and glacier views. The main building also houses Toastworks Museum, a repository of antique toasters and other kitchen gadgets. Guests have access to bicycles for exploring the small mining town. The inn's restaurant, the Bitter Creek Café, serves seafood and burgers. **Pros:** Nice decks and views from rooms. **Con:** Somewhat noisy. ⊡ *Box 625, Stewart* ☎ *250/636–2344* ⊕ *www.ripleycreekinn. com* ⇦ *32 rooms* ⚲ *In-room: no phone (some), kitchen (some), refrigerator (some), Wi-Fi. In-hotel: bicycles, no elevator, public Internet, public Wi-Fi, some pets allowed, no-smoking rooms* ☐ *AE, MC, V.*

HYDER TIPS

The town of Hyder is small and has only a handful of tourist-oriented businesses, a post office, and a library. Nearby Stewart has more to offer, including a museum, hotels, restaurants, and camping. You will need to check in at Canadian customs (open 24 hours) before crossing the border from Hyder into Stewart. Canadian money is primarily used in Hyder, but greenbacks are certainly accepted.

PRINCE OF WALES ISLAND

15 mi northwest of Ketchikan.

Prince of Wales Island stretches more than 130 mi from north to south, making it the largest island in Southeast Alaska. Only two American islands—Kodiak in Alaska and Hawaii in the Hawaiian chain—are larger. Prince of Wales (or "P.O.W." as locals call it) has a diversity of landforms, a plethora of wildlife, and exceptional sportfishing. The island has long been a major source of timber, both from Tongass National Forest lands and those owned by native corporations. While much of the native land has been cut over, environmental restrictions on public lands have greatly reduced logging activity. The island's economy is now supported by small-scale logging operations, tourism, and commercial fishing.

Approximately 4,500 people live full-time on Prince of Wales Island, scattered in small villages and towns. A network of 1,500 mi of roads—nearly all built to access clear-cuts—crisscrosses the island, providing connections to even the smallest settlement.

GETTING HERE & AROUND

The **Inter-Island Ferry Authority** operates a daily vehicle and passenger ferry between Ketchikan and Prince of Wales Island. The ferry terminal is in the tiny settlement of Hollis, 31 mi from Craig on a paved road. Another IFA ferry connects Coffman Cove—located on the north end of Prince of Wales—with Wrangell and Petersburg; it calls at South Mitkof Island, 25 mi of paved and gravel road from Petersburg proper.

Paved roads link Craig, Klawock, Hollis, Thorne Bay, Hydaburg, and Coffman Cove. The prevalence of roads, combined with ferry and air access from Ketchikan, makes it easy to explore this island, though few people choose to do so.

ESSENTIALS

Ferry Info **Inter-Island Ferry Authority** (☎ *907/826–4848 or 866/308–4848* ⊕ *www.interislandferry.com).*

Visitor Info **Prince of Wales Chamber of Commerce** (✉ *Box 490, Klawock 99921* ☎ *907/775-2626* ⊕ *www.princeofwalescoc.org).*

WHAT TO SEE

The primary commercial center for Prince of Wales is **Craig,** on the island's western shore. This town of 1,500 retains a hard-edged aura fast disappearing in many Inside Passage towns, where tourism now holds sway. Although sightseeing attractions are slim, the town exudes a frontier spirit, and its small-boat harbors buzz with activity.

A half-dozen miles from Craig is the Tlingit village of **Klawock,** with a sawmill, cannery, hatchery, and the island's only airport. The town is best known for its striking 21 totem poles in **Totem Park.** Several of these colorful poles were moved here in the 1930s; others are more-recent carvings. You can watch carvers restoring old totems at the carving shed, across the road from the grocery store. Klawock is also home to **Prince of Wales Hatchery** (☎ *907/755-2231* ⊕ *www.powhasalmon. org* ☾ *Tours June–Aug., Mon.–Sat. 1–5),* one of the state's most effective hatcheries. It's open for summertime tours ($2), and it also has a small visitor center with an aquarium full of young coho salmon. Along the bay, you'll find **St. John's by the Sea Catholic Church** (☎ *907/755-2345)* with stained-glass windows picturing native Alaskans.

The Haida village of **Hydaburg,** approximately 40 mi south of Klawock (via chip-sealed road), lies along scenic Sukkwan Strait. A small collection of **totem poles** occupies the center of this Haida settlement, the only one in Alaska. Originally from British Columbia's Queen Charlotte Island, the Haida settled here around 1700.

A number of large natural caverns pockmark northern Prince of Wales Island. The best known of these, **El Capitan Cave,** has one of the deepest pits in the United States and is open to the public. Paleontologists have found a wealth of black bear, brown bear, and other mammal fossils in the cave, including some that date back more than 12,000 years. The Forest Service leads free two-hour El Capitan tours several times a week in summer. Reservations are required, and no children under age seven are permitted. Rubber boots and a light jacket are a good idea for spelunkers. ⊠*Mi 51 along North Prince of Wales Rd.* ☎*907/828–3304 Forest Service.*

WHERE TO STAY

$–$$ 🏨**Inn of the Little Blue Heron.** With sweeping water views, cozy rooms, and outdoor decks tailored for simultaneous coffee drinking and wild-life viewing, the Little Blue Heron is a favorite among regular visitors to Craig. Two locations in town cater to your desired luxury factor: the South Cove Boat Harbor outpost features four small but well-appointed rooms (two with water views), while the Bucareli Bay Suite, built in 2005, offers two spacious rooms with unimpeded bay views, queen-size Tempur-Pedic mattresses, and satellite TV. **Pros:** Both locations offer wireless Internet, can rent out whole inn or suite for large groups. **Con:** Rooms at the South Cove location are small. ⊠*406 9th St. and 403 Beach Rd., Craig* ☎*907/826–3608* ⊕*www.littleblueheroninn.com* ⮑*6 rooms, 1 suite* ⌂*In-room: no phone (some), kitchen (some), refrigerator, Wi-Fi. In-hotel: no elevator, public Wi-Fi, no kids under 5 (Bucareli Bay location), no-smoking rooms* ▭*MC, V* ⍣*CP.*

$$$$ 🏨**McFarland's Floatel.** You'll need a boat or floatplane to access this quiet resort 2 mi across the bay from the logging town of Thorne Bay on the eastern side of Prince of Wales. Each of the four beachfront log cabins sleeps up to six people and includes a loft, woodstove, full kitchen, and private bath. A 200-foot walkway leads to the floating main lodge, which was built in Ketchikan but floated by raft to its present location in 1981. The lodge now acts as a gathering place for Floatel guests and visitors. A bait and food store is also located on the property. Co-owner Jeannie McFarland teaches basketry workshops and sells her pine-needle raffia baskets here. Charter-fishing trips are available, or you can rent a skiff and fishing gear and head out on your own. **Pro:** Nightly rate covers up to four guests. **Con:** Restaurant has closed. ⍔*Box 19149, Thorne Bay, 99919* ☎*907/828–3335 or 888/828–3335* ⊕*www.mcfarlandsfloatel.com* ⮑*4 cabins* ⌂*In-room: no phone, kitchen, refrigerator, no TV, Wi-Fi. In-hotel: no elevator, laundry facilities, public Internet, public Wi-Fi, airport shuttle, no-smoking rooms* ▭*MC, V* ⍣*Closed mid-Sept.–mid-Apr.*

$–$$ 🏨**Ruth Ann's Hotel.** Victorian-style furnishings and details flavor this tasteful gingerbread hotel. The honeymoon suite includes a double shower, large hot tub, and kitchenette. Across the street, the popular Ruth Ann's Restaurant serves home-style food with seafood and steaks at dinner, and burgers, sandwiches, and fish-and-chips at lunch. Ask for a table in the back room, where picture windows face the harbor; a tiny bar at the front of the restaurant fills up most nights. **Pro:** Honeymoon suite is perfect for romantic travelers. **Con:** Rooms are up the hill and not on the water. ⊠*505 Water St., Craig* ☎*907/826–3378* ⮑*17 rooms, 1 suite* ⌂*In-room: kitchen (some), refrigerator. In-hotel: restaurant, bar, no elevator, some pets allowed, no-smoking rooms* ▭*AE, MC, V* ⍣*Restaurant closed Jan.*

$$$$ 🏨**Shelter Cove Lodge.** Tall windows front the water at this modern lodge along the South Boat Harbor in Craig. The lodge here, renovated in 2008, runs all-inclusive fishing packages starting at $2,150 per person for three days and four nights. Rooms are modern, and each contains a queen and twin bed. Six of them face the harbor. Fresh seafood tops the restaurant's menu, along with steaks, delectable desserts, Alaska beers, and nightly specials. Prime rib attracts the locals on Friday and Saturday nights. **Pro:** Price is all-inclusive. **Con:** Expensive rate in comparison to similar properties. ✉ *703 Hamilton Dr., Craig* ☎ *907/826–2939 or 888/826–3474* ⊕ *www.sheltercovelodge.com* ⤢ *10 rooms* △ *In-room: refrigerator, Wi-Fi. In-hotel: restaurant, bar, water sports, no elevator, laundry facilities, public Wi-Fi, airport shuttle, no-smoking rooms* ▭ *AE, D, MC, V* ⊘ *Restaurant closed Sept.–May AI.*

$$$$
Fodor's Choice
★

🏨 **Waterfall Resort.** At this upscale fishing lodge, guests can choose from several accommodation styles, eat bountiful meals with all the trimmings, and fish from custom-built 25-foot cabin cruisers under the care of expert fishing guides. ■**TIP**→ Fish processing and packaging is included in the package pricing—there's no better Alaska souvenir. A three-night minimum stay with all meals, including floatplane fare from Ketchikan, comes to around $3,795 per person. **Pros:** Plenty of saltwater fishing, opportunity to spot whales, sea lions, and eagles. **Con:** Most kitchens in the condos aren't used, as meals are provided by the resort. 🖂 *Box 6440, Ketchikan , 99901* ☎ *907/225–9461 or 800/544–5125* ⊕ *www.waterfallresort.com* ⤢ *10 lodge rooms, 4 suites, 4 condos, 26 cabins* △ *In-room: no phone, kitchen (some), refrigerator (some), no TV. In-hotel: restaurant, bar, no elevator, laundry facilities, public Internet, no kids under 10* ▭ *AE, D, MC, V* ⊘ *Closed Sept.–late May* ❢⊙❢ *FAP.*

WRANGELL

87 mi north of Ketchikan.

A small, unassuming timber and fishing community, Wrangell sits on the northern tip of Wrangell Island, near the mouth of the fast-flowing Stikine River—North America's largest un-dammed river. Like much of the Southeast, the town has suffered in recent years from a declining resource-based economy. Wrangell has flown three different national flags in its time. Russia established Redoubt St. Dionysius here in 1834. Five years later, Great Britain's Hudson's Bay Company leased the southern Alaska coastline, renaming the settlement Fort Stikine. It was rechristened Wrangell when the Americans took over in 1867; the name came from Baron Ferdinand Petrovich von Wrangel, governor of the Russian-American Company.

EXPLORING WRANGELL

The rough-around-the-edges town of Wrangell is off the track of the larger cruise ships, so it does not suffer from tourist invasions to the degree that Ketchikan and Juneau do. Hence, it is nearly devoid of tourist-targeted shops that dominate so many other nearby downtown areas.

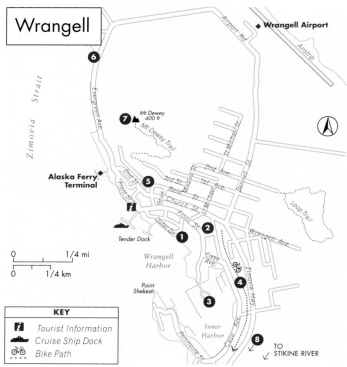

KEY

ℹ️ *Tourist Information*
🚢 *Cruise Ship Dock*
🚲 *Bike Path*

GETTING HERE & AROUND

While you probably won't get to Wrangell on a cruise ship, ferries connect the town to other Southeast Alaska ports via the **Alaska Marine Highway,** and the **Inter-Island Ferry Authority** runs between Wrangell and Coffman Cove on Prince of Wales Island. The town is fairly compact, and most sights are within walking distance of the city dock or ferry terminal.

ESSENTIALS

Ferry Contact The **Alaska Marine Highway System** (☎ 907/465-3941 or 800/642-0066 ⊕ www.dot.state.ak.us/amhs). **Inter-Island Ferry Authority** (☎ 907/826-4848 or 866/308-4848 ⊕ www.interislandferry.com).

Medical Center **Wrangell Medical Center** (✉ 310 Bennett St. ☎ 907/874-7000 ⊕ www.wrangellmedicalcenter.com).

Pharmacy **Stikine Drug** (✉ 202 Front St. ☎ 907/874-3422).

Visitor Info **Wrangell Visitor Center** (✉ 296 Campbell Dr., in the Nolan Center ⌂ Box 1350, Wrangell 99929 ☎ 907/874-2829 or 800/367-9745 ⊕ www. wrangell.com).

A GOOD WALK

Bone up on local history and biology at the **Nolan Center**, which houses informative and surprisingly entertaining exhibits, a well-stocked gift shop, and a helpful visitor center. Farther along Front Street, check out **Kiksetti Totem Park** before turning onto Shakes Street to see the town's prized attraction, **Chief Shakes Island**. You may want to spend time here just soaking in the harbor view and examining the old totem poles. **Chief Shakes's grave site** is on the hill overlooking Wrangell Harbor. Get there from Chief Shakes Island by turning right on Case Avenue. From the grave site, head up Church Street to the **Irene Ingle Public Library**.

About 0.6 mi north of the ferry terminal along Evergreen Avenue, you'll find **Petroglyph Beach**, where ancient etchings are visible along the shore. Be prepared to leave the observation deck behind: most of the best petroglyphs are scattered across the rocky beach. For a woodsy hike, climb **Mt. Dewey**, the hill right behind town. Farther afield (5 mi south of town) is the fun hike to **Rainbow Falls**.

It is a 1.5-mi walk between Petroglyph Beach and Chief Shakes Island, so you should plan at least three hours to complete the walk and sightseeing around town.

4

WHAT TO SEE

❸ ★ **Chief Shakes Island.** This small island sits in the center of Wrangell's protected harbor and is accessible by a footbridge from the bottom of Front Street. Seven totem poles surround a traditionally styled tribal house, built in the 1930s as a replica of one that was home to many of the various Shakes and their peoples. ⊠ *Off Shakes St.* ☎ *907/874–3481* 🏷 *$3.50* ⊗ *Daily when cruise ships are in port (ask at Wrangell Visitor Center) or by appointment.*

❹ **Chief Shakes's grave site.** Buried here is Shakes V, who led the local Tlingit during the first half of the 19th century. A white picket fence surrounds the grave, and two killer-whale totem poles mark his resting spot overlooking the harbor. Find the grave on Case Avenue. ⊠ *Case Ave.*

❺ **Irene Ingle Public Library.** The library, behind the post office, has two ancient petroglyphs out front, and is home to a large collection of Alaskan books, computers with free Internet access, and a helpful staff. ⊠ *124 2nd St.* ☎ *907/874–3535.*

❷ **Kiksetti Totem Park.** You'll find a couple of recently carved totem poles at this pocket-size park with Alaska greenery. ⊠ *Front St.*

❼ **Mt. Dewey.** Despite the name, this landmark is more of a hill than a peak. Still, it's a steep 15-minute climb from town to the top through a second-growth forest. The trail begins from 3rd Street behind the high school, and an observation platform on top provides a viewpoint for protected waterways and quirkily named islands, including Zarembo, Vank, and Woronkofski.

❶ **Nolan Center.** Wrangell's museum moved into a building that acts as a
🕐 centerpiece for cultural life in Wrangell. Exhibits provide a window on
★ the region's rich history. Featured pieces include decorative posts from
Chief Shakes's clan house, petroglyphs, century-old spruce-root and
cedar-bark baskets, masks, gold-rush memorabilia, and a fascinating
photo collection. If you're spending any time in town, don't pass this
up. Also in the building are the town's **Civic Center,** a 200-seat movie
theater/performance space/convention center, and the **Wrangell Visitor
Center** (☎907/874–2829 or 800/367–9745 ⊕www.wrangell.com).
The latter is staffed when the museum is open, and has details on local
adventure options. ✉296 Outer Dr. ☎907/874–3770 💲$5 ⊙May–
Sept., Tues.–Sat. 10–5, and when ferry or cruise ships are in port; Oct.–
Apr., Tues.–Sat. 1–5.

❻ **Petroglyph Beach.** Scattered among other rocks at this public beach are
three dozen or more large stones bearing designs and pictures chiseled
by unknown, ancient artists. No one knows why the rocks at this curious site were etched the way they were, or even exactly how old these
etchings are. You can access the beach via a boardwalk, where you'll
find signs describing the site along with carved replicas of the petroglyphs. Most of the petroglyphs are to the right between the viewing
deck and a large outcropping of rock in the tidal beach area. Because
the original petroglyphs can be damaged by physical contact, only photographs are permitted. But you are welcome to use the replicas to
make a rubbing from rice paper and charcoal or crayons (available in
local stores). ✉0.6 mi north of ferry terminal off Evergreen Ave.

❽ **Rainbow Falls.** The trail to this scenic waterfall starts across the road
from Shoemaker Bay, 5 mi south of Wrangell. A 0.75-mi trail climbs
uphill through the rain forest, with long stretches of boardwalk steps,
ending at an overlook just below the falls. Hikers with more stamina
can continue another 3 mi and 1,500 vertical feet to Shoemaker Bay
Overlook.

OUTDOOR ACTIVITIES & GUIDED TOURS

AIR CHARTER

Sunrise Aviation (☎907/874–2319 or 800/874–2311 ⊕www.sunrise-
flights.com) is a charter-only air carrier that flies to the Anan Creek
Wildlife Observatory, LeConte Glacier, or Forest Service cabins.

BICYCLING

A waterfront trail connects Wrangell with Shoemaker Bay Recreation
Area, 4.5 mi south of town. The trail is mainly flat; moreadventur-
ous souls can brave the dozens of miles of logging roads that criss-
cross the island. Bicycle rentals are available from several suppliers,
including **Rainwalker Expeditions** (☎907/874–2549 or 888/276–2549
⊕www.rainwalkerexpeditions.com), which provides helmets and
island maps.

WORTH THE DETOUR

Anan Creek Wildlife Observatory. About 30 mi southeast of Wrangell in the Tongass National Forest, Anan is one of Alaska's premier black- and brown-bear viewing areas. Each summer, from early July to mid-August, as many as 30 to 40 bears gather at this Southeast stream to feed on huge runs of pink salmon. On an average visit of about three hours you might spot up to 16 bears while strolling the 0.5-mi viewing boardwalk. There is a photo blind which affords the opportunity to view and photograph bears at eye level while they catch and eat salmon. Forest Service interpreters are on hand to answer questions. The site is accessible only by boat or floatplane. **Alaska Waters** (☎ *907/874–2378 or 800/347–4462* ⊕ *www.alaskawaters.com*) is one of several local companies that offer day trips there. For additional details, contact the **Tongass National Forest Wrangell Ranger District** (☎ *907/874–2323* ⊕ *www.fs.fed.us/r10/tongass*).

BOATING

Mark Galla of **Alaska Peak & Seas** (☎ *907/874–2454* ⊕ *www.wedo-alaska.com*) guides wildlife trips, Stikine jet-boat tours, and boat trips to surrounding areas. **Alaska Vistas and Stikine Wilderness Adventures** (☎ *907/874–3006 or 866/874–3006* ⊕ *www.alaskavistas.com*) has jet-boat trips to Anan Creek Wildlife Observatory that depart from Wrangell, plus a variety of guided sea-kayak adventures and rafting trips. They also offer custom tours and itinerary planning. **Breakaway Adventures** (☎ *907/874–2488 or 888/385–2488* ⊕ *www.breakawayadventures.com*) leads a variety of jet-boat trips, including a tour to Chief Shakes Glacier and the nearby hot springs. You can catch one of their water taxis to Petersburg or Prince of Wales Island.

FISHING

Numerous companies schedule salmon- and trout-fishing excursions ranging in length from an afternoon to a week. Contact the **Wrangell Visitor Center** (☎ *907/874–2829 or 800/367–9745* ⊕ *www.wrangell.com*) for information on guide services and locations.

GOLF

Muskeg Meadows Golf Course (☎ *907/874–4653* ⊕ *www.wrangellalaskagolf.com*), Southeast Alaska's first USGA regulation links, is a well-maintained, 2,950-yard 9-hole course with a driving range. Situated in a wooded area 0.5 mi from town, the course is easily accessible, and golf clubs and pull carts can be rented on-site.

NATURAL HISTORY

Alaska Charters and Adventures (☎ *888/993–2750* ⊕ *www.alaskaupclose.com*) offers wildlife viewing, bear photography trips, fishing, glacier tours, and a Stikine River jet-boat wilderness tour.

Rainwalker Expeditions (☎ *907/874–2549 or 888/276–2549* ⊕ *www.rainwalkerexpeditions.com*) leads two-hour, half-day, and full-day guided natural-history, botany, wildlife, and bird-watching tours of wild places near Wrangell. The company also rents bikes, canoes, and sea kayaks if you want to head out on your own.

WHERE TO EAT

$–$$$ AMERICAN **Zak's Cafe.** Despite its simple, no-nonsense atmosphere, Zak's is a standout among Wrangell's limited dining choices, with good food and reasonable prices. Check out the day's specials or try their steaks, chicken, seafood, and salads. At lunch, the menu includes burgers, sandwiches, fish-and-chips, and wraps. *✉314 Front St. ☎907/874–3355 ▭MC, V.*

WHERE TO STAY

$–$$$ **Alaskan Sourdough Lodge.** This rambling lodge on the south side of the harbor began life as a construction camp, and traces of its rough-hewn origins remain today. The hallways are tight, but rooms are modestly furnished, and a private suite (handicap-accessible and large enough for six people) has a large bathroom with a heated floor and a hot tub. Hardy home-style meals, including fresh seafood, are also available for those not staying here (advance reservations required). The lodge offers a courtesy van to the airport and ferries. **Pro:** Excellent home-style dining. **Cons:** Tight hallways and sparse furnishings. *✉1104 Peninsula St., Box 1062 ☎907/874–3613 or 800/874–3613 🌐www.akgetaway.com 15 rooms, 1 suite In-room: no TV (some), Ethernet, Wi-Fi (some). In-hotel: restaurant, bar, water sports, no elevator, laundry facilities, public Internet, public Wi-Fi, airport shuttle, some pets allowed, no-smoking rooms ▭AE, D, DC, MC, V CP.*

$ **Grand View Bed & Breakfast.** Two miles from town—perhaps within walking distance for avid pedestrians—this unassuming beachside home provides spectacular views across Zimovia Strait. Rooms, some with antiques and some decorated Alaska style, have private baths and entrances, plus access to a large common area, a library of Alaska travel books, and a fully stocked kitchen. Friendly owners John and Judy Baker, who have lived in Alaska for more than 50 years, take guests sightseeing and prepare delectable breakfasts. **Pro:** Expert sightseeing tours provided by owners. **Con:** Location is 2 mi from town. *✉Mi 2, Zimovia Hwy. Box 927, 99929 ☎907/874–3225 🌐www.grandviewbnb.com 3 rooms In-room: VCR (some). In-hotel: no elevator, laundry facilities, public Internet, airport shuttle, no-smoking rooms ▭No credit cards BP.*

$$$$ **Rain Haven.** This one-bedroom floating houseboat is perfect for those in search of a peaceful retreat with up-close wildlife viewing. In July and August, the houseboat is anchored in a remote cove 30 mi south of Wrangell, with canoes and kayaks for access to Anan Creek Wildlife Observatory. It's perfect for couples and small families, with a double bed, a pullout couch, and a single bed. The galley is stocked with staples, and there's a sunny atrium at the stern and a covered deck on the bow. Package stays include transportation from Wrangell. In May,

June, and September, the houseboat is docked in town and goes for $85 per night. Owner Marie Oboczky, a former Forest Service naturalist, leads local tours, and is very knowledgeable about the area. **Pro:** Excellent property for private retreats. **Cons:** Few amenities, no television, and no telephone. ✉ *Box 2074, 99929* ☎ *907/874–2549 or 888/276–2549* ⊕ *www.rainwalkerexpeditions.com* ⬅ *1 room* ♿ *In-room: no phone, kitchen, refrigerator, no TV. In-hotel: water sports (remote), bicycles (in town), no-smoking rooms* ⊟ *No credit cards.*

$ ⊡ **Rooney's Roost Bed & Breakfast.** This century-old home—easily Wrangell's most charming digs—is just a block from downtown. Decorated with a country theme that includes an amusing collection of rooster art, the Roost's cozy quarters are filled with the scent of freshly baked cookies every afternoon. Each of its six rooms has been decorated with a different theme. Friendly owners, a large-screen television, and a filling breakfast (featuring such heavenly fare as poached pears with raspberry sauce) add to its homey appeal. Ask for the room with a private bathroom, as the shared bathroom tends to be busy. **Pro:** Large, delicious breakfast. **Con:** Crowded communal bathroom. ✉ *206 McKinnon St.* ✉ *Box 552, Wrangell 99929* ☎ *907/874–2026* ⊕ *www. rooneysroost.com* ⬅ *6 rooms* ♿ *In-room: Wi-Fi. In-hotel: no elevator, public Wi-Fi, airport shuttle, no-smoking rooms* ⊟ *MC, V* ⏐◯⏐ *BP.*

¢ ⊡ **Shakes Slough Cabins.** If you're a hot-springs or hot-tub enthusiast, these Forest Service cabins on the Stikine River, accessible from Wrangell, are worth checking out. Shakes Slough Hot Springs are a short, 4-mi boat ride away from the cabins. Here you can soak in both an open-air hot tub and an enclosed version. Guests may spot the brown and black bears, goats, and moose that frequent the area. These remote and very rustic cabins—which feature views of the Popof Glacier and Mt. Basargin—sleep six on plywood bunks, and feature basic facilities, including outhouses and woodstoves, but no water or electricity. Bring your own sleeping bag, food, and cooking utensils. Reservations are required for the cabins; request details from the Forest Service office in Wrangell or make reservations by calling the **National Recreation Reservation Service. Pro:** Open-air hot tub. **Cons:** Cabins have no electricity or water. *Forest Service,* ✉ *525 Bennett St., Wrangell* ☎ *907/874–2323, 877/444–6777 National Recreation Reservation Service* ⊕ *www.recreation.gov* ⬅ *2 cabins* ⊟ *AE, D, MC, V.*

$–$$ ⊡ **Stikine Inn.** After some down years, Wrangell's largest inn is on the upswing; rooms are still basic, but the bathrooms have been remodeled, and the Stikine Inn's in-house restaurant may be the best in town. Located on the waterfront in downtown Wrangell, half of the inn's rooms have excellent ocean views. One suite includes a kitchen; all rooms have pillow-top beds. **Pro:** Scenic waterfront location. **Con:** Rooms are sparsely furnished. ✉ *107 Front St.* ☎ *907/874–3388 or 888/874–3388* ⊕ *www.stikineinn.com* ⬅ *33 rooms, 3 suites* ♿ *In-room: kitchen (some), refrigerator (some), Wi-Fi. In-hotel: restaurant, no elevator, public Wi-Fi, airport shuttle, some pets allowed, no-smoking rooms* ⊟ *AE, D, DC, MC, V.*

SHOPPING

A rocky ledge near the Stikine River is the source for **garnets** sold by local children for 25¢ to $50. The site was deeded to the Boy Scouts in 1962 and to the Presbyteria of Alaska in 2006, so only children can collect these colorful but imperfect stones, the largest of which are an inch across. At a few covered shelters near the city dock when cruise ships are in, or at the ferry terminal when a ferry is in port, you can purchase garnets. Local artist **Brenda Schwartz** (⊠7 *Front St.* ☎*907/874–3508* ⊕*www.marine-artist.com*)   creates   watercolor scenes of the Alaskan coast on navigational charts of the region.

FOR STARTERS

Sourdough is a nickname for a longtime resident of Alaska. Prospectors who trekked here in search of gold often carried sourdough starter for pancakes and bread. To this day, you'll find sourdough goods on hundreds of menus throughout the state.

PETERSBURG

22 mi north of Wrangell.

Getting to Petersburg is an experience, whether you take the "high road" by air or the "low road" by sea. Alaska Airlines claims the shortest jet flight in the world, from takeoff at Wrangell to landing at Petersburg. The schedule calls for 20 minutes of flying, but it's usually more like 15. At sea level only ferries and smaller cruisers can squeak through Wrangell Narrows with the aid of more than 50 buoys and range markers along the 22-mi waterway, which takes almost four hours. But the inaccessibility of Petersburg is also part of its charm: you'll never be overwhelmed here by hordes of cruise passengers; only smaller ships can reach the town.

The Scandinavian heritage is gradually being submerged by the larger American culture, but you can occasionally hear Norwegian spoken, especially during the Little Norway Festival, held here each year on the weekend closest to May 17. If you're in town during the festival, be sure to take part in one of the fish feeds that highlight the Norwegian Independence Day celebration. You won't find better folk dancing and beer-batter halibut outside Norway.

One of the most pleasant things to do in Petersburg is to roam among the fishing vessels tied up dockside in the town's expanding harbor. This is one of Alaska's busiest, most prosperous fishing communities, with an enormous variety of seacraft. You'll see small trollers, big halibut vessels, and sleek pleasure craft. By watching shrimp, salmon, or halibut catches being brought ashore (though be prepared for the pungent aroma), you can get a real appreciation for this industry.

On clear days Petersburg's scenery is second to none. Across Frederick Sound the sawlike peaks of the Stikine Ice Cap scrape clouds from the sky, looking every bit as malevolent as their monikers suggest. (Some of the most wickedly named summits include Devil's Thumb, Kate's Needle, and Witch's Tit.) **LeConte Glacier,** Petersburg's biggest draw, lies at the foot of the ice cap, about 25 mi east of town. Accessible only by water or air, the LeConte is the continent's southernmost tidewater glacier and one of its most active, often calving off so many icebergs that the tidewater bay at its face is carpeted shore to shore with floating bergs.

4

EXPLORING PETERSBURG

Although Petersburg is nice to explore, commercial fishing is more important than tourism—in other words, you'll find more hardware stores than jewel merchants. The main attractions are the town's Norwegian heritage, vibrant community, and its magnificent mountain-backed setting. The country around Petersburg provides an array of outdoor fun, from whale-watching and glacier-gazing to hiking and fishing.

GETTING HERE & AROUND

Once you arrive in Petersburg by ferry on the **Alaska Marine Highway** or by airplane, a host of outdoor activities await you. **Kaleidoscope Cruises** conducts whale-watching and glacier-ecology boat tours led by a professional naturalist, and **Tongass Kayak Adventures** leads multiday sea-kayak trips to the Stikine River and LeConte Glacier and half-day trips up Petersburg Creek. You can also see the Stikine River and LeConte Glacier from above on a flightseeing tour with the locally popular air-taxi operator **Pacific Wing.** For help finding more tours of the environs, contact travel agency **Viking Travel,** or visit the **Petersburg Visitor Information Center.**

ESSENTIALS

Ferry Contact **Alaska Marine Highway System** (☎ *907/465–3941 or 800/642–0066* ⊕ *www.dot.state.ak.us/amhs*).

Medical Assistance **Petersburg Medical Center** (✉ *103 Fram St.* ☎ *907/772–4291*).

Pharmacy **Rexall Drugs** (✉ *215 N. Nordic Dr.* ☎ *907/772–3265* ⊕ *www.petersburgrexall.com*).

Tour Info **Kaleidoscope Cruises** (☎ *907/772–3736 or 800/868–4373* ⊕ *www.petersburglodgingandtours.com*). **Pacific Wing** (✉ *1500 Haugen Dr.* ☎ *907/772–9258* ⊕ *www.pacificwing.com*). **Tongass Kayak Adventures** (☎ *907/772–4600* ⊕ *www.tongasskayak.com*). **Viking Travel** (☎ *907/772–3818 or 800/327–2571* ⊕ *www.alaskaferry.com*).

Petersburg

TO SANDY BEACH ↗

Wrangell Narrows

⑥

1st St.

Dolphin St.

Excel St.

⑤

Fram St.

③ ④

Gjoa St.

Haugen Dr.

Harbor
Way

Main St.

Nordic Dr.

**Floatplane
Base**

*Sing Lee
Alley*

①

②

2nd St.

3rd St.

4th St.

5th St.

**Ferry
Terminal**

Nordic Dr.

Mitkof Hwy.

TO CRYSTAL LAKE HATCHERY,
BLIND SLOUGH RECREATION AREA &
FALL'S CREEK FISH LADDER

0   1/4 mile

0   1/4 kilometer

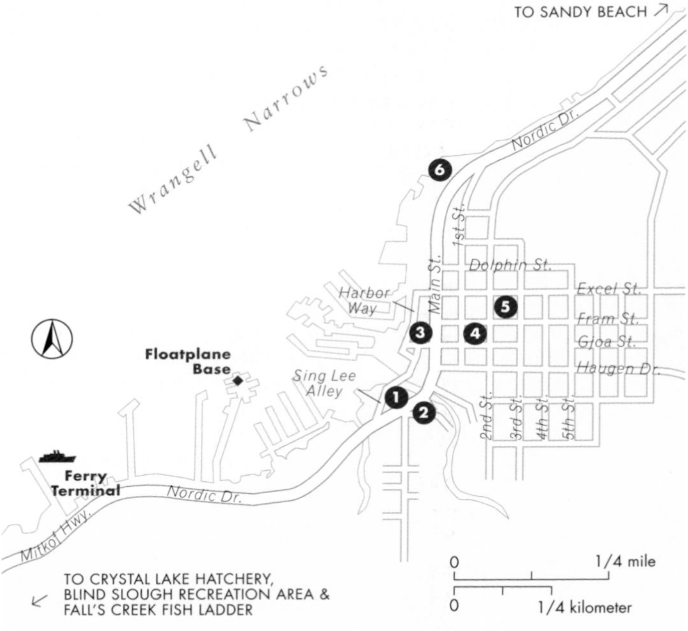

Visitor Info **Petersburg Visitor Information Center** (⊠ *1st and Fram Sts.* ⌂ *Box 649, Petersburg 99833* ☎ *907/772–4636* ⊕ *www.petersburg.org*).

WHAT TO SEE

❺ Clausen Memorial Museum. The museum's exhibits explore the commercial fishing and the cannery industry, the era of fish traps, the social life of Petersburg, and Tlingit culture. Don't miss the museum shop; the 126.5-pound king salmon—the largest ever caught commercially—as well as the Tlingit dugout canoe; the Cape Decision lighthouse station lens; and *Earth, Sea and Sky,* a 3-D wall mural outside. ⊠ *203 Fram St.* ☎ *907/772–3598* ⊕ *www.clausenmuseum.net* ⊡ *$3* ⊙ *May–early Sept., Mon.–Sat. 10–5; mid-Sept.–Apr. by appointment.*

❻ Eagle's Roost Park. Just north of the Petersburg Fisheries cannery, this small roadside park is a great place to spot eagles, especially at low tide. On a clear day you will also discover dramatic views of the sharp-edged Coast Range, including the 9,077-foot summit of Devil's Thumb.

❷ Hammer Slough. Houses on high stilts and the historic Sons of Norway Hall border this creek that floods with each high tide, creating a photogenic reflecting pool in the still waters.

③ Petersburg Marine Mammal Center. Visitors to this nonprofit research and learning center can share and gather information on marine mammal sightings, pick up reference material, and have fun with the interactive educational kiosk. ⊠ *Gjoa St. and Sing Lee Alley, behind Viking Travel* ☎ *907/772–4170 summer only* ⊕ *www.psgmmc.org* ▰ *Free* ☉ *Mid-June–Aug., Mon.–Sat. 9–5.*

④ Petersburg Visitor Information Center. This small office is a good source for local information, including maps and details on tours, charters, and nearby outdoor recreation opportunities. ⊠ *1st and Fram Sts.* ☎ *907/772–4636* ⊕ *www.petersburg.org* ☉ *May–Sept., Mon.–Sat. 9–5, Sun. noon–4; Oct.–Apr., weekdays 10–2.*

① Sons of Norway Hall. Built in 1912, this large, barnlike structure that stands just south of the Hammer Slough is the headquarters of an organization devoted to keeping alive the traditions and culture of Norway. The window shutters are decorated with colorful Norwegian rosemaling designs. Outside sits a replica of a Viking ship that is a featured attraction in the annual Little Norway Festival each May. On the south side of the building is the **Bojer Wikan Fisherman's Memorial,** where deceased local fishermen are honored with a bronze statue. ⊠ *23 S. Sing Lee Alley* ☎ *907/772–4575.*

OFF THE BEATEN PATH

Falls Creek Fish Ladder. Coho and pink salmon migrate upstream in late summer and early fall at this fish ladder south of town. Fish head up the ladder to get around a small falls. ⊠ *Mi 10.8, Mitkof Hwy.*

Blind Slough Recreation Area. This recreation area includes a number of sites scattered along the Mitkof Highway 15–20 mi south of Petersburg. **Blind River Rapids Trail** is a wheelchair-accessible, 1-mi boardwalk that leads to a three-sided shelter overlooking the river—one of the Southeast's most popular fishing spots—before looping back through the muskeg. Not far away is a bird-viewing area where several dozen trumpeter swans spend the winter. In summer you're likely to see many ducks and other waterfowl. At Mile 18, the state-run **Crystal Lake Hatchery** releases thousands of king and coho salmon each year. The kings return in June and July, the coho in August and September. Nearby is a popular picnic area. Four miles south of the hatchery is a Forest Service campground. ☎ *907/772–4772.*

OUTDOOR ACTIVITIES

HIKING

For an enjoyable loop hike from town, follow Dolphin Street uphill from the center of town. At the intersection with 5th Street, a boardwalk path leads 900 feet through forested wetlands to the baseball fields, where a second boardwalk takes you to 12th Street and Haugen Drive. Turn left on Haugen and follow it past the airport to **Sandy Beach Park,** where picnickers can sit under log shelters, and low tide reveals remnants of ancient fish traps and a number of petroglyphs. From here you can return to town via Sandy Beach Road, or hike the beach when the tide is out. Along the way is the charming **Outlook Park,** a covered observatory with binoculars to scan for marine life. A pull-out at Hungry Point provides views to the Coast Range and Frederick Sound. Across the road, the half-mile **Hungry Point Trail** takes you back to the baseball fields—a great spot for panoramic views of the mountains—where you can return downtown on the nature boardwalk. Plan on an hour and a half for this walk.

For something more strenuous, a 4-mi trail begins at the airport and climbs 1,600 feet in elevation to **Raven's Roost Cabin.** Along the way you take in a panorama that reaches from the ice-bound Coast Range to the protected waters and forested islands of the Inside Passage far below. The two-story Forest Service cabin is available for rent ($35 per night); contact the **National Recreation Reservation Service** (☎ *518/885–3639 or 877/444–6777* ⊕ *www.recreation.gov*). Get details on these and other hikes from the Petersburg Visitor Information Center or from the **Petersburg Ranger District** (✉ *12 N. Nordic Dr.* ☎ *907/772–3871* ⊕ *www.fs.fed.us/r10/tongass*).

WHERE TO EAT

¢–$ ✕**Coastal Cold Storage.** This busy little seafood deli in the heart of Peters-
SEAFOOD   burg serves daily lunch specials, including fish chowders and halibut beer bits (a local favorite), along with grilled-chicken wraps, steak sandwiches, breakfast omelets, and waffles. It's a great place for a quick bite en route to your next adventure; there isn't much seating in the shop's cramped interior. Live or cooked crab is available for takeout, and the shop can process your sport-caught fish. ✉ *306 N. Nordic Dr.* ☎ *907/772–4177 or 877/257–4746* ⊟ *AE, D, DC, MC, V.*

¢   ✕**Helse Restaurant.** Locals flock to this modest mom-and-pop place for
AMERICAN   lunch. It's the closest thing to home cooking Petersburg has to offer, and most days it's open from 8 to 5, even in winter. A couple of dozen sandwiches grace the menu, as do rotating soups and homemade bread. The daily specials are a good bet, and the gyros are decent as well. Helse also doubles as an ice cream and espresso stand. ✉ *13 Sing Lee Alley* ☎ *907/772–3444* ⊟ *MC, V.*

$ ✕**Papa Bear's Pizza.** Although it has a few tables, this oft-crowded pizza
PIZZA   joint primarily specializes in take-out pizzas, pizza by the slice, wraps, and giant calzones. It also serves ice cream and espresso. ✉ *306 N. Nordic Dr., upstairs from Coastal Cold Storage* ☎ *907/772–3727* ⊟ *MC, V.*

WHERE TO STAY

$ ▦**A Guest House at Water's Edge.** Along the shore of Frederick Sound, 2 mi north of Petersburg, this family-run B&B offers one creek- and one beachside room. Seals, eagles, deer, and whales are often seen just outside the door. A substantial continental breakfast is served, and the small library is stocked with books on Alaska and natural history. The property is available as a vacation rental for three or more nights. Take advantage of the owners' Kaleidoscope Cruises—lodging-cruise packages are available—or borrow bikes to explore on your own. **Pro:** Available as a vacation rental for three or more nights. **Con:** Property is not disability-friendly. ✉*705 Sandy Beach Rd., Box 1201* ☎*907/772–3736 or 800/868–4373* ⊕*www.petersburglodgingandtours.com* ↪*2 rooms* ⚲*In-room: no phone (some), kitchen (some), refrigerator (some), VCR (some), no TV (some), Wi-Fi. In-hotel: bicycles, laundry facilities, public Wi-Fi, airport shuttle, no children under 12, no-smoking rooms* ▭*MC, V* ❄|*CP.*

$–$$$ 🏨 **Scandia House.** This hotel on Petersburg's main drag, a fixture since 1910, was rebuilt following a 1995 fire. You won't find much of the original charm, but what the Scandia lacks in quirky character it makes up for in hospitality. Some rooms have kitchenettes, king-size beds, or in-room hot tubs and harbor views. Fourth-floor rooms, including the suites, aren't accessible by elevator. Guests can get their caffeine fix in the coffee shop adjoining the hotel, take care of those split ends at the hair salon, or rent a car to explore "out the road." You'll find homemade muffins and coffee in the small but inviting lobby each morning. **Pro:** Some pets allowed. **Con:** Fourth-floor rooms aren't accessible by elevator. ✉*110 Nordic Dr., Box 689,* ☎*907/772–4281 or 800/722–5006* ⊕*www.scandiahousehotel.com* ↪*33 rooms, 3 suites* ⚲*In-room: kitchen (some), Wi-Fi. In-hotel: water sports, public Wi-Fi, airport and ferry shuttle, some pets allowed, no-smoking rooms* ▭*AE, D, DC, MC, V* ❄|*CP.*

$ 🏨 **Sea Level B&B.** The views from the large picture windows at this small B&B, a home on stilts above the Wrangell Narrows, are worth the 10 or 15 minutes it takes to walk to town. The smaller room, with one queen bed, is already a better deal than most hotel rooms. The larger room has fantastic views of the narrows, where guests can watch boats go by and birds fight over their breakfast. When it's not raining, the small deck outside is the perfect place to take in some afternoon sun, binoculars close at hand. Humpback and orca whales sometimes frolic in front of the B&B. **Pro:** Excellent view of narrows. **Con:** B&B is a 10–15 minute walk from downtown. ✉*913 N. Nordic Dr. 99833* ☎*907/772–3240* ⊕*www.sealevelbnb.com* ↪*2 rooms* ⚲*In-room: kitchen (some), VCR (some), Wi-Fi. In-hotel: airport shuttle* ▭*No credit cards* ❄|*CP.*

$ 🏨 **Tides Inn.** The Tides, Petersburg's largest hotel, is a block uphill from the town's main thoroughfare. Rooms have comfortable, but timeworn furnishings; some have kitchenettes. Rooms in the newer wing—nicer than the motel-style rooms in the old wing—have views of the boat harbor. The coffee is always on in the lobby, and in the morning there are complimentary juices, muffins, and pastries. Car rental is available on-site, but parking is limited. **Pro:** Views of the boat harbor from the newer rooms. **Con:** Rooms in the old wing are dark and dated. ✉*307 N. 1st St. 99833* ☎*907/772–4288 or 800/665–8433* ⊕*www.tidesinnalaska.com* ↪*45 rooms* ⚲*In-room: kitchen (some), Wi-Fi. In-hotel: no elevator, public Wi-Fi, airport shuttle, some pets allowed, no-smoking rooms* ▭*AE, D, DC, MC, V* ❄|*CP.*

NIGHTLIFE

The **Harbor Bar** (✉*310 N. Nordic Dr.* ☎*907/772–4526*), with ships' wheels, nautical pictures, and a mounted red snapper, is true to the town's seafaring spirit. A separate outside entrance leads to the bar's liquor store. Sample the brew and blasting music at the smoky **Kito's Kave** (✉*Sing Lee Alley* ☎*907/772–3207*), a popular hangout among rowdy local fishermen. La Fonda, a Mexican restaurant, leases space inside the bar.

SHOPPING

BOOKSTORE

Off an alley in a beautiful big white house that served as a boardinghouse to fishermen and schoolteachers, **Sing Lee Alley Books** stocks books on Alaska, best sellers, cards, and gifts. ✉*11 Sing Lee Alley* ☎*907/772–4440.*

SEAFOOD

At **Tonka Seafoods,** across the street from the Sons of Norway Hall, you can tour the small custom seafood plant, check out the gift shop, and sample smoked or canned halibut and salmon. Be sure to taste the white king salmon—an especially flavorful type of Chinook that the locals swear by. Tonka will also ship. ✉*22 Sing Lee Alley* ☎*907/772–3662 or 888/560–3662* ⊕*www.tonkaseafoods.com* ✉*Free, tours $15* ☉*June–Aug., daily 8–5; Sept.–May, Mon.–Sat. 8–5; tours at 1* PM *(minimum 5 people).*

SITKA

110 mi west of Petersburg.

Sitka was home to the Kiksádi clan of the Tlingit people for centuries prior to the 18th-century arrival of the Russians under the direction of territorial governor Alexander Baranof. Baranof believed the region was ideal for the fur trade. The governor also coveted the Sitka site for its beauty, mild climate, and economic potential; in the island's massive timber forests he saw raw materials for shipbuilding. Its location offered trading routes as far west as Asia and as far south as California and Hawaii. In 1799 Baranof built St. Michael Archangel—a wooden fort and trading post 6 mi north of the present town.

Strong disagreements arose shortly after the settlement. The Tlingits attacked the settlers and burned their buildings in 1802. Baranof, however, was away in Kodiak at the time. He returned in 1804 with a formidable force—including shipboard cannons—and attacked the Tlingits at their fort near Indian River, site of the present-day 105-acre Sitka National Historical Park, forcing many of them north to Chichagof Island.

By 1821 the Tlingits had reached an accord with the Russians, who were happy to benefit from the tribe's hunting skills. Under Baranof and succeeding managers, the Russian-American Company and the town prospered, becoming known as the Paris of the Pacific. The community built a major shipbuilding and repair facility, sawmills, and forges and even initiated an ice industry, shipping blocks of ice from nearby Swan Lake to the booming San Francisco market. The settlement that was the site of the 1802 conflict is now called Old Sitka. It is a state park and listed as a National Historic Landmark.

> ## NORWEGIAN CRAFTS
>
> The appropriately named **Cubby Hole** sells items decorated by Norwegian-style rosemaling, including plates, trays, key chains, and other items. They also offer day classes, available to visitors, in rosemaling design. ✉ *14 Sing Lee Alley* ☎ *907/772-2717.*

4

The town declined after its 1867 transfer from Russia to the United States, but became prosperous again during World War II, when it served as a base for the U.S. effort to drive the Japanese from the Aleutian Islands. Today its most important industries are fishing, government, and tourism.

EXPLORING SITKA

It's hard not to like Sitka, with its eclectic blend of native Alaskan, Russian, and American history and its dramatic and beautiful open-ocean setting. This is one of the best Inside Passage towns to explore on foot, with such sights as St. Michael's Cathedral, Sheldon Jackson Museum, Castle Hill, Sitka National Historical Park, and the Alaska Raptor Center topping the town's must-see list.

GETTING HERE & AROUND

Sitka is a common stop on cruise routes and a regular stop along the **Alaska Marine Highway System. Alaska Airlines** also operates flights from Seattle and other Pacific Coast and southwestern cities to Sitka. The best way to see the town's sights is on foot.

ESSENTIALS

Airline Contact **Alaska Airlines** (☎ *800/252-7522* ⊕ *www.alaskaair.com*).

Ferry Contact The **Alaska Marine Highway System** (☎ *907/465-3941 or 800/642-0066* ⊕ *www.dot.state.ak.us/amhs*).

Internet **Highliner Café** (✉ *327 Seward St., in the Seward Square Mall* ☎ *907/747-4924*).

Medical Assistance **Sitka Community Hospital** (✉ *209 Moller Ave.* ☎ *907/747-3241* ⊕ *www.sitkahospital.org*).

Pharmacy **Harry Race Pharmacy** (✉ *106 Lincoln St.* ☎ *907/747-8006*). **White's Pharmacy** (✉ *705 Halibut Point Rd.* ☎ *907/747-5755*).

Visitor Info **Sitka Convention and Visitors Bureau** (✉ *303 Lincoln St.* ✉ *Box 1226, Sitka, 99835* ☎ *907/747-5940* ⊕ *www.sitka.org*).

WHAT TO SEE

⓿ Alaska Raptor Center. The only full-service avian hospital in Alaska, the Raptor Center rehabilitates 100 to 200 birds each year. Situated just above Indian Creek, the center is a 20-minute walk from downtown. Well-versed guides provide an introduction to the rehabilitation center (including a short video), and guests are able to visit with one of these majestic birds. The Raptor Center's primary attraction is an enclosed 20,000-square-foot flight training center, built to replicate the rain forest, where injured eagles relearn survival skills, including flying and catching salmon. Visitors watch through one-way glass windows. A large deck out back faces an open-air enclosure for eagles and other raptors whose injuries prevent them from returning to the wild. Additional mews with hawks, owls, and other birds are along a rain-forest path. The gift shop sells all sorts of eagle paraphernalia, the proceeds from which fund the center's programs. ✉ *1000 Raptor Way, off Sawmill Creek Rd.* ☎ *907/747–8662 or 800/643–9425* ⊕ *www.alaskaraptor.org* ⌑ *$12* ⊙ *Mid-May–Sept., daily 8–4.*

❶ Castle Hill. On this hill Alaska was formally handed over to the United States on October 18, 1867, and the first 49-star U.S. flag was flown on January 3, 1959, signifying Alaska's statehood. To reach the hill, take the first right off Harbor Drive just before O'Connell Bridge; then go into the **Baranof Castle Hill State Historic Site** entrance. A paved path switchbacks to the top, where you can read the interpretive signs on the area's Tlingit and Russian history and take in the views of Crescent Harbor and downtown Sitka. On a clear day, look for the volcanic flanks of Mt. Edgecumbe on the horizon.

⓬ Harbor Mountain. During World War II the U.S. Army constructed a road to the 2,000-foot level of Harbor Mountain, providing the perfect vantage point to watch for invading Japanese subs or ships (none were seen). This road has been improved over the years, and those with vehicles can drive 5 mi to a spectacular summit viewpoint across Sitka Sound. A trail climbs uphill from the parking lot, and then follows the ridge 2.5 mi to a Forest Service shelter. From there, ambitious hikers could continue downhill another 3.5 mi to Sitka via the **Gavan Hill Trail.**

❻ Harrigan Centennial Hall. A Tlingit war canoe sits to the side of this brick building, which houses the **Sitka Historical Museum.** Check out its collection of Tlingit, Victorian-era, and Alaska-purchase historical artifacts; there's an auditorium for New Archangel Dancers performances, which take place when cruise ships are in port. ✉ *330 Harbor Dr.* ☎ *907/747–6455 museum, 907/747–5940 Visitors Bureau* ⊕ *www.sitkahistory.org* ⌑ *$1* ⊙ *Museum mid-May–mid-Sept., daily 8–5; mid-Sept.–mid-May, Tues.–Sat. 10–4. Information desk May–Sept., 8–5 when cruise ships are in port.*

❹ Russian and Lutheran cemeteries. Most of Sitka's Russian dignitaries are buried in these sites off Marine Street, which, thanks to their wooded locations, require a bit of exploring to locate. The most distinctive (and easily accessible) grave belongs to Princess Maksoutoff (died 1862),

Continued on page 172

MADE IN ALASKA

Intricate Aleut baskets, Athabascan birch-bark wonders, Inupiaq ivory carvings, and towering Tlingit totems are just some of the eye-opening crafts you'll encounter as you explore the 49th state. Alaska's native peoples—who live across 570,000 square miles of tundra, boreal forest, arctic plains, and coastal rain forest—are undeniably hardy, and their unique artistic traditions are just as resilient and enduring.

TIPS ON FINDING AN AUTHENTIC ITEM

1 The Federal Trade Commission has enacted strict regulations to combat the sale of falsely marketed goods; it's illegal for anything made by non-native Alaskans to be labeled as INDIAN, NATIVE AMERICAN, or ALASKA NATIVE.

2 Some authentic goods are marked by a silver hand symbol or are labeled as an AUTHENTIC NATIVE HANDICRAFT FROM ALASKA.

3 The Alaska State Council on the Arts, in Anchorage, is a great resource if you have additional questions or want to confirm a permit number. Call 907/269–6610 or 888/278–7424 in Alaska.

4 The MADE IN ALASKA label, often accompanied by an image of a polar bear with cub, simply denotes that the handicraft was made in the state.

5 Be sure to ask for written proof of authenticity with your purchase, as well as the artist's name. You can also request the artist's permit number, which may be available.

6 Materials should be legal. For example, only some feathers, such as ptarmigan and pheasant feathers, comply with the Migratory Bird Act. Only native artisans are permitted to carve new walrus ivory. The seller should be able to answer your questions about material and technique.

THE NATIVE PEOPLE OF ALASKA

There are many opportunities to see the making of traditional crafts in native environments, including the Southeast Alaska Indian Cultural Center in Sitka and Anchorage's Alaska Native Heritage Center.

After chatting with the artisans, pop into the gift shops to peruse the handmade items. Also check out prominent galleries and museum shops.

RUSSIA

Inupiaq

Athabascan

CANADA

Yup'ik, Cup'ik

Eyak, Tlingit, Haida, Tsimshian

Aleut, Alutiiq

NORTHWEST COAST INDIANS: TLINGIT, HAIDA & TSIMSHIAN

Scattered throughout Southeast Alaska's rain forests, these highly social tribes traditionally benefited from the region's mild climate and abundant salmon, which afforded them a rare luxury: leisure time. They put this time to good use by cultivating highly detailed crafts, including ceremonial masks, elaborate woven robes, and, most famously, totem poles.

(left) A wagging tongue at the Juneau-Douglas City Museum
(right) A Tlingit totem reaches for the skies in Ketchikan

TOWERING TOTEM POLES

Throughout the Inside Passage's braided channels and forested islands, Native peoples use the wood of the abundant cedar trees to carve totem poles, which illustrate history, pay reverence, commemorate a potlatch, or cast shame on a misbehaving person.

Every totem pole tells a story with a series of animal and human figures arranged vertically. Traditionally the totem poles of this area feature ravens, eagles, killer whales, wolves, bears, frogs, the mythic thunderbird, and the likenesses of ancestors.

K'alyaan Totem Pole

Carved in 1999, the K'alyaan totem pole is a tribute to the Tlingits who lost their lives in the 1804 Battle of Sitka between invading Russians and Tlingit warriors. Tommy Joseph, a venerated Tlingit artist from Sitka, and an apprentice spent three months carving the pole from a 35-ft western red cedar. It now stands at the very site of the skirmish, in Sitka National Historical Park.

Raven: Atop the pole sits the striking raven, the emblem of one of the two moieties (large multi-clan groups) of Tlingit culture.

Sockeye Salmon (above) and Dog/ Chum Salmon (below): These two symbols signify the contributions of the Sockeye and Dog Salmon Clans to the 1804 battle. They also illustrate the symbolic connection to the tribe's traditional food sources.

Woodworm: The woodworm—a Tlingit clan symbol—is a wood-boring beetle that leaves a distinctive mark on timber.

Beaver: Sporting a fearsome pair of front teeth, this beaver symbol cradles a child in its arms, signifying the strength of Tlingit family bonds.

Frog: This animal represents the Kik.-sádi Clan, which was very instrumental in organizing the Tlingit's revolt against the Russian trespassers. Here, the frog holds a raven helmet—a tribute to the Kik.sádi warrior who wore a similar headpiece into battle.

Tools and Materials

As do most modern carvers, Joseph used a steel adz to carve the cedar. Prior to European contact—and the accompanying introduction of metal tools—Tlingit artists carved with jade adzes. Totem poles are traditionally decorated with paint made from salmon-liver oil, charcoal, and iron and copper oxides.

ALEUT & ALUTIIQ

The Aleut inhabit the Alaska Peninsula and the windswept Aleutian Islands. Historically they lived and died by the sea, surviving on a diet of seals, sea lions, whales, and walruses, which they hunted in the tumultuous waters of the Gulf of Alaska and the Bering Sea. Hunters pursued their prey in *Sugpiaq*, kayaklike boats made of seal skin stretched over a driftwood frame.

WATERPROOF *KAMLEIKAS*

The Aleut prize seal intestine for its remarkable waterproof properties; they use it to create sturdy cloaks, shelter walls, and boat hulls. To make their famous cloaks, called *kamleikas*, intestine is washed, soaked in salt water, and arduously scraped clean. It is then stretched and dried before being stitched into hooded, waterproof pullovers.

FINE BASKETRY

Owing to the region's profusion of wild rye grass, Aleutian women are some of the planet's most skilled weavers, capable of creating baskets with more than 2,500 fibers per square inch. They also create hats, socks, mittens, and multipurpose mats. A long, sharpened thumbnail is their only tool.

ATHABASCANS

Inhabiting Alaska's rugged interior for 8,000 to 20,000 years, Athabascans followed a seasonally nomadic hunter-gatherer lifestyle, subsisting off of caribou, moose, bear, and snowshoe hare. They populate areas from the Brooks Range to Cook Inlet, a vast expanse that encompasses five significant rivers: the Tanana, the Kuskwin, the Copper, the Susitna, and the Yukon.

FUNCTIONAL & ORNAMENTED PIECES

Much like that of the neighboring Eskimos, Athabascan craftwork traditionally served functional purposes. But tools, weapons, and clothing were often highly decorated with colorful embroidery and shells. Athabascans are especially well known for ornamenting their caribou-skin clothing with porcupine quills and animal hair—both of which were later replaced by imported western beads.

BIRCH BARK: WATERPROOF WONDER

Aside from annual salmon runs, the Athabascans had no access to marine mammals—or to the intestines that made for such effective boat hulls and garments. They turned to the region's birch, the bark of which was used to create canoes. Also common were birch-bark baskets and baby carriers.

INUPIAQ, YUP'IK & CUP'IK

Residing in Alaska's remote northern and northwestern regions, these groups are often collectively known as Eskimos or Inupiaq. They winter in coastal villages, relying on migrating marine mammals for sustenance, and spend summers at inland fish amps. Ongoing artistic traditions include ceremonial mask carving, ivory carving (not to be confused with scrimshaw), sewn skin garments, basket weaving, and soapstone carvings.

Thanks to the sheer volume of ivory art in Alaska's marketplace, you're bound to find a piece of ivory that fits your fancy—regardless of whether you prefer traditional ivory carvings, scrimshaw, or a piece that blends both artistic traditions.

IVORY CARVING

While in Alaska, you'll likely see carved ivory pieces, scrimshaw, and some fake ivory carvings (generally plastic). Ivory carving has been an Eskimo art form for thousands of years. After harvesting ivory from migrating walrus herds in the Bering Sea, artisans age tusks for up to one year before shaping it with adzes and bow drills.

KEEP IN MIND

The Marine Mammal Protection Act states that only native peoples are allowed to harvest fresh walrus ivory, which is legal to buy after it's been carved by a native person. How can you tell if a piece is real and made by a native artisan? Real ivory is likely to be pricey; be suspect of anything too cheaply priced. It should also be hard (plastic will be softer) and cool to the touch. Keep an eye out for mastery of carving technique, and be sure to ask questions when you've found a piece you're interested in buying.

WHAT IS SCRIMSHAW?

The invention of scrimshaw is attributed to 18th-century American whalers who etched the surfaces of whale bone and scrap ivory. The etchings were filled with ink, bringing the designs into stark relief.

More recently the line between traditional Eskimo ivory carving and scrimshaw has become somewhat blurred, with many native artisans incorporating both techniques.

TIPS

Ivory carving is a highly specialized native craft that is closely regulated. As it is a by-product of subsistence hunting, all meat and skin from a walrus hunt is used.

Ivory from extinct mammoths and mastodons (usually found buried underground or washed up on beaches) is also legal to buy in Alaska; many native groups keep large stores of it, as well as antique walrus tusk, for craft purposes. Many of the older pieces have a caramelized color.

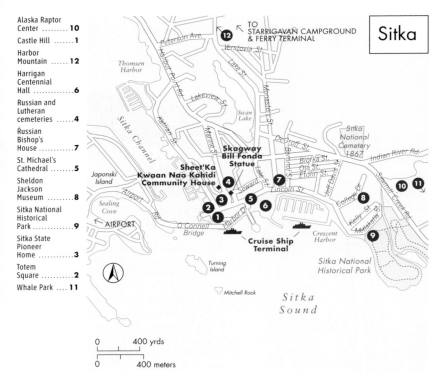

wife of the last Russian governor and one of the most illustrious members of the Russian royal family to be buried on Alaska soil.

7 **Russian Bishop's House.** A registered historic landmark, this house facing the harbor was constructed by the Russian-American Company for Bishop Innocent Veniaminov in 1842 and completed in 1843. Inside the house, one of the few remaining Russian-built log structures in Alaska, are exhibits on the history of Russian America, including several places where portions of the house's structure are peeled away to expose Russian building techniques. The ground level is a free museum, and Park Service rangers lead guided tours of the second floor, which houses the residential quarters and a chapel. ✉*501 Lincoln St.* ☎*907/747–6281* ⊕*www.nps.gov/sitk* ✉*Tours $5* ⊙*May–Sept., 9–5; Oct.–Apr. by appointment.*

5 **St. Michael's Cathedral.** This cathedral, one of Southeast Alaska's best-★ known national landmarks, is treasured by visitors and locals alike—so treasured that in 1966, as a fire engulfed the building, townspeople risked their lives and rushed inside to rescue the cathedral's precious Russian icons, religious objects, and vestments. Using original blueprints, an almost exact replica of onion-dome St. Michael's was completed in 1976. Today you can see what could possibly be the largest

A GOOD WALK

Most folks begin their tours of Sitka under the distinctive onion dome of **St. Michael's Cathedral**, right in the town center. A block behind the cathedral along Harbor Drive is **Harrigan Centennial Hall**, a low-slung convention hall that houses the smallish **Sitka Historical Museum** and an information desk that opens when cruise ships are in port. A block east, along Lincoln Street, you'll find the **Russian Bishop's House**, one of the symbols of Russian rule. Continue out on Lincoln Street along the bustling boat harbor to Sheldon Jackson College, where the worthwhile **Sheldon Jackson Museum** is packed with native cultural artifacts. Another 0.5 mi out along gently curving Metlakatla Street is the **Sitka National Historical Park**, where you can chat with native artisans as they craft carvings and silver jewelry. Behind the main building a network of well-signed paths takes you through the rain forest past more than a dozen totem poles and to the site of a Tlingit fort from the battle of 1804. A signed trail crosses the Indian River (watch for spawning salmon in late summer) and heads across busy Sawmill Creek Road to the **Alaska Raptor Center**, for an up-close look at bald eagles.

Return to town along Sawmill Creek Road. On your right, you'll see the white headstones of the small Sitka National Cemetery. Back downtown, you can browse the many shops or walk along Harbor Drive and take the path to the summit of **Castle Hill**, where Russia transferred Alaska to American hands—these are the best views in town. If you follow the path down the other side of the hill, check out the impressive **Sitka State Pioneers Home**, with the statue of pioneer "Skagway Bill" Fonda. Across the street is **Totem Square**, with its tall totem pole and three ancient anchors. Adjacent to the Pioneers Home is the **Sheet'ka Kwaan Naa Kahidi** community house. Native dances take place here in summer. End your walk at the haunting (not haunted) **Russian and Lutheran cemeteries** which fill the dark woods along Marine Street a block from the blockhouse. The grave of Princess Maksoutoff, a member of the Russian royal family, is here.

Sitka has many attractions, and you can easily spend a full day exploring this culturally rich area. You can accomplish the walk in two to three hours if you do not spend much time at each stop. You can pound the pavement around town in an hour or so.

collection of Russian icons in the United States, among them the much-prized *Our Lady of Sitka* (also known as the *Sitka Madonna*) and the *Christ Pantocrator* (*Christ the Judge*) on either side of the doors of the interior altar screen. ⊠*Lincoln St.* ☎*907/747–8120* ☜*$2 requested donation* ⊙*May–Sept., daily 8:30–4; Oct.–Apr., hrs vary.*

8 ★ **Sheldon Jackson Museum.** Near the campus of **Sheldon Jackson College**, this octagonal museum, which dates from 1895, contains priceless Aleut and Eskimo items collected by Dr. Sheldon Jackson (1834–1909), who traveled the remote regions of Alaska as an educator and missionary. This state-run museum features artifacts from every native Alaska culture; on display are carved masks, Chilkat blankets, dogsleds, kayaks, and even the impressive helmet worn by Chief Katlean during the 1804 battle against the Russians. The museum's gift shop, operated by the Friends of the Sheldon Jackson Museum, carries books, paper goods, and handicrafts created by Alaska native artists.■TIP➡ Native artisans are here all summer, creating baskets, carvings, or masks. ⊠ *104 College Dr.* ☏*907/747–8981* ⊕*www.museums.state.ak.us* ⌕*$4 mid-May–mid-Sept., $3 mid-Sept.–mid-May* ⊙*Mid-May–mid-Sept., daily 9–5; mid-Sept.–mid-May, Tues.–Sat. 10–4.*

❾
Fodor'sChoice
★
Sitka National Historical Park. The main building at this 113-acre park houses a small museum with fascinating historical exhibits and photos of Tlingit native culture. Highlights include a brass peace hat given to the Sitka Kiksádi by Russian traders in the early 1800s and Chilkat robes. Head to the theater to watch a 12-minute video about Russian-Tlingit conflict in the 19th century. Also here is the **Southeast Alaska Indian Cultural Center,** where native artisans demonstrate silversmithing, weaving, wood carving, and basketry. Don't be afraid to strike up a conversation; the artisans are happy to talk about their work and Tlingit cultural traditions. At the far end of the building are seven totems (some more than a century old) that have been brought indoors to protect them from decay. Behind the center, a wide, 2-mi path takes you through the forest and along the shore of Sitka Sound. Scattered along the way are some of the most skillfully carved native totem poles in Alaska. Keep going on the trail to see spawning salmon from the footbridge over Indian River. Park Service rangers lead themed walks in summer, which focus on the Russian-Tlingit conflict, the area's natural history, and the park's totem poles. ⊠ *106 Metlakatla St.* ☏*907/747–6281, 907/747–8061 gift shop* ⊕*www.nps.gov/sitk* ⌕*$3* ⊙*Mid-May–Sept., daily 8–5; Oct.–mid-May, Mon.–Sat. 8–5.*

❸ **Sitka State Pioneers Home.** This large, red-roof home for elder Alaskans has an imposing 14-foot statue in front, symbolizing Alaska's frontier sourdough spirit ("sourdough" generally refers to Alaska's American pioneers and prospectors); it was modeled by an authentic prospector, William "Skagway Bill" Fonda. Adjacent to the Pioneers Home is **Sheet'ka Kwaan Naa Kahidi** community house, where you can watch native dance performances throughout the summer. ⊠*Lincoln and Katlian Sts.* ☏*907/747–3213.*

❷ **Totem Square.** On this grassy square directly across the street from the Pioneers Home are three anchors discovered in local waters and believed to be of 19th-century British origin. Look for the double-headed eagle of czarist Russia carved into the cedar of the totem pole in the park.

⓫ Whale Park. This small waterside park sits in the trees 4 mi east of Sitka
out by Sawmill Creek Road. Boardwalk paths lead to five viewing platforms and steps take you down to the rocky shoreline. A gazebo next
to the parking area contains signs describing the whales that visit Silver
Bay, and you can listen to their sounds from recordings and an offshore
hydrophone here. ■TIP➔ Tune your radio to FM 88.1 anywhere in Sitka
to hear a broadcast of humpback whale sounds picked up by the
hydrophone.

SPORTS, THE OUTDOORS & GUIDED TOURS

BICYCLING

If it isn't raining, rent a high-quality mountain bike from **Yellow Jersey
Cycle Shop** (⊠*329 Harbor Dr.* ☎*907/747–6317* ⊕*www.yellowjersey-
cycles.com*) and head out on the nearby dirt roads and trails. Staffers
know Sitka's many mountain- and road-bike routes well.

BOAT & KAYAK TOURS

Alaska Travel Adventures (☎*800/478–0052, 800/791–2673 outside
Alaska* ⊕*www.bestofalaskatravel.com*) leads a three-hour kayaking
tour in protected waters south of Sitka. The tour includes friendly
guides, basic kayak instruction, and snacks at a remote cabin on the
water.

Allen Marine Tours (☎*907/747–8100 or 888/747–8101* ⊕*www.allen-
marinetours.com*), one of the Southeast's largest and best-known tour
operators, leads different boat-based Sitka Sound tours throughout
the summer. Their Wildlife Quest tours are a fine opportunity to view
humpback whales, sea otters, puffins, and eagles in a spectacular setting. When seas are calm enough, they offer a tour to the bird sanctuary
at **St. Lazaria Islands National Wildlife Refuge.**

BUS TOURS & HISTORICAL WALKS

Sitka Tours (☎*907/747–8443*) meets ferries and cruise ships and leads
both bus tours and historical walks. **Tribal Tours** (☎*907/747–7290 or
888/270–8687* ⊕*www.sitkatours.com*) emphasizes Sitka's rich native
culture, with bus or walking tours and dance performances at the
Tribal Community House.

FISHING

Sitka is home to a growing fleet of
charter boats. The Sitka Convention and Visitors Bureau Web site
(⊕*www.sitka.org*) has descriptions
of and Web links to several dozen
sportfishing operators. A good one
is **Sitka's Secrets** (⊠*500 Lincoln
St., Unit B-9* ☎*907/747–5089*
⊕*www.sitkasecret.com*), operated
by naturalists who combine wildlife viewing with fishing.

NEED ADVICE?

The Harrigan Centennial Hall has
a volunteer-staffed information
desk provided by the **Sitka Convention and Visitors Bureau**
(⊠*303 Lincoln St.* ☎*907/747–
5940* ⊕*www.sitka.org*), whose
headquarters are a short walk
away on Lincoln Street.

FOUR-WHEELED FUN

Alaska ATV Tours (☎ *907/966–2301 or 877/966–2301* ⊕ *www.alaskaatvtours.com*) offers half-day tours of remote Kruzof Island aboard two-person Yamaha ATVs. Stops include Iris Meadows Estuary, a black-sand beach, and one of Kruzof's numerous salmon-laden creeks. The tour, which departs from Sitka, includes a scenic 30-minute boat transfer through the islands and channels of Sitka Sound.

HIKING & BIRD-WATCHING

Seven miles north of Sitka, **Starrigavan Recreation Area** is a peaceful, end-of-the-road place to explore the rain forest. The state ferry terminal is less than a mile from Starrigavan, and a popular Forest Service campground is also here. Several easy trails lead hikers through the area, including the 0.25-mi boardwalk **Estuary Life Trail.** It circles a small estuary and includes a bird-viewing shelter and access to a nearby artesian well. The 0.75-mi **Forest and Muskeg Trail** winds through a spruce-hemlock forest and traverses a muskeg, with interpretive signs along the way. Across the road is the delightful 1.25-mi loop **Mosquito Cove Trail,** which skirts the rocky shoreline to Mosquito Cove before returning through thickly forested hills. Get a map of local trails from **Sitka Trail Works** (⊠ *801 Halibut Point Rd.* ☎ *907/747–7244* ⊕ *www. sitkatrailworks.org*).

UNDERWATER ACTION

Discovery Tours (☎ *907/966–2301 or 877/966–2301* ⊕ *www.sealifediscoverytours.com*) operates a semisubmersible tour vessel with large underwater windows that provide views of kelp forests, fish, crab, sea urchins, anemones, and starfish. Divers with underwater cameras zoom in for close-up views via the video monitor.

WHERE TO EAT

$–$$$
JAPANESE

✕ **Little Tokyo.** Sitka probably isn't the first place you expect to find Japanese food, but Little Tokyo delivers great rolls and *nigiri.* It's not fancy, but this small restaurant has a sushi bar where the chefs prepare all the standards, plus Alaska rolls (with smoked salmon and avocado). Udon noodle soups are popular on rainy afternoons, and bento-box dinners—complete with katsu entrées, California rolls, tempura, pot stickers, miso soup, and salad—are only $11. ⊠ *315 Lincoln St.* ☎ *907/747–5699* ▤ *MC, V.*

$–$$$$
MEDITERRANEAN
Fodor's Choice
★

✕ **Ludvig's Bistro.** This remarkably creative eatery used to escape detection by most tourists (much to the pleasure of Sitkans). It's now almost always packed with food lovers from all corners of the globe, so be prepared for a wait—but rest assured that Ludvig's is worth it. The interior evokes an Italian bistro, with rich yellow walls and copper-topped tables. Seafood (particularly king salmon and scallops) is the specialty, and organic ingredients are used whenever possible. You'll also find Caesar salads, vegetarian specials, prime rib, and one of the state's best wine lists. From 2 to 5 the café serves Spanish-style tapas with house wine for $13–$17. ⊠ *256 Katlian St.* ☎ *907/966–3663* ▤ *AE, MC, V* ⊘ *Closed mid-Feb.–Apr.*

$–$$ ✕**Nugget Restaurant.** Travelers flying out from Sitka head here while
AMERICAN hoping their jet will make it through the pea-soup fog outside. The setting is standard, and the menu encompasses burgers (15 kinds), sandwiches, tuna melts, salads, steaks, pasta, seafood, and Friday-night
prime rib. There's a big breakfast menu, too, but the real attraction is
their range of homemade pies, which are known throughout Southeast
Alaska. ■TIP➔ Get a slice à la mode, or buy a whole pie to take with you.
The lemon custard is a local favorite. Reservations are recommended.
⊠*Sitka Airport Terminal* ☎*907/966–2480* ⊟*AE, D, DC, MC, V.*

¢–$$$ ✕**Van Winkle & Sons.** This restaurant's somewhat lackluster ambience
SEAFOOD (Formica tabletops, paper napkins, vinyl swivel-chair seating) is incon-
gruous with its gorgeous water views and upscale fare. One of Sitka's
largest eateries, it bills itself as "Frontier Cuisine," which translates to
a seafood-heavy menu. But Van Winkle also serves pizzas and chicken,
duck, and veal. The create-your-own pastas are excellent (a half order
is plenty for normal-size appetites), and the rich desserts necessitate
sharing. There's no elevator to the restaurant's second-floor location,
but a stair lift assists disabled customers. The water view is good, but
cars often block it at lunch. ⊠*205 Harbor Dr.* ☎*907/747–7652*
⊟*AE, D, DC, MC, V.*

WHERE TO STAY

$$–$$$$ 🏠**Alaska Ocean View Bed & Breakfast.** Carole Denkinger, who runs this
★ cozy B&B out of the home she shares with her husband Bill, is an
extremely personable host who enjoys talking about the area and prides
herself on never serving anyone the same breakfast twice. In one of the
upstairs rooms, guests can take advantage of a deep, jetted tub; a comfortable king bed facing an ambient fireplace; and a small balcony overlooking the harbor. The double queen room downstairs has a sliding
glass door leading out to a hot tub. Guests can borrow a laptop to
check their e-mail, binoculars to scan the water for whales, and Alaska
videos to take to their rooms. **Pro:** Large, varied breakfasts. **Con:** Only
three rooms. ⊠*1101 Edgecumbe Dr.* ☎*907/747–8310* or *888/811–
6870* ⊕*www.sitka-alaska-lodging.com* ⟿*3 rooms* ♿*In-room: refrigerator, DVD, VCR, dial-up, Wi-Fi. In-hotel: no elevator, laundry
service, concierge, public Internet, public Wi-Fi, some pets allowed,
no-smoking rooms* ⊟*AE, D, DC, MC, V* ⊚*BP.*

$ 🏠**Alaska Swan Lake Bed & Breakfast.** This is one of the best B&Bs in
♨ town, with a quiet, lakeside setting, attractively appointed rooms with
private baths, and friendly owners. Two downstairs rooms share a
comfortable sitting room, as do the two rooms upstairs. Private
entrances provide access. Children have fun with the play equipment
on the lawn that drops down to Swan Lake. The B&B is six blocks
from the center of town. **Pros:** Quiet, convenient location. **Con:** Bathrooms are small. ⊠*206½ Lakeview Dr.,* ☎*907/747–5746* ⟿*4 rooms*
♿*In-room: no phone (some), refrigerator (some), VCR (some), Wi-Fi.
In-hotel: no elevator, laundry facilities, public Wi-Fi, no-smoking
rooms* ⊟*MC, V* ⊚*CP.*

$$$$ 🖵 **Baranof Wilderness Lodge.** This cozy fishing lodge is nestled in Warm Springs Bay, 20 air mi from Sitka on the wild east side of Baranof Island. Guest cabins have pine paneling, private baths, and electricity from a small hydroelectric plant. Packages range from two-night stays ($585 per person) to seven-night fishing adventures ($4,850 per person). All include floatplane transport from Sitka, boats and guide service, lodging in cabins with private baths, plus gourmet food and wines served at communal meals. Special wildlife photography seminars and fly-fishing classes are offered throughout summer. The lodge has two wood-fired hot tubs, and nearby is a natural hot spring that pours 108°F water into a series of pools overlooking a waterfall. Most of the surrounding land is within Tongass National Forest. **Pro:** Rate is all-inclusive from Sitka. **Con:** Rate is expensive in comparison to similar accommodations. *Box 2187, 99835* ☎*907/738–3597 or 800/613–6551* *www.flyfishalaska.com* *1 room, 7 cabins* *In-room: no phone, no TV. In-hotel: water sports, airport shuttle, some pets allowed, no-smoking rooms* *No credit cards* *Closed Oct.–May* *AI.*

$$–$$$$ 🖵 **Rockwell Lighthouse.** On an island 1 mi from town, Burgess Bauder (a
★ local veterinarian and loveable curmudgeon) rents out his 1,600-square-foot four-story lighthouse, which was hand-built in the 1980s with coastal woods and a light at the top installed to Coast Guard specifications. The lighthouse can accommodate eight people in four rooms ($200 for four, plus $35 per person for extra guests); you must rent the whole property. The price includes motorboat transportation to and from the island; it's $35 per day extra for use of the hot tub, which is only available when Burgess feels like going to the trouble. The Ritz Carlton it isn't, but the views are unmatched, and laid-back visitors who don't care how old the carpet is have the time of their lives. ■TIP→ Call up to a year ahead of time for midsummer reservations. **Pros:** Accommodations are private, group must rent entire property. **Con:** Proprietor is not always friendly. *Box 277, 99835* ☎*907/747–3056* *4 rooms* *In-room: no phone (some), kitchen, refrigerator. In-hotel: no elevator, laundry facilities, some pets allowed, no-smoking rooms* *No credit cards.*

$$ 🖵 **Shee Atiká Totem Square Inn.** On Totem Square in downtown Sitka, this inn lacks character, but it's one of the town's better-run outfits. The rooms are clean and well furnished, and some have town and/or harbor views. Pay the extra $10 for a room with a harbor view. It's a popular choice for the fishing and corporate types. Salmon-fishing charters are available nearby. **Pro:** Convenient location for fishermen. **Con:** Rooms without harbor view overlook a particularly unattractive parking lot. ✉*201 Katlian St.,* ☎*907/747–3693 or 866/300–1353* *www.totem-squareinn.com* *67 rooms* *In-room: Ethernet, Wi-Fi. In-hotel: gym, laundry facilities, public Internet, public Wi-Fi, airport shuttle, some pets allowed, no-smoking rooms* *AE, D, DC, MC, V* *CP.*

$ 🖵 **Sitka Hotel.** This noisy but comfortable, old-fashioned downtown hotel was built in 1939. A 2006 fire destroyed about half of the original building, and the hotel has been restored although some rooms still smell smoky. Walls are thin and rooms are fairly spartan—no coffee-pots, microwaves, hair dryers, writing desks, closet space, and so on—but the price is right. A pub-style lounge, Victoria's Pour House, provides a comfy place to relax, and Victoria's Restaurant opens early (4:30 AM in summer) to feed the charter-fishing crowd. Check bedding accommodations when making a reservation, as some rooms feature twin beds. **Pro:** Good views from most rooms. **Cons:** Noisy location, some rooms smell of smoke. ⊠ *118 Lincoln St.,* ☎ *907/747–3288* ⊕ *www.sitkahotel.com* ⟿ *45 rooms* ⟐ *In-room: refrigerator (some), Wi-Fi. In-hotel: restaurant, bar, laundry facilities, public Internet, public Wi-Fi, some pets allowed, no-smoking rooms* ⊟ *AE, MC, V.*

¢ ⚠ **Starrigavan Recreation Area.** Seven miles north of town, and just 0.75 mi from the ferry terminal, this popular Tongass National Forest campground has a mix of sites for car campers, backpackers, and RV travelers. All sites have tree cover, and facilities include tables, grills, potable water, and vault restrooms. Everything is fully ADA accessible, and group sites include a covered cooking shelter. Campsites are open year-round, though snow may limit vehicle access in the winter months. ☎ *907/747–4216 information, 877/444–6777 reservations* ⊕ *www. recreation.gov* ⊟ *AE, D, MC, V.*

$$–$$$$ 🖳 **Westmark Sitka.** Sitka's nicest hotel has large rooms, many overlooking Crescent Harbor; the best are the corner suites. Downstairs, the Raven Dining Room is open for three meals a day, with seafood (including beer-batter halibut), pasta, chicken, pork, and steak. Adjacent to the Raven, the Kadataan Lounge serves up a diverse menu of bar food. The property offers a complimentary continental breakfast featuring fresh bagels and muffins, but arrive before 8 AM for the best selection. **Pro:** Continental breakfast is good. **Con:** No airport/ferry shuttle. ⊠ *330 Seward St.* ☎ *907/747–6241 or 800/544–0970 in U.S., 800/999–2570 in Canada* ⊕ *www.westmarkhotels.com* ⟿ *100 rooms, 4 suites* ⟐ *In-room: kitchen (some), refrigerator (some), Wi-Fi. In-hotel: restaurant, room service, bar, laundry service, public Internet, public Wi-Fi, no-smoking rooms* ⊟ *AE, D, DC, MC, V.*

¢ 🖳 **White Sulphur Springs Cabin.** This Tongass National Forest public-use cabin is 65 mi northwest of Sitka. Like many other Forest Service cabins, this cabin sleeps four (bring your own sleeping bags) and has bunk beds, a woodstove, a table, and an outhouse. No mattresses, cooking utensils, or any services are provided, so you must bring all your own supplies. The cabin, which faces the Pacific Ocean, has incredible views. With proximity to a hot-springs bathhouse, this isolated retreat is one of the Southeast's most prized cabins. ■TIP➜ Cabin guests don't have exclusive access to the bathhouse, so think twice before taking a skinny-dip. Access is by boat only (you'll need to walk in from a nearby cove). **Pro:** Good views of Pacific Ocean. **Cons:** Guests must bring own bedding and cooking utensils. ☎ *907/747–6671 information, 877/444–6777 reservations* ⊕ *www.recreation.gov* ⟿ *1 cabin* ⊟ *AE, D, MC, V.*

NIGHTLIFE & THE ARTS

BARS
As far as the locals are concerned, a spot in one of the limited green-and-white-vinyl booths at **Pioneer Bar** (✉*212 Katlian St.* ☎*907/747–3456*), across from the harbor, is a fine destination. It's vintage Alaska, with hundreds of pictures of local fishing boats, rough-hewn locals clad in Carhartts and Xtra-Tuff boots, occasional live music, and pool tables. Regulars, mostly local fishermen, swear by the submarine sandwiches and hot dogs.

DANCE
★ The **New Archangel Dancers of Sitka** perform authentic Russian folk dances whenever cruise ships are in port. This all-female troupe tours extensively, with a mix of traditional dance styles. Tickets are $8, and are sold a half hour before performances. A **recorded message** (☎*907/747–5516* ⊕*www.newarchangeldancers.com*) gives the schedule a week in advance. Performances are 30 minutes long and take place in Harrigan Centennial Hall. **Sheet'ka Kwaan Naa Kahidi Dancers** (☎*907/747–7290 or 888/270–8687* ⊕*www.sitkatours.com)* perform Tlingit dances in full native regalia at the Sheet'ka Kwaan Naa Kahidi community house on Katlian Street. The dance schedule is listed on the board at Harrigan Centennial Hall.

FESTIVALS
Southeast Alaska's major chamber-music festival is the annual **Sitka Summer Music Festival** (☎*907/277–4852* ⊕*www.sitkamusicfestival. org)*, a three-week June celebration of concerts and special events that attracts musicians from as far away as Europe and Asia. All performances are held in Harrigan Centennial Hall. The **Sitka WhaleFest** (☎*907/747–7964* ⊕*www.sitkawhalefest.org*) is held around town in early November, when the whales are plentiful (as many as 80) and tourists are not.

SHOPPING

ART GALLERIES
Fairweather Gallery and Gifts (✉*209 Lincoln St.* ☎*907/747–8677* ⊕*www.fairweatherprints.com*) sells shirts, dresses, and other clothing featuring hand-printed Alaska designs. The shop also has two back rooms packed with works by local artisans. **Fishermen's Eye Fine Art Gallery** (✉*239 Lincoln St.* ☎*907/747–6080* ⊕*www.fishermenseye. com*) is a tasteful downtown gallery that prides itself on its vibrant collection of made-in-Sitka art. Housed within a Victorian-style 1895 home next to the Bishop's House, **Sitka Rose Gallery** (✉*419 Lincoln St.* ☎*907/747–3030 or 888/236–1536* ⊕*www.sitkarosegallery.com*) is the town's most charming shop, and features Alaskan paintings, sculptures, native art, and jewelry.

BOOKSTORE

Old Harbor Books (✉ *201 Lincoln St.* ☎ *907/747–8808*) has an impressive collection of Alaska titles, along with a knowledgeable staff. Directly behind the bookstore is a cozy left-wing hangout called the **Backdoor Café** (☎ *907/747–8856*), with excellent espresso and fresh-baked pastries.

GIFTS

Fresh Fish Company (✉ *411 DeGroff St.* ☎ *907/747–5565, 888/747–5565 outside Alaska* ⊕ *www.akfreshfish.com*) sells fresh locally caught salmon, halibut, and shrimp. Located in the old pulp mill building 5 mi east of Sitka, **Theobroma Chocolate Company** (☎ *907/966–2345 or 888/985–2345* ⊕ *www.theobromachocolate.com*) produces a range of rich treats, including chocolates shaped like halibut and salmon. Tours of this gourmet chocolate factory are available daily. Behind the Sitka Rose Gallery, **WinterSong Soap Company** (✉ *419 Lincoln St.* ☎ *907/747–8949 or 888/819–8949* ⊕ *www.wintersongsoap.com*) sells colorful and scented soaps that are handcrafted on the premises.

JUNEAU

100 mi northeast of Sitka.

Juneau, Alaska's capital and third-largest city, is on the North American mainland but can't be reached by road. The city owes its origins to two colorful sourdoughs (Alaskan pioneers)—Joe Juneau and Richard Harris—and to a Tlingit chief named Kowee, who led the two men to rich reserves of gold at Snow Slide Gulch, the drainage of Gold Creek around which the town was eventually built. That was in 1880, and shortly thereafter a modest stampede resulted in the formation of a mining camp, which quickly grew to become the Alaska district government capital in 1906. The city may well have continued under its original appellation—Harrisburg, after Richard Harris—were it not for Joe Juneau's political jockeying at a miner's meeting in 1881.

For some 60 years after Juneau's founding, gold was the mainstay of the economy. In its heyday, the AJ (for Alaska Juneau) Gold Mine was the biggest low-grade ore mine in the world. It was not until World War II, when the government decided it needed Juneau's manpower for the war effort, that the AJ and other mines in the area ceased operations. After the war, mining failed to start up again, and government became the city's principal employer. Juneau's mines leave a rich legacy, though; the AJ Gold Mine alone produced more than $80 million in gold.

Perhaps because of its colorful history, Juneau is full of contrasts. Its dramatic hillside location and historical downtown buildings provide a frontier feeling, but the city's cosmopolitan nature comes through in fine museums, noteworthy restaurants, and a literate and outdoorsy populace. Here you can enjoy the Mt. Roberts Tramway, plenty of densely forested wilderness areas, quiet bays for sea kayaking, and even a famous drive-up glacier.

EXPLORING JUNEAU

Along with the Alaska State Museum and Mt. Roberts Tramway, make time for a tour to Mendenhall Glacier and the Macaulay Salmon Hatchery. Douglas (which at one point was a bigger outpost than Juneau) is across the Gastineau Channel to the west. For goings on, pick up the *Juneau Empire* (⊕ *www.juneauempire. com)*, which keeps tabs on state politics, business, sports, and local news.

GETTING HERE & AROUND

Juneau is an obligatory stop on the Inside Passage cruise and ferry circuit. Hence, the town has an overabundance of visitors in midsummer. **Alaska Airlines** also flies here. Downtown Juneau is compact enough so that most of its main attractions are within walking distance of one another. Note, however, that the city is very hilly, so your legs will get a real workout. Look for the 20 signs around downtown that detail Juneau's fascinating history.

ESSENTIALS

Airline Contact **Alaska Airlines** (☎ *800/252–7522* ⊕ *www.alaskaair.com*).

Internet **Heritage Coffee Company** (⊠ *174 S. Franklin St. and 216 2nd S.* ☎ *907/586–1087* ⊕ *www.heritagecoffee.com*). **Juneau Public Library** (⊠ *292 Marine Way* ☎ *907/586–5249* ⊕ *www.ccl.lib.ak.us*)

Medical Assistance **Bartlett Regional Hospital** (⊠ *3260 Hospital Dr.* ☎ *907/586–2611* ⊕ *www.bartletthospital.org*)

Post Office & Shipping **U.S. Postal Service** (⊠ *709 W. 9th St.* ⊠ *9491 Vintage Blvd.* ⊕ *www.usps.gov*). **DHL** (⊠ *Drop box: 8th-fl. lobby, State Office Bldg., 333 Willoughby Ave.* ☎ *800/225–5345* ⊕ *www.dhl-usa.com*). **FedEx** (⊠ *9203 Bonnett Way* ☎ *800/463–3339* ⊕ *www.fedex.com*). **UPS** (⊠ *1900 Renshaw Way* ☎ *800/742–5877* ⊕ *www.ups.com*).

Pharmacy **Juneau Drug Co.** (⊠ *202 Front St.* ☎ *907/586–1233*). **Ron's Apothecary Shoppe** (⊠ *9101 Mendenhall Mall Rd., in Mendenhall Mall next to Super Bear market* ☎ *907/789–0458* ⊕ *www.ronsapothecary.com*).

Visitor Info **Juneau Convention and Visitors Bureau** (⊠ *1 Sealaska Plaza, Suite 305* ☎ *907/586–1737 or 800/587–2201* ⊕ *www.traveljuneau.com*).**Alaska Department of Fish & Game** (✆ *Box 115526, Juneau 99811-5526* ☎ *907/465–4100, 907/465–4180 sportfishing seasons and regulations, 907/465–2376 license information* ⊕ *www.state.ak.us/adfg*). **Alaska Division of Parks** (⊠ *400 Willoughby Ave.99811* ☎ *907/465–4563* ⊕ *www.alaskastateparks.org*).

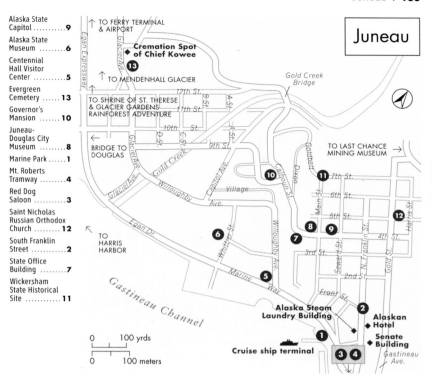

WHAT TO SEE

❾ Alaska State Capitol. Completed in 1931 and remodeled in 2006, this rather unassuming building houses the governor's office and hosts state legislature meetings in winter, placing it at the epicenter of Alaska's increasingly animated political discourse. Historical photos line the upstairs walls. Feel free to stroll right in. ■TIP→ You can pick up a self-guided tour brochure as you enter. ⊠ *Corner of Seward and 4th Sts.* ☎ *907/465–4648* ⊙ *Weekdays 8–5.*

❻ Alaska State Museum. This is one of Alaska's finest museums. Native-Alaskan buffs will enjoy examining the 38-foot walrus-hide *umiak* (an open, skin-covered Eskimo boat). Natural-history exhibits include preserved brown bears and a two-story-high eagle nesting tree. Russian-American and gold-rush displays and contemporary art complete the collection. ■TIP→ Be sure to visit the cramped gift shop with its extraordinary selection of native art, including baskets, carvings, and masks. ⊠ *395 Whittier St.* ☎ *907/465–2901* ⊕ *www.museums.state.ak.us* ⊠ *$5* ⊙ *Mid-May–mid-Sept., daily 8:30–5:30; mid-Sept.–mid-May, Tues.–Sat. 10–4.*

❺ Centennial Hall Visitor Center. Here you can get complete details on Juneau sights and activities, plus walking-tour maps. You can find out about hiking trails and other activities on nearby Tongass National Forest

A GOOD WALK

The most common starting spot is **Marine Park**, situated right along the cruise-ship dock. For an introduction to Alaska's human and natural history, head to the engaging **Alaska State Museum**. From here, circle back along Willoughby Avenue to the **State Office Building**. Catch the elevator to the eighth-floor atrium, which features an observation deck with vistas across the Gastineau Channel. The snug but cheery **Juneau-Douglas City Museum**, a local treasure that's slightly off the beaten path, sits a short distance away at 4th and Main streets. The looming, banklike building across the street is the **Alaska State Capitol**. For a far more attractive example of governmental architecture, walk past the **Governor's Mansion**, a few minutes uphill on Calhoun Street. If you have the time and energy, you may want to continue along Calhoun, across the Gold Creek Bridge, and then down along 12th Street to the quiet **Evergreen**

Cemetery, where town fathers Joe Juneau and Richard Harris, as well as Chief Kowee, are buried.

Back in downtown, the **Centennial Hall Visitor Center** isn't far from the historic buildings and busy shops of downtown Juneau, particularly those along **South Franklin Street**. Check out the Alaskan Hotel, the Alaska Steam Laundry Building, and the Senate Building before dipping inside the terminally crowded **Red Dog Saloon** at the intersection of South Franklin Street and Admiralty Way. Try a microbrew, and then continue down the street to the **Mt. Roberts Tramway**, a popular way to reach alpine country for a hike overlooking Juneau and the Gastineau Channel.

To cover downtown Juneau's many interesting sights, you should allow at least three or four hours for exploring. Add at least another hour if you're a museum fan, or if you plan to ride the Mt. Roberts Tramway.

lands. ✉*101 Egan Dr.* ☎*907/586–2201 or 888/581–2201* ⊕*www.traveljuneau.com* ⊗*May–Sept., weekdays 8:30–5, weekends 9–5; Oct.–Apr., weekdays 9–4.*

⑬ Evergreen Cemetery. Many Juneau pioneers, including Joe Juneau and Richard Harris, are buried here. Juneau (1836–99), a Canadian by birth, died in Dawson City, Yukon, but his body was returned to the city that bears his name. Harris (1833–1907), whose name can be found on downtown's Harris Street, died here. A meandering gravel path leads through the graveyard, and at the end of it is the monument commemorating the cremation spot of Chief Kowee.

⑩ Governor's Mansion. Completed in 1912, this stately colonial-style home overlooks downtown Juneau. With 14,400 square feet, six bedrooms, and 10 bathrooms, it's no miner's cabin. Out front is a totem pole that tells three tales: the history of man, the cause of ocean tides, and the origin of Alaska's ubiquitous mosquitoes. Alaska's first female and youngest governor, Sarah Palin, lives here with her husband ("First Dude" Todd Palin) and their children. Tours of the residence are, unfortunately, not permitted. ✉*716 Calhoun Ave.*

Mendenhall Glacier, Juneau. Kayak along this receding glacier just 13 mi outside of the city.

⑧ Juneau-Douglas City Museum. Among the exhibits interpreting local mining and Tlingit history are old mining equipment, a reconstructed Tlingit fish trap, a three-dimensional model of the Treadwell Mine, historic photos, a diorama of an Assay Lab, and an interactive exhibit on Juneau as Alaska's Capital City. Youngsters will appreciate the hands-on room where they can try on clothes similar to ones worn by the miners or look at gold-rush stereoscopes. Guided historic walking tours are offered May to September. ⊠ *114 4th St.* ☎ *907/586-3572* ⊕ *www. juneau.org/parksrec/museum* ☑ *$4* ☉ *May–Sept., weekdays 9–5, weekends 10–5; Oct.-Apr., Tues.-Sat. 10–4.*

OFF THE BEATEN PATH

Last Chance Mining Museum. A 1.5-mi hike or taxi ride behind town, this small museum is housed in the former compressor building of Juneau's historic AJ Gold Mine. The collection includes old mining tools, railcars, minerals, and a 3-D map of the ore body. The surrounding country is steep and wooded, with trails leading in all directions, including one to the summit of Mt. Juneau. ⊠ *1001 Basin Rd.* ☎ *907/586-5338* ☑ *$4–$5* ☉ *Mid-May–mid-Sept., daily 9:30–12:30 and 3:30–6:30.*

① Marine Park. On the dock where the cruise ships "tie up" is a little urban oasis with benches, shade trees, and shelter. It's a great place to enjoy an outdoor meal from one of Juneau's street vendors, and, on Friday evenings in summer, it features live performances by Juneau musicians. A visitor kiosk is staffed according to cruise-ship schedules.

④ Mt. Roberts Tramway. One of Southeast Alaska's most popular tourist attractions, this tram whisks you from the cruise terminal 1,800 feet up the side of Mt. Roberts. After the six-minute ride you can take in a film on the history and legends of the Tlingits, visit the nature center, go for an alpine walk on hiking trails (including the 5-mi round-trip hike to Mt. Roberts's 3,819-foot summit), purchase native crafts, or chow down while enjoying mountain views. A local company leads guided wilderness hikes from the summit, and the bar serves locally brewed beers. ☎*907/463–3412 or 888/461–8726* ⊕*www.goldbelttours.com* ☞*$25* ☉*May–Sept., daily 9–9.*

❸ **Red Dog Saloon.** The frontierish quarters of the Red Dog have housed an infamous Juneau watering hole since 1890. Nearly every conceivable surface in this two-story bar is cluttered with graffiti, business cards, and memorabilia, including a pistol that reputedly belonged to Wyatt Earp, who failed to reclaim the piece after checking it in at the U.S. Marshall's office on June 27, 1900. A little atmospheric sawdust covers the floor as well. Bands pump out dance tunes when cruise ships are docked; the most notable (and bawdy) local performer is a legendary piano man named Phinneus Poon. ✉*278 S. Franklin St.* ☎*907/463–3658* ⊕*www.reddogsaloon.com.*

⑫ **St. Nicholas Russian Orthodox Church.** It's the oldest Russian church in Southeast Alaska—but it was actually built in Siberia in 1894. It was subsequently disassembled, shipped to Juneau, and reassembled by Tlingits and Slavic immigrants. The quaint, onion-dome white-and-blue church has services sung in Slavonic, English, and Tlingit on Saturday and Sunday, though it may be closed for renovations. ✉*326 5th St.* ☎*907/845–2288*

❷ **South Franklin Street.** The buildings on South Franklin Street (and neighboring Front Street), among the oldest and most-inviting structures in the city, house curio and crafts shops, snack shops, and two salmon shops. Many reflect the architecture of the 1920s and 1930s. When the small **Alaskan Hotel** opened in 1913, Juneau was home to 30 saloons; the Alaskan gives today's visitors the most authentic glimpse of the town's whiskey-rich history. The barroom's massive, mirrored, oak back bar is accented by Tiffany lights and panels. Topped by a wood-shingled turret, the 1901 **Alaska Steam Laundry Building** now houses a coffeehouse and other stores. The **Senate Building,** another of South Franklin's treasured landmarks, is across the street.

❼ **State Office Building.** The building's sprawling eighth-floor patio, which faces the Gastineau Channel and Douglas Island, is a popular lunch destination for state workers and assorted residents. On most Fridays at noon, concerts inside the four-story atrium feature a grand old theater pipe organ, a veteran of the silent-movie era. Also here is the historic old witch totem pole; the Alaska State Library, with a fine collection of historical photos; and computers with public Internet access. If you're having trouble finding the building, just ask for directions to the "S.O.B."—the locals are fond of acronyms. ⊠*4th and Calhoun Sts.*

⓫ Wickersham State Historical Site. At the top of the hill behind the capitol, on a rise sometimes known as "Chicken Ridge," stands the former residence of James Wickersham, pioneer judge, delegate to Congress, prolific author, and gutsy outdoorsman. The white New England–style home, constructed in 1898, contains memorabilia from the judge's travels throughout Alaska—from rare native basketry and ivory carvings to historic photos and a Chickering grand piano that came "'round the Horn" to Alaska in the 1870s. The tour provides a glimpse into the life of this dynamic man and also includes tea and sourdough cookies. ⊠*213 7th St.* ☎*907/586–9001* ⊕*www.dnr.state.ak.us/parks* ⊠*$2* ☉*Mid-May–Sept., Thurs.–Tues. 10–noon and 1–5, additional hrs when cruise ships are in port; Oct.–mid- May by appointment.*

4

WHERE TO EAT

¢–$$$
AMERICAN
✕**Douglas Café.** In the heart of quiet Douglas, across the bridge and a couple of miles from downtown Juneau, this family eatery has Formica tables and a three-meals-a-day menu (breakfast on weekends only) that includes omelets, sandwiches, kids' favorites, and 15 types of burgers, which are often cited as the best in the city. It's a good choice for those seeking an alternative to downtown Juneau's occasionally nutty midsummer pace. ⊠*916 3rd St., Douglas* ☎*907/364–3307* ▭*MC, V.*

$$$$
SEAFOOD
✕**Gold Creek Salmon Bake.** Trees, mountains, and the rushing water of Salmon Creek surround the comfortable, canopy-covered benches and tables at this authentic salmon bake. Fresh-caught salmon is cooked over an alder fire and served with a succulent sauce. For $35 there are all-you-can-eat salmon, pork spareribs, and chicken along with baked beans, rice pilaf, salad bar, corn bread, and blueberry cake. Wine and beer are extra. After dinner you can pan for gold in the stream, wander up the hill to explore the remains of the Wagner gold mine, or roast marshmallows over the fire. A round-trip bus ride from downtown is included. ⊠*1061 Salmon Lane Rd.* ☎*907/789–0052 or 800/323–5757* ▭*AE, MC, V* ☉*Closed Oct.–Apr.*

$–$$$
ECLECTIC
✕**Hangar on the Wharf.** Crowded with locals and travelers, the Hangar occupies the building where Alaska Airlines started business. Flight-theme puns dominate the menu (i.e. "Pre-flight Snacks" and the "Plane Caesar"), but the comfortably worn wood and vintage airplane photos create a casual dining experience that overcomes the kitsch. Every seat has views of the Gastineau Channel and Doug-

WORD OF MOUTH

"Our favorite local hangout is Hangar on the Wharf, with its huge selection of microbrews; it has the same owners as Twisted Fish. It's quieter and has a more-varied menu and the best coconut shrimp I've had. It's fun to sit at the big windows and watch the harbor activity while you eat."

—klondike

las Island. This Juneau hot spot makes a wide selection of entrées, including locally caught halibut and salmon, filet mignon, great burgers, and daily specials. Two dozen beers are on tap. On Friday and Saturday nights jazz or rock bands take the stage, and prime rib arrives on the menu. ⊠*2 Marine Way, Merchants Wharf Mall* ☎*907/586–5018* ⊕*www.hangaronthewharf.com* ☰*AE, D, MC, V.*

¢ ✕**Heritage Coffee Company.** Juneau's favorite coffee shop is a downtown
CAFÉ   institution, with locally roasted coffees, gelato, fresh pastries, and all sorts of specialty drinks. ■**TIP**➜ **The window-front bar is good for people-watching while you sip a chai latte.** The same folks also operate several other coffee outposts, including the **Glacier Cafe** in Mendenhall Valley, which boasts a bigger menu that includes breakfast burritos and omelets, along with lunchtime paninis, wraps, soups, salads, and burgers, plus various vegetarian dishes. ⊠*174 S. Franklin St.* ☎*907/586–1087* ⊠*216 2nd S.* ☎*907/586–1752* ⊠*Mendenhall Mall Rd.* ☎*907/789–0692* ⊕*www.heritagecoffee.com* ☰*AE, D, MC, V* ⊗*No dinner.*

¢–$$ ✕**Island Pub.** The Island Pub in Douglas has fast service, views of the
PIZZA   Gastineau Channel, a full bar, occasional live music, and good times, making it one of the area's coolest restaurants. There are salads, sandwiches, and wraps, but the real draw is the pizza: thin, 13-inch focaccia crusts are prepared fresh daily, topped with creative ingredients, and baked in a copper wood-fired oven. Customers are encouraged to build their own pizzas, and the best of their creations end up on the menu. The menu is therefore in a state of constant flux. If you've got room, try one of the chef's dessert pizzas—bizarre, but surprisingly good. ⊠*1102 2nd St., Douglas* ☎*907/364–1595* ⊕*www.theislandpub.com* ☰*AE, D, DC, MC, V.*

¢ ✕**Rainbow Foods.** Housed upstairs in a building that began life as an
VEGETARIAN   Assembly of God church, this crunchy natural foods market is a popular lunch-break destination for downtown workers. Organic produce, soy ice cream, and vitamin supplements fill the shelves, but the real attraction is the weekday buffet, with various hot entrées, salads, soups, and deep-dish pizzas. Arrive before 11 AM for the best choices. Self-serve coffee and freshly baked breads are available, along with a few inside tables. ⊠*224 4th St.* ☎*907/586–6476* ⊕*www.rainbow-foods. org* ☰*MC, V.*

$–$$$ ✕**Twisted Fish.** Juneau's liveliest downtown eatery serves up creative
SEAFOOD   pan-Asian seafood and Alaska classics. Housed in a log-frame waterfront building adjacent to the Taku Store and the base of the Mt. Roberts Tramway, Twisted's fish is as fresh as you'll find. Grab a seat on the deck for prime-time Gastineau Channel–gazing and a bowl of Captain Ron's chowder. Inside, you'll find a dining room with a roaring river-rock hearth and flame-painted salmon, porpoises, marlin, and tuna decorating the walls. ⊠*550 S. Franklin St.* ☎*907/463–5033* ☰*AE, D, MC, V* ⊗*Closed Oct.–Mar.*

¢–$$$ ✕**Wild Spice.** In addition to a full menu with sandwiches, soups and
ECLECTIC   salads, seafood entrées, and an extensive wine list, this trendy downtown eatery also offers a Mongolian-style barbecue. Customers assemble their own entrées from an assortment of meats, vegetables, rice,

noodles, and sauces, then hand them to the chef to cook on an open, circular flat-top grill. Quick and (usually) delicious, this is a good mid-walk lunch or dinner stop. ⊠ *140 Seward St.* ☎ *907/523–0444* ⊕ *www. thewildspice.com* ▤ *AE, MC, V.*

$–$$$$

MEDITERRANEAN ✕ **Zephyr.** One of Juneau's more-upscale restaurants, Zephyr distinguishes itself by remaining faithfully Mediterranean. The Greco-Roman menu features Spanish, Greek, Italian, and Middle Eastern specialties such as hummus spread on pita toast points, lamb kebabs, and Aegean pasta with feta and sun-dried tomatoes. The restaurant's excellent beer and wine list, along with its two bars—one on the ground floor and another on the upstairs mezzanine level—make it a great place to meet friends for an aperitif. ⊠ *200 Seward St.* ☎ *907/780–2221* ▤ *MC, V.*

4

WHERE TO STAY

¢–$
★ 🛏 **Alaskan Hotel.** This historic 1913 hotel in the heart of downtown Juneau sits over the popular bar of the same name; be prepared for noise Thursday through Saturday nights when bands are playing. Ask staff for a less-noisy room on the northeast side. The older but well-maintained Queen Anne–style guest rooms ramble across three floors and include pedestal sinks, old-fashioned radiators, bay windows, and a smattering of antiques. The flocked wallpaper, red floral carpets, and Tiffany windows are reminiscent of the hotel's original gold rush–era opulence. The least-expensive rooms share a bath down the hall. The hotel plans to add a restaurant downstairs. **Pro:** Historic property with quaint furnishings. **Cons:** Some rooms are noisy and smell musty. ⊠ *167 S. Franklin St.* ☎ *907/586–1000 or 800/327–9347* ⊕ *www. thealaskanhotel.com* ⇋ *44 rooms, 22 with bath* 🛏 *In-room: kitchen (some), no TV (some), Wi-Fi (some). In-hotel: bar, no elevator, laundry facilities, public Wi-Fi, some pets allowed, no-smoking rooms* ▤ *AE, D, DC, MC, V.*

$$–$$$$
Fodor's Choice
★ 🛏 **Alaska's Capital Inn.** Gold-rush pioneer John Olds built this American foursquare home in 1906, and a major restoration transformed it into Juneau's most elegant B&B. Owners Linda Wendeborn and Mark Thorson are laid-back and accommodating, and guests can expect lively conversation with their gourmet breakfasts and afternoon wine and treats. Rooms are tastefully decorated with handcrafted antiques. The fourth-floor Governor's Suite includes a king-size oak bed, a fireplace, a hot tub, and a 180-degree view of downtown Juneau. Two rooms on the bottom level have private entrances and look out on a lush garden, where the hot tub sits under a gazebo. **Pro:** Beautiful restoration to 1906 mansion. **Con:** Governor's Suite no longer offers popular sleigh bed. ⊠ *113 W. 5th St.* ☎ *907/586–6507 or 888/588–6507* ⊕ *www.alaskacapitalinn.com* ⇋ *5 rooms, 2 suites* 🛏 *In-room: refrigerator (some), DVD, VCR, Ethernet, Wi-Fi. In-hotel: no elevator, concierge, public Internet, public Wi-Fi, no kids under 12, no-smoking rooms* ▤ *AE, D, DC, MC, V* ⏼ *BP.*

$$–$$$$
🛏 **Baranof Hotel.** The Baranof has long been Juneau's most prestigious address; it's as close to a big-city downtown boutique hotel as you're going to find in Southeast Alaska. Tasteful woods and period lamps in

the dark art-deco lobby create an old-money atmosphere reminiscent of 1939, when the hotel first opened. Upscale dining is available in the Gold Room, known for its embroidered chairs. Rooms on the front side have the best views, but street noise may keep you awake at the lower levels. The best are spacious corner suites on the upper floors, which overlook the busy harbor to the forested mountains of Douglas Island. Some of the other rooms are fairly small. **Pros:** Elegant art-deco public areas. **Con:** Lower floors are noisy. ⊠ *127 N. Franklin St.* ☎ *907/586–2660 or 800/544–0970* ⊕ *www.westmarkhotels.com* ↩ *196 rooms, 17 suites* ⋄ *In-room: kitchen (some), Wi-Fi. In-hotel: 2 restaurants, room service, bar, gym, laundry service, concierge, public Wi-Fi, parking (no fee), some pets allowed, no-smoking rooms* ⊟ *AE, D, DC, MC, V.*

$–$$ ⬚ **Driftwood Lodge.** This workaday downtown motel is one of Juneau's best values for the money, with a central location and well-maintained rooms, some of which include kitchenettes stocked with dishes, silverware, pots, and pans. The one- and two-bedroom units have more space than the efficiencies and standard rooms, but cost just a few extra dollars. **Pro:** Most units are spacious. **Con:** Not handicapped-accessible. ⊠ *435 Willoughby Ave.* ☎ *907/586–2280 or 800/544–2239* ⊕ *www.driftwoodalaska.com* ↩ *62 rooms, 31 suites* ⋄ *In-room: kitchen (some), refrigerator (some), dial-up. In-hotel: bicycles, no elevator, laundry facilities, laundry service, public Internet, airport shuttle, parking (no fee), some pets allowed, no-smoking rooms* ⊟ *AE, D, DC, MC, V.*

$–$$ ⬚ **Extended Stay Deluxe.** This corporate-style inn, within walking distance of the airport and 9 mi from downtown, is a popular choice with business travelers and families; what it lacks in charm and personality it makes up for in space and amenities. Rooms are large, with kitchenettes and big TVs. This is also one of the few Juneau lodging options with an indoor pool, fitness center, and hot tub. **Pro:** All rooms have kitchenettes. **Con:** Rooms are not as clean as they could be. ⊠ *1800 Shell Simmons Dr.* ☎ *907/790–6435 or 800/398–7829* ⊕ *extendedstayhotels.com* ↩ *94 rooms* ⋄ *In-room: kitchen, refrigerator, DVD, Wi-Fi. In-hotel: pool, gym, laundry facilities, laundry service, public Internet, public Wi-Fi, airport shuttle, some pets allowed, no-smoking rooms* ⊟ *AE, D, DC, MC, V* ⫧*CP.*

$$ ⬚ **Frontier Suites Airport Hotel.** Near the airport in Mendenhall Valley, 9 mi from Juneau, this rambling hotel is a great for families. The property's large rooms have comfortable furniture and full kitchens with a stove, refrigerator, dishwasher, microwave, dishes, silverware, and pans. Suites have separate bedrooms and living rooms (with sleeper sofas) and two televisions. Two bunk rooms include a mini-loft for older children. The **Pasta Garden,** downstairs, serves American, Asian, Mexican, and Mediterranean fare three meals a day. The hotel offers a shuttle to the airport and ferry. **Pros:** Large rooms, full kitchens. **Con:** Long distance from downtown. ⊠ *9400 Glacier Hwy.* ☎ *907/790–6600 or 800/544–2250* ⊕ *www.frontiersuites.com* ↩ *104 rooms, 32 suites* ⋄ *In-room: safe, kitchen, refrigerator, DVD (some), VCR (some), Ethernet. In-hotel: restaurant, room service, bar, gym, laundry*

facilities, laundry service, airport shuttle, some pets allowed, no-smoking rooms ☰*AE, D, DC, MC, V.*

$$$ 🏨 **Goldbelt Hotel Juneau.** A high-rise by local standards, the seven-story Goldbelt is one of Juneau's better lodging places, with decent (if somewhat overpriced) rooms with basic amenities including local coffee. Waterside rooms on the upper level have views across the Gastineau Channel, and some rooms have king-size beds. Zen, the restaurant adjacent to the hotel, offers an Asian fusion menu; Jaded, the adjoining bar, has one of Juneau's best wine lists and live music on weekends. **Pro:** Large rooms. **Con:** Street-side rooms are very noisy. ⊠*51 W. Egan Dr.* ☎*907/586–6900 or 888/478–6909* ⊕*www.goldbelt.com* ⇆*105 rooms, 1 suite* ⌂*In-room: Wi-Fi. In-hotel: restaurant, room service, bar, laundry service, public Wi-Fi, airport shuttle, parking (no fee), no-smoking rooms* ☰*AE, D, DC, MC, V.*

$$–$$$ 🏨**Grandma's Feather Bed.** This charming Victorian-style hotel—the smallest property in the Best Western chain—is less than a mile from the airport in Mendenhall Valley. Cheerful colors brighten each of the spacious and homey rooms, which come with jetted bathtubs and, as the name would suggest, beds topped with voluminous feather comforters. Guests especially appreciate the big breakfast buffet that includes omelets, pancakes, and hot cereals. Dinners are also available Tuesday through Saturday. The hotel is not really set up for children. **Pro:** Delicious breakfasts. **Con:** Hotel is the smallest in chain. ⊠*2348 Mendenhall Loop Rd.* ☎*907/789–5566 or 888/781–5005* ⇆*14 rooms* ⌂*In-room: refrigerator (some), Wi-Fi. In-hotel: restaurant, room service, no elevator, laundry facilities, public Wi-Fi, airport shuttle, no-smoking rooms* ☰*AE, D, DC, MC, V* ⎮⊙⎮*BP.*

$$$$ 🏨**Pearson's Pond Luxury Inn and Adventure Spa.** On a small pond near Mendenhall Glacier, this large, jaw-droppingly landscaped home may be Alaska's finest B&B. Owners Diane and Steven Pearson pull out all the stops for guests, with two outdoor hot tubs; ambient fireplaces; jetted bathtubs; a library full of books, DVDs, and videotapes; four-poster beds with high-end mattresses; private balconies; and a well-stocked breakfast nook. Diane Pearson is an itinerary planner extraordinaire, and she's even licensed to teach yoga and perform weddings. Guests can borrow a rowboat, paddleboats, kayaks, fishing poles, hiking gear, and cross-country skis. There's yoga on the deck each morning and wine and cheese in the evening, and there's never a shortage of friendly conversation. The Pearsons also have two condos ($199–$249 per night, one-week minimum) closer to town, which sleep four people each. **Pro:** Private balconies offer excellent views. **Con:** Property no longer offers canoes. ⊠*4541 Sawa Circle* ☎*907/789–3772* ⊕*www.pearsonspond.com* ⇆*5 suites* ⌂*In-room: kitchen, refrigerator, DVD, VCR*

Fodor's Choice
★

WORD OF MOUTH

"In Juneau we always stay at Grandma's Feather Bed, closer to the airport than to the downtown area (Juneau is very spread out). The hotel is wonderfully appointed (all rooms have a Jacuzzi), plus breakfast buffet or breakfast cooked to order included in price."
—klondike

4

(some), Ethernet, Wi-Fi. In-hotel: room service, gym, spa, water sports, bicycles, no elevator, laundry facilities, concierge, public Internet, public Wi-Fi, no kids under 12, no-smoking rooms ▭AE, D, DC, MC, V ⦿|BP.

$$–$$$ 🖼 **Prospector Hotel.** A short walk west of downtown and next door to the Alaska State Museum, this nicely appointed but visually unremarkable hotel is frequented by business travelers and legislators during the winter legislative session. Rooms are spacious and have cherrywood furnishings, leather chairs, and ottomans. T.K. McGuire's dining room and lounge, which sits just off the lobby, serves prime rib, steaks, and seafood, along with Juneau's best Sunday brunch. **Pro:** Convenient location. **Con:** Very lackluster exterior and lobby. ✉*375 Whittier St.* ☎*907/586–3737, 800/331–2711 outside Alaska, 800/478–5866 in Alaska* ⊕*www.prospectorhotel.com* ⇆*56 rooms, 7 suites* ⟐*In-room: refrigerator, Wi-Fi. In-hotel: restaurant, bar, laundry service, public Wi-Fi, parking (no fee), some pets allowed, no-smoking rooms* ▭AE, D, DC, MC, V.

$ 🖼 **Sentinel Island Lighthouse.** A few miles north of Juneau and adjacent to a rock where Steller sea lions haul out, this operating lighthouse, complete with a lantern visible from 17 mi away, provides a spectacular spot to watch whales and eagles. You have the entire cliff-bordered 6-acre island to roam around on. Simple accommodations include bunks in the lighthouse and in an adjacent building; you can also pitch a tent on a platform facing the water. Water and cooking facilities are provided for all accommodations. The lighthouse is managed by the Gastineau Channel Historical Society, and access is by charter boat, sea kayak, or helicopter. **Pro:** Excellent nature viewing. **Con:** Remote location. ✍*Box 21264, 99802* ☎*907/586–5338* ⇆*6 bunks in 2 bldgs.* ⟐*In-room: no phone, kitchen. In-hotel: no elevator, no-smoking rooms* ▭*No credit cards* ⊗*Closed mid-Sept.–mid-May.*

$$–$$$ 🖼 **Silverbow Inn.** Conveniently located in Juneau's historic downtown, the expanded Silverbow combines a downstairs bakery and café with 11 contemporary hotel rooms, on the two upper levels. Four of the rooms are tiny, but they're all comfortable and feature new flat-screen televisions, and include homey touches like rubber duckies for the tub. Guests stroll downstairs each morning for a filling breakfast, and each evening for wine and cheese. Owned by former New Yorkers, the bakery makes bagels and serves deli sandwiches on homemade bread, salads, soups, and pastries. The popular eatery added an outside awning to expand seating capacity, and the back room hosts live jazz and free films throughout the year. **Pro:** New flat-screen televisions in rooms. **Con:** No laundry facilities. ✉*120 2nd St.* ☎*907/586–4146 or 800/586–4146* ⊕*www.silverbowinn.com* ⇆*11 rooms* ⟐*In-room: DVD, VCR, Wi-Fi. In-hotel: restaurant, room service, bar, no elevator, public Wi-Fi, parking (no fee), no-smoking rooms* ▭AE, D, MC, V ⦿|BP.

¢ 🖼 **U.S. Forest Service Cabins.** Scattered throughout Tongass National

Fodor'sChoice

★ Forest, these rustic cabins offer a charming and cheap escape. Most are fly-in units, accessible by floatplanes, with bunks for six to eight occupants, tables, stoves, and outdoor privies but no electricity or running water. You provide your own sleeping bag, food, and cooking utensils. ✉*Juneau Ranger District, 8465 Old Dairy Rd., Juneau* ☎*907/586–8800, 877/444–6777 reservations* ⊕*www.recreation.gov* ⤴*150 cabins* ▤*AE, D, MC, V.*

¢ ⚠ **U.S. Forest Service Campgrounds.** Six Forest Service–maintained campgrounds are scattered around Tongass National Forest and are accessible from Juneau, Sitka, Ketchikan, Hollis, and Klawock. All have pit toilets and sites for RVs and tents, but not all provide drinking water. Reservations are possible for some of these campgrounds, but space is generally available without a reservation. ✉*Juneau Ranger District, 8465 Old Dairy Rd.* ☎*907/586–8800, 877/444–6777 reservations* ⊕*www.recreation.gov* ▤*D, MC, V.*

NIGHTLIFE & THE ARTS

BARS

The **Alaskan Hotel Bar** (✉*167 S. Franklin St.* ☎*907/586–1000*) is Juneau's most historically authentic watering hole, with flocked-velvet walls, antique chandeliers, and vintage Alaska frontier-brothel decor. The atmosphere, however, is anything but dated, and the bar's live music and open mike night draw high-spirited crowds. Past visitors to Juneau may recall the **Imperial Saloon** (✉*241 Front St.* ☎*907/586–1960*) as one of the downtown dives, but a major remodeling transformed it into a favorite place to drink, shoot pool, and meet singles. The divey decor hasn't all disappeared—the walls still feature mounted moose and bison heads. There's also the original pressed-tin ceiling. When the ships are in, the music at **Red Dog Saloon** (✉*278 S. Franklin St.* ☎*907/463–3658*) is live and the crowd gets livelier. Just down Front Street is the **Viking Lounge** (✉*218 Front St.* ☎*907/586–2159*), which sells more alcohol than any other bar in the Southeast. Cruise-ship workers love it for its DJ, dance floor, karaoke nights, and general rowdy vibe, and billiards enthusiasts appreciate the bar's eight pool tables.

If you're a beer fan, look for **Alaskan Brewing Company** (✉*5429 Shaune Dr.* ☎*907/780–5866* ⊕*www.alaskanbeer.com*). These tasty brews, including Alaskan Amber, Pale Ale, Stout, Alaskan Summer Ale and Smoked Porter, are brewed and bottled in Juneau. You can visit the microbrewery (and get free samples of the goods) 11 to 5 daily May through September, with 20-minute tours every half hour. Between October and April, tours take place Thursday through Saturday 11 to 4. ■TIP→ This is no designer brewery—it's in Juneau's industrial area and there is no upscale café/bar attached—but the gift shop sells T-shirts and beer paraphernalia.

MUSIC FESTIVALS

The annual weeklong **Alaska Folk Festival** (✉*Box 21748, 99802* ☎*907/463–3316* ⊕*www.akfolkfest.org*) is staged each April in Juneau, drawing singers, banjo masters, fiddlers, and even cloggers from all over the state and beyond, many of whom congregate at the Alaskan Hotel, the Festival's unofficial rallying point. During the last week of May, Juneau is the scene of **Juneau Jazz & Classics** (☎*Box 22152, 99802* ☎*907/463-3378* ⊕*www.jazzandclassics.org*), which celebrates music from Bach to Brubeck.

SYMPHONY

The **Juneau Symphony** (☎*907/586-4676* ⊕*www.juneausymphony.org*), directed by maestro Kyle Wiley Pickett, performs classical works October through June in the high school auditorium and local churches.

THEATER

Alaska's only professional theater company, the nationally renowned **Perseverance Theatre** (✉*914 3rd St., Douglas* ☎*907/463–TIXS* ⊕*www. perseverancetheatre.org*) performs a wide range of classics and new productions, regularly promoting Alaska artists and staging world premieres. The company tours extensively, bringing its unique productions (such as its all-Tlingit version of Shakespeare's "Macbeth") to audiences everywhere. Perseverance's season runs from September through May, giving travelers another good reason to visit Alaska during shoulder season.

SHOPPING

ART GALLERIES

Annie Kaill's Gallery (✉*244 Front St.* ☎*907/586–2880* ⊕*anniekaills. com*) displays a mix of playful and whimsical original prints, pottery, jewelry, and other arts and crafts from Alaska artists. A surprising exception to the cheesy-airport-gift-shop epidemic, Juneau's airport gift shop, **Hummingbird Hollow** (☎*907/789–4672* ⊕*www.humming-birdhollow.net*), is another fine place for authentic native art, including a diverse selection of jewelry, baskets, and Eskimo dolls. The cooperatively run **Juneau Artists Gallery** (☎*907/586–9891* ⊕*www.juneau-artistsgallery.com*), on the first floor of the old Senate Building at 175 South Franklin Street, sells a nice mix of watercolors, jewelry, etchings, photographs, art glass, ceramics, Ukrainian-style decorated eggs, and pottery from more than 20 artists. Across from the tram, the **Raven's Journey** (✉*435 S. Franklin St.* ☎*907/463–4686*) specializes in high-quality native Alaskan masks, grass baskets, carvings, dolls, ivory and silver jewelry, and more.

Rie Muñoz, of the **Rie Muñoz Gallery** (✉*2101 N. Jordan Ave.* ☎*907/789–7449 or 800/247–3151* ⊕*www.riemunoz.com*) is one of Alaska's best-known artists. She's the creator of a stylized, simple, and colorful design technique that is much copied but rarely equaled. The gallery is located in Mendenhall Valley, a convenient 10-minute walk from the airport. In downtown Juneau, see Rie Muñoz's paintings and tapestries at **Decker Gallery** (✉*233 S. Franklin St.* ☎*907/463–5536 or 800/463–5536*). Next door to Heritage Coffee, climb the stairs to **Wm. Spear Design** (✉*174 S. Franklin St.* ☎*907/586–2209* ⊕*www.wmspear. com*), where this lawyer-turned-artist produces a fun and colorful collection of enameled pins and zipper pulls.

SEAFOOD

Taku Store (✉ *550 S. Franklin St.* ☎*907/463–5319 or 800/582–5122* ⊕*www.takustore.com*), at the south end of town near the cruise-ship docks and Mt. Roberts Tramway, processes nearly 6 million pounds of fish a year, mostly salmon. ■TIP➜ Their smoked sockeye fillets make excellent gifts. You can view the smoking procedure through large windows and then purchase the packaged fish in the deli-style gift shop or have some shipped back home.

SIDE TRIPS FROM JUNEAU

Just a few miles outside of this ever-expanding city are some great day trips. The area's undisputed champion of visitor attractions is Mendenhall Glacier. Admiralty Island is also very popular—it has hikes through rain forest, excellent bear viewing, and secluded sea kayaking.

NATIVE CULTURE NEARBY

If you're interested in seeing how many native Alaskans of Southeast Alaska live today, you can fly or take one of the Alaska Marine Highway's ferries (☎*907/465–3941 or 800/642–0066*) to **Kake, Angoon,** or **Hoonah.** Hoonah's historic cannery building has been beautifully restored. Independent travelers won't find much organized touring in any of these communities, but you will find hotels (advance reservations strongly suggested), and guided fishing and natural-history trips can be arranged by asking around.

In Kake, contact the **Keex' Kwaan Lodge** (☎*907/785–3434* ⊕*www.kakealaska.com*).

In Angoon, try the all-inclusive **Favorite Bay Luxury Wilderness Resort** (☎*907/788–3344 or 866/788–3344* ⊕*www.favoritebay.com*).

In Hoonah, **Icy Strait Lodge** (☎*866/645–3636* ⊕*icystraitnow.com*) provides very comfortable on-the-water accommodations.

MACAULAY SALMON HATCHERY
3 mi northwest of downtown Juneau.

Watch through an underwater window as salmon fight their way up a fish ladder, from mid-June to mid-October. Inside the busy hatchery, which produces almost 125 million young salmon annually, you will learn about the environmental considerations of commercial fishermen and the lives of salmon. A retail shop sells gifts and salmon products. ✉*2697 Channel Dr.* ☎*907/463–4810 or 877/463–2486* ⊕*www. dipac.net* ✉*$3.25 including short tour* ⊙*Mid-May–mid-Sept., weekdays 10–6, weekends 10–5; Oct.–mid-May by appointment.*

GLACIER GARDENS RAINFOREST ADVENTURE
6.5 mi northwest of Juneau.

Spread over 50 acres of rain forest, Glacier Gardens has ponds, waterfalls, hiking paths, a large atrium, and gardens. The roots of fallen trees, turned upside down and buried in the ground, act as bowls to hold planters that overflow with begonias, fuchsias, and petunias. Guided tours in covered golf carts lead you along the 4 mi of paved paths, and a 580-foot-high overlook provides dramatic views of the Mendenhall wetlands wildlife refuge, Chilkat mountains, and downtown Juneau. A café and gift shop are here, and the conservatory is a popular wedding spot. ■TIP→ The Juneau city bus, which departs from multiple locations in downtown Juneau, stops right in front of Glacier Gardens. ✉7600 Glacier Hwy. ☎907/790–3377 ⊕www.glaciergardens.com ☞$22 including guided tour ☉May–Sept., daily 9–6.

FINDING THE RIGHT GUIDE

See the next section in this chapter ("Outdoor Activities & Guided Tours") for our favorite tour operators and guides who operate in and around Juneau.

MENDENHALL GLACIER
↻ *13 mi north of Juneau.*

Fodor'sChoice ★

Juneau's famous drive-up glacier spans 12 mi and is fed by the massive Juneau Icefield. Like many other Alaska glaciers, it is retreating up the valley, losing more than 100 feet a year as massive chunks of ice calve into the small lake separating Mendenhall from the **Mendenhall Visitor Center**. The center has highly interactive exhibits on the glacier, a theater and bookstore, educational exhibits, and panoramic views. It's a great place for children to learn the basics of glacier dynamics. Nature trails lead along Mendenhall Lake and into the mountains overlooking Mendenhall Glacier; the trails are marked by posts and paint stripes delineating the historical location of the glacier, providing a sharp reminder of the Mendenhall's hasty retreat. Look for spawning sockeye and coho salmon in Steep Creek, 0.5 mi south of the visitor center along the Moraine Ecology Trail. Several companies lead bus tours to the glacier. A glacier express bus leaves from the cruise-ship terminal and heads right out to Mendenhall Glacier; ask at the visitor information center there. ✉*End of Glacier Spur Rd. off Mendenhall Loop Rd.* ☎*907/789–0097* ⊕*www.fs.fed.us/r10/tongass/districts/mendenhall* ☞*Visitor center $3 in summer, free in winter* ☉*May–Sept., daily 8–7:30; Oct.–Apr., Thurs.–Sun. 10–4.*

SHRINE OF ST. THERESE
23 mi northwest of downtown Juneau.

A self-guided pilgrimage to the shrine is well worth the 23-mi journey from downtown Juneau (a taxi costs at least $50 round-trip). Built in the 1930s, this beautiful stone church and its 15 stations of the cross are the only inhabitants of a serene tiny island that is accessible via a 400-foot-long pedestrian causeway. Visitors enjoy the Merciful Love Labyrinth, the black-granite Shrine Columbarium, and the floral gardens along the Good Shepherd Rosary Trail. Sunday services are held at 1:30 PM from June through August. For those wishing to explore the area for more than a few hours, the shrine offers a lodge and four rental cabins that run the gamut from rustic to resplendent. ✉*5933 Lund St.* ☎*907/780–6112* ⊕*www.shrineofsainttherese.org.*

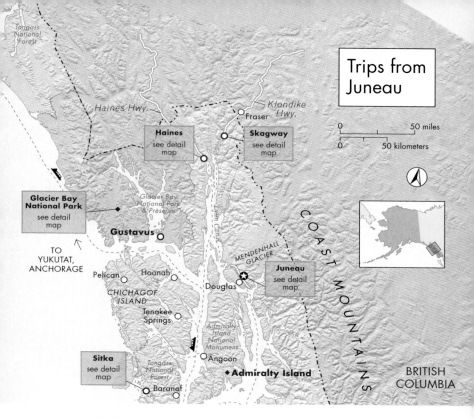

Haines see detail map

Skagway see detail map

Glacier Bay National Park see detail map

Juneau see detail map

Sitka see detail map

Trips from Juneau

Tongass National Forest

Haines Hwy.

Klondike Hwy.

Fraser

Glacier Bay National Park & Preserve

Gustavus

TO YUKUTAT, ANCHORAGE

Pelican

Hoonah

CHICHAGOF ISLAND

Tenakee Springs

Douglas

MENDENHALL GLACIER

Lynn Canal

Admiralty Island National Monument

Angoon

Tongass National Forest

Baranof

Admiralty Island

COAST MOUNTAINS

BRITISH COLUMBIA

0   50 miles
0   50 kilometers

ADMIRALTY ISLAND
10 mi south of Juneau.

The island is famous for its lush rain forests and abundant wildlife, including one of the largest concentrations of brown bears anywhere on the planet. Tlingit inhabitants called it Kootznoowoo, meaning "fortress of the bears." Ninety miles long, with 678 mi of coastline, Admiralty—the second-largest island in Southeast Alaska—is home to an estimated 1,500 bears, almost one per square mile.

The Forest Service's **Admiralty Island National Monument** has a system of public-use cabins, a canoe route that crosses the island via a chain of lakes and trails, the world's highest density of nesting bald eagles, large concentrations of humpback whales, and some of the region's best sea kayaking and sportfishing.

Fodor'sChoice
★
More than 90% of Admiralty Island is preserved within the Kootznoowoo Wilderness. Its chief attraction is **Pack Creek**, where you can watch brown bears feeding on salmon. One of Alaska's premier bear-viewing sites, Pack Creek is co-managed by the U.S. Forest Service and the Alaska Department of Fish and Game. Permits are required during

DID YOU KNOW?

On the Trail of Time see
the physical signs of
Mendenhall Glacier's history.
Dark (old) and light (new)
green vegetation meet at
the highest point reached
by the glacier's ice.

the main viewing season, from June 1 through September 10, and only 24 people per day are allowed to visit Pack Creek from July 5 through August 25. If you're headed to Pack Creek without a guide or an experienced visitor, be sure to cover the basics of bear safety before your trip. ■TIP➔ Applications can be mailed to the Forest Service beginning February 20. ☎907/586–8800 ⊕*www.fs.fed.us/r10/tongass/districts/ admiralty* ▰*$10–$50.*

OUTDOOR ACTIVITIES & GUIDED TOURS

BOATING, CANOEING & KAYAKING

Above & Beyond Alaska (☎*907/364–2333* ⊕*www.beyondak.com*) guides day and overnight camping, ice climbing, Mendenhall Glacier trips, and sea-kayaking trips in the Juneau area.

★ **Adventure Bound** (☎*907/463–2509 or 800/228–3875* ⊕*www.adventureboundalaska.com*) offers all-day trips to Sawyer Glacier within Tracy Arm in summer. **Alaska Boat and Kayak Rental** (☎*907/789–6886* ⊕*www.juneaukayak.com*) rents kayaks, canoes, and camping equipment at the Auke Bay boat harbor 12 mi north of Juneau. The company also provides water-taxi services for kayakers looking to access remote paddling terrain. **Alaska Discovery** (☎*510/594–6000 or 800/586–1911* ⊕*www.akdiscovery.com*) leads 9- and 12-day trips down the Tatshenshini and Alsek rivers. **Alaska Travel Adventures** (☎*800/478–0052, 800/791–2673 outside Alaska* ⊕*www.bestofalaskatravel.com*) leads Mendenhall River floats and numerous other tours throughout the Juneau area. The **Juneau Steamboat Company** (☎*907/723–0372* ⊕*www.juneausteamboat.com*) offers scenic tours of the Gastineau Channel aboard an authentic wood-fired steam launch, similar to those used around Juneau in the late 1800s and early 1900s. Tours come with entertaining narration about the historic mines of the area.

CLIMBING GYM

If it's pouring down rain—and in Juneau, it often is—head south of town to the **Rock Dump** (✉*1310 Eastaugh Way* ☎*907/586–4982* ⊕*www.rockdump.com*). The Dump has climbing walls for all abilities from beginner to expert; day passes are $10.

CROSS-COUNTRY SKIING

Find groomed cross-country ski trails near the Eaglecrest Ski Area and at Mendenhall Campground in the winter. You can rent skis and get advice about touring the trails and ridges around town from **Foggy Mountain Shop** (✉*134 N. Franklin St.* ☎*907/586–6780* ⊕*www.foggymountainshop.com*) In winter, the **Parks and Recreation Department** (☎*907/586–5226, 907/586–0428 24-hr info* ⊕*www.juneau.org/parksrec*) sponsors a group ski and snowshoe outing each Wednesday and Saturday when there's sufficient snow.

DOWNHILL SKIING

Southeast Alaska's only downhill ski area, **Eaglecrest** (☎*907/790–2000, 907/586–5330 recorded ski information* ⊕*www.juneau.org/eaglecrest*), is located on Douglas Island, just 30 minutes from downtown

Juneau. The resort typically offers late-November to mid-April skiing and snowboarding on 1,600 acres of well-groomed and off-piste terrain. Amenities include two double chairlifts, cross-country trails, a beginner's platter pull, a ski school, a ski-rental shop, a cafeteria, and a tri-level day lodge. Enjoy the northern lights while you night ski from January through mid-March.

FISHING

Sportfishing is an exceedingly popular activity in the Juneau area, and many charter boats depart from local harbors. **Alaska Trophy Fishing** (☎907/321–5859 or 866/934–7466 ⊕*www.alaskatrophyfishing.com*) offers tailor-made fishing vacations and charters. **Juneau Sportfishing & Sightseeing** (☎907/586–1887 ⊕*www.juneausportfishing.com*) has fishing trips aboard luxury boats.

The **Juneau Convention and Visitors Bureau** (☎907/586–1737 or 800/587–2201 ⊕*www.traveljuneau.com*) Web site has a complete list of operators, and several companies lead whale-watching trips from Juneau.

FLIGHTSEEING

Several local companies operate helicopter flightseeing trips to the spectacular glaciers flowing from Juneau Icefield. Most have booths along the downtown cruise-ship dock. All include a touchdown on a glacier, providing guests of almost all ages and abilities a chance to romp on these rivers of ice. Some also lead trips that include a dogsled ride on the glacier, an increasingly popular tourist pastime. Note that though we recommend the best companies, even some of the most-experienced pilots have been killed in helicopter accidents; always ask a carrier about their recent safety record before booking a trip.

Coastal Helicopters (☎907/789–5600 or 800/789–5610 ⊕*www.coastalhelicopters.com*) lands on several glaciers within the Juneau Icefield. Flying out of Douglas, **ERA Helicopters** (☎907/586–2030 or 800/843–1947 ⊕*www.flightseeingtours.com*) has a fully narrated one-hour trip that includes landing on the Norris or Taku Glacier. **NorthStar Trekking** (☎907/790–4530 ⊕*www.northstartrekking.com*) has three levels of excellent glacier hikes, starting with a one-hour interpretive walk, up to a four-hour hike that includes the chance to practice basic climbing and rope techniques. No experience is necessary.

Temsco Helicopters (☎907/789–9501 or 877/789–9501 ⊕*www.temscoair.com*), the self-proclaimed pioneers of Alaska glacier helicopter touring, offers glacier tours, dogsled adventures, and year-round flightseeing. **Ward Air** (☎907/789–9150 or 800/478–9150 ⊕*www.wardair.com*) conducts flightseeing trips to Glacier Bay, the Juneau Icefield, Tracy Arm, and Pack Creek.

GOLD PANNING

Gold panning is fun, especially for children, and Juneau is one of the Southeast's best-known gold-panning towns. Sometimes you actually uncover a few flecks of the precious metal in the bottom of your pan. You can buy a pan at almost any Alaska hardware or sporting-goods store. **Alaska Travel Adventures** (☎800/478–0052, 800/791–2673 *outside*

Alaska ⊕www.bestofalaskatravel. com) has gold-panning tours near the famous Alaska-Juneau Mine.

GOLF
Juneau's par-3, 9-hole **Mendenhall Golf Course** (⊠*2101 Industrial Blvd.* ☎*907/789–1221*) is a modest layout but has views that any exclusive private course would die for. Club rentals are available.

HIKING
Gastineau Guiding (☎*907/586– 8231* ⊕*www.stepintoalaska.com*) leads a variety of hikes in the Juneau area. Especially popular are their walks from the top of the tram on Mt. Roberts. The **Parks and Recreation Department** (☎*907/586– 5226, 907/586–0428 24-hr info* ⊕*www.juneau.org/parksrec*) in

> ### A BREATHTAKING JOURNEY
>
> **Taku Glacier Lodge** (☎*907/586–6275* ⊕*www.taku-glacierlodge.com*) is a remote, historic lodge south of Juneau along Taku Inlet. Hole-in-the-Wall Glacier is directly across the inlet from the lodge, and nature trails wind through the surrounding country, where black bears and bald eagles are frequently sighted. Floatplanes fly from Juneau on a scenic trip to the lodge, where you are served a delicious lunch or dinner and then flown back two hours later. No overnight stays are available.

Juneau sponsors a group hike each Wednesday morning and on Saturday in summer. Hikers can contact the **U.S. Forest Service** (☎*907/586– 8790*) for trail books and maps.

BIKING
Drop by the Centennial Hall Visitor Center for details on local trails open to bikes. Nearby is **Driftwood Lodge** (⊠*435 Willoughby Ave.* ☎*907/586–2280* ⊕*www.driftwoodalaska.com*), which has basic bikes for rent.

PACK CREEK BEAR VIEWING
Alaska Discovery (☎*510/594–6000 or 800/586–1911* ⊕*www.akdiscovery.com*) leads single- and multiday trips to Pack Creek that include a floatplane trip, sea kayaking, and guided bear viewing.

SIGHTSEEING & GLACIERS
Former miners lead three-hour tours of the historic **AJ Gold Mine** (☎*907/463–5017*) south of Juneau. A gold-panning demonstration is included, and approximately 45 minutes of the tour take place inside the old tunnels that lace the mountains. Mine tours depart from downtown by bus. The **Juneau Convention and Visitors Bureau** (☎*907/586– 1737 or 800/587–2201* ⊕*www.traveljuneau.com*) has a list of other companies that provide tours to Mendenhall Glacier. **Juneau Trolley Car Company** (☎*907/586–7433 or 877/774–8687* ⊕*www.juneautrolley. com*) conducts narrated tours, stopping at several of Juneau's historic and shopping attractions. An all-day pass is $19. **Mighty Great Trips** (☎*907/789–5460* ⊕*www.mightygreattrips.com*) leads guided bus tours that include a visit to Mendenhall Glacier. The company also offers helicopter tours, river rafting, and whale-watching.

WHALE-WATCHING

Alaska Whale Watching (☎907/321–5859 or 888/432–6722 ⊕*www. akwhalewatching.com*) offers small-group excursions (up to 12 guests) aboard a luxury yacht with an onboard naturalist. The company also offers a whale-watching/fishing combination tour, which is popular with multigenerational groups. **Four Seasons Marine** (☎907/790–6671 or 877/774–8687) combines whale-watching with an hour at Orca Point Lodge on Colt Island, where guests are served a grilled salmon lunch. The boat departs from Auke Bay with a free shuttle from Juneau. Several companies lead whale-watching trips from Juneau. **Juneau Sportfishing & Sightseeing** (☎907/586–1887 ⊕*www.juneausportfishing.com*) has been around for many years, and its boats carry a maximum of six passengers, providing a personalized trip.

★ **Orca Enterprises (with Captain Larry)** (☎907/789–6801 or 888/733–6722 ⊕*www.orcaenterprises.com*) offers whale-watching tours via jet-boats designed for comfort and speed. The operator boasts a whale-sighting success rate of 99.9% between May 1 and October 15.

4

GLACIER BAY NATIONAL PARK & PRESERVE

Fodor'sChoice *60 mi northwest of Juneau.*
★

Near the northern end of the Inside Passage, Glacier Bay National Park and Preserve is one of America's most magnificent national parks. Visiting Glacier Bay is like stepping back into the Little Ice Age—it's one of the few places in the world where you can approach such a variety of massive tidewater glaciers. Sounding like cannon fire, bergs the size of 10-story office buildings come crashing from the "snout" of a glacier, each cannon blast signifying another step in the glacier's steady retreat. The calving iceberg sends tons of water and spray skyward, propelling mini–tidal waves outward from the point of impact. **Johns Hopkins Glacier** calves so often and with such volume that large cruise ships can seldom come within 2 mi of its face.

Glacier Bay is a still-forming body of water fed by the runoff of the ice fields, glaciers, and mountains that surround it. In the mid-18th century, ice floes so covered the bay that Captain James Cook and then Captain George Vancouver sailed by and didn't even know it. At the time of Vancouver's sailing in 1794, the bay was still hidden behind and beneath a vast glacial wall of ice, which was more than 20 mi across and in places more than 4,000 feet in depth. It extended more than 100 mi north to its origins in the St. Elias Mountain Range, the world's tallest coastal mountains. Since then, the face of the glacial ice has melted and retreated with amazing speed, exposing 65 mi of fjords, islands, and inlets.

WORD OF MOUTH

"Did we see whales or did we see whales with Captain Larry!! We saw group after group of whales. They were blowing, chasing, flipping, breaching. I was elated. I shot a roll and a half of film. The folks on my boat were great."

—OaklandTraveler

Glacier Bay National Park & Preserve

KEY

Historical extent of glaciation
1794

ALASKA

BRITISH COLUMBIA

CANADA
UNITED STATES

Muir Glacier

Riggs Glacier

Carroll Glacier

Rendu Glacier

1907

1966

1966
1892

1976
1972
1960
1948

1929

Casement Glacier

1907
1892

Russell Island

1892

1880

Queen Inlet

1966
1892

Wachusett

1929
1949

East Arm Muir Inlet

Adams Inlet

West Arm

1907

1907

1907

Reid Glacier

1892
1907
1892
1879

1892

1907
1919

1892
1907

Tidal Inlet

1892

1907

1860

1860

Glacier Bay

1857

1845

Beartrack River

Lamplugh Glacier

Brady Icefield

1966
1892

Geikie Inlet

DRAKE ISLAND

WILLOUGHBY ISLAND

Beartrack Cove

BEARDSLEE ISLANDS

Visitor Center / Glacier Bay Lodge

Wood Lake

Berg Bay

Bartlett Cove

1794

Airport

Gustavus

Brady Glacier

1794

1961

Dundas River

Bartlett Cove

1750-80

PLEASANT ISLAND

Palma Bay

Dixon Harbor

Graves Bay

Taylor Bay

Dundas Bay

North Passage

LEMESURIER ISLAND

Icy Strait

INIAN ISLANDS

South Passage

0   10 mile

0   10 kilometer

Cross Sound

CHICHAGOF ISLAND

In 1879, about a century after Vancouver's sail-by, one of the earliest white visitors to what is now Glacier Bay National Park and Preserve came calling. The ever-curious naturalist John Muir, who would become one of the region's earliest proponents, was drawn by the flora and fauna that had followed in the wake of glacial withdrawals; he was also fascinated by the vast ice rivers that descended from the mountains to tidewater. Today the naturalist's namesake glacier, like others in the park, continues to retreat dramatically: the Muir Glacier's terminus is now scores of miles farther up the bay from the small cabin he built at its face during his time there.

> **FAIRWEATHER FOLLY**
>
> It was Vancouver who named the magnificent snow-clad **Mt. Fairweather**, which towers over the head of the bay. Legend has it that Vancouver named Fairweather on one of the Southeast's most beautiful blue days—and the mountain was not seen again during the following century. Overcast, rainy weather is certainly the norm here.

Glacier Bay is a marvelous laboratory for naturalists of all persuasions. Glaciologists, of course, can have a field day. Animal lovers can hope to see the rare glacial "blue" bears of the area, a variation of the black bear, which is here along with the brown bear; whales feasting on krill; mountain goats in late spring and early summer; and seals on floating icebergs. Birders can look for the more than 200 species that have already been spotted in the park, and if you're lucky, you may witness bald eagles engaging in aerobatics.

A remarkable panorama of plants unfolds from the head of the bay, which is just emerging from the ice, to the mouth, which has been ice-free for more than 200 years. In between, the primitive plants—algae, lichens, and mosses—that are the first to take hold of the bare, wet ground give way to more-complex species: flowering plants such as the magenta dwarf fireweed and the creamy dryas, which in turn merge with willows, alders, and cottonwood. As the living plants mature and die, they enrich the soil and prepare it for new species to follow. The climax of the plant community is the lush spruce-and-hemlock rain forest, rich in life and blanketing the land around **Bartlett Cove**. ☎*907/697–2230, 907/697–2627 boating info* ⊕*www.nps.gov/glba.*

GUSTAVUS

50 mi west of Juneau, 75 mi south of Skagway.

For airborne visitors, Gustavus is the gateway to Glacier Bay National Park and Preserve. The long, paved jet airport, built as a refueling strip during World War II, is one of the best and longest in Southeast Alaska, all the more impressive because of its limited facilities at the field. Alaska Airlines, which serves Gustavus daily in summer, has a large, rustic terminal at the site. Just down the road at the Gustavus Dray, from a free phone you can call any of the local hostelries for a courtesy pickup or taxi. Smaller, light-aircraft companies that serve the community out of Juneau also have on-site shelters. A summer ferry, operated by Aramark (☎*907/264–4600 or 888/229–8687* ⊕*www. visitglacierbay.com*), runs between Juneau and Bartlett Cove.

■TIP→ Before you get too excited about visiting this remote outpost, be forewarned: Gustavus has no downtown. In fact, Gustavus is not really a town at all. Instead, it's a scattering of homes, farmsteads, a craft studio, fishing and guiding charters, an art gallery, and other tiny enterprises peopled by hospitable individualists.

OUTDOOR ACTIVITIES & GUIDED TOURS

Glacier Bay is best experienced from the water, whether from the deck of a cruise ship, on a tour boat, or from the level of a sea kayak. National Park Service naturalists often come aboard to explain the great glaciers and to help spot bears, mountain goats, whales, porpoises, and birds.

BOATING & LOCAL INTEREST **Huna Totem Corporation/Aramark** (☎*907/264–4600 or 888/229–8687* ⊕*www.visitglacierbay.com*) provides daily summertime boat tours from the dock at Bartlett Cove, near Glacier Bay Lodge. These eight-hour trips into Glacier Bay have a Park Service naturalist aboard a high-speed 155-passenger catamaran. A light lunch is included. Campers and sea kayakers heading up the bay ride the same boat.

FLIGHTSEEING **Air Excursions** (☎*907/697–2375, 800/354–2479 in Alaska* ⊕*www.air-excursions.com*) operates Glacier Bay flightseeing tours and charter flights from Gustavus, plus scheduled flights to Juneau, Haines, Skagway, and Hoonah several times a day in summer.

HIKING Glacier Bay's steep and heavily forested slopes aren't the most conducive to hiking, but there are several short hikes that begin at the Glacier Bay Lodge. Among the most popular is the **Forest Loop Trail**, a pleasant 1-mi jaunt that begins in a forest of spruce and hemlock and finishes on the beach. Also beginning at the lodge is the **Bartlett River Trail**—a 5-mi round-trip hike that borders an intertidal lagoon, culminating at the Bartlett River estuary. The **Bartlett Lake Trail**, part of a 6-mi walk that meanders through rain forest, ends at the quiet lakeshore. The entire Gustavus beachfront was set aside by the Nature Conservancy, enabling visitors to hike the shoreline for miles without getting lost. The beachfront is part of the **Alaska Coastal Wildlife Viewing Trail** (⊕*wildlife.alaska.gov*). The spring and fall bird migrations are exceptional on Gustavus estuaries, including Dude Creek Critical Habitat Area, which provides a stopover before crossing the ice fields for sandhill cranes. Maps and wildlife viewing information are available from the **Alaska Division of Wildlife Conservation** (⊕*wildlife.alaska.gov*).

SEA KAYAKING The most adventurous way to explore Glacier Bay is by paddling your own kayak through the bay's icy waters and inlets. But unless you're an expert, you're better off signing on with the guided tours. You can book a five-day guided expedition through **Alaska Discovery** (☎*510/594–6000 or 800/586–1911* ⊕*www.akdiscovery.com*). Alaska Discovery provides safe, seaworthy kayaks and tents, gear, and food. Its guides are tough, knowledgeable Alaskans, and they've spent enough time in

DID YOU KNOW?

Glacier Bay National Park, along with Wrangell-St. Elias National Park in Alaska and Kluane National Park Reserve and Tatshenshini-Alsek Provincial Park in Canada, became the largest UNESCO World Heritage Site in 1992.

QUAKE HAPPY IN GLACIER BAY

Glacier Bay's impressive landscape is the result of plate tectonics. The region sits directly above a chaotic intersection of fault lines—resulting in a 100-million-year-old crunch-fest. While this movement can be credited for creating the region's stunning topography, it has also wreaked some havoc. On September 10, 1899, the area was rocked by a massive temblor registering 8.4 on the Richter scale. The quake, which had its epicenter in Yakutat Bay, rattled Glacier Bay so much that the entire bay was choked with icebergs. And on July 9, 1958, a tremendous earthquake—a 7.9 on the Richter scale—triggered a landslide of epic proportions in nearby Lituya Bay: 40 million cubic yards of rock tumbled into the bay, and created a tidal wave that reached 1,720 feet.

Glacier Bay's wild country to know what's safe and what's not. **Spirit Walker Expeditions** (☎907/697–2266 or 800/529–2537 ⊕*www.seak-ayakalaska.com*) leads 1- to 10-day sea-kayaking trips from Gustavus to various parts of Icy Strait. Trips to Glacier Bay and other remote areas of Southeast Alaska are also offered on a limited basis.

Alaska Mountain Guides (☎907/766–3396 or 800/766–3396 ⊕*www.alaskamountainguides.com*) offers day kayaking trips for whale-watching at Point Adolphus, a premier humpback gathering spot, as well as multiday sea-kayaking expeditions next to tidewater glaciers in Glacier Bay National Park.

Kayak rentals for Glacier Bay exploring and camping can be arranged through **Glacier Bay Sea Kayaks** (✉*Bartlett Cove* ☎907/697–2257 ⊕*www.glacierbayseakayaks.com*). You will be given instructions on handling the craft plus camping and routing suggestions for unescorted trips. Guided day trips are available in Bartlett Cove.

WHERE TO STAY

$$–$$$$ ☷ **Annie Mae Lodge.** This quiet two-story lodge, one of the few Gustavus places open year-round, faces the Good River, has beautiful grounds, and is a five-minute walk from the beach. Seven quiet guest rooms have doors that open to a wraparound veranda. Lodging includes at least a continental breakfast and ground transportation, but guests can tack on a full meal plan. Kayaking, flightseeing, and Glacier Bay cruises are arranged by the owner. **Pro:** Beautiful grounds. **Con:** Property is not on the beach. ☐*Box 55, 99826* ☎907/697–2346 or 800/478–2346 ⊕*www.anniemae.com* ➷*11 rooms, 9 with bath* ⚑*In-room: no phone, no TV. In-hotel: bicycles, no elevator, laundry facilities, no-smoking rooms* ▤*AE, D, MC, V* ❑*BP, CP, FAP.*

$$$$ ☷ **Bear Track Inn.** Built of spruce logs, this inn sits on a 97-acre property facing Icy Strait. Soaring ceilings open up the lobby, where a central fireplace and moose-antler chandeliers invite relaxation. Spacious guest rooms are luxuriously furnished, and a full-service restaurant (open to the public for dinner) specializes in seafood but also serves steak, vegetarian entrées, and wild game. All meals are made from scratch, and the inn is known for its fresh dressings, rolls, bread, ice cream, sorbet, and other desserts. The Bear Track doesn't cater to the light-walleted set: room rates start at $544 per person per night; the price includes meals and air transport from Juneau. (There are better deals for multiple-night packages.) **Pro:** Delicious meals at restaurant, a favorite with locals. **Cons:** High room rate, rooms do not have phones or TVs. ⊠*255 Rink Creek Rd.* ☎*907/697–3017 or 888/697–2284* ⊕*www.beartrackinn.com* ⌐*14 rooms* △*In-room: no phone, no TV. In-hotel: restaurant, water sports, bicycles, no elevator, laundry service, concierge, public Internet, airport shuttle, no-smoking rooms* ⊟*D, MC, V* ⊗*Closed Oct.–Apr.* ⍟*FAP.*

$$–$$$$ ⚏ **Glacier Bay Lodge.** Within the national park, this lodge is constructed of massive timbers and blends well into the thick rain forest surrounding it on three sides. The modern yet rustic rooms are accessible by boardwalk, and a large porch overlooks Glacier Bay. If it swims or crawls in the sea hereabouts, you'll find it on the menu in the dining room, which is open to non–lodge guests as well. Activities include whale-watching, kayaking, naturalist-led hikes, and tours of Glacier Bay. The lodge pushes package reservations, which include all meals, transfers, and a boat tour of Glacier Bay on your first day. **Pro:** Ample hiking trails nearby. **Con:** No hair dryers in bathrooms. ⊠*199 Bartlett Cove Rd.* ☎*907/264–4600 or 888/229–8687* ⊕*www.visitglacierbay.com* ⌐*49 rooms* △*In-room: no TV. In-hotel: restaurant, bar, water sports, bicycles, airport shuttle, some pets allowed, no-smoking rooms* ⊟*AE, D, DC, MC, V* ⊗*Closed mid-Sept.–mid-May* ⍟*FAP (optional).*

$$$ ⚏ **Gustavus Inn.** Built in 1928 and established as a hotel in 1965, this
Fodor's Choice inn continues a tradition of gracious Alaska rural living. In the remod-
★ eled original homestead building, rooms are decorated in New England–farmhouse style. Outside, a large vegetable garden provides much of the dining room's food. Here you can indulge in Glacier Bay sightseeing trips, fishing expeditions, bicycle rides, and berry picking in season. The hosts heap bountiful servings of seafood on the plates of overnight guests (all meals are included in the price) and others who reserve for family-style meals in the cozy dining room in advance. The hosts plan to expand the dining room to allow for more gracious serving and to open up views of the Icy Strait and the Salmon River meadows. Dinnertime is at 6:30 sharp. **Pro:** Wonderful food in the dining room. **Con:** Only one dinner seating. ⊠*Mi 1, Gustavus Rd.* ⚏*Box 60, Gustavus, 99826* ☎*907/697–2254 or 800/649–5220* ⊕*www.gustavusinn.com* ⌐*13 rooms, 11 with bath* △*In-room: no phone, no TV, Wi-Fi. In-hotel: restaurant, water sports, bicycles, no elevator, laundry facilities, public Internet, public Wi-Fi, airport shuttle, no-smoking rooms* ⊟*AE, MC, V* ⊗*Closed mid-Sept.–mid-May* ⍟*FAP.*

4

HAINES

75 mi north of Gustavus, 80 mi northwest of Juneau.

Haines encompasses an area that has been occupied by Tlingit peoples for centuries on the collar of the Chilkat Peninsula, a narrow strip of land that divides the Chilkat and Chilkoot inlets. Missionary S. Hall Young and famed naturalist John Muir were intent on establishing a Presbyterian mission in the area, and, with the blessing of local chiefs they chose the site that later became Haines. It's hard to imagine a more beautiful setting—a heavily wooded peninsula with magnificent views of Portage Cove and the snowy Coast Range. Unlike most other towns in Southeast Alaska, Haines can be reached by the 152-mi Haines Highway, which connects at Haines Junction with the Alaska Highway. It's also accessible by the state ferry (☎ *907/465–3941 or 800/642–0066*) and by scheduled plane service from Juneau. The Haines ferry terminal is 4.5 mi northwest of downtown, and the airport is 4 mi west.

Haines is an interesting community: its history contains equal parts enterprising gold-rush boomtown and regimented military outpost. The former is evidenced by Jack Dalton, who, in the 1890s, maintained a toll route from the settlement of Haines into the Yukon, charging $1 for foot passengers and $2.50 per horse. His Dalton Trail later provided access for miners during the 1897 gold rush to the Klondike.

The town's military roots are visible at Ft. William Henry Seward, located at Portage Cove just south of town. For 17 years (1923–39) prior to World War II, the post, renamed Chilkoot Barracks in commemoration of the gold-rush route, was the only military base in the territory. The fort's buildings and grounds are now part of a National Historic Landmark.

Today, the Haines–Fort Seward community is recognized for the native dance and art center at Fort Seward; the Haines Public Library (which, in 2005, was named Best Small Library in the United States); as well as for the superb fishing, camping, and outdoor recreation to be found at Chilkoot Lake, Portage Cove, Mosquito Lake, and Chilkat State Park on the shores of Chilkat Inlet. Northwest of the city is the Alaska Chilkat Bald Eagle Preserve. Thousands of eagles come here each winter to feed on a late run of chum salmon, making it one of Alaska's premier bird-watching sites.

EXPLORING HAINES

The downtown area feels as small as a postage stamp, and the town exudes a down-home friendliness. Perhaps this is because Haines sees fewer cruise ships, or maybe it's the grand landscape and ease of access to the mountains and sea. Whatever the cause, visitors should be prepared for a relative lack of souvenir and T-shirt shops compared to other ports. Local weather is drier than in much of Southeast Alaska.

GETTING HERE & AROUND

Haines is connected to other towns in Southeast Alaska by the **Alaska Marine Highway,** and from here you can connect with smaller vessels serving Bush communities. It is also one of the few towns in Southeast Alaska that is accessible by road; be aware that the weather and wildlife in this area present hazards on the highway. Take the Alaska Highway to Haines Junction and then drive on southwest on the Haines High-

way to the Alaska Panhandle. The town is a delightful place to explore on foot. In addition to regional connections, **L.A.B. Flying Service** offers flightseeing tours of Glacier Bay. Housed a few doors up the street from the visitor center, **Mountain Flying Service** leads flightseeing trips to nearby Glacier Bay National Park. **Wings of Alaska** has scheduled service to Juneau and Skagway.

ESSENTIALS

Medical Assistance **Haines Medical Clinic** (⊠ *131 1st Ave. N, next to the Convention and Visitors Bureau* ☎ *907/766–6300*).

Tour Info **L.A.B. Flying Service** (☎ *907/766–2222* ⊕ *www.labflying.com*). **Mountain Flying Service** (☎ *907/766–3007 or 800/954–8747* ⊕ *www.flyglacierbay. com*). **Wings of Alaska** (☎ *907/789–0790* ⊕ *www.wingsofalaska.com*).

Visitor Info **Haines Convention and Visitors Bureau** (⊠ *2nd Ave. near Willard St.* ⏏ *Box 530, Haines 99827* ☎ *907/766–2234 or 800/458–3579* ⊕ *www. haines.ak.us*).

WHAT TO SEE

❻ Alaska Indian Arts. Dedicated to the revival of Tlingit art, this nonprofit organization is housed in the former fort hospital, on the south side of the parade ground. You can watch artists carving totem poles and metalsmiths working in silver. ⊠ *Fort Seward* ☎ *907/766–2160* ⊕ *www. alaskaindianarts.com* ▣ *Free* ☺ *Weekdays 9–5.*

❸ American Bald Eagle Foundation. The main focuses here are bald eagles and associated fauna of the Chilkat Preserve, explored in lectures, displays, and videos. A taxidermy-heavy diorama also shows examples of local animals. The gift shop sells natural-history items. ⊠ *Haines Hwy. at 2nd Ave., Box 49* ☎ *907/766–3094* ⊕ *www.baldeagles.org* ▣ *$3* ☺ *May–Nov., weekdays 9–6, weekends 1–4.*

❺ Ft. William H. Seward National Historic Landmark. Circle the sloping parade ground of Alaska's first U.S. army post, where stately clapboard homes stand against a mountain backdrop. The Haines Convention and Visitors Bureau provides a walking-tour brochure of the fort.

❶ Haines Convention and Visitors Bureau. At this helpful tourist office you can pick up hiking- and walking-tour brochures, learn about lodging and attractions, and check out menus from local restaurants. ⊠ *122*

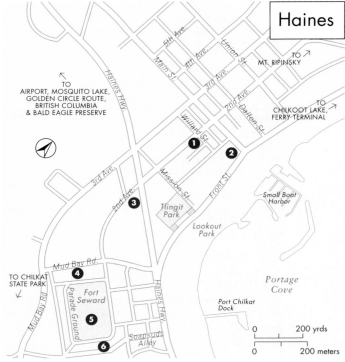

Haines

TO
AIRPORT, MOSQUITO LAKE,
GOLDEN CIRCLE ROUTE,
BRITISH COLUMBIA
& BALD EAGLE PRESERVE

TO ↗
MT. RIPINSKY

TO ↗
CHILKOOT LAKE,
FERRY TERMINAL

5th Ave.
Main St.
4th Ave.
Union St.
Haines Hwy.
3rd Ave.
2nd Ave.
Dalton St.
Willard St.
Mission St.
Front St.
3rd Ave.
2nd Ave.

❶
❷

Small Boat
Harbor

❸
Tlingit
Park

Lookout
Park

Mud Bay Rd.

TO CHILKAT
STATE PARK

❹

*Portage
Cove*

Mud Bay Rd.

Parade Ground

Fort
Seward

Haines Hwy.

❺

Port Chilkat
Dock

Soapsuds
Alley

❻

0		200 yrds
0		200 meters

2nd Ave. S, Box 530 ☏*907/766–2234 or 800/458–3579* ⊕*www.
haines.ak.us* ⊙ *Mid-May–mid-Sept., weekdays 8–5, weekends 9–4;
mid-Sept.–mid-May, weekdays 8–5.*

❹ **Hotel Halsingland.** In Fort Seward, wander past the huge, gallant, white-
columned former commanding officers' home, now a part of the hotel
on Officers' Row.

❷ **Sheldon Museum and Cultural Center.** Steve Sheldon began assembling
native artifacts, items from historic Ft. Seward, and gold-rush memorabilia, such as Jack Dalton's sawed-off shotgun, in the 1880s, and
started an exhibit of his finds in 1925. Today, the Alaska family's personal collection anchors an impressive array of artifacts, including an
18th-century carved ceremonial hat from the Murrelet Clan, Chilkat
blankets, and a model of a Tlingit tribal house. The museum also displays an impressive lens that came from Eldred Rock Lighthouse, a
sentinel located just south along Lynn Canal. ⊠ *11 Main St.* ☏*907/766–
2366* ⊕*www.sheldonmuseum.org* 🎟*$3* ⊙ *Mid-May–mid-Sept., week-
days 10–5, weekends 1–4; mid-Sept.–mid-May, weekdays 1–4.*

**OFF THE
BEATEN
PATH**

Chilkat State Park. This park on the Chilkat Inlet has beautiful and accessible viewing of both the Davidson and Rainbow glaciers along with
public campgrounds. The Seduction Point Trail, about 7 mi one-way,

A SCENIC DRIVE

The breathtaking **Haines Highway** starts at Mile 0 in Haines and continues 152 mi to Haines Junction. You don't have to drive the entire length to experience its beauty, as worthwhile stops are all along the route. At about Mile 6 a delightful picnic spot is near the Chilkat River. At Mile 9.5 the view of Cathedral Peaks, part of the Chilkat Range, is magnificent. Though at Mile 9 the Alaska Chilkat Bald Eagle Preserve begins, the best viewing is between Mile 19 and Mile 21. At Mile 33 is a roadside restaurant called, aptly, **33-Mile Roadhouse** (☎907/767–5510), where you fill your tank and coffee mug and grab a burger and home-baked goods. The United States–Canada border lies at Mile 42; stop at Canadian customs and set your clock ahead one hour.

In winter, the **Alaska Chilkat Bald Eagle Preserve** (☎907/766–2292), on Mile 19–Mile 21 of the Haines Highway, harbors the largest concentration of bald eagles in the world. Thousands come to feast on the late run of salmon in the clear, ice-free waters of the Chilkat River, heated by underground warm springs. November and December are the best months for viewing.

takes hikers to the very tip of the peninsula upon which Haines sits. ☎907/766–2292 ⊕*www.dnr.state.ak.us/parks.*

Dalton City. An 1890s gold-rush town was re-created for the movie *White Fang* and moved to the **Southeast Alaska State Fairgrounds** (☎907/766–2476), less than a mile from downtown. The movie-set buildings now house local businesses, including the **Haines Brewing Company** (☎907/766–3823). The four-day-long **Southeast Alaska State Fair,** held the last week of July, is one of several official regional blowouts, and thanks to its homespun feel, it's a must for state fair fans. In addition to the usual collection of barnyard animals, the fair has live music, rides on a vintage 1920 Herschal-Spillman carousel, local culinary arts, native dances, totemic crafts, art, and photography. ☎907/766–2476 ⊕*www.seakfair.org* ✑$7.

SPORTS, THE OUTDOORS & GUIDED TOURS

BICYCLING

Sockeye Cycle Company (✉*24 Portage St., Box 829* ☎*907/766–2869 or 877/292–4154* ⊕*www.cyclealaska.com*) specializes in guided mountain- and road-bike tours along the roads and trails of Haines, including the breathtaking 360-mi Golden Circle route that connects Haines and Skagway via the Yukon Territory. The outfit also rents, services, and sells bikes.

BOATING & FISHING

Alaska Fjordlines (☎*907/766–3395 or 800/320–0146* ⊕*www.alaskafjordlines.com*) operates a high-speed catamaran from Skagway and Haines to Juneau and back throughout the summer, stopping along the way to watch sea lions, humpbacks, and other marine mammals. **Chilkat Cruises** (☎*907/766–2100 or 888/766–2103* ⊕*www.chilkatcruises.com*)

provides a passenger catamaran ferry between Skagway and Haines, with special package rates for visitors who book a ride on Skagway's White Pass Summit Train. The service is offered up to 20 times a day in summer, and the trip takes 35 minutes each way. Chilkat also conducts guided kayak tours.

The jet-boat tours offered by **River Adventures** (☎907/766–2050 or 800/478–9827) are a great way to experience the bald eagle preserve in majestic Chilkat River valley.

For information on numerous sportfishing charter boats in Haines, contact the **Haines Convention and Visitors Bureau** (☎907/766–2234 or 800/458–3579 ⊕www.haines.ak.us).

HIKING

Battery Point Trail is a fairly level path that hugs the shoreline for 2 mi, providing fine views across Lynn Canal. The trail begins a mile east of town, and a campsite can be found at Kelgaya Point near the end. For other hikes, pick up a copy of "Haines Is for Hikers" at the Haines Convention and Visitors Bureau. **Alaska Mountain Guides** (☎907/766–3396 or 800/766–3396 ⊕www.alaskamountainguides. com), a guide service and climbing school, leads a variety of hiking and mountaineering trips from Haines, ranging from half-day trips to 90-day expeditionary courses for hiking, sea kayaking, fly-fishing, ice climbing, rock climbing, skiing, and mountaineering. Sea-kayak rentals are also available.

NATURE & SKI TOURS

FodorsChoice **Alaska Nature Tours** (☎907/766–2876 ⊕www.alaskanaturetours.net)
★ conducts bird-watching and natural-history tours through the Alaska Chilkat Bald Eagle Preserve and leads hiking treks in summer and ski tours in winter. The Chilkat Valley is a powdery heli-skiier's paradise, and **Southeast Alaska Backcountry Adventures** (☎907/767–5745 or 877/617–3418 ⊕www.skiseaba.com) lifts skiers and snowboarders by helicopter and Sno-Cat. The company also offers packages that include lodging.

WHERE TO EAT

¢–$$$ ✕**Bamboo Room.** Pop culture meets greasy spoon in this unassuming
AMERICAN coffee shop with red-vinyl booths, which has been in the same family for more than 50 years. The menu doesn't cater to light appetites—it includes sandwiches, burgers, fried chicken, chili, and halibut fish-and-chips, but the place really is at its best for an all-American breakfast (available until 3 PM). The adjacent bar has pool, darts, a big-screen TV, and a jukebox. ⊠2nd Ave. near Main St. ☎907/766–2800 ⊟AE, D, DC, MC, V.

¢–$$ ✕**Mosey's.** The fare at this Mexican restaurant just one block up from
MEXICAN the cruise-ship dock is on the spicy side—owner Martha Stewart (yes, that's her real name) travels to New Mexico each year and brings back bushels of roasted green chilies, the signature ingredient. If your taste buds can handle the kick, you'll be rewarded: the food is bursting with

fresh flavors, and the atmosphere is a cheery south-of-the-border alternative to the rest of Haines's more-mainstream offerings. Order lunch at the counter or sit down for table service in the evening. ⊠*Soap Suds Alley, Fort Seward* ☎*907/766–2320* ▤*MC, V.*

¢–$ ✕**Mountain Market.** Meet the locals over espresso and a fresh-baked
AMERICAN pastry at this busy corner natural-foods store, deli, café, wine-and-spirits shop, de facto meeting hall, and hitching post—the only thing missing is Wi-Fi connectivity. But Mountain Market is great for lunchtime sandwiches, wraps, soups, and salads. Friday is pizza day, but come early, since it's often gone by early afternoon. ⊠*3rd Ave. and Haines Hwy.* ☎*907/766–3340* ▤*AE, D, MC, V.*

WHERE TO STAY

4

$ ▦**Alaska Guardhouse.** Conveniently located near the docks, this unpre-
☺ tentious B&B in the Fort Seward area used to be the area's jail. Now it's a comfortable home with large picture windows, friendly dogs, common areas for visiting and dining, and a community room with videos, games, and an indoor hot tub. Two guest rooms on the ground floor have inlet views, and the basement apartment has a full kitchen. Airport shuttle is available on a limited basis. **Pro:** Conveniently located near the docks. **Con:** Limited amenities. ⊠*15 Seward Dr., Fort Seward* ☎*907/766–2566 or 866/290–7445* ⊕*www.alaskaguardhouse.com* ⬎*3 rooms, 2 with bath* &*In-room: no phone, kitchen (some), refrigerator (some), Wi-Fi. In-hotel: no elevator, no airport shuttle (some), public Wi-Fi, some pets allowed, no-smoking rooms* ▤*MC, V* ¶*CP.*

$ ▦**Captain's Choice Motel.** In summer, overflowing flower boxes surround this downtown Haines motel. While the accommodations are relatively plain, the staff is helpful; you can even have meals delivered to your door courtesy of the Bamboo Room restaurant. The second floor opens onto a deck with tables and chairs, and the patio down below serves as a nightly meeting place where guests can enjoy libations and conversation. Most rooms have great views; the honeymoon suite has a hot tub. **Pros:** Beautiful grounds, continental breakfast includes locally made raisin bread and muffins. **Con:** The hotel's airport shuttle is unreliable. ⊠*108 2nd Ave. N, Box 392* ☎*907/766–3111 or 800/478–2345* ⊕*www.capchoice.com* ⬎*40 rooms, 4 suites* &*In-room: refrigerator, VCR (some), Wi-Fi. In-hotel: room service, no elevator, laundry facilities, public Wi-Fi, airport shuttle, some pets allowed, no-smoking rooms* ▤*AE, D, DC, MC, V* ¶*CP.*

¢–$ ▦**Hotel Halsingland.** Ft. Seward's commanding officers once lived in the big white Victorian building that today houses this gracious hotel. On the National Register of Historic Places, the hotel has original claw-foot bathtubs and nonworking fireplaces decorated with Belgian tiles. Rooms are charming and nicely maintained, but not large. A few inexpensive ones share a hall bath. The **Commander's Room Restaurant** is one of the finest in the area, with a menu that includes locally caught halibut and salmon, steaks, and delicious desserts. Rental cars are available on-site, and a courtesy van to the ferry is available. **Pro:** Elegant, historic property. **Con:** Small showers. ⊠*Fort Seward, Box 1649* ☎*907/766–2000 or 800/542–6363* ⊕*www.hotelhalsingland.com* ⇨*58 rooms, 52 with bath* ⚙*In-room: Wi-Fi (some). In-hotel: restaurant, bar, no elevator, public Wi-Fi, airport shuttle, some pets allowed, no-smoking rooms* ⊟*AE, D, DC, MC, V* ⊘*Closed mid-Nov.–Mar.*

NIGHTLIFE & THE ARTS

THE ARTS

The **Chilkat Dancers' Storytelling Theater** (☎907/766–2540) performs at the tribal house on the fort's parade grounds in summer. This unique theatrical production includes elaborate carved masks and impressive costumes as dancers act out ancient Tlingit legends. Performances cost $12 and are held most weekdays at 4:30 PM. Call ahead for details.

The **Hammer Museum** (⊠*108 Main St.* ☎907/766–2374 ⊕*www.hammermuseum.org*) is Haines at its most peculiar; check out this one-of-a-kind shrine to hammers on Main Street. The owner started his collection decades ago and founded the Hammer Museum—the world's first—in 2001. Among his impressive collection of 1,800 hammers are a Roman battle hammer and 6-foot-long farming hammers used to secure posts into the sides of barns.

NIGHTLIFE

Locals might rule the pool tables at **Fogcutter Bar** (⊠*122 Main St.* ☎907/766–2555), but they always appreciate a little friendly competition. Like many bars in Southeast Alaska, the Fogcutter sells drink tokens that patrons often purchase for their friends; you'll notice folks sitting at the bar with a small stack of these tokens next to their beverage. The Fogcutter's embossed metal tokens are among the Southeast's most ornate. Purchase one for a keepsake—or for later use. **Haines Brewing Company** (⊠*108 Whitefang Way* ☎907/766–3823), a microbrewery among the Dalton City buildings at the fairgrounds, sells sample trays for $5. Commercial fisherfolk gather nightly at **Harbor Bar** (⊠*Front St. at the harbor* ☎907/766–2444), which dates from 1907. You might catch some live music here in summer, or take in one of their poker tournaments. Inside one of the oldest buildings in town (it was once a brothel), the **Pioneer Bar** (⊠*2nd Ave. near Main St.* ☎907/766–3443) has historical photographs on the walls, a large-screen television for sports, and occasional bands.

SHOPPING

GALLERIES & GIFTS

A surprising number of artists live in the Haines area, and you will find their works in several local galleries. Tresham Gregg's **Sea Wolf Gallery** (⊠*Fort Seward* ☎907/766–2540 ⊕*www.tresham.com*) sells wood carvings, silver jewelry, prints, and T-shirts with his native-inspired designs. Haines's most charming gallery, the **Wild Iris Gallery** (⊠*Portage St.* ☎907/766–2300) displays attractive jewelry, prints, and fashion wear created by owners Madeleine and Fred Shields. It's just up from the cruise-ship dock, and its summer gardens are to die for.

Birch Boy Products (☎ *907/767–5660 or 877/769–5660* ⊕ *www.birchboy.com*) produces tart and tasty birch syrup; it's sold in local gift shops.

SKAGWAY

14 mi northeast of Haines.

Located at the northern terminus of the Inside Passage, Skagway is only a one-hour ferry ride from Haines. By road, the distance is 359 mi, as you have to take the Haines Highway up to Haines Junction, Yukon, then take the Alaska Highway 100 mi south to Whitehorse, and then drive a final 100 mi south on the Klondike Highway to Skagway. North-country folk call this sightseeing route the Golden Horseshoe or Golden Circle tour, because it passes a lot of gold-rush country in addition to spectacular lake, forest, and mountain scenery.

However you get to Skagway, you'll find the town an amazingly preserved artifact from North America's biggest, most-storied gold rush. Most of the downtown district forms part of the Klondike Gold Rush National Historical Park, a unit of the national park system dedicated to commemorating and interpreting the frenzied stampede of 1897 that extended to Dawson City in Canada's Yukon.

EXPLORING SKAGWAY

Nearly all the historic sights are within a few blocks of the cruiseship and ferry dock, allowing visitors to meander through the town's attractions at whatever pace they choose. Whether you're disembarking from a cruise ship, a ferry, or a dusty automobile fresh from the Golden Circle, you'll quickly discover that tourism is the lifeblood of this town. Unless you're visiting in winter or hiking into the backcountry on the Chilkoot Trail, you aren't likely to find a quiet Alaska experience around Skagway.

GETTING HERE & AROUND

Skagway offers one of the few opportunities to drive in the region. Take the Alaska Highway to the Canadian Yukon's Whitehorse and then drive on Klondike Highway to the Alaska Panhandle. Southeast Alaska's only railroad, the **White Pass & Yukon Route,** operates several different tours between Skagway and Carcross, Yukon. The tracks follow the historic path over the White Pass summit—a mountain-climbing, cliff-hanging route of as far as 67.5 mi each way. Shorter trips to the summit or Fraser and back are available, and bus connections are available at Fraser to Whitehorse, Yukon. This route is far and away a tourist activity, though, and is rarely used for non-recreational transportation.

ESSENTIALS

Internet **Glacial Smoothies and Espresso** (✉ *3rd Ave. between Main and State Sts.* ☎ *907/983–3223*).

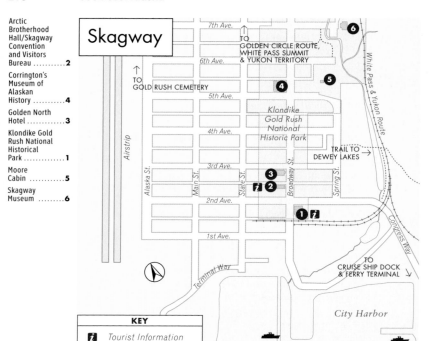

Skagway

7th Ave.

TO
GOLDEN CIRCLE ROUTE,
WHITE PASS SUMMIT
& YUKON TERRITORY

6th Ave.

TO
GOLD RUSH CEMETERY

5th Ave.

Klondike
Gold Rush
National
Historic Park

4th Ave.

3rd Ave.

2nd Ave.

1st Ave.

TRAIL TO
DEWEY LAKES →

TO
CRUISE SHIP DOCK
& FERRY TERMINAL

City Harbor

White Pass & Yukon Route

Airstrip

Alaska St.

Main St.

State St.

Broadway St.

Spring St.

Congress Way

Terminal Way

KEY

🛈 *Tourist Information*

Cruise Ship and Ferry Terminals

0   100 yds

0   100 m

Medical Assistance Skagway Dahl Memorial Clinic (✉ *310 11th Ave., at Broadway* ☎ *907/983–2255*).

Visitor and Tour Info Skagway Convention and Visitors Bureau (🖂 *Box 1029, Skagway 99840* ☎ *907/983–2854 or 888/762–1898* ⊕ *www.skagway.com*). **Klondike Gold Rush National Historical Park** (*Visitor center* ✉ *2nd Ave. and Broadway* 🖂 *Box 517, Skagway 99840* ☎ *907/983–2921* ⊕ *www.nps.gov/klgo*). **White Pass & Yukon Route** (☎ *907/983–2217 or 800/343–7373* ⊕ *www.wpyr.com*).

WHAT TO SEE

❷ **Arctic Brotherhood Hall.** The Arctic Brotherhood was a fraternal organi-
★ zation of Alaska and Yukon pioneers. Local members of the Brotherhood built the building's (now renovated) false front out of 8,833
pieces of driftwood and flotsam gathered from local beaches. The
result: one of the most unusual buildings in all of Alaska. The AB Hall
now houses the **Skagway Convention and Visitors Bureau,** along with
public restrooms. ✉ *Broadway between 2nd and 3rd Aves., Box 1029*
☎ *907/983–2854, 888/762–1898 message only* ⊕ *www.skagway.com*
🕙 *May–Sept., daily 8–6; Oct.–Apr., weekdays 8–noon and 1–5.*

❹ **Corrington's Museum of Alaskan History.** Inside a gift shop, this impressive
(and free) scrimshaw museum highlights more than 40 exquisitely
carved walrus tusks and other exhibits that detail Alaska's history. A

Continued on page 224

GOLD! GOLD! GOLD!

At the end of the 19th Century, scoundrels and starry-eyed gold seekers alike made their way from Alaska's Inside Passage to Canada's Yukon Territory, with high hopes for heavy returns.

> "There are strange things done in the midnight sun By the men who moil for gold. . . ."
>
> —*Robert Service, "The Cremation of Sam McGee"*

Miners have moiled for gold in the Yukon for many centuries, but the Klondike Gold Rush was a particularly strange and intense period of history. Within a decade, the towns of Skagway, Dyea, and Dawson City appeared out of nowhere, mushroomed to accommodate tens of thousands of people, and just about disappeared again. At the peak of the rush, Dawson City was the largest metropolis north of San Francisco. Although only a few people found enough gold even to pay for their trip, the rush left an indelible mark on the nation's imagination.

An 1898 photograph shows bearded miners using a gold pan and sluice as they search for riches.

A GREAT STAMPEDE

Historians squabble over who first saw the glint of Yukon gold. All agree that it was a member of a family including "Skookum" Jim Mason (of the Tagish tribe), Kate and George Carmack, and Dawson Charlie, who were prospecting off the Klondike River in 1896. Over the following months, word spread and claims were quickly staked. When the first boatload of gold reached Seattle in July 1897, gold fever ignited with the *Seattle Post-Intelligencer's* headline: "GOLD! GOLD! GOLD! Sixty-Eight Rich Men On the Steamer Portland." Within six months, 100,000 people had arrived in Southeast Alaska, intent upon making their way to the untold riches.

Skagway had only a single cabin standing when the gold rush began. Three months after the first boat landed, 20,000 people swarmed its raucous hotels, saloons, gambling houses, and dance halls. By spring 1898, the town was labeled "little better than a hell on earth." When gold was discovered in Nome the next year and in Fairbanks in the early 1900s, Skagway's population dwindled to 700 souls.

(above) Rush hour on Broadway, Skagway, 1898.

A GRITTY REALITY

To reach the mining hub of Dawson City, prospectors had to choose between two risky routes from the Inside Passage. From Dyea, the Chilkoot Trail was steep and bitterly cold. The longer, bandit-ridden White Pass Trail from Skagway killed so many pack animals that it earned the nickname Dead Horse Trail. After the mountains, there were still over 500 mi to travel. For those who arrived, dreams were quickly washed away, as most promising claims had already been staked by the Klondike Kings. Many ended up working as labor. The disappointment was unbearable.

KLONDIKE KATE

The gold rush was profitable for clever entrepreneurs. Stragglers, outfitters, and outlaws took advantage of every opportunity to make a buck. Klondike Kate, a brothel keeper and dance-hall gal, had an elaborate song-and-dance routine that involved 200 yards of bright red chiffon.

TWO ENEMIES DIE IN A SKAGWAY SHOWDOWN

CON ARTIST "SOAPY" SMITH

Claim to Fame: Skagway's best-known gold-rush criminal, Soapy was the de facto leader of the town's loosely organized network of criminals and spies.

Cold-Hearted Snake: Euphemistically referred to as "colorful," he ruthlessly capitalized on the naïveté of prospectors.

Famous Scheme: Soapy charged homesick miners $5 to wire a message home in his counterfeit Telegraph Office (the wires ended in a tangled pile behind a shed).

Shot Through the Heart: In 1898, just days after he served as grand marshal of Skagway's 4th of July parade, Soapy barged in on a meeting set up by his rival, Frank Reid. There was a scuffle, and they shot each other.

Famous Last Words: When he saw Reid draw his gun, Soapy shouted, "My God, don't shoot!"

R.I.P.: Soapy's tombstone was continually stolen by vandals and souvenir seekers; today's grave marker is a simple wooden plank in Skagway's Gold Rush Cemetery.

GOOD GUY FRANK REID

Claim to Fame: Skagway surveyor and all-around good fellow, Frank Reid was known for defending the town against bad guys.

The Grid Man: A civil engineer, Reid helped to make Skagway's streets wide and gridlike.

Thorn in My Side: Reid set up a secret vigilante meeting to discuss one very thorny topic: Soapy Smith.

In Skagway's Honor: Reid killed Soapy during the shootout on the city docks, breaking up Soapy's gang and freeing the town from its grip.

Dyin' Tryin': Reid's heroics cost him his life—he died some days later from the injuries he sustained.

R.I.P.: The town built a substantial monument in Reid's memory in the Gold Rush Cemetery, which you can visit to this day; the inscription reads: HE GAVE HIS LIFE FOR THE HONOR OF SKAGWAY.

(above) Soapy Smith (front), so named for his first con, which involved selling "lucky soap," stands with five friends at his infamous saloon.

FOLLOWING THE GOLD TRAIL TODAY

KEY

↘ 2.2 mi Cumulative distance in miles from Dyea

Bennett ↑ TO WHITEHORSE, YUKON
33.0 mi
Log Cabin
Lindeman City ● **Warden Station**
26.0 mi
BRITISH COLUMBIA
20.5 mi ○ Happy Camp ○ Fraser
16.5 mi ● **Chilkoot Pass**
CANADA US
Station
The Scales ○
16.0 mi
Ranger Station ● Sheep Camp
11.75 mi ○
White Pass
10.5 mi ○ Pleasant Camp
White Pass City
7.8 mi ○ Canyon City
4.8 mi ○ Finnigans Point
ALASKA
White Pass & Yukon RR
Klondike Hwy
White Pass Trail
Chilkoot Trail
98
Ranger Station ● 0.0 mi
Dyea ○
Dyea Rd.
0 ___ 4 mi
0 ___ 4 km
Skagway | Taiya Inlet

Alaska Hwy. 1
Haines Junction 1 ✦ Whitehorse
1
Carcross
Yukon
British Columbia 2
CANADA US
3 **GOLDEN CIRCLE** Klondike Hwy.
Alaska Hwy. Haines Hwy. Fraser 98
7 Skagway
Haines

Golden Circle Route

THE HISTORIC CHILKOOT TRAIL

If you're an experienced backpacker, consider hiking the highly scenic Chilkoot Trail, the 33-mi route of the 1897–98 prospectors from Skagway into Canada. Most hikers will need four to five days. The trail is generally in good condition, with primitive campsites strategically located along the way. Expect steep slopes and wet weather, along with exhilarating vistas at the summit. Deep snow often covers the pass until late summer. The trail stretches from Dyea (just outside of Skagway) to Lake Bennett. The National Park Service maintains the American side of the pass as part of **Klondike Gold Rush National Historical Park;** the Canadian side is part of the **Chilkoot Trail National Historic Park.** A backcountry permit is required.

■TIP→To return to Skagway, hikers usually catch the White Pass & Yukon Route train from Lake Bennett. The fare is $165 to Skagway; the train runs Sunday through Friday and Monday in the summer, departing at 2 PM.

For more details, including backcountry permits (C$55), contact the summer-only **Chilkoot Trail Center** ☎ 907/983–9234 ⊕ www.nps.gov/klgo. Or you can call Parks Canada ☎ 800/661–0486 ⊕ www.pc.gc.ca/chilkoot.

GOLDEN DRIVES

The Golden Circle Route starts in Skagway on the Klondike Highway, then travels to Whitehorse. The route continues to Haines Junction, and then south to Haines. On the much longer Klondike Loop, you'll hop on the Klondike Highway, following the White Pass railway as it travels toward Whitehorse. The highway meets the Alaska Highway, ending at Dawson City on the banks of the Klondike River. From start to finish, it covers 435 mi. If you're taking the Klondike Highway north from Skagway,

4

(top left) Trekking the Chilkoot Trail (right) White Pass & Yukon Route (bottom left) A bridge on Chilkoot Trail

you must stop at Canadian customs, Mile 22. If you're traveling south to Skagway, check in at U.S. Customs, Mile 6.

WHITE PASS & YUKON ROUTE

You can travel the gold-rush route aboard the historic White Pass & Yukon Route (WP & YR) narrow-gauge railroad. The diesel locomotives tow vintage-style viewing cars up steep inclines, hugging the walls of precipitous cliffs with views of craggy peaks, forests, and plummeting waterfalls. It's open mid-May to late September only, and reservations are highly recommended.

■TIP→ Most of the commentary is during the first half of the trip and relates to sights out of the left side of the train, so sit on this side. A "seat exchange" at the summit allows all guests a canyonside view.

Several options are available, including a fully narrated 3-hour round-trip excursion to White Pass summit (fare: $103). Sights along the way include Bridal Veil Falls, Inspiration Point, and Dead Horse Gulch. Through service to Whitehorse, Yukon (4 hours), is offered daily as well—in the form of a train trip to Fraser, where bus connections are possible on to Whitehorse (entire one-way fare to Whitehorse: $110). Also offered are the Chilkoot Trail hikers' service and a 4-hour roundtrip to Fraser Meadows on Saturday and Sunday (fare: $125).

Call ahead or check online for details and schedules. ☎ 907/983–2217 or 800/343–7373 ⊕ www.wpyr.com.

bright flower garden decorates the exterior. ✉ *5th Ave. and Broadway* ☎ *907/983–2579* 🌐 *Free* ⊙ *Open when cruise ships are in port.*

❸ **Golden North Hotel.** Built during the 1898 gold rush, the Golden North Hotel was—until closing in 2002—Alaska's oldest hotel. Despite the closure, the building has been lovingly maintained, and still retains its gold rush–era appearance; a golden dome tops the corner cupola. Today the downstairs houses shops. ✉ *3rd Ave. and Broadway.*

❶ **Klondike Gold Rush National Historical** ★ **Park.** Housed in the former White Pass & Yukon Route Depot, this wonderful museum contains exhibits, photos, and artifacts from the

White Pass and Chilkoot trails. It's a must-see for anyone planning on taking a White Pass train ride, driving the nearby Klondike Highway, or hiking the Chilkoot Trail. Films, ranger talks, and walking tours are offered. Special free Robert Service poetry performances by Buckwheat Donahue—a beloved local character and head of the Skagway Convention and Visitors Bureau—occasionally take place at the visitor center. ✉ *2nd Ave. at Broadway* ☎ *907/983–2921 or 907/983–9224* 🌐 *www.nps.gov/klgo* 🌐 *Free* ⊙ *May–Sept., daily 8–6; Oct.–Apr., weekdays 8–5.*

❺ **Moore Cabin.** Built in 1887 by Captain William Moore and his son Ben Moore, the tiny cabin was the first structure built in Skagway. An early homesteader, Captain Moore prospered from the flood of miners, constructing a dock, warehouse, and sawmill to supply them, and selling land for other ventures. Next door, the larger **Moore House** (1897–98) contains interesting exhibits on the Moore family. Both structures are maintained by the Park Service, and the main house is open daily in summer. ✉ *5th Ave. between Broadway and Spring St.* ☎ *907/983–2921* ⊙ *Memorial Day–Labor Day, daily 10–5.*

❻ **Skagway Museum.** This nicely designed museum occupies the ground floor of the beautiful building that also houses Skagway City Hall. Inside, you'll find a 19th-century Tlingit canoe (one of only two like it on the West Coast), historic photos, a red-and-black sleigh, and other gold rush–era artifacts, along with a healthy collection of contemporary local art and post–gold rush history exhibits. ✉ *7th Ave. and Spring St.* ☎ *907/983–2420* 🌐 *$2* ⊙ *Mid-May–Sept., weekdays 9–5, weekends 10–4; Oct.–mid-May, hrs vary.*

OUTDOOR ACTIVITIES & GUIDED TOURS

BIKING

Sockeye Cycle Company (☎907/983–2851 ⊕*www.cyclealaska.com*), based in Haines, and, in summertime, in Skagway, specializes in guided bike tours in the area, including a train/bike ride combo. Sockeye also rents bikes for independent explorers.

BOATING

Alaska Fjordlines (☎907/766–3395 or 800/320–0146 ⊕*www.alaskaf-jordlines.com*) operates a popular day tour from Skagway and Haines to Juneau and back. Passengers board a high-speed catamaran at 8 AM and stop along the way to watch sea lions and other marine mammals. The boat gets to Juneau at 11:45 AM, where a bus transports visitors into town and to Mendenhall Glacier, returning to the boat at 4:45 PM for the ride back to Skagway, where the boat returns at 8:15 PM. **Chilkat Cruises** (☎907/766–2100 or 888/766–2103 ⊕*www.chilkatcruises. com*) provides a fast passenger catamaran ferry between Skagway and Haines, with service up to 20 times a day in summer.

LOCAL INTEREST BY BUS

Skagway Street Car Company (☎907/983–2908 ⊕*www.skagwaystreet-car.com*) revisits the gold-rush days in lovingly renovated, bright-yellow 1920s sightseeing buses. Costumed conductors lead these popular two-hour tours, but advance reservations are recommended for independent travelers, since most seats are sold aboard cruise ships. Call a week ahead in peak season to reserve a space.

OUTDOOR ADVENTURE

Alaska Excursions (☎907/983–4444 ⊕*www.alaskaexcursions.com*) leads wheeled (no snow) sled-dog tours, horseback-riding tours, and golfing day trips. Booking independently with this service can be difficult, as cruise ship groups reserve the bulk of available slots. **Packer Expeditions** (☎907/983–2544 ⊕*www.packerexpeditions.com*) guides several day trips that include a helicopter flight from Skagway, a 5-mi hike to Laughton Glacier, and a train ride back to town. **Temsco Helicopters** (☎907/789–9501 or 877/789–9501 ⊕*www.temscoair.com*) will fly you to Denver Glacier for an hour of learning about mushing and riding on a dogsled.

WHERE TO EAT

¢ CAFÉ ✕ **Glacial Smoothies and Espresso.** This local hangout is the place to go for a breakfast bagel or a lunchtime soup-and-sandwich combo. Prices are steeper than at some coffee shops—a 12-ounce mocha goes for $4—but the ingredients are fresh and local, and nearly everything on the menu is made on-site. Customers can cool down with a Mango Madness or Blueberry Blues smoothie, and soft-serve ice cream in summer. ✉*3rd Ave. between Main and State Sts.* ☎907/983–3223 ▭MC, V ⊘*No dinner.*

¢–$$$ PIZZA ✕ **Skagway Pizza Station.** Housed in a former gas station, this year-round restaurant is known for its comfort-food specials, such as meat loaf or stuffed pork chops with mashed potatoes and gravy. (Friday is prime-rib day.) The huge calzones are stuffed and served piping hot with sides of house marinara and ranch dressing—build your own or choose one of the chef's creations, like the Chicken Hawk Squawk with pineapple and jalapeños. Or do like the Skagwegians do and wash down one of the 14-inch pizzas with a pint or two of Alaskan Summer Ale. For dog-tired travelers who can't walk another block, the Pizza Station delivers for free. ⊠ *4th Ave. between Main and State Sts.* ☎ *907/983–2200* ▤ *MC, V.*

$–$$$
CAFÉ
× **Stowaway Cafe.** Always crowded, this noisy little harborside café is just a few steps from the cruise-ship dock. Seafood is the attraction—including wasabi salmon and glacé de poisson—but you can also eat steaks, chicken, or smoked ribs. The café is open daily for dinner only. ⊠ *205 Congress Way* ☎ *907/983–3463* ▤ *AE, MC, V* ⊗ *Closed Oct.–Apr. No lunch.*

> **OUT & ABOUT**
>
> If you are up for a long walk, head 2 mi out of town along Alaska Street to the **Gold Rush Cemetery**, where you'll find the graves of combatants Soapy Smith and Frank Reid. The cemetery is also the trailhead for the short walk to Lower Reid Falls, an enjoyable jaunt through the valley's lush forest. (A city bus takes you most of the way to the cemetery for $2 each direction.) No tour of Skagway is complete without a train ride on the famed **White Pass & Yukon Route**. Trains depart from the corner of 2nd Street and Broadway several times a day in summer.

WHERE TO STAY

$–$$
⊞ **Mile Zero Bed & Breakfast.** In a quiet residential area a few blocks from downtown, this comfortable B&B has spacious and well-insulated guest rooms, all with private entrances, phones, and baths. Most have two queen beds, and one room is entirely handicap-accessible. The owner, Tara Mallory, is a born-and-raised Alaskan who knows the Skagway area inside out. Local travel tips and hilarious anecdotes are commonplace in the communal dining and living rooms. A buffet-style breakfast is served each morning. **Pro:** All rooms now have televisions. **Con:** Limited hotel amenities. ⊠ *9th Ave. and Main St.* ☎ *907/983–3045* ⊕ *www.mile-zero.com* ⇆ *6 rooms* & *In-room: refrigerator, DVD (some), VCR (some), Wi-Fi. In-hotel: public Internet, public Wi-Fi, no-smoking rooms* ▤ *MC, V* ⦿ *CP.*

$
⊞ **Sgt. Preston's Lodge.** This four-building lodge—which feels more like a motel—occupies a former army barracks. Some rooms are spacious and revamped, while others feel dated and cramped, with very small sinks in the bathrooms. The property offers one of the few handicapped-accessible rooms in Skagway. All are priced accordingly, and the lodge's downtown location and proximity to the cruise ship and ferry docks (a short walk to each) make it a good choice for budget-conscious travelers. The owners plan to renovate the building's exterior in 2009. **Pros:** Convenient to the cruise ship and ferry docks, has a handicapped-accessible room. **Con:** Small sinks in the bathrooms.

✉*370 6th Ave., Box 538* ☎*907/983–2521 or 866/983–2521* ⊕*sgt-prestonslodge.com* ⇘*40 rooms* ⌂*In-room: refrigerator (some), DVD (some), Wi-Fi. In-hotel: public Internet, public Wi-Fi, airport shuttle, some pets allowed, no-smoking rooms* ☰*AE, D, MC, V* ♟|*EP.*

$–$$$ 🏨 **Skagway Inn Bed & Breakfast.** Each room in this family-friendly downtown Victorian inn (once a not-so-family-friendly bordello) is named after a different gold-rush gal. The creaky building, one of Skagway's oldest, was built in 1897 and has been lovingly restored. The small rooms have no televisions and share a Victorian motif, with period antiques and cast-iron beds. A big homemade breakfast is served downstairs each morning from 7 to 8 AM in Olivia's Restaurant, and the restaurant is open for lunch and dinner to anyone in the mood for "Alaskan tapas." Outdoor seating is next to the gardens. Chilkoot Trail hikers who spend two nights at the hotel get free transport to the trailhead, Coleman stove fuel, and storage of their gear while hiking. **Pro:** Large breakfast served. **Cons:** Floors are creaky, walls are thin. ✉*655 Broadway, Box 500* ☎*907/983–2289 or 888/752–4929* ⊕*www.skagwayinn.com* ⇘*10 rooms, 4 with bath* ⌂*In-room: no TV, Wi-Fi. In-hotel: restaurant, no elevator, public Wi-Fi, public Internet, airport shuttle, no-smoking rooms* ☰*AE, D, MC, V* ✸*Closed Oct.–Apr.* ♟|*BP.*

$–$$ 🏨 **White House.** This B&B is about two blocks from downtown Skagway. Built in 1902 by Lee Guthrie, a gambler and owner of one of the town's most profitable gold-rush saloons, the white-clapboard two-story house is furnished with original Skagway antiques and hand-crafted quilts. Light breakfasts are served, and children are welcome. **Pro:** Conveniently located. **Con:** No pets allowed. ✉*8th Ave. and Main St., Box 41* ☎*907/983–9000* ⊕*www.atthewhitehouse.com* ⇘*10 rooms* ⌂*In-room: refrigerator, Wi-Fi. In-hotel: no elevator, laundry facilities, public Wi-Fi, no-smoking rooms* ☰*AE, D, MC, V* ♟|*CP.*

NIGHTLIFE & THE ARTS

BARS

Whereas Skagway was once host to dozens upon dozens of watering holes in its gold-rush days, the **Red Onion Saloon** (✉*Broadway at 2nd Ave.* ☎*907/983–2222* ⊕*www.redonion1898.com*) is pretty much the sole survivor among them. The upstairs was Skagway's first bordello, and you'll find a convivial crowd of Skagway locals and visitors among the scantily clad mannequins who represent the building's former illustrious tenants. A ragtime pianist tickles the keys in the afternoons, and local musicians strut their stuff on Thursday nights. The saloon closes up shop for winter.

THEATER

★ Since 1927 locals have performed a show called *The Days of '98 with Soapy Smith* at Eagles Hall. You'll see cancan dancers (including Molly Fewclothes, Belle Davenport, and Squirrel Tooth Alice), learn a little local history, and watch desperado Soapy Smith being sent to his reward. At the evening show, you can enjoy a few warm-up rounds of mock gambling with Soapy's money. Performances of Robert Service poetry start a half hour before showtime. ⊠ *Broadway and 6th Ave.* ☎ *907/983–2545 May–mid-Sept., 808/328–9132 mid-Sept.–Apr.* 💳 *$16* ⊙ *Mid-May–mid-Sept., daily at 10:30, 2:30, and 8.*

SHOPPING

Corrington's Alaskan Ivory (⊠ *525 Broadway* ☎ *907/983–2579*) is the destination of choice for scrimshaw seekers; it has one the state's best collection of ivory art. For those in search of locally produced silver jewelry, watercolor prints, and other handmade crafts, the artist-owned **Skagway Artworks** (⊠ *555C Broadway* ☎ *907/983–3443* ⊕ *www.skag-wayartworks.com*) can't be beat. **Skaguay News Depot & Books** (⊠ *264 Broadway* ☎ *907/983–3354*), its moniker a throwback to the town's old spelling, is a small but quaint bookstore that carries books on Alaska, magazines, children's books, maps, and gifts.

Anchorage

WORD OF MOUTH

"I had a weekend in Anchorage following a business trip and I rented a bike . . . the Tony Knowles Coastal Trail . . . was fabulous. Denali (Mt. McKinley) was visible, and I saw several moose along the ride. I followed up with a drink/meal at the Glacier BrewHouse."

—lindsyb

WELCOME TO ANCHORAGE

TOP REASONS TO GO

★ **Tackling a 50-pound salmon:** Anglers can cast for huge king salmon or feisty silvers while wading among reflections of skyscrapers. The spot is Ship Creek; derbies here offer cash prizes to anglers who haul in the biggest fish.

★ **Winter celebrations:** In late February, locals put on their best parkas and step outside to celebrate Fur Rendezvous, Alaska's answer to Mardi Gras. Events up to the start of the Iditarod Trail Sled Dog Race in early March.

★ **Shopping:** Shops sell gold pans, mini totem poles, and native Alaskan handicrafts. Check for the Silver Hand emblem for native-made items.

★ **Seafood:** Dining out in Anchorage is a delight. Many restaurants offer dishes featuring local halibut, salmon, king-crab legs, scallops, and oysters.

★ **Hiking and biking:** Laced with rugged paths and paved trails, Anchorage is a paradise for hikers and bicyclists.

1 **Downtown.** The city's cultural center has a festive atmosphere on summer afternoons with flowers hung from street lamps and the smell of grilled onions and hot dogs in the air along 4th Avenue. The streets are lined with art galleries and shops; the weekend markets promise good hunting for shoppers seeking souvenirs.

Downtown Anchorage

2 **Midtown.** Some 3 mi east of the airport, midtown is a newer neighborhood with an assortment of restaurants, shopping centers, and large hotels. The city's main library branch and a major movie theater complex are located a short walk from most hotels.

3 Tony Knowles Coastal Trail & Kincaid Park. An 11-mi ribbon of asphalt beginning downtown and stretching to Kincaid Park, the popular Tony Knowles Coastal Trail traverses tidal marshes, moose-inhabited greenbelts, and bluffs overlooking the inlet, Mt. Susitna, and the distant Alaska Range. Kincaid Park offers 40 mi of trails for biking, hiking, and cross-country skiing.

Anchorage Museum of History & Art

GETTING ORIENTED

Founded in 1915 as a railroad camp, Anchorage has grown into Alaska's largest city and main travel hub. It's connected to the state's road network by the Seward and Glenn highways and remains the headquarters for the Alaska Railroad, which runs from Seward to Fairbanks. The city is bordered to the east by the Chugach foothills, to the west by Cook Inlet, to the south by Potter Marsh, and to the north by military bases. Sled-dog races are still revered; moose and occasionally bears roam city bike trails, and spectacular wilderness is a short drive away.

5

A native dancer in traditional moccasins

ANCHORAGE PLANNER

How's the Weather?

Located between the coast and several mountain ranges, Anchorage is a meteorologist's nightmare. Fickle weather patterns change less by the day than by the hour. Generally, fair-weather visitors should plan trips between the last week of May and mid-August.

Of the snow-free months, May is typically driest, August and September the wettest. July is the warmest month, with an average temperature of 58.4°F, and May the coolest at 46.6°F. But don't be fooled by statistics. Late-May temperatures can exceed 70°F, and "hot" July and August days sometimes break 80°F. Of course, rainy low-pressure systems from the Gulf of Alaska can skulk in at any time, bringing wet and cool weather.

So how to plan for such vagaries? Do as the locals do: come prepared to go with the flow. That means packing umbrellas and light rain jackets as well as tank tops and sunblock, and allowing for some flexibility with your planning.

Getting Here

By Air: Ted Stevens Anchorage International Airport (☎ 907/266-2529 ⊕ www.anchorageairport.com) is 6 mi from downtown Anchorage on International Airport Road. Several carriers, including ERA, Frontier Flying Service, and PenAir, connect Anchorage with smaller Alaskan communities. Floatplane operators and helicopters serve the area from Lake Hood, which is adjacent to and part of Anchorage International Airport. A number of smaller air taxis and air-charter operations are at Merrill Field, 2 mi east of downtown on 5th Avenue.

Taxis queue up at the lower level of the airport terminals outside the baggage-claim areas. They are on a meter system, and it costs about $20, not including tip, for a ride downtown. An Alaska Railroad station in the airport has direct service to downtown. Most of the larger hotels provide free airport shuttle services.

By Sea: Cruise ships sailing the Gulf of Alaska and the Alaska Marine ferries call in Seward, two hours by train or bus south of Anchorage. The **Alaska Railroad** (☎ 907/265-2494 or 800/544-0552 ☎ 907/265-2323 ⊕ www.akrr.com) runs between Anchorage and Seward, daily, mid-May through September, and also to Fairbanks via Denali National Park and Preserve during the same period. Year-round passenger service is available from Anchorage north to Talkeetna. Call for schedule and fare information.

Getting Around

The Glenn Highway enters Anchorage from the north and becomes 5th Avenue near Merrill Field; this route will lead you directly into downtown. Gambell Street leads out of town to the south, becoming New Seward Highway at about 20th Avenue. South of town, it becomes the Seward Highway. If you bring your RV or rent one on arrival, know that parking an RV downtown on weekdays is challenging. There's a big parking lot on 3rd Avenue between C and E streets. Parking is usually not a problem in other parts of town.

Tours

Tour Anchorage and the surrounding mountains and glaciers of South Central Alaska by land or by air with one of the many sightseeing companies in the region. The Log Cabin and Visitor Information Centers have brochures for Anchorage bus tours, and for a one-hour overview, hop on a trolley with **Anchorage City Trolley Tours** (☎ 907/276–5603). **Gray Line of Alaska** (☎ 907/277–5581 or 800/312–5581 ⊕ www.graylineofalaska.com) has a city tour ($48) that lasts three hours.

Any air-taxi company can arrange for a flightseeing trip over Anchorage and environs. The fee is determined by the length of time you are airborne and the size of the plane. Tours of about an hour and a half generally cost around $200 per person. Three-hour flights over Mt. McKinley from **Regal Air** (☎ 907/243–8535 ⊕ www.regal-air.com), including a landing on a remote backcountry lake, run about $330 per person.

About the Hotels & Restaurants

Anchorage's ethnic diversity lends vibrant flavor to the restaurant scene. Smoking is not allowed in Anchorage restaurants.

For a listing of hotels, contact the Anchorage Convention & Visitors Bureau. Reservations are a must for the major hotels.

Anchorage B&Bs lists a range of accommodations on its Web site. For campgrounds, contact the Alaska Public Lands Information Center.

Girdwood, 40 mi south of downtown, has ski-resort amenities amid mountains.

WHAT IT COSTS

¢	$	$$	$$$	$$$$
RESTAURANTS				
under $10	$10–$15	$15–$20	$20–$25	over $25
HOTELS				
under $100	$100–$150	$150–$200	$200–$250	over $250

Restaurant prices are per person for a main course at dinner. Hotel prices are for two people in a standard double room in high season.

Emergency Contacts

Police, fire, and ambulance (☎ 911). **Alaska Regional Hospital** (✉ 2801 DeBarr Rd., East Anchorage ☎ 907/276–1131 ⊕ www.alaskaregional. com). **Physician-referral service** (☎ 888/254–7884 Alaska Regional Hospital, 907/261–2945 Providence Alaska Medical Center). **Providence Alaska Medical Center** (✉ 3200 Providence Dr., East Anchorage ☎ 907/562–2211 ⊕ www. providence.org/alaska).

Visitor Information

Anchorage Convention and Visitors Bureau (ACVB ✉ 524 W. 4th Ave., Downtown ☎ 907/276–4118, 800/478–1255 to order visitor guides ᕹ 907/278–5559 ⊕ www. anchorage.net). **Log Cabin and Visitor Information Centers** (✉ 4th Ave. and F St., Downtown ☎ 907/274–3531 ⊕ www.anchorage.net).

5

Updated by
Tom Reale

By far Alaska's largest and most sophisticated city, Anchorage is backed by the Chugach Range to the east, and bordered by the tides of Cook Inlet and Turnagain Arm to the west and south. Anchorage is Alaska's medical, financial, and banking center, and home to the executive offices of most of the native corporations. The city has a population of roughly 283,000, approximately 40%, of the people in the state.

The relative affluence of this white-collar city—with a sprinkling of olive drab from nearby military bases—fosters fine restaurants and pricey shops, first-rate entertainment, and sporting events. Incorporated in 1920, Anchorage is a young city. Nearly everything has been built since the 1970s—an Anchorage home dating from the 1950s almost merits historic status. The city got its start with the construction of the federally built Alaska Railroad, completed in 1917, and traces of its railroad heritage remain today.

Boom and bust periods followed major events: an influx of military bases during World War II; a massive buildup of Arctic missile-warning stations during the Cold War; reconstruction following the devastating Good Friday earthquake of 1964; and in the late 1960s the biggest jackpot of all—the discovery of oil at Prudhoe Bay and the construction of the trans-Alaska pipeline. Not surprisingly, Anchorage positioned itself as the perfect home for the trans-Alaska pipeline administrators and support industries, and it continues to attract a large share of the state's oil-tax dollars.

EXPLORING ANCHORAGE

Anchorage is a pedestrian- and bike-friendly city. Downtown Anchorage's flower-lined streets are easily explored on foot, and several businesses rent bicycles. The grid plan was laid out by the Army Corps of Engineers, and streets and avenues run exactly east–west and north–south, with numbers in the first direction and letters of the alphabet or

Alaska place-names (Barrow, Cordova, Denali, etc.) in the other. The only aberration is the absence of a J Street—a concession, some say, to the city's early Swedish settlers, who had difficulty pronouncing the letter. You'll need a car for longer stays and for expeditions.

Outside downtown, Anchorage is composed of widely scattered neighborhoods and large shopping malls clustered along busy thoroughfares. And while there's no shortage of excellent restaurants downtown, many of the town's best places are found in cheesy strip malls. Also, you're never more than a block or two from a good espresso stand or cart.

The municipal **People Mover** (☎907/343–6543 ⊕www.peoplemover. org) bus system covers the whole Anchorage Bowl. A one-way fare is $1.75 for rides outside the downtown area; rides within downtown are free. ■TIP→Get schedules and information from the central bus depot at 6th Avenue and G Street.

If you need a taxi, call one of the cab companies; it's not common to hail one. Prices are $2 to $3 for pick-up, plus an additional $2.50 for each mile. Allow 20 minutes for arrival of the cab during morning and evening rush hours. **Alaska Cab** (☎907/563–5353) has taxis with wheelchair lifts. In the snow-free months a network of paved trails provides good avenues for in-city travel for bicyclists and walkers.

You'll find plenty to do year-round in Anchorage, though most visitors, particularly first-timers, might be happiest in June, July, or August, when the days are longer—up to 19 hours, 21 minutes during the summer solstice—and the temperatures warmer. If you must choose one of the shoulder seasons, choose fall. There's less chance of rain; the snow has not yet arrived on trails, except in the highest mountain passes; and there's an excellent chance for warm, sunny days, cool nights, and dazzling color changes in the trees and tundra.

DOWNTOWN ANCHORAGE

WHAT TO SEE

⓾ Alaska Center for the Performing Arts. The distinctive stone-and-glass building overlooks an expansive park filled with brilliant flowers all summer. Look inside for upcoming events, or relax amid the blossoms on a sunny afternoon. ⊠621 W. 6th Ave., at G St., Downtown ☎907/ 263–2900, 800/478–7328 tickets ⊕www.alaskapac.org ☜Tours free ⊙Daily 8–5; tours Wed. at 1.

➏ Alaska Public Lands Information Center. Stop here for information on all of ★ Alaska's public lands, including national and state parks, national for-
☯ ests, and wildlife refuges. You can make reservations for a state ferry; plan a hiking, sea-kayaking, bear-viewing, or fishing trip; find out about public-use cabins; learn about Alaska's plants and animals; or head to the theater for films highlighting different parts of the state. The bookstore sells maps and nature books. Guided walks to historic downtown sights depart daily. ⊠605 W. 4th Ave., No. 105, at F St., Downtown ☎907/271–2737 ☎907/271–2744 ⊕www.nps.gov/aplic

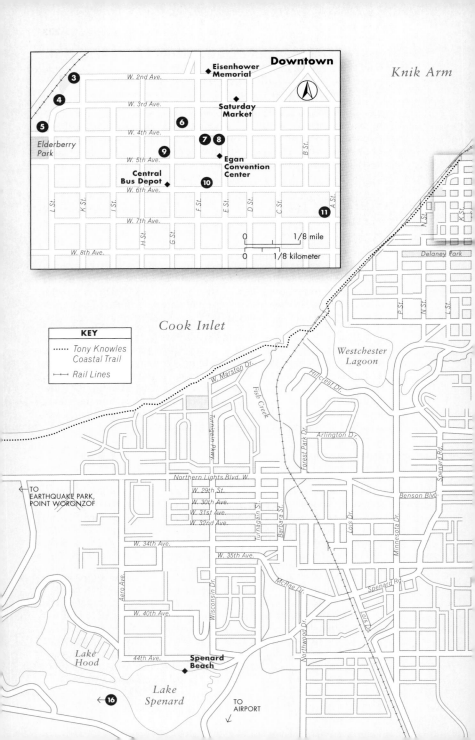

Downtown

Knik Arm

W. 2nd Ave.

Eisenhower Memorial

❸

❹

W. 3rd Ave.

Saturday Market

❺

W. 4th Ave.

❻

Elderberry Park

❼ ❽

W. 5th Ave.

❾

Egan Convention Center

Central Bus Depot

❿

W. 6th Ave.

L St.

K St.

I St.

H St.

G St.

F St.

E St.

D St.

C St.

B St.

A St.

⓫

W. 7th Ave.

0   1/8 mile

W. 8th Ave.

0   1/8 kilometer

Delaney Park

Cook Inlet

KEY

······ Tony Knowles Coastal Trail

⊢—⊣ Rail Lines

Westchester Lagoon

W. Marston Dr.

Fish Creek

Hillcrest Dr.

Forest Park Dr.

Turnagain Pkwy.

Arlington Dr.

Spenard Rd.

P St.

N St.

L St.

Northern Lights Blvd. W.

W. 29th St.

W. 30th Ave.

W. 31st Ave.

W. 32nd Ave.

Turnagain St.

Barbara St.

Lois Dr.

Benson Blvd.

Minnesota Dr.

→ TO
EARTHQUAKE PARK,
POINT WORONZOF

W. 34th Ave.

W. 35th Ave.

Aero Ave.

Wisconsin Dr.

McRae Dr.

Lois Dr.

Spenard Rd.

I St.

W. 40th Ave.

Lake Hood

44th Ave.

Spenard Beach

Northwood Dr.

← ⓰

Lake Spenard

TO
AIRPORT
↓

Anchorage

5

A GOOD WALK

A pleasant two- or three-hour walk starts at 4th Avenue and F Street at the **Log Cabin and Visitor Information Centers.** Next door, the **Historic City Hall** is fronted by a marble statue honoring William Seward. Many of Anchorage's original buildings, dating from 1920 when the city was incorporated, still stand along 4th Avenue.

A walk down F Street to 2nd Avenue takes you to the site of original town-site homes built by the Alaska Engineering Commission, which also built the Alaska Railroad in the early 1900s. Continue east along 2nd Avenue—toward the Chugach Mountains that form Anchorage's backdrop—to a set of stairs leading down to the **Alaska Railroad Historic Depot.** From here you will overlook **Ship Creek,** where salmon run from early June through August, attracting hundreds of anglers and curious visitors alike, all amid an unlikely setting of industrial dock facilities and adjacent skyscrapers.

Turning around and walking to the far west end of 2nd Avenue, you can step onto the **Tony Knowles Coastal Trail,** which curls along between the city's edge and Cook Inlet, offering views of Mt. Susitna (locally called "Sleeping Lady" after

a Dena'ina Indian legend of uncertain provenance), Mt. McKinley, and the Alaska Range. Popular among walkers, runners, bicyclists, and in-line skaters, the Coastal Trail passes by the **Oscar Anderson House Museum.** Set off the trail at the north end of Elderberry Park, the Oscar Anderson House was Anchorage's first permanent frame house, built in 1915 by city butcher Oscar Anderson. From Elderberry Park, head back up 5th and continue past the Egan Convention Center, whose lobby has several modern native Alaskan sculptures and a beaded curtain that evokes the northern lights. Across the street, next door to the **Alaska Center for the Performing Arts,** is Town Square Park, packed with sculptures, fountains, and flowers in summer. Walk on to A Street and 7th Avenue for the entrance to the **Anchorage Museum of History and Art,** which occupies the whole block between 6th and 7th avenues. The red metal sculpture out front is a favorite hide-and-seek site for children.

Volunteers from **Anchorage Historic Properties** (☎ *907/274–3600*) lead historic walking tours on weekdays in summer. These depart from the Historic City Hall at 524 West 4th Avenue and cost $5.

⊗ *Memorial Day–Labor Day, daily 9–5; Labor Day–Memorial Day, weekdays 10–5.*

❷ Alaska Railroad Historic Depot. Totem poles and a locomotive built in 1907 are outside the station, the headquarters of the Alaska Railroad since 1915. A monument in front of the depot relates the history of the railroad, which brought an influx of people into the city during the early 1900s. During February's Fur Rendezvous festival, model-train buffs set up their displays here. ⊠ *411 W. 1st Ave., Downtown* ☎ *907/ 265–2494* ⊕ *www.akrr.com* ⊗ *Daily, depending on train schedules.*

⓫ **Anchorage Museum of History and Art.** An impressive collection of historic and contemporary Alaskan art is exhibited along with dioramas and displays on Alaskan history and village life. You can join an informative 45-minute tour (given several times daily) or step into the theater to watch a film on Alaska. In July the first-floor atrium is the site of free daily presentations by local artists and authors. A café spills out into the atrium, serving delicious lunches from the Marx Bros. Cafe, and the gift shop sells Alaska native art and souvenirs. ⊠*121 W. 7th Ave., at C St., Downtown* ☎*907/343–4326, 907/343–6173 recorded information* ⊕*www.anchoragemuseum.org* ⊠*$8* ⊙*Mid-May–mid-Sept., daily 9–6 (Thurs. 9–9); winter, Tues. –Sat. 10–6, Sun. noon–5.*

Fodor's Choice
★

⑧ **Historic City Hall.** Offices of the Anchorage Convention and Visitors Bureau now occupy this 1936 building. A few exhibits and historic photos are right inside the lobby. Out front, take a look at the marble sculpture of William Seward, the secretary of state who engineered the purchase of Alaska from Russia. ⊠*524 W. 4th Ave., Downtown.*

⑨ **The Imaginarium.** Children can stand inside a giant soap bubble at the bubble lab, visit a sea star in the intertidal marine exhibit, check out the creepy insects, learn about the northern lights, take a galaxy tour in the planetarium, or learn how planes fly at this experiential science museum. Other attractions include such "radical reptiles" as an alligator, a bearded dragon, and a Chinese water dragon. The gift shop features all sorts of unusual science toys. ⊠*737 W. 5th Ave., in Glacier BrewHouse Mall, Downtown* ☎*907/276–3179* ⊕*www.imaginarium. org* ⊠*$5.50* ⊙*Mon.–Sat. 10–6, Sun. noon–5.*

⑦ **Log Cabin and Visitor Information Centers.** A giant jade boulder stands outside this bush-style log cabin, whose sod roof is festooned with huge hanging baskets of flowers. Anchorage calls itself the "Air Crossroads of the World." It's a major stopping point for cargo jets en route to Asia, and a signpost out front marks the mileage to many international destinations. ■TIP➡After a stop in the cabin, step out the back door to the more spacious visitor center stocked with brochures. ⊠*4th Ave. and F St., Downtown* ☎*907/274–3531* ⊕*www.anchorage.net* ⊙*June– Aug., daily 7:30–7; May and Sept., daily 8–6; Oct.–Apr., daily 9–4.*

⑤ **Oscar Anderson House Museum.** City butcher Oscar Anderson built Anchorage's first permanent frame house in 1915, at a time when most of Anchorage consisted of tents. Swedish Christmas tours are held the first two weekends of December. Guided 45-minute tours are available whenever the museum is open. ⊠*420 M St., Downtown* ✛ *in Elderberry Park* ☎*907/274–2336* ⊠*$3* ⊙*June–mid-Sept., weekdays. noon–5; group tours (maximum 10 participants per group) must be arranged in advance.*

④ **Resolution Park.** This tiny park has a cantilevered viewing platform dominated by a monument to Captain Cook, whose explorations in 1778 led to the naming of Cook Inlet and many other geographic features in Alaska. Mt. Susitna, known as the Sleeping Lady, is the prominent low mountain to the northwest and Mts. Spurr and Redoubt, active

5

volcanoes, are just south of Mt. Susitna. Mt. McKinley, Mt. Foraker, and other peaks of the Alaska Range are often visible from more than 100 mi away. ⊠*3rd Ave. at L St., Downtown.*

❶ **Ship Creek.** The creek is dammed here, with a footbridge across the dam. ☾ You'll see a waterfall; salmon running upstream from June through August; anglers; and, above it all, downtown Anchorage. Farther upstream (follow Whitney Road and turn left on Post Road) is the Elmendorf salmon hatchery—during the runs you can see salmon in the clear, shallow water as they try to leap up the falls. ⊠ *Whitney Rd., Downtown.*

❸ **Tony Knowles Coastal Trail.** Strollers, runners, bikers, dog walkers, and in-line skaters cram this recreation trail on sunny summer evenings, particularly around Westchester Lagoon. In winter, cross-country skiers take to it by storm. The trail begins off 2nd Avenue, west of Christensen Drive, and curls along Cook Inlet for approximately 11 mi to Kincaid Park, beyond the airport. In summer you might spot beluga whales offshore in Cook Inlet. Access points are on the waterfront at the ends of 2nd, 5th, and 9th avenues and at Westchester Lagoon.

Fodor'sChoice ★

MIDTOWN & BEYOND

WHAT TO SEE

⑯ **Alaska Aviation Heritage Museum.** The state's unique aviation history is presented with 25 vintage aircraft—seven have been completely restored—a theater, an observation deck along **Lake Hood,** the world's busiest seaplane base, a flight simulator, and a gift shop. Highlights include a historic Fairchild American Pilgrim and a Stearman C2B, the first plane to land on Mt. McKinley, back in the early 1930s. Volunteers are working to restore a 1931 Pilgrim aircraft and are eager to talk shop. ⊠*4721 Aircraft Dr., West Anchorage* ☎*907/248–5325* ⊕*www.alaskaairmuseum.org* ⊠*$10* ☉*May 15–Sept. 15, daily 9–5; Sept. 15–May 14, Wed.–Sun. 9–5.*

⑭ **Alaska Botanical Garden.** The garden showcases perennials hardy enough to make it in South Central Alaska in several large display gardens, a pergola-enclosed herb garden, and a rock garden among 110 acres of mixed boreal forest. There's a 1-mi nature trail loop to Campbell Creek, with views of the Chugach Range and a wildflower trail between the display gardens. Interpretive signs guide visitors and identify plants along the trail. Children can explore the garden with an activity-filled duffel bag Tuesday–Saturday, 1–4 PM. Docent tours are available between June and August on Wednesday and Saturday at 1 PM, and the gift shop and retail nursery are open Tuesday–Sunday June–September. An information kiosk is at the entrance. ⊠*4601 Campbell Airstrip Rd., East Anchorage* ⊹*off Tudor Rd. (park at Benny Benson School)*

THREE DAYS IN ANCHORAGE

Make the most of your time in Anchorage with this itinerary:

Day 1. Above Cook Inlet and backed by the Chugach Mountains, Anchorage's distinctive setting is part of its allure. After breakfast at a downtown eatery, a walk along the **Tony Knowles Coastal Trail** provides views of the inlet, Mt. Susitna, and the Alaska Range. Afterward, check out some shops and galleries, historic sites, museums, and parks downtown. By car, visit the **Alaska Aviation Heritage Museum** and the **Alaska Native Heritage Center.**

Day 2. Head down the Seward Highway for views of **Potter Marsh** and Turnagain Arm. Keep an eye out for Dall sheep along the cliffs and

beluga whales in Turnagain Arm. If you time your trip for one to two hours after a very low tide, you may catch sight of a tidal bore flooding Turnagain Arm between McHugh Creek and Girdwood.

Continue farther down the highway to Alyeska Resort at Girdwood and ride the tram 2,300 feet up the mountain for lunch with a spectacular alpine view. Next, continue south to Portage Glacier and the Begich-Boggs Visitor Center for educational displays and lectures on area glaciers

Day 3. Take in a baseball game at Mulcahy Stadium or get a bird's-eye view of the city with a hike into the Chugach Mountains.

☎907/770–3692 ⊕*www.alaskabg.org* 🖃*$5, $10 families* ⊙Daily during daylight hrs.

⑬ ★ Alaska Heritage Museum at Wells Fargo. More than 900 Alaska native artifacts are the main draw in the quiet, unassuming lobby of a large midtown bank—it's reputed to be the largest private collection of native artworks in the country. You'll also find paintings by Alaskan artists, a library of rare books, and a 46-troy-ounce gold nugget. ⊠ *Wells Fargo Bank, 301 W. Northern Lights Blvd., at C St., Midtown* ☎907/265–2834 ⊕www.wellsfargohistory.com/museums/museums_an.htm 🖃*Free* ⊙*Late May–early Sept., weekdays noon–5; early Sept.–late May, weekdays noon–4.*

⑫ ★ Alaska Native Heritage Center. On a 26-acre site facing the Chugach Mountains, this facility provides an introduction to Alaska's native peoples. The spacious Welcome House has interpretive displays, artifacts, photographs, demonstrations, native dances, storytelling and films, along with a café and gift shop. Step outside for a stroll around the adjacent lake, where you will pass five village exhibits representing native cultural groups through traditional structures and exhibitions. ■TIP→ The Heritage Center provides a free shuttle from the downtown Log Cabin and Visitor Information Centers several times a day in summer. You can also hop a bus at the downtown transit center; Route 4 will take you to the Heritage Center's front door. ⊠*8800 Heritage Center Dr. (Glenn Hwy. at Muldoon Rd.), East Anchorage* ☎907/330–8000 or 800/315–6608 ⊕*www.alaskanative.net* 🖃*$23.50, $10 Alaska residents* ⊙*Mid-May–Sept., daily 9–5; Oct.–mid-May, Sat. 10–5.*

Fodor'sChoice

⓯ **Potter Marsh.** Sandhill cranes, trumpeter swans, and other migratory birds, as well as the occasional moose or beaver, frequent this marsh about 10 mi south of downtown on the Seward Highway. An elevated boardwalk makes viewing easy, and in summer there are salmon runs in the creek beneath the bridge. The **Potter Section House,** an old railroad service building just south of the marsh, operates as a state park office. Out front is an old engine with a rotary snowplow that was used to clear avalanches. ⊠*Seward Hwy., South Anchorage* ☎*907/345–5014* ⊕*www.wc.adfg.state.ak.us/index.cfm?adfg=alaska_guide.potter* ⊗ *Weekdays 8–noon and 1–4:30.*

OUTDOOR ACTIVITIES & GUIDED TOURS

BICYCLING, RUNNING & WALKING

Anchorage has more than 120 mi of paved bicycle trails, and many streets have marked bike lanes. Although busy during the day, downtown streets are uncrowded and safe for cyclists in the evening. ■ TIP➜ Pick up a guide to local trails at the **Alaska Public Lands Information Center** (⊠*4th Ave. and F St., Downtown* ☎*907/271–2737* 🖷*907/271–2744* ⊕*www.nps.gov/aplic*) or at area bookstores. At the far west end of Raspberry Road in South Anchorage, the 40 mi of trails at **Kincaid Park** (☎*907/343–6397* ⊕*www.muni.org/parks/parkdistrictsw.cfm*) wind through 1,400 acres of mixed spruce and birch forest. Mountain bikers will find easy-to-moderate riding along with some challenging hills. Be advised that Kincaid Park is home to a sizable moose population, so stay alert at all times. Parking lots are open 6 AM–11 PM daily. The Kincaid Outdoor Center—locally called Kincaid Chalet—is available for a fee for social functions such as weddings, receptions, and meetings. The **Tony Knowles Coastal Trail** (⊕*www.trailsofanchorage.com*) and other bike trails in Anchorage are used by runners, cyclists, in-line skaters, and walkers. It begins downtown off 2nd Avenue and is also easily accessible from Westchester Lagoon near the west end of 15th Avenue. The trail runs from the lagoon 2 mi to Earthquake Park and then continues an additional 7 mi to Kincaid Park, where a series of unpaved trails provides for more adventurous biking and hiking. A number of popular running events are held annually in Anchorage, including the **Alaska Run for Women** (⊕*www.akrfw.org*) in early June, which raises money for the fight against breast cancer. The late-April **Heart Run** is a fund-raiser for the American Heart Association's work to

GIRDWOOD

A ski resort, summer vacation spot, and home to an eclectic collection of locals, the town of Girdwood, 40 mi southeast of Anchorage, sits in a deep valley and is surrounded by tall mountains on three sides. The main attraction is the Mt. Alyeska Ski Resort, the largest ski area in Alaska. Besides enjoying the obvious winter attractions, you can hike up the mountain, rent a bike, or visit several restaurants (our favorite is Seven Glaciers) and gift shops open all year. Girdwood is wetter than Anchorage; it often rains or snows here while the sun shines to the north.

Uniquely Alaska

Alaska has more than its share of odd and unexpected attractions, including the handful of offbeat destinations described below. This is just a sampling; see elsewhere in this book for infamous bars (such as the Red Dog Saloon in Juneau and the Salty Dawg Saloon in Homer) and Alaskan thrills, including the world-famous 1,100-mi-long Iditarod Trail Sled Dog Race.

HAMMERS IN HAINES

Alaska's most peculiar museum is owned by Dave Pahl, whose collection of more than 1,400 hammers is on display in the crowded little **Hammer Museum** (108 Main St., Haines 907/766–2374 www.hammer-museum.org) in downtown Haines.

LAST TRAIN TO NOWHERE, NOME

Among Alaska's most interesting bush settlements, Nome was founded following a major gold discovery in 1898, and is still home to summertime gold-dredging operations. During the gold rush, the Council City and Solomon River Railroad envisioned a rail system connecting Nome with the Lower 48—thousands of miles away. Construction only reached 35 mi before storms destroyed the tracks along the Bering Sea in 1907, and the project was abandoned. The company went under, but visitors marvel at the engines and several railcars rusting away on the tundra south of Nome.

NORTH POLE, ALASKA

The world's tallest St. Nick (40 feet in all his wooden splendor) welcomes you to **Santa Claus House** (101 St. Nicholas Dr., North Pole 907/488–2200) in the town of North Pole just southeast of Fairbanks. Inside this large red-and-white store, kids can sit on Santa's lap any time of the year, while parents shop for all sorts of Christmas paraphernalia, from ornaments and CDs to certificates that grant you 1 square inch of land in the Santa Claus subdivision of North Pole. The town was started by Con Miller, who built a trading post here in the 1950s. He and his neighbors incorporated the new town as North Pole.

SURFING IN SOUTHEAST

The remote town of Yakutat lies along the Gulf of Alaska halfway between Juneau and Cordova. It isn't a major tourist destination, but it does have the state's longest beach, a 70-mi stretch that starts just outside town. It's never crowded, but local surfers and beach bums ride the swells that roll off the Gulf of Alaska throughout the year. There's even a surf shop, aptly named Icy Waves.

—Don Pitcher

prevent heart disease. It's been taking place for more than 25 years. Alaska's biggest and most famous running event is the **Mayor's Midnight Sun Marathon** (*www.mayorsmarathon.com*), held on the summer solstice in late June. **Downtown Bicycle Rental** (*333 W. 4th Ave., Downtown* 907/279–5293 *www.alaska-bike-rentals.com*) rents mountain bikes and provides trail recommendations, and can provide shuttle service for hikers to the parking lot at Flattop Mountain in Chugach State Park. The **Arctic Bicycle Club** (907/566–0177 *www.arcticbike.org*) organizes races and tours.

BIRD-WATCHING

Popular bird-watching places include the Tony Knowles Coastal Trail, which provides access to Westchester Lagoon and nearby tide flats, along with Potter Marsh on the south end of Anchorage. The Anchorage chapter of the **Audubon Society** (⊕ *www.anchorageaudubon.org*) refers you to local birders who will advise you on the best bird-watching spots. You can also sign up for bird-watching classes and field trips. The society's **bird hot line** (☎ *907/338–2473*) tracks the latest sightings in town. Naturalists Lisa Moorehead and Bob Dittrick of **Wilderness Birding Adventures** (☎ *907/694–7442* ⊕ *www.wildernessbirding.com*) offer backcountry birding, wildlife, and natural history trips to remote parts of Alaska, as well as village-based, birding-focused trips to some of Alaska's birding hot spots.

> ## CRUISE KENAI
>
> Give your arms a rest, soak up glacier views, and spot the abundant wildlife of Kenai Fjords National Park from a cruise boat. Alaska Heritage Tours Reservations (⊠ *509 W. 4th Ave., Downtown* ☎ 877/777--2805 ⊕ *www.kenaifjords.com*), with Kenai Fjord Tours, offers day packages to Kenai Fjords National Park April through November. The company offers transportation via coach and train between Anchorage and Seward. ■TIP→Check the Web site for special deals.

CANOEING & KAYAKING

Local lakes and lagoons, such as Westchester Lagoon, Goose Lake, and Jewel Lake, have favorable conditions for canoeing and kayaking. More adventurous paddlers should head to Whittier or Seward for sea kayaking. Take a guided trip in sea kayaks from **Kayak Adventures Worldwide** (⊠ Box 2249,, *Seward* ☎ *907/224–3960* ⊕ *www.kayakak.com*), which offers half-day trips to Resurrection Bay and a variety of full-day trips to Resurrection Bay, Aialik Bay, and Bear Glacier. They also run multiday trips in Kenai Fjords, and offer customized booking dates. Better known as REI, **Recreational Equipment Inc.** (⊠ *1200 W. Northern Lights Blvd., Spenard* ☎ *907/272–4565* ⊕ *www.rei.com*) sells and rents all sorts of outdoor gear, including canoes and sea kayaks.

FISHING

Nearly 30 local lakes are stocked with catchable game fish. ■TIP→ You must have a valid Alaska sportfishing license to fish in the state. Fishing licenses may be purchased at any Fred Meyer or Carr's/Safeway grocery or local sporting goods store. Nonresidents can buy an annual license for extended stays, or a 1-, 3-, 7-, or 14-day permit. A separate king salmon stamp is required to fish for the big guys. Rainbow trout, arctic char, landlocked salmon, Dolly Varden, grayling, and northern pike are among the species found in waters like Jewel Lake in South Anchorage and Mirror and Fire lakes near Eagle River. Coho salmon return to Ship Creek (downtown) in August, and king salmon are caught there between late May and early July. Campbell Creek and Bird Creek just south of town are also good spots for coho—locally called silver—salmon. Lately Bird Creek has had some issues with local brown bears encroaching on anglers, so be bear aware if you fish or hike near

Flattop Mountain, Anchorage. "This picture harnesses the energy from my first hike to the top of Flattop Mountain just outside of Anchorage. The hike is great for all skill levels." —Clay W. Padgett, Fodors.com photo contest winner

there. Contact the **Alaska Department of Fish and Game** (☎907/267–2218 ⊕*www.state.ak.us/adfg*) for licensing information. For maps showing locations and public access to Anchorage-area lakes, visit ⊕ www. sf.adfg.state.ak.us and click on Region II, then Lake Maps.

GOLF

Anchorage is Alaska's golfing capital, with several public courses. They won't compare to offerings in Phoenix or San Diego, but courses are open until 10 PM on long summer days. **Anchorage Golf Course** (✉*O'Malley Rd., South Anchorage* ☎*907/522–3363*) has 18 holes. Golf carts and clubs are available for rent. The city-run **Russian Jack Springs Park** (✉*5200 DeBarr Rd., South Anchorage* ☎*907/343–6992*) is generally open May through September. It has 9 holes and clubs for rent. **Tanglewood Lakes Golf Club** (✉*11701 Brayton Dr., South Anchorage* ☎*907/345–4600*) is a 9-hole course in South Anchorage, and home to an indoor driving range. For info on other courses around the state, check out ⊕*www.alaskagolflinks.com*.

ICE SKATING

Ice skating is a favorite wintertime activity in Anchorage, with several indoor ice arenas, outdoor hockey rinks, and local ponds opening when temperatures drop.

Ben Boeke Ice Arena (✉*334 E. 16th Ave., Midtown* ☎*907/274–5715* ⊕*www.benboeke.com*) is a city-run indoor ice arena with open skating and skate rentals year-round. The **Dimond Ice Chalet** (✉*800 E. Dimond Blvd., South Anchorage* ☎*907/344–1212* ⊕*www.dimondcenter.com*)

has an indoor ice rink at Dimond Mall that is open to the public daily, with lessons and skate rentals. In winter, **Westchester Lagoon**, 1 mi south of downtown, is a favorite outdoor family (and competitive) skating area, with smooth ice and piles of firewood next to the warming barrels.

RAFTING

Based in Girdwood, **Chugach Adventure Guides** (⌂ *Box 641, Girdwood 99587* ☎ *907/783–4354* ⊕ *www.alaskanrafting.com*) leads scenic floats on the Placer, Twentymile, and Portage rivers, along with white-water trips on the Talkeetna River and summerTordrillo mountain packages Alaska's oldest adventure and wilderness guiding company (in business since 1975), **Nova** (⌂ *Box 1129, Chickaloon 99674* ☎ *907/745–5753 or 800/746–5753* ⊕ *www.novalaska.com*), provides both scenic and white-water wilderness rafting trips statewide, including day trips in the Anchorage and Mat-Su areas, multiday trips in remote areas, and glacier hikes on the Mat-Su Glacier.

SKIING

★ Cross-country skiing is extremely popular in Anchorage. Locals ski on trails in town at Kincaid Park or Hillside and farther away at Girdwood Valley, Turnagain Pass, and Chugach State Park. Downhill skiing is convenient to downtown. A number of cross-country ski events are held annually in Anchorage. The **Alaska Ski for Women** (⊕ *www.alaskaskiforwomen.org*), held on Super Bowl Sunday in early February, is the biggest women's ski race in North America, attracting more than 1,500 skiers. The **Nordic Skiing Association of Anchorage** (⊕ *www.anchoragenordicski.com*) sponsors many other ski races and events throughout winter, from wooden ski classics to the highly competitive Besh Cup series. Biggest of all is the **Tour of Anchorage** (⊕ *www.tourofanchorage. com*), a grueling 50-km (31-mi) race in early March. If you're not up to doing 50k, there are 25k (16-mi) and 40k (25-mi) competitions as well. **Alyeska Ski Resort** (☎ *907/754–1111, 800/880–3880, 907/754–7669 recorded information and snow conditions, 907/753–2275 ticket office* ⊕ *www.alyeskaresort.com*), at Girdwood, 40 mi south of the city, is Alaska's premier destination resort, where snowfall averages 742 inches annually. Alyeska features a day lodge, hotel, restaurants, nine lifts, a tram, a vertical drop of 2,500 feet, and 68 runs for all abilities. Lift tickets cost $50 for adults; $30 for night skiing. The tram ($16) is open in summer, providing access to the Seven Glaciers restaurant and hiking trails. **Alyeska Accommodations** (☎ *907/783–2000 or 888/783–2001* ⊕ *www.alyeskaaccommodations.com*) can set you up in a privately owned cabin or condo. **Alpenglow at Arctic Valley** (✉ *Mi 7, Arctic Valley Rd. off Glenn Hwy., just past Muldoon Exit* ☎ *907/428–1208* ⊕ *www.skialpenglow.com*) is a small ski area just north of Anchorage. On the eastern edge of town, **Hilltop Ski Area** (✉ *Abbott Rd. near Hillside Dr., East Anchorage* ☎ *907/346–1446* ⊕ *www.hilltopski-area.org*) is a favorite ski area with families.

On 1,400 acres of rolling, timbered hills and bordered on the west by Cook Inlet, **Kincaid Park** (✉ *Main entrance at far west end of Rasp-*

berry Rd., Southwest Anchorage ☎907/343–6397 ⊕www.muni.org/
parks/parkdistrictsw.cfm) is a scenic treasure with maintained trails
groomed for diagonal and skate-skiing. National cross-country skiing
events (including U.S. Olympic team qualifying events and national
masters championships) are held each winter along the 60 km (37 mi)
of interwoven trails—including 20 km (12 mi) that are lighted for night
skiing. The park is open year-round: for skiing in winter; and for mountain biking, hiking, and other outdoor activities in summer. The Raspberry Road parking lot is open 6 AM–11 PM daily; lots inside the park
are open 10 AM–10 PM daily. The locally owned **Alaska Mountaineering
and Hiking** (⊠2633 Spenard Rd., Midtown ☎907/272–1811 ⊕www.
alaskamountaineering.com) outdoors shop has a highly experienced
staff and plenty of cross-country skis for sale or rent. Ski sales and rentals are available from **Recreational Equipment Inc.** (⊠1200 W. Northern
Lights Blvd., Midtown ☎907/272–4565 ⊕www.rei.com).

WHERE TO EAT

DOWNTOWN

¢–$
AMERICAN
✕**Arctic Roadrunner.** Every year when locals vote for Anchorage's best
burger joint, Arctic Roadrunner comes out on top. Forget McDonald's—these cheeseburgers are the real thing. Eat in or drive through at
the Arctic Boulevard location and head to nearby Valley of the Moon
Park for a sack lunch with the kids. Ultrathick milk shakes and crunchy
onion rings are also on everybody's list of favorites. The South Anchorage location has an outdoor deck on Campbell Creek, and in midsummer you can watch spawning salmon swim past. ⊠2477 Arctic Blvd.,
Downtown ☎907/279–7311 ⊠5300 Old Seward Hwy., South
Anchorage ☎907/561–1245 ☰No credit cards ⊗Closed Sun. ✛F4

$$$–$$$$
STEAK
✕**Club Paris.** Alaska's oldest steak house has barely changed since open-
ing in 1957. The restaurant has dark wood and an old-fashioned feel and
serves tender, flavorful steaks of all kinds, including a 4-inch-thick filet
mignon. If you have to wait for a table, have a martini at the bar and
order the hors d'oeuvres platter ($29)—a sampler of top sirloin steak,
cheese, and prawns that could be a meal for two. For dessert, try a tart
key lime pie or a chocolate sweet-potato pie. Dinner reservations are
advised. ⊠417 W. 5th Ave., Downtown ☎907/277–6332 ⊕www.club-
parisrestaurant.com ☰AE, D, DC, MC, V ⊗No lunch Sun. ✛C2

$$$–$$$$
CONTINENTAL
✕**Corsair Restaurant.** This fine-dining establishment specializes in conti-
nental and American cuisine with an emphasis on traditional French
haute cuisine, and has earned an international reputation for its steak
and seafood. More than 800 wine selections from its 10,000-bottle cel-
lar have won the Corsair recognition from Wine Spectator magazine.
⊠944 W. 5th Ave., Downtown ☎907/278–4502 ⊕www.corsairres-
taurant.com ☰AE, D, DC, MC, V ⊗Closed Sun. ✛A2

$$$$
CONTINENTAL
✕**Crow's Nest Restaurant.** In the Hotel Captain Cook, American and
French cuisine is the order of the day, along with the best view in
Anchorage—the Chugach Mountains to the east, the Alaska Range to

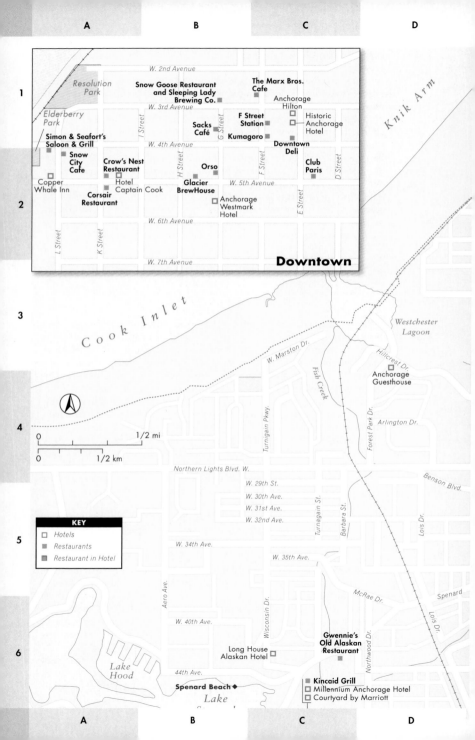

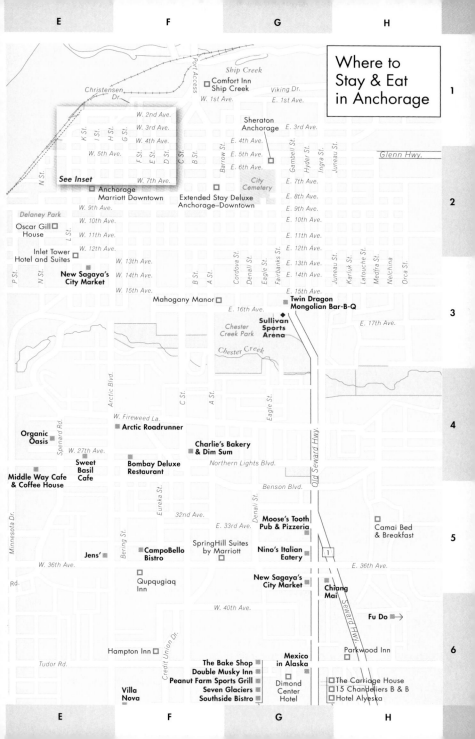

Where to Stay & Eat in Anchorage

E | F | G | H

1

Ship Creek
Comfort Inn Ship Creek
Christensen Dr.
W. 1st Ave.
Viking Dr.
E. 1st Ave.
Port Access

Sheraton Anchorage
E. 3rd Ave.
W. 2nd Ave.
W. 3rd Ave.
W. 4th Ave.
E. 4th Ave.
E. 5th Ave.
W. 5th Ave.
E. 6th Ave.
Glenn Hwy.
Gambell St.
Hyder St.
Ingra St.
Juneau St.

See Inset
W. 7th Ave.
City Cemetery
E. 7th Ave.

2

Anchorage Marriott Downtown
W. 9th Ave.
Extended Stay Deluxe Anchorage–Downtown
E. 8th Ave.
E. 9th Ave.

Delaney Park
Oscar Gill House
W. 10th Ave.
W. 11th Ave.
E. 10th Ave.
E. 11th Ave.

Inlet Tower Hotel and Suites
W. 12th Ave.
E. 12th Ave.

New Sagaya's City Market
W. 13th Ave.
W. 14th Ave.
W. 15th Ave.
E. 13th Ave.
E. 14th Ave.
E. 15th Ave.

Juneau St.
Karluk St.
Latouche St.
Medfra St.
Nelchina St.
Orca St.

3

Mahogany Manor
E. 16th Ave.
Twin Dragon Mongolian Bar-B-Q

Chester Creek Park
Sullivan Sports Arena
E. 17th Ave.

Chester Creek

4

Arctic Blvd.
C St.
A St.
Eagle St.

W. Fireweed La.
Arctic Roadrunner

Organic Oasis
Spenard Rd.
W. 27th Ave.
Charlie's Bakery & Dim Sum

Sweet Basil Cafe
Bombay Deluxe Restaurant
Northern Lights Blvd.

Middle Way Cafe & Coffee House
Benson Blvd.

5

Minnesota Dr.
Eureka St.
32nd Ave.
Denali St.

E. 33rd Ave.
Moose's Tooth Pub & Pizzeria
Camai Bed & Breakfast

Jens'
Bering St.
CampoBello Bistro
SpringHill Suites by Marriott
Nino's Italian Eatery
Old Seward Hwy.

W. 36th Ave.
Qupqugiaq Inn
E. 36th Ave.

Rd.
New Sagaya's City Market
Chiang Mai

6

W. 40th Ave.
Fu Do

Hampton Inn
Parkwood Inn

Tudor Rd.
Credit Union Dr.

Villa Nova
The Bake Shop
Double Musky Inn
Peanut Farm Sports Grill
Seven Glaciers
Southside Bistro
Mexico in Alaska
Dimond Center Hotel
The Carriage House
15 Chandeliers B & B
Hotel Alyeska
Seward Hwy.

E | F | G | H

the north, and the sprawling city of Anchorage 20 stories below. Equally impressive are the 10,000-bottle wine cellar and hefty portions. The expert waitstaff presents a menu of seafood, along with game and other meats, served in an elegant setting with plenty of starched linen, brass, and teak. It's best known for a leisurely five-course set chef's tasting menu: $70 per person or $110 with wine pairings. ⊠*Hotel Captain Cook, 20th fl., 5th Ave. and K St., Downtown* ☎*907/343–2217* ⌖*Reservations essential* ⊟*AE, D, DC, MC, V* ☽*Closed Sun. and Mon. in winter. No lunch.* ✢*A2*

¢–$

AMERICAN

✕**Downtown Deli.** A longtime favorite, this café is across the street from the Log Cabin and Visitor Information Centers. Although you can choose from familiar sandwiches, like the French dip or the chicken teriyaki, this deli also has Alaskan favorites, like grilled halibut and reindeer stew. The dark, rich chicken soup comes with either noodles or homemade matzo balls, and breakfasts range from omelets and homemade granola to cheese blintzes. You can sit in one of the wooden booths for some privacy or out front at the sidewalk tables for some summertime people-watching. ⊠*525 W. 4th Ave., Downtown* ☎*907/276–7116* ⌖*Reservations not accepted* ⊟*AE, D, DC, MC, V.* ✢*C1*

$–$$

AMERICAN

✕**F Street Station.** Space is at a premium in this minuscule downtown bar where the business crowd heads for a light meal. It isn't for kids, but the food is always delicious. The steak sandwiches and cheeseburgers are good bets, but also check out the board for the day's seafood specials. A giant block of cheese occupies one corner of the bar, and the TVs are usually tuned to sports in this Cheers-type gathering place. ⊠*325 F St., Downtown* ☎*907/272–5196* ⊟*AE, DC, MC, V.* ✢*C1*

$–$$$$

AMERICAN

Fodor'sChoice

★

✕**Glacier BrewHouse.** The scent of hops permeates the cavernous, wood-beam BrewHouse, where a dozen or so ales, stouts, lagers, and pilsners are brewed on the premises. Locals mingle with visitors in this noisy, always-busy heart-of-town restaurant where dinner selections range from thin-crust, 10-inch pizzas to seafood chowder and from whiskey barbecue pork ribs to jambalaya fettuccine. For dessert, don't miss the wood-oven roasted-apple-and-currant bread pudding. You can watch the hardworking chefs in the open kitchen. The brewery sits behind a glass wall, and the same owners operate the equally popular Orso, next door. ⊠*737 W. 5th Ave., Downtown* ☎*907/274–2739* ⊕*www.glacierbrewhouse.com* ⊟*AE, D, MC, V.* ✢*B2*

$$–$$$$

JAPANESE

✕**Kumagoro.** A favorite of the suit-and-tie lunch crowd, Kumagoro has traditional Japanese lunches and a take-out deli with such specialties as herring roe on kelp, and a sleek sushi bar (dinner only). The best items on the dinner menu are the sizzling salmon or beef teriyaki, both served with miso soup and a salad. With the shabu-shabu dinner ($39 for two people), you cook your own meats and vegetables in a stockpot of boiling broth. Inexpensive homemade ramen soups are also available. All entrée prices include a 10% gratuity. ⊠*533 W. 4th Ave., Downtown* ☎*907/272–9905* ⊟*AE, D, DC, MC, V.* ✢*C1*

$$$–$$$$

CONTINENTAL

Fodor'sChoice

★

✕**Marx Bros. Cafe.** Inside a little frame house built in 1916, this nationally recognized 46-seat café opened in 1979 and is still going strong. The menu changes every week, and the wine list encompasses more than 700 international choices. For an appetizer, try the king crab–

Alaska's Well-Worn Trail

Since 1973 mushers and their sled-dog teams have raced more than 1,000 mi across Alaska in a marathon unlike any other: the Iditarod Trail Sled Dog Race, the longest sled-dog race in the world. After a ceremonial start in downtown Anchorage on the first Saturday in March, dog teams wind through Alaska, battling almost every imaginable winter challenge. Iditarod mushers and dogs endure extreme cold, deep snow, gale-force winds, whiteouts, river overflow, and moose attacks, not to mention fraying tempers. Less than 10 days later, the "Last Great Race" ends (at least for the front-runners) with spectacular fanfare in Nome, on the Bering Sea coast.

The Iditarod's origins can be traced to two events: an early 1900s long-distance race called the All-Alaska Sweepstakes and the delivery of a lifesaving serum to Nome by dog mushers during a diphtheria outbreak in 1925. Fascinated with the trail's history, Alaskan sled-dog enthusiasts Dorothy Page and Joe Redington Sr. staged the first race in 1967 to celebrate the role of mushing in Alaska's history. Only 50 mi long and with a purse of $25,000—no small amount at that time—it attracted the best of Alaska's competitive mushers. Enthusiasm waned in 1969, however, when the available winnings fell to $1,000. Instead of giving up, Redington expanded the race.

In 1973, after three years without a race, he organized a 1,000-mi race from Anchorage to Nome, with a then-outrageous purse of $50,000. Critics scoffed, but 34 racers entered. First place went to a little-known musher named Dick Wilmarth, who finished in 20 days. Redington then billed the Iditarod as a 1,049-mi race to symbolize Alaska, the 49th state. While still the official distance, the race really covers 1,100 mi.

The race actually begins in Wasilla, home of the Iditarod headquarters, a 50-mi drive north of Anchorage. The first few hundred miles take mushers and dogs through wooded lowlands and hills, including a stretch known as Moose Alley. Teams then cross the Alaska Range and enter Interior Alaska, with Athabascan villages and gold-rush ghost towns, including Iditarod. Next, the trail follows the frozen Yukon River, then cuts over to the Bering Sea coast for the final 270-mi "sprint" to Nome. It was here, in 1985, that Libby Riddles drove her team into a blinding blizzard, en route to a victory that made her the first woman to win the race. After that, Susan Butcher won the race four times, but the all-time record holder is Rick Swenson, with five victories. The fastest time was recorded in 2002, when Swiss-born musher Martin Buser finished in just under nine days.

5

stuffed squash blossoms or fresh Kachemak Bay oysters. The outstanding made-at-your-table Caesar salad is a superb opener for the baked halibut with a macadamia-nut crust served with coconut curry sauce and fresh mango chutney. ✉ *627 W. 3rd Ave., Downtown* ☎ *907/278–2133* ⊕ *www.marxcafe.com* ✑ *Reservations essential* ▤ *AE, DC, MC, V* ✆ *Closed Sun. and Mon. No lunch.* ✛ *C1*

¢–$
ECLECTIC
✗ **New Sagaya's City Market.** Stop here for quick lunches and Kaladi Brothers espresso. The in-house bakery, L'Aroma, cranks out specialty breads and pastries of all types, and the international deli and grocery

Alaska Wildlife Conservation Center, Anchorage. "These reindeer enjoy their home at the Alaska Wildlife Conservation Center. Along with native bears, moose and other animals, all of the residents at the sanctuary are native to Alaska." —Amy Dawson, Fodors.com photo contest participant

serves California-style pizzas, Chinese food, lasagna, rotisserie chicken, salads, and even stuffed cabbage. You can eat inside on the sheltered patio or grab an outside table on a summer afternoon. New Sagaya's has one of the best seafood counters in town and will even box and ship your fish. The grocery stores carry an extensive selection of Asian foodstuffs, and the produce and meat selections are excellent. ⊠ *900 W. 13th Ave., Downtown* ☎ *907/274–6173, 907/274–9797, or 800/764–1001* ⊠ *3700 Old Seward Hwy., Midtown* ☎ *907/562–9797* ⊕ *www. newsagaya.com* ▭ *AE, D, DC, MC, V.* ♧ *E3, G5*

$$–$$$$ ✕ **Orso.** One of Anchorage's culinary stars, Orso ("bear" in Italian),
ITALIAN evokes the earthiness of a Tuscan villa. Alaskan touches flavor rustic Mediterranean dishes that include traditional pastas, fresh seafood, and locally famous desserts—most notably a delicious molten chocolate cake. Be sure to ask about the daily specials. If you can't get a table at dinner (reservations are advised), you can select from the same menu at the large bar. Upstairs you'll find a cozier, quieter space. ⊠ *737 W. 5th Ave., at G St., Downtown* ☎ *907/222–3232* ⊕ *www.orsoalaska. com* ▭ *AE, D, MC, V* ☉ *No lunch weekends.* ♧ *B2*

$$–$$$$ ✕ **Sacks Café.** This colorful restaurant serves light American cuisine such
AMERICAN as chicken and scallops over udon noodles, and local produce when available. They also feature monthly wine flights, normally with three different selections of 3-ounce pours with information sheets on each wine. Be sure to ask about the daily specials, particularly the fresh king salmon and halibut. Flowers adorn the tables, and singles congregate along a small bar, sampling wines from California, Australia, and France.

The café is especially crowded during lunch, served from 11 to 2:30, and dinner begins at 5. The weekend brunch menu includes eggs Benedict, a Mexican scrambled egg dish called *migas,* and various salads and sandwiches. ✉*328 G St., Downtown* ☎*907/276–3546 or 907/274–4022* ⊕*www.sackscafe.com* ◿*Reservations essential* ▭*AE, MC, V.* ✛*B1*

$$–$$$$ ╳**Simon & Seafort's Saloon & Grill.** Windows overlooking Cook Inlet vistas, along with the high ceilings and a classic brass-and-wood interior, have long made this an Anchorage favorite. The menu includes prime rib (aged 28 days), pasta, and sesame chicken salad, but the main attraction is seafood: fish is blackened, grilled, fried, or prepared any other way you like it. Try the king crab legs or the grilled ahi tuna with ginger-and-mango salsa, and, for dessert, the Brandy Ice: vanilla ice cream whipped with brandy, Kahlúa, and crème de cacao. The bar is a great spot for microbrews, single-malt Scotch, and martinis; the best tables are adjacent to tall windows facing the water. ✉*420 L St., Downtown* ☎*907/274–3502* ⊕*www.r-u-i.com/sim* ◿*Reservations essential* ▭*AE, DC, MC, V* ◷*No lunch weekends.* ✛*A1*

JAPANESE

¢–$ ╳**Snow City Cafe.** At this unassuming café along "lawyer row" you'll find dependably good and reasonably priced breakfasts and lunches. Service is fast, and the setting, formerly a funky mix of mismatched chairs and Formica tables, has been upgraded and remodeled, but there's still a great mix of families and singles enjoying some of the best breakfasts in Anchorage. Snow City is consistently voted the best breakfast in a local poll. Breakfast is served all day, but arrive early on the weekend or be prepared to wait. Snow City's lunch menu consists of hot or cold sandwiches, fresh soups, and salads, and has lots of vegetarian-friendly options. The kitchen closes at 3 PM weekdays and 4 PM weekends. ✉*4th Ave. at L St., Downtown* ☎*907/272–2489* ⊕*www.snowcitycafe.com* ▭*AE, D, DC, MC, V* ◷*No dinner.* ✛*A1*

ECLECTIC

$–$$$$ ╳**Snow Goose Restaurant and Sleeping Lady Brewing Company.** Although you can dine indoors at this comfortable edge-of-downtown eatery, the real attraction in summer is alfresco dining on the back deck and on the rooftop. On clear days you can see Mt. McKinley on the northern horizon and the Chugach Mountains to the east. The menu emphasizes Alaskan fare, but the beer and the view are the best reasons to visit. To sample the specialty beers, gather around oak tables in the upstairs bar for a brewed-on-the-premises ale, India Pale Ale, stout, barley wine, or porter. ✉*717 W. 3rd Ave., Downtown* ☎*907/277–7727* ⊕*www.alaskabeers.com* ▭*AE, D, DC, MC, V.* ✛*B1*

AMERICAN

MIDTOWN

$–$$ ╳**Bombay Deluxe Restaurant.** Anchorage's only Indian restaurant is housed in a collection of international shops at the Valhalla Center strip mall, flanked by a Korean restaurant on one side and an Asian market on the other. Dinners include such spicy standards as lamb korma, chicken vindaloo, *palak paneer* (spinach and cheese), and 10 different types of Indian breads—from tandoori roti to garlic naan. The restaurant is especially popular for weekday lunch, when the big buffet ($10) provides a sampling of Indian favorites, including several vegetarian

INDIAN

offerings. ⊠*555 W. Northern Lights Blvd., Midtown* ☎*907/277–1200* ⊕*www.bombaydeluxe.com* ⊟*AE, D, DC, MC, V.* ✛*F4*

$$–$$$ ✕**CampoBello Bistro.** Tucked into a midtown mall, CampoBello has sur-
ITALIAN   prisingly sophisticated Italian entrées and sinful desserts. Step inside for
a romantic lunch or dinner surrounded by splashes of modern art on the
walls and candles on the tables. Specialties include ample servings of
seafood crepes, wild-mushroom cannelloni, veal saltimbocca, homemade four-cheese ravioli, and shrimp and scallops Florentine. Service is
attentive, and the wine list—particularly the Italian choices—is impressive. Dinner reservations are advised. ⊠*601 W. 36th Ave., Midtown*
☎*907/563–2040* ⊟*DC, MC, V* ⊘*Closed Sun. No lunch Sat.* ✛*F5*

¢–$ ✕**Charlie's Bakery & Dim Sum.** Tucked away in a midtown strip mall, this
CHINESE   little gem serves some of the finest authentic Chinese food in Anchorage—and at bargain prices. The atmosphere at this popular lunch spot
is casual; order at the counter, take a number for your table, and wait
for your meal to be delivered. Dinner is served from 5 to 8:30, and the
place closes at 9. Dishes like the vibrant Spicy Shrimp, loaded with
vegetables and hot sauce, make this eatery worth a visit. ⊠*2729 C St.,
Midtown* ☎*907/677–7777* ⊟*AE, D, MC, V* ⊘*Closed Sun.* ✛*F4*

¢–$ ✕**Chiang Mai.** Among the Thai restaurants scattered around Anchor-
THAI   age, this is one of the best, with authentic Thai cooking and friendly
service. You will find fare such as fresh spring rolls (an order of eight,
a house specialty), pad thai (spicy cooked noodles with shrimp, chicken,
and eggs), and *tom kha gai* (a flavorful soup of coconut milk, chicken,
lemongrass, and ginger). Vegetarians have a number of choices, and
unique Thai desserts are on the menu board. The restaurant closes at
9 PM. ⊠*3637 Old Seward Hwy., Midtown* ☎*907/563–8900* ⊟*AE,
MC, V* ⊘*Closed Sun.* ✛*G5*

$ ✕**Fu Do.** This is one of the oldest and best Chinese restaurants in Alaska.
CHINESE   Although it's surrounded by fast-food spots and gas stations, when you
step inside Fu Do, the flame-red Chinese wallpaper and lanterns, ultraf-
riendly staff, and Asian music take you to another continent. All the
standards are available, including beef with oyster sauce, kung pao
chicken, sweet-and-sour pork, and various vegetable entrées. Portions
are enormous and include soup, kimchi, rice, egg roll, and tea. Lunch
specials are an even better deal, and free delivery is offered if you don't
want to leave your hotel. ⊠*2600 E. Tudor Rd., Midtown* ☎*907/561–
6610* ⊕*www.fudochineserestaurant.net* ⊟*AE, MC, V.* ✛*H6*

$$–$$$$ ✕**Jens'.** Despite its being in a midtown strip mall, Jens' is a playful res-
CONTINENTAL   taurant where the menu changes daily. Colorful paintings grace red
walls, and friendly gray-haired waiters greet new arrivals. The dinner
menu usually includes Alaskan salmon, halibut, and rockfish, along
with such specialties as rack of lamb, tenderloin of veal, and an "almost
world-famous" pepper steak. Head chef Jens Haagen Hansen's heritage
reveals itself at lunch when the Danish specials appear. For a lighter
evening meal, sample the appetizers at the wine bar, where Jens holds
court. Reservations are suggested, but they can usually accommodate
drop-ins. ⊠*701 W. 36th Ave., at Arctic Blvd., Midtown* ☎*907/561–
5367* ⊕*www.jensrestaurant.com* ⊟*AE, D, DC, MC, V* ⊘*Closed Sun.
and Jan. No lunch Sat., no dinner Mon.* ✛*E5*

¢–$$$ ✕**Moose's Tooth Pub & Pizzeria.** Always the top pick when local newspa-
PIZZA pers rate Anchorage pizzerias, Moose's Tooth is packed all week, even
though a building addition was completed in 2006, and the place now
seats 300 diners. The reason for the popularity is obvious: creative piz-
zas and handcrafted beers from their own brewery. More than a dozen
ales, ambers, porters, and stouts are the order of the day, and home-
made root beers, cream sodas, and ginger ales are also available. You
can match these brews with one of the 40 different pizzas with such
varied toppings as roasted red peppers, jalapeños, cream cheese, hali-
but, and capers. Check out the daily pizza specials for some pretty
exotic topping combinations such as southern pork barbecue and
Samui shrimp if you're so inclined. Weekday lunches start at $5 for a
slice of pizza and a salad. ✉*3300 Old Seward Hwy., Midtown*
☎*907/258–2537* ⊕*www.moosestooth.net* ▭*D, DC, MC, V.* ✛*G5*

$–$$$ ✕**Nino's Italian Eatery.** One of the newest players in the Anchorage res-
ITALIAN taurant scene, Nino's achieved near-instant success with their excellent
southern Italian dishes at reasonable prices. There isn't a bad choice on
the menu of chicken, veal, seafood, pastas, heroes, and pizza. They also
have a good selection of Italian wines, imported bottled beer, and local
drafts. No reservations are taken, but it's worth the wait. ✉*831 36th
Ave., Midtown* ☎*907/336–6466* ⊕*www.ninositalianeatery.com*
▭*AE, MC, V* ⌦ *No reservations.* ✛*G5*

¢–$ ✕**Sweet Basil Cafe.** Recently moved from its downtown location to mid-
CAFÉ town, this family-run café has hot and cold lunchtime sandwiches on
freshly baked sweet basil bread accompanied by a choice of homemade
soups. Fresh pastas, salads, wraps, fish tacos, smoothies, pastries, and
light breakfasts fill out the menu, but the daily specials are often your
best bet. They also sell a nice variety of dinners to go, including wild
mushroom- and chicken-filled crepes and a roasted-veggie-and-goat-
cheese lasagna. ■TIP➜The juice bar is one of a handful in Anchorage.
✉ *1021 W. Northern Lights Blvd., Midtown* ☎*907/274–0070* ▭*AE,
D, MC, V* ☽*Closed Sun. No dinner.* ✛*E4*

¢–$$ ✕**Twin Dragon Mongolian Bar-B-Q.** If you haven't eaten Mongolian bar-
CHINESE becue before, you're in for a treat. Choose your stir-fry ingredients and
sauces, then watch as the chefs cook your meal with a flourish in the
giant wok. The restaurant also has an impressive Chinese buffet with
a multitude of choices; it's $8 for lunch or $13 for dinner—for one
price you can have as much from the buffet and the stir-fry selections
as you like. There's also a slim selection of beers and wines. ✉*612 E.
15th Ave., Midtown* ☎*907/276–7535* ▭*D, MC, V.* ✛*G3*

$–$$$ ✕**Villa Nova.** This standby restaurant is popular for its authentic Italian
ITALIAN cuisine including veal, lamb, chicken, steak, and seafood entrées.
Dim lighting, linen tablecloths, and fresh flowers create a romantic

5

ambience (though dress is casual). The bar has domestic and imported liquors, wines, and beers. Make reservations for dinner. ⊠ *5121 Arctic Blvd., Midtown* ☎ *907/561–1660* ☐ *AE, D, DC, MC, V* ☼ *Closed Sun. and Mon.* ✛ *F6*

GREATER ANCHORAGE

SPENAND

✕ **Gwennie's Old Alaskan Restaurant.**

¢–$$$ Historic Alaskan photos, stuffed
AMERICAN animals, and memorabilia adorn this old family favorite, just south of city center toward the airport. Lunch and dinners are available— including an all-you-can-eat beef barbecue for $17—but the res- taurant is best known for its old- fashioned breakfasts, available all day. Try the sourdough pancakes, reindeer sausage and eggs, or crab omelets. Portions are very gener- ous—a serving of fries alone can feed a small family. Start the morning with Anchorage's best Bloody Mary. ⊠ *4333 Spenard Rd., Spenard* ☎ *907/243–2090* ⊕ *www.gwenniesrestaurant.com* ☐ *AE, D, DC, MC, V.* ✛ *C6*

> ### WORD OF MOUTH
>
> "Gwennie's has the best all-around meals in town. The fresh halibut steak and fried-in-beer-batter hali- but & chips are fantastic!"
>
> —Paul

¢ ✕ **Middle Way Cafe & Coffee House.** This lunchtime nook next to the REI
VEGETARIAN store has gussied-up grain-and-soy burgers, turkey-cranberry sand- wiches, avocado melts, vegan baked goods, jumbo whole-grain tortillas wrapped around combinations of organic veggies, falafel, brown rice, and beans, and daily specials. A kids' menu has smaller portions. You can get a fruit smoothie at the juice bar, choose from 35 different teas, or enjoy an espresso, made from 100% organic, Fair Trade coffees. The service is perfunctory at times. According to the owner, "We invented the 'wrap' sandwich back in '94, which led to World Wraps opening in a Seattle REI, and the rest is history." ⊠ *1200 W. Northern Lights Blvd., Spenard* ☎ *907/272–6433* ⊕ *middlewaycafe.com* ☖ *Reserva- tions not accepted* ☐ *AE, MC, V.* ✛ *E4*

¢–$$ ✕ **Organic Oasis.** Next to a yoga studio and just up the street from
CAFÉ Chilkoot Charlie's, this popular café specializes in fresh-squeezed juices, smoothies, organic sandwiches, and tofu burgers. For the omni- vore, the menu also includes buffalo burgers, chicken, and fresh mus- sels. They've even got organic beer. There's live music Tuesday through Saturday nights and free wireless Internet access anytime. Service can be slow at times. ⊠ *2610 Spenard Rd., Spenard* ☎ *907/277–7882* ⊕ *www.alaska.net/~organicoasis* ☐ *AE, D, MC, V.* ✛ *E4*

SOUTH ANCHORAGE

$$$$ ✕ **Kincaid Grill.** This out-of-the-way restaurant provides a respite after
CONTINENTAL a summertime hike or wintertime ski in nearby Kincaid Park. Chef and owner Al Levinsohn worked his way up through some of Alaska's finest restaurants, and the experience shines through in his diverse and cre- ative menu. The upscale setting is lively, with old-time jazz spilling from the speakers, the buzz of conversations, and artistically presented

meals. Low-backed metal stools line the wine bar, where you can sample a microbrew or vintages from around the globe. The menu changes every few weeks, but always includes filet mignon, grilled Hawaiian game fish, Alaskan salmon or halibut, and a rich seafood gumbo. ⊠*6700 Jewel Lake Rd., South Anchorage* ☎*907/243–0507* ⊕*www. kincaidgrill.com* ⌲*Reservations essential* ▭*AE, MC, V* ⊗*Closed Sun. and Mon. No lunch.* ⊹*C6*

$$

MEXICAN

✕**Mexico in Alaska.** This not your standard Tex-Mex or Mexican-American fare, but the most authentic Mexican food in town and maybe even in Alaska. Owner Maria Elena Ball befriends everyone, particularly young children. Favorite dishes include lime-marinated fried chicken, *chilaquiles* (tortilla casserole with mole sauce), and *entremesa de queso* (melted cheese, jalapeños, and onions with homemade tortillas). Weekday lunch buffets ($10) and Sunday dinner buffets ($12) are popular, and a vegetarian menu is available. The restaurant is several miles south of downtown, so you'll need to drive or catch the city bus. ⊠*7305 Old Seward Hwy., South Anchorage* ☎*907/349–1528* ▭*AE, D, MC, V* ⊗*No lunch Sun.* ⊹*G6*

$–$$$

AMERICAN

✕**Peanut Farm Sports Grill.** Alaska's largest sports bar has 70 TV screens, pool tables, darts, an outdoor deck on the bank of Campbell Creek, a heated deck overlooking the creek, and a large and varied menu. The hot wings are the best in town, and you can slake your thirst with one of 30 draft beers. They open at 6 for breakfast every day, and they have live entertainment on weekends and Wednesday nights. It's a happenin' place, and the food's always good. ⊠*5227 Old Seward Hwy., South Anchorage* ☎*907/563–3283* ⊕*http://peanutfarmbarandgrill.com* ▭*AE, D, MC, V.* ⊹*G6*

$–$$$$

CONTINENTAL

✕**Southside Bistro.** Established in South Anchorage, the Southside (another in a long list of great Anchorage restaurants tucked away in nondescript strip malls) quickly became a local favorite for its Alaska seafood, veal, venison, and rack of lamb. A hardwood brick oven produces flat breads and pizzas; cheesecakes, pastries, and ice creams are decorated with hand-painted designs. The wine list includes more than 100 mostly American wines, and several local beers on tap. If you're watching your budget, grab a seat on the bistro side of the restaurant and order from the bar menu—they've got burgers, pizzas, appetizers, and one of our favorites, an excellent angel-hair pasta. Reservations are highly recommended. ⊠*1320 Huffman Park Dr., South Anchorage* ☎*907/348–0088* ⊕*www.southsidebistro.com* ▭*AE, D, MC, V* ⊗*Closed Sun. and Mon.* ⊹*G6*

GIRDWOOD

¢–$

AMERICAN

✕**The Bake Shop.** The atmosphere is vintage 1975 at this old-time Girdwood favorite where you order at the counter and wait for servers to bring your meal. Breakfasts are filling, with piles of sourdough pancakes, fluffy omelets (we heartily recommend the Farmer's omelet), and homemade pastries. Skiers and snowboarders drop by for a fast lunch or dinner of homemade soups, sandwiches, or garden-fresh pizzas. Get a loaf of their hearty sourdough or one of their huge cinnamon buns to go. Dine out front in summer, surrounded by hanging baskets filled with begonias, lobelia, and impatiens. ⊠*Alyeska*

Boardwalk, Girdwood ☎ *907/783–2831* ⊕ *www.thebakeshop.com* ⊟ *No credit cards.* ✛ *G6*

$$$$
SOUTHERN

✕ **Double Musky Inn.** Anchorage residents say eating at this award-winning spot is well worth the one-hour drive south to Girdwood and the inevitable wait for dinner—you can usually find a spot at the bar, order an appetizer while you wait, and choose from one of their 22 martinis or a local draft beer. It's very noisy, and the interior is completely covered with tacky art and Mardi Gras souvenirs of all types, but the windows frame views of huge Sitka spruce trees. The diverse menu mixes hearty Cajun-style meals with such favorites as garlic seafood pasta, rack of lamb, French pepper steak, and lobster kebabs. For dessert lovers, the biggest attraction is the gooey, chocolate-rich Double Musky pie. The restaurant and lounge are smoke-free. ✉ *Crow Creek Rd., Girdwood* ☎ *907/783–2822* ⊕ *www.doublemuskyinn.com* ♨ *Reservations not accepted* ⊟ *D, DC, MC, V* ☾ *Closed Mon. and late Oct.– Dec. 10. No lunch.* ✛ *G6*

$$$$
CONTINENTAL

✕ **Seven Glaciers.** A 60-passenger aerial tram (free with dinner reservations, otherwise $16 round-trip) carries you to this refined yet relaxing mountainside Girdwood restaurant, perched at the 2,300-foot level on Mt. Alyeska. The comfortable dining room overlooks seven glaciers. Try the artfully presented smoked and grilled salmon or mesquite-grilled strip loin of buffalo and fresh Alaska king crab in season. Appetizers—particularly the peppered crab cakes—are extraordinary. À la carte prices are high, but a four-course menu ($70 per person, including a matched wine) is available nightly in summer. Both tram and restaurant are wheelchair accessible. Dinner seatings are from 5:30 to 9:30 PM. ✉ *Hotel Alyeska, 1000 Arlberg Rd., Girdwood* ☎ *907/754–2237* ⊕ *www.alyeskaresort.com* ♨ *Reservations essential* ⊟ *AE, D, MC, V* ☾ *Closed Sun.–Thurs. Nov.–May.* ✛ *G6*

WHERE TO STAY

DOWNTOWN

$$$$

⌂ **Anchorage Hilton.** Alaska's largest hotel is just a block from city center and fills with cruise-ship tourists all summer long. The lobby includes full-size mounted Kodiak and polar bears, a gift shop with Alaskan native-made art and crafts, a café, and a sports bar. Well-maintained rooms, decorated in a contemporary style with oak and maple furnishings, are in two towers, one of which is 22 floors. Request a corner north-facing suite on the upper levels for Mt. McKinley vistas. **Pros:** Downtown location close to shopping and restaurants, great views from upper floors. **Cons:** Parking fee can add up if you're driving, not a great value for your travel dollar, facilities can be overrun with cruise-ship crowds at times. ✉ *500 W. 3rd Ave., Downtown* ☎ *907/ 272–7411 or 800/245–2527* ⊕ *www.hilton.com* ⇋ *592 rooms, 14 suites* ♿ *In-room: safe, Ethernet. In-hotel: 3 restaurants, bars, pool, gym, public Wi-Fi, room service, concierge, no-smoking rooms* ⊟ *AE, D, DC, MC, V.* ✛ *C1*

$$$$ ⊤**Anchorage Marriott Downtown.** One of Anchorage's biggest lodgings, the brightly decorated Marriott appeals to business travelers, tourists, and corporate clients. The hotel's Cafe Promenade serves American cuisine with an Alaskan flair. All guest rooms have huge windows; views are breathtaking from the top floors. If you stay on one of the top three levels of this 20-story hotel, you have access to a concierge lounge and are served a light breakfast as well as evening hors d'oeuvres and desserts. **Pros:** One of the newest hotels in town, modern, up-to-date facilities. **Cons:** No Wi-Fi, cruise-ship crowds at times in summer. ⊠*820 W. 7th Ave., Downtown* ☎*907/279–8000 or 800/228–9290* ⊕*www.marriott. com* ⬅*392 rooms, 3 suites* ⌂*In-room: Ethernet. In-hotel: restaurant, room service, bar, pool, gym, concierge* ▭*AE, D, DC, MC, V.* ⚓*E2*

$$$–$$$$ ⊤**Anchorage Westmark Hotel.** Each comfortable room in this 13-story hotel has a small private balcony and modern furnishings. Reserve a room or suite on the higher floors for the best mountain views. The downstairs restaurant, Solstice Bar & Grill, serves three meals a day, and several notable eateries are nearby, including Orso and Glacier BrewHouse. **Pros:** The restaurant gets high marks, central downtown location gives you walking access to other great eating spots and tourist attractions. **Cons:** Noise, both from other rooms and outside, is a problem, few frills, no airport shuttle. ⊠*720 W. 5th Ave., Downtown* ☎*907/276–7676 or 800/544–0970* ⊕*www.westmarkhotels.com* ⬅*188 rooms, 12 suites* ⌂*In-hotel: 2 restaurants, room service, public Internet, public Wi-Fi* ▭*AE, D, DC, MC, V.* ⚓*B2*

$$–$$$ ⊤**Comfort Inn Ship Creek.** The namesake Ship Creek gurgles past this popular family hotel, a short walk northeast of the Alaska Railroad Historic Depot. Rooms come in a variety of configurations, including with kitchenette and two-room suites. A substantial continental breakfast is served each morning, and the lobby has an enormous stuffed brown bear. The hotel stocks a limited number of fishing rods for those who want to try their luck catching salmon in Ship Creek. **Pros:** Pet-friendly, pool, good location to fish or watch the fisherfolk. **Cons:** If you're not into the fishing opportunity at Ship Creek, the location is a problem, the walk into the downtown area is an uphill climb, rooms are a bit noisy at times. ⊠*111 Ship Creek Ave., Downtown* ☎*907/277–6887 or 800/424–6423* ⊕*www.comfortinn.com* ⬅*88 rooms, 12 suites* ⌂*In-room: kitchen (some), refrigerator, Wi-Fi. In-hotel: pool, gym, some pets allowed (fee)* ▭*AE, D, DC, MC, V* ⦿*CP.* ⚓*F1*

$$–$$$ ⊤**Copper Whale Inn.** A view across Cook Inlet to Sleeping Lady and other mountains is a bonus at this small inn on the edge of downtown. New owners remodeled in 2006, and the rooms offer a simple yet elegant ambience. A hearty continental breakfast is served in the comfortable living room, and a dozen good restaurants, including several of Alaska's finest, are within 10 minutes' walk. Profuse gardens grace the property. The 11-mi Coastal Trail is just down the hill. **Pros:** Excellent breakfast, convenient downtown location, responsive and attentive staff. **Cons:** Some rooms are small, some shared baths, some rooms do not have TVs. ⊠*440 L St., Downtown* ☎*907/258–7999* ⊕*www. copperwhale.com* ⬅*14 rooms, 12 with bath* ⌂*In-room: no TV*

5

DID YOU KNOW?

The Tongass and Chugach national forests—Alaska's only ones—are the two largest in the U.S. At 17 million acres, the Tongass is three times the size of the Chugach.

(some), Wi-Fi. In-hotel: bicycles, no elevator, public Internet, no-smoking rooms. ▤*AE, D, DC, MC, V* ❏❘*CP.* ✛*A2*

$$–$$$ ⬚ **Extended Stay Deluxe Anchorage—Downtown.** Formerly the Aspen Hotel, this is one of Anchorage's newest downtown hotels. Rooms are large and comfortably furnished with a single king or two queen beds, a writing table, 27-inch TV, DVD player, mini-refrigerator, and microwave. Two-room suites include a larger refrigerator, stovetop, and pull-out sofa; some also have hot tubs. The hotel is a block from the Anchorage Museum of History and Art and Delaney Park Strip, and has limited off-street parking plus a pool and hot tub downstairs. Nightly, weekly, and monthly rates are available. **Pros:** Very good rates available on-line, nice facilities for long stays. **Cons:** Fee for Internet and laundry use, parking can be a hassle. ✉*108 E. 8th Ave., Downtown* ☎*907/868–1605* ⊕*www.extendedstay.com* ⟿*75 rooms, 14 suites* ⌂*In-room: kitchen, refrigerator, DVD, Wi-Fi. In-hotel: pool, gym, laundry service, public Internet, airport shuttle* ▤*AE, D, MC, V* ❏❘*CP.* ✛*F2*

$$$–$$$$ ⬚ **Historic Anchorage Hotel.** The little building has been around since
★ 1916. Experienced travelers call it the only hotel in Anchorage with charm: the original sinks and tubs have been restored, and upstairs hallways are lined with old Anchorage photos. The rooms are nicely updated with dark cherrywood furnishings and HD flat-screen TVs. The small lobby, its fireplace crackling in chilly weather, has a quaint European feel, and the staff is adept at meeting your needs. Request a corner room if possible; rooms facing the street may have traffic noise. The junior suites include sitting areas. **Pros:** Excellent staff, new TVs, very convenient downtown location. **Cons:** Rooms are small, no airport shuttle, Wi-Fi can be spotty. ✉*330 E St., Downtown* ☎*907/272–4553 or 800/544–0988* ⊕*www.historicanchoragehotel.com* ⟿*16 rooms, 10 junior suites* ⌂*In-room: refrigerator, Wi-Fi. In-hotel: no-smoking rooms* ▤*AE, D, DC, MC, V* ❏❘*CP.* ✛*C1*

$$–$$$$ ⬚ **Hotel Captain Cook.** Recalling Captain Cook's voyages to Alaska and
★ the South Pacific, dark teak paneling lines the hotel's interior and a nautical theme continues into the guest rooms. All rooms have ceiling fans, and guests can use the separate men's and women's athletic clubs with shared indoor heated pool, business center, and other facilities, including three restaurants and a coffee, wine, and martini bar. The hotel occupies an entire city block with three towers, the tallest of which is capped by the **Crow's Nest Restaurant.** The most luxurious accommodation is found on the 19th floor of Tower III—a sprawling, 1,600-square-foot two-bedroom suite, which costs a mere $1,500 per night. **Pros:** Staff very well trained and accommodating, generally considered the nicest hotel in town. **Cons:** Fixtures and furnishings a bit dated, hallways can be dark. ✉*4th Ave. and K St., Downtown* ☎*907/276–6000 or 800/843–1950* ⊕*www.captaincook.com* ⟿*457 rooms, including 96 suites* ⌂*In-room: Wi-Fi. In-hotel: 3 restaurants, room service, pool, gym, concierge, executive floors* ▤*AE, D, DC, MC, V.* ✛*A2*

$$$–$$$$
★ ⊡ **Inlet Tower Hotel and Suites.** Windows overlook either the Chugach Mountains, the Cook Inlet, or downtown Anchorage. Built in 1952 in a residential area a few blocks south of downtown, this 14-story building was Alaska's first high-rise. A major remodeling brought spacious rooms and suites, uniquely Alaskan wallpaper, high-end linens, large televisions, high-speed Internet lines and wireless Internet in the lobby, kitchenettes, and blackout curtains for summer mornings when the sun comes up at 3 AM. The Mixx Grill Restaurant & Bar, serves fresh seafood, steaks, vegetables, and other local favorites. **Pros:** Excellent restaurant on-site, the New Sagaya store and restaurant is but a stone's throw away. **Cons:** Downtown attractions a bit of a hike, hallways narrow and can be dark. ⊠ *1200 L St., Downtown* ☎ *907/276–0110 or 800/544–0786* ⊕ *www.inlettower.com* ⇆ *156 rooms, 24 suites* ⊿ *In-room: kitchen (some), refrigerator, Wi-Fi. In-hotel: restaurant, gym, laundry facilities, public Internet, executive floor, no-smoking rooms, airport shuttle, parking (no fee)* ▤ *AE, D, DC, MC, V.* ✛ *E2*

$ ⊡ **Oscar Gill House.** Gill originally built his home in the settlement of Knik (north of Anchorage) in 1913. Three years later he floated it by boat to Anchorage, where he later served as the mayor for three terms and then speaker of the Territorial House. The home has been transformed into a comfortable B&B in a quiet neighborhood along Delaney Park Strip, with downtown attractions a short walk away. Two rooms share a bath with a classic claw-foot tub, and the third contains a private bath and hot tub. Little touches include down comforters, free use of bicycles, and a delicious breakfast. **Pros:** Great breakfast, very hospitable owners in a bit of Old Anchorage history. **Cons:** Shared bath in two of the rooms, walk to downtown might be a bit of a hike for some. ⊠ *1344 W. 10th Ave., Downtown* ☎ *907/279–1344* ⊕ *www.oscargill. com* ⇆ *3 rooms, 1 with bath* ⊿ *In-room: Wi-Fi. In-hotel: no-smoking rooms* ▤ *AE, MC, V* ⍾ *BP.* ✛ *E2*

$$$–$$$$ ⊡ **Sheraton Anchorage.** A glass-canopy lobby with a jade-tile staircase, acres of new marble, and guest rooms where you can pick up voice mail, iron a suit, and brew your own coffee make this 16-story hotel one of the city's best, despite its marginal neighborhood. Get a room high up on the north side to watch F-22 Raptors and other jets flying tight patterns over nearby Elmendorf Air Force Base. A downstairs restaurant serves three meals a day, and Josephine's, on the 15th floor, open Sunday only, serves a brunch with a view all summer. **Pros:** Nice, modern renovation, great views from the upper floors. **Cons:** Neighborhood a bit dodgy, fees for parking and Internet access. ⊠ *401 E. 6th Ave., Downtown* ☎ *907/276–8700 or 800/325–3535* ⊕ *www.sheraton.com* ⇆ *375 rooms, 5 suites* ⊿ *In-hotel: 2 restaurants, room service, bar, gym, public Internet* ▤ *AE, D, DC, MC, V.* ✛ *G2*

$$$$ ⊡ **SpringHill Suites by Marriott.** The city's main public library and a 16-plex movie theater are near this midtown Anchorage hotel. Spacious one-room suites have separate living and sleeping areas and either a king bed or two double beds with a pullout sofa, plus two televisions. With no extra charge, up to five people can stay in these suites, and breakfast is included. **Pros:** Great breakfast included, 24-hour airport shuttle. **Cons:** Small laundry facilities for such a large hotel, only res-

5

taurants within easy walking distance are national chains. ✉ *3401 A St., Downtown* ☎ *907/562–3247 or 888/287–9400* ⊕ *www.springhill-suites.com* ⇆ *101 suites* ♿ *In-room: refrigerator, Wi-Fi. In-hotel: pool, gym, airport shuttle, no-smoking rooms* ☰ *AE, D, DC, MC, V* ⬤|CP. ✛ *F5*

GREATER ANCHORAGE

¢   ⬚ **Anchorage Guesthouse.** Popular with young outdoorsy travelers, this adventure travel accommodation in a residential neighborhood near downtown has private rooms as well as dorm-style accommodations with bunks. All rooms share three bathrooms. You can rent bikes here, then head out for the Tony Knowles Coastal Trail, or store your gear in the garage before taking off for extended trips into the wilderness. The glassed-in sunroom has a computer and wireless Internet to check your e-mail while you sip coffee on a chilly morning. Make-it-yourself breakfasts of fresh fruit, cereal, orange juice, coffee, and tea are included with the price. Book well in advance for the summer season. **Pros:** Affordable rooms for adventurous travelers, great chance to meet an eclectic clientele. **Cons:** Basic, no-frills accommodations not for everyone, shared baths. ✉ *2001 Hillcrest Dr., Midtown* ☎ *907/274–0408* ⊕ *www.akhouse.com* ⇆ *2 rooms, 1 dorm room, all without bath* ♿ *In-room: no phone, kitchen, no TV. In-hotel: bicycles, laundry facilities, public Internet, public Wi-Fi, no-smoking rooms* ☰ *AE, MC, V* ⬤|CP. ✛ *D3*

$ ⬚ **Camai Bed & Breakfast.** This elegant B&B is Anchorage's oldest. Two of the suites have private entries and plenty of space for families. All suites have private baths and in-room DVD and phones. Moose frequently visit the yard, and the B&B is adjacent to Chester Creek. Breakfast is a high point, with specials like French toast stuffed with peaches and cream and vegetable quiche. **Pros:** Private entries a real plus, quiet residential neighborhood, very experienced hosts. **Cons:** It's a relatively long way from the downtown restaurants, lack of credit-card payment option can be a bother. ✉ *3838 Westminster Way, East Anchorage* ☎ *907/333–2219 or 800/659–8763* ⊕ *www.camaibnb.com* ⇆ *3 suites* ♿ *In-room: DVD, Wi-Fi. In-hotel: public Internet, no-smoking rooms* ☰ *No credit cards* ⬤|BP. ✛ *H5*

$ ⬚ **The Carriage House.** This Girdwood bed-and-breakfast is across from the Double Musky restaurant and close to Alyeska Resort's downhill ski slopes. Horse-drawn carriage tours are given of the spruce-studded, mountain-flanked resort area, about a 40-minute drive south of Anchorage. Rooms are accessed through a private entrance and patios; the rooms in the back have a view of Mt. Alyeska, and the purling of nearby California Creek can be heard through open windows on warm summer evenings. **Pros:** Elegant furnishings, very nice breakfast spread. **Cons:** Location can be a bit remote for some, restaurant traffic is bothersome. ✉ *Mi 0.2, Crow Creek Rd., Girdwood* ☎ *907/783–9464 or 888/961–9464* ⊕ *www.thecarriagehousebandb.com* ⇆ *4 rooms* ♿ *In-room: kitchen, Ethernet* ☰ *AE, D, MC, V* ⬤|BP. ✛ *H6*

$$$ 🖵 **Courtyard by Marriott.** Business travelers pack this modern hotel near the airport. The restaurant serves breakfast and dinner and offers limited room service in the evening. Some rooms have a whirlpool bath and king-size bed; all have two phones, coffeemakers, and hair dryers. **Pros:** Close to airport, free Wi-Fi and shuttle. **Cons:** There's a fee for breakfast, location is noisy, not convenient for restaurants and sights. ✉ *4901 Spenard Rd., Midtown* ☎ *907/245–0322 or 877/729–0197* ⊕ *www.marriott.com* 🛏 *148 rooms, 6 suites* ⚓ *In-hotel: restaurant, room service, pool, laundry service, airport shuttle, no-smoking rooms* ▭ *AE, D, DC, MC, V.* ✛ *C6*

$$$–$$$$ 🖵 **Dimond Center Hotel.** Owned by the Seldovia Native Association, this modern hotel is popular with Alaskans from the bush who appreciate nearby shopping (along with ice-skating and bowling) at Dimond Center Mall, Wal-Mart, Costco, and other big stores. The surprisingly plush facility has custom-designed furnishings and a huge lobby with tall windows. Spacious high-ceiling rooms include 36-inch TVs, relaxing soaking tubs, goose-down comforters on the queen or king beds, and Wi-Fi. Stuff yourself at the breakfast bar, which includes Belgian waffles, fresh fruit, yogurt, and pastries. Guests receive a pass to an adjacent fitness center that includes two pools, Nautilus, steam rooms, hot tubs, and more. There's even a big freezer if you're bringing home fish from your trip. Check the Web site for special rates. **Pros:** Excellent beds, helpful staff, breakfast draws rave reviews. **Cons:** Setting not great for most travelers—you're in a mall parking lot near the railroad tracks. ✉ *700 E. Dimond Blvd., South Anchorage* ☎ *907/770–5000 or 866/770–5002* ⊕ *www.dimondcenterhotel.com* 🛏 *109 rooms* ⚓ *In-room: refrigerator, Wi-Fi. In-hotel: airport shuttle, no-smoking rooms* ▭ *AE, D, DC, MC, V* �📖 *CP.* ✛ *G6*

$$–$$$$ 🖵 **15 Chandeliers Bed & Breakfast.** One of Alaska's premier B&Bs, 15 Chandeliers is a 7,500-square-foot, three-story Victorian-style mansion with a spacious front lawn, private patio, and floral gardens. Owners Max and Peggy Espeland have five theme rooms, all with private baths, antique furnishings, high ceilings, chandeliers, queen beds, televisions, high-speed Internet, theater room, and access to common areas. A deluxe four-course breakfast is served buffet style. **Pros:** Elegant, stylish property, great spread for breakfast. **Cons:** No restaurants or other attractions within walking distance, near highway and busy side road. ✉ *14020 Sabine St., Hillside* ☎ *907/345–3032* ⊕ *www.15chandeliers. com* 🛏 *5 rooms* ⚓ *In-room: Wi-Fi. In-hotel: no-smoking rooms* ▭ *MC, V* �📖 *BP.* ✛ *H6*

$$$$ 🖵 **Hampton Inn.** Midway between the airport and downtown, the Hampton has all the standard features, and a few that are better than average, such as designer furnishings, an indoor swimming pool, and a spa. All rooms have exceptionally comfortable, supportive mattresses. **Pros:** Shuttle will take you into town, great beds, excellent breakfast. **Cons:** Some rooms near the pool can be noisy and smell of chlorine, basic chain-hotel ambience. ✉ *4301 Credit Union Dr., Midtown* ☎ *907/550–7000 or 800/426–7866* ⊕ *www.stonebridgecompanies. com* 🛏 *101 rooms* ⚓ *In-room: refrigerator, dial-up. In-hotel: pool, spa, laundry service* ▭ *AE, D, DC, MC, V* ⓞ *CP.* ✛ *F6*

$$$$
Fodor'sChoice
★

⊡ **The Hotel Alyeska.** Lush forests surround this large and luxurious hotel at the base of Alyeska Ski Resort, in Girdwood, an hour south of Anchorage. Some rooms have views of the Chugach Mountains. Rooms are on the small side, but all have heated towel racks, ski-boot storage lockers, bathrobes, and slippers, plus phones in both the bathrooms and bedrooms. All the rooms were renovated in 2008 with new mattresses, artwork, carpeting, and furniture. Guests relax in front of the big lobby fireplace, with tall windows facing the mountains. The large heated saltwater pool is a major attraction for families, and the hot tub is a hit after a day on the slopes. Dining choices include a family-style restaurant; a gourmet Japanese grill, Teppanyaki Sakura ($$$$); and a new sushi bar. A spectacular aerial tram (free if you have dinner reservations) transports diners to the Seven Glaciers Restaurant at the 2,300-foot level on the mountain. **Pros:** Great views, recent remodeling of all rooms a definite plus. **Cons:** Smallish rooms, service can be uneven. ⊠*1000 Arlberg Rd., Box 249, Girdwood* ☎*907/754–1111 or 800/880–3880* ⊕*www.alyeskaresort.com* ⇗*304 rooms, 12 suites* ⌂*In-room: safe, refrigerator. In-hotel: 5 restaurants, room service, bar, pool, gym, concierge, public Wi-Fi, no-smoking rooms* ⊟*AE, D, DC, MC, V.* ⊹*H6*

$$

⊡ **Long House Alaskan Hotel.** Just five minutes from the airport, this hotel consists of three log-covered two-story buildings. Rooms are large, modern, and comfortable, with two televisions in the suites (where no door separates the rooms). Anglers appreciate the big walk-in freezer to store their catch. **Pros:** Free shuttle, close to airport, friendly staff. **Cons:** No elevator to second-floor rooms, pretty basic amenities. ⊠*4335 Wisconsin St., Midtown* ☎*907/243–2133 or 800/243–2133* ⊕*www.longhousehotel.com* ⇗*54 rooms, 3 suites* ⌂*In-room: Wi-Fi, refrigerator. In-hotel: airport shuttle, free parking* ⊟*AE, D, DC, MC, V* ⓣⓞⓛ*CP.* ⊹*C6*

$$$

⊡ **Mahogany Manor.** Escape from city life at this rambling B&B hidden behind a tall fence along busy 15th Avenue and decorated with Alaska native art throughout. Unwind with the expansive decks, large picture windows, indoor waterfall, fireplaces, and big-screen television. An unusual 19-foot hot tub and jetted lap pool occupies a lower deck, with a solarium to hold in the heat. The spacious three-room suite is perfect for families and small groups. A hearty continental breakfast is served anytime, and guests have access to a separate kitchen and a computer with high-speed Internet. **Pros:** Gorgeous property and rooms, very helpful and accommodating hosts. **Cons:** Property is up for sale, so ownership is in question, not within walking distance of tourist attractions. ⊠*204 E. 15th Ave., Midtown* ☎*907/278–1111 or 888/777–0346* ⊕*www.mahoganymanor.com* ⇗*3 rooms, 1 suite* ⌂*In-hotel: restaurant, pool, public Internet, no-smoking rooms* ⊟*AE, D, MC, V* ⓣⓞⓛ*CP.* ⊹*F3*

$$$$
★

⊡ **Millennium Anchorage Hotel.** Perched on the shore of Lake Spenard, the extensively renovated Millennium Anchorage Hotel is one of the city's best spots to watch planes come and go. The lobby resembles a hunting lodge with its stone fireplace, trophy heads, and mounted fish on every wall. The luxurious guest rooms continue the inviting Alaskan theme. The **Flying Machine Restaurant** is known for its enormous Sunday brunch buffets ($29). **Pros:** Close to the airport, old Alaska hunting-lodge feel. **Cons:** Furnishings and facilities getting worn, airplane noise from Lake Hood can be a problem in summer, fee for Wi-Fi use. ✉*4800 Spenard Rd., Midtown* ☎*907/243–2300 or 800/544–0553* ⊕*www.millennium-hotels.com/anchorage* ↘*243 rooms, 5 suites* ⚐*In-room: refrigerator. In-hotel: restaurant, room service, bar, gym, laundry service, public Internet, airport shuttle, some pets allowed* ▭*AE, D, DC, MC, V.* ⊹*C6*

¢–$ ▯**Qupqugiaq Inn.** A bland, boxy exterior disguises this cross between a motel and a hostel with an unpronounceable name. The interior architecture of "Q Inn" is distinctive, with flowing, asymetrical curves, handmade tiles, handcrafted furniture, and an international theme in each room. This is a good option for budget travelers who can tolerate small quarters and a no-alcohol policy but appreciate clean and well-maintained facilities, including antique English beds. You have access to a communal kitchen and sitting room. A pleasant café serving authentic Turkish food is downstairs, and Europa Bakery is across the street. **Pros:** Good value for your travel dollar, unique architecture and ambience. **Cons:** Eco-hippie vibe could be a problem for some, room quality varies considerably. ✉*640 W. 36th Ave., Midtown* ☎*907/563–5633* ⊕*www.qupq.com* ↘*25 rooms, 12 with bath* ⚐*In-room: Wi-Fi. In-hotel: kitchen, restaurant, public Internet, no-smoking rooms* ▭*AE, MC, V.* ⊹*F5*

NIGHTLIFE & THE ARTS

NIGHTLIFE

Anchorage does not shut down when it gets dark. Bars here—and throughout Alaska—open early (in the morning) and close as late as 3 AM on weekends. There's a ban on smoking in bars and bingo parlors, as well as restaurants. The listings in the *Anchorage Daily News* entertainment section, published on Friday, and in the free weekly *Anchorage Press* (⊕*www.anchoragepress.com*) range from concerts and theater performances to movies and a roundup of nightspots featuring live music.

BARS & NIGHTCLUBS

Anchorage's favorite martini bar, **Bernie's Bungalow Lounge** (✉*626 D St., Downtown* ☎*907/276–8808*) is a hipster spot, with retro furnishings, splashy art, and a DJ most weekends. The cocktail to order here is a cosmopolitan. **Chilkoot Charlie's** (✉*2435 Spenard Rd., Spenard* ☎*907/272–1010* ⊕*www.koots.com*), a rambling timber building with sawdust floors, 11 bars (including one made of ice), three dance floors, loud music (rock or swing bands and DJs) nightly, 2 DJs every Thursday, Friday, and Saturday, and rowdy customers, is where young Alaskans go to get crazy. This legendary bar has many unusual nooks and crannies, including a room filled with Russian artifacts and serving the

Fodor'sChoice
★

finest vodka drinks, plus a reconstructed version of Alaska's infamous Birdhouse Bar. If you haven't been to 'Koots, you haven't seen Anchorage nightlife at its wildest.

Lots of old-timers favor the dark bar of **Club Paris** (⌧*417 W. 5th Ave., Downtown* ☎*907/277–6332* ⊕*www.clubparisrestaurant.com*). The Paris mural and French street lamps hanging behind the bar have lost some luster, but there's still a faithful clientele. The jukebox favors swing. **F Street Station** (⌧*325 F St., Downtown* ☎*907/272–5196*), a crowded little downtown bar, is a delightful spot for a perfectly prepared and reasonably priced lunch or dinner. Check the board for the day's specials, or just enjoy a beer and appetizers with the suit-and-tie crowd. A half-dozen small tables are available, or you can eat at the bar and chat with the chefs as they work. **Rumrunners** (⌧*501 W. 4th Ave., Downtown* ☎*907/278–4493,* ⊕*www.rumrunnersak.com*) is right across from Old City Hall in the center of town. A pub-grub menu brings the lunch crowd, but when evening comes the big dance floor gets packed as DJs spin the tunes. A trendy place for the dressy "in" crowd, the bar at **Simon & Seafort's Saloon & Grill** (⌧*420 L St., Downtown* ☎*907/274–3502* ⊕*www.r-u-i.com/sim*) has stunning views of Cook Inlet, a special single-malt Scotch menu, and a wide selection of imported beers. **Snow Goose Restaurant** (⌧*717 W. 3rd Ave., Downtown* ☎*907/277–7727* ⊕*www.alaskabeers.com*) is a good place to unwind with a beer inside or on the airy outside deck overlooking Cook Inlet. There's decent food, too.

GAY & LESBIAN BARS

Anchorage's gay nightlife centers on a pair of bars, both of which attract a mixed crowd. **Mad Myrna's** (⌧*530 E. 5th Ave., Downtown* ☎*907/276–9762* ⊕*www.alaska.net/~madmyrna*) has karaoke on Wednesday, country dancing (with lessons) on Thursday, and drag shows every Friday. The **Raven** (⌧*708 E. 4th Ave., Downtown* ☎*907/276–9672*) is a neighborhood hangout where you'll meet regulars over a game of billiards or darts.

COFFEE INSTEAD? Looking for one of the best cups of coffee in town? Kaladi Brothers Coffee has espresso, lattes, baked goods, and more. They've got seven other locations in town, most with free Wi-Fi access. For a list, go to ⊕*www.kaladi.com*. ⌧*621 W. 6th Ave.* ☎*907/277–1881*.

LIVE MUSIC

See the "Play" section in Friday editions of the *Anchorage Daily News* for complete listings of upcoming concerts and other performances, or get the same entertainment info online at ⊕*www.adn.com*.

Fodor'sChoice ★ **Blues Central/Chef's Inn** (⌧*825 W. Northern Lights Blvd., Spenard* ☎*907/272–1341*), a modest eatery, is also a blues mecca that stages bands seven nights a week. **Chilkoot Charlie's** (⇨*Bars & Nightclubs*) is an exceptionally popular party place, with live music every night of the week. Fans of salsa, merengue, and other music crowd the dance floor at the downtown **Club Soraya** (⌧*333 W. 4th Ave., Downtown* ☎*907/276–0670*). There are dance classes several nights a week, followed by live bands. Check ⊕ *www.akswing.com* for current info. One of Anchorage's favorite bars, **Humpy's Great Alaskan Alehouse** (✉*610 W. 6th Ave., Downtown* ☎*907/276–2337* ⊕*www.humpys. com*) serves up rock, blues, and folk five nights a week, including open mike on Monday, along with dozens of microbrews (more than 40 beers are on tap) and surprisingly tasty pub grub—we especially like the smoked salmon spread. It's noisy and always packed. **Latitude 61** (✉*4848 Old Seward Hwy., Midtown* ☎*907/562–5701*) has country music Wednesday and poker tournaments Monday through Thursday; Friday and Saturday are dance nights. Downtown's **Snow City Cafe** (✉*4th Ave. at L St., Downtown* ☎*907/272–2489* ⊕*www.snowcity-cafe.com*) has Irish music jam sessions on Wednesday evening.

THE ARTS

Anchorage often surprises visitors with its variety—and high quality—of cultural activities. In addition to top-name touring groups and performers, a sampling of local productions, including provocative theater, children's shows, improvisational troupes, Buddhist lectures, photography exhibits, poetry readings, and native Alaskan dance performances, is always going on around town. The Friday entertainment section of the *Anchorage Daily News* is packed with events and activities. Tickets for many cultural events can be purchased at any Carrs or Safeway grocery store. **Carrs Tix** (☎*907/263–2787 or 800/478–7328* ⊕*http://tickets.com/search.cgi?q=anchorage*) has recorded information on cultural events of the week and the option to buy tickets by phone or from the Web site.

The **Alaska Center for the Performing Arts** (✉*621 W. 6th Ave., at G St., Downtown* ☎*907/263–2900, 800/478–7328 tickets* ⊕*www.alaska-pac.org*) has three theaters and hosts local performing groups and traveling production companies that have brought *Rent, Les Misérables,* and *Lord of the Dance.* The lobby box office (Monday–Saturday 10–6) sells tickets to the productions and is a good all-around source of cultural information.

FILM
The popular **Bear Tooth Theatre Pub** (✉*1230 W. 27th Ave., Spenard* ☎*907/276–4200* ⊕*www.beartooththeatre.net*) screens second-run and art films for only $3 and also serves tasty pizzas, sandwiches, burritos, salads, and beer while you watch.

OPERA & CLASSICAL MUSIC
The **Anchorage Opera** (☎*907/279–2557* ⊕*www.anchorageopera.org*) produces three operas during its November through March season. The **Anchorage Symphony Orchestra** (☎*907/274–8668* ⊕*www.anchoragesymphony.org*) performs classical concerts October through April. The box office of the Alaska Center for the Performing Arts sells tickets for both.

Continued on page 273

THE GLORIOUS AND RELENTLESS MIDNIGHT SUN

The side-lit afternoons seeping into late evening. The unforgettable sunsets streaking the sky with swaths of neon. The 9PM golf tee offs and midnight baseball games. The black-out curtains and sleep masks. The bloodshot eyes. The madness of it all: Alaska's tilted life.

The light (and lack thereof) is one of Alaska's most dramatic characteristics. Long summer days goad visitors to sightsee well into the evening, while record-breaking vegetables (read: cabbages the size of coffee tables) grow in the fields. The feeble, or just plain absent, winter sun allows snow to recharge glaciers while the aurora borealis (a.k.a. the northern lights) dances above hibernating bears and humans alike.

Remember that the farther north you go in Alaska, the more pronounced the midnight sun will be. If you make it to Barrow, you'll experience nightless days in summer. Heading south means a less extreme case of the midnight sun, but often just as much revelry celebrating its presence. Summertime simply has a different feeling in Alaska—enjoy the local fairs and festivals, and the stunning mixture of persistent daylight, snow-capped mountains, and miles of vibrant wildland.

(above) A brave Midnight Sun runner (right) How does *your* garden grow?

THE MIDNIGHT SUN: HOW IT WORKS

The Earth spins on a slightly tilted axis as it rotates around the sun. The northern hemisphere is tilted toward the sun in summer and away from it in winter. So how does this explain Alaska's midnight sun? The globe's most northern areas, including much of Alaska, are tilted so far toward the sun in summer that there's continuous light.

In **Barrow**, at the top of the world, the sun rises in mid-May and doesn't set until August.

Summer Solstice: June 22.

Summer

In winter the northern hemisphere faces away from the sun and Alaska has several months of darkness.

Spring Equinox: March 22.

Spring

Winter Solstice: December 22.

Winter

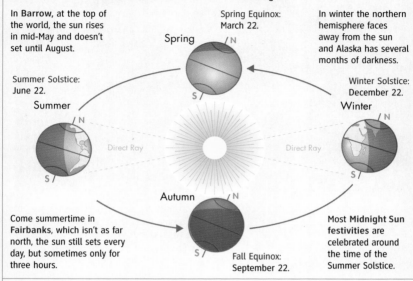

Come summertime in **Fairbanks**, which isn't as far north, the sun still sets every day, but sometimes only for three hours.

Fall Equinox: September 22.

Autumn

Most **Midnight Sun** festivities are celebrated around the time of the Summer Solstice.

TIPS FROM AN ALASKAN

Coping with the Midnight Sun

■ Close your shades a few hours before bedtime. Bring a sleep mask or use the black-out curtains in your hotel room!

■ Bring antihistamines to soothe the mosquito bites we *promise* you'll get—the added bonus is the drowsiness.

■ You can always count sheep. Or count microbrews! Alaska has many to enjoy, including Silver Gulch, Sleeping Lady, Kodiak Brewery, and Moose's Tooth.

■ If all else fails, go out and enjoy the eerie light. Many people find that they simply need less sleep in summer.

Surviving the Polar Winter

■ Get what sunlight you can. Make sure you're up and at 'em whenever the sun is.

■ Take your vitamins, especially vitamin D, and eat plenty of fruit.

■ Some Alaskans go that extra step and visit tanning salons to boost their mood—and, of course, for a little color!

■ Fool your body into thinking the sun is out: sip your morning coffee near a lamp (preferably full-spectrum).

■ Did we mention Alaska's many excellent microbrews?

MIDNIGHT SUN REVELRY

During the peak of the midnight sun season, June and early July, there's almost no end to the special activities and festivals celebrating the light. It's a good thing, too—you may have trouble falling asleep!

■ Taking place the Saturday closest to the summer solstice, the **Mayor's Marathon and Half Marathon in Anchorage** attract runners from all over the country. (⊕ www.mayorsmarathon.com)

■ The much less formal 10-km **Midnight Sun Run is held in Fairbanks** every June on the weekend closest to the summer solstice. The run starts at 10 PM. (⊕ fairbanks-alaska.com/midnight-sun-run.htm)

■ The **midnight sun baseball game in Fairbanks** is the best-known midnight sun activity in Alaska. The Alaska Goldpanners are the stars of the Alaska League, comprised of college athletes from around the country. Every summer solstice, the Goldpanners host the "high noon at midnight" classic, a tradition since 1906. The first pitch is thrown at 10:30 PM, and the entire game is played without the use of artificial lights. (They haven't worked since they were struck by lightning years ago!) (⊕ www.goldpanners.com)

■ If you'd rather steer clear of festivals and find a spot of your own, **drive out of Fairbanks** along Steese Highway or Chena Hot Springs Road for the unforgettable nighttime view.

■ Almost every Alaskan town has a special event on or near the summer solstice, but one of the best is the **Nome Midnight Sun Festival**, which celebrates 22 hours of direct sunlight with parades, barbecues, and folk music. (⊕ www.nomealaska.org/vc)

■ The **Alaska State Fair** runs for 12 days before Labor Day in the town of Palmer, 40 mi northeast of Anchorage. Check out the giant midnight sun–grown vegetables on display and colorful vending booths selling an array of goods from cookies to jewelry. (⊕ www.alaskastatefair.org)

THEATER

The **Alaska Center for the Performing Arts** stages major theater performances, and hosts the Anchorage Opera and the Anchorage Symphony Orchestra. The Anchorage Community Theater (✉ *1133 E. 70th Ave.* ☎ *907/344-4713* ⊕ *http://actalaska.org*) has a year-around schedule of locally produced plays, and also offers training for prospective thespians of all ages and skill levels. **Cyrano's Off-Center Playhouse** (✉ *4th Ave. and D St., Downtown* ☎ *907/274-2599* ⊕ *www.cyranos.org*) mounts innovative productions in a cozy theater connected to a namesake café and bookstore. **Out North Contemporary Art House** (✉ *1325 Primrose St., just west of Bragaw Rd. off DeBarr Rd., East Anchorage* ☎ *907/279–3800* ⊕ *www.outnorth.org*), whose productions are thought-provoking and, at times, controversial, often earns critical acclaim from local reviewers. Student productions from the **University of Alaska Anchorage Theater** (✉ *3211 Providence Dr., East Anchorage* ☎ *907/786–4849*) are timely and well done. The theater is intimate, with seating on three sides.

MUSIC ALFRESCO

On most summertime Fridays, open-air concerts are performed at noon on the stage in front of the **Old City Hall** (✉ *524 W. 4th Ave., Downtown*). A range of performers play at the **Saturday Market** (✉ *3rd Ave. and E St., Downtown* ☎ *907/272-5634* ⊕ *www.anchoragemarkets.com*) every Saturday from late May to mid-September. The music includes everything from family bands (with daughter on violin and dad on guitar and vocals) to Peruvian panpipe musicians.

5

SHOPPING

Stock up for your travels around Alaska in Anchorage, where there's no sales tax. The Saturday and Sunday markets are packed with Alaskan-made products of all types, and you're likely to meet local artisans.

MALLS & DEPARTMENT STORES

Anchorage's **5th Avenue Mall** occupies a city block at 5th Avenue and A Street, and contains dozens of stores, including JC Penney, Banana Republic, and other popular chains, spread over several levels. The top level houses a food court. Just across 6th Avenue, and connected by a skywalk to the 5th Avenue Mall, is Alaska's only **Nordstrom.** The city's largest shopping mall, **Dimond Center,** is on the south end of town at Dimond Boulevard and Old Seward Highway. In addition to dozens of shops, Dimond Center has a movie theater and an ice-skating rink. Nearby are several big-box discount stores, including Costco, Best Buy, and Wal-Mart.

MARKETS

In summer, Anchorage's **Saturday and Sunday Markets** (☎907/272–5634 ⊕*www.anchoragemarkets.com*) are open in the parking lot at 3rd Avenue and E Street. More than 300 vendors offer Alaskan-made crafts, ethnic imports, and deliciously fattening food. The open-air markets run from mid-May to mid-September, weekends 10–6. A smaller market sells local produce and crafts July through August, on Wednesday from 11 to 5, at Northway Mall in East Anchorage.

SPECIALTY SHOPS

ART

Anchorage's **First Friday** art openings are a popular monthly event, with 15 or so galleries offering a chance to sample hors d'oeuvres while looking over the latest works by regional artists.

Artic Rose Gallery (⊠*420 L St., Downtown* ☎907/279–3911 ⊕*www. articrosegallery.com*) is in the same building as Simon and Seafort's restaurant. Alaska's oldest gallery, **Artique** (⊠*314 G St., Downtown* ☎907/277–1663 ⊕*www.artiqueltd.com*), sells paintings, prints, and jewelry by prominent Alaskan artists.The **International Gallery of Contemporary Art** (⊠*427 D St., Downtown* ☎907/279–1116 ⊕*www. igcaalaska.org*) is Anchorage's premier fine arts gallery, with changing exhibits monthly. **One People** (⊠*425 D St., Downtown* ☎907/274–4063) offers the works of Alaskan artists and crafts workers, including an excellent selection of native pieces.

BOOKS & MUSIC

Barnes & Noble Booksellers (⊠*200 E. Northern Lights Blvd., at A St., Midtown* ☎907/279–7323 ⊕*www.bn.com*) is one of Anchorage's most popular bookstores. The store stays open late, with literary events some nights. **Borders Books & Music** (⊠*1100 E. Dimond Blvd., west of Seward Hwy., South Anchorage* ☎907/344–4099 ⊕*www.borders. com*) also stocks a diverse selection of titles and has a café. **Metro Music & Book Store** (⊠*530 E. Benson Blvd., Spenard* ☎907/279–8622) carries a well-thought-out inventory of fiction and nonfiction, but the main draw is the impressive collection of CDs. You can listen to any of them before buying. Inside, Felix Cafe serves crepes, espresso, and housemade yogurt. Easily the largest independent bookstore in Alaska, **Title Wave Books** (⊠*1360 W. Northern Lights Blvd., Midtown* ☎907/278–9283 or 888/598–9283 ⊕*www.wavebooks.com*) fills a sprawling store at the other end of the REI strip mall. The shelves are filled with new and used titles, and a large section of Alaska stuff, and the staff is very knowledgeable. Also here is **Kaladi Brothers Coffee Shop** (⊠415 W. 5th Ave., *Downtown* ☎907/258–9283) with Wi-Fi access for Web surfers. They recently opened a downtown location inside the Alaska Center for Performing Arts as well.

GIFTS

Several downtown shops sell quality native Alaskan artwork, but the best buys can be found in the gift

★ shop at the **Alaska Native Medical Center** (✉ *4315 Diplomacy Dr., at Tudor and Bragaw Rds., East Anchorage* ☎ *907/563–2662),* which is open weekdays 10–2 and 11–2 on the first and third Saturday of the month. They don't take credit cards. The gift shop at **Alaska Native Heritage Center** (✉ *8800 Heritage Center Dr., Glenn Hwy. at Muldoon Rd., East Anchorage* ☎ *907/330–8000 or 800/315–6608* ⊕ *www.alaskanative.net*) sells native crafts. **Laura Wright Alaskan Parkys** sells distinctive Eskimo-style "parkys" (parkas) and will custom sew one for you. They're available at **Heritage Gifts** (✉ *333 W. 4th Ave., No. 227, at D St., Downtown* ☎ *907/274–4215).* **Oomingmak** (✉ *6th Ave. and H St., Downtown* ☎ *907/272–9225 or 888/360–9665* ⊕ *www.qiviut. com*), a native-owned cooperative, sells items made of qiviut, the warm undercoat of the musk ox. Scarves, shawls, and tunics are knitted in traditional patterns.

Get smoked reindeer meat and salmon products at **Alaska Sausage and Seafood Company** (✉ *2914 Arctic Blvd., Midtown* ☎ *907/562–3636 or 800/798–3636* ⊕ *www.alaskasausage.com*).**New Sagaya's City Market** (✉ *900 W. 13th Ave., Downtown* ☎ *907/274–6173*) sells an excellent selection of fresh seafood. If you don't want to carry the fish with you, the market will pack and ship it.

Although furs may not be to everyone's taste or ethics, a number of Alaska fur companies have stores and factories in Anchorage. One of the city's largest and best-known furriers is **David Green Master Furrier** (✉ *130 W. 4th Ave., Downtown* ☎ *907/277–9595* ⊕ *www.davidgreenfurs.com).* **Alaska Fur Exchange** (✉ *4417 Old Seward Hwy., Midtown* ☎ *907/563–3877* ⊕ *www.alaskafurexchange.com*) has a large midtown store that sells both furs and native artwork.

JEWELRY

The **Kobuk Valley Jade Co.** (✉ *Olympic Circle, Girdwood* ☎ *907/783–2764),* at the base of Mt. Alyeska, sells hand-polished jade pieces as well as native masks, baskets, and jewelry.

GREEN GIANTS

Can you heft a 105-pound cabbage? Ever seen a 942-pound pumpkin? Produce gets big in South Central Alaska, as those two state records suggest. There are about 900 commercial vegetable farms in the state, reaping annual revenues of about $52 million. Growing seasons in South Central are short but intense. Still, seeing is believing at the Saturday and Sunday Markets, which feature the large vegetables. The biggest produce is saved for show at the annual Alaska State Fair in Palmer.

5

Finger Lake Checkpoint. Sled dogs start the Iditarod in Anchorage and stop here, 194 mi into the 1,131 mi trek.

SPORTS & OUTDOORS EQUIPMENT

If you get to Alaska and discover you've left some critical camping or outdoor recreation gear behind, **REI** (✉*1200 W. Northern Lights Blvd., Spenard* ☎*907/272–4565* ⊕*www.rei.com*) rents camping, skiing, and paddling equipment. They also give weekly seminars on season-specific outdoors subjects, and the salespeople are very knowledgeable about local conditions and activities, and the gear required to get you out and back safely. **Sportsman's Warehouse** (✉*8681 Old Seward Hwy., South Anchorage* ☎*907/644–1400* ⊕*www.sportsmanswarehouse.com*) is a big-box outdoors store with all manner of fishing, hiking, and camping gear. Prices are lower than at most places in town, and the selection is great, but you won't find the personal attention and knowledgeable staff that the more high-end places specialize in. And speaking of high-end, there's **Mt. View Sports Center** (✉*3838 Old Seward Hwy., Midtown* ☎*907/563–8600* ⊕*www.mtviewsports.com*). If you're looking for brand names like Abel, Sims, Filson, Patagonia, Kimber, and Mountain Hardwear, Mt. View is your place. They are pretty much fly-fishing central in Anchorage, and you can find expert advice and guidance for your prospective fishing and hunting adventures. They've also got an excellent book section that covers all sorts of outdoor activities in Alaska.

SLED DOG RACES & WINTER FUN

World-championship races are run in February, with three consecutive 25-mi heats through downtown Anchorage, out into the foothills, and back. People line the route with cups of coffee in hand to cheer on their favorite mushers. The three-day races are part of the annual **Fur Rendezvous**, one of the largest winter festivals in the United States. Other attractions include a snow-sculpture competition, car races, Eskimo blanket toss (a holdover from earlier days when dozens of people would team up to grasp a round walrus hide blanket and launch a hunter high into the air, trampoline-style, in an effort to spot distant seals, walrus, and whales), dog weight–pulling contests (where canines of all breeds and sizes compete to see which can pull the most weight piled on a sled), a carnival, and even snowshoe softball. Fur Rondy (or Fur Rendezvous Festival) events take place from late February to the start of the Iditarod in early March. The **Fur Rondy office** (✉ *400 D St., No. 200, Downtown* ☎ *907/274-1270* ⊕ *www.furrondy.net*) has a guide to the festival's events. In March, mushers and their dogs compete in the 1,100-mi **Iditarod Trail Sled Dog Race** (☎ *907/376-5155, 800/545-6874 Iditarod Trail Headquarters* ⊕ *www.iditarod.com*). The race commemorates the delivery of serum to Nome by dog mushers during the diphtheria epidemic of 1925. The serum run was the inspiration for the animated family film *Balto*. Dog teams leave downtown Anchorage and wind through the Alaska Range, across the Interior, out to the Bering Sea coast, and on to Nome. Depending on weather and trail conditions, winners can complete the race in nine days (⇨ *Alaska's Well-Worn Trail Close-Up box*).

SPORTS

Wintertime brings hockey, dog mushing, and ski races, and the long summer days provide the chance to watch a semipro baseball game and still have time to watch the sun go down at midnight. **Sullivan Arena** (✉ *334 E. 16th Ave., Midtown* ☎ *907/566-1596*) is Anchorage's primary venue for large events, from ice hockey to boat shows. **Mulcahy Stadium** (✉ *E. 16th Ave. at Cordova St., Midtown*) is the center for semipro baseball in Anchorage.

BASEBALL

Two summer collegiate baseball teams play at Mulcahy Stadium next to the Sullivan Arena. The games played here are intense—many players have gone on to star in the major leagues. The **Anchorage Bucs** (☎ *907/561-2827* ⊕ *www.anchoragebucs.com*) have a dozen or so former players who went on to the majors, including standouts Wally Joyner, Jeff Kent, and Bobby Jones. The most famous player on the **Glacier Pilots** (☎ *907/274-3627* ⊕ *www.glacierpilots.com*) was Mark McGwire, but many other pre–major leaguers have played for them over the years, including Dave Winfield, Randy Johnson, and Reggie Jackson.

FOOTBALL

Alaska's entry in the Intense Football League playing indoor arena-style ball is the Alaska Wild (☎*907/771–9400* ⊕*www.goakwild.com*). Their season runs from March through June, playing their home games in Anchorage.

HOCKEY

Hockey is in the blood of any true Alaskan, and kids as young as age four crowd local ice rinks in hopes of becoming the next Scott Gomez (who still lives in Anchorage when he's not playing for the New York Rangers).

The East Coast Hockey League's **Alaska Aces** (☎*907/258–2237* ⊕*www.alaskaaces.com*) play minor-league professional hockey in the Sullivan Arena. The **University of Alaska Anchorage** (☎*907/786–1293* ⊕*www.goseawolves.com*) has a Division I NCAA hockey team that draws several thousand loyal fans to home games at the Sullivan Arena.

South Central Alaska

INCLUDING PRINCE WILLIAM SOUND, HOMER & THE KENAI PENINSULA

WORD OF MOUTH

"I did make the trip on the Alaska Railroad from Anchorage to Seward specifically to visit the Kenai Fjords. It was FANTASTIC! Lots of birds and sealife, glaciers abound, and the weather was absolutely gorgeous the day I went. It started my whole Alaska vacation on a wonderful note."

—hpeabody

WELCOME TO SOUTH CENTRAL ALASKA

A dancer displays a native costume

TOP REASONS TO GO

★ **The fishing:** In summer salmon fill the rivers, which you can fish with a guide, from your own boat, or from the bank. Fish for halibut and rockfish charter boats out of Homer or Seward.

★ **The wildlife:** Urban moose, black and brown bears, sea lions, Dall sheep, gray whales, and bald eagles are all common sights in the region. Keep your eyes open and you're likely to see numerous animals, whether in a town or the backcountry.

★ **The scenery:** South Central doesn't scrimp on grandiose scenes. Boasting views of volcanoes and mountains that fall right into the water, the Kenai Peninsula is a buffet for the eyes, while Prince William Sound offers calving glaciers and narrow inlets uninhabited by anything but sea life.

★ **The access:** With a network of roads and ferries, all the above are easily accessible. No matter where you go in the region, you're always only a few steps away from the wilderness.

1 **Prince William Sound.** Spanning 15,000 mi, Prince William Sound is made up of remote coves, glaciers that curve right into the sea, and small islands topped with sea lions and puffins. The sound is easily accessible from Anchorage via Whittier or Valdez.

3 **Homer.** Literally the end of the road, Homer has an alluring blend of commercial fishermen, artists, bohemians, and tourists. With bluffs sloping down to Kachemak Bay, it's hard to find a spot in town without a view of the ocean or mountains. Be sure to try the excellent restaurants and sip a local beer.

GETTING ORIENTED

South Central is the population and commercial center of Alaska, and its attractions are relatively road accessible. The region includes the Kenai Peninsula south of Anchorage, Prince William Sound and Wrangell–St. Elias National Park to the east, and the Interior gateway town of Talkeetna to the north. Geographic features include four mountain ranges, three national parks, the country's second-largest national forest, Cook Inlet, and more glaciers, rivers, and lakes than you could visit in a lifetime.

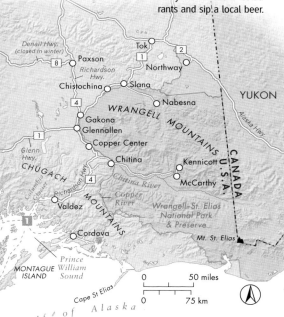

A Russian Orthodox Church in Kenai

2 **Kenai Peninsula.** A look at Friday-afternoon traffic pouring out of Anchorage in summer onto the single road south to the Kenai is all the evidence you need that the peninsula's nickname "Anchorage's playground" is accurate. The Kenai has world-class recreation options that include fishing, hiking, canoeing, and whale-watching.

4 **Mat-Su Valley and Beyond.** Just north of Anchorage, the Matanuska-Susitna Valley is a mixture of bedroom communities, agricultural concerns, and recreation options, and it's the gateway to the Interior. Several spectacular mountain ranges converge here: the Chugach, the Talkeetna, and the Alaska, with rivers and streams full of trophy-class salmon and trout.

SOUTH CENTRAL ALASKA PLANNER

How's the Weather?

Summer is peak season, with the major population influx coinciding with the end of the school year and the beginning of the salmon runs. Long daylight hours make it easy to burn the candle at both ends. Some of this can be avoided by using the shoulder seasons, but spring and fall can be a bit iffy, weather-wise. Autumn starts early here, the tundra plants and the deciduous trees beginning to show color in mid-August. The animals are actively getting ready for winter, there are plenty of fish to catch, and most of the visitor services stay open into September.

Pack Right

Carry a day pack with an extra layer (or two) of clothing, rain gear, water, and snacks as a bare minimum. Everyone should have his or her own pair of binoculars, even if it's just an inexpensive set. There are few things more frustrating than having the wildlife sighting of a lifetime with everyone grabbing for the same set of field glasses.

Water Ways

Ferries are a great way to explore the South Central coast, with its glaciers, mountains, fjords, and sea mammals. The ferries between Valdez and Whittier run by way of Columbia Glacier in summer, where it is not unusual to witness giant fragments of ice calving from the face of the glacier into Prince William Sound.

The **Alaska Marine Highway** (☎ *907/465–3941 or 800/642–0066* ⊕ *www.dot.state.ak.us/amhs*), the state-run ferry operator, has scheduled service to Valdez, Cordova, Whittier, Homer, and Seldovia on the mainland; to Kodiak and Port Lions on Kodiak Island; and to the port of Dutch Harbor in the Aleutian Islands. These connect to the ferries that operate in Southeast Alaska, but the two systems connect only on once-a-month sailings. Ferries operate on two schedules; summer (May–September) sailings are considerably more frequent than fall and winter service. Check your schedules carefully: ferries do not stop at all ports every day. Reservations are required on all routes and should be made as far in advance as possible.

Travel Times from Anchorage

DESTINATION	TIME
Chugach State Park	20 mins–1 hr by car, depending on section of park
Cordova	1 hr to Whittier by car, then 3 hrs by ferry
Denali State Park	3 hrs by car
Glennallen	4 hrs by car
Homer	4–5 hrs by car
Kenai/Soldotna	2–3 hrs by car
Lake Clark	1–2 hrs by air taxi
Portage Glacier	50 mins by car
Seward	2-2.5 hrs by car
Wrangell–St. Elias	6–8 hrs by car

Getting Around

Anchorage is the region's hub, connected by rail and road to major ports in South Central. To the east, you can reach McCarthy and Valdez by an indirect but scenic drive on the Glenn and Richardson highways. The Seward and Sterling highways connect to nearly every town on the Kenai Peninsula. South Central's other "highway," the ferry-driven Alaska Marine Highway, connects with Kodiak, Whittier, Valdez, Homer, Seldovia, and Cordova and other ports throughout the Southeast and the Aleutians.

The **Alaska Railroad Corporation** (☎ 800/544–0552 ⊕ www.akrr.com) operates the Alaska Railroad, which runs 470 mi between Seward and Fairbanks via Anchorage. There's daily service between Anchorage and Fairbanks in summer, and in winter there's one round-trip per week. Service to Seward from Anchorage only runs mid-May to September.

For bus service, contact **Alaska Direct Bus Lines** (☎ 907/277–6652 or 800/770–6652).**Homer Stage Line** (☎ 907/362–3644 or 907/235–2252). **Park Connection** (☎ 800/208–0200, 907/224–7116 for Seward, 907/683–1240 for Denali). **Seward Bus Line** (☎ 907/563–0800 or 907/224–3608).

About the Hotels & Restaurants

The best way to describe the hospitality industry in Alaska is "informal," so don't worry if you still have your hiking clothes on when you go out to eat. Every kind of food is available, especially in larger towns, but options decline considerably from mid-September through April. Any time you're traveling the road system, carry a copy of *The Milepost* (⊕ www.themilepost.com), which covers the roads mile by mile.

WHAT IT COSTS

¢	$	$$	$$$	$$$$
RESTAURANTS				
under $10	$10–$15	$15–$20	$20–$25	over $25
HOTELS				
under $75	$75–$125	$125–$175	$175–$225	over $225

Restaurant prices are per person for a main course at dinner. Hotel prices are for two people in a standard double room in high season.

Making the Most of Your Time

For a weeklong trip in South Central, begin by driving northeast on the Glenn Highway to Valdez out of Anchorage. Take the whole day to drive, stopping for lunch at the Matanuska Glacier and a short hike at Thompson Pass. Spend the night in Valdez, and then drive on to the ferry to Cordova. Have breakfast downtown, reserving the afternoon for driving the Copper River Highway. The next morning, drive back on the ferry to Whittier, continue through the tunnel to Portage, and take a left on the Seward Highway. Keep going until you reach Seward, and unpack your bags for at least a two-night stay. Take a glacier cruise or fishing charter on the middle day, and spend an evening walking around Exit Glacier and sipping a brew on the Resurrection Roadhouse's riverfront· deck. If you'd like to slow down, use Seward as a base for exploring Kenai Fjords National Park and the Chugach. Otherwise roll across the peninsula to Homer, and spend several days there halibut fishing, kayaking Kachemak Bay, shopping on the spit, and taking a day trip to Seldovia.

6

Updated by
Catherine
Bodry

With mountains, wildlife, rivers, glaciers, and the sea, South Central offers nearly every sight you'd want on an Alaskan vacation. Even better, there are roads! It's easy to travel from point to point, and it's possible to make a loop in and out of Anchorage by driving onto ferries in Prince William Sound. Whichever route you take, it's sure to be memorable.

South Central Alaska is bordered on the south and west by the port towns on the Gulf of Alaska, Prince William Sound, and Cook Inlet—Cordova, Valdez, Whittier, Seward, Seldovia, Kodiak, Homer, and Kenai—with their harbors, ferries, glaciers, and ocean life, and at its center is Anchorage. South Central towns and cities have very different personalities. Kodiak is a busy commercial-fishing port, whereas Homer is a funky tourist town and artists' colony on beautiful Kachemak Bay. Talkeetna, the northern edge of the region, is where mountaineers gather to launch their assaults on towering Mt. McKinley. On the eastern border, the defunct copper mine outside McCarthy lies at the foot of the Wrangell Mountains. South Central is also Alaska's farm country. In the Matanuska-Susitna Valley (often just referred to as the "Mat-Su Valley" or simply "the Valley"), under an ever-present summertime sun, 75-pound cabbages are common.

Then come those mountains, curled like an arm embracing the region. To the east of Anchorage and sweeping on to the southwest are the Chugach Mountains, a young, active, and impressively rugged range notable for its high coastal relief. Near-mile-high valley walls and peaks rise almost directly from the sea. Across Cook Inlet to the southwest march the high volcanic peaks of the Alaska Range, part of the Pacific Ocean's great Ring of Fire, but snowcapped nonetheless. Farther north in the Alaska Range shimmers Mt. McKinley, with Mt. Foraker at its shoulder—the towering granite giants of the North American continent. No matter which of Alaska's climate zones or ecosystems you wish to explore, you'll find it somewhere nearby—from the coastal rain forests near Seward and Kodiak to the Arctic environment of the glaciers flowing off the Harding Icefield, to the tundra and taiga of the mountain ranges, to the near-ubiquitous wetlands and riparian habitats of the countless stream drainages.

Most visitors to South Central start and end their visit in Anchorage, the region's transportation hub. From here you can branch out by car, bus, train or plane to sample the area's varied attractions. South Central Alaska can be broken down into three general subregions—the towns and bays of Prince William Sound, communities on the Kenai Peninsula, and communities north of Anchorage in the Matanuska-Susitna (Mat-Su) Valley and beyond. The region is ideal for exploring by boat, train, car, RV, or plane. For the most part, roads have two lanes and are paved. Traffic, especially on the Kenai Peninsula, can be frustrating on summer weekends, so allow plenty of time. Be wary of impatient drivers passing in inappropriate places—this is a perpetual problem on Alaska's rudimentary road system.

PRINCE WILLIAM SOUND

6

With steep fjords, mossy waterfalls, calving glaciers, and hidden coves perfect for camping, Prince William Sound is an accessible escape from the highway crowds. The sound covers some 15,000 square mi—15 times the size of San Francisco Bay—and is home to more than 150 glaciers. In addition to hosting brown and black bears, gray wolves, and Sitka black-tailed deer, the sound thrives with a variety of birds and all manner of marine life, including salmon, halibut, humpback and killer whales, sea otters, sea lions, and porpoises. Bald eagles often soar overhead or perch in tall trees.

The *Exxon Valdez* oil spill in 1989 heavily damaged parts of the sound, and oil is still uncovered after storms and high tides. What lasting effect this lurking oil will have on the area is still being studied and remains the topic of much debate. ■TIP➡Bring your rain gear—Prince William Sounds receives more than 150 inches of rain per year.

The sound is best explored by charter boat or guided excursion out of Whittier, Cordova, or Valdez. Even though the waters are mostly protected, open stretches are common, and the fickle Alaska weather can fool even experienced boaters. From the road system, Whittier and Valdez are your best bets for finding charter outfits.

CHUGACH STATE PARK

Bordering Anchorage to the east.

Chugach State Park is Alaska's most accessible wilderness. Nearly half a million acres in size, the park rises from the coast to more than 8,000 feet, with mountains bearing such colorful names as Williwaw Peak, Temptation Peak, Mt. Magnificent, and Mt. Rumble. The park has nearly 30 trails—from 2 mi to 30 mi long—totaling more than 150 mi, suitable for shorter hikes, weeklong backpacking, and mountain biking. Easy-to-follow cross-country routes extend from one park

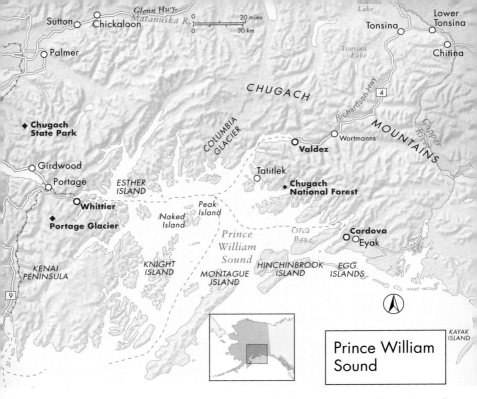

entrance to another, allowing multiday excursions and a variety of loop trips.

But this is not your typical urban park—it's real wilderness, home to Dall sheep, mountain goats, brown bears, and several packs of wolves that reside on the edge of Anchorage. Many of the trails were blazed by early miners who usually sought the easiest passes. There are also some comfortable roadside campgrounds for people traveling by car or bicycle. Trailheads are scattered around the park's perimeter from Eklutna Lake, 30 mi north of Anchorage, to the trailhead for the Crow Pass Trail near Girdwood, 37 mi to the south. Some of the more-popular trailheads charge a daily parking fee of $5. The Eagle River Nature Center or the park headquarters near Potter Marsh 12 mi south of town has park information.

The views from high perches in this park are intoxicating. You can look down on Anchorage, observe the great tides in Cook Inlet, gaze north toward Mt. McKinley, or delineate the grand procession of snowy peaks across the inlet, marching down the Alaska Peninsula, including Mt. Spurr, Mt. Redoubt, and Mt. Iliamna, all active volcanoes. The most frequently climbed alpine perch in Alaska is Flattop Mountain, on Chugach Park's western edge, ascended by hikers of all abilities. The trailhead is at the Glen Alps parking lot on the hillside above town. Even though you might see hikers heading up the trail in everything from full-on climbing gear to flip-flops, be advised that a trek to the peak can be challenging. Wear sturdy hiking footwear and attire, carry water and a snack, and prepare for sudden weather changes. Every year people are rescued from this trail because they underestimated its potential for calamity, so be prepared.

GETTING HERE & AROUND

Visitor Info **Park Headquarters** (✉ *Mi 115, Seward Hwy.* ☞ *HC 52, Box 8999, Indian 99540* ☎ *907/345–5014* ⊕ *www.dnr.state.ak.us/parks/units/chugach*) .

WHAT TO SEE

Eagle River Road leads 12 mi into the mountains from the bedroom community of Eagle River. The **Eagle River Nature Center,** at the end of Eagle River Road, has wildlife displays, telescopes for wildlife spotting, hiking trails, and volunteers to answer questions, lead hikes, and host naturalist programs throughout the year. A cabin that sleeps eight, and a pair of yurts (insulated tents) that sleep four and six are available to rent. Cost is $65 per night, and a hike in of about 1.5 mi is required. Amenities include woodstoves, firewood, and outdoor latrines. ✉ *32750 Eagle River Rd.* ☎ *907/694–2108* ⊕ *www.ernc.org* ✉ *Parking $5* ⊙ *May and Sept., Tues.–Sun. 10–5; June–Aug., Sun.–Thurs. 10–5, Fri. and Sat. 10–7; Oct.–Apr., Fri.–Sun. 10–5.*

OUTDOOR ACTIVITIES & GUIDED TOURS

The **Little Rodak Trail** is less than 1 mi long and has a viewing platform that overlooks the Eagle River valley. **Albert Loop Trail** behind the nature center has markers that coordinate with a self-guided hike along its 3-mi route; pick up a brochure at the Eagle River Nature Center.

HIKING Several trailheads along the edge of Anchorage lead into the park and its 3,000- to 5,000-foot-tall peaks. The park's most popular day climb is **Flattop Mountain,** which towers 3,500 feet above sea level. It's reached via the Glen Alps Trailhead off Upper Huffman Road on Anchorage's Hillside. A 1-mi trail climbs 1,300 feet from the Glen Alps parking area to the top. On a bright summer day you'll encounter plenty of company. Bring along a day pack with plenty of water and energy bars, a rainproof jacket, and good hiking boots.

MOUNTAIN BIKING Mountain biking has become very popular in the park, and most, but not all, trails are open to bikes; check the signs and symbols at the trailheads if in doubt. The Powerline Pass trail from the Glen Alps parking lot is wide and well maintained for bikes and offers a great view from the pass, as well as opportunities to spot moose, Dall sheep, bears, and maybe even wolves. **Sunshine Sports** (✉ *1231 W. Northern Lights Blvd.* ☎ *907/272–6444*) rents mountain bikes.

WHERE TO STAY

⚠ **Alaska State Park Campgrounds.** You'll find three road-accessible campgrounds in Chugach Park: at Eklutna Lake, Bird Creek, and Eagle River. All are within a short drive from Anchorage, and sites are available on a first-come, first-served basis. The Eklutna Lake site has a ranger station, and hiking trails of varying degrees abound in the area. Eagle River has running water and a dump station. Fishing is best at

Bird Creek during the annual silver salmon run in July and August, but be prepared for crowds. Online reservations are available. ⚇ *Pit toilets, drinking water, fire grates, picnic tables* ⟿ *135 sites* ⚐ *Alaska State Parks, HC 52, Box 8999, Indian, 99540* ☎ *907/345–5014* ⊕ *www. dnr.state.ak.us/parks/units/chugach/facility.htm* ⊟*MC, V* ⊘ *Closed roughly Oct.–Apr.*

CHUGACH NATIONAL FOREST

40 mi east of Anchorage.

Sprawling east of Chugach State Park, Chugach National Forest encompasses nearly 6 million acres to embrace a major part of the Kenai Peninsula as well as parts of Prince William Sound. It's the second-largest national forest in the United States, exceeded in size only by the Tongass in Southeast Alaska.

Recreational opportunities include hiking, camping, backpacking, fishing, boating, mountain biking, horseback riding, hunting, rock climbing, flightseeing, and, in winter, snowshoeing, cross-country skiing, ice climbing, snowmobiling, and dog mushing. Hiking trails offer easy access into the heart of the forest. You can go for a hike looking for birds and wildlife or embark on a multiday backpacking excursion. You can also fish a backcountry lake or just indulge yourself in a part of Alaska that's seldom seen by visitors. At all but the most popular trailheads, even a five-minute stroll down a wooded trail leads you to the sights, smells, and tranquillity of backcountry Alaska.

CLIMB IT

Every summer solstice (June 21), locals climb to the top of Flattop Mountain to celebrate the longest day of the year. If you're in town for this event, it's great fun; there's even an impromptu concert by musicians who lug their instruments to the top of the mountain. Parking spots are at a premium, so arrive early.

The Seward Highway between Anchorage and Seward has a number of trail access points. (Check the highway for mile markers, with the distance measured from Seward.) At Mile 63.7, just south of Turnagain Pass, is the turnoff to the Johnson Pass Trail, a relatively flat trail to walk. Seven miles farther south, take the Hope Highway 18 mi to its end and find the Porcupine Campground. From there, the Gull Rock Trail follows the shore of Turnagain Arm for 5 mi, offering scenic views across the arm and the chance to spot beluga whales foraging for salmon. Farther south on the Seward Highway at Mile 23.1, the Ptarmigan Creek Trail starts at the campground and climbs 3.5 mi into the mountains, ending next to a lake surrounded by snowy peaks.

⚠ **Be prepared to be self-sufficient when entering Chugach Forest. Trailheads typically offer nothing more than a place to park and perhaps an outhouse. Running water, trail maps, and other amenities are not available.**

Also, be "bear aware" whenever you travel in bear country—and all of Alaska is bear country (⇨ *Welcome to Bear Country, Chapter 8*). Pay attention to your surroundings, and make noise when traveling, especially in areas of reduced visibility. Bears will most likely make themselves scarce with some advance warning of your arrival.

ESSENTIALS

Visitor Info Alaska Public Lands Information Center (☎ *907/644–3661 or 866/869–6887* ⊕ *www.nps.gov/aplic*).**Forest Headquarters** (☎ *907/743–9500 Anchorage* ⊕ *www.fs.fed.us/r10/chugach*).

OUTDOOR ACTIVITIES

★ **Resurrection Pass Trail,** a 38-mi-long backpacking trail through the Chugach National Forest, draws hikers and backpackers for its colorful wildflowers in summer. There's also a chance to spot wildlife: moose, caribou, Dall sheep, mountain goats, black and brown bears, wolves, coyotes, and lynx all traverse the forest. Carry binoculars for the best wildlife-viewing opportunities.

The northern end of the trail starts south of the town of Hope, following an old mining trail through the Kenai Mountains to its end near Cooper Landing. A side trail leads to the Devil's Pass trailhead along the Seward Highway. Besides cabins, the U.S. Forest Service has provided several "official" campsites along the trail, where you'll find a cleared patch of ground and a fire ring; however, you're free to pitch your tent wherever you like.

WHERE TO STAY

¢ **U.S. Forest Service Cabins.** Along trails, near wilderness alpine lakes, in coastal forests, and on saltwater beaches, these rustic cabins offer retreats for the solo hiker or a group of friends. Some cabins are built of logs, and some are A-frames. Most have tables, chairs, wood-burning stoves, and bunks, but no electricity, running water, or bedding. Many require a fly-in or boat ride, although some can be reached by car and then on foot. If you're suitably equipped and sufficiently adventurous, these cabins are Alaska's best bargain for getting away from town and enjoying backcountry wilderness with a roof over your head. **Pros:** Remote, cheap, beautiful. **Cons:** Too remote for some, extremely basic, often booked months in advance in summer. ☎*877/444–6777 reservations* ⊕*www.recreation.gov* ⌂*41 cabins* ▤*AE, D, MC, V.*

U.S. Forest Service Campgrounds. The Forest Service maintains 18 campgrounds, 14 of them road accessible, within Chugach National Forest. The campgrounds do not have hookups for RVs. The Russian River Campground has a three-day limit during salmon-fishing season in June and July. Most have sites suitable for RVs and tents. Reservations (for a fee) are accepted at five campgrounds—Cooper Creek South, Ptarmigan Creek, Russian River, Trail River, and Williwaw. ⌂*Pit toilets, drinking water, fire grates, picnic tables* ⌂*414 RV/tent sites* ☎*877/444–6777* ⊕*www.recreation.gov* ▤*AE, D, MC, V.*

PORTAGE GLACIER

54 mi southeast of Anchorage.

Portage Glacier is one of Alaska's most frequently visited tourist destinations. A 6-mi side road off the Seward Highway leads to the Begich-Boggs Visitor Center, on the shore of Portage Lake and named after two U.S. congressmen who disappeared on a small-plane journey out of Anchorage in 1972. The center is staffed by Forest Service personnel, who can help plan your trip and explain the natural history of the area. A film on glaciers is shown hourly, and icebergs sometimes drift down to the center from Portage Glacier. The glacier has receded from view in recent years, as have most of the glaciers in Alaska.

GETTING HERE & AROUND

Gray Line of Alaska leads summer boat tours (from mid-May to mid-September) along the face of Portage Glacier aboard the 200-passenger *Ptarmigan* for $29. The view of Portage Lake and the surrounding peaks and hanging glaciers (the ones high up that terminate at the tops of cliffs) is spectacular, especially on a sunny day when the icy blue hues of the glaciers shine through.

ESSENTIALS

Visitor & Tour Info **Begich-Boggs Visitor Center** (☎ *907/783–2326* ⊕ *www. fs.fed.us/r10/chugach/chugach_pages/bbvc* ☉ *Oct. 1–May 3*). **Gray Line of Alaska** (☎ *907/277–5581 or 800/478–6388* ⊕ *www.graylinealaska.com*).

WHAT TO SEE

The mountains surrounding Portage Glacier are covered with smaller glaciers. A 1-mi hike west brings you to the **Byron Glacier** overlook. The glacier is notable for its accessibility—it's one of the few places where you can hike onto a glacier from the road system. In summer, naturalists lead free weekly treks in search of microscopic ice worms.

Several hiking trails are accessible from the Seward Highway, including the steep paths up Falls Creek and Bird Ridge. Both offer spectacular views of **Turnagain Arm,** where explorer Captain Cook searched for the Northwest Passage. Local lore has it that the arm is so named because Cook entered it repeatedly, only to be forced to turn back by the huge tide. The tide is so powerful it sometimes rushes up the arm as a tidal bore—a wall of water that goes up an inlet—that locals occasionally surf. To view the bore tide, station yourself at one of the turnoffs along the arm about 2½ hours after low tide in Anchorage—tide books are available at sporting goods and book stores, or you can find tide info on the Web.

During the summer months, beluga whales are frequent visitors to the arm as they patrol the muddy waters in search of salmon and hooligan, a variety of smelt. The whales travel in pods of adult and juvenile animals, the adults distinguishable by their bright white color. They're smaller than other whales that frequent Alaska's coastal waters, reaching only 15 feet in length and weighing up to a ton. When the tide is high and the surface of the water is calm, belugas are often spotted from the highway, frequently causing traffic jams as tourists and residents pull off the road for a chance to view the whales as they travel up and down the shoreline.

Alaska Wildlife Conservation Center is a 144-acre drive-through wildlife center just before the Portage Glacier turnoff. Moose, bison, elk, caribou, Sitka black-tailed deer, musk ox, great horned owls, a brown bear, and a bald eagle, many of them orphaned in the wild, now live in the park. There are also snack and gift shops. ⊠ *Mi 79, Seward Hwy.* ☏ *907/783–2025* ⊕ *www.alaskawildlife.org* ⊠ *$7.50* ⊙ *May–Sept., daily 8–8; Oct.–Apr., daily 10–6.*

Little remains of the community of **Portage** as a result of the 1964 earthquake. The ghost forest of dead spruce in the area was created when the land subsided by 6 to 10 feet after the quake and saltwater penetrated inland from Turnagain Arm, killing the trees.

EN ROUTE On your way to Portage, look for **Indian Valley Meats** (⊠ *Huot Circle, 23 mi south of Anchorage on Seward Hwy. at Mi 103.9* ☏ *907/653–7511* ⊕ *www.indianvalleymeats.com*), where workers sell the smoked salmon and musk ox, reindeer, and buffalo sausage made on the premises. They'll also smoke, can, and package the fish you've caught and arrange for shipping.

OUTDOOR ACTIVITIES & GUIDED TOURS

NOVA (⊠ *Mi 76.2, Glenn Hwy., Chickaloon, 99674* ☏ *800/746–5753* ⊕ *www.novalaska.com*) has been guiding residents and visitors since 1975. The company conducts river rafting, glacier hiking, fishing, and backcountry combo trips from its office in tiny Chickaloon between Palmer and Glennallen.

ROCK & ICE CLIMBING For information about rock- and ice-climbing activities, check with the **Alaska Rock Gym** (⊠ *4840 Fairbanks St., Anchorage* ☏ *907/562–7265* ⊕ *www.alaskarockgym.com*). They've got a great indoor gym, and they can point you to where local climbers have set routes along the Seward Highway south of town that are close to Anchorage.

WHITTIER

60 mi south of Anchorage.

Drive through the 2.5-mi Anton Anderson Memorial Tunnel in the mountains off Portage Glacier Road, and you'll emerge in tiny and mysterious Whittier, a town developed by the military during World War II to be cut off from the rest of the world. In years past, the only way to get to the town was by boat or through the railroad tunnel, but in 2000 the tunnel was opened to vehicle traffic.

Although the town itself isn't much to look at, the location is unbeatable. Surrounding peaks cradle alpine glaciers, and when the summer weather melts off the huge winter snow load, you can catch glimpses of the brilliant blue ice underneath. Sheer cliffs drop into Passage Canal and provide nesting places for flocks of black-legged kittiwakes, while sea otters and harbor seals cavort in the small-boat harbor, and salmon

return to spawn in nearby streams. A short boat ride out into the sound reveals tidewater glaciers, and an alert wildlife watcher can catch sight of mountain goats clinging to the mountainsides and black bears patrolling the beaches and hillsides in their constant search for food.

Nearly all the residents of Whittier live in one building—a large World War II–era apartment building known as Begich Towers. Many B&Bs are run out of the Towers as well. There's a small-boat harbor; a cruiseship terminal and dock; a ferry terminal for trips to Valdez and Cordova; fishing and sightseeing charter companies; and sea-kayak rentals and tours. A few restaurants and shops surround the harbor, but lodging facilities are limited.

■ TIP➔ Many companies' phones in Whittier are disconnected from October through April. If you can't get through to a number with prefix 472, check the company's Web site for an alternate number.

GETTING HERE & AROUND

Unless you come in on a cruise ship, ferry, or other boat, your only way in and out of Whittier is through the tunnel. Its access, however, is limited by the railroad schedule, so it's not always possible to just breeze in and out of town. (*For current tunnel info and schedules, check* ⊕ *www.tunnel.alaska.gov.*) Tolls are $12 for passenger vehicles and $20 to $35 for RVs and trailers; waits of up to an hour are possible, and summer hours are from 6 AM until 11 PM.

OUTDOOR ACTIVITIES & GUIDED TOURS

BOATING & WILDLIFE VIEWING **Alaska Sea Kayakers** (☎877/472–2534 ⊕*www.alaskaseakayakers. com*) can supply sea kayaks and gear for exploring Prince William Sound and also conducts guided day trips, multiday tours, instruction, and boat-assisted and boat live-aboard kayaking trips. The company practices a leave-no-trace camping ethos, and is very conscientious about avoiding bear problems. All guides are experienced Alaskan paddlers, and group sizes are kept small. Trips are May through September 15.

The small fleet of boats at **Honey Charters** (☎907/472–2493 ⊕*www. honeycharters.com*) is available for private charter, sightseeing, and sea-kayak drop-offs. Groups of up to 30 people can join trips through Prince William Sound; you can also get transport to Cordova and Valdez. Standard sightseeing trips run from three to six hours.

Major Marine Tours (☎ 907/274–7300 or 800/764–7300 ⊕*www.major-marine.com*) runs a five-hour cruise from Whittier that visits two tidewater glaciers. The waters of Prince William Sound are well protected and relatively calm, making this a good option if you're inclined toward queasiness. Seabirds, waterfowl, and bald eagles are always present, and the chance to get close to the enormous walls of ice of the glaciers is not to be missed. The cruise is $107 per person, and runs from mid-May to mid-September. For an additional $15, every cruise features a freshly prepared all-you-can-eat salmon and prime rib meal and reserved table seating for every guest inside the heated cabin.

From Whittier, tours with **Prince William Sound Glacier Cruises** (✉*Pier 1, Whittier* ☎ *907/277–2131 or 800/992–1297* ⊕*www.princewilliam-sound.com*) travel through the sheltered bays, fjords, and canals of Prince William Sound. You can view glaciers, seabirds, and wildlife such as seals, sea lions, sea otters, whales, bears, and mountain goats. The company can arrange transportation from Anchorage to Whittier by bus or rail, or you can drive to Whittier in your own vehicle. Prices vary according to length of trip and travel options; cruises take place mid-May through mid-September.

Retired marine biologist Gerry Sanger runs a number of tours in his six-passenger, 30-foot boat with **Sound Eco Adventures** (☎ *907/472–2312 or 888/471–2312* ⊕*www.soundecoadventure.com*) from March through October. He'll take you whale-watching or glacier viewing or on a general wildlife-viewing trip for anywhere from 5 to 10 hours. He can also transport sea kayakers, cabin renters, and anyone else needing a charter boat out of Whittier. Longer trips include a beach stop. Gorp and fresh veggie snacks are provided, but bring your own lunch.

Phillips' Cruises & Tours has been running the **26 Glacier Cruise** (☎ *907/276–8023 or 800/544–0529* ⊕*www.26glaciers.com*) through Prince William Sound for many years. The high-speed catamaran covers 135 mi of territory in 4½ hours, leaving Whittier and visiting Port Wells, Barry Arm, and College and Harriman fjords. The boat is a very stable platform, and even visitors prone to seasickness can take this cruise with no ill effects. The heated cabin has large windows, upholstered booths, and wide aisles, and all seats are pre-reserved. There's a snack bar and a saloon on board, and wildlife encounters are commonplace. You can drive to Whittier and catch the boat at the dock, or you can arrange with the company to travel from Anchorage by rail or bus. The trip is $139 per person plus tax, and includes a hot lunch of cod or chicken; tours are given May through September.

WHERE TO STAY & EAT

¢–$
AMERICAN

✗**Frankie's Deli & Café.** Frankie's is a busy little spot on the Whittier waterfront, and the outside seating area overlooks the sound and the ferry dock area. Deli sandwiches, seafood, and numerous burgers made from beef, chicken, and seafood fill the menu. Buffalo chili is a specialty of the house. ✉*Harbor Loop* ☎*907/472–2477* ▭*MC, V.*

¢–$$$$
SEAFOOD

✗**Varly's Swiftwater Seafood Café.** Place your order at the window and then grab a seat at the counter and wait for your food. There's outdoor seating that overlooks the small-boat harbor. Menu items include homemade chowders, hand-battered seafood, peel-and-eat shrimp, burgers, and chicken. A smoked prime rib dinner is served on Friday and Saturday nights. ✉*Harbor Loop* ☎*907/472–2550* ▭*MC, V* ☻*Closed mid-Sept.–May.*

$–$$$$

🛏**June's Whittier Condo Suites.** June's rents out 10 condominiums in the Begich Towers building, half with bay views, half with mountain views. There's a large variety of room sizes and types—some that can accommodate large groups. June's also operates Bread-n-Butter Charters, which can arrange fishing or sightseeing tours and even overnight trips into the sound. **Pro:** Private condos in Penthouse area of Begich Towers.

6

Con: Old building is a little rough outside. ⊠*Begich Towers, Kenai St.* ⌂*Box 715 99693* ☎*888/472–2396* ⊕*www.breadnbuttercharters. com* ⚓*10 rooms* ⌂*In-room: kitchen, refrigerator, VCR. In-hotel: parking, no-smoking rooms* ⊟*AE, MC, V* ⦿*CP.*

$ ⛱**Soundview Getaway.** When the Begich Towers building was used by the military during the war, the Bachelor Officer's Quarters were home to soldiers stationed in Whittier. Today this building has been refurbished as B&B condos with full kitchens and full baths. The larger rooms sleep four, and two smaller rooms can be joined as a suite sleeping up to six. **Pros:** Family-friendly, kitchen amenities makes this lodging an affordable option. **Con:** Few amenities. ⊠*Whittier Manor Condos, Blackstone Rd., Whittier* ⌂*5800 E. 142nd Ave., Anchorage 99516* ☎ *907/472–2358 or 800/515–2358 in summer, 907/345–1335, 907/440–9114* ⊕*www.soundviewalaska.com* ⚓*4 rooms* ⌂*In-room: VCR. In-hotel: public Wi-Fi, no-smoking rooms* ⊟*MC, V* ⦿*CP.*

VALDEZ

6 hrs northeast of Whittier by water, 304 mi east of Anchorage.

Valdez (pronounced val-*deez*) is the largest of the Prince William Sound communities. This year-round ice-free port was the entry point for people and goods going to the Interior during the gold rush. Today that flow has been reversed, as Valdez Harbor is the southern terminus of the trans-Alaska pipeline, which carries crude oil from Prudhoe Bay and surrounding oil fields nearly 800 mi to the north. This region, with its dependence on commercial fishing, is still feeling the aftereffects of the massive oil spill in 1989. Much of Valdez looks modern, because the business area was relocated and rebuilt after its destruction by the 1964 Good Friday earthquake. Even though the town is younger than the rest of developed Alaska, it's acquiring a lived-in look.

Many Alaskan communities have summer fishing derbies, but Valdez may hold the record for the number of such contests, stretching from late May into September for halibut and various runs of salmon. If you go fishing, by all means enter the appropriate derby. Every summer the newspapers run sob stories about tourists who landed possible prizewinners but couldn't share in the glory (or sizable cash rewards) because they hadn't forked over the five bucks to officially enter the contest. The **Valdez Silver Salmon Derby** is held the entire month of August. Fishing charters abound in this area of Prince William Sound, and for good reason: these fertile waters provide some of the best saltwater sportfishing in all of Alaska.

GETTING HERE & AROUND

Valdez is road-accessible, and the 304-mi drive from Anchorage is stunning if a bit long to do in one day. The Richardson Highway portion of the drive takes you through Thompson Pass, high alpine country with 360-degree views. As you approach the town, the road descends into a steep canyon with rushing waterfalls—a popular ice-climbing destination in winter. Valdez's port is a stop on the Alaska Marine

Highway, a great way to travel to Cordova and Whittier. There's also a commercial airport.

The downtown is above the harbor and two main avenues—Hazelet and Meals—run north–south with smaller streets branching off.

ESSENTIALS

Medical Assistance **Community Hospital** (✉ *911 Meals Ave.* ☎ *907/835–2249*)

Visitor & Tour Info **Valdez Convention and Visitors Bureau** (✉ *200 Fairbanks St.* ✆ *Box 1603, Valdez 99686* ☎ *907/835–2984* ⊕ *www.valdezalaska.org*).

WHAT TO SEE

The **Valdez Museum** explores the lives, livelihoods, and events significant to Valdez and surrounding regions. Exhibits include a restored 1880s Gleason & Baily hand-pump fire engine, a 1907 Ahrens steam fire engine, a 19th-century saloon, information on the local native peoples, and an exhibit on the 1989 oil spill. Every summer the museum hosts an exhibit of quilts and fiber arts made by local and regional artisans. At a separate site, a 35-by-40-foot model of **Historical Old Town Valdez** (✉ *436 Hazlet Ave.*) depicts the original town, which was devastated by the 1964 earthquake. There's also an operating seismograph and an exhibit on local seismic activity. A Valdez History Exhibits Pass includes admission to both the museum and the annex. ✉ *217 Egan Dr.* ☎ *907/835–2764* ⊕ *www.valdezmuseum.org* 🕮 *$5* ☉ *June–Aug., daily 9–6; Sept.–May, weekdays 1–5, Sat. noon–4.*

NEED A BREAK? A visit to **Columbia Glacier**, which flows from the surrounding Chugach Mountains, should certainly be on the agenda. Its deep aquamarine face is 5 mi across, and it calves icebergs with resounding cannonades. This glacier is one of the largest and most readily accessible of Alaska's coastal glaciers. The state ferry travels past the face of the glacier, and scheduled tours of the glaciers and the rest of the sound are available by boat and aircraft from Valdez, Cordova, and Whittier.

OUTDOOR ACTIVITIES & GUIDED TOURS

ADVENTURE If you want a taste of backcountry snowmobiling action, **Alaska Snow Safaris** (✉ *6543 Brayton Dr., Anchorage* ☎ *907/868–7669 or 888/414–7669* ⊕ *www.snowmobile-alaska.com*) has an enormous winter playground near Valdez. From November to the end of April, they'll take you into the wilderness on your machine or theirs to explore mile after mile of untouched, ungroomed snow. The trips are tailored to all levels of experience.

Anadyr Adventures (☎ *907/835–2814 or 800/865–2925* ⊕ *www.anadyradventures.com*), a sea-kayaking and hiking company, has 17 years of experience leading sea-kayak trips into Alaska's most spectacular wilderness, Prince William Sound. Guides will escort you on day trips, multiday camping trips, "mother ship" adventures based in a remote anchorage, or lodge-based trips for the ultimate combination of adventure by day and comfort by night. If you're already an experienced kayaker, they'll outfit you and you can travel on your own. Also available are guided hiking and glacier trips, ice caving at Valdez Glacier, soft-adventure charter-boat trips in the sound, and water-taxi service to or from anyplace on the eastern side of the sound.

Whether you're looking for a full-on winter backcountry heli-ski excursion or a half-day walk on a glacier, **H2O Guides** (✉ *100 Meals Ave.* ☎ *907/835–8418* ⊕ *www.h2oguides.com*) can hook you up. For most visitors, their day trips to Worthington Glacier State Park will suffice. They can set up any level of icy adventure you desire, from a half-day walk on the glacier to a multiday ice-climbing trip. Their office is in the Mountain Sky hotel, and they can also arrange fishing, flightseeing, and multiday, multisport trips as well.

BOATING &
WILDLIFE
VIEWING

Valdez-based **Columbia Glacier Wildlife Cruises/Lu-Lu Belle** (☎ *907/835– 5141 or 800/411–0090* ⊕ *www.lulubelletours.com*) leads small-group whale-watching, wildlife-viewing, and Columbia Glacier cruises.

Stan Stephens Glacier & Wildlife Cruises (☎ *907/835–4731 or 866/867– 1297* ⊕ *www.stanstephenscruises.com*) leads Prince William Sound glacier and wildlife-viewing cruises to Columbia and Meares glaciers from mid-May through mid-September. Their trips include narration on local commercial fishing operations as well as commentary on the Alyeska Pipeline terminal and history of defunct gold mines.

WHERE TO EAT

¢–$$$
SEAFOOD

✕ **Alaska Halibut House.** At this very casual place you order at the counter, sit at the Formica-covered tables, and check out the photos of local fishing boats. The battered halibut is excellent—light and not greasy. Other menu items include homemade clam chowder, but if you're eating at the Halibut House, why try anything else? ✉ *208 Meals Ave.* ☎ *907/835–2788* ▭ *MC, V.*

$$–$$$$
SEAFOOD

✕ **Alaska's Bistro.** The nautically themed two-tier dining room guarantees a view of the small-boat harbor. Local seafood dominates the menu and the house specialty is paella for two. There's also a large selection of appetizers, salads, poultry, pork, steaks, and pizza. The wine cellar includes more than 250 selections. ✉ *100 Fidalgo Dr.* ☎ *907/835– 5688* ▭ *AE, D, MC, V.*

$–$$$
AMERICAN

✕ **Mike's Palace.** On the harbor, this convivial restaurant with Italian-diner decor is a local favorite. The pizza is terrific, but the menu also includes veal, beer-batter halibut, steaks, Mexican food, and Greek gyros. ✉ *201 N. Harbor Dr.* ☎ *907/835–2365* ▭ *MC, V.*

WHERE TO STAY

If you roll into town without reservations, especially if it's after hours, stop at the Valdez Convention and Visitor's Bureau on the corner of Fairbanks. They post vacancies in bed-and-breakfasts on the window when they close for the day.

¢   ⚠ **Bayside RV Park.** This full-service RV park with a few tent sites has a panoramic view of the mountains. The staff can help you book fishing and sightseeing trips with local charter outfits. ♿ *Flush toilets, full hookups, dump station, drinking water, guest laundry, showers, picnic tables, electricity, public telephone, public Internet* ⇌ *110 RV/tent sites* ⊠ *230 E. Egan Dr.,* ☎ *907/835–4425 or 888/835–4425* ⊕ *www.baysiderv.com* ⊟ *MC, V* ⊗ *Closed Sept. 11–Apr.*

$$ 🖾 **Best Western Valdez Harbor Inn.** Near the harbor, this hotel has an inlet from the sound, complete with sea otters, seals, and waterfowl, right outside the lobby windows and visible from some of the rooms. **Pros:** On an inlet, very clean. **Con:** Just like any Best Western elsewhere. ⊠ *100 Harbor Dr., Box 468* ☎ *907/835–3434 or 888/222–3440* ⊕ *www.bestwestern.com* ⇌ *88 rooms* ♿ *In-room: refrigerator, dial-up, Wi-Fi. In-hotel: restaurant, room service, gym, no elevator, laundry facilities, some pets allowed, no-smoking rooms* ⊟ *AE, D, DC, MC, V* ℣⊙℣ *CP.*

$$ 🖾 **Mountain Sky Hotel and Suites.** The hotel is within easy walking distance of shops, restaurants, and the small-boat harbor—the center of summertime activity. The business center and pool are noteworthy for small-town Alaska. **Pros:** Has all amenities, very clean. **Con:** Not much personality. ⊠ *100 Meals Ave.* ☎ *907/835–4445* ⊕ *www.mountainskyhotelsuite.com* ⇌ *101 rooms* ♿ *In-room: refrigerator, Wi-Fi. In-hotel: pool, gym, spa, no elevator, laundry facilities, no-smoking rooms* ⊟ *AE, D, DC, MC, V* ℣⊙℣ *CP.*

$$$$ 🖾 **Prince William Sound Lodge.** This fly-in lodge on a remote shore of northeastern Prince William Sound offers a wide range of vacation activities, including hiking, bird-watching, wildlife-viewing, exploring nearby Alaska native villages, and the chance for some of the best silver salmon fishing in the state. You can also go halibut fishing, take seaplane rides, or join boat trips on a converted commercial fishing boat. Gourmet meals add to the attractions. Lodging price does not include the $150 (round-trip) per person floatplane flight to the lodge. **Pros:** Delicious meals, incredible location. **Cons:** Remote, fly-in location. ⊠ *Ellamar* ⊕ *3900 Clay Products Dr.,Anchorage 99517* ☎ *907/248–0909 or 907/440–0909* ⊕ *www.princewilliamsound.us* ⇌ *5 rooms* ♿ *In-room: no phone, no TV. In-hotel: restaurant, beachfront, public Wi-Fi, no-smoking rooms* ⊟ *No credit cards* ⊗ *Closed late Sept.–mid-May* ℣⊙℣ *FAP.*

$$ 🖾 **Thompson Pass Mountain Chalet.** This rustic cabin in subalpine forest sits just off the trans-Alaska pipeline and within minutes of skiing and hiking at Thompson Pass. Open year-round, the chalet has a small kitchen and facilities for four, and the owners can direct you to the local hiking and ski trails, or, for an additional fee, guide you on backcountry excursions. The views from the upstairs window are unbeatable. **Pros:** Clean, comfortable, and cozy—and right on a babbling brook. **Con:** Narrow spiral staircase to sleeping loft demands some agility. ⊠ *Mi 19, Richardson Hwy.* ☎ *907/835–4817* ⊕ *www.thompsonpass.com* ⇌ *1 cabin* ♿ *In-room: kitchen, no TV, Wi-Fi. In-hotel: no-smoking rooms* ⊟ *No credit cards* ℣⊙℣ *CP.*

6

CORDOVA

6 hrs southeast of Valdez by water, 150 mi east of Anchorage by air.

A small town with the spectacular backdrop of snowy Mt. Eccles, Cordova is the gateway to the Copper River delta—one of the great birding areas of North America. Perched on Orca Inlet in eastern Prince William Sound, Cordova began life early in the 20th century as the port city for the Copper River and Northwestern Railway, which was built to serve the Kennicott copper mines 191 mi away in the Wrangell Mountains. Since the mines and the railroad shut down in 1938, Cordova's economy has depended heavily on fishing. Attempts to develop a road along the abandoned railroad line connecting to the state highway system were dashed by the 1964 earthquake, so Cordova remains isolated. Access is limited to airplane or ferry.

GETTING HERE & AROUND

Take the scenic ferry from either Whittier or Valdez along the **Alaska Marine Highway,** or catch a commercial flight from Anchorage. Once in town, the center is foot-friendly, but you'll want some wheels for heading down the Copper River Highway.

Though there isn't much in the way of paved road in Cordova, you can still drive the remnants of the scenic Copper River Highway, which takes you past Childs Glacier and the Million Dollar Bridge.

ESSENTIALS

Ferry Info Alaska Marine Highway (⊠ *6858 Glacier Hwy., Juneau* ☎ *907/465–3941 or 800/642-0066* 🖨 *907/277-4829* ⊕ *http://www.dot.state.ak.us/amhs*).

Medical Assistance Cordova Medical Center (⊠ *602 Chase Ave.* ☎ *907/424-8000*).

Rental Cars Chinook Auto Rentals (⊠ *Cordova Airport* ☎ *877/424-5279*).

Visitor Info Cordova Chamber of Commerce (🖂 *Box 99, Cordova 99574* ☎ *907/424-7260* ⊕ *www.cordovachamber.com*).

WHAT TO SEE

The **Cordova Museum** emphasizes the unique Cordova community history through native, pioneer, mining, and fishing artifacts and stories. Exhibits tell of early explorers to the area, native culture, the Copper River and Northwestern Railway/Kennicott Mine era, and the growth of the commercial fishing industry. An informative brochure outlines a self-guided walking tour of the town's historic buildings. Evening programs and regional art exhibits such as "Fish Follies" and "Bird Flew" are sponsored by the Historical Society. The gift shop features a selection of local postcards, Cordova and Alaskan gifts, and local history books. ⊠ *622 1st St.* ☎ *907/424-6665* ⊕ *www.cordovamuseum.org* 🖼 *$1* ⊗ *Memorial Day–Labor Day, Mon.–Sat. 10–6, Sun. 2–4; Labor Day–Memorial Day, Tues.–Fri. 10–5, Sat. 1–5.*

Drive out of town along the Copper River Highway and visit the **Copper River delta.** This 700,000-acre wetland is one of North America's most spectacular vistas. The two-lane highway crosses marshes, forests, streams, lakes, and ponds that are home to countless shorebirds, waterfowl, and other bird species. Numerous terrestrial mammals including moose, wolves, lynx, mink, and beavers live here, too, and the Copper River salmon runs are world famous. When the red and king salmon hit the river in spring, there's a frantic rush to net the tasty fish and rush them off to waiting markets and restaurants all over the country.

The **Million Dollar Bridge,** at Mile 48, was a railroad project completed in 1910 for the Copper River and Northwestern Railway to carry copper ore to market from the mines at Kennicott. Soon after construction was completed, the nearby Childs and Miles glaciers threatened to overrun the railroad and bridge. Although the glaciers stopped short of the railroad, the copper market collapsed in 1938, making the route economically obsolete. The far span of the bridge was toppled by the Good Friday earthquake in 1964 and was not rebuilt until 2005.

From the end of the road you can view the **Childs Glacier.** Although there is no visitor center, there is a covered viewing area next to the bridge, where you can see the face of the glacier and wait for a huge chunk of ice to topple into the river. The waves produced by falling ice frequently wash migrating salmon onto the riverbank; the local brown bears have been known to patrol the river's edge looking for an easy meal, so keep your eyes peeled.

OUTDOOR ACTIVITIES & GUIDED TOURS

Spring migration to the **Copper River delta** provides some of the finest avian spectacles in the world. Species include the western sandpiper, American dipper, orange-crowned warbler, and short-billed dowitcher. Trumpeter swans and dusky Canada geese can also be seen. The **Copper River Delta Shorebird Festival** (☎*907/424–7260* ⊕*www.cordovachamber.com*), held the first week of May, includes five days of workshops and guided field trips. As many as 5 million birds, mostly western sandpipers and dunlins, descend on the Copper River delta, feeding and resting on their long migration to their northern nesting grounds. This migration respite is critical for these birds, and the food they gather from the rich mudflats of the delta keeps them alive and healthy.

Alaskan Wilderness Outfitting Co. (☎*907/424–5552* ⊕*www.alaskawilderness.com*) operates an air-taxi service out of Cordova and arranges fresh- and saltwater fly-out fishing experiences, from drop-offs to guided tours with lodge accommodations. They also offer floating cabins in Prince William Sound and a full-service lodge for silver salmon on the Tsiu River.

Cordova Air Service (☎*907/424–3289*) leads aerial tours of Prince William Sound on planes with wheels or floats.

Cordova Coastal Outfitters (☎ *907/424–7424* ⊕*www.cordovacoastal.com*) conducts half- and full-day sea-kayak tours. They rent kayaks, canoes, bikes, small motorboats, and camping and fishing gear, and can arrange custom tours to fit your desired level of activity. They also run half- and full-day wildlife/natural history tours on their 32-foot commercial fishing boat, as well as a water taxi. If you rent a kayak or bring your own, they'll provide pick-up and drop-off service anywhere on the road system.

FOR BIRDERS **At Mile 17 there's a turnoff to Alaganik Slough. This 5-mi road leads to a wheelchair-accessible boardwalk as well as covered viewing shelters, restrooms, and picnic areas. A dedicated bird-watcher can spend hours peering into the vegetation, seeking out interesting avian species.**

WHERE TO EAT

¢–$$
AMERICAN
✕**Ambrosia.** Pastas, hamburgers, and steaks are served behind the storefront, but it's the hearty pizzas that have earned this place its reputation among locals. ⌂*410 1st St.* ☎*907/424–7175* ▤*AE, MC, V* ⊘*Closed Nov.–Jan.*

¢–$
CAFÉ
✕**Killer Whale Café.** Have a breakfast of espresso and baked goods or an omelet at this café. For lunch you can choose from a deli menu of soups, salads, and sandwiches, followed by a fresh, homemade dessert. ⌂*507 1st St.* ☎*907/424–7733* ▤*MC, V* ⊘*No dinner.*

$–$$$
AMERICAN
✕**Powder House Bar & Restaurant.** On clear summer evenings you can relax on the deck overlooking Eyak Lake at this roadside bar and enjoy whatever the cook's in the mood to fix: homemade soups, sandwiches, sushi, and seasonal seafood are all possibilities. If you're lucky or skillful in your fishing endeavors, the kitchen staff will cook your catch. Steak and seasonal seafood, including shrimp, scallops, razor clams, and whatever else is fresh, are available every night. ⌂*Mi 2.1, Copper River Hwy.* ☎*907/424–3529* ▤*AE, D, MC, V.*

WHERE TO STAY

$
🏠**Cordova Lighthouse Inn.** Two of the rooms have mountain views, but if at all possible, get one of the two with harbor views for the full Alaskan fishing-village ambience. **Pro:** In-town location. **Con:** Must climb steep stairs to access the four rooms at the top. ⌂*112 Nicholoff Way, Box 2206* ☎*907/424–7080* ⊕*www.cordovalighthouseinn.com* ⬦*8 rooms* ⛄*In-room: no phone, Wi-Fi. In-hotel: laundry facility, no-smoking rooms* ▤*MC, V.*

$–$$
🏠**Cordova Rose Lodge.** This truly unique lodge sits on a barge on the Prince William Sound breakwater. There's a working lighthouse on the site, used by boats transiting the channel. The accommodations range from cabins to semiprivate to private rooms, and families and groups are welcome. A large, hot breakfast is the order of the day, and dinner is arranged if enough guests request it. Vacation packages including hiking, fishing, bird-watching, and wildlife viewing are also available. **Pros:** Delicious breakfast, waterfront location. **Cons:** Short walk from town, some folks might want a vehicle. ⌂*1315 Whitshed, Box 1494* ☎*907/424–7673* ⊕*www.cordovarose.com* ⬦*11 rooms, 2 cabins* ⛄*In-room: no phone (some), kitchen, no TV (some), Wi-Fi. In-hotel: public Internet, airport shuttle, no-smoking rooms* ▤*MC, V* ⦿*BP.*

¢–$
🏠**Northern Nights Inn B&B.** Commanding a dramatic view of Orca Inlet just a couple of blocks from downtown Cordova, this turn-of-the-20th-century bed-and-breakfast has roomy suites furnished with antiques. If

owner Becky Chapek doesn't have room for you, she'll serve as a valuable source of information on other B&Bs in town. She operates bus tours around town and to the Million Dollar Bridge, and she can transport you to and from the airport as well. She also operates Chinook Auto Rentals (☎907/424–5279 or 877/424–5279) at the airport. **Pro:** Big, bright rooms are a great value. **Con:** Only one ground-floor room for those who have trouble with stairs. ✉500 3rd St., Box 1564 ☎907/424–5356 ⊕www.northernnightsinn.com ➲1 room, 3 suites ⟨In-room: kitchen, DVD, VCR, Wi-Fi. In-hotel: no elevator, laundry facilities, no-smoking rooms ⊟AE, D, MC, V.

$$ **Orca Adventure Lodge.** The list of activities at the lodge goes on and on: fishing, kayaking, river rafting, hiking, bear viewing, and flightseeing. There's also the opportunity to fly out to one of Orca's remote wilderness camps for fishing or just relaxing. The lodge is a converted cannery on the Cordova waterfront. **Pros:** Spectacular views with sea otters congregating outside. **Con:** About 2 mi from town, so some folks might want a vehicle. ✉301 Orca Rd. ⌂Box 2105, 99574 ☎907/424–7249 or 866/424–6722 ⊕www.orcaadventurelodge.com ➲23 rooms, 4 suites ⟨In-room: no phone (some), no TV, Wi-Fi. In-hotel: restaurant, no elevator, airport shuttle, no-smoking rooms ⊟AE, MC, V ⊗Restaurant closed Oct.–May.

$–$$ **Reluctant Fisherman Inn.** At this waterfront hotel and restaurant you can watch the commercial-fishing fleet and other maritime traffic sail by. Comfortable, nautical-theme rooms were remodeled in 2008, and all overlook the harbor. The restaurant serves local seafood, as well as pastas and espresso. A large, south-facing deck for alfresco dining overlooks the harbor. **Pro:** Perfect location in the heart of Cordova. **Con:** Microwaves and refrigerators are only available for a small charge. ✉407 Railroad Ave. ☎907/424–3272 or 877/770–3272 ⊕www.reluctantfisherman.com ➲41 rooms ⟨In-room: dial-up, Wi-Fi. In-hotel: restaurant, bar, laundry facilities, airport shuttle, no smoking rooms ⊟AE, D, MC, V ⊟◎CP.

¢ **U.S. Forest Service Cabins.** The Cordova Ranger District of the Chugach National Forest maintains a series of 18 backcountry cabins for rent. These cabins are very basic: four walls, roof, floor, wooden bunks, usually a woodstove, table, benches, counter space for preparing meals, and a pit toilet out back. There's no bedding, cooking utensils, electricity, or running water. Most of the cabins are accessible only by boat or floatplane, although the McKinley Trail cabin is accessible by motor vehicle on the Copper River Highway. Two others can be reached by hiking from the road. ■TIP➜Rentals are arranged through the national parks Web site up to six months in advance. **Pros:** Beautiful and remote. **Con:** You must be self-sufficient and comfortable in the wilderness. ➲17 cabins ☎877/444–6777 ⊕www.recreation.gov ⊟AE, D, MC, V.

SHOPPING

Orca Book & Sound Co. (✉507 1st St. ☎907/424–5305 Closed Sun.) is much more than a bookstore. In addition to books, it sells music, art supplies, children's toys, and locally produced art. The walls often double as a gallery for local works or traveling exhibits, and the store

specializes in old, rare, out-of-print, and first-edition books, especially Alaskana. ■TIP➡ In the back is an espresso/smoothie bar; the upstairs area has wireless Internet access for a small fee.

KENAI PENINSULA

The Kenai Peninsula, thrusting into the Gulf of Alaska south of Anchorage, is South Central's playground, offering salmon and halibut fishing, spectacular scenery, and wildlife viewing. Commercial fishing is important to the area's economy; five species of Pacific salmon run up the aqua-color Kenai River every summer. Campgrounds and trailheads for backwoods hiking are strung along the roads. Along the way, you can explore three major federal holdings on the peninsula—the western end of the sprawling Chugach National Forest, Kenai National Wildlife Refuge, and Kenai Fjords National Park.

HOPE

39 mi west of Portage, 87 mi south of Anchorage.

The little gold-mining community of Hope sits just across Turnagain Arm from Anchorage. To visit, however, you must drive the 87 mi all the way around the arm. Your reward is a quiet little community that is accessible to but not overrun by tourists. Hope was founded by miners in 1896, and the old log cabins and weathered frame buildings in the town center are favorite photography subjects. You'll find lots of gold-panning, fishing, and hiking opportunities, and the northern trailhead for the 38-mi-long Resurrection Pass Trail is nearby. Contact the U.S. Forest Service for information on campgrounds, cabin rentals, and hikes in the area.

WHERE TO STAY & EAT

$
AMERICAN

🍴 **Bowman's Bear Creek Lodge.** Of the five cabins, four are around a pond and one is down by the creek. Each has a woodstove and an electric heater. Interior walls are chinked logs, beds have colorful quilts, and the lighting fixtures are modeled after gold rush–era styles. The cabins vary in size, but the largest sleeps up to six. A central bathhouse has hot showers and toilets. The excellent lodge café ($–$$$) serves dinner, with nightly specials, local seafood, and smoked-salmon chowder (the house specialty) every day. The food is reason enough to make the 16-mi side trip to Hope from the Seward Highway. ■TIP➡ Bowman's runs guided fishing and rafting trips; all-inclusive packages with rooms, meals, and guided excursions to Whittier, Seward, or Cooper Landing. **Pros:** Great café on site, nightly campfire around the pond. **Con:** Shared bath. ⊠*Mi 15.9, Hope Hwy.* 🅿*Box 4 99605* 🕾*907/782–3141* ⊕*www.bowmansbearcreeklodge.com* 🛏*5 cabins with shared bath* 🔧*In-room: no phone, no TV. In-hotel: restaurant, no-smoking rooms* 🖃*MC, V.*

¢

⚠ **Coeur d'Alene Campground.** If you really want to get away from civilization, come here. It sits high above the Resurrection Creek valley, quite literally in mountain-goat country. The drive is up a twisty 6-mi

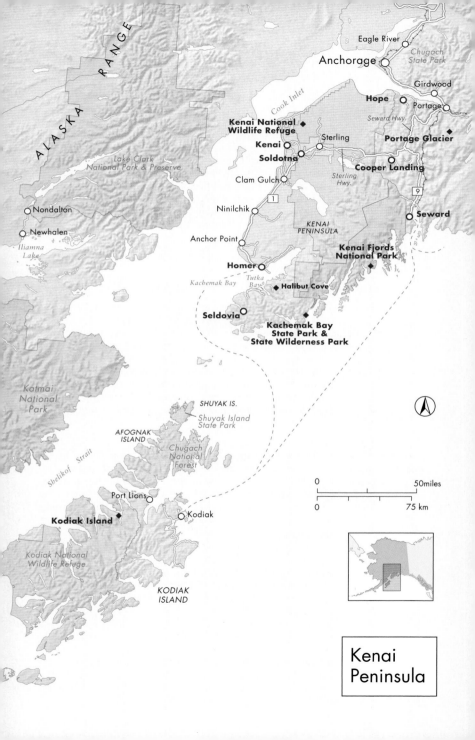

road over areas not recommended for RVs or trailers. There's no water at the site, no reservations are taken, and there's no charge for camping. From Hope take the Resurrection Creek road for 1.6 mi to the Palmer Creek Road, and head up the mountain. The road is frequently closed due to avalanches until mid- to late May. ⊠ *Mi 2 Palmer Creek Rd.* ⚱ *Pit toilets, fire pits, picnic tables* ⚑ *6 tent sites* 🕾 *No phone* ⊘ *Closed Oct.–Apr.*

¢ 🏔 **Porcupine Campground.** The highway dead-ends into this campground: you're right on the shore of Turnagain Arm, with access to the 5 mi Gull Rock Trail, which runs along the shoreline. Occasionally you can spot the bore tide and beluga whales as they hunt for salmon up and down the coast. Some of the campsites overlook the arm, but you'll have to be quick or lucky to snag one of these. Although the mudflats look tempting at low tide, under no circumstances should you venture onto them—it's very dangerous out there, and chances for rescue if you're stranded are nil. ⚱ *Pit toilets, drinking water, fire pits, picnic tables* ⚑ *24 RV/tent sites* ⊠ *Mi 17.8, Hope Hwy.* 🕾 *No phone* ▤ *No credit cards* ⊘ *Closed mid-Sept.–Apr.,*

¢–$$ ✕ **Tito's Discovery Cafe.** When the original Tito's restaurant burned down,
AMERICAN uninsured, in 1999, the owner was faced with financial ruin. But this tiny community got together and put Tito back on his feet and rebuilt the restaurant. Today Tito's serves basic American roadhouse food, along with seafood pasta, the ubiquitous halibut, and fresh-baked pies. ⊠ *Mi 16.5, Hope Hwy.* 🕾 *907/782–3274* ▤ *MC, V.*

SEWARD

74 mi south of Hope, 127 mi south of Anchorage.

Fodor'sChoice Completely encircled by Kenai Fjords National Park to the south and
★ west, the Chugach National Forest to the northeast, and Resurrection Bay to the south, Seward offers all the delights of a small railroad town with the bonus of jaw-dropping scenery. Seward was founded in 1903, when survey crews arrived at this ice-free port to begin planning for a railroad to the Interior. Since then the town has relied heavily on tourism and commercial fishing, and its harbor is important for loading coal bound for Asia. Seward is also the launching point for excursions into Kenai Fjords National Park, where you can spy calving glaciers, sea lions, whales, and otters.

GETTING HERE & AROUND

As a cruise-ship port, Seward has several routes in and out. Arrive by boat via the Alaska Marine Highway or, from Anchorage, take a luxury Ultradome railcar, or drive the 126 mi from Anchorage. Although there's a small airport, only private planes use it. It's possible to walk around town or from the harbor to downtown, but there's also trolley service in summer; for a dollar, the Seward Trolley Car Company will take you from the cruise-ship terminal, train station, and harbor area to downtown and back.

6

ESSENTIALS

Medical Assistance Providence Seward Medical Center (⊠ *417 1st Ave.* ☎ *907/224–5205.*

Trolley Info Seward Trolley Car Co. (☎907/224-4378 ⊕www.sewardtrolley. com).

Visitor & Tour Info Seward Visitors Bureau (⊠ *Mi 2, Seward Hwy.* ⌂ *Box 749, Seward 99664* ☎ *907/224–8051* ⊕ *www.sewardak.org*).

WHAT TO SEE

☉ Spend an afternoon at the **Alaska SeaLife Center,** with massive cold-water
Fodor's Choice tanks and outdoor viewing decks, as well as interactive displays of
★ cold-water fish, seabirds, and marine mammals, including harbor seals and a 2000-pound sea lion. A research center as well as visitor center, it also rehabilitates injured marine wildlife and provides educational experiences for the general public. Appropriately, the center was partially funded with reparations money from the *Exxon Valdez* oil spill. Films, hands-on activities, a gift shop, and behind-the-scenes tours ($12 and up) complete the offerings. ⊠ *301 Railway Ave.* ☎ *907/224–6300 or 888/378–2525* ⊕ *www.alaskasealife.org* ⊠ *$15* ☉ *May 1–Sept. 15, daily 8–7; Sept. 16–Apr., Thurs. –Mon. 10–5.*

★ A short walk from the parking lot along a paved path will bring you face to face with **Exit Glacier** (⊳ *Kenai Fjords National Park*), just outside Seward. Look for the marked turnoff at Mile 3.7 as you enter town or ask locals for directions. There's a small walk-in campground here, a ranger station, and access to the glacier. This mass of ice caps the Kenai Mountains, covering more than 1,100 square mi, and it oozes more than 40 glaciers from its edges and down the mountainsides. From Mile 3.7 you can also access **Harding Icefield.** The hike to the ice field from the parking lot is a 9-mi round-trip that gains 3,000 feet in elevation, so it's not for the timid or out of shape. But if you're feeling up to the task, the hike and views are breathtaking. Local wildlife includes mountain goats and bears both black and brown, so keep a sharp eye out for them. Once you reach the ice, don't travel across it unless you have the gear and experience with glacier travel. Glacier ice is notoriously deceptive—the surface can look solid and unbroken, while underneath a thin crust of snow, crevasses lie in wait for the unwary.

Seward, like Valdez, was badly damaged by the 1964 earthquake. A movie illustrating the upheaval is shown from Memorial Day until Labor Day, Monday through Saturday at 2 PM in the **Seward Community Library.** Russian icons and paintings by prominent Alaskan artists are on exhibit. ⊠ *5th Ave. and Adams St.* ☎ *907/224–4082* ⊠ *Movie $3* ☉ *Mon.–Thurs. 10–8, Fri. and Sat. 10–6,* Sun. 1-6.

The **Seward Museum** displays photographs of the quake's damage, model rooms and artifacts from the early pioneers, and historical and current information on the Seward area. ⊠ *336 3rd Ave., at Jefferson St.* ☎ *907/224–3902* ⊠ *$3* ☉ *Mid-May–Sept., daily 10–5; Oct.–mid-May, weekends noon–4. Hrs may vary; call for recorded information.*

The first mile of the historic original **Iditarod Trail** runs along the beach and makes for a nice, easy stroll, as does the city's printed walking tour—available at the visitor bureau, the converted railcar at the corner of 3rd Avenue and Jefferson Street, or the Seward Chamber of Commerce Visitor Center at Mile 2 on the Seward Highway.

For a different view of the town, drive out **Nash Road,** around Resurrection Bay, and see Seward as it appears nestled at the base of the surrounding mountains.If you drive south from the SeaLife Center for about 10 minutes, you'll reach **Lowell Point,** a wooded stretch of land along the bay with great access to camping, beach walking, hiking, and kayaking; the spot is great for a day trip.

OUTDOOR ACTIVITIES & GUIDED TOURS
■TIP→ For more details on Kenai Fjords, flip to the next section.

ADVENTURE
AND WILDLIFE
VIEWING

Exit Glacier Guides (✉*Small-boat harbor* ☏*907/224-5569 or 605/759-8525* ⊕*www.exitglacierguides.com)* offers guided tours to Exit Glacier—and not just to the moraine where most tourists stop. The experienced guides lead travelers onto the glacier. They also offer guided hikes to viewpoints and the Harding Icefield. For those wanting to visit the glacier independently, Exit Glacier Guides runs an hourly shuttle from downtown to the glacier for $9 round-trip.

6

BOATING

Kenai Fjords Tours (☏*907/276–6249, 800/478–8068, 907/224–8068 in Seward* ⊕*www.kenaifjords.com)* is the oldest and largest company running tours through the park. From March through November, it leads 3- to 10-hour cruises, priced from $69 to $169, which include lunch. In 2007 and 2008 they added catamarans to their fleet—cats are less susceptible to the rolling motion that can cause seasickness. Cruise options include exclusive visits to Fox Island, interpretive programs by National Park Service rangers, cruise and kayak combinations, glacier viewing, and opportunities to see whales, puffins, otters, and Steller sea lions. Transportation and overnight options are also available. **Mariah Tours** (☏*907/224–8068 or 800/270–1238* ⊕*www.mariahtours.com)* operates smaller boats through the park and into the Chiswell Islands, with a maximum of 16 passengers per boat mid-May through mid-September. This is a great option for birders or groups.

Major Marine Tours (☏*907/274–7300 or 800/764–7300* ⊕*www.major-marine.com)* conducts half-day and full-day cruises of Resurrection Bay and Kenai Fjords National Park. Park cruises are narrated by a national park ranger, and meals of salmon and prime rib are an option. They can also arrange transportation between Anchorage and Seward.

Renown Tours (☏*907/272–1961 or 888/514–8687* ⊕*www.renowncharters.com)* operates its custom-built catamaran daily from March through September. Summer cruises include a three-hour whale-watching tour and a six-hour Kenai Fjords trip, featuring narration by a national park ranger. Transportation packages from Anchorage are available.

DEEP-SEA
FISHING

Crackerjack Sportfishing (✉*Box 2794 Small-boat harbor* ☏*907/224-2606 or 800/566-3912* ⊕*www.crackerjackcharters.com)* offers full- and half-day fishing charters as well as two- to five-day fishing expeditions in the Kenai Fjords National Park and beyond. The local captains have been guiding in Seward for 15 years and offer trips year-round.

Fish House (✉ *Small-boat harbor* ☎ *907/224–3674 or 800/257–7760* ⊕ *www.thefishhouse.net*) is Seward's oldest booking agency for deep-sea fishing.

HIKING   The **Caines Head Trail** allows easy, flat hiking along the coast, but a large portion of the hike is over tidal mudflats, so care must be taken to time the hike correctly—with tides here running in the 10- to 20-foot range, bad planning isn't just a case of getting your feet wet. It's officially advised that the trail only be hiked when there's a "plus 4-foot tide or greater" in summer. The trail is 4.5 mi, starting from Lowell Point, and two cabins can be rented at Derby Cove and Callisto Canyon.

The **Lost Lake/Primrose Trail** is a 16-mi end-to-end loop through spruce forests and up into the high alpine area. The Lost Lake trailhead is near Mile 5 of the Seward Highway, and the other end is at the Primrose campground at Mile 17. The trails are steep and usually snow-covered through late June, but the views along the Lost Lake valley are worth the climb. Above the tree line you're in mountain-goat country—look for white, blocky figures perched on the precarious cliffs. The lake is a prime spot for rainbow trout fishing. As usual, be bear aware. The Dale Clemens cabin, at Mile 4.5 from the Lost Lake trailhead, has propane heat and a stunning view of Resurrection Bay.

For a comprehensive listing of all the trails, cabins, and campgrounds in the Seward Ranger District of Chugach National Forest, check the Web site of the U.S. Forest Service.

The footrace best known among Alaskans is Seward's annual **Mt. Marathon Race,** run on July 4 since 1915. It doesn't take the winners very long—44 minutes or so—but the route is straight up the mountain (3,022 feet) and back down to the center of town. Ambitious hikers can hit the Runner's Trail behind Providence Medical Center on Jefferson, while those who prefer a more-leisurely (though still steep) climb can take the Hiker's Trail from 1st Avenue. For more information, contact the **Seward Chamber of Commerce** (✉ *Box 749, Seward, 99664* ☎ *907/224–8051* ⊕ *www.sewardak.org*).

WHERE TO EAT

$–$$$$ ✕ **Chinooks Waterfront Restaurant.** On the waterfront in the small-boat
SEAFOOD   harbor, Chinooks has a dazzling selection of fresh seafood items, brews on tap, and a great view from the upstairs window seats. Pasta dishes and a few beef specialties round out the menu. ✉ *1404 4th Ave.* ☎ *907/224–2207* ▭ *MC, V* ☉ *Closed mid-Sept.–May.*

¢–$$$$ ✕ **Christo's Palace.** Serving Greek, Italian, Mexican, and seafood meals,
ECLECTIC   this ornately furnished downtown restaurant is a surprisingly elegant hidden treasure. The nondescript facade belies the high, beamed ceilings, dark-wood accents, ornate chandeliers, and a large, gorgeous mahogany bar reputedly built in the mid-1800s and imported from San Francisco. Portions are generous, desserts are tempting, and there is a

small selection of after-dinner cognacs. ✉*133 4th Ave.* ☎*907/224–5255* ⊟*AE, D, MC, V.*

¢–$
MEXICAN

✕**Railway Cantina.** This little hole-in-the-wall in the harbor area is a local favorite. A wide selection of burritos, quesadillas, and tacos incorporates local seafood and is supplemented by an array of hot sauces, many contributed by customers who brought them from their travels. ✉*1401 4th Ave.* ☎*907/224–8226* ⊟*MC, V.*

$$–$$$
SEAFOOD

✕**Ray's Waterfront.** True to its name, Ray's has views of the bay and small-boat harbor. Seafood is the specialty; the chowder is a must-try. The walls are lined with stuffed and mounted fish, so you can point to your order. ✉*Small-boat harbor* ☎*907/224–5606* ⊟*AE, D, MC, V* ☉*Closed Nov.–Apr.*

$$$
AMERICAN

✕ **Resurrection Roadhouse.** On a sunny summer evening you'll have to fight locals for seats on the Roadhouse's deck, which overlooks the Resurrection River and the mountains surrounding it. Tucked off Exit Glacier/Herman Leirer Road, the Roadhouse gets warm afternoon light that goes well with beers on tap and excellent pizzas and sweet-potato fries. ■TIP→The bar and restaurant have different menus—ask to see both and then decide where to sit. ✉ *Mi 0.5, Herman Leirer Rd.* ☎*907/224–7116* ⊟*AE, D, MC, V.*

$–$$
ECLECTIC

✕ **Yoly's Bistro.** One of Seward's newest restaurants, Yoly's offers casual bistro dining with Asian-infused dishes, burgers, an affordable wine list, and live jazz on weekends. Local art covers the walls, and it's one of the few smoke-free restaurants in town. ✉*220 4th Ave* ☎*907/224–3295* ⊟*MC, V* ☉*Closed Oct–Apr.*

WHERE TO STAY

$

▦ **Alaska Paddle Inn.** A brand-new building offers beachfront panoramic views out at Lowell Point. Two rooms—"Low Tide" is downstairs and "High Tide" is upstairs—come with 9-foot ceilings, fireplaces, and walk-in tiled showers. Soothing earth tones round out the experience. Proprietor Alison also runs Chugach Mountain Massage (907/362–2321) on-site. **Pros:** Unobstructed views, clean accommodation. **Con:** Twenty stairs to the High Tide room. ✉*13745 Beach Dr.* ☎*907/224–4440 or 907/362–2628* ⊕*www.alaskapaddleinn.com* ⤺*2 rooms* ⌂*In-room: kitchen, Wi-Fi* ⊟*D, MC, V* ⓧ*CP.*

$–$$
★

▦**Alaska's Treehouse B&B.** Enjoy spectacular views of the Chugach Mountains from the solarium and from the hot tub on the tiered deck at this quiet, rustic retreat. This wood-crafter's house has vaulted cedar ceilings and skylights. The hand-built wood-fired sauna is perfect for relaxing in after a hike or ski along nearby trails. Breakfast includes sourdough pancakes with homemade wild-berry sauces. A two-bedroom suite sleeps five comfortably, and occupants of the Forest Room can also rent the adjoining Loft Room for the kids. **Pros:** Silence, solitude and nature, modern amenities. **Con:** A bit out of town; you'll need a car. ✉*0.5 mi off Seward Hwy., at Mi 7* ✑*Box 861 99664* ☎*907/224–3867* ⊕*www.virtualcities.com/ak/treehouse.htm* ⤺*2 suites* ⌂*In-hotel: restaurant* ⊟*No credit cards* ⓧ*BP.*

$$

▦ **Breeze Inn.** Across the street from the small-boat harbor, this modern hotel is very convenient if you're planning an early-morning fishing trip. Some rooms in the annex building overlook the harbor and a new deluxe wing opened in 2008, offering suites with jetted tubs. **Pros:** Directly across from the harbor, walking distance to downtown. **Con:** Rooms are bland and chain-motel-like. ✉*1306 Seward Hwy.* ☏*Box 2147 99664* ☎*907/224–5237 or 888/224–5237* ⊕*www.breezeinn. com* ⇨*100 rooms* ☕*In-room: refrigerator, Wi-Fi. In-hotel: 2 restaurants, bar, laundry facilities, some pets allowed, no-smoking rooms* ▤*AE, D, MC, V.*

$$$–$$$$ ⊡**Hotel Edgewater.** The rooms at Seward's newest and snazziest hotel overlook Resurrection Bay, and on clear days the panorama of mountains, glaciers, and the bay is breathtaking. Continental breakfast is served in the lobby, a three-story atrium complete with a small waterfall, lots of plants, plus plush seating. A side room has a fireplace and a selection of works by local artists. Rooms are decorated with warm colors, artwork, and wooden crown moldings that complement the cabinetwork. **Pro:** The downtown location is convenient to the SeaLife Center, restaurants, and shops. **Con:** It's not the cheapest waterfront lodging in town. ✉*202 5th Ave.* ☎*907/224–2700 or 888/793–6800* ⊕*www.hoteledgewater.com* ⇨*76 rooms* ☕*In-room: refrigerator, DVD, dial-up. In-hotel: bar, laundry service, concierge, no-smoking rooms* ▤*AE, D, MC, V* ☾*Closed Sept.–Mar.* ⑩*CP.*

$$$
Fodor's Choice
★ ⊡**Hotel Seward.** This historic downtown hotel is convenient to restaurants, shopping, and the Alaska SeaLife Center. In each of its rooms you'll find a king- or queen-size pillow-top bed; some rooms have bay windows and views. **Pros:** Cool historic building, excellent downtown location. **Con:** No elevator in one wing. ✉*221 5th Ave., Box 670* ☎*907/224–2378 or 800/655–8785* ⊕*www.hotelsewardalaska.com* ⇨*38 rooms* ☕*In-room: refrigerator, dial-up. In-hotel: no-smoking rooms* ▤*AE, D, DC, MC, V.*

$$$$ ⊡**Kenai Fjords Wilderness Lodge.** An hour's boat ride from Seward, this wilderness lodge sits within a quiet, forest-lined cove on Fox Island in Resurrection Bay. Built of local wood, each cabin has two beds, private bath with shower, propane stoves, and expansive views of the bay and mountains. Lodging rates include meals, boat transportation to the island, and a cruise of Kenai Fjords National Park. Meals are served family style in the main lodge. Hiking trails make it possible to explore the island. Guided kayak trips and coastal wildlife tours can also be arranged. **Pros:** Solitude, great views, everything's included. **Con:** Its location makes it pricey. ✉*Fox Island* ☏*1304 4th Ave. 99664* ☎*907/224–8068 or 800/478–8068* ⊕*www.kenaifjordslodge.com* ⇨*8 cabins* ☕*In-room: no phone, kitchen, no TV. In-hotel: restaurant, no-smoking rooms* ▤*AE, D, MC, V* ☾*Closed Sept.–May* ⑩*FAP.*

¢–$$$$ ⊡ **Miller's Landing.** This sprawling waterfront complex offers cabins, campsites for tents and RVs, water-taxi service to remote sites, sea-kayak and boat and motor rentals, and a booking service for area B&Bs, fishing trips, dogsled rides, hiking expeditions, sailing tours, and wildlife cruises. The lodgings run the gamut from one-room cabins with no running water and a woodstove for heat to a full-service cottage that sleeps 12. The campground has wooded sites and full hookups for motor homes, laundry, showers, Internet and Wi-Fi, bait, ice, and fishing-tackle sales and rental. To reach Miller's, take the road to

Seward. Fishing is an important industry and popular recreational activity in Seward.

Lowell Point from the SeaLife Center and follow the shoreline for 3.5 mi until you hit its parking lot on the beach. **Pros:** One-stop shopping for all your travel needs, a great location. **Cons:** Some cabins are very, very basic; the campground can be overcrowded. ⊠ *Lowell Point Rd., Box 81* ☎ *907/224–5739 or 866/541–5739* ⊕ *www.millerslandingak. com* ⊅ *13 cabins, 3 rooms, 29 tent sites, 31 RV sites with hookups* ⊟ *AE, D, MC, V.*

$$$ ⛰ **Seward Windsong Lodge.** In a forested setting near the banks of the Resurrection River, the Seward Windsong has rooms and deluxe balcony suites decorated in warm plaids, pine furniture, and Alaskan prints. The lodge is just down the road from Exit Glacier, and a full-service restaurant is on the premises. **Pros:** Incredible views of the river valley, Resurrection Roadhouse is right next door. **Con:** Outside town, so you'll need a car. ⊠ *Mi 0.5, Exit Glacier Rd., about 2 mi north of Seward* ⊅ *2525 C St., Anchorage 99503* ☎ *907/265–4501 or 888/959–9590* ⊕ *www.sewardwindsong.com* ⊅ *180 rooms, 16 suites* ⌖ *In-room: VCR, Wi-Fi. In-hotel: restaurant, bar, no-smoking rooms* ⊟ *AE, D, MC, V.*

$$ ⛰ **Stoney Creek Inn.** Sandwiched between two streams—one glacial, the other salmon-spawning—this bed-and-breakfast about 6 mi out of Seward offers a quiet respite from the summer buzz. Detox in the sauna or watch salmon migrate while soaking in the wooded streamside hot tub. A common area has games and books. **Pros:** Quiet location a perfect distance from town. **Con:** Far enough from town that you'll want a car. ⊠ *33422 Stoney Creek Ave.* ☎ *907/224–3940* ⊕ *www.stoney-creekinn.net* ⊅ *5 rooms* ⊟ *MC, V* ⥢ *CP.*

$–$$ ⊡ **Van Gilder Hotel.** Built in 1916 and listed on the National Register of Historic Places, the Van Gilder is an elegant building steeped in local history. Photos of Seward from the early 20th century adorn the walls, beds are brass or carved wood, and the common rooms foster a cozy, B&B feel. This is definitely not a mass-market chain hotel, and the staff gives tours of the property, pointing out interesting historical information. There's a common kitchen area, a sitting room with books of local interest, and a player piano in the lobby. **Pro:** Oldest hotel in Seward. **Con:** Shared kitchen. ⊠*308 Adams St.* ☎*907/224–3079 or 800/204–6835* ⊕*www.vangilderhotel.com* ⟟*20 rooms, 4 suites* ♿ *In-hotel: no elevator, no-smoking rooms* ▤*AE, D, MC, V* ℠*CP.*

¢   ⚠ **Waterfront Park.** The city of Seward operates Waterfront Park, a sprawling facility that occupies some of the town's premier real estate. Campsites are all first-come, first-served except for "caravans" of 10 units or more. The payoff is camping on the shore of Resurrection Bay with an unparalleled view of the waterfront and the mountains across the way. Fishing boats, cruise ships, ferries, pleasure craft, and work boats parade past the park day and night; seals, sea lions, and sea otters cruise past; seabirds, waterfowl, and bald eagles glide overhead; and the fishing from the beach is very good during the silver salmon run that peaks in July. Expect crowds and a limited selection of sites on holiday and salmon derby weekends, and any time the fishing is especially hot. ♿*Pit toilets, full hookups, drinking water, fire pits, picnic tables* ⟟*500 spaces, 99 with hookups* ⊠*Ballaine Blvd.* ☏*City of Seward, SPRD/Parks & Campgrounds, Box 167 99664-0167* ☎*907/224–4055* ⊕*www.cityofseward.net/sprd/campgrounds.htm* ▤*No credit cards.*

SHOPPING

☼   The **Ranting Raven** (⊠*224 4th Ave.* ☎*907/224–2228*) is a combination gift shop, bakery, and lunch spot, adorned with raven murals on the side of the building. You can indulge in fresh-baked goods, espresso drinks, and daily lunch specials such as quiche, focaccia, and home-made soups while perusing the packed shelves of artwork, native crafts, and jewelry.**Resurrect Art Coffeehouse** (⊠*320 3rd Ave.* ☎*907/224–7161* ⊕*www.resurrectart.com*) is a darling coffeehouse and gallery/gift shop. It is housed in a 1932 church, and the ambience and views from the old choir loft are reason enough to stop by. Local art is showcased, and it's a good place to find Alaskan gifts that aren't mass-produced.

KENAI FJORDS NATIONAL PARK

125 mi south of Anchorage.

★   Photogenic Seward is the gateway to the 670,000-acre Kenai Fjords National Park. This is spectacular coastal parkland incised with sheer, dark slate cliffs rising from the sea, ribboned with white waterfalls, and tufted with deep-green spruce. Kenai Fjords presents a rare opportunity for an up-close view of blue tidewater glaciers as well as some remarkable ocean wildlife.

GETTING HERE & AROUND

The only land route to the park is via Herman Leirer (Exit Glacier) Road, which ends at Exit Glacier. Boats leaving Seward for half-day tours and beyond are ample. Beyond that access is limited unless you charter a boat or airplane, or arrange for a tour with one of the local companies. If you take a day trip on a tour boat out of Seward, you can be pretty sure of seeing sea otters, crowds of Steller sea lions lazing on the rocky shelves along the shore, a porpoise or two, bald eagles, and tens of thousands of seabirds. Humpback whales and orcas are sighted occasionally, and mountain goats mull about the seaside cliffs. The park's coastal fjords are a favorite of sea kayakers, who can camp or stay in reserved public-use cabins.

One of the park's chief attractions is Exit Glacier, which can be reached only by the one road that passes into Kenai Fjords. Trails inside the park lead to an overlook of the vast Harding Icefield.

Before venturing out into the far reaches of the park, gather as much data as possible from the locals concerning the weather, tides, and dangerous beaches. Once you leave Seward, you're a long way from help. Backcountry travelers should also be aware that some of the park's coastline has been claimed by local native organizations and is now private property. Check with park headquarters to avoid trespassing on native property.

ESSENTIALS

Visitor Info Kenai Fjords Park Office ☎*907/224–7500* ⊕*www.nps.gov/kefj.*

OUTDOOR ACTIVITIES & GUIDED TOURS

BOATING **Major Marine Tours** (☎*907/274–7300 or 800/764–7300* ⊕*www.major-marine.com*) runs ranger-led boat tours through the park, with both half- and full-day excursions available.

COMBO TOURS **Kenai Coastal Tours** (☎*907/277–2131 or 800/478–8068*) leads day trips into Kenai Fjords National Park. It also conducts combination train-cruise–motor-coach trips from Anchorage.**Exit Glacier Guides** (✉*Small-boat harbor* ☎*907/224–5569* ⊕*www.exitglacierguides.com*) provides a $9 shuttle from town to Exit Glacier, and offers guided hikes to the glacier and Harding Icefield.

WHERE TO STAY

¢ **National Park Service Cabins.** The Kenai Fjords National Park manages four cabins, including three along the coast, favored by sea kayakers and for summer use only. The cabins cost $50 per night: three have a three-night limit, and the North Arm cabin can be reserved for up to nine nights, since it's considerably farther out than the others. Cabins have wooden bunks, heating stoves, and tables. There's no electricity, running water, indoor plumbing, or bedding. **Pro:** You'll get all the nature you want. **Con:** A few are accessible by boat or floatplane only. ✉*1212 4th Ave.* ✆*Box 1727, Seward 99664* ☎*907/224–7500 to reserve winter cabin, 907/271–2737 in Anchorage for summer rentals* ⊕*www.nps.gov/kefj/trip_planning/backcountry/puc/puc.htm* ⇋*4 cabins* ▤*MC, V.*

Continued on page 320

ALASKA'S GLACIERS
NOTORIOUS LANDSCAPE ARCHITECTS

(opposite) Facing the Taku Glacier challenge outside of Juneau. (top) River of ice

Glaciers—those massive, blue-hued tongues of ice that issue forth from Alaska's mountain ranges—perfectly embody the harsh climate, unforgiving terrain, and haunting beauty that make this state one of the world's wildest places. Alaska is home to roughly 100,000 glaciers, which cover almost 5% of the state's land.

FROZEN GIANTS

A glacier occurs where annual snowfall exceeds annual snowmelt. Snow accumulates over thousands of years, forming massive sheets of compacted ice. (Southeast Alaska's **Taku Glacier**, popular with flightseeing devotees, is one of Earth's meatiest: some sections measure over 4,500 feet thick.) Under the pressure of its own weight, the glacier succumbs to gravity and begins to flow downhill. This movement results in sprawling masses of rippled ice (Alaska's **Bering Glacier**, at 127 miles, is North America's longest). When glaciers reach the tidewaters of the coast, icebergs calve, or break off from the glacier's face, plunging dramatically into the sea.

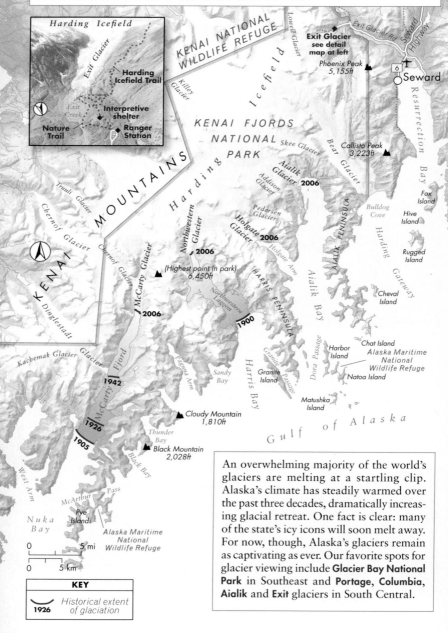

THE RAPIDLY RETREATING GLACIERS IN KENAI FJORDS NATIONAL PARK

Detail map (upper left):

Harding Icefield

Exit Glacier

Killey Glacier

Harding Icefield Trail

Interpretive shelter

Exit Creek

Nature Trail

Ranger Station

Main map labels:

KENAI NATIONAL WILDLIFE REFUGE

Lowell Glacier

Exit Glacier Rd

Seward Highway

Exit Glacier see detail map at left

Phoenix Peak 5,155ft

Seward

6

Icefield

Resurrection Bay

KENAI FJORDS NATIONAL PARK

Skee Glacier

Bear Glacier

Callisto Peak 3,223ft

Fox Island

Truuli Glacier

Aialik Glacier 2006

Addison Glacier

Pedersen Glacier

Holgate Glacier 2006

Holgate Arm

AIALIK PENINSULA

Bulldog Cove

Hive Island

Harding

Rugged Island

Gateway

Chernof Glacier

Chernof Glacier

Northwestern Glacier

2006

(Highest point in park) 6,450ft

Northwestern Lagoon

HARRIS PENINSULA

Aialik Bay

Cheval Island

H A R D I N G

M O U N T A I N S

K E N A I

McCarty Glacier

2006

1900

Dinglestadt Glacier

Kachemak Glacier

McCarty Fjord

Tasma Arm

Sandy Bay

Harris Bay

Granite Passage

Granite Island

Dora Passage

Harbor Island

Chat Island

Alaska Maritime National Wildlife Refuge

Natoa Island

1942

Cloudy Mountain 1,810ft

Matushka Island

1926

Thunder Bay

Black Mountain 2,028ft

1905

Black Bay

Gulf of Alaska

West Arm

McArthur Pass

Pye Islands

Nuka Bay

Alaska Maritime National Wildlife Refuge

0 5 mi

0 5 km

KEY

1926 Historical extent of glaciation

An overwhelming majority of the world's glaciers are melting at a startling clip. Alaska's climate has steadily warmed over the past three decades, dramatically increasing glacial retreat. One fact is clear: many of the state's icy icons will soon melt away. For now, though, Alaska's glaciers remain as captivating as ever. Our favorite spots for glacier viewing include **Glacier Bay National Park** in Southeast and **Portage, Columbia, Aialik** and **Exit** glaciers in South Central.

ICY BLUE HIKES & THUNDEROUS BOATING EXCURSIONS

Glaciers enchant us with their size and astonishing power to shape the landscape. But let's face it: nothing rivals the sheer excitement of watching a bus-size block of ice burst from a glacier's face, creating an unholy thunderclap that resounds across an isolated Alaskan bay.

Most frequently undertaken with a seasoned guide, **glacier trekking** is becoming increasingly popular. Many guides transport visitors to and from glaciers (in some cases by helicopter or small plane), and provide ski excursions, dogsled tours, or guided hikes on the glacier's surface. Striding through the surreal landscape of a glacier, ice crunching underfoot, can be an otherworldly experience. Whether you're whooping it up on a dogsled tour, learning the fundamentals of glacier travel, or simply poking about on a massive field of ice, you're sure to gain an acute appreciation for the massive scale of the state's natural environment.

You can also experience glaciers **via boat**, such as the Alaska Marine Highway, a cruise ship, a small chartered boat, or even your own bobbing kayak. Our favorite out of Seward is the ride with Kenai Fjords Tours. Don't be discouraged by rainy weather. Glaciers often appear even bluer on overcast days. When piloting your own vessel, be sure to keep your distance from the glacier's face.

■TIP➔ For more information about viewing Alaska's glaciers, see Chapter 1: Sports & Wilderness Adventures.

Taking in the sights at Mendenhall Glacier

DID YOU KNOW?

What do glaciers and cows have in common? They both *calve*. While bovine calving refers to actual calf-birth, the word is also used to describe a tidewater glacier's stunning habit of rupturing icebergs from its terminus. When glacier ice meets the sea, steady tidal movement and warmer temperatures cause these frequent, booming deposits.

GLACIER-VIEWING TIPS

- The most important rule of thumb is never to venture onto a glacier without proper training or the help of a guide.

- Not surprisingly, glaciers have a cooling effect on their surroundings, so wear layers and bring gloves and rain gear.

- Glaciers can powerfully reflect sunlight, even on cloudy days. Sunscreen, sunglasses, and a brimmed hat are essential.

- Warm, thick-soled waterproof footwear is a must.

- Don't forget to bring a camera and binoculars (preferably waterproof).

COOPER LANDING

100 mi south of Anchorage.

Centrally located on the Kenai Peninsula, Cooper Landing is within striking distance of some of Alaska's most popular fishing locations. Here the Russian River flows into the Kenai River, and spectacular fishing opportunities abound. Solid lines of traffic head south from Anchorage every summer weekend, and the confluence of the two rivers gets so crowded with enthusiastic anglers that the pursuit of salmon is often referred to as "combat fishing." However, a short walk upstream will separate you from the crowds and afford a chance to enjoy these gorgeous blue rivers.

The Russian River supports two runs of red (sockeye) salmon every summer, and it's the most popular fishery in the state. The Kenai River is famous for its runs of king (chinook), red, pink, and silver (coho) salmon, as well as large rainbow trout and Dolly Varden char. A number of nearby freshwater lakes, accessible only by hiking trail, also provide excellent fishing for rainbow trout and Dolly Varden.

Don't let the presence of dozens if not hundreds of fellow anglers lull you into a sense of complacency: in recent years the amount of brown bear activity at the Russian River has increased noticeably. This needn't deter you from enjoying yourself, though. Be aware of the posted signs warning of recent bear sightings, observe the local "rules of the road" about fishing and disposing of carcasses, and keep your senses tuned.

Cooper Landing serves as a trailhead for the 38-mi-long Resurrection Pass Trail, which connects to the village of Hope, and the Russian Lakes/Resurrection River trails, which run south to Exit Glacier near Seward. The town's central location also affords easy access to saltwater recreation in Seward and Homer.

GETTING HERE & AROUND

Follow the line of traffic flowing south out of Anchorage on the Seward Highway every Friday; take a right at the "Y" onto the Sterling Highway and soon you'll be there. Lodges and tackle shops dot either side of the highway. Cooper Landing does not operate a commercial airport.

SPORTS, THE OUTDOORS & GUIDED TOURS

FISHING For fly-fishing for trout and salmon, **Alaska Troutfitters** (☎*907/595–1212 ⊕www.aktroutfitters.com*) accommodates every level of fisherperson, from rank amateur to seasoned veteran. The company conducts a school covering everything from casting technique to fishing entomology and can arrange package deals with instruction, fishing, transportation, and accommodations.

WHERE TO EAT

¢–$ ✕**Sunrise Inn.** On the shore of Kenai Lake, this cheerful little restaurant
AMERICAN dishes up homemade soups, chowders, and salsas. The eclectic and very reasonably priced menu includes wraps and vegetarian items. Daily specials made from scratch and hand-grated French fries feature prominently in what the owners describe as a "backwoods bistro." There's a

spotting scope in the parking lot for spying on the Dall sheep and mountain goats in the surrounding peaks. The bar hosts live music on Saturday in summer, and there's a great deck for when the weather's warm. ⊠ *Mi 45, Sterling Hwy.* ☎ *907/595–1222* ⊕ *www.alaskasunriseinn.com* ⊟ *D, MC, V.*

WHERE TO STAY

$$ 🍴 **Alaska Wildland Adventures' Kenai Riverside Lodge.** This collection of buildings on the bank of the Kenai River offers a "roughing it in authentic comfort" all-inclusive package with renovated cabins that have private baths. Whether you choose to hike, raft, fish, attend a naturalist program, or stroll the nature trail, in the evening your most difficult decision is whether to venture into the wood-fired sauna or to pour yourself into a rocking chair on the deck overlooking the Kenai River. **Pros:** Beautiful wooded location, all-inclusive. **Con:** Cabins are a bit small. ⊠ *Mi 50.1, Sterling Hwy.* ✏ *Box 389, Girdwood 99587* ☎ *907/783–2928 or 800/478–4100* ⊕ *www.alaskasportfish.com* ⇱ *8 cabins* ♨ *In-room: no phone, no TV. In-hotel: restaurant, no-smoking rooms* ⊟ *D, DC, MC, V* ⊘ *Closed Oct.–mid-May* ⌢ *CP.*

$$$$ 🍴 **Great Alaska Adventure Lodge.** Midway between Seward and Homer,
★ this lodge lives up to its name. Activities include natural history, soft-adventure options, and a remote bear-viewing camp. The fishing guides are top-notch, and seven world records have been set along the camp's riverbanks. They offer 2- to 10-day trips with any-day arrivals and free Anchorage pick-up. Rates include lodging, meals, and most activities, and the basic fishing package—two days and one night, all expenses covered, including a fishing guide—runs $995 per person. They also offer group packages, plus a fly-out bear-viewing camp and boat-in kayaking camp. Rooms, which are in the main lodge or in riverside cabins, have fireplaces, artwork, and comfortable seating. Some of the cabins are two stories with spiral staircases. **Pros:** All-inclusive, right on the Sterling Highway. **Con:** Right on the Sterling Highway. ⊠ *Mi 82.5, 33881 Sterling Hwy., Sterling* ✏ *Box 2670, Poulsbo, WA 98370* ☎ *907/262–4515, 800/544–2261, 360/697–6454 in winter* ⊕ *www.greatalaska.com* ⇱ *25 rooms* ♨ *In-room: no phone, no TV. In-hotel: restaurant, airport shuttle* ⊟ *AE, MC, V* ⊘ *Closed Oct.–mid-May* ⌢ *FAP.*

$–$$$$ 🍴 **Gwin's Lodge.** Gwin's is the epicenter of much of the activity on the peninsula. This roadside establishment is a one-stop shop for visitors and locals alike, providing food, lodging, and fishing tackle around the clock in summer. ■ **TIP→** The travel agency can book fishing, hiking, rafting, and other adventure travel anywhere on the peninsula. The lodge is the fishing headquarters of prospective anglers during the annual salmon runs on the nearby Russian and Kenai rivers. Cabins vary in configuration from standard log cabin with beds and private baths to deluxe chalets with lofts, vaulted ceilings, and full kitchens. The restaurant ($–$$) serves a full menu of fresh fish when available, sandwiches, steaks, and hearty breakfasts. A giant salmon bake was constructed in 2008, serving grilled salmon and live music against the backdrop of the steep mountains. **Pro:** Get everything you need in one place. **Con:** Some cabins are actually trailers with a log facade. ⊠ *Mi 52, Sterling Hwy.*

6

☎ *907/595–1266* ⊕ *www.gwinslodge.com* ⇨ *17 rooms* ⌂ *In-room: no phone, no TV, Wi-Fi. In-hotel: restaurant, bar, no-smoking rooms* ⊟ *AE, D, MC, V* ⊘ *Restaurant closed Oct.–Mar.*

$–$$$$ ⊡ **Ingram's Base Camp.** Cabins come in three variations—regular, deluxe, and riverfront, all with private baths, heat, and kitchens. One cabin has a gourmet kitchen and private hot tub. You can arrange for a remote guided or unguided fishing trip, a backpacking drop-off, or air transportation to one of the Forest Service cabins in the area. Ingram's also offer guided drift-boat fishing on the Kenai and Kasilof rivers, walk-in guided fishing to many local streams; fly-out guiding can be arranged from the camp. All tackle can be provided, or bring your own. **Pros:** Accommodations fit any budget, great views. **Cons:** Some staircases are steep (although most also have bedrooms downstairs), some upstairs rooms are only semiprivate. ⊠ *Mi 48.1, Sterling Hwy., Box 748* ☎ *907/595–1213 or 866/595–1213* ⊕ *www.ingramsbasecamp.com* ⇨ *12 cabins* ⌂ *In-room: no phone, kitchen, refrigerator, no TV, Wi-Fi. In-hotel: public Wi-Fi, no-smoking rooms* ⊟ *MC, V.*

$$ ⊡ **The Inn at Tern Lake.** Although the address is technically in Moose Pass, the Inn at Tern Lake sits right between Cooper Landing and Moose Pass a few miles south of the "Y" where the Sterling Highway branches off the Seward. The inn is nestled in a valley of spruce trees between the jagged peaks of the Kenai Mountains. Walk (or, in winter, cross-country ski) through the woods to the shore of Tern Lake, soak in the hot tub, practice your tennis or putting (on the landing strip), or just scan the mountainsides for Dall sheep, mountain goats, or bears. The rooms and common areas have antiques and Alaskan artifacts, and the Hetricks will help you book any other adventures. **Pros:** Babbling springs and, of course, terns on the lake complete the Alaska experience. **Con:** Its unique location also means it's a bit far from any amenities. ⊠ *Mi 36, Seward Hwy.* ⌂ *Box 7, Moose Pass 99631* ☎ *907/288–3667* ⊕ *www.ternlakeinn.com* ⇨ *4 rooms* ⌂ *In-room: kitchen, refrigerator, dial-up. In-hotel: tennis court, public Internet, no-smoking rooms* ⊟ *AE, D, MC, V* ⊘|*CP.*

$$$$ ⊡ **Kenai Princess Wilderness Lodge.** "Elegantly rustic" might best describe
Fodor's Choice   this sprawling complex approximately 45 mi from Seward, on a bluff
★   overlooking the Kenai River. Paths lead from the main lodge to charming bungalows, each containing four spacious units. Buildings higher on the bluff house eight units. Each has a king or two double beds, a wood-burning fireplace, a comfortable sitting area, and a porch. Vaulted ceilings of natural-finish wood complement the Alaskan art prints on the walls. Staff can arrange for fishing, flightseeing, horseback riding, and river rafting. There's also a nature trail. The Eagle's Crest Restaurant serves a variety of Alaska fare, including seafood, and the Rafter's Lounge offers a good menu of bar food and local beers that can be enjoyed from the spacious deck overlooking the river. **Pros:** Cozy rooms have fireplaces and manage to escape a corporate feel. **Con:** Rooms don't have views of the river, even though the lodge sits right on top of it. ⊠ *Mi 47.7, Sterling Hwy.* ⌂ *Box 676, Cooper Landing 99572* ☎ *907/595–1425 or 800/426–0500* ⊕ *www.princessalaskalodges.com* ⇨ *86 rooms* ⌂ *In-hotel: 2 restaurants, bar, gym, laundry facilities* ⊟ *AE, DC, MC, V* ⊘ *Closed mid-Sept.–May.*

KENAI NATIONAL WILDLIFE REFUGE

95 mi northwest of Kenai Fjords National Park, 150 mi southwest of Anchorage.

The Kenai National Wildlife Refuge, in its nearly 2 million acres, takes in a portion of the Harding Icefield as well as two large and scenic lakes, Skilak and Tustumena. The refuge is not only the finest moose habitat in the region, but its waterways are great for canoeing and kayaking. The refuge maintains two visitor centers. The main center, in Soldotna, has wildlife dioramas, free films and information, and a bookstore and gift shop. There's also a seasonal "contact" center at Mile 57.8 of the Sterling Highway, open from mid-June to mid-August.

Wildlife is plentiful even by Alaskan standards: the refuge was originally established to protect the Kenai moose. Although caribou seldom appear near the road, Dall sheep and mountain goats live on the peaks near Cooper Landing, and black and brown bears, wolves, coyotes, lynx, beavers, and lots of birds abide here as well.

The refuge also contains a canoe trail system through the Swan Lake and Swanson River areas. Covering more than 140 mi on 100 lakes and the Swanson River, this route is an underused portion of the refuge that escapes the notice of most visitors and residents alike. This series of lakes linked by overland portages offers fantastic access to the remote backcountry, well away from what passes for civilization in the subarctic. The fishing improves exponentially with distance from the road system, and opportunities for undisturbed wildlife viewing are nearly unlimited.

GETTING HERE & AROUND

■TIP➜ You must paddle into the refuge; access is generally by canoe. Road access to the canoe trailheads is off the Swanson River Road at Mile 83.4 of the Sterling Highway. Other than canoeing, the only other way to get into the far reaches of the refuge is by airplane. Floatplane services in Soldotna, where the refuge is headquartered, can fly you into the backcountry. The refuge office maintains lists of transporters, air taxis, canoe rentals, and big-game guides that are permitted to operate on refuge lands. To reach the main visitor center/refuge office on Ski Hill Road, turn south on Funny River Road in Soldotna just west of the Kenai River bridge, and follow the signs.

ESSENTIALS

Visitor Info **Kenai National Wildlife Refuge Visitor Center** (⊠ *Ski Hill Rd., Soldotna* ☎ *907/262–7021* ⊕ *kenai.fws.gov*).

SPORTS, THE OUTDOORS & GUIDED TOURS

CANOEING The best way to experience the refuge's backcountry is by canoe. The **Swan Lake Canoe System** and the **Swanson River Canoe System** are accessed from the road system at the turnoff at Mile 83.4 of the Sterling Highway. Several loop trips enable visitors to fish, hike, and camp away from the road system and motorized boat traffic. Fishing for trout, salmon, and Dolly Varden is excellent, and the series of lakes and portages offer access to more than 100 mi of waterways. The **Kenai National Wildlife Refuge Visitor Center** has a list of canoeing outfitters.

HIKING   Hiking trails branch off from the Sterling Highway and the Skilak Lake Loop. Degree of difficulty ranges from easy half-mile walks to

> **MOOSE ALERT**
>
> Moose are the most commonly seen large animal on the refuge— it was originally named the Kenai National Moose Range.

strenuous climbs to mountain lakes. Bring topographic maps, water, food, insect repellent, and bear awareness. You won't find toilets, water fountains, or signposts. Remember: brown and black bears are numerous on the Kenai Peninsula. ⇨ *Check out "Welcome to Bear Country," in Chapter 8.*

WHERE TO STAY

$$$$ 🏨 **Kenai Backcountry Lodge.** A trip to the Kenai Backcountry Lodge involves much more than driving up to the door and booking a room— in fact, that's not even an option. Access is by boat across Skilak Lake. There you can stay in a traditional Alaskan tent cabin or a log cabin, taking all your meals, included in the price, at the main lodge. Hot water and showers are at the shared bathhouse, and the company stresses a low-impact, environmentally friendly facility. Trip cost includes all guided activities, such as hiking, kayaking, a Kenai River Canyon raft trip, motorboat tours, and wildlife viewing. With all the moose, caribou, wolves, bears, eagles, and spawning salmon, chances are you'll see more animals than people during your stay. There's a two-night minimum. **Pro:** Gets you to the backcountry without roughing it too much. **Con:** Shared bathrooms. ⌂ *Box 389, Girdwood 99587* ☎ *907/783–2928 or 800/334–8730* ⊕ *www.alaskawildland. com/kenaibackcountrylodge.htm* ⇝ *4 log cabins, 6 tent cabins* ♿ *In-room: no phone, no TV. In-hotel: restaurant, airport shuttle, no-smoking rooms* ▤ *D, DC, MC, V* ⊙ *Closed Sept.–May* ❄*FAP.*

¢   ⚠ **Kenai National Wildlife Refuge Campgrounds.** The U.S. Fish and Wildlife Service maintains 14 road-accessible campgrounds in the Kenai Refuge. None have hookups, and only two of the campgrounds (Hidden Lake and Upper Skilak Lake) charge fees for camping. All but three campgrounds have drinking water; all have nearby hiking trails and fishing. The maximum length of stay is 14 consecutive days, with a few exceptions—the Russian River Ferry site limit is 3 days, and the Hidden Lake and Upper Skilak limit is 7 days. ♿ *Flush toilets, drinking water (some), fire pits, picnic tables* ⇝ *130 sites (110 suitable for RVs)* ⌂ *Kenai National Wildlife Refuge, Box 2139, Soldotna 99669-2139* ☎ *907/262–7021* ⊕ *kenai.fws.gov* ⚠ *Reservations not accepted* ▤*No credit cards.*

¢   ⚠ **USFWS Cabins.** These cabins are in remote areas of the refuge accessible only by air or boat. The reservation system is a bit cumbersome, but can be done over the phone. However, if you're willing to overcome these hurdles, you'll find tranquillity and true wilderness, and won't have to worry about your tent springing a leak. ⇝ *11 cabins* ⌂ *Kenai National Wildlife Refuge, Attn: Cabin Reservation, Box 2139, Soldotna, 99669*

☎907/262–7021 or 877/285–5628 🖷907/262–3599 ⊕*kenai.fws.gov/ visitorseducators/cabin/reserve.htm* ▬D, MC, V.

KENAI & SOLDOTNA

116 mi northwest of Seward, 148 mi southwest of Anchorage.

The towns of Kenai and Soldotna are mentioned almost interchangeably due to their proximity. Soldotna, with its strategic location on the peninsula's northwest coast, is the commercial and sportfishing hub of the Kenai Peninsula. Along with its sister city, Kenai, whose onion-dome Holy Assumption Russian Orthodox Church highlights the city's old town, it is home to Cook Inlet oil-field workers and their families. Soldotna's commercial center stretches along the Sterling Highway, making this a stopping point for those traveling up and down the peninsula. The town of Kenai lies near the end of the road that branches off the Sterling Highway in Soldotna. Near Kenai is Captain Cook State Recreation Area, one of the least-visited state parks on the road system. This portion of the peninsula is level and forested, with numerous lakes and streams pocking and crisscrossing the area. Trumpeter swans return here in spring, and sightings of moose are common.

6

GETTING HERE & AROUND

As you're driving either north or south on the Sterling Highway from Cooper Landing or Homer, you'll know you've hit Soldotna when you're suddenly stuck in traffic in between strip malls. Kenai is 11 mi up the Kenai Spur Highway, which originates in central Soldotna. Commercial flights are available to Kenai from Anchorage and around.

ESSENTIALS

Medical Assistance Central Peninsula General Hospital (⊠ *250 Hospital Pl., Soldotna* ☎ *907/714–4404*).

Visitor Info Kenai Visitor and Convention Bureau (⊠ *11471 Kenai Spur Hwy., Kenai* ☎ *907/283–1991*).

WHAT TO SEE

☺ In addition to fishing, clam digging is also popular at **Clam Gulch,** 24 mi south of Soldotna on the Sterling Highway. This is a favorite of local children, who love any excuse to dig in the muddy, sloppy goo. Ask locals on the beach how to find the giant razor clams (recognized by their dimples in the sand). Ask for advice on how to clean the clams—cleaning is pretty labor intensive, and it's easy to get into a clam-digging frenzy when the conditions are favorable, only to regret your efforts when cleaning time arrives. The clam digging is best when tides are minus 4 or 5 feet. ■TIP➔ A sportfishing license, available at grocery, sporting-goods, and drugstores, is required for clam diggers 16 years old and over.

OUTDOOR ACTIVITIES & GUIDED TOURS

FISHING Anglers from around the world come for the salmon-choked streams and rivers, most notably the Kenai River and its companion, the Russian River. Knowledgeable fishery professionals figure it's only a matter of time before someone with sportfishing gear catches a 100-pounder. There are two runs of kings up the Kenai every summer. The first run starts in mid-May and tapers off in early July, and the second run is from early July until the season closure on July 31. Generally speaking, the first run has more fish, but they tend to be smaller than second-run fish. Smaller, of course, has a whole different meaning when it comes to these fish. Fifty- and 60-pounders are unremarkable here, and 40-pound fish are routinely tossed back as being "too small." The limit is one king kept per day, five per season, no more than two of which can be from the Kenai. The river also supports two runs of red (sockeye) salmon every year, as well as runs of silver (coho) and pink (humpback) salmon. Rainbow trout of near-mythic proportions inhabit the river, as do Dolly Varden char. Fishing pressure is heavy, so don't expect a wilderness experience, especially in the lower river near Soldotna.

Farther up the river, between Kenai Lake in Cooper Landing and Skilak Lake, motorboats are banned, so a more idyllic experience can be had. Scores of guide services ply the river, and if you're inexperienced at the game, consider hiring a guide for a half-day or full-day trip. Deep-sea fishing for salmon and halibut out of Deep Creek is challenging Homer's position as the preeminent fishing destination on the southern Kenai Peninsula. This fishery is unusual in that tractors launch boats off the beach and into the Cook Inlet surf. The local campground and RV lot is packed on summer weekends.

Area phone books list some 300 fishing charters and guides, all of whom stay busy during the hectic summer fishing season. **Hi Lo Charters** (☎ 907/283–9691 or 800/757–9333 ⊕ www.hilofishing.com) runs salmon-fishing trips on the world-famous Kenai River. The **Sports Den** (☎ 907/262–7491 ⊕ www.alaskasportsden.com) arranges fishing trips on the river, on the saltwater, or to a remote fly-in location for salmon, trout, or halibut.

DID YOU KNOW? The Kenai River is home to the world's largest king salmon. In 1985 a local resident, Les Anderson, caught a 97-pound, 4-ounce fish. That record still stands.

WHERE TO EAT

$–$$$
AMERICAN
✕ **The Duck Inn.** With pizzas, burgers, chicken, steaks, and seafood, there's something for everyone. Portions are generous and the prices are reasonable. Locally caught halibut is a specialty, prepared in enough different ways to stave off halibut overload. There's also lots of artwork featuring ducks. ✉ 43187 Kalifornsky Beach Rd., Soldotna ☎ 907/262–1849 ▭ D, MC, V.

¢–$
AMERICAN
✕ **Sal's Klondike Diner.** In Sterling, between Cooper Landing and Soldotna, Sal's has a true diner atmosphere. It's open 24 hours and the portions are large; there's even a sign on the wall that says, "If you're still hungry, tell us." Burgers, sandwiches, fish-and-chips, halibut, salmon, and some steaks are available, and they bake their own bread and pies every day. You can buy loaves of sourdough, white, or wheat bread. It's a favorite spot for locals. ✉ 44619 Sterling Hwy., Sterling ☎ 907/262–2220 ▭ AE, MC, V.

¢–$ ✕**Suzie's Cafe.** This Sterling roadside café is a cut above most roadside
AMERICAN cafés in Alaska. There's a deck for outside dining, the interior has
antiques, and fresh flowers liven up the tables. Food is homemade, and
you won't go hungry. Main courses include burgers, seafood, pot roast,
real mashed potatoes with a choice of gravies, and homemade soups
and desserts. The coffee is excellent, another rarity on the road system.
✉*Mi 82.7, Sterling Hwy., Sterling* ☎*907/260–5751* 🖃*MC, V.*

WHERE TO STAY

$$ 🛏**Aspen Hotel Soldotna.** The Soldotna facility sits on a bluff overlooking
the Kenai River, and if you get a river-view room you'll have a front-
row seat for the fishing action during salmon runs. In addition to regu-
lar rooms, the Aspen also offers two family suites with bunk beds, and
several executive suites. **Pros:** Hot tub, swimming pool, and river front-
age. **Con:** Bland, corporate feel. ✉*326 Binkley Circle, Soldotna*
☎*907/260–7736 or 888/308–7848* ⊕*www.aspenhotelsak.com* ⇆*63
rooms* ⚷*In-room: refrigerator, DVD, Wi-Fi. In-hotel: pool, spa, laun-
dry facilities, public Internet* 🖃*AE, D, DC, MC, V* ⎁*CP.*

$–$$ 🛏**Best Western King Salmon Motel.** This Best Western has large rooms,
including some with kitchenettes. If you're traveling by RV, you can
take advantage of the park with full hookups, available for $35 per
night. **Pro:** Meticulously cleaned. **Con:** Surrounded by strip malls.
✉*35546-A Kenai Spur Hwy., Soldotna* ☎*907/262–5857 or 888/
262–5857* ⊕*www.bestwestern.com* ⇆*49 rooms* ⚷*In-room: kitchen
(some), dial-up. In-hotel: restaurant, laundry facilities* 🖃*AE, D, DC,
MC, V.*

$$$–$$$$ 🛏**Timber Wolf Lodge.** The lodge sits on the bank of the Kenai River and
has a small fleet of fishing boats and guides. The rooms are all two-
bedroom, two-bathroom condos, some of which are brand new. They
also offer bear-viewing trips, sightseeing, overnight halibut fishing, and
rafting and kayaking adventures. Patios overlook the river, and barbe-
cue grills are available for fortunate fishermen. **Pros:** Centrally located
and right on the river. **Con:** Right on the highway. ✉*44485 Sterling
Hwy., Soldotna* ☎*907/260–5752 or 888/352–3888* ⊕*www.timber-
wolflodgeak.com* ⇆*28 rooms* ⚷*In-room: kitchen, refrigerator. In-
hotel: no-smoking rooms* 🖃*AE, D, DC, MC, V.*

HOMER

77 mi south of Soldotna, 226 mi south of Anchorage.

At the southern end of the Sterling Highway lies the city of Homer, at
the base of a narrow spit that juts 4 mi into beautiful Kachemak Bay.
Glaciers and snowcapped mountains form a dramatic backdrop across
the water.

Founded in the late 1800s as a gold-prospecting camp, this commu-
nity was later used as a coal-mining headquarters. Chunks of coal are
still common along local beaches; they wash into the bay from nearby
slopes where the coal seams are exposed. Today the town of Homer
is an eclectic community filled with tacky tourist paraphernalia; com-
mercial-fishing boats, canneries, and repair yards; and a thriving group

of local artists, sculptors, actors, and writers. Much of the commercial fishing centers on halibut, and the popular Homer Jackpot Halibut Derby is often won by enormous fish weighing more than 300 pounds. The local architecture includes everything from dwellings that are little more than assemblages of driftwood, flotsam, and jetsam to steel commercial buildings and magnificent homes on the hillside overlooking the surrounding bay, mountains, forests, and glaciers.

GETTING HERE & AROUND
The Sterling Highway ends in Homer, and the drive in is beautiful. Once there, you'll see signs on your left for Pioneer Avenue, Homer's commercial district. On the right is the historic town center, and if you keep to the road you'll hit the spit. Homer also operates a commercial airport, with flights daily to and from Anchorage, Seldovia, and elsewhere. If you're traveling on the marine highway system, ferries to Kodiak and beyond dock several times a week in summer.

ESSENTIALS
Medical Assistance **South Peninsula Hospital** (⊠ *4300 Bartlett St.* ☎ *907/235–8101*).

Visitor Info **Homer Chamber of Commerce** (⊠ *201 Sterling Hwy.* ⬝ *Box 541, Homer 99603* ☎ *907/235–7740* ⊕ *www.homeralaska.org*).

EXPLORING HOMER

WHAT TO SEE
Start your visit with a stop at the Homer Chamber of Commerce's **Visitor Information Center**, where racks are filled with brochures from local businesses and attractions. ⊠ *201 Sterling Hwy.* ☎ *907/235–7740* ⊕ *www.homeralaska.org* ☉ *Memorial Day–Labor Day, weekdays 9–7, weekends 10–6; early Sept.–late May, weekdays 9–5.*

☺ Protruding into Kachemak Bay, **Homer Spit** provides a sandy focal point
Fodor'sChoice for visitors and locals. A paved path stretches most of the 4 mi and is
★ great for biking or walking. A commercial-fishing-boat harbor at the end of the path has restaurants, hotels, charter fishing businesses, sea-kayaking outfitters, art galleries, and on-the-beach camping spots. Fly a kite, walk the beaches, drop a line in the Fishing Hole, or just wander through the shops looking for something interesting; this is one of Alaska's favorite summertime destinations.

☺ The **Pratt Museum** is an art gallery and natural history museum rolled
★ into one. It has a saltwater aquarium; an exhibit on the 1989 Exxon Valdez oil spill; a wildflower garden; a gift shop; and pioneer, Russian, and Alaska native displays. You can spy on wildlife with robotic video cameras set up on a seabird rookery and at the McNeil River Bear Sanctuary. A refurbished homestead cabin and outdoor summer exhibits are along the trail out back. ⊠ *Bartlett St. off Pioneer Ave.* ☎ *907/235–8635* ⊕ *www.prattmuseum.org* ⬚ *$6* ☉ *Mid-May–mid-Sept., daily 10–6; mid-Sept.–mid-May, Tues.–Sun. noon–5.*

⟳ **Islands and Ocean Center** provides a wonderful introduction to the
★ Alaska Maritime National Wildlife Refuge. The refuge covers some 3.5
million acres spread across some 2,500 Alaskan islands, from Prince of
Wales Island in the south to Barrow in the north. Opened in 2003, this
37,000-square-foot facility with towering windows facing Kachemak
Bay is a must-see for anyone interested in wild places—and it's free! A
film takes visitors along on a voyage of the Fish and Wildlife Service's
research ship, the MV *Tiglax*. Interactive exhibits detail the birds and
marine mammals of the refuge (the largest seabird refuge in America),
and one room even re-creates the noisy sounds and pungent smells of
a bird rookery. In summer, guided bird-watching treks and beach walks
are offered. ✉ *95 Sterling Hwy.* ☎ *907/235–6961* ⊕ *www.islandsand-
ocean.org* ⮐ *Free* ☉ *Memorial Day–Labor Day, daily 9–6; Labor
Day–Memorial Day, Tues. –Sat. noon–5.*

Kachemak Bay abounds in wildlife, including a large population of puffins and eagles. Tour operators take you past bird rookeries or across
the bay to gravel beaches for clam digging. Most fishing charters include
an opportunity to view whales, seals, porpoises, and birds close up. At
the end of the day, walk along the docks on Homer Spit and watch
commercial-fishing boats and charter boats unload their catch.

Directly across from the end of Homer Spit is **Halibut Cove**, a small
artists community. Spend a relaxing afternoon or evening meandering
along the boardwalk and visiting galleries. The cove is lovely, especially during salmon runs, when fish leap and splash in the clear water.
Several lodges are on this side of the bay, on pristine coves away from
summer crowds. The *Danny J* ferries people across from Homer Spit,
with a stop at the rookery at Gull Island and two or three hours to walk
around Halibut Cove, for $47 apiece. The ferry makes two trips daily:
the first leaves Homer at noon and returns at 5 PM, and the second
leaves at 5 PM and returns at 10 PM. Central Charters handles all book-
ings. *(⇨ See " Outdoor Activities & Guided Tours," below.)*

Across Kachemak Bay from Homer Spit lies one of the largest coastal
parks in America, the 400,000-acre **Kachemak Bay State Park** (☎ *907/
235–7024* ⊕ *www.alaskastate-
parks.org*). Flip ahead to the next
section of this chapter for more
information about this park. The
park encompasses a line of snowcapped mountains and several large
glaciers; the prominent one visible
from the spit is called Grewingk
Glacier. One of the most popular
trails leads 2 mi, ending at the lake
in front of Grewingk Glacier. Several state park cabins can be rented
for $50–$65 a night, and a number

HOMER FESTIVALS

Early-summer visitors to Homer
join thousands of migrating
shorebirds for the **Kachemak Bay
Shorebird Festival** on the first
weekend of May. Experts offer
bird-watching trips and photography demonstrations, and a simul-
taneous Wooden Boat Festival
provides a chance to meet some
of Alaska's finest boatbuilders.
Various kids' events add to the
fun. In late July the KBBI Concerts on the Lawn (☎ *907/235–
7721* ⊕ *www.kbbi.org*) bring a
weekend of folk and rock music to
Karen Hornaday Park.

of luxurious private lodges occupy remote coves. Park access is primarily by water taxi from the spit; contact **Mako's Water Taxi** (☎ *907/235–9055* ⊕ *www.makoswatertaxi.com*).

OUTDOOR ACTIVITIES & GUIDED TOURS

BOATING & FISHING

Homer is a major commercial fishing port (especially for halibut) and a popular destination for sport anglers in search of giant halibut or feisty king and silver salmon. Near the end of the spit, Homer's famous **Fishing Hole** is a small bight stocked with king and silver salmon smolt (baby fish) by the Alaska Department of Fish and Game. The salmon then head out to sea, returning several years later to the Fishing Hole, where they are easy targets for wall-to-wall bankside anglers throughout summer. The Fishing Hole isn't anything like casting for salmon along a remote stream, but your chances are good and you don't need to drop $800 for a flight into the wilderness. Fishing licenses and rental poles are available from fishing-supply stores on the spit.

Quite a few companies offer charter fishing in summer, for around $175 per person per day (including bait and tackle). **Central Charters** (✉ *4241 Homer Spit Rd.*, ☎ *907/235–7847 or 800/478–7847* ⊕ *www. centralcharter.com*) arranges fishing and ferry trips to Halibut Cove, around Kachemak Bay, and across to Seldovia.

Homer Ocean Charters (☎ *907/235–6212 or 800/426–6212* ⊕ *www. homerocean.com*) on the spit sets up fishing and sightseeing trips, as well as sea-kayaking and water-taxi services and remote-cabin rentals. Some of their most-popular cruises go to the **Rookery Restaurant** at Otter Cove Resort. The narrated wildlife lunch cruise ($60) leaves at noon, and dinner trips to the restaurant leave at 6 PM; the ferry trip is $20, and dinner main courses run $18–$35. Also try **Inlet Charters** (☎ *907/235–6126 or 800/770–6126* ⊕ *www.halibutcharters.com*) for fishing charters, water-taxi services, and wildlife cruises.

Anyone heading out on a halibut charter is advised to buy a $10 ticket for the **Homer Jackpot Halibut Derby** (☎ *907/235–7740* ⊕ *www. homerhalibutderby.com*); first prize for the largest halibut is more than $40,000.

BEAR WATCH

Homer is a favorite departure point for viewing Alaska's famous brown bears in Katmai National Park. **Emerald Air Service** (☎ *907/235–6993* ⊕ *www. emeraldairservice.com*) is one of several companies offering all-day and custom photography trips starting around $595 per person. **Hallo Bay Wilderness** (☎ *907/235–2237 or 888/535–2237* ⊕ *www.hallobay.com*) offers guided close-range viewing without the crowds. Day trips are offered, but it's the two- to seven-day stays at this comfortable coastal location that provide the ultimate in world-class bear- and wildlife-viewing.

SEA KAYAKING

Several local companies offer guided sea-kayaking trips to protected coves within Kachemak Bay State Park and nearby islands. **True North Kayak Adventures** (☎907/235–0708 ⊕*www.truenorthkayak.com*) has a range of such adventures, including a six-hour paddle to Elephant Rock for $125 and an all-day boat and kayak trip to Yukon Island for $145 (both trips include round-trip water taxi to the island base camp, guide, all kayak equipment, and bakery lunch). For something more unusual, book an overnight trip to Kasitsna Bay through the beautiful **Across the Bay Tent & Breakfast** (☎907/235–3633, 907/345–2571 Sept.–May ⊕*www.tentandbreakfastalaska.com*). Grounds are gorgeous, facilities are basic, and guests can take kayak tours, rent a mountain bike, or just hang out on the shore.

WHERE TO EAT

$–$$$$
ECLECTIC

✕**Café Cups.** It's hard to miss this place as you drive down Pioneer Avenue—look for the huge namesake cups on the building's facade. A longtime Homer favorite, this café serves dinners that make the most of the locally abundant seafood, complemented by a terrific wine list. The menu includes hand-cut steaks, a "twisted fettuccine" that blends seafood, raspberries, and chipotle in an Alfredo cream sauce. ■TIP→ Locals know to ignore the menu and just ask to hear the day's specials. Vegetarian options are also offered, and singles mix at the hand-carved wine bar. ⊠*162 W. Pioneer Ave.* ☎*907/235–8330* ▤*MC, V* ☺*Closed Sun. and Mon.*

$$–$$$$
SEAFOOD

Captain Pattie's Seafood Restaurant. A favorite with hard-to-please locals, Captain Pattie's offers a wide array of fresh local seafood, along with beachfront views of Kachemak Bay. The appetizer menu alone is worth the wait, which can be considerable during the summer rush. The clam chowder is excellent, and the staff is friendly and efficient. There's a good wine selection, and local beer on tap. If you get lucky on your fishing excursion, the restaurant will cook your catch to your liking. Try the great desserts, too. ⊠*4241 Homer Spit Rd.* ☎*907/235–5135* ▤*D, MC, V* ☺*Closed Oct.–Mar.*

$$
MEDITERRANEAN

✕**Fat Olives Restaurant.** Pumpkin-color walls, light streaming through tall front windows, and a playful collection of Italian posters add to the appeal of this fine Tuscany-inspired bistro. The menu encompasses enticing appetizers, salads, sandwiches, calzones, and pizzas throughout the day, along with oven-roasted chicken, fresh seafood, pork loin, and other fare in the evening. If you're in a hurry, just get a giant slice of the thin-crust pizza to go for $3.75. You can order meals at the bar, and there's always something decadent for dessert. ⊠*276 Olson La.* ☎*907/235–8488* ▤ *MC, V.*

$–$$$$
CAFÉ
☺

✕**Fresh Sourdough Express Bakery & Café.** This place was the first certified green restaurant in Alaska, and they're proud of it. They feature regional, organic ingredients, baked goods made with hand-ground grain, and fresh seafood in season. They also package box lunches for customers going on all-day fishing or sightseeing trips—you can order them online for next-day pickup. There's a small gift shop and a play

6

area outside for kids. ⊠*1316 Ocean Dr.* ☎*907/235–7571* ⊕*www. freshsourdoughexpress.com* ☰*MC, V.* ⊗ *Closed Nov.–Feb.*

¢ ✕**Fritz Creek Store.** Directly across the road from Homestead Restaurant
ECLECTIC is this old-fashioned country store, gas station, liquor store, post office,
video-rental shop, and deli. The last of these is the main reason for a
visit, and the food is amazingly good, from the hot and fattening turkey
sandwiches to freshly baked breads and pastries, pizza by the slice, veggie burritos, tamales, and ribs to go. Pull up a chair at a table crafted
from an old cable spool and join the back-to-the-land crowd as they
drink espresso, talk Alaskan politics, and pet the cats. ⊠*Mi 8.2, E. End
Rd.* ☎*907/235–6521* ☰*AE, D, MC, V.*

$$–$$$$ ✕**Homestead Restaurant.** This former log roadhouse 8 mi from town is
CONTINENTAL a favorite of locals who appreciate artfully presented food served amid
Fodor'sChoice contemporary art. The Homestead specializes in seasonal fish and shell-
★ fish prepared with garlic, citrus fruits, or spicy ethnic sauces, as well as
steak, rack of lamb, and prime rib. Epic views of the bay, mountains,
and hanging glaciers are yours for the looking. Homestead has an
extensive wine list and locally brewed beer on tap. ⊠*Mi 8.2, E. End
Rd.* ⊘*Box 3041, Homer* ☎*907/235–8723* ☰*AE, MC, V* ⊗*Closed
Jan. and Feb.*

$$–$$$$ ✕**Saltry Restaurant.** On a hill overlooking Halibut Cove, this is a won-
SEAFOOD derful place to soak up a summer afternoon. Local seafood is the main
Fodor'sChoice attraction, prepared in everything from curries and pastas to sushi. The
★ restaurant is small, and although the tables aren't exactly crowded
together, it's definitely intimate. When weather permits, get a table on
the deck. Dinner seatings are at 6 and 7:30; before or after dinner you
can stroll around the boardwalks at Halibut Cove and visit the art galleries or just relax on the dock. Sea otters often play just offshore. Reservations are essential for the ferry ($28 round-trip), which leaves
Homer Spit at 5 PM. A noon ferry ($48) will take you to the Saltry for
lunch (¢–$), stopping along the way for wildlife-viewing. ⊠ *4241
Homer Spit Rd., Main Deck* ☎*907/235–7847, 800/478–7847 Central
Charters* ⚲*Reservations essential* ☰*D, MC, V* ⊗*Closed Labor Day–
Memorial Day.*

¢ ✕**Two Sisters Bakery.** This very popular café is just a short walk from
CAFÉ both Bishops Beach and the Islands and Ocean Center. In addition to
fresh breads and pastries, Two Sisters specializes in deliciously healthful
lunches, such as vegetarian focaccia sandwiches, homemade soups,
quiche, and salads. Sit on the wraparound porch on a summer afternoon, or take your espresso and scone down to the beach to watch the
waves roll in. **Upstairs are three comfortable guest rooms ($), all with pri-
vate baths.** Your latte and Danish pastry breakfast is served in the café.
⊠*233 E. Bunnell Ave.* ☎*907/235–2280* ⊕*www.twosistersbakery.net*
☰*MC, V.*

WHERE TO STAY

$$$ ⊡**Alaskan Suites.** These modern log cabins offer million-dollar views
from a hilltop on the west side of Homer. Each contains two queen beds
and a kitchenette, and there's a gas barbecue grill on the deck. Every

cabin is equipped with a 42-inch flat-screen plasma TV with DVD, satellite connections, and surround sound. Guests can soak in a large hot tub with Kachemak Bay, mountains, glaciers, and three volcanoes as the backdrop. **Pros:** Crow's-nest views, highway location with no highway noise. **Con:** Not within walking distance of anything. ✉ *3255 Sterling Hwy.* ☏ *907/235–1972 or 888/239–1972* ⊕ *www.alaskan-suites.com* ⬅ *5 cabins* ♿ *In-room: kitchen, DVD. In-hotel: public Wi-Fi, some pets allowed, no-smoking rooms* ☰ *AE, D, MC, V.*

¢-$$ 🏨 **Driftwood Inn.** The Driftwood seeks to accommodate all travelers, with an RV park, deluxe lodge, and inn. There are standard hotel-type bedrooms; a "ship's quarters," with cedar walls and a pull-down bed; and a family-friendly "deluxe room," with queen-size beds, dining room table, microwave, refrigerator, full private bath, and private outside entrance. Downstairs is a comfortable sitting room with fireplace, TV, books, and videos. A small eating area has self-service coffee, tea, pastries, and cereal. The bluff-front Lodge, which sleeps up to 12, has spacious rooms overlooking Kachemak Bay, with private bathrooms and king-size beds; the Cottage—which sleeps up to 8 and overlooks the bay—consists of two bedrooms, a loft, and a full and half bath. You have full access to the inn's facilities if you stay at the on-site campground and full-hookup RV park. **Pro:** Accommodation for every budget. **Con:** The ship's quarters are tight. ✉ *135 W. Bunnell St.* ☏ *907/235–8019 or 800/478–8019* ⊕ *www.thedriftwoodinn.com* ⬅ *21 rooms, 11 with bath; 1 cottage* ♿ *In-room: no phone (some), Wi-Fi. In-hotel: no elevator, laundry facilities, some pets allowed, no-smoking rooms* ☰ *D, MC, V.*

¢ ⛺ **Homer Spit Campground.** Homer's 4-mi-long spit is popular not just as a jumping-off point for fishing, kayaking, and other adventures, but also because it provides great camping with a view. Find a spot on the sand between the other tents and RVs and pay your fee at the city's camping office. The beach is often windy—make sure your tent poles are sturdy—and it's not far from the road. Still, it's hard to beat the spectacular setting. A few campsites are open year-round. ♿ *Flush toilets, partial hookups, dump station, drinking water, guest laundry, showers, grills, picnic tables, electricity, public telephone* ⬅ *122 RV sites, 25 tent sites* ✉ *4535 Homer Spit Rd.,99603* ☏ *907/235–8206* ☰ *MC, V.*

$$ 🏨 **Land's End Resort and Lodges.** This sprawling complex at the end of Homer Spit has wide-open views of the bay. Most of the rooms face the bay; some have nautical decor, and others are more floral. Some are perfect for a couple; the five rooms with lofts are big enough for a family. Eighteen lodges (or condos) sleep six comfortably, and some have four bedrooms. If you're traveling with a large group, the condos can be economical, especially because they include kitchens and a private beach. Land's End's restaurant ($$–$$$$) specializes in seafood, including salmon, halibut, scallops, and oysters; burgers and steak are also served. ■**TIP→** Call ahead to reserve a window table with views of Kachemak Bay and the Kenai Mountains. In winter, chefs craft a special once-a-month "Uncorked" theme dinner with paired wines for $70 per person. **Pro:** The spit-end location puts you 5 mi out into the bay. **Con:** You

might be disappointed if you get a room without a view. ✉*4786 Homer Spit Rd.* ☎*907/235–0400 or 800/478–0400* ⊕*www.lands-end-resort.com, www.landsendlodges.com* ⟲*107 rooms, 18 lodges* ⟳ *In-room: kitchen (some), refrigerator, Wi-Fi. In-hotel: restaurant, bar, pool, spa, no elevator, laundry facilities.* ⊟*AE, D, DC, MC, V.*

$ ⌂**Old Town Bed & Breakfast.** Bright and cozy, the Old Town B&B is housed in the oldest commercial building in Homer. It's in an excellent location, and not just because it's in the old town—it's also above the Bunnell Street Art Gallery and Panarelli's Deli. Rooms are elegantly appointed with period furnishings and fixtures, and the second-story setting provides sweeping views of the bay and mountains. The art gallery hosts occasional evening music, poetry, or arts programs, and breakfast is served in the parlor upstairs. **Pros:** Warm, inviting, and friendly. **Con:** Some rooms have shared baths. ✉*106 W. Bunnell St.* ☎*907/235–7558* ⊕*www.oldtownbedandbreakfast.com* ⟲*3 rooms, 1 with bath* ⟳*In-room: no phone, no TV. In-hotel: no elevator, public Wi-Fi, no-smoking rooms* ⊟*MC, V* ⏀*BP.*

$$$$ ⌂**Tutka Bay Wilderness Lodge.** On a small cove 9 mi by boat from Homer Spit, this luxurious small resort is adjacent to Kachemak Bay State Park. The deluxe modern cabins have private baths and comfortable beds. Other facilities include a cozy main lodge, sauna, beachfront open-air hot tub, and three hearty meals a day. Hikers can head into the park from the lodge for day trips, watch eagles and otters just off-shore, or pay extra for guided sea-kayaking, charter fishing trips, and other activities. Access is by water taxi ($90 extra) from Homer. **Pro:** Location, location, location. **Con:** Because of its location, it's a bit pricey. ⌂*Box 960, 99603* ☎*907/235–3905 or 800/606–3909* ⊕*www.tutkabaylodge.com* ⟲*4 cabins, 2 suites* ⟳*In-room: no phone, no TV (some), Wi-Fi. In-hotel: no-smoking rooms* ⊟*AE, MC, V* ⏀*FAP.*

NIGHTLIFE

★ Dance to lively bands on weekends at **Alice's Champagne Palace** (✉*195 E. Pioneer Ave.* ☎*907/235–6909*). The bar attracts nationally known singer-songwriters on a regular basis. The members of **Pier One Theater** (☎*907/235–7333* ⊕*www.pieronetheatre.org*) perform plays on weekends throughout the summer. Find them in the old barnlike building on the spit.

The spit's infamous **Salty Dawg Saloon** (☎*907/235–6718*) is a tumble-down lighthouse of sorts, sure to be frequented by a carousing fisherman or two, along with half the tourists in town.

SHOPPING

ART & GIFTS

A variety of art by the town's residents can be found in the galleries on and around Pioneer Avenue. The **Bunnell Street Gallery** (✉*Main St. and Bunnell Ave.* ☎*907/235–2662* ⊕*www.bunnellstreetgallery.org*) displays innovative contemporary art, all of it produced in Alaska. The gallery, which occupies the first floor of a historic trading post, also hosts workshops, lectures, musical performances, and other community events.

The gift shop at the **Pratt Museum** (⌧*Bartlett St. off Pioneer Ave.* ☎*907/235–8635*) stocks natural-history books, locally crafted or inspired jewelry, note cards, and gifts for children. **Ptarmigan Arts** (⌧*471 E. Pioneer Ave.* ☎*907/235–5345*) is a cooperative gallery, with photographs, paintings, pottery, jewelry, woodworking, and other pieces by local artisans.

CLOTHING

Homer's Jeans (⌧*564 E. Pioneer Ave., Suite 1,* ☎*907/235–6234*) offers name-brand outdoor wear in addition to more utilitarian gear. Buy your cute shoes or your hiking boots here. **Nomar** (⌧*104 E. Pioneer Ave.* ☎*907/235–8363 or 800/478–8364* ⊕*www.nomaralaska.com*) creates Polarfleece garments and other rugged Alaskan outerwear, plus duffels, rain gear, and children's clothing. The company manufactures equipment and clothing for commercial fishermen.

FOOD

Alaska Wild Berry Products (⌧*528 E. Pioneer Ave.* ☎*907/235–8858* ⊕*www.alaskawildberryproducts.com*) sells chocolate-covered candies, jams, jellies, sauces, and syrups made from wild berries handpicked on the Kenai Peninsula, as well as Alaska-theme gifts and clothing. Drop by for free samples of the chocolates. Homer is famous for its halibut, salmon, and Kachemak Bay oysters. For fresh fish, head to **Coal Point Trading Company** (☎*907/235–3877 or 800/325–3877* ⊕*www.welove-fish.com*) on the spit. Coal Point can also package and ship fish that you catch.

Fritz Creek Store (⌧*Mi 8.2, E. End Rd.* ☎*907/235–6521*) sells fresh, homemade food in an old log building. **Two Sisters Bakery** (⌧*235 E. Bunnell Ave.* ☎*907/235–2280*) serves fresh-baked bread as well as coffee, muffins, soup, and pizza.

KACHEMAK BAY STATE PARK & STATE WILDERNESS PARK

10 mi southeast of Homer.

Kachemak Bay State Park & State Wilderness Park, accessible by boat or bush plane, protects more than 350,000 acres of coast, mountains, glaciers, forests, and wildlife on the lower Kenai Peninsula. Recreational opportunities include boating, sea-kayaking, fishing, hiking, and beachcombing. Facilities are minimal but include 20 primitive campsites, five public-use cabins, and a system of trails accessible from Kachemak Bay.

ESSENTIALS

Visitor Info **Kenai State Parks Office** (☎*907/262–5581 or 907/235–7024* ⊕*www.dnr.state.ak.us/parks/units/kbay/kbay.htm*).

WHERE TO STAY

¢   ⛺ **Alaska State Parks Cabins.** Three public-use cabins are within Kachemak Bay's Halibut Cove Lagoon area, another is near Tutka Bay Lagoon, and a fifth is at China Poot Lake. All but the lakeside cabin are accessible by boat; China Poot can be reached only on foot from the boat landing on the beach or by floatplane to the lake. The cabin furnishings are spartan, but include wooden bunks and sleeping platforms, a table, and chairs; there's no running water or electricity. Four of the five cabins sleep up to six people (the other, the Overlook cabin at Halibut Cove, sleeps eight), and all can be reserved up to six months in advance. **Pros:** Solitude and views. **Con:** Remote locations with no amenities. ✉ *Alaska State Parks Kenai Office, Box 1247, Soldotna* ☎ *907/262–5581* ⊕ *www.dnr.state.ak.us/parks/cabins/kenai.htm* 🛏 *5 cabins* ▭ *No credit cards.*

¢   🏕 **Alaska State Parks Campsites.** Twenty primitive, free campsites with pit toilets and fire rings are scattered along the shores of Kachemak Bay across from Homer and are accessible by boat (water taxis operate here daily in summer). The sites are available on a first-come, first-served basis, and camping is allowed nearly everywhere in the park, not restricted to developed sites. ♿ *Pit toilets (some), fire pits (some), picnic tables (some)* 🛏 *6 campgrounds with 20 tent sites* 🏛 *Alaska State Parks Kenai Office, Box 1247, Soldotna 99669* ☎ *907/235–7024 or 907/262–5581* ⊕ *www.dnr.state.ak.us/parks/units/kbay/kbay.htm* ⟲ *Reservations not accepted.*

$$$$ 🏨 **Kachemak Bay Wilderness Lodge.** Across Kachemak Bay from Homer, ★   this luxurious lodge provides wildlife-viewing opportunities and panoramic mountain and bay vistas in an intimate setting for up to 14 guests. The main log building has a piano and a big stone fireplace to warm you after a day of hiking, fishing, kayaking, or touring in one of the lodge's five guided boats (some of the guided fly-out trips may cost extra). Scattered throughthe woods, the rustic cabins, all with electricity, full baths, and decks, are decorated with antiques, original artworks, and homemade quilts. Cabin layouts differ slightly; some are suited for couples, some for groups or families. Dinners spotlight seafood—clams, mussels, and fish—caught in the bay. There's a three-day/three-night package for $2,100 per person and a six-day/six-night package for $3,800 per person; kids 13 and under are about two-thirds the price. **Pros:** Extraordinary facility in a stunning location, sauna and hot tub. **Con:** Its remote location makes the lodge fairly pricey. 🏠 *Box 956,Homer 99603* ☎ *907/235–8910* ⊕ *www.alaskawildernesslodge. com* 🛏 *4 cabins, 1 room in lodge* ♿ *In-room: no phone, no TV. In-hotel: restaurant, public Internet, no-smoking rooms* ▭ *V* ⊘ *Closed Oct.–Apr.* 🍴 *FAP.*

SELDOVIA

16 mi south of Homer.

The town of Seldovia is another off-the-road-system settlement on the south side of Kachemak Bay and retains the charm of an earlier Alaska.

The town's Russian bloodline shows in its onion-dome church and its name, which means "herring bay." For many years this was the primary fishing town on the bay, but today the focus is on tourism. The town was heavily damaged in the 1964 earthquake, but a few stretches of old boardwalk still exist and houses stand on stilts along Seldovia Slough. Access is via the Alaska Marine Highway ferry (twice weekly from Homer), aboard a water taxi ($35–$45), or by air from Homer ($50). Seldovia has several restaurants and lodging places, plus a small museum and a hilltop Russian Orthodox church. The area abounds with hiking, mountain-biking, and sea-kayaking options.

WHERE TO STAY

$$–$$$ ⬚ **Across the Bay Tent & Breakfast Adventure Co.** A step up the comfort ladder from camping, this beachfront establishment is reachable via water taxi from Homer. You stay in sturdy canvas-wall tents with carpeted floors and twin beds, and a large common room has hardwood floors and a piano. Prices vary depending on whether you do your own cooking or eat the gourmet seafood meals prepared by the staff. A propane stove and grill, as well as pots, pans, and picnic tables, are provided. Otherwise, host-prepared meals are hearty and served family style, and include garden-grown greens. A beach is great for walking and beachcombing; guided kayak trips and mountain bikes are available for an extra charge. **Pros:** Friendly owners, excellent food, beautiful grounds. **Con:** Although comfortable, you're still sleeping in a tent. ✉ *Mi 8, Jakalof Bay Rd., 8 mi east of Seldovia* ✆ *In winter:Box 112054, Anchorage 99511* ✆ *In summer:Box 81, Seldovia 99663* ☎ *907/235–3633 in summer, 907/345–2571 in winter* ⊕ *www.tentand-breakfastalaska.com* ⇆ *6 tents* ⟡ *In-room: no phone, no TV. In-hotel: restaurant, beachfront, bicycles, public Wi-Fi* ▬*MC, V* ⊘ *Closed Labor Day–Memorial Day.*

$–$$ ⬚ **Seldovia Boardwalk Hotel.** This hotel with a fabulous view of the harbor has immaculate modern rooms, half of which face the water. The rooms are bright, with white walls and ceilings, lots of plants, and locally produced artwork and Alaskana. A large, sunlit parlor downstairs has a woodstove and coffee service. The proprietors can also arrange charter-fishing or sea-kayaking trips; one-night, two-night, or two-nights-plus-all-day kayaking tour packages are also an option. You can also rent bikes and fishing tackle here. **Pro:** In-town location. **Con:** Few on-site amenities. ✉ *Main St.* ✆ *Box 72 99663* ☎ *907/234–7816* ⊕ *www.alaskaone.com/boardwalkhotel* ⇆ *14 rooms* ⟡ *In-room: no TV, Wi-Fi. In-hotel: no-smoking rooms* ▬*MC, V* ⦿*CP.*

KODIAK ISLAND

248 mi southwest of Anchorage by air.

Russian explorers discovered Kodiak Island in 1763, and Kodiak served as Alaska's first capital until 1804, when the government was moved to Sitka. Situated as it is in the northwestern Gulf of Alaska, Kodiak has been subjected to several natural disasters. In 1912 a volcanic eruption on the nearby Alaska Peninsula covered the town site in knee-deep drifts of ash and pumice. The 1964 earthquake and resulting tsunami destroyed the island's large fishing fleet and smashed Kodiak's low-lying downtown area.

Today commercial fishing is king in Kodiak. Despite its small population—about 15,000 people scattered among the several islands in the Kodiak group—the city is among the busiest fishing ports in the United States. The harbor is also an important supply point for small communities on the Aleutian Islands and the Alaska Peninsula.

Visitors to the island tend to follow one of two agendas: either immediately fly out to a remote lodge for fishing, kayaking, or bear viewing; or stay in town and access whatever pursuits they can reach from the limited road system. If the former is too pricey an option, consider combining the two: driving the road system to see what can be seen inexpensively, then adding a fly-out or charter-boat excursion to a remote lodge or wilderness access point.

GETTING HERE & AROUND
Access to the island is via the Alaska Marine Highway (which makes several stops a week) or by plane. A few roads stretch out of town, perfect for a day of sightseeing. The action, however, is in town.

Your first stop in exploring the island should be the Kodiak Island Convention & Visitors Bureau. Here you can pick up brochures, pamphlets, and lists of all the visitor services on Kodiak and the surrounding islands, and get help with planning your adventures. If you want to strike out and hike the local trails, there's an informative *Hiking and Birding Guide* published by the Kodiak Audubon Society.

ESSENTIALS
Medical Assistance **Providence Kodiak Island Medical Center** (✉ *1915 E. Rezanof Dr.* ☎ *907/486–3281*).

Visitor Info **Kodiak Island Convention & Visitors Bureau** (✉ *100 Marine Way, Suite 20099615* ☎ *907/486–4782* or *800/789-4782* ⊕ *www.kodiak.org*).

WHAT TO SEE
Floatplane and boat charters are available from Kodiak to numerous remote attractions. Chief among these areas is the 1.6-million-acre **Kodiak National Wildlife Refuge,** lying partly on Kodiak Island and partly on Afognak Island to the north, where spotting the enormous Kodiak brown bears is the main goal of a trip. Seeing the bears, which weigh a pound at birth but up to 1,500 pounds when fully grown, is worth the trip to this rugged country. The bears are spotted easily in July and August, feeding along salmon-spawning streams. Chartered flightseeing trips go to the area, and exaggerated tales of encounters with these impressive beasts are frequently heard. ✉ *1390 Buskin River Rd.* ☎ *907/487–2600* ⊕ *http://kodiak.fws.gov.*

★ The **Alutiiq Museum and Archaeological Repository** is home to one of the largest collections of Eskimo materials in the world, and contains archaeological and ethnographic items dating back 7,500 years. The museum displays only a fraction of its more than 150,000 artifacts, including harpoons, masks, dolls, stone tools, seal-gut parkas, grass baskets, and pottery fragments. The museum store sells native arts and educational materials. ⊠ *215 Mission Rd., Suite 101* ☎ *907/486–7004* ⊕ *www.alutiiqmuseum.org* ✉ *$3 donation requested* ⊙ *June–Aug., weekdays 9–5, Sat. 10–5, Sun. by appointment; Sept.-May, Tues.–Fri. 9–5, Sat. 10:30–4:30.*

The **Baranov Museum** presents artifacts from the area's Russian past. On the National Register of Historic Places, the building was built in 1808 by Alexander Baranov to warehouse precious sea-otter pelts. W.J. Erskine made it his home in 1911. On display are samovars, a collection of intricate native basketry, and other relics from the early native Koniags and the later Russian settlers. A collection of 40 albums of archival photography portrays various aspects of the island's history. Contact the museum for a calendar of events. ⊠ *101 Marine Way* ☎ *907/486–5920* ⊕ *www.baranov.us* ✉ *$3* ⊙ *May–Sept., Mon.–Sat. 10–4, Sun. noon–4; Oct.–Jan., Mar., and Apr., Tues.–Sat. 10–3.*

↻ As part of America's North Pacific defense in World War II, Kodiak was the site of an important naval station, now occupied by the Coast Guard fleet that patrols the surrounding fishing grounds. Part of the old military installation has been incorporated into **Fort Abercrombie State Historical Park,** 3.5 mi north of Kodiak on Rezanof Drive. Self-guided tours take you past concrete bunkers and gun emplacements. There's a spectacular scenic overlook, great for bird- and whale-watching, and there are 13 campsites suitable for tents or RVs (no hookups), with pit toilets, drinking water, fire grates, and picnic tables. ⊠ *Mi 3.7, Rezanof Dr.* ⌂ *Alaska State Parks, Kodiak District Office, 1400 Abercrombie Dr. 99615* ☎ *907/486–6339* ⊕ *http://www.dnr.state.ak.us/parks/units/kodiak/ftaber.htm* ✉ *Park free, campsites $10* ⊟ *No credit cards.*

The ornate **Holy Resurrection Russian Orthodox Church** is a visual feast, both inside and out. The cross-shape building is topped by two onion-shape blue domes, and the interior contains brass candle stands, distinctive chandeliers, and numerous icons representing Orthodox saints. Three different churches have stood on this site since 1794. Built in 1945, the present structure is on the National Register of Historic Places. ⊠ *Mission and Kashevaroff Rds.* ☎ *907/486–3854 parish priest* ✉ *Donations accepted* ⊙ *By appointment.*

OUTDOOR ACTIVITIES & GUIDED TOURS
Kodiak Adventures Unlimited (☎ *907/486–8766 or 800/575–5380* ⊕ *www.kodiakadventuresunlimited.com*) books charter and tour operators for all of Kodiak. Find them in St. Paul Harbor across from Wells Fargo.

WHERE TO EAT
$–$$$$ ✗ **Henry's Great Alaskan Restaurant.** Henry's is a big, boisterous, friendly
AMERICAN place at the mall near the small-boat harbor. The menu is equally big, ranging from fresh local seafood and barbecue to pastas and even some Cajun dishes. Dinner specials, a long list of appetizers, salads, rack of

lamb, and a tasty dessert list round out the choices. ⌧*512 Marine Way* ☎*907/486–8844* ▭*AE, MC, V.*

¢–$

CAFÉ

✕**Mill Bay Coffee & Pastries.** Serving lunches and fabulous pastries, this charming little shop is well worth the trip. The coffee is fresh roasted on-site every other day. Inside, elegant antique furnishings are complemented by local artwork and handicrafts. ⌧*3833 Rezanof Dr. E* ☎*907/486–4411* ⊕*www.millbaycoffee.com* ▭*MC, V* ⊘*No dinner.*

$–$$$

SEAFOOD

✕**Old Powerhouse Restaurant.** This converted powerhouse facility allows a close-up view of Near Island and the channel connecting the boat harbors with the Gulf of Alaska. Enjoy fresh sushi and sashimi while watching the procession of fishing boats gliding past on their way to catch or deliver your next meal. Keep your eyes peeled for sea otters, seals, sea lions, and eagles, too. The menu also features tempura, *yakisoba* (fried noodles), and rice specials; there's live music on occasion. ⌧*516 E. Marine Way* ☎*907/481–1088* ▭*MC, V.*

WHERE TO STAY

$$

🏨 **Best Western Kodiak Inn.** Rooms here have soothing floral decor, and some overlook the harbor. The Chartroom Restaurant has harbor views and serves local seafood and American fare, including steak and pasta. **Pro:** Downtown location. **Con:** Harbor-view rooms are on the street, quieter rooms are in the back. ⌧*236 W. Rezanof Dr.99615* ☎*907/486–5712 or 888/563–4254* ⊕*www.kodiakinn.com* ⇄*81 rooms* ⌂*In-room: refrigerator, Wi-Fi. In-hotel: restaurant, bar, some pets allowed (fee)* ▭*AE, D, DC, MC, V* ⫪*CP.*

$$

★

🏨 **Comfort Inn Kodiak.** This modern lodge is a five-minute walk from the main terminal at the airport, about 4.5 mi from downtown. The Buskin Riverside Restaurant ($$–$$$$) serves local seafood, including king crab, scallops, Cajun prawns, pasta, and steaks. The atmosphere is semiformal (in Alaska that means hip waders would be a bit out of place). **Pro:** Fish for salmon in the river out back. **Con:** A bit out of town, so you might want a vehicle. ⌧*1395 Airport Way* ☎*907/487–2700 or 800/544–2202* ⇄*50 rooms* ⌂*In-room: refrigerator, Wi-Fi. In-hotel: restaurant, bar, public Internet, airport shuttle, some pets allowed (fee), no-smoking rooms* ▭*AE, D, DC, MC, V* ⫪*CP.*

$

🏨 **Kodiak B&B.** Kodiak's first B&B commands a view of the St. Paul harbor and the waterways beyond. It's a short walk from downtown and most of the town's businesses. Owner Mary Monroe is a gracious and knowledgeable host, and can help you make the most of your Kodiak stay with plenty of helpful local information. The guest rooms share a bath and common sitting area, and bookshelves are loaded with local histories. **Pros:** Right downtown, great view. **Con:** Twenty steps up to house from the street. ⌧*308 Cope St.* ☎*907/486–5367* ⇄*2 rooms share 1 bath* ⌂*In-room: refrigerator, Wi-Fi. In-hotel: some pets allowed, no-smoking rooms* ▭*MC, V* ⊘*Closed Dec. and Jan.* ⫪*BP.*

MAT-SU VALLEY & BEYOND

Giant homegrown vegetables and the headquarters of the best-known dogsled race in the world are among the most prominent attractions of the Matanuska-Susitna (Mat-Su) Valley. The valley, lying an hour north of Anchorage by road, draws its name from its two largest rivers, the Matanuska and the Susitna, and is bisected by the Parks and Glenn highways. Major cities are Wasilla on the Parks Highway and Palmer on the Glenn Highway. To the east, the Glenn Highway connects to the Richardson Highway by way of several high mountain passes sandwiched between the Chugach Mountains to the south and the Talkeetnas to the north. ■TIP→ At Mile 103 of the Glenn Highway, you can view the massive Matanuska Glacier from the road.

LOCAL BREW

The **Kodiak Island Brewing Co.** (✉ *338 Shelikof Ave.* ☎ *907/486–2537* ⊕ *www.kodiakbrewery.com*) sells fresh-brewed, unfiltered beer in a variety of styles and sizes of containers, from 20-ounce bottles up to full kegs, so you can stock up for your wilderness expedition without suffering from beer withdrawal. Brewer Ben Millstein will also give you a tour of the facility on request. It's open from noon to 7 daily in summer and noon to 6 Monday through Saturday in winter. Due to a change in state liquor laws, some on-premise sales and consumption are now allowed.

6

LAKE CLARK NATIONAL PARK & PRESERVE

100 mi west of Anchorage by air.

When the weather is good, an idyllic choice beyond the Mat-Su Valley is the 3.4-million-acre Lake Clark National Park and Preserve, on the Alaska Peninsula and a short flight from Anchorage or Kenai and Soldotna. There's no road access to the park, so all visits are via small plane. The parklands stretch from the coast to the heights of two grand volcanoes: Mt. Iliamna and Mt. Redoubt, both topping out above 10,000 feet. The country in between holds glaciers, waterfalls, and turquoise-tinted lakes. The 50-mi-long Lake Clark, filled by runoff waters from the mountains that surround it, is an important spawning ground for thousands of red (sockeye) salmon.

The river running is superb in this park. You can make your way through dark forests of spruce and balsam poplars or you can hike over the high, easy-to-travel tundra. The animal life is profuse: look for bears, moose, Dall sheep, wolves, wolverines, foxes, beavers, and minks on land; seals, sea otters, and white (or beluga) whales offshore. Wildflowers embroider the meadows and tundra in spring, and wild roses bloom in the shadows of the forests. Plan your trip to Lake Clark for the end of June or early July, when the insects may be less plentiful. Or consider late August or early September, when the tundra glows with fall colors.

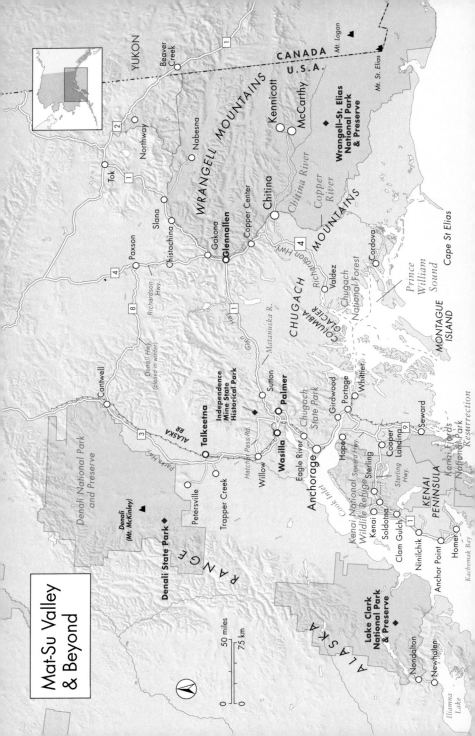

Mat-Su Valley & Beyond

YUKON

CANADA
U.S.A.

Beaver
Creek

Mt. Logan

Mt. St. Elias

Northway

Nabesna

WRANGELL MOUNTAINS

Kennicott

McCarthy

Wrangell–St. Elias
National Park
& Preserve

Tok

Slana

Chistochina

Gakona

Copper Center

Chitina

Chitina River

Copper River

Paxson

Richardson Hwy.

Glennallen

CHUGACH MOUNTAINS

Cordova

Richardson Hwy.

Valdez

Chugach
National Forest

Prince
William
Sound

Cape St Elias

Denali Hwy.
(closed in winter)

Matanuska R.

Glenn Hwy.

COLUMBIA GLACIER

Cantwell

Sutton

Palmer

Chugach
State Park

Girdwood

Portage

Whittier

MONTAGUE
ISLAND

Independence
Mine State
Historical Park

Talkeetna

Hatcher Pass Rd.

Wasilla

Seward

Denali National Park
and Preserve

ALASKA RR

Parks Hwy.

Willow

Eagle River

Anchorage

Hope

Cooper
Landing

Kenai Fjords
National Park

Resurrection

Denali
(Mt. McKinley)

Petersville

Trapper Creek

Kenai National
Wildlife Refuge

Seward Hwy.

Sterling

Sterling
Hwy.

KENAI
PENINSULA

Denali State Park ◆

R A N G E

Kenai

Soldotna

Cook Inlet

A L A S K A

Clam Gulch

Ninilchik

Anchor Point

Homer

Kachemak Bay

Lake Clark
National Park
& Preserve

Nondalton

Newhalen

Iliamna
Lake

50 miles

75 km

0

ESSENTIALS

Visitor Info **Lake Clark Administrative Headquarters** *Administrative Headquarters: 240 W. 5th Ave., Suite 236, Anchorage 99501* 🕾*907/644-3626* ✉*Park visitor center: 1 Park Pl., Port Alsworth* 🕾*907/781-2218* ⊕*www.nps.gov/lacl.*

WHERE TO STAY

$$$$ ☲**Farm Lodge.** Near park headquarters in Port Alsworth, the farm was built as a homestead back in the 1940s and has been a lodge since 1977. Five modern duplexes house as many as 40 guests in private rooms that have either bunk or double beds. A large, manicured, and fenced lawn with flower and vegetable gardens surrounds the main lodge, where home-cooked meals including fresh vegetables, salmon, and domestic meats are served. The lodge also provides flight services and guided trips. **Pros:** At the headquarters of Lake Clark National Park, commercial standard aircraft and pilots, family-friendly. **Con:** Removed from road system. *Box 1, Port Alsworth 99653* 🕾*907/781-2208 or 888/440-2281* ⊕*www.lakeclarkair.com/farm_lodge.html* ⏎*13 rooms* ♿*In-room: no TV. In-hotel: restaurant, no-smoking rooms* ▤*AE, D, MC, V* �‖*FAP.*

PALMER

40 mi northeast of Anchorage.

With mountain-ringed farms, Palmer is charming and photogenic. This is the place to search for 100-pound cabbages and fresh farm cheese. Historic buildings are scattered throughout the Matanuska-Susitna Valley (often just referred to as the "Mat-Su Valley" or simply "the Valley"); in 1935 the federal government relocated about 200 farm families from the Depression-ridden Midwest to the Mat-Su Valley. Now it has developed into the state's major agricultural region. Good growing conditions of rich soil combined with long hours of summer sunlight result in some huge vegetables.

GETTING HERE & AROUND

The Glenn Highway heads north out of Anchorage and heads right through Palmer. The Chugach Range lines both sides of Palmer's valley, and if you continue past the town you'll find yourself smack in the middle of the mountains.

ESSENTIALS

Medical Assistance **Mat-Su Regional Medical Center** (✉*2500 S. Woodworth Loop* 🕾*907/861-6000*).

Visitor Info **Mat-Su Convention & Visitors Bureau** (✉*7744 E. Visitors View Ct., 99645* 🕾*907/746-5000* ⊕*www.alaskavisit.com*). **Palmer Chamber of Commerce** (✉*723 S. Valley Way, 99645* 🕾*907/745-2880* ⊕*www.palmerchamber.org*).

WHAT TO SEE

☼ On a sunny day the town of Palmer looks like a Swiss calendar photo, with its old barns and log houses silhouetted against craggy Pioneer Peak. On nearby farms (on the Bodenburg Loop off the old Palmer Highway) you can pay to pick your own raspberries and other fruits

Independence Mine. "The Hatcher Pass road was paved a little way off Highway 3, then became a narrow gravel road, which led to the abandoned Independence Mine. The scenery was awesome." – Tom Wells, Fodors.com photo contest participant

and vegetables. The peak picking time at **Pyrah's Pioneer Peak Farm** (⊠ *Mi 2.6, Bodenburg Loop* ☎ *907/745–4511*), which cultivates 35 kinds of fruits and vegetables, occurs around mid-July.

Fifty or so animals roam at the **Musk Ox Farm**, which conducts 30-minute guided tours from May to September. There's a hands-on museum and a gift shop featuring hand-knitted items made from the cashmere-like underfur (qiviut) combed from the musk ox. The scarves, caps, and more are made by Oomingmak, an Alaskan native collective. ⊠ *Mi 50.1, Glenn Hwy.* ☎ *907/745–4151* ⊕ *www.muskoxfarm.org* ⊠ *$8.50* ☉ *May–Sept., daily 10–6; Oct.–Apr., by appointment.*

★ Gold mining was an early mainstay of the Mat-Su Valley's economy. You can tour the long-dormant **Independence Mine** on the Hatcher Pass Road, a loop that in summer connects the Parks Highway just north of Willow to the Glenn Highway near Palmer. The road to Independence Mine from the Palmer side was paved in the summer of 2003. The remainder of the roadway to Willow is gravel. In the 1940s as many as 200 workers were employed by the mine. Today it is a 271-acre state park and a cross-country ski area in winter. Only the wooden buildings remain; one of them, the red-roof manager's house, is now used as a visitor center. Guided tours are given on weekdays at 1:30 and 3:30. ⊠ *Independence Mine State Historical Park, 19 mi from Glenn Hwy. on Hatcher Pass Rd.* ☎ *907/745–3975* ⊕ *www.dnr.state.ak.us/parks/units/indmine.htm* ⊠ *$5 per vehicle, $3 tours* ☉ *Visitor center early June–Labor Day, daily 11–7; grounds year-round. Guided tours start*

June 14 at 1 and 3 daily weekdays. On weekends and holidays an additional tour is offered at 4:30. There is a day-use parking fee and a separate tour fee.

WHERE TO STAY

$ 🏨 **Colony Inn.** All guest rooms in this lovingly restored historic building are tastefully decorated with antiques and quilts. The building was used as a women's dormitory during the farm colonization of the 1930s. The small café ($–$$) serves light breakfasts, lunches, and Friday-night dinners. Be sure to try one of the homemade pies; the recipes have won blue ribbons at the Alaska State Fair. Inn reservations and check-in are handled at the Valley Hotel at 606 South Alaska Street. **Pros:** Quiet, charming, centrally located. **Cons:** Front desk a five-minute walk away at Valley Hotel, rooms are small. ⊠*325 E. Elmwood Ave.* ☎*907/745–3330, 800/478–7666 in Alaska* 🛏*12 rooms* ☐*In-room: Wi-Fi. In-hotel: restaurant, no elevator, laundry facilities, no-smoking rooms* ▭*AE, D, MC, V.*

$–$$ 🏨 **Hatcher Pass Lodge.** This lodge has spectacular views and can serve as base camp for hiking, berry picking, and—in fall and winter—skiing. Most rooms and cabins have queen-size beds. Three dormer-style rooms provide cozy accommodations for one or two guests. The cabins, some with lofts, are carpeted and have large picture windows with views of Hatcher Pass Valley. The cabins' half baths have chemical toilets and water coolers; showers are in the lodge. The restaurant's continental menu includes fondues, halibut, and pizzas. The bar serves cappuccinos and hot buttered rum for chilly nights. **Pros:** Views and nature right out your door. **Cons:** No kitchens and a bit far from town, so dining options are limited. ⊠*Mi 17, Hatcher Pass Rd., Box 763* ☎*907/745–5897 or 907/745–1200* ⊕*www.hatcherpasslodge.com* 🛏*3 rooms, 9 cabins with shared showers* ☐*In-room: no phone, no TV, Wi-Fi. In-hotel: restaurant, bar, some pets allowed (fee), no-smoking rooms* ▭*AE, D, MC, V.*

$ 🏨 **Valley Hotel.** Built in 1948 and run by the same folks as the Colony Inn, this three-story budget hotel was remodeled in 2008. Small, well-kept rooms have quilts and carpets. The hotel is close to shopping, the library, and the local tourist information center. The restaurant—which serves all homemade desserts—is the only 24-hour operation in the area. **Pro:** Centrally located. **Con:** Small rooms make the hotel less family-friendly than other venues. ⊠*606 S. Alaska St.* ☎*907/745–3330, 800/478–7666 in Alaska* 🛏*43 rooms* ☐*In-room: Wi-Fi. In-hotel: restaurant, bar, no elevator, laundry facilities, no-smoking rooms* ▭*AE, D, MC, V.*

MEGA STATE FAIR

Giant vegetables (a 105-pound cabbage, a 300-plus-pound summer squash that took four people to carry) are big attractions at Palmer's Alaska State Fair (⊠ *Mi 40.2, Glenn Hwy.* ☎ *907/745–4827 or 800/850–3247* ⊕ *www. alaskastatefair.org*). Shop for Alaskan-made gifts and crafts, and whoop it up with midway rides, livestock and 4-H shows, bake-offs, home-preserved produce contests, food, and live music. The fair runs 12 days, ending on Labor Day. Admission is $10.

6

WASILLA

42 mi north of Anchorage, 10 mi west of Palmer.

Wasilla is one of the valley's original pioneer communities, and over time has served as a supply center for farmers, gold miners, and mushers. Today fast-food restaurants and strip malls line the Parks Highway. It's the best place to stock up if you're heading north to Talkeetna or Denali. Rolling hills and more-scenic vistas can be found by wandering the area's back roads.

ESSENTIALS

Visitor Info **Wasilla Chamber of Commerce** (⊠*415 E. Railroad Ave.,99654* ☎*907/376–1299* ⊕*www.wasillachamber.org*).

WHAT TO SEE

On a 20-acre site, the **Museum of Alaska Transportation and Industry** exhibits some of the machines that helped develop Alaska, from dogsleds to jet aircraft and everything in between. The Don Sheldon Building houses aviation artifacts as well as antique autos and photographic displays. There is also a snowmachine (Alaskan for snowmobile) exhibit. ⊠*From Parks Hwy., turn south onto Neuser Rd. at Mi 47, follow road 0.75 mi to end* ☎*907/376–1211* ⊕*www.museumofalaska.org* ☜*$8* ⊙*May–Sept., Tues.–Sun. 10–5.*

☾ The **Iditarod Trail Headquarters** displays dogsleds, mushers' clothing, and trail gear, and you can catch video highlights of past races. The gift shop sells Iditarod items. Dogsled rides are available year-round; in summer, rides on wheels are available for $10. ⊠*Mi 2.2, Knik Rd.* ☎*907/376–5155* ⊕*www.iditarod.com* ☜*Free* ⊙*Mid-May–mid-Sept., daily 8–7; mid-Sept.–mid-May, weekdays 8–5.*

WHERE TO EAT

$–$$ ✕ **Cadillac Café.** Hearty fare fills the menu at this diner-style café, includ-
CAFÉ ing homemade pies; big, hand-pressed burgers; exotic pizzas turned out of a stone, wood-fired oven; and Southwestern-style Mexican food. The owner describes the decor as "Alaska minimalist," but the booths are plush and comfortable and hand-rubbed wood is evident. Breakfast is served only on weekends. ⊠*Mi 49, Parks Hwy. at Pittman St.* ☎*907/357–5533* ▤*MC, V.*

$–$$$ ✕ **Evangelo's Restaurant.** The food is good and the servings are ample at
ITALIAN this spacious local favorite on the Parks Highway. Try the garlic-sautéed shrimp in a white-wine butter sauce or a mammoth calzone. The pizzas are loaded with goodies, and a salad bar provides a fresh selection. ⊠*2530 E. Parks Hwy.* ☎*907/376–1212* ▤*AE, MC, V.*

WHERE TO STAY

$$ ▣ **Best Western Lake Lucille Inn.** This well-maintained resort on Lake Lucille provides easy access to several recreational activities, including boating in summer and ice-skating and snowmobiling in winter. Half of the inn's bright and cheery rooms have private balconies overlooking the lake. **Pro:** Beautiful lakefront property. **Con:** The sound of power-boats whizzing by. ⊠*1300 W. Lake Lucille Dr., Mi 43.5, Parks Hwy.*

☎*907/373–1776 or 800/528–1234* ⊕*www.bestwestern.com/lakelucilleinn* ⇌*50 rooms, 4 suites* ☂*In-room: Wi-Fi. In-hotel: gym, laundry facilities, some pets allowed, no-smoking rooms* ⊟*AE, D, DC, MC, V* ⦿*CP.*

$–$$
★
🛏**Pioneer Ridge Bed and Breakfast Inn.** Each of the spacious, log-partitioned rooms in this converted barn and award-winning inn is decorated according to a theme. The Denali Room has posters of the mountain, snowshoes, crampons, and other climbing gear. A dogsled and other race paraphernalia mark the Iditarod Room. A rooftop common room has a spectacular 360-degree panorama of the mountains and river valleys. **Pros:** Cozy and warm, with views you can't stop staring at. **Con:** Not handicapped friendly—although it's only one story, the hotel has many steps. ⊠*2221 Yukon Circle, HC31, Box 5083K* ☎*907/376–7472 or 800/478–7472* ⊕*www.pioneerridge.com* ⇌*1 suite; 1 cabin; 4 rooms with private baths; 1 room with separate, unshared bath* ☂*In-room: no TV, Wi-Fi* ⊟*AE, D, MC, V* ⦿*BP.*

TALKEETNA

56 mi north of Wasilla, 112 mi north of Anchorage.

Talkeetna lies at the end of a spur road near Mile 99 of the Parks Highway. The town maintains a Wild West vibe with a small, unpaved downtown area surrounding a central green. Lucky is the traveler who gets a few sunny days—Denali looms over the town, begging you to take dramatic photos. Mountaineers congregate here to begin their assaults on Mt. McKinley in Denali National Park; those just off the mountain are recognizable by their tanned faces with sunglasses lines. The Denali mountain rangers have their climbing headquarters here, as do most glacier pilots who fly climbing parties to the mountain. A carved pole at the town cemetery honors deceased mountaineers.

WHAT TO SEE

The **Talkeetna Historical Society Museum,** across from the Fairview Inn, explores the history of Mt. McKinley climbs. The museum has a scale model of Mt. McKinley and features information on the history of climbing attempts on the continent's highest peak. A Talkeetna walking-tour map points out sites of historical interest. ⊠*1st Alley and D St.* ☎*907/733–2487* ⊕*www.talkeetnahistoricalsociety.org* ⇌*$3* ⊗*May 15–Sept. 15, daily 10–6.*

OUTDOOR ACTIVITIES & GUIDED TOURS

BOATING,
FLOATING &
FISHING
Mahay's Riverboat Service (☎*907/733–2223 or 800/736–2210* ⊕*www.mahaysriverboat.com*) conducts scenic jet-boat tours and guided fishing charters on the Susitna and Talkeetna rivers.

Tri-River Charters (⌂*Box 312, 99676* ☎*907/733–2400* ⊕*www.tririvercharters.com*) operates fishing trips out of Talkeetna and on the nearby Deshka River, and can provide all the necessary tackle and gear.

6

WHERE TO STAY

$ Swiss-Alaska Inn. Family-run since 1976, this rustic-style property is well known among those who come to fish in the Talkeetna, Susitna, and Chulitna rivers. Menu selections at the restaurant (¢–$$) include halibut, salmon, buffalo burgers, and the owner's secret-recipe Swiss-style French toast. **Pro:** Very quiet. **Con:** About a half-mile from town, so some folks might want a car. ✉ *East Talkeetna, by boat launch,* ⬠ *Box 565* ☎ *907/733–2424* ⊕ *www.swissalaska.com* ↝*20 rooms* ⟍*In-room: DVD, no TV. In-hotel: restaurant, public Internet, no-smoking rooms* ⊟*AE, D, MC, V.*

$$$$ Talkeetna Alaskan Lodge. This ★ luxury hotel has excellent views of Mt. McKinley as well as access to nature trails. Rooms are modern, in the style of an Alaskan lodge, and mountainside room upgrades are available. The Great Room has comfortable seating, a 46-foot river-rock fireplace in the center of the room, and an espresso bar. The tour desk can arrange flightseeing, river trips, or any other Alaska adventure you can imagine. **Pro:** The restaurant is the place to watch the sun set while you also gaze at Mt. McKinley. **Cons:** Large and lacking much personality. ✉ *Mi 12.5, Talkeetna Spur Rd.* ⬠ *2525 C St., Suite 405, Anchorage 99503* ☎ *907/265–4501 or 888/959–9590* ⊕ *www.talkeetnalodge.com* ↝*212 rooms, 3 suites* ⟍*In-room: Wi-Fi. In-hotel: restaurant, bar, no-smoking rooms* ⊟*AE, D, MC, V.*

¢–$ Talkeetna Roadhouse. This circa-1917 log roadhouse has a common ★ sitting area and rooms in a variety of sizes, including a bunk room with four beds ($21). Rooms are very basic: bed, table, window, period. Sizable breakfasts—with sourdough pancakes from a 1902 starter and famous cinnamon rolls—are the order of the day at the restaurant (¢), along with soup, desserts, and pies, all made from scratch daily. It's a popular place with locals and with climbers who use Talkeetna's air taxis to reach Mt. McKinley. In winter the café is open only on weekends and evenings. **Pro:** This is true, down-home Alaska at its best. **Con:** Shared bath. ✉ *13550 E. Main St., Box 604* ☎ *907/733–1351* ⊕ *www.talkeetnaroadhouse.com* ↝*5 rooms, 2 cabins, share 5 baths* ⟍*In-room: no phone, no TV, Wi-Fi. In-hotel: restaurant, laundry facilities, public Internet, some pets allowed, no-smoking rooms* ⊟*MC, V.*

SMALL-TOWN FLAVOR

Talkeetna is a must-visit if you're driving between Anchorage and Denali or Fairbanks. A true small town, Talkeetna has a genuine roadhouse (with delicious homemade berry pies), quirky locals, and a pebbly shore along the Susitna with fantastic views of Mt. McKinley on a clear day. If you do come through town, be sure to check out the West Rib Restaurant (☎ 907/733–3354), which is in the back of historic Nagley's Store on Main Street (a mini-museum of sorts). Grab a seat out back and wash down the delicious chili, burgers, and fries with a local microbrew.

A Privileged Communion

Between 1903 and 1912, eight expeditions walked the slopes of 20,320-foot Mt. McKinley. But none had reached the absolute top of North America's highest peak. Thus the stage was set for Hudson Stuck, a self-described American amateur mountaineer.

Stuck came to Alaska in 1904, drawn not by mountains but by a missionary calling. As the Episcopal Church's archdeacon for the Yukon River region, he visited native villages year-round. His passion for climbing was unexpectedly rekindled in 1906, when he saw from afar the "glorious, broad, massive uplift" of McKinley, the "father of mountains." Five years after that wondrous view, Stuck pledged to reach McKinley's summit—or at least try. For his climbing party he picked three Alaskans experienced in snow and ice travel, though not in mountaineering: Harry Karstens, a well-known explorer and backcountry guide who would later become the first superintendent of Mt. McKinley National Park; Robert Tatum, Stuck's missionary assistant; and Walter Harper, part native, who served as Stuck's interpreter.

Assisted by two sled-dog teams, the group began its expedition on St. Patrick's Day, 1913, at Nenana, a village 90 mi northeast of McKinley. A month later they began their actual ascent of the great peak's northern side, via the Muldrow Glacier. The glacier's surface proved to be a maze of crevasses, some of them wide chasms with no apparent bottom. Carefully working their way up-glacier, the climbers established a camp at 11,500 feet. From there, the team chopped a staircase up several miles—and 3,000 vertical feet—of rock, snow, and ice.

Their progress was delayed several times by high winds, heavy snow, and near-zero visibility.

By May 30 the climbers had reached the top of the ridge (later named in Karstens's honor) and moved into a high glacial basin. Despite temperatures ranging from subzero to 21°F, they kept warm at night by sleeping on sheep and caribou skins and covering themselves with down quilts, camel's-hair blankets, and a wolf robe.

On June 6 the team established its high camp at 18,000 feet. The following morning was bright, cloudless, and windy. Three of the climbers suffered headaches and stomach pains, but given the clear weather everyone agreed to make an attempt. They left camp at 5 AM and by 1:30 PM stood within a few yards of McKinley's summit. Harper, who had been leading all day, was the first to reach the top, soon followed by the others. After catching their breath, the teammates shook hands, said a prayer of thanks, made some scientific measurements, and reveled in their magnificent surroundings. In his classic book *The Ascent of Denali*, Hudson Stuck later reflected, "There was no pride of conquest, no trace of that exultation of victory some enjoy upon the first ascent of a lofty peak, no gloating over good fortune that had hoisted us a few hundred feet higher than others who had struggled and been discomfited. Rather, was the feeling that a privileged communion with the high places of the earth had been granted."

6

DENALI STATE PARK

34 mi north of Talkeetna, 132 mi north of Anchorage.

Overshadowed by the larger and more-charismatic Denali National Park and Preserve in the Interior, "Little Denali" offers excellent access (it's bisected by the Parks Highway), beautiful views of Mt. McKinley, scenic campgrounds, and prime wilderness hiking and backpacking opportunities within a few miles of the road system. Between the Talkeetna Mountains and the Alaska Range, Denali State Park combines wooded lowlands and forested foothills topped by alpine tundra.

ESSENTIALS

Visitor Information Alaska State Parks, Mat-Su Area Office ⊠*HC 32, Box 6706, Wasilla 99687* ☎*907/745–3975.*

OUTDOOR ACTIVITIES

The park's chief attraction, other than McKinley views, is the 35-mi-long **Curry-Kesugi Ridge,** which forms a rugged spine through the heart of the park that is ideal backpacking terrain. The initial climb to get to the ridge is strenuous, but once you get up high, it's mostly gentle up-and-down terrain. The trail runs from the Troublesome Creek trailhead at Mile 137.3 to the Little Coal Creek trailhead at Mile 163.9. The Byers Lake campground at Mile 147 has a trailhead for a spur trail that intersects the Kesugi Ridge trail, offering an alternative to hiking the entire trail. Views of Mt. McKinley and the Alaska Range from the ridge trail are stunning. ■TIP→ This is a bear-intensive area, especially the Troublesome Creek area in late summer when the salmon runs are in full force.

Another destination favored by backcountry travelers is the **Peters Hills,** accessible from Petersville Road in Trapper Creek. Denali State Park borders the hills, and primitive trails and campgrounds are used year-round. It's especially popular with snowmobilers in winter and mountain bikers in summer.

WHERE TO STAY

¢ 🛖 **Alaska State Parks Cabins.** Three public-use cabins are in Denali State Park, along the shores of Byers Lake. One cabin is on a gravel road, 1 mi from the highway, and the other two are accessible by canoe or by a 0.5-mi walk-in trail. All are equipped with bunks to sleep six, wood-burning stove, table, and benches. **Pro:** More accessible than most wilderness cabins. **Cons:** Very basic, no running water or electricity. ✑*Alaska State Parks Information Center, 550 W. 7th Ave., Suite 1260, Anchorage 99501-3557* ⊠*Mi 43.5, Parks Hwy.* ☎*907/269–8400* ⊕*www.dnr.state.ak.us/parks/cabins/matsu.cfm* ⊷*3 cabins* ⊟*No credit cards.*

¢ ⛺ **Alaska State Parks Campgrounds.** Four roadside campgrounds are within Denali State Park—two at Byers Lake, Lower Troublesome Creek, and Denali Viewpoint North. All are easily accessible from the Parks Highway. The Byers Lake campground has a boat launch, canoe and kayak rentals, and nearby hiking trails. Sites are on a first-come, first-served basis, and there aren't any hookups. ⚡ *Pit toilets, drinking water, fire pits, picnic tables* ⟋ *143 tent/RV sites* ⊡ *Alaska State Parks, HC 32, Box 6706, Wasilla 99654* ☎ *907/745–3975* ⊕ *www.dnr.state. ak.us/parks/units/denali2.htm* ⚒ *Reservations not accepted* ⊟ *No credit cards* ⊘ *Closed Oct.–May.*

$$-$$$ 📺 **McKinley Princess Wilderness Lodge.** When the sky is clear and Mt. McKinley is visible, this lodge has excellent views of North America's highest peak, especially from the lobby, with its large stone fireplace. On private land inside Denali State Park, this hillside lodge overlooks the Chulitna River. You stay in bungalow-style guest rooms with separate sitting rooms. The tour desk can arrange any kind of tour. **Pros:** Clean, with everything you might need. **Cons:** Huge, somewhat bland. ⊠ *Mi 133, Parks Hwy., Trapper Creek* ☎ *907/733–2900 or 800/426– 0500* ⊕ *www.princessalaskalodges.com* ⟋ *460 rooms, 4 suites* ⚡ *In-hotel: 3 restaurants, bars, gym, laundry service* ⊟ *AE, D, DC, MC, V* ⊘ *Closed mid-Sept.–mid-May.*

GLENNALLEN

187 mi northeast of Anchorage.

This community of 900 residents is the gateway to Wrangell–St. Elias National Park and Preserve. It's 124 mi from Glennallen to McCarthy, the last 58 mi on unpaved gravel. This town is also the service center for the Copper River Basin and is a fly-in base for several wilderness outfitters.

ESSENTIALS

Medical Assistance Crossroads Medical Center (⊠ *Mi 187.5, Glenn Hwy.* ☎ *907/822–3203*).

Visitor Info Bureau of Land Management (⊡ *Box 147, Glennallen 99588* ☎ *907/822–3217* ⊕ *www.glennallen.ak.blm.gov*).

WHERE TO STAY

$$ 📺 **Caribou Hotel.** Mauve and sea-green rooms fill this modern hotel. ■ TIP→ **Unless you're on a strict budget, ask for a room in the main building and not in the trailerlike annex out front, where rooms are spartan and share a bath.** A pair of rustic cabins is available for those who want to get a taste of living in "Bush Alaska." Several rooms in the main building have hot tubs. The owners own property with several apartments. **Pro:** Several rooms have hot tubs. **Cons:** Rooms can be basic, some have shared bath. ⊠ *Mi 186.5, Glenn Hwy.* ⊡ *Box 329 99588* ☎ *907/822–3302 or 800/478–3302* ⊕ *www.caribouhotel.com* ⟋ *83 rooms, 63 with bath; 3 suites; 2 cabins* ⚡ *In-room: kitchen (some), refrigerator (some), Wi-Fi. In-hotel: some pets allowed* ⊟ *AE, D, DC, MC, V.*

WRANGELL–ST. ELIAS NATIONAL PARK & PRESERVE

77 mi southeast of Glennallen, 264 mi east of Anchorage.

In a land of many grand and spectacularly beautiful mountains, those in the 9.2-million-acre Wrangell–St. Elias National Park and Preserve are possibly the finest of them all. This extraordinarily compact cluster of immense peaks belongs to four different mountain ranges.

ESSENTIALS

Visitor Info **Wrangell–St. Elias Parks Office** ✉ *Mi 106.8, Richardson Hwy.* 🗐 *Box 439, Copper Center 99573* ☎ *907/822–5234* ⊕ *www.nps.gov/wrst.*

WHAT TO SEE

Covering a 100 mi by 70 mi area, the **Wrangells** tower above the 2,500-foot-high Copper River Plateau, and the peaks of Mts. Jarvis, Drum, Blackburn, Sanford, and Wrangell rise 15,000 feet to 16,000 feet from sea level.

The white-iced spire of **Mt. St. Elias,** in the St. Elias Range, reaches more than 18,000 feet. It's the fourth-tallest mountain on the North American continent and the crown of the planet's highest coastal range.

The park's coastal mountains are frequently wreathed in snow-filled clouds, their massive height making a giant wall that contains the great storms brewed in the Gulf of Alaska. As a consequence, they bear some of the continent's largest ice fields, with more than 100 glaciers radiating from them. One of these, the **Malaspina Glacier,** is 1,500 square mi—larger than the state of Rhode Island. This tidewater glacier has an incredible pattern of black-and-white stripes made by the other glaciers that coalesced to form it. ■ TIP→ Look for Malaspina Glacier on the coast north of Yakutat if you fly between Juneau and Anchorage.

Rising through many life zones, the Wrangell–St. Elias Park and Preserve is largely undeveloped wilderness parkland on a grand scale. The area is perfect mountain-biking and hiking terrain, and the rivers invite rafting for those with expedition experience. The mountains attract climbers from around the world; most of them fly in from Glennallen or Yakutat.

★ The nearby abandoned **Kennicott Mine** is one of the park's main visitor attractions.

Limited services are available in the end-of-the-road town of **McCarthy.** Facilities include guest lodges, a B&B, and a restaurant. There's no gas station or post office.

The park is accessible from Alaska's highway system, via one of two gravel roads. The unpaved **Nabesna Road** leaves the Glenn Highway–Tok Cutoff at the village of Slana and takes you 45 mi into the park's northern foothills.

The better-known route is **McCarthy Road,** which stretches 60 mi as it follows an old railroad bed from Chitina to the Kennicott River. At the end of the road you must park and cross the river via a footbridge.

OUTDOOR ACTIVITIES & GUIDED TOURS

ADVENTURE TOURS

St. Elias Alpine Guides (☎ 907/345–9048 or 888/933–5427 ⊕*www.steliasguides.com*) gives introductory mountaineering lessons, leads excursions ranging from half-day glacier walks to monthlong backpacking trips, and is the only company contracted by the Park Service to conduct guided tours of historic Kennicott buildings. If you'd rather raft than hike, their Copper Oar

rafting outfit (www.copperoar.com) has river trips into the heart of the wilderness.

WHERE TO STAY

⚠ **Alaska State Parks Campgrounds.** The state maintains 23 road-accessible campgrounds in the Matanuska-Susitna–Copper River region. The allowed length of stay varies from 4 to 15 days. Although they can accommodate RVs of up to 35 feet, there aren't any hookups . ⚐ *Flush toilets, drinking water (some), fire pits (some), picnic table (some)* ☜ *23 campgrounds* ☐ *Alaska State Parks, Mat-Su Area Office, HC 32, Box 6706, Wasilla 99654* ☎ *907/745–3975* ☜ *Reservations not accepted* ▤ *No credit cards* ☉ *Closed Oct.–May.*

$$–$$$ ☷ **Copper River Princess Wilderness Lodge.** At the gateway to the park, this lodge has views of the Wrangell–St. Elias mountain range and the Copper and Klutina rivers. A wall of windows two stories high provides dramatic views of towering peaks and the Copper River. Dark-wood accents and Alaska wildlife and scenery prints, conveying the ambience of a well-appointed hunting lodge, adorn each room. **Pro:** Luxurious lodge in the wilderness. **Con:** Few amenities nearby except Princess's. ✉ *Brenwick Craig Rd., Mi 102, Richardson Hwy., Copper Center* ☎ *907/822–4000, 800/426–0500 reservations* ⊕ *www.princesslodges.com* ☜ *85 rooms* ⚐ *In-hotel: 2 restaurants, bar, airport shuttle, no-smoking rooms* ▤ *AE, DC, MC, V* ☉ *Closed mid-Sept.–mid-May.*

$$–$$$$ ☷ **Kennicott Glacier Lodge.** Artifacts and photos of the era when mining
★   was the main order of business in the ghost town of Kennicott adorn the small rooms in this modern wood lodge. Fresh-baked goods are favorites at the buffet breakfast. Sit-down lunches are served, or you can request a sack lunch to take with you. Dinner is a "wilderness gourmet" spread served family style. The front desk can arrange glacier trekking, flightseeing, rafting, and alpine hiking for additional fees. A vacation package that includes room and all meals is available. The lodge provides a shuttle from the end of the road in McCarthy. **Pros:** Lots of character, delicious food. **Con:** Some rooms have shared bath. ✉ *5 mi from McCarthy* ☐ *Box 103940, Anchorage 99510* ☎ *907/258–2350 or 800/582–5128* ⊕ *www.kennicottlodge.com* ☜ *35 rooms, 10 with bath* ⚐ *In-room: no phone, no TV. In-hotel: restaurant, no-smoking rooms* ▤ *AE, D, MC, V* ☉ *Closed mid-Sept.–mid-May.*

$$$$ ⚌ **Ultima Thule Outfitters.** This remote fly-in-only lodge on the Chitina
★ River in Wrangell–St. Elias National Park and Preserve provides a wonderful chance to experience an "air-safari adventure." The cost is
$1,000 per person per day, with a four-day minimum. Included in your
stay are breathtaking flightseeing, rafting, climbing, hiking, fishing,
mushing, and skiing excursions. Three generations of the family make
their home here, and their knowledge of the area is unsurpassed. The
family-style meals include local fish, game, and vegetables from the
garden as well as homemade bread, pies, and cakes. Oak floors, wallpaper, wood-burning stoves, and brass beds provide the comforts of
home, Bavarian style. **Pros:** Adventure and comfort at their best. **Con:**
Four-night minimum means it will be an expensive venture. ⌂ *Sum-*
mer: Box 109, Chitina 99566 ⌂ *Winter: Box 770361, Eagle River,*
99577 ☎ *907/688–1200* ⊕ *www.ultimathulelodge.com* ➷ *6 cabins*
⌂ *In-room: no phone, no TV. In-hotel: restaurant, public Internet, no-*
smoking rooms ⊟ *No credit cards* ⎮⊘⎮ *FAP.*

The Interior and Denali National Park & Preserve

WITH FAIRBANKS & THE YUKON

WORD OF MOUTH

"What a view! This Dall sheep was catching some rays, surveying his magnificent kingdom in Denali National Park."
—Chris Marlow, Photo Contest Winner

WELCOME TO THE INTERIOR

TOP REASONS TO GO

★ **Denali National Park & Preserve:** Denali's vertical relief, 18,000 feet, is greater than Mt. Everest's. The park itself is bigger than Massachusetts and is a stunning place to sample Alaska's natural wonders.

★ **Gold-rush heritage:** The frontier spirit of the richest gold rush in Alaska remains alive in Fairbanks. From exploring dredges to panning for gold, chances to participate in the past abound.

★ **Stern-wheeler cruises:** The riverboat *Discovery* is an authentic stern-wheeler that cruises the Chena and Tanana rivers, which served as highways long before there were roads.

★ **The gateway to the Arctic:** Fairbanks is an essential point for connections to northern Alaska—vast land of the midnight sun and the northern lights.

★ **Dog mushing:** The Interior is Alaska's prime mushing spot. Many people live here just so they can spend ever free winter moment running sled dogs.

A family of bears crosses the Denali Park Road.

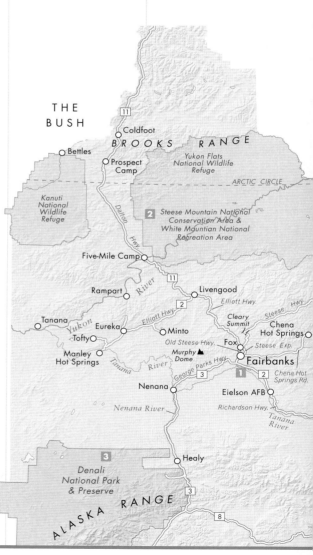

THE BUSH

BROOKS RANGE

Coldfoot
Bettles
Prospect Camp
Yukon Flats National Wildlife Refuge
ARCTIC CIRCLE
Kanuti National Wildlife Refuge
Dalton Hwy
Steese Mountain National Conservation Area & White Mountain National Recreation Area
Five-Mile Camp
11
Rampart
River
Livengood
Elliott Hwy.
Steese Hwy.
Tanana
Yukon
Eureka
Tofty
Elliott Hwy
Minto
Old Steese Hwy.
Cleary Summit
Chena Hot Springs
Manley Hot Springs
Tanana River
Murphy Dome
Fox
Steese Exp.
Fairbanks
George Parks Hwy.
Nenana
3
Chena Hot Springs Rd.
Eielson AFB
Richardson Hwy.
Nenana River
Tanana River
Denali National Park & Preserve
Healy
3
ALASKA RANGE
8

1 **Fairbanks.** With an area population of about 85,000, Fairbanks is home to the University of Alaska and is an important point along the trans-Alaska oil pipeline. This rough-edged town also has a vibrant arts scene.

2 **North of Fairbanks.** The Alaska wilderness is right at Fairbanks' door, with hundreds of miles of sub-arctic wilderness to explore. Hiking, canoeing, dog mushing, skiing, hot spring soaking, and fishing are part of daily life. A few roads and isolated villages are the extent of civilization here.

3 **Denali National Park & Preserve.** A 6-million-acre wonderland of wildlife, taiga, tundra, rushing rivers, and, of course, Mt. McKinley—the park's soaring crown jewel that we like to call the *High One.*

4 **Fortymile Country & the Yukon.** Fortymile Country yielded some of the first gold discoveries in the state. Mining operations can be seen along the Taylor Highway. Over the border is Dawson City, the Canadian Klondike Gold Rush boomtown. The Yukon offers countless outdoor activities such as paddling, climbing, backpacking, and cycling.

GETTING ORIENTED

Interior Alaska is the central part of the state, a vast and broad plateau bordered by the Alaska Range to the south and the Brooks Range to the north. The Yukon River and its many tributaries, including the Tanana River, are dominant features of the landscape. There are few roads and numerous widespread villages reached only by aircraft. Fairbanks is the major town in the Interior and serves as the transportation hub for northern and central Alaska.

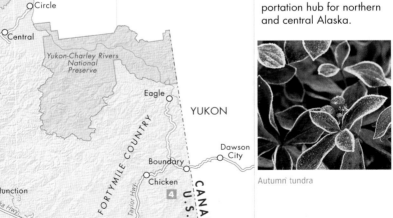

Autumn tundra

7

THE INTERIOR AND DENALI NATIONAL PARK & PRESERVE PLANNER

Making the Most of Your Time

If You Have 3 Days. Spend a day in Fairbanks taking in the trans-Alaska pipeline, University of Alaska Museum, and the riverboat Discovery tour. End your day at Pioneer Park so that you can have dinner at the Alaska Salmon Bake and catch a show at the park's Palace Theatre and Saloon. The next day head to Denali National Park and Preserve and hike or take a whitewater rafting trip down the nearby Nenana River. Spend the night in the park. Call ahead for room or campsite reservations; it's very crowded in summer. The third day get up early to take a shuttle bus (again, reserve!), and spend the third day exploring the national park. Stay in Fairbanks the last night; enjoy a dinner along the river at the Pump House Restaurant.

If You Have 5 Days. Follow the three-day itinerary; spend the fourth day in Fairbanks to take the tour of El Dorado Gold Mine, where you can pan for gold, and visit the Fairbanks Ice Museum. That afternoon, head out on the scenic Chena Hot Springs Road for a relaxing soak at Chena Hot Springs Resort. Spend the night at the resort or head back to town and consider stopping for dinner at Two Rivers Lodge.

Tour Options

Adventure: Go North Alaska Adventure Travel Center (☎907/479-7272 or 866/236-7272 ⊕www.paratours. net). Northern Alaska Tour Company (☎907/474-8600 or 800/474-1986 ⊕www.northernalaska.com). Trans Arctic Circle Treks (☎907/479-5451 or 800/336-8735 ⊕www.arctictreks.com).

Climbing: Alaska Mountaineering School (☎907/733-1016 ⊕www.climbalaska.org).

Sea & Land Tours: Denali Park Resorts (☎907/276-7234 or 800/276-7234 ⊕www.denaliparkresorts.com). Gray Line of Alaska (☎800/478-6388 ⊕www.graylinealaska. com). Northern Alaska Tour Company (☎907/474-8600 ⊕www.northernalaska.com). Princess Tours (☎907/479-9660 or 800/426-0442 ⊕www.princessalaskalodges. com). Trans Arctic Circle Treks (☎907/479-5451 ⊕www.arctictreks.com).

River Trips: Greatland River Tours (✉1020 Hoselton Rd., Fairbanks ☎907/452-8687 or 866/452-8687 ⊕www. greatlandrivertours.com). Riverboat Discovery (✉1975 Discovery Dr., near Fairbanks International Airport, Fairbanks ☎907/479-6673 or 866/479-6673 ⊕www. riverboatdiscovery.com).

Custom Sightseeing: Alpenglow Alaska/Yukon Tours (☎907/479-2277 or 800/770-7275 ⊕www.akalpenglow.com).

Fishing: NatureAlaska Tours (☎907/488-3746 ⊕www. naturealaska.com). Wilderness Enterprises (☎907/488-7517 ⊕www.wildernessenterprises.com).

Getting Around

Fairbanks is a sprawling city, with a layout that isn't ideal for pedestrians. There is public transportation, but service is limited. Hotels run shuttle buses to and from the airport, and you can get around by taxi. If you plan to spend more than a couple of days in the city, rent a car.

Alaska's Wild Rivers

Interior Alaska is thick with rivers, and the Delta and Nenana take particularly unusual routes—they cut right through the massive Alaska Range, creating important (though wet) mountain passes. Several theories address how these odd passes formed, but take a float on the Nenana and dream up your own hypothesis. The logistics of creating a trip to any remote river can be nightmarish, though, so go with an outfitter; they guide or rent gear for four-hour cruises up to weeklong forays hundreds of miles off the road system. If white water is more your style, numerous companies operate on the Nenana River outside Denali National Park. Be prepared for a wild ride; you'll need the dry suit provided.

About the Restaurants & Hotels

Even in the most elegant establishments, Alaskans sometimes don sweats or Carhartts. Most restaurants fly in fresh salmon and halibut from the coast. Meat-and-potatoes main courses and the occasional pasta dish fill menus, but most restaurants offer palatable vegetarian choices, too. The food isn't the only thing full of local flavor: walls are usually decked in some combination of snowshoes, caribou and bear hides, the state flag, and historic photos.

You won't find ultra-luxury hotels, but you can find a range of bed-and-breakfasts, rustic-chic lodges, and national chains, the best of which will please even the most discriminating travelers. For interaction with Alaskans, choose a bed-and-breakfast, as they're usually local-owned; proprietors tend to be eager to provide travel tips or an unforgettable story. Summer reservations for popular hotels and at campsites near Denali need to be made months in advance. The cheapest options are tents or RVs, and there is no shortage of campgrounds here.

Timing

June and July bring near-constant sun, sometimes punctuated by afternoon cloudbursts. In winter it gets so cold (−30°F or below) that boiling water flung out a window will land as ice particles.

Many attractions shut down in mid-September. A trip in May avoids the rush, but it can snow in Fairbanks in spring. Late August brings fall colors, ripe berries, active wildlife, and the start of northern-lights season. Winter sports fans should come in March, when the sun's back but there's still plenty of snow.

FROM FAIRBANKS TO:	
BY CAR	(HRS: MINS)
Anchorage	7:00
Dawson City	14:00
Denali	2:00
Seward	9:30
Skagway	15:00
Whitehorse	12:00

FROM FAIRBANKS TO:	
BY AIR	(HRS: MINS)
Anchorage	1:00
Barrow	1:30
Juneau	3:15
Nome	2:00
Prudhoe Bay	1:30
Seattle	3:30

7

WHAT IT COSTS

¢	$	$$	$$$	$$$$
RESTAURANTS				
under $10	$10–$15	$15–$20	$20–$25	over $25
HOTELS				
under $75	$75–$125	$125–$175	$175–$225	over $225

Restaurant prices are per person for a main course at dinner. Hotel prices are for two people in a standard double room in high season.

Updated
by Laurel
Schoenbohm

The gem of the Interior is Denali National Park, where the Alaska Range—the "great wall" dividing the Interior from the South Central region—rises more than 20,000 feet. If the peak remains shrouded in clouds during your stay, the rivers, tundra, and wildlife amaze and please as well. And there's an excellent chance you'll spot plenty of the last, because Denali's open tundra makes it difficult for the animals to hide or blend in with their surroundings.

There's a slice of heaven for outdoor athletes; ample biking, rafting, mountaineering, and backpacking opportunities abound. Be sure to journey into the heart of the park, since this is where you'll find the best views of Denali and wildlife-spotting opportunities.

Just as geologic forces shaped Denali and the Alaska Range, the geology of the Interior played a key role in human history at the turn of the 19th century. The image of 1900s Alaska, set to the harsh tunes of countless honky-tonk saloons and the clanging of pans, is rooted around the Interior's goldfields. The gold fever struck in Circle and Eagle in the 1890s, spread into Canada's Yukon Territory in the big Klondike Gold Rush of 1898, then came back to Alaska's Interior when Fairbanks hit pay dirt in 1903. The broad, swift Yukon River was the rush's main highway. Flowing almost 2,300 mi from Canada to the Bering Sea, just below the Arctic Circle, it carried prospectors across the border in search of instant fortune.

Although Fairbanks has grown into a small city, many towns and communities in the Interior seem little changed. While soaking in the water of the Chena Hot Springs Resort, you can almost hear the whispers of gold seekers exaggerating their finds and claims, ever alert

FAIRBANKS GOLD

The gold strike by Felix Pedro in 1902 is commemorated annually in late July with the celebration of Golden Days, marked by a parade and several days of gold rush–inspired activities.

for the newest strike. When early missionaries set up schools in the bush, the nomadic native Alaskan peoples were herded to these regional centers for schooling and "salvation," but Interior Alaska is still flecked with native villages. Fort Yukon, on the Arctic Circle, is the largest Athabascan village in the state.

Alaska's current gold rush—the pipeline carrying black gold from the oil fields in Prudhoe Bay south to the port of Valdez—snakes its way through the Interior. The Richardson Highway, which started as a gold stampeders' trail, parallels the trans-Alaska pipeline on its route south of Fairbanks. Actual gold still glitters in the Interior; Fairbanks, the site of the largest gold production in Alaska in pre–World War II days, is home to the Fort Knox Gold Mine, which has approximately doubled Alaska's gold production.

EXPLORING THE INTERIOR

Interior Alaska is sandwiched between two monumental mountain ranges: the Brooks Range to the north and the Alaska Range to the south. In such a vast wilderness, many of the region's residents define their area by a limited network of two-lane highways.

You need a car in the Interior, even if you're based in Fairbanks. The Steese Highway, the Dalton Highway, and the Taylor Highway (closed in winter) are well-maintained gravel roads. However, summer rain can make them slick and dangerous. ■ TIP→ Rental-car companies have varying policies on whether they allow travel on gravel roads, so check in advance.

The George Parks Highway runs south to Denali National Park and Preserve and on to Anchorage, the state's largest city, 360 mi away on the coast. The Richardson Highway extends to the southeast to Delta Junction before turning south to Valdez, which is 368 mi from Fairbanks.

There are two major routes to the north. You can take the Elliott Highway to the Dalton Highway, following the trans-Alaska pipeline to its origins at Prudhoe Bay on Alaska's North Slope. Alternatively, explore the Steese Highway to its termination at the Yukon River and the town of Circle.

Beyond the highways are many native villages reached by small airplanes making daily connections out of Fairbanks, which is the regional hub and the thriving commercial center of the Interior.

FAIRBANKS

At first glance, Fairbanks appears dominated by a sprawling conglomeration of strip malls, chain stores, and other evidence of suburbia (or, as a local writer once put it, "su-brrr-bia"). But look beyond the obvious in the Interior's biggest town and you'll discover why thousands insist that this is the best place to live in Alaska. Many of the old homes

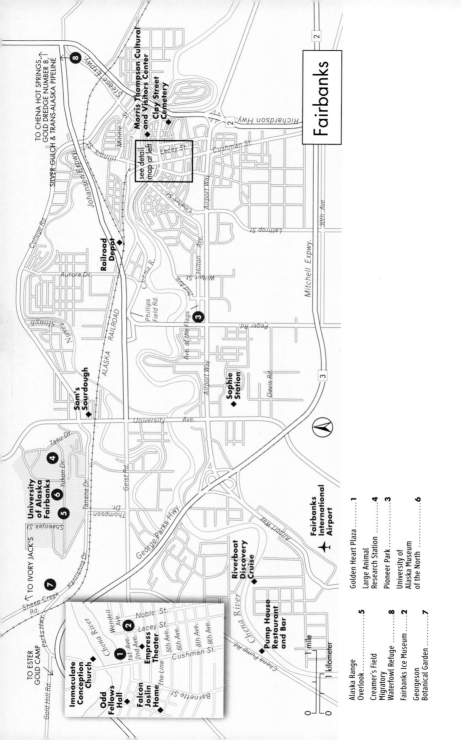

Fairbanks

TO CHENA HOT SPRINGS,
GOLD DREDGE NUMBER 8,
TRANS-ALASKA PIPELINE

SILVER GULCH

Morris Thompson Cultural
and Visitors Center

Clay Street
Cemetery

see detail
map at left

Richardson Hwy.

Steese Expwy.

Johansen Expwy.

Minnie St.

Illinois St.

Lacey St.

Cushman St.

Cowles St.

Airport Way

Chena R.

Phillips Field Rd.

Lathrop St.

Wilbur St.

2nd Ave.

Hilton Ave.

Mitchell Expwy.

30th Ave.

Peger Rd.

Ave. of the Flags

Railroad Depot

Aurora Dr.

Cottage Rd.

Noyes Slough

ALASKA RAILROAD

Sam's Sourdough

University Ave.

Sophie Station

Davis Rd.

University of
Alaska Fairbanks

Taku Dr.

Yukon Dr.

Sheenjek St.

Tanana Dr.

Thompson Dr.

Geist Rd.

George Parks Hwy.

Kazitsna Dr.

TO IVORY JACK'S

Sheep Creek Rd.

TO ESTER
GOLD CAMP

Gott Hill Rd.

Parks Hwy.

Riverboat
Discovery
Cruise

Chena River

Airport Way

Fairbanks International
Airport

Pump House
Restaurant
and Bar

Chena Pump Rd.

0   1 mile

0   1 kilometer

Detail map

Immaculate
Conception
Church

Odd
Fellows
Hall

Falcon
Joslin
Home

Wendell
Ave.

Noble St.

Lacey St.

Cushman St.

1st Ave.

2nd Ave.

5th Ave.

6th Ave.

8th Ave.

9th Ave.

The Line

Barnette St.

Empress
Theater

Chena River

and commercial buildings trace their history to the city's early days, especially in the downtown area, with its narrow, winding streets following the contours of the Chena River. Even if each year brings more chain stores, the beautiful hillsides and river valleys remain.

The hardy Alaskans who refuse to leave during the cold and dark winters bind together with strong camaraderie. The fight to stave off cabin fever leads to creative festivals, from winter solstice celebrations to outhouse and snowmachine tug-of-war during Chatanika Days in Chatanika, about 28 mi north of town. The other bonus? An average of 243 nights a year of aurora, or northern lights, viewing.

These magic lights were a common sight to the native Alaskans who lived and traveled through Interior Alaska for thousands of years. But it wasn't until the early 1900s that a permanent settlement took shape along the banks of the Chena River. In 1901, E.T. Barnette, a merchant traveling upstream, was forced to get off the boat with all of his trading goods at a wooded spot along the Chena River because the water was too low to pass. He was left for a year, awaiting passage farther east. His luck improved when an Italian prospector discovered gold 12 mi north of Barnette's settlement the next summer. The resulting gold rush created customers for Barnette's stockpile of goods and led to the birth of the city, which for a brief time became the largest and wealthiest settlement in Alaska.

EXPLORING FAIRBANKS

The city's nickname, the Golden Heart, reflects Fairbanks's gold-rush history and its location: it's the gateway to the Far North—the Arctic and the Bering Coast—and to Canada's Yukon Territory.

As you walk the streets of Fairbanks today, it takes a good imagination to envision the rough-and-tumble gold-mining camp that first took shape along the Chena River in the early 1900s. While a few older neighborhoods have weathered log cabins, the rest is a Western hodgepodge that reflects the urge to build whatever one wants, wherever one wants—a trait that has long been a community standard.

There are efforts to preserve some of the gold-rush past, most notably in the 44-acre Pioneer Park, where dozens of cabins and many other relics were moved out of the path of progress. For details on all local attractions, historical and otherwise, stop by the downtown Fairbanks Convention and Visitors Bureau in the Morris Thompson Cultural and Visitors Center. Downtown Fairbanks began to deteriorate in the 1970s, before and after the boom associated with the building of the trans-Alaska pipeline. But the downward spiral ended and most of downtown has been rebuilt.

We highly recommend a trip to the campus of the University of Alaska Fairbanks, where the University of Alaska Museum of the North got a makeover in 2006; the new building is full of soothing, swooping lines that evoke glaciers, mountains, and sealife. A good complement to the

TOURING THE OLD TOWN

Points of interest on the Convention and Visitors Bureau's self-guided walking tour include the nearby **Golden Heart Plaza**, home of the *Unknown First Family* statue; the **Clay Street Cemetery**, with its marked and unmarked graves of early pioneers; the **Empress Theater**, the first concrete structure in Interior Alaska; the stately **Falcon Joslin Home**, the oldest frame house in Fairbanks still at its original location; the **Line**, home of the red-light district until the mid-1950s;

Odd Fellows Hall, a bathhouse for gold miners (until the pipes froze in the winter of 1910–11) that is now a museum; and the historic **Immaculate Conception Church**, which was raised off its foundation in 1911 and rolled across the frozen Chena River on logs pulled by horses.

museum is the Fairbanks Convention and Visitors Bureau's 90 minute walking tour of downtown; it gives a good overview of local history.

Make **Morris Thompson Cultural and Visitors Center** your first stop, and take the time to browse the 10,000-foot exhibit space; partake in the theater, films, dancing, storytelling, and art exhibitions; and peruse the gift shop. This new facility is shared by several organizations: the Alaska Public Lands Information Center, Tanana Chiefs Conference, and the Denakkanaaga, Inc. (the Interior Alaska Regional Elders and Youth Organization). ⊠ *101 Dunkel St., Downtown* ☎ *907/459–3880* ⊕ *www.morristhompsoncenter.org*

Located in the new Morris Thompson Cultural and Visitors Center, at the **Fairbanks Convention and Visitors Bureau** you can receive trip-planning information, check e-mail, and pick up a map for a self-guided 90-minute walking tour through the historic downtown area. ⊠ *101 Dunkel St., Downtown* ☎ *907/456–5774, 800/327–5774 recording* ⊕ *www.explorefairbanks.com.*

GETTING HERE & AROUND

Delta and Northwest Airlines offer seasonal nonstop service from Fairbanks to the Lower 48. Alaska Airlines, ERA Aviation, and Frontier Flying Service fly the Anchorage–Fairbanks route. There are hotel shuttles, rental cars, and taxis available at the Fairbanks airport.

As for ground transportation, the Alaska Park Connection provides regularly scheduled shuttle service between Seward, Anchorage, and Denali National Park from mid-May to mid-September. Denali Overland Transportation serves Anchorage, Talkeetna, and Denali National Park with charter bus and van service. Alaska/Yukon Trails runs between Fairbanks, Denali, Anchorage, Talkeetna, Whitehorse, and Dawson City (⇨ *See* Essentials, *below*).

Between late May and early September, Alaska Railroad's daily passenger service runs between Seward, Anchorage, and Fairbanks, with stops at Talkeetna and Denali National Park and Preserve. Standard trains have dining, lounge, and dome cars, plus the only outdoor viewing platform of its kind. Holland America and Princess offer luxurious travel packages as well.

ESSENTIALS

Airline Contacts Alaska Airlines (☎ *800/252–7522* ⊕ *www.alaskaair.com*). **ERA Aviation** (☎ *907/266–8394 or 800/866–8394* ⊕ *www.flyera.com*). **Frontier Flying Service** (☎ *800/478–6779* ⊕ *www.frontierflying.com*).

City Bus Fairbanks MACS Bus System (☎ *907/459–1011* ⊕ *www.co.fairbanks.ak.us/transportation,* ➔ *$1.50 a ride or $3 a day*).

Commuter Buses Alaska Park Connection (☎ *907/245–0200 or 800/208–0200* ⊕ *www.alaskatravel.com*). **Alaska/Yukon Trails** (☎ *800/770–7275* ⊕ *www.alaskashuttle.com*).

Internet College Coffeehouse (✉ *3677 College Rd.* ☎ *907/374–0468* ⊕ *www.collegecoffeehousefairbanks.com*). **Fairbanks Convention and Visitors Bureau** (✉ *101 Dunkel St.* ☎ *907/456–5774 or 800/327–5774* ⊕ *www.explorefairbanks.com*). **Noel Wien Library** (✉ *1215 Cowles St.* ☎ *907/459–1020* ⊕ *library.fnsb.lib.ak.us*).

Medical Assistance Fairbanks Memorial Hospital (✉ *1650 Cowles St.* ☎ *907/452–8181*). **Fairbanks Urgent Care Center** (✉ *1867 Airport Way* ☎ *907/452–2178*).**Tanana Valley Clinic**(✉ *1001 Noble St.* ☎ *907/459–3500* ⊕ *www.tvcclinic.com*.

Post Offices & Shipping U.S. Postal Service (✉ *315 Barnette St.* ☎ *907/452–3223* ✉ *4024 Geist Rd.* ☎ *907/479–6021* ⊕ *www.usps.gov*). **FedEx** (✉ *418 3rd St., 5A* ☎ *907/456–7348 or 800/463–3339* ⊕ *www.fedex.com*).

Rail Alaska Railroad (☎ *907/458–6025 or 800/544–0552* ⊕ *www.akrr.com*). **Holland America Tours/Gray Line of Alaska** (☎ *907/451–6835 or 888/452–1737* ⊕ *www.graylinealaska.com*). **Princess Tours** (☎ *800/426–0500* ⊕ *www.princesslodges.com*).

Rental Cars Budget Rent-A-Car (☎ *907/474–0855, 800/474–0855 in Alaska* ⊕ *www.budget.com*). **Dollar Rent A Car** (☎ *907/451–4360 or 800/800–4000* ⊕ *www.dollar.com*). **Hertz** (☎ *907/452–4444 or 800/654–3131* ⊕ *www.hertz.com*).

Visitor & Tour Info Alaska Department of Fish and Game (✉ *1300 College Rd.* ☎ *907/459–7207*). **Morris Thompson Cultural and Visitors Center** (✉ *101 Dunkel St.* ☎ *907/459–3880* ⊕ *www.morristhompsoncenter.org*).

WHAT TO SEE

❺ Alaska Range Overlook. Much of the north side of the Alaska Range is visible from this overlook, a favor-

---

SIGHTSEEING TOURS

Gray Line of Alaska (☎ *800/478–6388* ⊕ *www.graylinealaska.com*) runs scenic and informative trips through the Fairbanks area, including a four-hour Discover the Gold sightseeing tour of the *Gold Dredge Number 8* with a lunch of miner's stew for $60.

Princess Tours (☎ *800/426–0442* ⊕ *www.princesslodges.com*) has city bus tours.

ite spot for time-lapse photography of the midwinter sun just peeking over the southern horizon on a low arc. The three major peaks, called the Three Sisters, are nearly always distinguishable on a clear day. From your left are **Mt. Hayes,** 13,832 feet; **Mt. Hess,** 11,940 feet; and **Mt. Deborah,** 12,339 feet. Much farther to the right, toward the southwest, hulks **Mt. McKinley,** the highest peak in North America. On some seemingly clear days it's not visible at all. At other times the base is easy to see but the peak is lost in cloud cover. ⊠ *West Ridge, University of Alaska Fairbanks campus, Yukon Dr.; look for parking area just east of University of Alaska Museum.*

GARDENS FOR GIANTS

Interior Alaska gets an extra-large helping of sunlight between May and August. The growing season is short in days, but every day counts because the sun is rarely out of sight. The long daylight hours create intense, vivid colors in flowers, while allowing vegetables to grow to gargantuan dimensions. Cabbages that top 50 pounds and zucchini with telephone-pole diameters are common.

8 **Creamer's Field Migratory Waterfowl Refuge.** Thousands of migrating ducks, geese, and sandhill cranes stop here in spring as they head north to nesting grounds, and in late summer, as they head south before the cold hits. This is also a great place to view songbirds and moose. Five miles of nature trails lead through fields, forest, and wetlands, and are open year-round. Don't miss the Wednesday naturalist walks. The barns and buildings of **Creamer's Dairy** still stand here. Now on the National Register of Historic Places, Creamer's Dairy was the northernmost dairy in North America from 1910 to 1966. The farmhouse is now a visitor center and gift shop open daily Memorial Day–Labor Day and Saturday the rest of the year. ⊠ *1300 College Rd., Lemeta* ☎ *907/459–7307 or 907/452–5162* ⊕ *www.creamersfield.org.*

9 **Fairbanks Ice Museum.** You'd think that the last thing Fairbanksans would want to hang onto through the too-brief summer is a reminder of the brutal winters. However, the folks at the Ice Museum do just that. Sculptors work behind glass in large freezers where they create intricate sculptures from ice. About 25 sculptures are usually on display. Billed as "the coolest show in town," the Ice Showcase, a large glass-wall display, is kept at 20°F. *Freeze Frame* is a large-screen film demonstrating the techniques of ice sculpture. The museum is in the historic Lacey Street Theater, on the corner of 2nd Avenue and Lacey Street. ⊠ *500 2nd Ave., Downtown* ☎ *907/451–8222* ⊕ *www.ice-museum.com* ☑ *$12* ⊗ *May–Sept., daily 10–9; Oct. –Apr., daily noon–5.*

7 **Georgeson Botanical Garden of the Agricultural and Forestry Experiment Station Farm.** When most people think of Alaska vegetation, they conjure up images of flat, treeless tundra, so the amazing variety of native and cultivated flowers on exhibit here is often unexpected. This is where researchers at the University of Alaska Fairbanks study Interior Alaska's unique, short, but intense midnight-sun growing season. The

Just Outside Fairbanks: Liquid Gold

Trans-Alaska Pipeline. Just north of Fairbanks you can see and touch the famous trans-Alaska pipeline. This 48-inch-diameter pipe travels 800 mi from the oil fields on the North Slope of the Brooks Range over three mountain ranges and over more than 800 rivers and streams to the terminal in Valdez. There the crude oil is pumped onto tanker ships and transported to oil refineries in the Lower 48 states. Since the pipeline began operations in 1977, more than 15 billion barrels of North Slope crude have been pumped. Currently the pipe is carrying about 700,000 gallons per day. The parking lot is right off the Steese Highway and has a sign loaded with information. Informative guides staff a small visitor center, and there's a gift shop with pipeline-company memorabilia. ⊠ *Mi 8.4, Steese Hwy.* ☎ *907/457-3344* ☜ *Free* ⊗ *Visitor center mid-May–Sept., daily 8:30–6.*

results are spectacular. There are about 300 perennials and 300 new annuals on the grounds. The nonstop daylight brings out rich and vibrant colors. The best times to visit are from mid-June to late August. ⊠ *117 W. Tanana Dr., west end of campus, 4 mi west of downtown* ☎ *907/474–6921* ☜ *$2* ⊗ *May–Sept., daily 8–8; tours Fri. at 2.*

❶ **Golden Heart Plaza.** This riverside park is the hub of downtown celebrations, including free evening concerts in the park. The plaza is dominated by the towering statue of the Unknown First Family, encircled by plaques containing the names of 4,500 local families who contributed to the building of the plaza.

❹ **Large Animal Research Station.** Out on the fringes of the University of
☾ Alaska campus is a 134-acre home to about 45 musk ox, 15 caribou,
★ and 40 domestic reindeer. Resident and visiting scientists study these large ungulates to better understand their physiologies and how they adapt to Arctic conditions. The station also serves as a valuable outreach program. Most people have little chance to see these animals in their natural habitats, especially the musk ox. Once nearly eradicated from Alaska, these shaggy, prehistoric-looking beasts are marvels of adaptive physiques and behaviors. They are also being studied for potential commercial uses: qiviut, the soft, delicate musk-ox undercoat, is combed out (without harming the animals) and made into scarves, hats, and gloves by Alaska native women. It has the feel of cashmere and is remarkably warm. The station has unprocessed wool for sale at about $25 an ounce. On tours you visit the pens for close-up looks at the animals and their young, while learning about the biology and ecology of the animals from a naturalist. ⊠ *Yankovich Rd. off Ballaine Rd., behind University of Alaska Fairbanks* ☎ *907/474–7207 tour information* ⊕ *www.uaf.edu/lars* ☜ *Tours $10* ⊗ *Memorial Day–Labor Day by tour only; 45-min tours daily beginning at 10 am.*

❸ **Pioneer Park.** The 44-acre park is along the Chena River near downtown
☾ Fairbanks and has several museums, an art gallery, theater, civic center,
★ native village, large children's playground, miniature-golf course,

7

antique merry-go-round, and restaurants. The park also has a re-created gold-rush town with historic buildings saved from urban renewal, log-cabin gift shops, and **Mining Valley,** an outdoor museum of mining artifacts surrounding an indoor–outdoor Alaska salmon-bake restaurant. The 227-foot stern-wheeler *Nenana* is the second-largest wooden vessel in existence and a national historic landmark. A diorama inside the stern-wheeler details the course the riverboat took on the Yukon and Tanana rivers around the turn of the 20th century. The **Crooked Creek and Whiskey Island Railroad,** a narrow-gauge train, circles the park. The newest addition to the park is a museum housing the first railroad locomotive in Fairbanks, which has been restored to its 1905 condition and is run on special occasions. ■TIP➔ No-frills RV camping is available for $12 a night in the west end of the large parking lot on Airport Way. ⊠*Airport Way and Peger Rd.* ☎*907/459–1087* ⊕*http://co.fairbanks.ak.us/parksandrecreation* ⊠*Free* ☉*Park 24 hrs; museum and shops Memorial Day–Labor Day, daily noon–8.*

❻ University of Alaska Museum of the North. This museum has become the

FodorśChoice　most distinctive architectural landmark in the state, with sweeping

★　curves and graceful lines, suggesting glaciers, mountains, and a fluke of a diving whale. Inside, two-story viewing windows look out on the Alaska Range and the Tanana Valley. Otto, the 8-foot, 9-inch brown bear, greets visitors to the entrance of the Gallery of Alaska, featuring the state's largest display of gold, Alaska native art and artifacts, and Blue Babe, a mummified steppe bison that lived 36,000 years ago during the Pleistocene epoch. The museum has several "please touch" items, including the molars of a mammoth and a mastodon, a gray-whale skull, and a 5,495-pound copper nugget. In the Place Where You Go to Listen, ever-changing light and sound, composed by the real-time movements of the sun, moon, aurora, and seismic activity, create a mesmerizing effect. And don't miss the year-round special exhibits or the Rose Berry Alaska Art Gallery, representing 2,000 years of Alaska's art, from ancient to modern. ⊠*University of Alaska Fairbanks, 907 Yukon Dr.* ☎*907/474–7505* ⊕*www.uaf.edu/museum* ⊠*$15 mid-May–mid-Sept.; $10 in winter* ☉*Mid-May–mid-Sept., daily 9–9; Mon.–Sat. 9–5 in winter.*

OUTDOORS ACTIVITIES & GUIDED TOURS

ADVENTURE TOURS

Northern Alaska Tour Company (☎*907/474–8600 or 800/474–1986* ⊕*www.northernalaska.com*) leads year-round half- and full-day excursions to the Arctic Circle and the Yukon River and two- and three-day fly-drive tours to Prudhoe Bay, Barrow, and the Brooks Range. They also have winter aurora-watching trips.

BICYCLING

Bicyclists in Fairbanks use the paved paths from the University of Alaska campus around Farmers Loop to the Steese Highway. Another path follows Geist and Chena Pump roads into downtown Fairbanks. Be warned that many of the trails are in rough shape and suffer from lack of maintenance. A shorter, less-strenuous route is the bike path between downtown and Pioneer Park along the south side of the Chena River. Maps showing all the bike paths are available at the **Fairbanks Convention and Visitors Bureau** (⇨ *above*). Mountain bikers can test their skills in summer on the ski trails of the University of Alaska Fairbanks and the Birch Hill Recreation Area or on many of the trails and dirt roads around Fairbanks. Stop by the **Alaska Public Lands Information Center** (⊠ *101 Dunkel St.* ☎ *907/456–0527*) for mountain-biking information.

BOATING

For relaxing boating in or near Fairbanks, use Chena River access points at Nordale Road east of the city, the Cushman and Wendell Street bridges near downtown, Pioneer Park above the Peger River Bridge, the state campground, and the University Avenue Bridge.

The Tanana River, with a current that is fast and often shallow, is ideally suited for riverboats. On this river and others in the Yukon River drainage, Alaskans use long, wide, flat-bottom boats powered by one or two large outboard engines. The boats include a lift to raise the engine a few inches, allowing passage through the shallows, and some of the engines come equipped with a jet unit instead of a propeller to allow more bottom clearance. Arrangements for riverboat charters can be made in almost any river community. Ask at the Fairbanks Convention and Visitors Bureau.

CRUISING & CANOEING TOURS
Fodor'sChoice ★

Alaska Outdoor Rentals & Guides (⊠ *Pioneer Park Boat Dock, along Chena River next to Peger Rd.* ☎ *907/457–2453* ⊕ *www.2paddle1. com*) organizes canoeing and kayaking tours for groups of up to 50 on Class I waters of the lower Chena River. The only real challenge for canoeists on the lower river is watching out for powerboats. You can rent canoes and kayaks independent of any organized tour; they also rent bicycles and climbing supplies. **Greatland River Tours** (⊠ *1020 Hoselton Rd., University Ave.* ☎ *907/452–8687 or 866/452–8687* ⊕ *www.greatlandrivertours.com*) provides nightly dinner cruises on the Chena River aboard the stern-wheeler *Tanana Chief,* a replica of the riverboats that once plied Interior rivers. The dinner cruise costs $49.95 and boards at 6:30 PM.

Fodor'sChoice ★

The city's riverboat history and the Interior's cultural heritage are relived each summer aboard the **Riverboat Discovery** (⊠ *1975 Discovery Dr.,* ☎ *907/479–6673 or 866/479–6673* ⊕ *www.riverboatdiscovery. com*), a 3½-hour narrated trip by stern-wheeler along the Chena and Tanana rivers to a rustic native village on the Tanana River. The cruise provides a glimpse of the lifestyle of the dog mushers, subsistence fishermen, traders, and native Alaskans who populate the Yukon River drainage. Sights along the way include operating fish wheels, a bush airfield, floatplanes, a smokehouse and cache, log cabins, and dog kennels once tended to by the late Iditarod champion Susan Butcher. The Binkley family, with four generations of river pilots, has run the great rivers of the north for more than 100 years. Cruises are $49.95 and run twice daily (at 8:45 and 2) mid-May to mid-September.

DOG MUSHING

From November to March, a constant string of sled-dog races is held throughout the region, culminating in the **North American Open Sled-Dog Championship,** which attracts international competition to Fairbanks. Throughout Alaska, sprint races, freight hauling, and long-distance endurance runs are held in late February and March, during the season when longer days afford enjoyment of the remaining winter snow. Men and women often compete in the same classes in the major races. For children, various racing classes are based on age, starting with the one-dog category for the youngest.

In Fairbanks many of the sprint races are organized by the **Alaska Dog Mushers Association** (☎ *907/457–6874* ⊕ *www.sleddog.org*), one of the oldest organizations of its kind in Alaska, and held at its Jeff Studdert Sled Dog Racegrounds at Mile 4, Farmers Loop. The **Yukon Quest International Sled-Dog Race** (☎ *907/452–7954* ⊕ *www.yukonquest.org*) is an endurance race held in February that covers more than 1,000 mi between Fairbanks and Whitehorse, Yukon Territory, via Dawson and the Yukon River. You can get more details from the visitor center in either city or by checking in with the Fairbanks Yukon Quest office, located in the log cabin at 550 1st Avenue.

★ If you want to experience dog mushing for yourself, **Sun Dog Express Dog Sled Tours** (☎ *907/479–6983* ⊕ *www.mosquitonet.com/~sleddog*), with more than 20 years of mushing experience, offers summer and winter tours and demonstrations. When there is no snow, the dogs pull a wheeled cart.

Offering a mix of trips, **Paws for Adventure Sled Dog Tours** (☎ *907/378– 3630* ⊕ *www.pawsforadventure.com* ☉ *Oct. –Apr.*) is a good choice. The most adventurous can embark on multiday trips, but other options include a mushing school or a short sled. For night owls, try the dinner and aurora-viewing option. Located at the same site is **Alaska Iron Dog Adventures** (☎ *907/378–3228* ⊕ *www.irondogadventures.com*), featuring snowmachine adventures.

FISHING

Although a few fish can be caught right in town from the Chena River, avid fishermen can find outstanding angling by hopping a plane or riverboat. Fishing trips include air charters to **Lake Minchumina** (an hour's flight from Fairbanks), known for good pike fishing and a rare view of the north sides of Mt. McKinley and Mt. Foraker. Another charter trip by riverboat or floatplane will take you pike fishing in the **Minto Flats,** west of Fairbanks off the Tanana River, where the mouth of the Chatanika River spreads through miles of marsh and sloughs.

Salmon run up the **Tanana River** most of the summer, but they're not usually caught on hook-and-line gear. Residents take them from the river with gill nets and fish wheels, using special commercial and subsistence permits. Check the "Outdoors" section in the Friday *Fairbanks Daily News–Miner* for weekly updates on fishing in the Interior.

PANNING FOR GOLD

The gold information center for Interior Alaska, **Alaskan Prospectors** (✉ *504 College Rd., Lemeta* ☎ *907/452–7398* ⊕ *www.alaskagoldinformationcenter.com*) is the oldest mining and prospecting supply store in the state, also featured on the Travel Channel. Stop here for gold pans and books or videos, or to peruse the rocks and minerals museum. Employees have valuable advice for the neophyte gold bug.

El Dorado Gold Mine (✉ *Mi 3, Elliott Hwy.,* ☎ *907/479–6673 or 866/479–6673* ⊕ *www.eldoradogoldmine.com*) conducts two-hour tours ($34.95) of a seasonal mining operation with a ride on a narrow-gauge railroad. Experienced miners Dexter Clark and his wife "Yukon Yonda" demonstrate modern and historical mining techniques and help you pan for gold.

Gold Dredge Number 8 (✉ *Mi 9, 1755 Old Steese Hwy. N,* ☎ *907/457–6058* ⊕ *www.golddredgeno8.com* 🎫 *$25* 🕑 *Mid-May–mid-Sept., daily 9:30–3:30.*) a five-deck workhorse of a ship, was built in 1928 and is more than 250 feet long. It processed millions of dollars' worth of gold out of the Goldstream and Engineer creeks north of Fairbanks until its retirement in 1959. This dredge has been declared a National Historic District, one of the few privately owned districts in the nation. After a guided tour of the dredge, admission entitles you to the necessary tools, gold-panning instructions, and a chance to find "colors" at the sluice. A sit-down, family-style, all-you-can-eat, miner's beef stew is served from 11 AM to 3 PM for an additional $9.75. The dredge (and the miner's stew) is a featured stop on Holland America's tours operated by Gray Line of Alaska.

■TIP→ You can purchase fishing licenses (good for one day or longer; $20 and up) at many sporting-goods stores and online at www.admin.adfg.state.ak.us/license.

Arctic Grayling Guide Service (☎ *907/479–0479* or *907/322–8004* ⊕ *www.wildernessfishing.com*) offers guided and unguided fishing trips via jet boat to a remote fishing spot 60 mi south of Fairbanks to fish for grayling and salmon. Cabins are available.

GOLF

Chena Bend (☎ *907/353–6223*), a well-maintained Army course open to civilians, is an 18-hole spread on nearby Ft. Wainwright. The 9-hole course at the **Fairbanks Golf and Country Club** (☎ *907/479–6555*) straddles Farmers Loop just north of the university. Summertime midnight golf with a 3 AM tee time is considered normal at this course. The 18-hole course at the **North Star Golf Club** (☎ *907/457–4653, 907/455–8362 in winter* ⊕ *www.northstargolf.com*) is on the Old Steese Highway, 0.7 mi past Chena Hot Springs Road. It is the northernmost course in the United States and perhaps the only one where you are encouraged to mark your scorecard with a tally of the wildlife you see.

HIKING

Creamer's Field Migratory Waterfowl Refuge (⇨ *Exploring Fairbanks*) has three nature trails within its 1,800 acres on the edge of Fairbanks. The longest trail is 2 mi, and one is wheelchair accessible.

SKIING

CROSS-COUNTRY The Interior has some of the best weather and terrain in the nation for cross-country skiing, especially in late fall and early spring. Among the developed trails in the Fairbanks area, the ones at the **Birch Hill Recreation Area,** on the city's north side, and the **University of Alaska Fairbanks** are lighted to extend their use into winter nights. Cross-country ski racing is a staple at several courses on winter weekends. The season stretches from October to late March or early April. Other developed trails can be found at **Chena Hot Springs Resort, White Mountains National Recreation Area,** the **Chena Lakes Recreation Area,** and the **Two Rivers Recreation Area.** For more information, check with the **Alaska Public Lands Information Center** (☎907/456–0527).

DOWNHILL **Birch Hill** (☎907/353–7053), in Ft. Wainwright, has a chairlift and beginner and intermediate runs; it's open November through April, Thursday through Sunday. **Mt. Aurora/Skiland** (☎907/389–2314 ⊕*www.skiland.org*), on the Steese Highway about 20 mi from Fairbanks at Cleary Summit, has a chairlift, more than 20 runs ranked intermediate to expert, and a 1,100-foot vertical drop. There's lodging in an old gold-camp bunkhouse and aurora viewing. It's open weekends from December to mid-April. **Moose Mountain** (☎907/479–4732, 907/459–8132 *for ski report* ⊕*www.shredthemoose.com*), off Murphy Dome Road, has 42 runs from two summits for all skiing levels, all accessed by a bus lift system; it's open November through April, Friday through Sunday, plus school and government holidays.

WHERE TO EAT

¢ CAFÉ ✕ **Alaska Coffee Roasting Company.** Fuel up with the university folk, where green coffee beans from around the world are roasted and blended. The scratch kitchen also offers flat bread, perfect for one or two, and pastries and desserts like tiramisu, scones, and cheesecake. With its inviting hardwood floors, wood oven, and tasteful artwork, this hangout is so popular that a line often curls out the door. ⊠ *4001 Geist Rd., Suite 2, University West* ☎907/457–5282 ⊕*www.alaskacoffeeroasting.com* ▭*AE, D, MC, V.*

$$$$ SEAFOOD ★ ✕ **Alaska Salmon Bake.** Salmon cooked over an open fire with a lemon-and-brown-sugar sauce is a favorite at this indoor-outdoor restaurant in Pioneer Park's Mining Valley. Halibut, cod, prime rib, a salad bar, and dessert are also for eating at the all-you-can-eat dinner. ⊠*Airport Way and Peger Rd., Pioneer Park* ☎907/452–7274 *or* 800/354–7274 ⊕*www.akvisit.com/salmon.html* ▭MC, V ⊗ *No lunch mid-May–mid-Sept.*

$–$$$ AMERICAN ★ ✕**Cookie Jar.** Tucked away in a nondescript neighborhood on a street not found on most Fairbanks maps, this restaurant is worth tracking down. The open space features lots of cookie jars, along with plants and artwork. Spanning breakfast, lunch, and dinner, the huge menu includes scads of homemade items, an extensive kids' menu, and vegetarian selections. Entrées range from steak and shrimp to coq au vin. For dessert, try the homemade tortes or cookies to match anything your grandma ever baked. Weekend breakfasts are especially popular, so allow extra time. Take Danby Street off the Johansen Expressway; the restaurant is behind Aurora Motors. ⊠*1006 Cadillac Ct., Aurora* ☎*907/479–8319* ⊟*AE, D, MC, V.*

$–$$$
ITALIAN
★

✕**Gambardella's Pasta Bella.** Locals crowd the family-run Italian restaurant, which has earned a reputation as one of the best restaurants in town. The menu includes salads, pasta, pizza, vegetarian entrées, and submarine sandwiches on homemade bread. Its specialties are lasagna, which the *Seattle Times* aptly described as "the mother of all lasagnas," the seafood *fra diavolo,* and the tiramisu. The two-story restaurant has outdoor seating on a balcony and at street level. It feels as close to a romantic back-alley restaurant in Italy as you can get in Interior Alaska. ⊠*706 2nd Ave., Downtown* ☎*907/456–3417* ⊟*AE, MC, V* ⊗*No lunch Sun.*

$$–$$$$
ITALIAN

✕**Geraldo's.** The sign outside will likely contain a plug for the virtues of garlic. Rightly so, for no one in Fairbanks puts fresh chopped garlic to better use than Geraldo's, which has gourmet pizza, seafood, pasta, and veal dishes. A painting of Don Corleone hangs on the wall, and Frank Sinatra and Dean Martin provide background music for this cozy and often crowded spot. ⊠*701 College Rd., Lemeta* ☎*907/452–2299* ⊟*AE, MC, V.*

$–$$$$
AMERICAN

✕**Ivory Jack's.** Jack "Ivory" O'Brien used to deal Alaskan ivory and whalebone out of this small restaurant tucked into the gold-rich hills of the Goldstream Valley on the outskirts of Fairbanks. Crab-stuffed mushrooms are a specialty of this large, open, and airy bar-restaurant. You can choose from more than 15 appetizers as well as burgers, pizza, and entrées such as halibut Dijon and Alaskan king crab. You'll catch live, local music on some weekends; the cover charge depends on the band. ⊠*2581 Goldstream Rd., Goldstream* ☎*907/455–6666* ⊟*AE, D, DC, MC, V.*

$$–$$$$
AMERICAN

✕**Lavelle's.** With offerings ranging from rack of lamb and lobster cakes to halibut and New York steaks, this impressive restaurant has won a loyal local following. Lavelle's features an extensive 3,000-bottle wine cellar, and holds regular wine tastings and other events that give the restaurant sophistication far removed from the frontier image cultivated elsewhere in Fairbanks. This is one of the few places where Fairbanksans dress up for dinner. ⊠*SpringHill Suites, 575 1st Ave., Downtown* ☎*907/450–0555* ⊟*AE, D, DC, MC, V* ⊗*No lunch.*

$$$–$$$$
AMERICAN
★

✕**Pike's Landing.** Enjoy lunch on a huge outside deck (it seats 420) overlooking the Chena River, or inside in the elegant dining room of an extended log cabin. The meals cost up to $40 for steak and lobster and rank with the best in the Interior. For a dinner in the $10 range, relax in the sports bar and catch a view of the river. The palate-pleasing Sunday brunch has an irresistible dessert table. ⊠*4438 Airport Way, near airport* ☎*907/479–7113* ⊟*AE, D, DC, MC, V.*

$$–$$$$
AMERICAN
★

✕**Pump House Restaurant.** Alongside the Chena River, this mining pump station–turned–restaurant claims it's the northernmost oyster bar in the world, and also turns out house specialties such as Alaskan wild-game

7

stew and seafood chowder. Listed on the National Register of Historic Places, this pump house, circa 1930s, now houses and utilizes antiques up to 150 years old. The furnishings and floor are made of rich, polished wood, the pool table dates from 1898, and an Alaskan grizzly bear in a glass case is on sentry next to the hostess station. Wednesday night is karaoke night in the bar. In summer, enjoy the midnight sun on the deck out back by the Chena River. ⊠ *Mi 2, Chena Pump Rd.* ☎ *907/479–8452* ⊟ *AE, D, MC, V* ⊘ *No lunch mid-Sept.–June 1.*

$-$$
AMERICAN
★
✕ **Sam's Sourdough Cafe.** Although Sam's serves meals all day, Fairbanksans know it as the best breakfast place in town. Sourdough recipes are a kind of minor religion in Alaska, and Sam's serves an extensive menu of sourdough specialties, including hotcakes and French toast, as well as standard meat-and-eggs items, all at reasonable prices. On weekends get here early or be prepared for a wait. The address is Cameron Street, but it's really fronted on University, just over the railroad tracks. ⊠ *3702 Cameron St., College* ☎ *907/479–0523* ⊟ *MC, V.*

¢-$$$
AMERICAN
✕ **Silver Gulch Brewing and Bottling Co.** You'll find some unique souvenirs and an interesting collection of Fairbanks citizens at North America's northernmost brewery. Founded in 1998, Silver Gulch is probably best known for its pilsner. Fairbanks and Anchorage are the major markets, but a few spots on the Kenai carry Silver Gulch as well. The brewery is in the Fox Roadhouse building. A preserved section of the old roadhouse's exterior still stands in the second floor of the restaurant. The rest of the original building is around to the right and through the side door of the main entrance. This hot spot is 10 mi north of Fairbanks on the Old Steese Highway. After your brewery tour, satisfy your hunger with I.P.A.-battered fish-and-chips or cedar-plank roasted salmon with hazelnut hollandaise. ⊠ *2195 Old Steese Hwy., Fox* ☎ *907/452– 2739* ⊕ *www.silvergulch.com* ⚲ *Free tours and beer tastings Fri. 5–7 pm or by appointment* ⊟ *AE, MC, V* ⊘ *No lunch weekdays.*

¢-$
THAI
★
✕ **Thai House.** Fairbanks is not known for a wide selection of international cuisine, but Thai food is an exception, and the Thai House is among the best of the bunch. The prices are astounding, the staff dress in elaborate Thai silks, and the atmosphere is elegant with hardwood floors and Thai decor on the walls. The restaurant has a loyal following because the food is authentic. ⊠ *412 5th Ave., Downtown* ☎ *907/452– 6123* ⊟ *MC, V.*

$$$-$$$$
AMERICAN
✕ **Turtle Club.** Don't go to this windowless and nondescript dining room expecting great variety. Do go if you are hungry for prime rib, lobster, or king crab and have a big appetite. There's a good salad bar, the service is prompt, and every order comes with homemade bread. The "Turtle Cut" serving of prime rib, advertised as a "medium portion," weighs a pound. Many of the patrons make this a regular stop. It's worth the 10-mi drive north of Fairbanks. ⊠ *Mi 10, Old Steese Hwy., Fox* ☎ *907/457–3883* ⊟ *AE, D, MC, V.*

WHERE TO STAY

$$–$$$ ⊡ **All Seasons Bed and Breakfast Inn.** In a quiet residential neighborhood within walking distance of downtown, this nicely furnished inn provides relaxation and privacy. With only eight rooms, this small B&B emphasizes hospitality, a trademark of owner Mary Richard's Southern roots. Breakfast in the dining room may feature apple pancakes, quiche, egg puffs, or lighter selections. Her recipes frequent a column in the Food Section of the *Fairbanks Daily News–Miner*. **Pros:** Close to downtown, clean rooms, sunroom. **Cons:** No elevator, lacks an Alaskan ambience. ⊠ *763 7th Ave., Downtown* ☎ *907/451–6649* ⊕ *www. allseasonsinn.com* ⬎ *8 rooms* ♿ *In-hotel: no elevator, laundry facilities, public Internet, public Wi-Fi, no-smoking rooms* ═ *AE, D, DC, MC, V* ⦿|*BP*.

$$$ ⊡ **A Taste of Alaska Lodge.** The Eberhardt family's lodge is just 20 minutes from Fairbanks, yet far enough away to make you feel like you're on a wilderness retreat. On 280 acres of fields and forested woodlands, the lodge has great views of the Alaska Range to the south. In winter you can see the northern lights. Stay in a remote cabin, a two-story log home, or the main lodge. The rooms are decorated with collectibles, and the resort owners strive to create the friendly atmosphere of an old-time roadhouse—and succeed. Breakfast is served at 8 AM sharp. **Pros:** Great view, eclectic collections, quiet location. **Cons:** Not close to town, no elevator. ⊠ *551 Eberhardt Rd., Two Rivers* ☎ *907/488–7855* ⊕ *www.atasteofalaska.com* ⬎ *8 rooms in lodge, 2 in log house, 1 in annex* ♿ *In-room: kitchen (some), DVD (some), VCR (some), Wi-Fi. In-hotel: no elevator, public Wi-Fi* ═ *AE, MC, V* ⦿|*BP*.

$$ ⊡ **Aurora Express.** It's off the beaten path, but this bed-and-breakfast is unforgettable, especially for railroad buffs. The private rooms with Victorian furnishings are in four renovated historic cars of the Alaska Railroad, parked on 700 feet of transplanted railroad tracks. The hillside setting offers panoramic views of the area. **Pros:** Most unique lodging in the area, sweeping views of the valley. **Cons:** Far from town, no phone or TV in some rooms. ⊠ *1540 Chena Ridge* ☎ *907/474–0949 or 800/221–0073* ⊕ *www.fairbanksalaskabedandbreakfast.com* ⬎ *7 rooms* ♿ *In-room: no phone (some), no TV (some). In-hotel: no-smoking rooms* ═ *MC, V* ⊘ *Closed early Sept.– end of May* ⦿|*BP*.

$$ ⊡ **Bridgewater Hotel.** In the heart of downtown Fairbanks, just above the Chena River, this hotel has gone through a number of incarnations and is now a thoroughly modern, European-style hotel. Its location is convenient to shops and restaurants. Flowers overflow the hanging baskets and wicker furniture adorns the light and airy lobby. The restaurant serves breakfast only. Glimpse the past through poster-size historical photos adorning the walls. **Pros:** Good location, dedicated staff, downtown hotel with the most character. **Cons:** Small and modest rooms, no kitchen or refrigerators. ⊠ *723 1st Ave., Downtown* ☎ *907/452–6661 or 800/528–4916* ⊕ *www.fountainheadhotels.com/ bridgewater/bridgewater.htm* ⬎ *94 rooms* ♿ *In-room: Wi-Fi. In-hotel: restaurant, laundry service, public Wi-Fi, airport shuttle, no-smoking rooms* ═ *AE, D, DC, MC, V* ⊘ *Closed mid-Sept.–mid-May* ⦿|*CP*.

7

$$$ ☎**Comfort Inn–Chena River.** Situated near the banks of the Chena River, directly across the water from Pioneer Park, this hotel has a great vantage point. With all the comforts of a modern hotel, this rest stop's location offers a woodsy feel in the midst of a city. Families will enjoy the moderate-size pool and the continental breakfasts. **Pros:** Surrounded by woods, the lounge is equipped with a cozy fireplace. **Cons:** Not within easy walking distance to most attractions, the rooms have a chain-hotel feeling. ✉*1908 Chena Landings Loop, Railroad Industrial Area* ☎*907/479–8080 or 800/228–5150* ⊕*www.choicehotels. com* ⌨*74 rooms* &*In-room: refrigerator, Wi-Fi. In-hotel: pool, public Wi-Fi, airport shuttle, some pets allowed, no-smoking rooms* ▭*AE, D, DC, MC, V* ¶⊙*CP.*

$$$ ☎**Fairbanks Princess Riverside Lodge.** An expansive wooden deck facing the Chena River draws a crowd at this luxury lodge in summer. Gold, russet, green, and burgundy accents warm the rustic decor. You can stop by the tour desk to book additional excursions around Fairbanks. The Edgewater Restaurant welcomes diners in suits and dresses or duct-tape-patched Carhartt's work clothes, and there's a daily breakfast buffet during the high season. The lodge is just off the road to Fairbanks International Airport. **Pros:** Grandiose halls and lounge, next to the Chena River, large gym to work off the steam. **Cons:** Caters to large tours, basic rooms lack refrigerators or kitchenettes. ✉*4477 Pikes Landing Rd., near airport* ☎*907/455–4477 or 800/426–0500* ⊕*www. princesslodges.com/fairbanks_lodge.cfm* ⌨*326 rooms* & *In-hotel: 2 restaurants, bar, gym, laundry facilities, public Wi-Fi, airport shuttle, no-smoking rooms* ▭*AE, D, DC, MC, V.*

$$–$$$$ ☎**Minnie Street Bed & Breakfast Inn.** Martha Stewart would approve of this B&B. With many room options, there's a choice for every traveler's needs. The classy rooms come equipped with fluffy bathrobes and makeup mirrors, for when you return from your massage or get out of the Jacuzzi. The location is central, and the breakfast is excellent. Sip your coffee on the deck that adjoins all four houses and enjoy the flowers. **Pros:** Luxurious decor, massage and Jacuzzi available, variety of room styles. **Cons:** Not directly downtown, no elevator. ✉*345 Minnie St., Downtown* ☎*907/456–1802 or 888/456–1849* ⊕*www.minniestreetbandb.com* ⌨*12 rooms, 3 suites, 1 stand-alone house* &*In-room: kitchen (some), refrigerator (some), DVD (some), VCR (some), Wi-Fi. In-hotel: spa, no elevator, laundry facilities* ▭*AE, D, MC, V* ¶⊙*BP.*

$$$ ☎**Pike's Waterfront Lodge.** Log columns and beams support the high-ceiling lobby of this hotel and conference center on the banks of the Chena River. The grounds are strewn with more than 20,000 flowering plants, and a 0.5-mi river walk borders the property. Other new innovations on the property include solar panels and a greenhouse that university students tend. Chefs sprinkle these locally grown herbs over dinner, while the produce is donated to the food bank. There are several warm and cozy common areas, including a piano room and a fireplace lounge, and in summer an ice-cream parlor operates on the premises. Upon request, riverfront rooms for an extra $10 offer scenic views. If you're looking for a more Alaskan experience, try one of the 28 rustic log cabins. **Pros:** Located on the banks of the Chena River; Pike's Land-

ing next door is a hot spot; close to the airport. **Cons:** Small gym, cabins are a walk from the restaurant. ⊠*1850 Hoselton Rd., near airport* ☎ *907/456–4500 or 877/774–2400* ⊕*www.pikeslodge.com* ⇆*180 rooms, 28 cabins* ⚲*In-room: refrigerator, Wi-Fi. In-hotel: restaurant, bar, gym, laundry facilities, concierge, public Wi-Fi, airport shuttle, no-smoking rooms* ⊟*AE, D, MC, V* ⋈*CP.*

$$$–$$$$ ⛺**River's Edge Resort.** If you want the privacy of a cottage, a bit of elbow room, and the amenities of a luxury hotel, you can find it along the banks of the Chena River at the River's Edge Resort. The individual cottages have patios or garden spaces, many fronting the river and surrounded by beautifully landscaped grounds. On summer evenings you can sit outside and watch canoes, rafts, and powerboats pass by. Chena's Restaurant serves breakfast, lunch, and dinner at the lodge, which has a banquet hall, meeting rooms, and executive suites. **Pros:** Prime location along the Chena River, private cabins. **Cons:** No kitchenettes, not within walking distance of nearby shops or restaurants. ⊠*4200 Boat St., University West* ☎*907/474–0286 or 800/770–3343* ⊕*www. riversedge.net* ⇆*94 cottages* ⚲*In room: Wi-Fi. In-hotel: restaurant, no elevator, laundry facilities, public Wi-Fi, airport shuttle* ⊟*AE, D, MC, V* ⊘*Closed mid-Sept.–mid-May.*

$$$$ ⛺**Sophie Station Hotel.** Its quiet location and helpful staff make this spa-
★ cious hotel near the airport one of Fairbanks's best. It has comfy furniture, rich upholstery, and Alaskan artwork throughout. Don't feel like dining out? These suites include full-size ranges and refrigerators. Or you can try a buffalo burger at Zach's, the hotel restaurant, which serves breakfast, lunch, and dinner. **Pros:** Complimentary newspaper upon arrival, separated rooms, walking distance to two grocery stores, equipped with full kitchens. **Cons:** Average interior decor, no DVD or VCR. ⊠*1717 University Ave., near airport* ☎*907/479–3650 or 800/528–4916* ⊕*www.fountainheadhotels.com* ⇆*149 suites* ⚲*In-room: kitchen, refrigerator, Wi-Fi. In-hotel: restaurant, bar, gym, public Wi-Fi, airport shuttle, no-smoking rooms* ⊟*AE, D, DC, MC, V.*

$$$ ⛺**SpringHill Suites by Marriott.** At the center of what was once the heart of the commercial district, the SpringHill Suites has 140 comfortable suites, each with a microwave, refrigerator, living-room furniture, and well-lighted work areas. The continental breakfast by the fireplace next to the lobby is a cut above standard fare, not to mention the restaurant, **Lavelle's.** Ask for a room facing the river, the scenic side of the hotel. **Pros:** Comfortable work areas within the rooms, a pool to relax in, home to one of Fairbanks's favorite restaurants. **Cons:** Small lounge, no DVD or VCR, moderate-size gym. ⊠*575 1st Ave., Downtown* ☎*907/451–6552 or 877/729–0197* ⊕*www.springhillsuites.com* ⇆*140 suites* ⚲*In-room: refrigerator, Ethernet, Wi-Fi. In-hotel: restaurant, pool, gym, public Wi-Fi, airport shuttle* ⊟*AE, D, DC, MC, V* ⋈*CP.*

$$$ ⛺**Wedgewood Resort.** Both wild and cultivated flowers adorn the land-
Fodor'sChoice scaped grounds of the Wedgewood Resort, which borders on Creamer's
★ Field Migratory Waterfowl Refuge. Headquartered on the resort is the Alaska Bird Observatory, a local nonprofit that researches and promotes the conservation of Alaska's birds. You'll also find a replica of a

COME WINTER

The temperature gets down to 40 below zero every winter in Fairbanks, but school is never canceled, no matter how cold it gets. In recent years, in fact, the only times schools have closed were when some rare winter warm spells created icy conditions on the roads that made it too hazardous for bus travel. Young Alaskans are so hardy that outdoor recess takes place down to 20 below zero.

The weather is a great unifying factor among Fairbanks residents.

Winter conditions freeze the pipes of university presidents as well as laborers. After a night of 40 below, it's common to see cars bumping along as if the tires were flat; the bottoms of the tires freeze flat, and it takes a quarter mile or so before they warm up and return to round. Every car has an electric plug hanging out front between the headlights because they need to be plugged in during winter to keep running.

miner's cabin, a bush plane, courtyards, and gazebos. Evenings feature free sled-dog presentations from Iditarod musher Ken Anderson, and Alaska movies. All rooms are suites with full kitchens. The Bear Lodge hotel—also part of the resort—has 157 large rooms available in summer. Shuttles go to downtown Fairbanks and local shopping spots. **Pros:** Courteous staff, 2 mi of trails through 76 acres of wildlife sanctuary, antique automobile museum, elegant banquet halls. **Cons:** Outdated rooms, although changes are on the way; no gym. ⊠ *212 Wedgewood Dr.* ☎ *907/456–3642 or 800/528–4916* ⊕ *www.fountainheadhotels.com* ⌖ *297 suites* ⌂ *In-room: kitchen, refrigerator, Wi-Fi. In-hotel: 2 restaurants, bar, laundry service, public Wi-Fi, airport shuttle, no-smoking rooms* ⊟ *AE, D, DC, MC, V.*

$$$ 🌐 **Westmark Fairbanks Hotel and Conference Center.** Built on a courtyard on a quiet street, this full-service and recently expanded complex is within easy walking distance of downtown. The decor leans toward modern and professional. All of the rose-and-burgundy rooms have a writing desk, but if access to the Internet is important, be sure to request a room in the North Tower. The Red Lantern Steak & Spirits restaurant serves steaks and seafood, and the Northern Latitudes room offers a buffet. **Pros:** On the outskirts of downtown, decent rooms without an overdose of "Alaskana." **Cons:** Modern and corporate ambience that does not feel intimate, no spa. ⊠ *813 Noble St., Downtown* ☎ *907/456–7722 or 800/544–0970* ⊕ *www.westmarkhotels.com* ⌖ *400 rooms* ⌂ *In-room: Wi-Fi (some). In-hotel: restaurant, bar, gym, laundry service, airport shuttle, no-smoking rooms* ⊟ *AE, D, DC, MC, V.*

NIGHTLIFE & THE ARTS

Check the "Kaleidoscope" section in the Thursday *Fairbanks Daily News–Miner* for current nightspots, plays, concerts, and art shows.

THE ARTS

FESTIVALS **Golden Days** (☎907/452–1105 ⊕*www.fairbankschamber.org*) is the annual celebration of Fairbanks's gold-rush past. Several days of events are capped by a big parade through the city in late July. **Tanana Valley State Fair** (✉*1800 College Rd., Aurora* ⊕*www.tananavalleyfair.org*) is Interior Alaska's largest annual gathering. It fills a week in early August with attractions such as giant vegetables and the handiwork of local artisans.

Winter is a festive time in Fairbanks, especially between February and March. The mid-February Yukon Quest (☎907/452–7954 ⊕*www.yukonquest.com*) calls itself the "toughest dogsled race in the world," passing through historical early-gold-rush territory. In odd-numbered years the 1,000-mi race starts in Whitehorse and in even-numbered years it starts in Fairbanks. The **World Ice Art Championships** (☎907/451–8250 ⊕*www.icealaska.com*) in late February to late March draw ice artists from around the world for an international ice-sculpting competition. Mid-March brings out a festival goofy enough to cure any case of cabin fever: Chatanika Days (☎907/389–2164) feature outhouse races and a snowmachine tug-of-war.

NIGHTLIFE

SALOONS The **Blue Loon** (✉ *Mi 353.5, Parks Hwy.* ☎907/457–5666 ⊕*www.theblueloon.com*), between Ester and Fairbanks, presents year-round entertainment and great grill food. Movies are nightly at 5:30 and 8. Catch national touring bands, comedy, outdoor summer concerts, DJ dancing late nights on weekends, and much more, including free wireless. The **Howling Dog Saloon** (✉*Mi 11, Old Steese Hwy.* ☎907/456–4695 ⊕*www.howlingdogsaloon.com* ☉*Closed Nov.–Mar.*) has live music, specializing in blues and rock and roll; bar food; a beer, wine, and liquor menu; and gobs of atmosphere. The clientele is a mix of college students, airline pilots, tourists, miners, and bikers. Out back, there are a volleyball court, horseshoe pit, and 10 rustic cabins for rent.

★ Don't be alarmed by the exterior of the **Midnight Mine** (✉*308 Wendell St.* ☎907/456–5348). It's a friendly neighborhood bar with darts, foosball, a pool, and a big-screen TV, and it's within walking distance of downtown. Sam the dog is likely to

ALL THAT JAZZ

Alaska's premier cultural gathering, the **Fairbanks Summer Arts Festival** (☎*907/474–8869* ⊕*www.fsaf.org*) takes place over two weeks in late July. It grew from a small jazz festival to a major University of Alaska–affiliated event attracting students and instructors worldwide. The festival presents music, dance, theater, opera, storytelling, creative writing, healing arts, visual arts, and ice-skating instruction. Visitors are encouraged to participate in one-week classes.

CLOSE UP

Celestial Rays of Light: Aurora Borealis

The light show often begins simply, as a pale yellow-green luminous band that arches across Alaska's night sky. Sometimes the band will quickly fade and disappear. Other nights, however, it may begin to waver, flicker, and pulsate. Or the quiescent band may explode and fill the sky with curtains of celestial light that ripple wildly above the northern landscape. Growing more intense, these dancing lights take on other colors: pink, red, blue, or purple. At times they appear to be heavenly flames, leaping across the sky, or perhaps they're exploding fireworks, or cannon fire.

The Fairbanks area is one of the best places in the world to see the aurora borealis—commonly called the northern lights. Here they may appear more than 200 nights per year; they're much less common in Anchorage, partly because of urban glare.

As you watch these dazzling lights spreading from horizon to horizon, it is easy to imagine why many northern cultures, including Alaska's native peoples, created myths to explain auroral displays. What start out as patches, arcs, or bands can be magically transformed into vaporous, human-like figures. Some of Alaska's native groups have traditionally believed the lights to be spirits of their ancestors. According to one belief, the spirits are celebrating with dance and drumming; another says they're playing games. Yet another tradition says the lights are torches, carried by spirits who lead the souls of recently deceased people to life in the "afterworld."

During Alaska's gold-rush era some nonnative stampeders supposed the aurora to be reflections of ore deposits. Even renowned wilderness explorer John Muir allowed the northern lights to spark his imagination.

Once while traveling through Southeast Alaska in 1890, Muir stayed up all night to watch a gigantic, glowing auroral bridge and bands of "restless electric auroral fairies" who danced to music "too fine for mortal ears."

Scientists have a more technical explanation for these heavenly apparitions. The aurora borealis is an atmospheric phenomenon that's tied to explosive events on the sun's surface, known as solar flares. Those flares produce a stream of charged particles, the "solar wind," which shoots off into space. When such a wind intersects with Earth's magnetic field, most of the particles are deflected; some, however, are sent into the upper atmosphere where they collide with gas molecules such as nitrogen and oxygen. The resulting reactions produce glowing colors. The aurora is most commonly a pale yellowish green, but its borders are sometimes tinged with pink, purple, or blue. Especially rare is the all-red aurora, which appears when charged solar particles collide with oxygen molecules from 50 to 200 mi above Earth's surface.

■ TIP➜ Alaska's long hours of daylight hide the aurora in summer, so the best viewing is from September through March. Scientists at the University of Alaska Geophysical Institute give a daily forecast from late fall to spring of when the lights will be the most intense at ⊕ *www.gedds.alaska.edu/auroraforecast* and in the *Fairbanks Daily News–Miner.*

WHERE AND HOW TO SEE THE NORTHERN LIGHTS

The **Aurora Borealis Lodge** (⊠ *Mi 20.5, Steese Hwy., Cleary Summit* ☎ *907/389–2812* ⊕ *www.auroracabin.com*) has late-night tours to a log lodge on Cleary Summit, with big picture windows to see the sky. The $65 tour includes hot drinks and transportation from Fairbanks. With independent transportation, admission is $20 per person. Four spacious rooms in two-story building are also available, each with large, north-facing windows, private baths, and kitchens. Call for availability of rooms in summer and for aurora tours. Depending on snow conditions, give a snowshoe tour a shot.

About 60 mi northeast of Fairbanks, the **Chena Hot Springs Resort** (⊠ *End of Chena Hot Springs Rd., Chena Hot Springs* ☎ *907/451–8104*) treats guests to a Sno-Cat ride to a yurt with a 360-degree panoramic vista of nothing but wilderness.

Visitors fill the two warm mountaintop lodges at **Mount Aurora Skiland** (⊠ *Mi 20.5, Steese Hwy., Cleary Summit* ☎ *907/389–2314* ⊕ *www.skiland. org*) after 10 PM on winter nights. Images from an aurora Web cam are shown on a large-screen TV. Admission is $25 and includes hot drinks.

Northern Alaska Tour Company (☎ *907/474–8600 or 800/474–1986* ⊕ *www.northernalaska.com*) has a variety of single or multiday winter aurora tours going north to the Arctic Circle and the Brooks Range.

greet you as you come in—be sure to ask to see her trick. It'll cost you a buck, but it's worth it.

The *Golden Heart Revue* ($18) at the **Palace Theatre and Saloon** (✉ *Pioneer Park, Airport Way and Peger Rd.* ☎ *907/456–5960 or 800/354–7274* ⊕ *www.akvisit.com*) is a musical-comedy show about the founding and building of Fairbanks. It begins at 8:15 nightly.

The **Senator's Saloon** (✉ *Mi 2.0, Chena Pump Rd.* ☎ *907/479–8452*) at the Pump House Restaurant is the place to hear easy-listening music alongside the Chena River on a warm summer evening.

SQUARE The square-dancing clubs in Fairbanks, North Pole, Delta Junction,
DANCING and Tok are all affiliated with the **Northern Lights Council of Dancers** (☎ *907/452–5699* ⊕ *www.fairnet.org/agencies/dancealaska/phpbb/portal.php*) and hold frequent dances.

SHOPPING

CRAFTS

Known for handwoven rugs, the **Alaska Rag Company** (✉ *603 Lacey St., Downtown* ☎ *907/451–4401* ⊕ *www.alaskaragco.com*) carries the work of many local artists. **The Artworks** (✉ *3677 College Rd., No. 3, College* ☎ *907/479–2563*) is known for high-quality fine art and crafts. **Beads and Things** (✉ *537 2nd Ave., Downtown* ☎ *907/456–2323*) sells native handicrafts from around the state. The **Great Alaskan Bowl Company** (✉ *4630 Old Airport Rd.* ☎ *907/474–9663* ⊕ *www.woodbowl.com*) sells lathe-turned bowls made out of Alaskan birch.

If Only . . . A Fine Store (✉ *215 Cushman St., Downtown* ☎ *907/457–6659*) carries a wide range of unique Alaska items. **New Horizons Gallery** (✉ *519 1st Ave., Downtown* ☎ *907/456–2063* ⊕ *www.newhorizonsgallery.com*) is one of Alaska's largest art galleries. **A Weaver's Yarn** (✉ *1810 Alaska Way, College* ☎ *907/374–1995*) has musk-ox qiviut to spin.

JEWELRY

In her small, eponymous shop **Judie Gumm Designs** (✉ *3600 Main St., Ester* ☎ *907/479–4568* ⊕ *www.judiegumm.com*), Ms. Gumm fashions stunning (and moderately priced) silver and gold designs best described as sculptural interpretations of northern images. Ester is 6 mi south of Fairbanks off the George Parks Highway.

Larson's Fine Jewelers (✉ *405 Noble St., Downtown* ☎ *907/456–4141*) has been making Alaskan gold-nugget jewelry and other contemporary designs for six decades. **Taylor's Gold-N-Stones** (✉ *3578-N Airport Way, University Avenue* ☎ *907/456–8369 or 800/306–3589*) uses gemstones mined in Alaska and creates unique gold designs.

OUTERWEAR & OUTDOOR GEAR

Apocalypse Design (✉*201 Minnie St.* ☎*907/451–7555 or 866/451–7555* ⊕*www.akgear.com*) makes its own specialized cold-weather clothing for dog mushers and other winter adventurers. Travelers from colder areas of the Lower 48 will appreciate the double-layer fleece mittens, among other items. **Beaver Sports** (✉*3480 College Rd., College* ☎*907/479-2494* ⊕*www.beaversports.com*) is equipped with a fine selection of quality backpacking, biking, paddling, and skiing gear; a big part of Beaver Sports is community involvement, from supporting high school sports teams to facilitating midnight sun runs.

SPORTS

BASEBALL

★ Scores of baseball players, including Tom Seaver, Dave Winfield, and Jason Giambi, have passed through Fairbanks on their way to the major leagues. The Interior is home to the **Alaska Goldpanners** (☎*907/451-0095* ⊕*www.goldpanners.com*), a member of the Alaska Baseball League, a string of amateur baseball organizations throughout the state. Players are recruited from college teams nationwide, and the summer season (mid-June–late July) generates top-caliber competition. Home games are played at Growden Field, along Lower 2nd Avenue at Wilbur Street, not far from Pioneer Park. The baseball park hosts the **Midnight Sun Baseball Game,** a Fairbanks tradition in which the Goldpanners play baseball at midnight of the summer solstice without benefit of artificial lights. This is thrilling (and possibly chilly) to watch on a clear, sunny night when the daylight never ends.

CURLING

Hundreds of Fairbanksans participate each year in curling, a game in which people with brooms play a giant version of shuffleboard on ice. Curlers have an almost fanatical devotion to their sport, and they're eager to explain its finer points to the uninitiated. The **Fairbanks Curling Club** (✉*1962 2nd Ave.* ☎*907/452-2875* ⊕*www.curlfairbanks.org*) hosts an annual international *bonspiel* (match) on the first weekend of April. The club season runs from early October through the middle of April.

RIVERBOAT RACING

Another summer highlight is riverboat racing sanctioned by the **Fairbanks Outboard Association** (☎*907/452-5377* ⊕*www.yukon800.com*). These specially built 24-foot racing boats are powered by 50-horsepower engines and reach speeds of 75 mph. Weekend races in summer and fall begin and end either at the Pump House Restaurant or at Pike's Landing, just off Airport Way near Fairbanks International Airport. The season's big event in late June is the **Yukon 800 Marathon,** a two-day, 800-mi race between Fairbanks and Galena by way of the Chena, Tanana, and Yukon rivers.

The **Roland Lord Memorial Race,** from Fairbanks to Nenana and back, is held in early August; the **Tanana 440** is held in late July.

7

NORTH OF FAIRBANKS

When you drive north of Fairbanks you enter territory where people are few and far between. Away from the highways spread hundreds of thousands of square miles with few signs of human habitation. Thus, driving in the north-country involves both nail-biting and jaw-dropping experiences. You may spot caribou, view spectacular scenery, and meet Alaskan characters along the way.

On the roads heading east, northeast, and northwest of Fairbanks, the going gets tougher the farther you drive. However, the gravel and other assorted surfaces are worth the trouble of navigating; these roads open up long slivers of the Alaskan wilderness. And since Alaska is so big, the more country you cover, the better your understanding of the place—and the better your chances of understanding the history of each unique road from the stories shared by the people you meet. ■ TIP➜ Road conditions can be rough, and if you break down, help may be a long way off, so be sure to check your fuel and spare tire before you go.

Follow the Chena Hot Springs Road to its end and you'll find a natural hot spring that is among the best in the state. The Steese Highway connects to historic goldfields in Central and Circle, while the Elliott Highway leads northwest and, before shifting to the southwest, connects to the roughly north–south Dalton Highway (built to assist construction of the trans-Alaska pipeline). All three roads give access to countless starting points for hiking, skiing, camping, fishing, canoeing, and other outdoor-oriented adventures.

CHENA HOT SPRINGS

62 mi northeast of Fairbanks.

The 57-mi paved Chena Hot Springs Road, which starts 5 mi outside Fairbanks, leads to Chena Hot Springs, a favorite playground of many Fairbanks residents. The road passes several attractions, including Chena River State Recreation Area and Chena Hot Springs Resort. If you're heading to the resort, don't skip the hiking, fishing, camping, and canoeing along the way. ■ TIP➜ The chances of spotting a moose are excellent if you keep a sharp eye on the roadside.

From Mile 26 to Mile 51, the road passes through the **Chena River State Recreation Area,** a diverse facility of nearly 400 square mi. You can also stop for a picnic, take a hike for an hour or an extended backpacking trip, fish for the beautiful yet gullible arctic grayling, or rent a rustic backcountry cabin and savor a truly wild Alaskan adventure. Grayling fishing in the Chena River is catch-and-release, single-hook, artificial lure only. There are several stocked lakes along the road affording catch-and-keep fishing for rainbow trout, which are well suited for the frying pan.

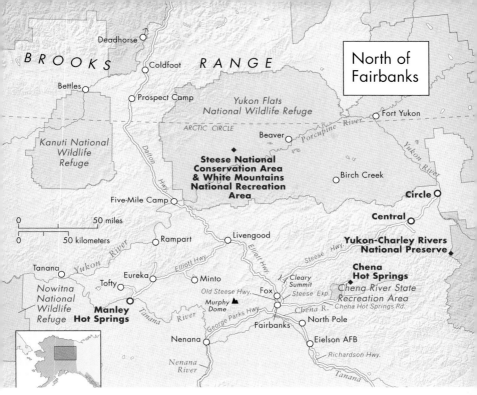

OUTDOOR ACTIVITIES & GUIDED TOURS

DOGSLEDDING **Chena Dog Sled Adventures** (⊠ *Mi 24, Chena Hot Springs Rd., Two Rivers* ☎ *907/488–5845* ⊕ *www.ptialaska.net/~sleddogs*) provides winter visitors a chance to drive a dog team or ride in a sled. Ice fishing and snowshoeing are also available.

HIKING **Granite Tors Trail,** a 15-mi loop, can be done in a day and offers a view of the upper Chena Valley and an opportunity to see dramatic "tors" (fingers of rock protruding through grassy meadow) which are reminiscent of the *maoi* monuments of Easter Island. The trail is steep, but the views at the top are worth it. Although the Interior landscapes lack the impressive mountain views of other parts of the state, the enormous expanse of rolling hills and seemingly endless tracts of forest are every bit as awe-inspiring. However, since there are no mountains here to collect snow and contribute to the water table, water sources along the way are unreliable. ■ TIP→ **Bring a couple of quarts of water per person, plus mosquito repellent.** Hiking uphill on a hot summer day requires it. Also, weather is fickle here, and a bright, sunny morning can easily turn into an overcast, rainy, and windy afternoon. Come with adequate clothing, including rain gear, no matter how promising the skies look in the morning. A shorter hike is the 3.5-mi Angel Rocks Trail, near the eastern boundary of the area.

Have Your Green & Eat It, Too

Don't feel guilty about leaving on the lights at Chena Hot Springs Resort; all the energy is geothermal. Since July 2006, the resort has been utilizing the 165°F springwater to power two turbines. This feat shocked geothermal experts who claimed that water temperatures must be at least 265 °F. This free source of power allows the resort to run greenhouses through the -40°F winters. The nightly free Alternative Energy tours end at these productive greenhouses, where row upon row of lettuce, up to 30 heads a day, and 17 varieties of tomatoes thrive off a hydroponic, or soil-free, system. Order a salad for dinner and taste the special flavor of local, fresh-picked greens.

PADDLING   The **Chena River State Recreation Area** has numerous well-marked river-access points (the Chena Hot Springs Road parallels the Chena River, and canoeists use several put-in points along the way). The lower sections of the river area are placid, but the area above the third bridge, at Mile 44.1, can be hazardous for inexperienced boaters.

Wilderness Enterprises (☎907/488–7517 ⊕ *www.wildernessenterprises. com*) has guided fishing for arctic grayling and scenic float trips on the Chena River. Half-day and full-day trips are available. When the temperatures drop, try your hand at ice fishing.

WHERE TO EAT

$$$–$$$$ ✕**Two Rivers Lodge.** Fairbanksans are known to make the 40-mi round-
SEAFOOD   trip for the delicious dinners here, including hand-cut, aged filet
★   mignon, prime rib, frequent crab specials, and other Alaskan seafood dishes. Don't be discouraged by the building's outward appearance—rustic logs belie the menu's elegance. For a study in Alaskan-style contrasts, stop in the Trapline Lounge first for a predinner refreshment. ⊠*Mi 16, Chena Hot Springs Rd.* ☎907/488–6815 ▭ D, MC, V ⊗ *No lunch*.

WHERE TO STAY

$$–$$$ 🛏 **Chena Hot Springs Resort.** People come in droves to soak in the hot
Fodor's Choice   springs via either the hot tubs, the indoor swimming pool, or the natu-
★   ral-rock lake. Just as many, if not more, flock to see the magnificent aurora. Miles from the nearest village, in winter you can snowmobile, dogsled, and "snow-coach" tour. Summer activities include gold panning, flightseeing, and mountain biking. ATV tours are year-round. The Aurorarium is a large, glassed-in room for viewing the northern lights in winter, and there's a snow-coach ride to a hilltop yurt offering a 360-degree panorama. Don't miss the world's only year-round Ice Museum complete with an ice bar, ice bedrooms, and a multitude of ice carvings created by world-class carvers. Tours for the ice museum are $15.

There are also sports-equipment rentals, camping sites, and yurts ($65) for rent. **Pros:** It's 100% powered by geothermal energy, there's an activity for every taste. **Cons:** With so many activities, basic services sometimes get neglected, like the pool locker rooms and the lone, fuzzy TV channel. ⊠*Mi 57, Chena Hot Springs Rd. 907/451–8104* ⊕*www. chenahotsprings.com* ↩*80 rooms* ⬩*In-room: no phone (some). In-hotel: restaurant, bar, bicycles, no elevator, laundry facilities, public Wi-Fi* ⊟*AE, D, DC, MC, V.*

¢ ⬩ **Department of Natural Resources Cabins.** Used by those with extensive backcountry experience, these cabins have woodstoves, bunks, and tools for cutting wood. You have to supply everything else—food, bedding, water, cooking utensils. This is basic Alaskan shelter, but it can't be beat for leaving the "real" world behind. Hiking distances range from 3 to 10 mi, but the North Fork and Chena River cabins are road-accessible. The nightly fee ranges from $25 for the Colorado and Angel Creek cabins to $50 per night for the larger North Fork and Chena River cabins. Wildlife in the area includes moose, porcupines, lynx, fox, pine marten, wolves, coyotes, black bears, and, occasionally, grizzly bears. Facilities vary with each cabin; potable water is available near some. ⊠*Mi 32 to 50, Chena Hot Springs Rd., Chena River State Recreation Area* ↩*5 cabins* ⬩*Pit toilets* 🖀*907/451–2705* ⊕*www. dnr.state.ak.us* ⬩*Reservations essential* ⊟*MC, V.*

¢ ⬩ **Red Squirrel Campground.** If you want to combine easy fishing access with your camping, the grassy Red Squirrel State Campground at Mile Marker 42.8 is your top choice: it's got a pond stocked with grayling. There are two pavilion shelters, and the low number of campsites means quiet evenings (though the fact that it's the farthest trek from Fairbanks out of all the Chena sites might have something to do with that, too). ⊠*Mi 42.8, Chena Hot Springs Rd.* ↩*12 RV and tent sites* ⬩*Pit toilets, drinking water, trash cans, fire pits, picnic tables, swimming (pond)* ⬩*Reservations not accepted* ⊟*No credit cards.*

¢ ⬩ **Rosehip Campground.** At Mile 27 you'll find these campgrounds are very basic but have the essentials for family camping. There's a trail that leads down to the river, which makes it a good put-in and take-out spot for paddlers. It's a shorter drive from Fairbanks than other campgrounds and has river access, but this has helped it grow into the biggest (and potentially most crowded) campground near here. ⊠*Mi 27, Chena Hot Springs Rd.* ↩*37 sites* ⬩*Pit toilets, drinking water, trash cans, fire pits, picnic tables* ⬩*Reservations not accepted* ⊟*No credit cards.*

¢ ⬩ **Tors Trail Campground.** Campers at Mile 39.5 are adjacent to the Granite Tors trailhead, a 15-mi loop into the high country. Also across from the campground you'll find a parking area (free for campers) and picnic spot near the river. There are no flush toilets here. ⊠*Mi 39.5, Chena Hot Springs Rd.* ↩*24 sites* ⬩*Pit toilets, drinking water, trash cans, fire pits, picnic tables* ⬩*Reservations not accepted* ⊟*No credit cards.*

CENTRAL & CIRCLE

From Fairbanks: 128 mi northeast on the Steese Hwy. to Central, 162 mi on Steese to Circle.

The Steese Highway follows the Chatanika River and several other creeks along the southern part of the White Mountains. It eventually climbs into weatherworn alpine mountains, peaking at Eagle Summit (3,624 feet), about 100 mi from Fairbanks, and drops back down into forested creek beds en route to Central. At Central you can drive the 30-plus mi on a winding gravel road to Circle, a small town on the Yukon River. The highway is paved to Mile 44 and usually in good shape. A possible exception is in winter, when Eagle Summit is sometimes closed due to drifting snow.

OUTDOOR ACTIVITIES

Tour companies aren't common in the area. Outdoor activities are generally do-it-yourself.

PADDLING   The **Chatanika River,** a choice spot for canoeists and kayakers, is still fairly close to Fairbanks. The most northerly **access point** is at Cripple Creek campground, near Mile 60, Steese Highway. Other commonly used access points are at Long Creek (Mile 45, Steese Highway); at the state campground, where the Chatanika River crosses the Steese Highway at Mile 39; and at the state's Whitefish Campground, where the river crosses the Elliott Highway at Mile 11. The stream flows into the Minto Flats below this point, and river access is more difficult.

Water in the Chatanika River may or may not be clear, depending on mining activities along its upper tributaries. In times of very low water, the upper Chatanika River is shallow and difficult to navigate. ⚠ Avoid the river in times of high water, especially after heavy rains, because of the danger of sweepers, floating debris, and hidden gravel bars. Contact the **Alaska Public Lands Information Center** (☎ 907/456–0527) for the status of the river.

WHERE TO STAY

¢   ⊡ **Chatanika Lodge.** Rocket scientists from the nearby Poker Flat Research Range gather at this cedar lodge, as do mushers (staff can arrange dogsled rides), snowmachiners, and local families. The eclecticism of the clientele is matched by the diamond willow lamps and a variety of wild-animal trophy heads and skins, including bear, lynx, and wolf. Most of the 20,000 Christmas lights at the lodge stay up year-round. The rooms generally have a double and single bed, sink, and TV. The bathrooms and showers are down the hall. **Pros:** A local favorite, Alaskan character. **Cons:** Long drive from Fairbanks, shared baths. ⊠ *Mi 28.5, 5760 Steese Hwy., Fairbanks* ☎ 907/389–2164 ⤶ *10 rooms with shared bath* ☾ *In-room: no phone. In-hotel: restaurant, bar, no elevator, some pets allowed* ▭ *MC, V.*

Native Alaska by Bush Plane

From Fairbanks you can catch a ride on regularly scheduled mail planes to small, predominantly Athabascan villages along the Yukon River or to Eskimo settlements on the Arctic coast. All of the smaller air services operate the mail runs on varying schedules. If you want to visit a particular village, or just have the desire to see a bit of native Alaska village life, contact any one of the services.

Frontier Flying Service
(☎ *907/450–7250, 800/478–6779*

in Alaska ⊕ *www.frontierflying.com*) has an extensive roster of scheduled flights to many of the bush villages in northwest Alaska, the Interior, and the North Slope of the Brooks Range. **Warbelow's Air Ventures** (☎ *907/474–0518 or 800/478–0812* ⊕ *www.warbelows.com*) serves approximately 20 villages. **Wright Air Service** (☎ *907/474–0502, 800/478–0502 in Alaska* ⊕ *www.wrightair.net*) flies from its Fairbanks base to Interior and Brooks Range villages.

STEESE & WHITE MOUNTAINS

30 mi north of Fairbanks via Elliott Hwy.

For those who want to immerse themselves in nature for several days at a time, the **Steese National Conservation Area and the White Mountains National Recreation Area** (☎ *907/474–2200 Bureau of Land Management, or BLM*) have opportunities for backcountry hiking and paddling. Both areas have road-accessible entry points, but you cannot drive into the Steese Conservation Area. The White Mountains Recreation Area has limited camping facilities from June to November; reservations are not accepted.

In the Steese National Conservation Area you can take a four- to five-day or 126-mi float trip on the lively, clear-water **Birch Creek**, a challenge with its several rapids; Mile 94 of the Steese Highway is the access point. Moose, caribou, and birds are easily spotted. This stream winds its way north through the historic mining country of the Circle District. The first take-out point is at the Steese Highway Bridge, 25 mi from Circle. Most people take out here to avoid the increasingly winding river and low water. From there, Birch Creek meanders on to the Yukon River well below the town. Fairbanks outfitter Alaska Outdoor Rentals and Guides *(⇨Boating, above)*, arranges these trips.

Rising out of the White Mountains National Recreation Area, **Beaver Creek** makes its easy way north. If you have enough time, it's possible to run its entire length to the Yukon, totaling 360 river mi if done from road to road. If you make a shorter run, you will have to exit via small plane. A lot of people make the trip in five or six days, starting from Nome Creek and taking out at Victoria Creek. Contact Alaska Outdoor Rentals and Guides *(⇨Boating, above)* to schedule a trip.

7

WHERE TO STAY

¢ **BLM Public-Use Cabins.** The BLM manages 12 public-use cabins in the White Mountains National Recreation Area, with 300 mi of interconnecting trails. Designed primarily for winter use by dog mushers, snowmachiners (snowmobilers), and cross-country skiers, cabins provide shelter for summer backpackers, although summer access is limited by mountainous and boggy terrain. The cabins have bunk beds, woodstoves, tables, and chairs. Permits are required and available up to 30 days in advance. **Pros:** Remote locations allow for an intimate experience with the land. **Cons:** Permits required, geared for winter use, no place to take a hot bath. ⊠*BLM Headquarters, 1150 University Ave., Fairbanks* ☎*907/474–2251 or 800/437–7021* ⊕ *www.blm.gov/ak* ♿*Pit toilets* ⛺*12 cabins* ▭*MC, V.*

¢ **BLM Campgrounds.** The BLM manages three road-accessible campgrounds in the Steese Highway area, off Mile 57 (7 mi up the U.S. Creek Road to Nome Creek Road) and at Mile 60, and two along the Dalton Highway at Mile 115 and Mile 180. The Cripple Creek Campground at Mile 60, Steese Highway, is the best for RVs, with a dozen sites and a half-dozen places for tents. The campgrounds are available on a first-come, first-served basis. In addition, you'll find several undeveloped campsites along the Dalton—old gravel pits with no facilities, available free of charge (though they might not be every visitor's first choice). These are really great sites for campfires—and you'll want them given the particular voraciousness of mosquitos in and around these parks. *5 campgrounds* ♿*Fire pits, picnic tables* ☎*907/474–2251 or 800/437–7021* ⚠*Reservations not accepted* ▭*No credit cards.*

YUKON–CHARLEY RIVERS NATIONAL PRESERVE

20 mi north of Eagle, 100 mi east of Fairbanks.

The 126-mi stretch of the Yukon River running between the small towns of Eagle and Circle—former gold-rush metropolises—is protected in the 2.5-million-acre **Yukon–Charley Rivers National Preserve.** In the pristine Charley River watershed, a crystalline white-water stream flows out of the Yukon-Tanana uplands, allowing for excellent river running for expert rafters.

In great contrast to the Charley River, the Yukon River is a powerful stream, dark with mud and glacial silt. The only bridge built across it in Alaska holds the trans-Alaska pipeline, north of Fairbanks. The river surges deep, and to travel on it in a small boat is a humbling and magnificent experience. You can drive from Fairbanks to Eagle (via the Taylor Highway off the Alaska Highway) and to Circle (via the Steese Highway) and from either of these arrange for a ground-transportation shuttle back to your starting city at the end of your Yukon River trip. Weeklong float trips down the river from Eagle to Circle, 150 mi away, are possible. For information contact the **National Park Service** (☎*907/547–2233*) in Eagle. ■**TIP→** Note that there are no developed campgrounds or other visitor facilities within the preserve itself, though low-impact backcountry camping is permitted. ⊠*National Park*

Service, 201 1st Ave., Doyon Bldg., Fairbanks ☎*907/457–5752* ⊕*www.nps.gov/yuch/index.htm.*

OUTDOOR ACTIVITIES & GUIDED TOURS

HIKING   The **Alaska Public Lands Information Center** (☎907/456–0527) has detailed information about the trails in the Yukon–Charley Rivers National Preserve.

The **Circle-Fairbanks Historic Trail** stretches 58 mi from the vicinity of Cleary Summit to Twelve-Mile Summit. This route, which is not for novices, follows the old summer trail used by gold miners; in winter they generally used the frozen Chatanika River to make this journey. The trail has been roughly marked and cleared, but there are no facilities and water is often scarce. Most of the trail is on state land, but it does cross valid mining claims that must be respected. Although you'll find rock cairns and mileposts while hiking, no well-defined tread exists, so it's easy to become disoriented. ■TIP→ The State Department of Natural Resources strongly recommends that backpackers on this trail equip themselves with the following USGS topographical maps: Livengood (A-1), Circle (A-6), Circle (A-5), and Circle (B-4).

The BLM maintains the **Pinnell Mountain National Recreation Trail,** connecting Twelve-Mile Summit and Eagle Summit on the Steese Highway. This 27-mi-long trail passes through alpine meadows and along mountain ridges, all above the tree line. It has two emergency shelters. No dependable water supply is available in the immediate vicinity. Most hikers spend three days making the trip.

RAFTING   Rafting trips on the Charley River are for experts only. With access via a small plane, you can put in a raft at the headwaters of the river and travel 88 mi down this exhilarating, bouncing waterway. Contact the National Park Service *(⇨above).* The river here is too rough for kayaks and open canoes.

WINTER   Once past Mile 20 of the Steese Highway you enter a countryside that
SPORTS   seems to have changed little in 100 years, even though you're only an hour from downtown Fairbanks. Mountains loom in the distance, and in winter, a solid snowpack of 4 to 5 feet makes the area great for snowshoeing, backcountry skiing, and snowmachine riding.

MANLEY HOT SPRINGS

From Fairbanks: 73 mi north on Elliott Hwy. to Livengood, then 79 mi west on Elliott Hwy. to Manley.

The Elliott Highway, which starts in Fox, takes you to the Tanana River and the small community of **Manley Hot Springs.** A colorful, close-knit, "end-of-the-road" place, this town was a trading center for placer miners who worked the nearby creeks. Residents maintain a small public campground, across from the Manley Roadhouse. Northern pike are caught in the nearby slough, and a dirt road leads to the Tanana River with its summer runs of salmon. The Manley Hot Springs Resort has closed, but the hot springs are only a short walk from the campground.

The Dalton Highway

Plenty of hardy, adventurous visitors are choosing to "do the Dalton," a 414-mi gravel highway that connects Interior Alaska to the oilfields at Prudhoe Bay on the Beaufort Sea. Alaska's northernmost highway, the Dalton was built in the mid-1970s, during the state's oil-boom days, so that trucks could haul supplies to Prudhoe and Trans-Alaska Pipeline construction camps in Alaska's northern reaches.

The pipeline is arguably the main attraction—or heated talking point—for many who make it up this way: stretching 800 mi across the 49th state from Prudhoe Bay to Valdez, it's both an engineering marvel and a reminder of Alaska's economic dependence on oil production. It carries crude oil across three mountain ranges, 34 major rivers—including the mighty Yukon—and hundreds of smaller creeks. It crosses permafrost regions and three major fault lines, too; half of the pipeline runs aboveground and is held aloft by 78,000 vertical supports that proved their ability to withstand sudden, violent ground shifts as recently as 2002 in a 7.9 magnitude quake along the Denali Fault.

Thousands of 18-wheelers still drive the formerly private Dalton each year, but since 1994 they've been sharing it with sightseers, anglers, and other travelers. That doesn't mean the Dalton has become an easy drive. The road is narrow, often winding, and has several steep grades. Sections may be heavily potholed, and its coarse gravel is easily kicked up into headlights and windshields by fast-moving trucks. If you drive it in your own car, make sure you have windshield replacement insurance, because you will be making a claim when you get home. Besides being tough on vehicles, the road has few visitor facilities. And with tow-truck charges of up to $5 per mi (both coming and going), a vehicle breakdown can cost hundreds of dollars even before repairs. Public access ends at Deadhorse, just shy of Prudhoe Bay.

Unless you're an experienced outdoorsperson, areas off the Dalton Highway are best explored on a guided adventure tour. Services and comforts are few and far between, and the only lodging options are down-at-the-heels motels or wilderness camping.

At **Coldfoot,** over 250 mi north of Fairbanks, a first-rate **visitor center** (☎ *907/678–5209*) provides information on backcountry conditions. A picnic area and a large, colorful sign mark the spot where the road crosses the Arctic Circle.⚠ There are no services between Coldfoot and Prudhoe Bay, a distance of nearly 250 mi.

Today the Dalton Highway is still used to carry oil-field supplies and is open all the way to **Deadhorse,** just shy of the Arctic coast. This town exists mainly to service the oil fields of Prudhoe Bay. **Oil-field tours** (☎ *907/659–2368 or 866/659–2368*) and shuttles to the Arctic Ocean leave daily from the Arctic Caribou Inn in Deadhorse. The tours include a video presentation of the oil field and a tour of the grounds with a stop at the Arctic Ocean, providing a good sense of how industrialization has come to Alaska's North Slope. A minimum 24-hour advance reservation is required to go on the tour. For security reasons, when making reservations you need a valid government ID number for everyone in your group (from either a driver's license, state ID, passport, Social Security card, or other government-issued document). Children are required to be with their legal guardian, and need only provide their date of birth.

TIPS FOR DOING THE DALTON:

- Slow down and move to the side of the road for trucks.
- Always leave your headlights on.
- Yield on one-lane bridges.
- Pull to the side of the road when stopping for pictures.
- Carry at least one spare tire.
- Consider bringing extra gas.
- Consider purchasing a citizens band radio.

Note: Car-rental companies have different policies on whether they allow customers to take vehicles on this rugged highway, so check in advance.

OUTDOOR ACTIVITIES & GUIDED TOURS

Although this is not a prime fishing area, fish, mostly grayling, populate the streams along the Dalton. You'll do better the farther you hike from the road, where fishing pressure is less. Lakes along the road contain grayling, and some have lake trout and arctic char. The Alaska Department of Fish and Game (⇨ *Fairbanks Essentials, above*) puts out a pamphlet titled "Sport Fishing along the Dalton Highway," which is also available at the Alaska Public Lands Information Center (⇨ *Fairbanks Essentials, above*).

Coyote Air (✉ *Mi 175, Dalton Hwy., Coldfoot* ☎ *907/678–5995 or 800/252–0603 mid-May–mid-Sept., 907/479–5995 in winter* ⊕ *www.fly-coyote.com*) is a family-run bush-plane service with three generations of flying experience. This outfit specializes in scenic flights, backcountry trip

support, and fall hunting trips in the Brooks Range.

Marina Air Fly-In Fishing (✉ *1195 Shypoke Dr., Fairbanks* ☎ *907/479–5684* ⊕ *www.akpikefishing.com*) has fly-in trips to remote lakes for northern pike, rainbow trout, grayling, and silver salmon. Overnight packages with a cabin are $190.

If all this sounds great except for the white-knuckled driving part, fear not: there are some great tour coompanies who will take some of the stress out of getting up to Prudhoe Bay. Here are some of the best ones that take you along the Dalton; for more on how to get here via air, see Let the Journey Begin *in* Ch. 1.

Alaskan Arctic Turtle Tours (☎ *907/457–1798 or 888/456–1798* ⊕ *www.wildalaska.info*) specializes in Dalton Highway–area trips, with tours in 15-passenger vans. Destinations include the Arctic Circle, Yukon River, Brooks Range, and Prudhoe Bay on the Arctic Coast.

Northern Alaska Tour Company (☎ *907/474–8600 or 800/474–1986* ⊕ *www.northernalaska.com*) is the most established tour company for the Dalton Highway. It has numerous trips to the Arctic Circle and beyond, some with fly/drive options that operate year-round. **Princess Tours** (☎ *907/479–9660 or 800/426–0442* ⊕ *www.princessalaskalodges.com*) runs tour buses on the Dalton from Fairbanks all the way to Prudhoe Bay, with a variety of services, including an overnight at Coldfoot, a tour of the oil field, and air service from Prudhoe Bay back to Fairbanks or Anchorage. Tours operate once a week from June through August.

7

The highway is paved for 28 mi outside Fairbanks. If you travel here over land, take a moment to reflect on how year-round access to Manley Hot Springs only began as recently as 1982, when the state decided to start plowing the Elliott highway in winter.

OUTDOOR ACTIVITIES

HIKING   The BLM maintains the moderately difficult 20-mi **Summit Trail,** from the Elliott Highway, near Wickersham Dome, north into the White Mountains National Recreation Area. This nonmotorized trail can be explored as a day hike or in an overnight backpacking trip. It quickly rises into alpine country with 360-degree vistas that include abundant wildflowers and bird-watching in summer with blueberry picking in fall. This is not a loop trail, but ends at Beaver Creek. Be sure to bring water, as sometimes the sources are bleak, and take advantage of the rest shelter at Mile 8. You'll find the parking lot at Mile 28.

WHERE TO STAY

¢–$ ⌨ **Manley Roadhouse.** Built in 1903 in the midst of the gold rush into the Interior, this roadhouse is among the oldest in Alaska. Today it caters to a diverse crowd of vacationers, miners, and road-maintenance crews. Not only is the roadhouse known for the food and the rooms, which occupy the original roadhouse and several cabins, but the bar earns bragging rights for its 250 brands of liquor and 20 varieties of beer. The restaurant serves breakfast, lunch, and dinner. Pros: Historic and authentic building, location near hot springs, decent prices. Cons: No rooms have phones and not all have TVs. ⌂ *Mi 152, Elliott Hwy., Manley Hot Springs* ☎ *907/672–3161* ⌫ *13 rooms, 6 with bath; 3 cabins* ⌖ *In-room: no phone, no TV (some). In-hotel: restaurant, bar, no elevator, some pets allowed* ▤ *AE, MC, V* ☻ *Closed Oct.–May.*

DENALI NATIONAL PARK & PRESERVE

Fodor'sChoice   *120 mi south of Fairbanks on the George Parks Hwy.; 240 mi north of*
★   *Anchorage on the George Parks Hwy.*

The most accessible of Alaska's national parks and one of only three connected to the state's highway system, 6-million-acre Denali National Park and Preserve is one of North America's most picturesque and easiest places to see wildlife in its natural environment.

McKinley, commonly known by its Athabascan name, *Denali,* meaning "the High One," is North America's tallest mountain, ringing in at 20,320 feet. Unfortunately for visitors on a tight schedule, McKinley is wreathed in clouds an average of two out of three days in summer and is not visible from the park entrance. If time permits, increase your odds of glimpsing Denali through a venture into the heart of the park or stay at a wilderness lodge at the western park boundary. Although most Denali visitors are content to contemplate Mt. McKinley from afar, more than 1,000 adventurers climb the mountain's slopes each summer.

You need not climb Mt. McKinley to appreciate the park; in fact, most people who visit Denali will never come closer than 35 mi to the mountain's snowy base. The 92-mi Denali Park Road (the park's only road) is unpaved after the first 15 mi. After that, private-vehicle access is limited, but you can travel into the heart of Denali on shuttle buses in summer. These rides present the best opportunity to observe grizzly bears, wolves, caribou, moose, and Dall sheep—often considered the

WELCOME TO DENALI

You are about the enter one of the country's most pristine, wildlife-rich parks. Explorers across the globe dream of visiting this vast wilderness. Comprised of healthy forests, great tundra expanses, the continent's tallest mountain, and a huge roster of resident wildlife, Denali is teeming with adventure and possibility.

"big five" of Alaska. And don't miss the soaring golden eagles, clucking ptarmigans, and chattering ground squirrels. If you prefer to take in the scenery by pedal, bikes with sturdy tires are allowed to cruise the park road. Flightseeing is one of the best ways to gain an eagle's-eye view of this mountainous landscape. Without wings, the bulk of the park is accessible only on foot in summer or by dog team or cross-country skis in winter.

For all the challenges of access and planning, those who explore Denali are certain to reap many rewards: wilderness solitude, a sense of discovery, wildlife encounters, and a greater appreciation for the landscape's immensity and the rigors of the subarctic climate.

7

EXPLORING DENALI

With a landmass larger than Massachusetts, Denali National Park and Preserve has too much area for even the most dedicated vacationer to explore in one go. It's wise to consider some important questions before you plan your trip: do you want to strike out on your own as a backcountry traveler, or do you want to stay at a lodge nearby and enjoy Denali as a day hiker with the help of a tour or shuttle bus?

PARK BASICS

Admission to Denali is $10 per person or $20 per family. The **Wilderness Access Center** (⊠*Mile 1, Park Rd.* ☎*907/683–9274*) near the park's entrance at Mile 237.3, George Parks Highway, is where you can handle reservations for roadside camping and bus trips into the park. A smaller building nearby is the **Backcountry Information Center,** for those visitors who want to travel and stay overnight in the wilderness. The Backcountry Information Center has backcountry permits and hiking information, including current data on animal sightings, river-crossing conditions, weather, and closed areas. It's closed in winter (mid-September through mid-May). ■TIP➔ Free permits are required for overnight backpacking trips, but you won't need one for day hiking.

Open from mid-May to mid-September, the **Denali Visitor Center**(⊠*Mi 1.5, Park Rd.* ☎*907/683–9532* ⊕ *www.nps.gov/dena*) exhibits beautiful displays about the park's natural and cultural history, and offers

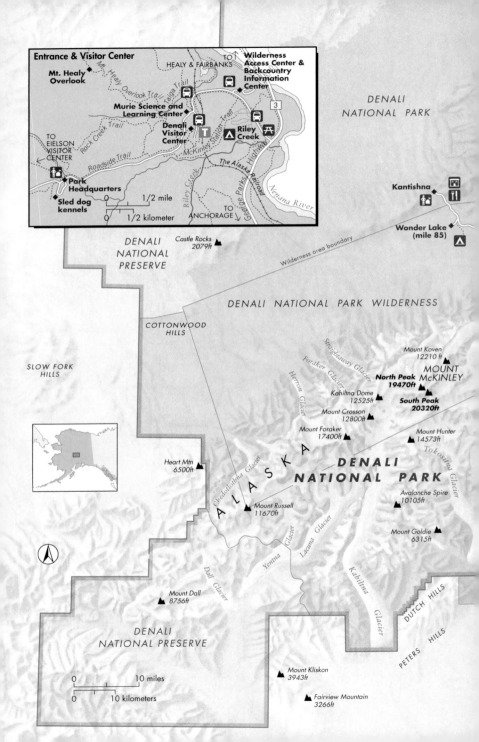

Entrance & Visitor Center

Mt. Healy Overlook

TO HEALY & FAIRBANKS

Wilderness Access Center & Backcountry Information Center

Mt. Healy Overlook Trail

Taiga Trail

Murie Science and Learning Center

Rock Creek Trail

Denali Visitor Center

3

Riley Creek

TO EIELSON VISITOR CENTER

Roadside Trail

McKinley Station Trail

The Alaska Railroad

George Parks Highway

Riley Creek

Nenana River

Park Headquarters

Sled dog kennels

1/2 mile

1/2 kilometer

TO ANCHORAGE

DENALI NATIONAL PARK

Castle Rocks 2079ft

Kantishna

Wonder Lake (mile 85)

DENALI NATIONAL PRESERVE

Wilderness area boundary

DENALI NATIONAL PARK WILDERNESS

COTTONWOOD HILLS

SLOW FORK HILLS

Straightaway Glacier

Foraker Glacier

Herron Glacier

Mount Koven 12210 ft

MOUNT McKINLEY

North Peak 19470ft

Kahiltna Dome 12525ft

Mount Crosson 12800ft

South Peak 20320ft

Mount Foraker 17400ft

Mount Hunter 14573ft

Heart Mtn 6500ft

A L A S K A

Chedotlothna Glacier

DENALI NATIONAL PARK

Tokositna Glacier

Avalanche Spire 10105ft

Mount Russell 11670ft

Yentna Glacier

Lacuna Glacier

Mount Goldie 6315ft

Dall Glacier

Kahiltna Glacier

DUTCH HILLS

Mount Dall 8756ft

DENALI NATIONAL PRESERVE

PETERS HILLS

10 miles

10 kilometers

Mount Kliskon 3943ft

Fairview Mountain 3266ft

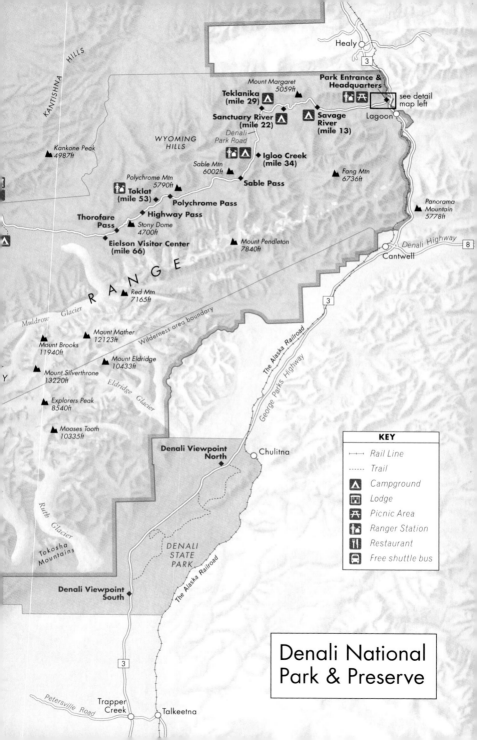

KANTISHNA HILLS

Healy

3

Mount Margaret
5059ft

Park Entrance &
Headquarters

see detail
map left

Teklanika
(mile 29)

Sanctuary River
(mile 22)

Savage
River
(mile 13)

Lagoon

WYOMING
HILLS

Denali
Park Road

Kankone Peak
4987ft

Igloo Creek
(mile 34)

Sable Mtn
6002ft

Fang Mtn
6736ft

Polychrome Mtn
5790ft

Toklat
(mile 53)

Sable Pass

Panorama
Mountain
5778ft

Polychrome Pass

Highway Pass

Thorofare
Pass

Stony Dome
4700ft

Denali Highway

8

Eielson Visitor Center
(mile 66)

Mount Pendleton
7840ft

Cantwell

R A N G E

Red Mtn
7165ft

3

Muldrow Glacier

Mount Mather
12123ft

Mount Brooks
11940ft

Mount Eldridge
10433ft

Wilderness area boundary

Mount Silverthrone
13220ft

Eldridge Glacier

The Alaska Railroad

George Parks Highway

Explorers Peak
8540ft

Mooses Tooth
10335ft

Denali Viewpoint
North

Chulitna

Ruth Glacier

DENALI
STATE
PARK

Tokosha
Mountains

Denali Viewpoint
South

The Alaska Railroad

KEY

⊢•⊣	*Rail Line*
----	*Trail*
◬	*Campground*
▣	*Lodge*
⊼	*Picnic Area*
⌁	*Ranger Station*
⍭	*Restaurant*
⛍	*Free shuttle bus*

3

Denali National
Park & Preserve

Petersville Road

Trapper
Creek

Talkeetna

regular showings of the *Heartbeats of Denali* in the Karsten's Theater. In addition, the center offers a wide variety of interpretive programs and a chance to browse the nearby Denali Bookstore.

RESERVING A SPOT

It's important to reserve tickets for buses ahead of time; call the numbers provided here or log on to ⊕ *www.reservedenali.com.*

The neighboring **Murie Science and Learning Center** (⊠ *P.O. Box 136* ☎ *907/683–1269* ⊕ *www.murieslc.com*) is the foundation of the park's science-based education programs, and also serves as the winter visitor center when the Denali Visitor Center is closed. ⟶ *Box 9, Denali Park99755* ☎ *907/683–2294* ⊕ *www.nps.gov/dena.*

GETTING HERE & AROUND

You can reach the park by bus or by car along the George Parks Highway. On its route between Anchorage and Fairbanks, the Alaska Railroad makes a stop at Denali (⟶ *See* Fairbanks, Getting Here & Around, *above*).

Only one road penetrates Denali's expansive wilderness: the 92-mi Denali Park Road, which winds from the park entrance to Wonder Lake and Kantishna, the historic mining district in the heart of the park. The first 15 mi of the road are paved and open to all vehicles, but beyond the checkpoint at Savage River access is limited.

Campers with permits for the Teklanika campground can drive into and back out from their campsites at Mile 29, but they cannot tour the park road in their vehicles. Except for a few permit-holding professional photographers, private vehicles with special permits, and community members of Kantishna, the only other vehicles past Mile 15 are tour buses, shuttle buses, camper buses, and Park Service vehicles.

Mountain bikes are currently allowed on the park road.

TOUR, SHUTTLE & CAMPER BUSES

Don't be alarmed by the crowded park entrance. Starting at the developed and semitamed entrance area, this adventure transports you into a wild landscape. From the bus, you'll have the opportunity to see Denali's wildlife in natural settings as the animals are habituated to the road and vehicles, and go about their daily routine with little bother.

Bus trips take time. The maximum speed limit is 35 mph. Add in rest stops, wildlife sightings, and slowdowns for passing, and it's an 8- to 11-hour day to reach the heart of the park and the best Denali views from Miles 62–85. All prices listed below are for adults and include the $10 park admission fee. ■ TIP→ If you decide to tour the park by bus, you have two choices: a sightseeing bus tour offered by a park concessionaire or a ride on the shuttle bus. The differences between the two are significant.

Tour buses (☎ *800/622–7275, 907/272–7275 in Alaska or outside the U.S.* ⊕ *www.reservedenali.com*) offer a guided introduction to the park. Reservations start on December 1. Advance reservations are required for the tour buses and are recommended for the park shuttles. Rides through the park include a 5-hour Natural History Tour ($69.96), a 6- to 8-hour Tundra Wilderness Tour ($103), and an 11- to 12-hour Kantishna Experience ($149). These trips are fully narrated by the driver-guides and include a snack or box lunch and hot drinks. Although the Natural History Tour lasts five hours, it only goes 17 mi into the park (2 mi beyond the private-vehicle turnaround), emphasizing Denali's human and natural history. Do not take the Natural History Tour if you seek the best wildlife or Denali viewing opportunities. ■ TIP→ The Tundra Wilderness Tour is a great way to go if you're a first-time visitor wanting a fun and thorough introduction to the park. The Kantishna Experience travels the whole length of the road, features an interpretive guide and ranger, lunch, and some walking. Another important consideration: these trips don't allow you to leave the bus and travel independently through the park.

The park's **shuttle buses** (☎ *800/622–7275 or 907/272–7275* ⊕ *www.reservedenali.com*) don't include a formal interpretive program or food and drink. ■ TIP→ They're less expensive, and you can get off the bus and take a hike or just stop and sightsee, then catch another bus along the road. Most of the drivers are well versed in the park's features and will point out plant, animal, and geologic sights. The shuttles are less formal than the tour buses. They do stop to watch and photograph wildlife, but with a schedule to keep, time is sometimes limited. Shuttle-bus round-trip fares are $22.75 to the Toklat River at Mile 53; $29.25 to Fish Creek or Eielson Visitor Center at Mile 63; and $40 to Wonder Lake at Mile 85.

If you decide to get off the shuttle bus and explore the tundra, just tell the driver ahead of time where you'd like to get out. Some areas are closed to hiking, so check with the rangers at the visitor center before you decide where to go. Some areas are closed permanently, such as Sable Pass, which is heavily traveled by bears; others close as conditions warrant.

When it's time to catch a ride back, just stand next to the road and wait; it's seldom more than 15 minutes or so between buses. The drivers stop if there is room on board. However, during the mid- and late-summer peak season, an hour or more may pass between stopping buses, as they are more likely to be full. Be prepared to split up if you are in a big group in order to fit on crowded buses during peak times.

Camper buses (☎ *800/622–7275 or 907/272–7275* ⊕ *www.reservedenali.com*) serve permitted backpackers and Wonder Lake campers. Seats in the back of the bus are removed for gear storage and there is no formal narration. The $29.95 pass includes transportation anywhere down the road for the length of the backpacker's stay. Get off and on in the same manner as the shuttle buses.

WHEN TO GO

Late May through early September is the prime visiting time for Denali—the area is loosed from winter's icy grip and the animals are awake, active, and browsing for food and companionship. In early summer, trails may be muddy and not all the trees will be fully leafed, but this leads to easier wildlife spotting. Most of the park lies above the tree line and gets 16 to 20 hours of daylight at this time of year—which means you'll have plenty of time to enjoy the expansive view of unspoiled landscape and catch a few glimpses of Alaskan wildlife in the open spaces.

Late spring and early autumn provide opportunities to see the area when visitor traffic is lighter, but be advised that the onset of winter and the appearance of spring are far different from those in the Lower 48 and even from the seasonal changes in Anchorage. Weather conditions can change in a hurry in Alaska, going from warm and sunny to blustery within hours. Snow squalls may occur at any time of year, particularly in the hills and mountains. Be prepared for all of weather's faces.

One advantage to early or late arrival is that before May 20 and sometime after the buses stop running around mid-September, visitors are allowed to drive their own vehicles as far as Teklanika for as long as the weather permits.

The park is open all winter, although services are curtailed and the road into the park is blocked by snow at Mile 3.1. Intrepid travelers can visit the park on dogsleds, snowshoes, or cross-country skis and get a glimpse of Denali that's seldom enjoyed by outsiders.

■TIP→ The farther into the park you venture and the longer you stay, the better your chances of seeing the park's charismatic megafauna (i.e., large animals). Getting an early start or making your way deep in the park doesn't guarantee that you'll see wildlife; the whereabouts of Denali's animals is almost always impossible to predict. Still, the possibility is always present, so stay alert.

MAKING THE MOST OF THE SCENERY

If you get on an early morning bus, you increase your wildlife-viewing opportunities. The animals are most active early in the morning and in the evening, but, as with all rules, this one is occasionally broken and a grizzly or caribou may show up along the road at midday.

On the way to the Savage River checkpoint, look for moose, black bears, and red foxes, which frequent the spruce forest areas near the road. From the parking lot at Savage River, scan the ridges to the west of the river with your binoculars for Dall sheep, usually visible as white specks on or near the skyline. Once you get above tree line, scan the open tundra for caribou and grizzlies.

Primrose Ridge, not far beyond the Savage River bridge, is favored by Dall sheep, especially in spring and early summer. Dall sheep are also commonly seen in the Igloo and Cathedral mountains (between Mile 34 and Mile 37) and Polychrome Pass area (Mile 43.5). Moose are best seen in the forested entrance area and along the stretch of road from Eielson to Wonder Lake (Miles 66 to 85). Grizzlies are where you find them, but alpine areas from Sable Pass (Mile 38) to Eielson (Mile 66) are especially worth noting. Caribou are true nomads, almost

Continued on page 405

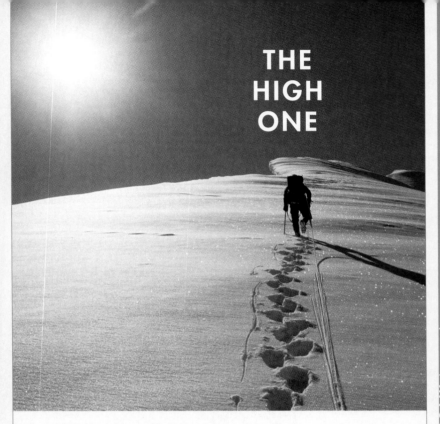

THE
HIGH
ONE

In the heart of mainland Alaska, within 6-million-acre Denali National Park & Preserve, the continent's most majestic peak rises into the heavens. Officially known as **Mount McKinley,** this 20,320-foot massif of ice, snow, and rock is most commonly referred to by its native name of Denali, or "the High One." Some simply call it "The Mountain." One thing is certain: It's a giant among giants, and the most dominant feature in a land of extremes and superlatives.

Those who have walked McKinley's slopes know it to be a wild, desolate place. As the highest peak in North America, McKinley is a target of mountaineers who aspire to ascend the "seven summits"—the tallest mountains on each continent. A foreboding and mysterious place, it was terra incognita—unclimbed and unknown to most people—as recently as the late 1890s. Among Athabascan tribes, however, the mountain was a revered landmark; many generations regarded it as a holy place and a point of reference.

NAMING TERRA INCOGNITA

Linguists have identified at least eight native Alaskan names for the mountain, including Deenaalee, Doleyka, Traleika, and Dghelay Ka'a. The essence of all the names is "the High One" or "Big Mountain." The first recorded sighting of Mt. McKinley by a foreign explorer was in 1794, when Captain George Vancouver spotted it in the distance. More than a century later, after a summer of gold-seeking, Ivy Leaguer William Dickey reported his experiences in the *New York Sun*. His most significant news was of a massive peak, which he dubbed "Mt. McKinley," after Republican William McKinley of Ohio. Mountaineer Hudson Stuck, who led the first mountaineering team to McKinley's summit, was just one in a long line of Alaskans to protest this name. In Stuck's view, the moniker was an affront to both the mountain and Alaska's native people. For these very reasons, a vast majority of Alaskans call the continent's highest peak by its original name, Denali.

Mount McKinley Facts & Figures

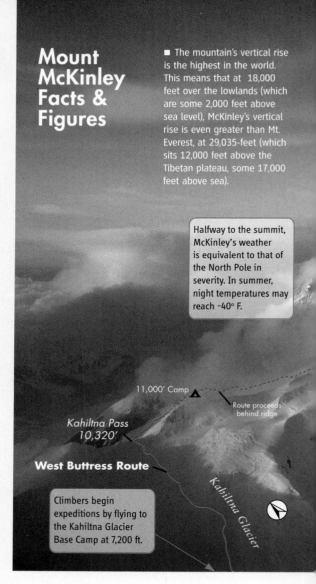

■ The mountain's vertical rise is the highest in the world. This means that at 18,000 feet over the lowlands (which are some 2,000 feet above sea level), McKinley's vertical rise is even greater than Mt. Everest, at 29,035-feet (which sits 12,000 feet above the Tibetan plateau, some 17,000 feet above sea).

Halfway to the summit, McKinley's weather is equivalent to that of the North Pole in severity. In summer, night temperatures may reach -40° F.

11,000' Camp ▲

Route proceeds behind ridge

Kahiltna Pass 10,320'

West Buttress Route

Climbers begin expeditions by flying to the Kahiltna Glacier Base Camp at 7,200 ft.

Kahiltna Glacier

THE WEST BUTTRESS ROUTE

■ The safest route to the summit is the West Buttress. Eighty to 90% of climbers attempting to ascend the peak take this route, with only about half reaching the top.

■ More than 30 people—including some world-class mountaineers—have been killed on the West Buttress.

■ From base camp to high camp, climbers must trek

some 16 miles and 10,000 vertical feet—a trip that takes two to three weeks.

■ The most technically challenging stretch is the ascent to 18,200-foot Denali

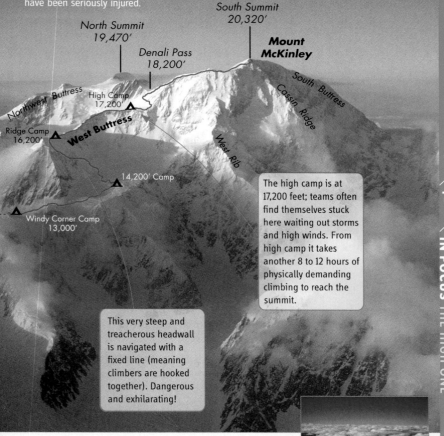

- In addition to coping with severe weather, climbers face avalanches, open crevasses, hypothermia, frostbite, and high-altitude illnesses. Nearly 100 people have died on the mountain and hundreds more have been seriously injured.

- McKinley's awesome height and its subarctic location make it one of the coldest mountains on Earth, if not the coldest.

- Primarily made of granite, McKinley undergoes continual shifting and uplift thanks to plate tectonics (the Pacific plate pushing against the North American Plate); it grows about 1 mm per year.

South Summit
20,320'

Mount McKinley

North Summit
19,470'

Denali Pass
18,200'

South Buttress

Cassin Ridge

Northwest Buttress

High Camp
17,200' △

West Buttress

Ridge Camp
16,200' △

West Rib

△ 14,200' Camp

Windy Corner Camp
13,000'

The high camp is at 17,200 feet; teams often find themselves stuck here waiting out storms and high winds. From high camp it takes another 8 to 12 hours of physically demanding climbing to reach the summit.

This very steep and treacherous headwall is navigated with a fixed line (meaning climbers are hooked together). Dangerous and exhilarating!

Pass; climbers must cross a steep snow-covered slope then a shallow bowl called the Football Field.

- Then, still roped together, climbers ascend an 800-foot snow-and-ice wall to reach the "top of the continent" itself.

Fearless climbers facing the icy challenge at 16,400 feet on the West Buttress Route.

EARLY MILESTONES

Climbing Mt. McKinley in the early 1900s

- In **1903**, two different expeditions made the first attempts to climb Mt. McKinley. The highest point reached? 11,000 feet. Over the next decade, other expeditions would try, and fail, to reach the top.

- Finally, in **1913**, a team led by Hudson Stuck reached the summit. The first person to the top was Walter Harper, a native Alaskan.

- After the Stuck party's success in **1913**, no attempts were made to climb the mountain until **1932**. That year, for the first time, a pilot landed a small plane on one of the mountain's massive glaciers. Another first: a party climbed both the 20,320-foot South Peak and 19,470-foot North Peak. More tragically, the first deaths occurred on the mountain.

- Alaskans Dave Johnston, Art Davidson, and Ray Genet completed the first winter ascent of McKinley in February **1967**. Japanese climber Naomi Uemura completed the first solo ascent of McKinley in **1970**.

A FLIGHT TO REMEMBER

Talkeetna is the home of the popular Denali Flyers. Pilots take you on a variety of air tours into the Alaska Range in small, ski-equipped planes. Flights usually include a passage through the Ruth Glacier's Great Gorge, which is bordered by breathtaking granite spires. Leaving the gorge, you'll enter immense glacial basins of the Don Sheldon Amphitheater (named in honor of the first Denali Flyer). Most trips also include flights past McKinley's southern flanks and show glimpses of its climbing routes. Longer tours circle the mountain, passing among the perennially ice-capped upper slopes, saw-toothed ridges, and vertical rock faces. Flights generally range from 30 minutes to 3 hours and cost $150 to $300 per person.

HUDSON AIR SERVICE has a fleet of four airplanes. In 2006, they celebrated their 60th anniversary in business. A 1-hour flight costs $180 per person. The McKinley Grand Tour is 90 minutes and costs $255 per person. A glacier landing adds 30 minutes to your flight and costs an additional $75.

☎ *907/733–2321 or 800/478–2321*
🌐 *www.hudsonair.com*

K2 AVIATION specializes in flightseeing and glacier landings in the Alaska Range. Prices range from $190 (for a 1-hour flightsee) to $340 (for a 90-minute flightsee with a glacier landing).

☎ *907/733–2291 or 800/764–2291*
🌐 *www.flyk2.com*

TALKEETNA AIR TAXI conducts a breathtaking exploration flight close to massive Mt. McKinley, as well as glacier landings. See Ruth Glacier and the South Face ($180); the base camp ($220); or the mountain summit, 20,000 ft in the air ($295).

☎ *907/733–2218 or 800/533–2219* 🌐 *www. talkeetnaair.com*

always on the move, but they tend to congregate along the Eielson–Wonder Lake stretch of road in August and September. Wolves are seen as often as Denali's other large mammals, but they may happen to pass near the road anywhere from the entrance area to Kantishna, as several different packs inhabit the park.

FAUNA & FLORA

Thirty-seven species of mammals reside here, from wolves and bears to little brown bats and pygmy shrews that weigh a fraction of an ounce. The park also has a surprisingly large avian population in summer of 160 identified species. Most of the birds migrate in fall, leaving only two dozen year-round resident species, including ravens, boreal chickadees, and hawk owls. Some of the summer birds travel thousands of miles to nest and breed in subarctic valleys, hills, and ponds. The northern wheatear migrates from southern Asia, warblers arrive from Central and South America, and the arctic tern annually travels 24,000 mi while commuting between Denali and Antarctica.

The most-sought-after species among visitors are the large mammals: grizzlies, wolves, Dall sheep, moose, and caribou. All inhabit the forest or tundra landscape that surrounds Denali Park Road. You can expect to see Dall sheep finding their way across high meadows, grizzlies and caribou frequenting stream bottoms and tundra, moose in the forested areas both near the park entrance and deep in the park, and the occasional wolf or fox that may dart across the road.

Vegetation in the park consists largely of taiga and tundra. Taiga is coniferous forest in moist areas below a tree line of 2,700 feet and consists mainly of white and black spruce trees. Due to the layer of permafrost that lies just under the surface of the land, the trees have shallow root systems. This subjects them to the vagaries of wind and land movements. The "drunken forest" is a phenomena of this, where the uppermost layer of soil shifted on the permafrost, yanking the black spruce trees around and leaving them in a disheveled state that suggests arboreal inebriation. Ground cover in the taiga forest includes dwarf birch, blueberry, and willow shrubs

The rest of the landmass not covered by ice and snow is carpeted by tundra, consisting of a variety of delicate plants like lichens, berries, bright wildflowers, and woody plants. This complex carpet of low-lying vegetation generates brilliant color, especially in August.

GEOLOGY & TERRAIN

The most prominent geological feature of the park is the Alaska Range, a 600-mi-long crescent of mountains that separates South Central Alaska from the Interior. Mt. Hunter (14,573 feet), Mt. Foraker

FINDING YOUR FOOTING IN DENALI

Denali's entrance area and road corridor (from the highway to Savage River) has plenty of adventure and learning. Besides the visitor and Murie centers, there are sled-dog demonstrations, interpretive walks, and the only maintained trails within the park. Keep an eye out for wildlife, especially moose.

7

(17,400 feet), and Mt. McKinley (20,320 feet) are the mammoths of the group. Glaciers flow from the entire Alaska Range.

Another, smaller group of mountains, the Outer Range, which is located north of Denali's park road, is a mix of volcanics and heavily metamorphosed sediments. Though not as breathtaking as the Alaska Range, the Outer Range is popular with hikers and backpackers because its summits and ridges are not as technically difficult to reach.

Several of Denali's most spectacular landforms are deep in the park, but are still visible from the park road. The multicolor volcanic rocks

DINOSAUR FOSSILS UNDER DENALI'S SHADOW

On June 27, 2005 a geologist discovered the track of a theropod, or a three-toed carnivorous dinosaur in 65- to 70-million-year-old Cretaceous sedimentary rock, just 35 mi west of the park entrance. This is the first "hard" evidence of dinosaurs in the Interior of Alaska. While the initial discoveries were made by geologists, subsequent finds were uncovered by participants in a teacher workshop with the Murie Science and Learning Center.

at Cathedral Mountain and Polychrome reflect the vivid hues of the American Southwest. The braided channels of glacially fed streams such as the Teklanika, Toklat, and McKinley rivers serve as "highway routes" for both animals and hikers. The debris- and tundra-covered ice of the Muldrow Glacier, one of the largest glaciers to flow out of Denali National Park's high mountains, is visible from Eielson Visitor Center, at Mile 66 of the park road. Wonder Lake, a dark and narrow "kettle pond" that's a remnant from Alaska's Ice Ages, lies at Mile 85, just a few miles from the former gold-boom camp of Kantishna.

HIKING TERRAIN & BACKCOUNTRY TRAVEL

You can have one of North America's premier hiking and wilderness experiences in Denali with the proper planning: know your goals; consult park staff before setting out to learn Leave No Trace and bear etiquette; carry proper clothing, food, and water; and don't try to cover too much ground in too short a time.

Most of Denali is "trail-less wilderness," so you have to make your own way across the landscape. Distances in the wide-open tundra can be deceiving; what looks like a 2-mi walk may in fact be 6 mi. Main lesson: be conservative in route planning. Also deceiving is the tundra; though it looks like a smooth carpet from a distance, it may have bogs and thickets of willow.

A big draw for more experienced hikers and backpackers are the foothills and ridges accessible from the park road. As long as you don't go deep into the Alaska Range, it's possible to reach some summits and high ridges without technical climbing expertise. Stamina and physical fitness are required. Once up high, hikers find easy walking and sweeping views of braided rivers, tundra benches and foothills, and ice-capped mountains.

Logistics and Details: If you're camping overnight in Denali's wilderness, you must obtain a special permit (free of charge) from rangers at the Backcountry Information Center. This must be done in person. Advance reservations are not accepted. Only experienced backpackers should try this option. At the center, you must also choose an area to backpack in. Denali's backcountry is divided into 87 units, and only a limited number of campers are allowed each night in most units. The most-desirable units are near the middle of the park, in areas with open tundra and wide-open vistas. These fill up faster than the low-lying areas, many of which are moist and are loaded with mosquito populations. To obtain the best backpacking areas, arrive a couple of days early, stay at one of the facilities near the park entrance (or at the Riley Creek Campground), and check in at the backcountry desk early each morning until the desired unit opens up. It is also wise to check the park's Web site in advance (⊕*www.nps.gov/dena*) and read up on bear and wildlife safety, clean camping, river crossings, and proper food storage; when you're at the park, talk with the rangers and tap into their local knowledge. For $29.95 you may ride a camper bus for the duration of your stay (⇨ Tour, Shuttle & Camper Buses, *above*).

NATURE TRAILS & SHORT WALKS

There are options for those who prefer to stay on marked and groomed pathways. The park's entrance area has a system of more than a half-dozen forest and tundra trails. These range from easy to challenging and are therefore suitable for all ages and hiking abilities. Some, like the **Taiga Loop Trail** and **McKinley Station Loop Trail,** are less than 1.5 mi; others, like the **Rock Creek Trail** and **Triple Lakes Trail,** are several miles round-trip, with an altitude gain of several hundred feet. Along these paths you may see beavers working on their lodges in Horseshoe Lake; red squirrels chattering in trees; red foxes hunting for rodents; sheep grazing on tundra; golden eagles gliding over alpine ridges; and moose feeding on willow.

The Savage River Trail, farthest from the park entrance and as far as private vehicles are allowed, offers a 1.75-mi round-trip hike along a raging river and under rocky cliffs. Be on the lookout for caribou, Dall sheep, foxes, and marmots.

The only relatively long, marked trail for hiking in the park, **Mt. Healy Overlook Trail,** is accessible from the entrance area; it gains 1,700 feet in 2.5 mi and takes about four hours round-trip, with outstanding views of the Nenana River below and the Alaska Range, including the upper slopes of Mt. McKinley.

TENT & RV CAMPING IN DENALI NATIONAL PARK

If you want to camp in the park, either in a tent or an RV, five campgrounds are available with varying levels of access and facilities. Two of the campgrounds—Riley Creek (near the park entrance) and Savage River (Mile 13)—have spaces that accommodate tents, RVs, and

LOCAL LINGO

Alaskans refer to snowmobiles as snowmachines; calling them snowmobiles automatically brands you as someone from "Outside."

UP CLOSE & PERSONAL

Enjoy moose from a distance! Weighing 1,000 pounds or more, they can get pretty mean despite their harmless appearance. Never get between a moose and its calf. If you encounter a moose at close range acting aggressively, leave the area immediately and quickly. If it decides to charge, either stand behind a tree or stand still with your arms raised but not waving and fingers spread to convince the moose that you are the bigger animal.

Tactics are a bit more clear-cut for one of Denali's other major megafauna: never run from a bear—you may trigger its predatory chase instincts and encourage the bear to respond to you as prey. Be loud as you hike so you don't inadvertently surprise them, stand next to your hiking partners if you come upon one to appear more threatening, and try to have rocks handy to throw if they do charge. A little caution and a large dose of common sense will assure you a safe trip in the park. A summary of bear-safety tips is available at the Denali Visitor Center. For more information, flip to "Welcome to Bear Country" in Chapter 8 of this book.

campers. Visitors with private vehicles can also drive to the Teklanika campsite (Mile 29), but they must first obtain park-road travel permits; in recent years no tent camping has been allowed at Teklanika, but visitors should check with park staff for updates. Sanctuary River (Mile 22), and Wonder Lake (Mile 85) have tent spaces only. The camper buses offer the only access to these camping areas.

Visitors to the Sanctuary and Igloo Creek campsites should come prepared: Sanctuary has no drinking water, and the water must be taken from a stream and treated. All sites have flush or chemical toilets and food lockers for proper storage of food. Individual sites are all beyond sight of the park road, though within easy walking distance.

Fees for individual sites range from $10 to $20 per night. ■ TIP→ Campsites can be reserved in advance several ways: online, through the Denali National Park Web site (⊕ *www.reservedenali.com*); by faxing a reservation form (form available at ⊕ *www.nps.gov/dena*; fax to 907/264–4684); by mailing in the reservation form; or by calling the reservation service (☎ *800/622–7275 or 907/272–7275*). Reservations can also be made in person at the park. It's best to visit Denali's Web site before making reservations, both to see the reservation form and to learn if any changes in the reservation system have been made. ⌂ *Denali National Park Headquarters, Box 9, Denali Park 99755* ☎ *907/683–2294 information, 907/272–7275, 800/622–7275 reservations* ⊕ *www.reservedenali.com* ☰ *AE, D, MC, V* ⊙ *All but Riley Creek (no visitor facilities) closed mid-Sept.–late May.*

SPORTS, THE OUTDOORS & GUIDED TOURS

FLIGHTSEEING

One of the best ways to get a sense of the Alaska Range's immensity, and also get some close-up views of Mt. McKinley and its neighboring giants, plus (if you choose) stand on a glacier without carrying gear and food, is a flightseeing tour of the park. Most Denali flightseeing is done out of Talkeetna, a small end-of-the-road town between Anchorage and Denali (⇨ *See "The High One" in this chapter for more information).*

GUIDED TOURS

In addition to exploring the park on your own, you can take free ranger-guided "discovery hikes" and learn more about the park's natural and human history. Rangers lead daily hikes throughout summer. Inquire at the visitor center.

Privately operated, narrated bus tours are available through **Denali Park Resorts** (☎ *907/276–7234 or 800/276–7234 ⊕www.denaliparkresorts. com).*

HORSEBACK RIDING

Get a taste of the real "frontier" by exploring the Stampede Trail area on horseback on one-, two-, or four-hour tours. Bonuses include panoramic views of the mountains and knowledgeable guides. The 50 draft cross horses are treated like royalty, and the owner knows their personalities well. **Denali Saddle Safaris** (✉ *Mi 3.9, Stampede Rd. 907/683–1200 ⊕www.denalisaddlesafaris.com)*

KAYAKING & RAFTING

Several privately owned raft and tour companies operate along the Parks Highway near the entrance to Denali, and they schedule daily rafting, both in the fairly placid areas on the Nenana and through the 10-mi-long Nenana River canyon, which contains some of the roughest white water in North America.

Alaska Raft Adventures books two-hour-long white-water and scenic raft trips along Nenana River through **Denali Park Resorts** (☎ *907/276–7234 or 800/276–7234 ⊕www.denaliparkresorts.com/activities/detail.cfm).* Those feeling adventurous on the white-water trip may choose to do the work and paddle. All others have the choice to sit back and let a guide do the work.

★ **Denali Outdoor Center** (✉ *Mi 240, Parks Hwy.* ⌁ *Denali Park 99755* ☎ *907/683–1925 or 888/303–1925 ⊕www.denalioutdoorcenter. com)* carries a respected reputation among locals. This organization takes visitors five years old and up, of all abilities, on scenic rafting trips on the Nenana River. It also leads more adventurous trips down the Nenana River canyon's rapids

WORDS OF WISDOM

Keep in mind that, as one park lover put it, "this ain't no zoo." You might hit an off day and have few viewings—enjoy the surroundings anyway. Of course, under no circumstances should you feed the animals (a mew gull or ground squirrel may very well try to share your lunch).

DID YOU KNOW?

Breathe deep when climbing Mt. McKinley. The high latitude means there's even less available oxygen at this altitude than at the same height closer to the equator.

in either rafts or inflatable kayaks. No river experience is necessary. The kayaks, called Duckies, are easy to get out of, stable, and self-bailing. The company also teaches white-water kayaking. All gear is provided, including full dry suits. Camping sites, rental cabins, and mountain-bike tours/ rentals are also available. Plus, there's a free local shuttle from hotels, lodges, the Alaska Railroad depot, the Denali visitor center, and elsewhere.

Denali Raft Adventures (☎*907/683–2234 or 888/683–2234* ⊕*www. denaliraft.com*) launches its rafts several times daily on two- or four-hour and all-day scenic and white-water raft trips on the Nenana River. Gore-Tex dry suits are provided. Guests under the age of 18 must have a release waiver signed by a parent or guardian. Contact the company for copies before the trip. Courtesy pickup at hotels and the train depot is available.

MOUNTAIN BIKING

Mountain biking is allowed on the park's dirt road, and no permit is required for day trips. The first 15 mi of the road are paved. Beyond the Savage River checkpoint the road is dirt and gravel, and during the day is traversed by the park buses, which can make for a dust-intensive experience. It can also be sloppy if it's raining. The most rewarding time to bike is late night, when the midnight sun is shining and buses have ceased shuttling passengers for the day. When biking on the road, you need to be aware of your surroundings and observe park rules if you decide to get off the road. Off-road riding is forbidden, and some sensitive wildlife areas are closed to hiking. The Sable Pass area is always closed to off-road excursions on foot because of the high bear population, and other sites are posted due to denning activity or recent signs of carcass scavenging. **Denali Outdoor Center** (✉*Mi 238.5, Parks Hwy.* ☎*907/683–1925 or 888/303–1925* ⊕*www.denalioutdoorcenter.com*) rents mountain bikes by the hour or day, and conducts guided 2- to 2½-hour tours of the park, complete with bike, helmet, water bottle, and shuttle-van transport.

MOUNTAINEERING

Alaska Mountaineering School (✉*3rd St., Talkeetna* ☎*907/733–1016* ⊕*www.climbalaska.org*) leads backpacking trips in Denali and elsewhere in the state, including the Brooks Range. It also conducts 6- and 12-day mountaineering courses, expeditions to Denali and other peaks in the Alaska Range, and climbs for all levels of climbing expertise. **Mountain Trip** (☎*866/886–8747 or 970/369–*

A HEALY HIGHLIGHT

One of Healy's greatest attractions is the **Stampede Trail,** perhaps most famous to today's traveler for being where Christopher McCandless of *Into the Wild* met his match. On the Stampede Trail, you can enter Denali by snowmobile, dogsled, cross-country skis, or mountain bike. This wide, well-traveled path leads all the way to Kantishna, 90 mi inside the park. To get here, take the George Parks Highway 2 mi north of Healy to Mile 251.1, where Stampede Road intersects the highway. Eight miles west on Stampede Road is a parking lot and the start of the trail.

1153 ⊕*www.mountaintrip.com*) has been guiding climbing expeditions on Mt. McKinley and other Alaska Range peaks since 1973, making it the most senior of the guide companies to operate on the High One. Though the company emphasizes climber safety, most McKinley expeditions reach the summit. Novice to experienced trip levels are offered.

WINTER SPORTS

Snowshoers and skiers generally arrive with their own gear and park or camp at the Riley Creek Campground at the park entrance. Dog mushing can also be done with your own team, or you can contact one of the park concessionaires that run day or multiday trips.

Denali West Lodge (☎ 907/674–3112 ⊕*www.denaliwest.com*) is located near the western park boundary, on the shores of Lake Minchumina. Run by Tonya Schlentner, a 1,000-mi Yukon Quest finisher, this fly-in lodge offers multiday expeditions in March. **Earthsong Lodge Dog Sled Adventures** (☎907/683–2863 ⊕*www.earthsonglodge.com*) is situated 4 mi up the Stampede Trail. This operation offers one- to four-hour trips, and up to 10-day excursions.

WHERE TO EAT

ALONG THE GEORGE PARKS HIGHWAY

$$–$$$$ AMERICAN Fodor'sChoice ★

✕ **229 Parks Restaurant and Tavern.** Even if this hot spot didn't serve amazing food, the graceful timber-frame design, inviting atmosphere, and elaborate elm etchings would be enough to draw in crowds. But just in case, chef and owner Laura Cole directs a scratch kitchen that serves local produce; grass-fed, free-range meat; homemade ice cream and breads; and delectable imports. This is as organic and local as you can get without doing the hunting and gathering yourself. Menus change daily, according to availability. From handmade pappardelle pasta with reindeer sausage and leeks to wild-caught Alaskan weathervane scallops with crisped prosciutto, Laura knows how to make food come to life. Be prepared to play boccie ball while you wait for a table at this hopping restaurant. ⊠ *Mi 229.7, Parks Hwy.99755* ☎907/683–2567 ⊕*www.229parks.com* ⚞*Reservations not accepted* ▭MC, V ◷*No lunch; closed weekdays mid-Sept.–mid-May.*

$ AMERICAN

✕ **Bub's Subs.** Loving care is poured into each and every sub that passes over the counter. They are so large you'll need a fork to clean up the overflowing scraps. The homemade soups draw a following, as do the Philly cheesesteaks, organic and locally grown salads, and grilled chicken, beef, or vegetarian Mediterranean pitas drizzled with tzatziki sauce, feta cheese, and kalamata olives. Don't forget to ask for the East Coast hots (crushed red-hot cherry peppers spread). For lunch on the go try the Italian sub full of deli meats, cheeses, and dressings.

✉ *Mi 238.6, Parks Hwy., Denali Drive* ☎*907/683–7827* ▭*MC, V* ◷*Closed Sept.–May.*

$$
SEAFOOD

✕**McKinley/Denali Salmon Bake.** Fresh salmon tops the menu at this rustic building, which looks as if it might blow away in a stiff wind, but is one of the oldest buildings in the developed strip north of the park entrance known locally as Glitter Gulch. Steaks, burgers, and chicken are available, and breakfast, lunch, and dinner are served. It's a hot spot with live music, 1 mi north of the park entrance. Shuttle service is provided to area hotels, and 12 cabins (8 tent cabins) with shared bath are for rent starting at $69. ✉*Mi 238.5, Parks Hwy.* ☎*907/683–2733 May–Sept.* ▭*AE, D, DC, MC, V* ◷*Closed Oct.–Apr.*

$$–$$$$
AMERICAN

The Perch. The bay windows of this fine-dining restaurant atop a forested hillside present a panoramic view of the surrounding Alaska Range foothills. The Perch serves breakfast, lunch, and dinner, offering home-baked breads and desserts along with steak and seafood; the **Panorama Pizza Pub** also serves soup and sandwiches. If you're looking for a quiet, quality sit-down meal away from the crowds of Glitter Gulch, this restaurant is about 13 mi south of the park entrance. **Cabin rentals** are available May–September ($125 with a private bath, $85 shared, with breakfast included). ✉*Mi 224, Parks Hwy.* ☎*907/683–2523 or 888/322–2523* ⊕*www.denaliperchresort.com/9.html* ▭*D, MC, V* ◷ *Closed mid-Sept.–mid-Apr.*

HEALY

$$–$$$$
AMERICAN

✕ **Black Diamond Grill.** For a casual and family-oriented atmosphere, dine with a view at this off-the-beaten-path local. The menu specializes in hand-pressed burgers, New York steaks, white-wine-poached halibut baked in parchment paper, salads with local and organic greens, and homemade foods. To make a day of it, give the ATV tours ($95), horse-drawn carriage rides with a full meal ($79), or 9-hole and minigolf course ($69) a shot. If you don't have three hours to spare for the activities, enjoy the fishing at nearby Otto Lake. ✉*1 mi up Otto Lake Rd, off Mi 247, Parks Hwy.* ☎*907/683–4653* ⊕*www.blackdiamondgolf.com* ▭*AE, D, MC, V* ◷*Closed mid-Sept.–mid-May.*

¢–$$
AMERICAN

Totem Inn. Travelers from the George Parks Highway, Healy, and Denali come here not so much for the lodging (which is modest at best) as for standard American food at reasonable prices. Steaks, sandwiches, and homemade pizzas are served year-round. An attached bar with pool table serves for swapping stories with the locals. The kitchen is open daily 7 AM–10 PM. ⊠*Mi 248.7, Parks Hwy.* ☎*907/683–6500* ⊕*www.thetoteminn.com* ⊟*D, MC, V.*

WHERE TO STAY

WITHIN THE PARK

If you can afford the price tag, it's worth it to book your stay at a wilderness lodge within Denali. Camp Denali/North Face Lodge and the Kantishna Roadhouse are in Kantishna, a private inholding at the end of the park road, in the heart of the wilderness, accessible only via plane or bus.

$$$$

Fodor'sChoice

★

⛺**Camp Denali and North Face Lodge.** The legendary, 30-year family-owned Camp Denali and North Face Lodge both provide stunning views of Mt. McKinley. At Camp Denali, guests stay in one of 17 quaint cabins that include a small wood-burning stove, wall-mounted propane lights, Alaskan artwork, and quilts crafted by members of the staff. Guests share bathing facilities, though each cabin also has its own outhouse. The North Face Lodge is a north country–style inn built on a tundra meadow. It has 15 rooms, each with private bath. The knowledgeable naturalists on staff offer outings during the three, four, or seven-night stays. Evening programs focus on the natural and cultural history of Denali, while the Special Emphasis Series brings in experts to Camp Denali for the whole stay. Each property has its own kitchen and dining room featuring local and organic food, and fresh-baked bread. Lodging costs include round-trip transport from the park entrance on custom buses, all meals, guided activities, and recreation gear such as canoes, mountain bikes, and fishing tackle. The rate is based on a three-night minimum stay at $1,365 per person. **Pros:** The only in-park lodge with a view of Denali and access to canoes, strong emphasis on learning, attention to detail, family-owned, dedicated staff. **Cons:** Alchohol is BYOB, Camp Denali cabins lack private baths (but you can't beat the view from the outhouse). ⌂*Box 67, Denali Park, 99755* ☎*907/683–2290* ⊕*www.campdenali.com* ⇌*17 cabins (Camp Denali) with shared bath, 15 rooms (North Face Lodge)* ♿*In-room: no a/c, no phone, no TV. In-hotel: 2 restaurants, water sports, bicycles* ⊟*No credit cards* ⊗*Closed mid-Sept.–early June* ⎟⊙*AI.*

$$$$

⛺ **Kantishna Roadhouse.** Run by the Athabascan Doyon Tourism, this establishment offers an enriching wilderness getaway. To make the most of your time, you must commit to at least two nights in an

THE RANGER KNOWS

You may choose to go on a guided "discovery" walk with one of Denali's rangers. Rangers will talk about the area's plants, animals, and geological features.

Before heading into the wilderness, even on a short hike, check in at the Backcountry Information Center. Rangers will update you on conditions and make route suggestions. Because this is bear country, the Park Service provides backpackers with bear-proof food containers. These containers are mandatory if you're staying overnight in the backcountry.

7

elegant log cabin duplex or fourplex. The Kantishna Roadhouse, a massive log lodge, is where you'll spend your time when not out on adventures. The Fannie Quigley dining room prepares family-style meals with fresh fruits, vegetables, and baked goods. If you plan on a full-day excursion, the kitchen will prepare a sack lunch. Activities range from two- to six-hour guided hikes, mountain biking, dog-mushing demos, gold panning, fishing, and, for an extra cost, flightseeing. Cozy up every night with a cup of cocoa and catch an evening program with guest speakers, artists, or Athabascan elders. **Pros:** Guided hikes with naturalists, all rooms have private baths, only saloon in the Denali backcountry. **Cons:** No connection to the outside world besides a phone booth, no elevator to library and evening program room, lacks a direct view of Denali. ⊠ *Box 130, Denali Park, Kantishna* ☎ *800/942–7420* ⊕ *www.kantishnaroadhouse.com/index.htm.* 📠 *32 rooms* ⌂ *In-room: no a/c, no phone, no TV. In-hotel: restaurant, bar, bicycles, no-smoking rooms* ▤ *MC, V* ⊙ *Closed mid-Sept. –early June* ⧖ *AI.*

ALONG THE GEORGE PARKS HIGHWAY

Hotels, motels, RV parks, campgrounds, and some restaurants are clustered along the highway near the park entrance, which is at Mile 237.3. You can judge distance from the park by mileage markers; numbers increase northward and decrease southward.

$$$–$$$$ **Denali Cabins.** Cedar cabins built within the taiga forest have all the basic amenities (including TV and phone), private baths, and shared hot tubs at this complex along the highway 8 mi south of the park entrance. Complimentary shuttle service to the park visitor center is provided. Stays at the cabins can be packaged with a Denali Backcountry Adventure, which is a full-day narrated trip along the park road to Kantishna, returning to the park entrance in the evening. The cost of that trip is $149 per person. **Pros:** Quiet location, offers National Park day trips, sauna and hot tub to relax in. **Cons:** Not located on the river, few amenities offered. ⊠ *Mi 229, Parks Hwy.* ☎ *907/644–9980 or 888/560–2489* ⊕ *www.denali-cabins.com* 📠 *45 cabins* ⌂ *In-hotel: no-smoking rooms* ▤ *MC, V* ⊙ *Closed mid-Sept.–June 1* ⧖ *CP.*

$$–$$$ **Denali River Cabins and Cedars Lodge.** The cabins, clustered along the glacially fed Nenana River, are next to McKinley Village Lodge, 6 mi south of the park entrance. A boardwalk connects the cedar-sided log cabins, most with double beds, and leads to spacious sundecks, as well as to the river. Cedars Lodge has standard, fully furnished hotel rooms. The management operates park excursions and a courtesy shuttle service to and from the train depot. **Pros:** River views and Finnish sauna, lodge or cabin options. **Cons:** Cabins crowded together; property is situated near other resorts. ⊠ *Mi 231.1, Parks Hwy.* *907/683–8000 in summer, 907/459–2121 in winter, 800/230–7275 year-round* ⊕ *www.denalirivercabins.com* 📠 *48 rooms, 54 cabins* ⌂ *In-hotel: restaurant, bar, no-smoking rooms* ▤ *MC, V* ⊙ *Closed mid-Sept.–mid-May.*

$$ **Denali Education Center.** Situated on 10 acres of forest across from
★   Denali National Park, this nonprofit offers something for everybody.
☾   Intensive learning experiences range from a variety of all-inclusive weeklong Elderhostel programs focused on providing quality educa-

tional experiences, to weeklong youth programs with hands-on research in conjunction with the National Park Service, to backpacking trips for high schoolers and 12-day trips for college-age students and older. If time is short, attend a Denali Community Series, which features workshops, art exhibits, slide shows, live music, or lecturers from around the world. In addition, the center sponsors the One World Film and Culture Festival in early June and the Fundraising Auction on the first weekend of August. The festival draws in hundreds of people and thousands of items, all for a good cause. **Pros:** Located on 10 acres, nature trail where you can search for owls, quality educational and immersion experiences. **Cons:** Bare-bones and outdated cabins with a summer-camp feel (but updates are planned). ⊠ *Mi 231, Parks Hwy., Box 212,* ☎*907/683–2597* ⊕*www.denali.org* ☞*12 cabins* ⚬*In room: no phone, no TV. In hotel: restaurant, no elevator* ☐*MC, V* ⊗*Closed mid-Sept.– mid-May.*

$$$ **Denali Crow's Nest Log Cabins.** These individually crafted log cabins 1 mi north of the park entrance are on a forested hillside with river and mountain views. Each has two double beds and its own bath, and a 180-degree view of the park entrance area. The **Overlook Bar and Grill** is a full-service restaurant featuring Alaskan seafood and steaks; it claims to have the largest beer selection in northern Alaska, with 16 taps and 70 varieties in bottles. There's also a courtesy park shuttle from the train. **Pros:** Best variety of beers and burgers around, located above the hustle and bustle of the highway and Glitter Gulch. **Cons:** Cabins are close together, no phone or TV. ⊠ *Mi 238.5, Parks Hwy. 907/683–2723 or 888/917–8130* ⊕*www.denalicrowsnest.com* ☞*39 rooms* ⚬*In-room: no phone, no TV. In-hotel: restaurant, bar, no-smoking rooms* ☐*MC, V* ⊗*Closed Oct.–mid-May.*

$$$$ **Denali Princess Wilderness Lodge.** This humongous lodge is located along the Parks Highway, in the Glitter Gulch community a mile north of the park entrance. Unlike the lodges at Kantishna, in the heart of the park, this one features rooms with TVs and telephones in case you want to catch up with the outside world. There is also a high-ceiling two-story main lodge with tour desk, sitting areas, gift shop, café, and dining room. Views from this hotel take in the Nenana River, and rich forest colors in rooms mimic the surroundings. Complimentary shuttle service is provided to the park and railroad station. The large **King Salmon Dining Room** offers an estimable view and fine dining featuring Alaskan seafood, and a dinner theater combines a meal with a musical comedy that recounts the first ascent of Mt. McKinley. If these don't suit your tastes, there are four other eating venues within the lodge property. **Pros:** Most grandiose lodge in Denali; gym, spa, and gift shop on-site. **Con:** With more than 600 rooms, too big to feel intimate. ⊠ *Mi 238.5, Parks Hwy., 1 mi north of park entrance 907/683–2282, 800/426–0500 reservations* ⊕*www.princesslodges.com/denali_lodge. cfm* ☞ *656 rooms* ⚬*In-room: refrigerator. In-hotel: restaurant, bar, gym, spa, laundry facilities, public Wi-Fi, no-smoking rooms* ☐*AE, D, DC, MC, V* ⊗*Closed mid-Sept.–mid-May.*

HEALY

$$$ [icon] **Denali Dome Home.** A 7,200-square-foot modified geodesic dome houses this year-round B&B. One room has a sauna and two rooms have jetted tubs. An inviting common room has a TV, a fireplace large enough for logs 3 feet long, and Alaska-related books and videos. Sit by the fireplace to take in spectacular views of nearby mountains through the tall windows. Rooms come equipped with any amenity you might need. **Pros:** Thoughtful and knowledgeable owners, unique architecture, attention to detail, DVD and VCR collection. **Cons:** Those with dog allergies beware of two Scottish Terriers, those squeamish of bear hides beware: the house is decorated with a few prize trophies. ⊠ *137 Healy Spur Rd. 99743* ☎ *907/683–1239 or 800/683–1239* ⊕ *www.denalidomehome.com* ➡ *7 rooms* ⚲ *In-room: DVD, VCR. In-hotel: no elevator, public Internet, no-smoking rooms* ⊟ *AE, D, MC, V* ⧖ *BP.*

$$–$$$ **Earthsong Lodge.** Above the tree line at the edge of Denali National Park, Earthsong yields views of open tundra backed by peaks of the Alaska Range. Each of a dozen hand-built cabins has a theme (Denali, Sled Dog, Mountaineering) and private bath, a rarity in such small cabins in remote settings. ■ TIP→ In winter, Earthsong Lodge is one of two concessionaires permitted to lead multiday dog-mushing tours into Denali. The restaurant, **Henry's Coffeehouse,** named after a beloved sled dog, serves a menu of soups, salads, sandwiches, and pastas, plus bagels, baked goods, and espresso drinks. Slide shows of Denali are a nightly treat; tours of the sled-dog kennel are offered as well. **Pros:** Each cabin has unique character; the owners offer a wealth of knowledge, as Jon Nierenberg worked many years at the park and wrote the *Backcountry Companion* hiking book for Denali. **Cons:** A 17-mi drive from the park entrance, barking and howling sled dogs at feeding time. ⊠ *Mi 4, Stampede Trail* ☎ *907/683–2863* ⊕ *www.earthsonglodge.com* ➡ *12 cabins* ⚲ *In-room: no phone, no TV. In-hotel: restaurant, public Wi-Fi, no-smoking rooms* ⊟ *MC, V* ⧖ *EP.*

¢ △ **McKinley RV Park and Campground.** This campground, about 11 mi north of the park entrance on the outskirts of Healy, has a variety of RV sites, from "basic" two-person tent sites to sites with full electricity, water, and sewer. A dump station, public showers, laundry facilities, deli, espresso bar, ice, and gasoline, diesel, and propane are also here. **Pros:** Some sites are wooded and off the highway, numerous services offered. **Cons:** Next to gas station, sites close together. ⊠ *Mi 248.5, Parks Hwy., Healy* ☎ *907/683–2379 or 800/478–2562* ⊕ *www.mckinleyrv.com.*

$$ [icon] **Motel Nord Haven.** Five wooded acres protect this motel from the road, providing a secluded feeling that other accommodations along the George Parks Highway lack. There's wood trim throughout, and rooms have one or two queen-size beds. Rooms with two queen beds can sleep up to five people at no additional charge. For a minimal

Mt. McKinley. Alaskans call Mt. McKinley by its original name, Denali, which means "the high one."

charge, box lunches can be prepared to carry along on your explorations. No breakfast is served in winter (mid-Sept.–mid-May). **Pros:** Reading and puzzle area with comfy couches, meeting/dining room with large deck and fireplace. **Cons:** Lacks character, no stove tops in kitchenettes. ⊠ *Mi 249.5, Parks Hwy. 907/683–4500 or 800/683–4501* ⊕ *www.motelnordhaven.com* ⇆ *28 rooms* ⚒ *In-room: kitchen (some). In-hotel: no elevator, public Wi-Fi, public Internet, no-smoking rooms* ⊟ *AE, D, MC, V* ⱺ *CP.*

FORTYMILE COUNTRY

A trip through the Fortymile Country up the Taylor Highway will take you back in time more than a century—when gold was the lure that drew hardy travelers to Interior Alaska. It's one of the few places to see active mining without leaving the road system. In addition, remote wilderness experiences and float trips abound.

The 160-mi **Taylor Highway** runs north from the Alaska Highway at Tetlin Junction, 12.5 mi south of Delta Junction. It's a narrow rough-gravel road that winds along mountain ridges and through valleys of the Fortymile River. The road passes the tiny community of Chicken and ends in Eagle at the Yukon River. This is one of only three places in Alaska where the Yukon River can be reached by road. A cutoff just south of Eagle connects to the Canadian Top of the World Highway leading to Dawson City in the Yukon Territory. This is the route many Alaskans take to Dawson City. ⚠ **The highway is not plowed in winter, so it is snowed shut from fall to spring.** Watch for road equipment. If you're roughing it, know that in addition to the lodging listed below, the Alaska Bureau of Land Management also maintains three first-come, first-served campsites (as all BLM campsites are) on the Taylor Highway between Tok and Eagle at Miles 48.5, 82, and 160.

TOK

12 mi west of Tetlin Junction, 175 mi southwest of Dawson City.

Loggers, miners, old sourdoughs (Alaskan for "colorful local curmudgeons"), and hunting guides who live and work along Tok's streams or in the millions of acres of spruce forest nearby come here for supplies, at the junction of the Glenn Highway and the Alaska Highway. Each summer the city, with a resident population of fewer than 1,500, becomes temporary home to thousands of travelers, including those journeying up the Alaska Highway from the Lower 48.

RUTH GLACIER

Even the shortest flightseeing trips usually include a passage through the Great Gorge of the Ruth Glacier, one of the major glaciers flowing off Denali's south side. Bordered by gray granite walls and gigantic spires, this spectacular chasm is North America's deepest gorge. Leaving the area, flightseers enter the immense, mountain-encircled glacial basins of Ruth Glacier's Don Sheldon Amphitheater. Among the enclosing peaks are some of the range's most rugged and descriptively named peaks, including Moose's Tooth and Rooster Comb.

After crossing into Alaska from the Yukon Territory on the Alaska Highway, the first vestiges of what passes for civilization in the Far North are found in the town of Tok. Here you'll find a visitor center, food, fuel, hotels, and a couple of restaurants, and the need to make a decision.

Staying on the Alaska Highway and heading roughly west will take you into the Interior and to Fairbanks, whereas heading south on the Tok Cutoff will aim you toward South Central Alaska and the population center of Anchorage. Or, you can make a huge loop tour, covering most of the paved highway in the state, taking in much of the terrific variety of landscapes and terrain that the 49th state has to offer. Head down the Tok Cutoff to the Richardson Highway (no one in Alaska uses the highway route numbers), and from there go south to Valdez. From there catch the ferry to Whittier, Cordova, or Seward, explore the Kenai and Anchorage, then head north on the Seward Highway to the parks, to Denali, Fairbanks, and beyond. Loop back to Tok and you've seen most of what can be seen from the road system.

The **Tetlin National Wildlife Refuge Visitor Center** parallels the Alaska Highway for the first 65 highway mi after leaving Canada and offers two seasonal campgrounds at Mileposts 1,249 and 1,256. This 700,000-acre refuge has most of the charismatic megafauna that visitors travel to Alaska to see, including black and grizzly bears, moose, Dall sheep, wolves, caribou, and tons of birds. The visitor center has a large deck with spotting scopes, and inside are maps, wildlife displays, books, and interpretive information. ✉ *Mi 1229, Alaska Hwy.* ☎ *907/883–5312*

WHERE TO PLAY ON THE WAY

If you're headed to Fortymile Country from Fairbanks, you'll drive along the historic Richardson Highway, once a pack-train (think mules with bags) trail and dogsled route for mail carriers and gold miners in the Interior. As quirky places to turn off a highway go, North Pole and Delta Junction are up there with the best of them.

NORTH POLE

It may be a featureless suburb of Fairbanks, but you'd have to be a Scrooge not to admit that this town's year-round acknowledgement of the December holiday season is at least a little bit fun to take in. If you stop in North Pole, don't skip the **Santa Claus House Gift Shop** (⊠ *Mi 349, Richardson Hwy.* ☎ *907/488–2200 or 800/588–4078* ⊕ *www.santaclaushouse.com*). Look for the giant Santa statue and the Christmas mural on the side of the building. You'll find toys, gifts, and Alaskan handicrafts; Santa is often on duty to talk to children.

The Knotty Shop (⊠ Mi 332, 6565 Richardson Hwy. , 32 mi south of Fairbanks ☎ 907/488–3014) has a large selection of Alaskan handicrafts as well as a mounted wildlife display and a yard full of spruce-burl sculptures, including a 6-foot mosquito and other wooden animals that photographers find hard to resist. Get served soft drinks and ice cream over a spruce burl counter.

DELTA JUNCTION

A good 100 mi southeast of Fairbanks, Delta is not only a handy stop on the Richardson Highway but is also the official western terminus of the Alaska Highway. It's no surprise, then, that in summer Delta becomes a bustling rest stop for road-weary travelers. On top of this, it's the largest agricultural center in Alaska, boasting a local farmers' market, meat-and-sausage company, and dairy. Delta is also known for its access to good fishing and its proximity to the Delta Bison Range. Don't expect to see the elusive 500-strong bison herd, though, as they roam free and generally avoid people.

At the actual junction of the Alaska and Richardson Hwys., stop in the **Delta Chamber of Commerce** (⊠ *Box 987, Delta Junction, 99737* ☎ *907/895–5068 or 877/895–5068* ⊕ *www.deltachamber.org*) for more information on the area. Across the street is the Sullivan Roadhouse Historical Museum and the Highway's End Farmer's Market, open on Wednesday and Saturday mid-May to early September. If you'd like to try local dairy and meat, check out the **Buffalo Center Drive-In** (☎ *907/895–4055* ⊙ *May–late Aug., Mon.–Sat. 11 am–10 pm, Sun. 12-10; closed winter*) just south of the Sullivan Roadhouse. Historic landmark **Rika's Roadhouse** (⊠ *Mi 275, Richardson Hwy.* ☎ *907/895–4201* ⊕ *www.rikas.com*), part of Big Delta State Historical Park, is a good detour for the free tours of the beautifully restored and meticulously maintained grounds, gardens, and historic buildings. Don't forget to try the delicious baked goods for lunch or breakfast.

7

⊕*tetlin.fws.gov* ✉*Free* ⊘*closed mid-Sept.–mid-May.*

To help with your planning, stop in at the **Tok Main Street Visitors Center** (⊠*Mi 1314, Alaska Hwy.* ☎*907 /883–5775*), which has travel information covering the entire state, as well as wildlife and natural-history exhibits. The staff is quite helpful.

ESSENTIALS

Medical Assistance **Public Health Clinic** (⊠*1314 Alaska Hwy.* ☎*907/883– 4101*).

WHERE TO EAT

$–$$$$
AMERICAN

✕**Fast Eddy's Restaurant.** It's much better than the name would indicate: the chef makes his own noodles for chicken noodle soup, and the homemade hoagies and pizza are a welcome relief from the roadhouse hamburgers served by most Alaska Highway restaurants. It's open 6 AM–11 PM (but the soup is usually gone by 5). ⊠*Mi 1,313.3, Alaska Hwy.* ☎*907/883–4411* ⊟*AE, D, MC, V.*

$–$$
SEAFOOD

✕**Gateway Salmon Bake & RV Park.** For highway travelers, Tok is the first stop in Alaska, and the Gateway is in turn the first stop in Tok. As an introduction to informal Alaska dining, it's tough to beat, with all-you-can-eat salmon, halibut, reindeer sausage, barbecue ribs, chicken, buffalo burgers, and salmon chowder. Seating is at picnic tables, either outdoors or under a covered pavilion. There's also a full-service RV park out back, and a very clean shower facility if you need to hose off the road dust from the long drive. ⊠*Mi 1,313.1, Alaska Hwy., ☎907/883–5555, 907/883–5578 in winter (mid-Sept.–mid-May)* ⊟ *AE, D, MC, V.*

WHERE TO STAY

$$

⌖ **Cleft of the Rock Bed & Breakfast.** With options for larger families and couples, this bed-and-breakfast offers either picturesque private cabins or comfortable rooms. **Pros:** Cabins with all the comforts of home, on-site basketball courts, close to town. **Cons:** No guided activities, no air-conditioning. ⊠ *Box 122, 0.5 Sundog Trail, off Mi 1,316.5 of the Alaska Hwy.* ☎*907/883–4219* ⊕*www.cleftoftherock.net* ⤴*5 cabins, 3 rooms* ㄴ*In room: no a/c, refrigerator, DVD (some), VCR (some), Wi-Fi. In hotel: no elevator, some pets allowed, no-smoking rooms* ⊟*D, MC, V* ⊘*Cabins closed mid-Sept.–mid-May* ⍓*BP.*

$

⌖**Westmark Tok.** Made up of a series of interconnected buildings, the hotel has been updated and has decent accommodations for this remote part of Alaska. The dining room serves standard fare, while the lounge makes a point of offering "Alaska's largest margaritas." The spacious dining room is a welcome respite when you are traveling the long stretches between civilization outposts along the Alaska Highway. **Pros:**

BORDER CROSSING

Crossing into Interior Alaska from the Lower 48 or from the ferry terminals in the Southeast requires border crossings into Canada and then into Alaska. Be very certain of all the requirements for crossing an international border before you travel, including restrictions on pets, firearms, and the need for adequate personal identification for every member of the party. Know that even citizens of Canada and the United States traveling between Alaska and Canada are now required to have a passport.

Internet access, margaritas to get lost in, some pets allowed. **Cons:** Not for those looking for lots of in-room character. ✉ *Junction of Alaska and Glenn Hwys.* 📬 *Box 130 Tok 99780* 🕾 *907/883–5174 or 800/544–0970* 🌐 *www.west-markhotels.com* 🖥 *92 rooms* ♿ *In-room: dial-up. In-hotel: restaurant, bar, no elevator, some pets allowed* 🟰 *AE, D, DC, MC, V* ☯ *Closed Oct.–May.*

SHOPPING

The **Burnt Paw** (✉ *Junction of Alaska and Glenn Hwys.* 🕾 *907/883–4121*

> **ON THE DEFENSIVE**
>
> Ft. Greely, which is 5 mi south of Tok toward Valdez, contains a growing number of underground silos with missiles that are part of the Ballistic Missile Defense System. The missiles are connected to tracking stations elsewhere and would be launched to try to shoot down enemy missiles in space if the United States were ever so attacked.

🌐 *www.burntpawcabins.com*) sells jade and ivory, Alaskan ceramics, crafts, paintings, smoked salmon—even sled-dog puppies. On display is a sled-dog equipment exhibit. There are also a B&B on the premises and log cabins with traditional Alaska sod roofs. In Northway, south of Tok, **Naabia Niign** (✉ *Mi 1264, Alaska Hwy.* 🕾 *907/778–2297*) is a native-owned crafts gallery with an excellent selection of authentic, locally made birch baskets, beadwork items, and fur moccasins and gloves.

7

CHICKEN

78 mi north of Tok, 109 mi west of Dawson City.

Chicken was, and still is, the heart of the southern Fortymile Mining District and many of these works are visible along the highway. Chicken has only a handful of permanent residents, mostly miners and trappers, creating an authentic frontier atmosphere. Do not trespass on private property, as miners rarely have a sense of humor about trespassing. Overland travel to Dawson City winds along a gravel road. Some drivers love it, some white-knuckle it. The road still closes for the entire winter, but in February and March snowmachiners hold a race on the road from Tok to Dawson City. Also, in June, Chicken hosts a music festival. There are only three businesses in town.

Get a feel for the past through a gold-mining adventure or tour of one of Chicken's three historical gold dredges at the Chicken Gold Camp & Outpost. The Gold Camp also provides meals, drinks, cabins, a campground/RV park, as well as gold panning, kayaking, and other activities.

Chicken Alaska, Inc. provides multiple services such as food, gifts, and gas at one location with Western-style wooden sidewalks connecting the buildings. The Chicken Creek Salmon Bake is open here from 4 to 8 pm. All in one establishment are the Goldpanner Gift Shop, Chicken Creek RV Park, the Old Town of Chicken, and the Chicken Creek Country Club. There is a gift shop with free wireless Internet, the RV park has gas and diesel, cabin rentals, and camping sites, and the Old Town provides daily tours of the Tisha's Schoolhouse at 9 AM and 2 PM.

SPORTS, THE OUTDOORS & GUIDED TOURS

CANOEING The beautiful **Fortymile River** offers everything from a 38-mi run to a lengthy journey to the Yukon and then down to Eagle. Its waters range from easy Class I to serious Class IV (possibly Class V) stretches. Only experienced canoeists should attempt boating on this river, and rapids should be scouted beforehand. Several access points can be found off the Taylor Highway.

Canoe Alaska (☎ *907/883–2628* ⊕ *canoealaska.net*) has been conducting guided canoe and raft trips on Interior Alaska rivers since 1980. Trips (mid-May–Labor Day) range from two to eight days on rivers that vary in difficulty and remoteness. Evening interpretive tours in the *Arctic Voyageur,* a replica of a 34-foot voyageur canoe, are offered on a lake. Multiday *Voyageur* trips, canoe instruction, and rentals to qualified paddlers are also available.

EAGLE

95 mi north of Chicken, 144 mi northwest of Dawson City. Road closed in winter.

Eagle was once a seat of government and commerce for the Interior. An Army post, Ft. Egbert, operated here until 1911, and territorial judge James Wickersham had his headquarters in Eagle until Fairbanks began to grow from its gold strike. The population peaked at 1,700 in 1898. Today it is fewer than 200. Although the majority of the population is gone, the town still retains its frontier and gold-rush facade.

The Yukon River has shaped Eagle in more ways than just geography. In earlier times, it provided a vital mode of transportation. Today vacationers use Eagle as a jumping-off point for journeys through the Yukon-Charley Rivers National Preserve.

The **Eagle Historical Society** (✉ *1st St.* ☎ *907/547–2325* ⊕ *www.eagleak. org*) has a two- to three-hour walking tour ($5) that visits six museum buildings while regaling participants with tales of the famous people (including arctic explorer Roald Amundsen) who have passed through this historic Yukon River border town. One daily tour begins at the courthouse at 9 AM, from Memorial Day to Labor Day. For the extra-curious traveler, there is an extensive archive and photo collection with staff available to help dig into the late 1800s. In addition, the Museum Store offers locally made items and locally oriented books.

The **National Park Service and BLM Visitor Center** (✉ *Yukon–Charley Rivers National Preserve* ☎ *907/547–2233* ⊕ *www.nps.gov/yuch*) is the headquarters for the 2.5-million-acre Yukon–Charley Rivers National Preserve. Informal interpretive programs, talks, and videos are available. Peruse the reference library, maps, and books for sale. It's located off 1st Avenue by the airstrip and the Yukon River, and is open Memorial to Labor Day.

YUKON TERRITORY

Gold! That's what called Canada's Yukon Territory to the world's attention with the Klondike Gold Rush of 1897–98. Although Yukon gold mining today is mainly in the hands of a few large companies that go almost unnoticed by the visitor, the territory's history is alive and thriving.

Though the international border divides Alaska from Yukon Territory, the Yukon River tends to unify the region. Early prospectors, miners, traders, and camp followers moved readily up and down the river with little regard to national boundaries. An earlier Alaska strike preceded the Klondike find by years, yet Circle was all but abandoned in the stampede to the creeks around Dawson City. Later gold discoveries in the Alaskan Fortymile Country, Nome, and Fairbanks reversed that flow across the border into Alaska.

DAWSON CITY

109 mi east of Chicken.

Dawson City is often considered one of the most prime specimens of a Yukon gold-rush town. Since the first swell of hopeful migrants more than 100 years ago, many of the original buildings have disappeared, victims of fire, flood, and weathering. But enough of them have been preserved and restored to give more than a hint of the city's former grandeur: in the years leading up to the turn of the 20th century, Dawson was transformed into the largest, most refined city north of San Francisco and west of Winnipeg. It had grand buildings with running water, telephones, and electricity. In 1899 the city's population numbered almost 30,000. Now home to about 1,500 people, Dawson City serves as a base from which to explore a region sometimes referred to as the "Patagonia of the northern hemisphere": there are plants and animals here the that aren't found anywhere else this side of the Equator.

GETTING HERE & AROUND

The Alaska Highway starts in Dawson Creek and goes almost 1,500 mi to Fairbanks. Drivers traveling north and southbound on the Alaska Highway can make a loop with the Taylor Highway route. This adds 100 mi to the trip, but is worth it. Part with the Alaska Highway at Tetlin Junction and wind through the Fortymile Country past the little communities of Chicken and Jack Wade Camp into Canada. The border is open 8 AM to 8 PM in summer. The Canadian section of the Taylor Highway is called Top of the World Highway. Broad views of range after range of tundra-covered mountains stretch in every direction. Join back with the Alaska Highway at Whitehorse.

Numerous bus companies offer package tours or simple shuttle services (⇨ Whitehorse Essentials, *below*). Regular air service to Dawson flies from Fairbanks in summer. **Air North** (☎ *800/661–0407* ⊕ *www. flyairnorth.com*), based in Whitehorse, offers direct air service from Whitehorse to Dawson City in summer.

ALASKA HIGHWAY HISTORY

It's hard to overestimate the importance of the Alaska Highway in the state's history. Before World War II there was no road connection between the Alaskan Interior and the rest of North America. Alaska's population center was in the coastal towns of the Southeast panhandle region, and most of the state's commerce was conducted along its waterways. Access to the Interior was via riverboat, until 1923 when the railroad connection from Seward through Anchorage and into Fairbanks was completed.

The onset of World War II changed everything. An overland route to the state was deemed a matter vital to national security in order to supply war material to the campaign in the Aleutians, and to fend off a potential invasion by Japan. In a feat of amazing engineering and construction prowess, the 1,500-mi-long route was carved out of the wilderness in eight months in 1942. The original road was crude but effective, and has been undergoing constant maintenance and upgrading ever since. Today the highway is easily traversed by every form of highway vehicle imaginable, from bicycles and motorcycles to the biggest, lumbering RVs known not so affectionately by locals as "road barns."

ESSENTIALS

Emergency Assistance **Royal Canadian Mounted Police** (☎ *867/993–2677*).

Internet **Tasty Byte Internet Cafe** (✉ Front and King Sts. ☎ *867/993–6100*).

Medical Assistance **Dawson City Nursing Station** (✉ *350 Church St.* ☎ *867/993–4444*).

Visitor & Tour Info **Visitor Information Centre** (✉ *1102 Front St.* ☎ *867/993–5566* ☉ *Early May–late Sept.*). **Klondike Visitors Association** (✉ *1102 Front St.* ☎ *867/993–5575*).

WHAT TO SEE

❷ The **Dawson City Museum,** housing the Yukon's largest collection, presents exhibits focusing on the gold rush, but also includes the geology and prehistory of the Klondike, as well as of the First Nations. Four restored locomotives from the Klondike Mines Railway are housed in an adjacent building. The museum also features a library and archives. Daily programs and costumed interpreters are featured during the summer season. ✉ *Territorial Administration Bldg., 5th Ave.* ☎ *867/993–5291* ⊕ *www.dawsonmuseum.ca* ✍ *C$9* ☉ *Mid-May–Labor Day, daily 10–6; call ahead for winter visits.*

❶ **Diamond Tooth Gertie's Gambling Hall** (✉ *Arctic Brotherhood Hall, Queen St.* ☎ *867/993–5575*), for adults 19 and over only, presents live entertainment and three different cancan shows three times a night, seven days a week from May until late September. It is the only authentic, legal gambling establishment operating in all of the north and the oldest in Canada. Yes, there really was a Diamond Tooth Gertie—Gertie Lovejoy, a prominent dance-hall queen who had a diamond between her two front teeth.

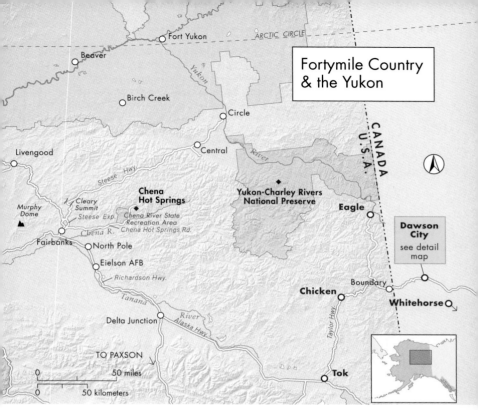

Fortymile Country & the Yukon

⑤ Parks Canada leads tours to **Gold Dredge Number 4**, along Bonanza Creek, a wooden-hull gold dredge about 20 minutes outside town. The one-hour walking tour takes you into what's billed as "the largest wooden hulled, bucket line gold dredge in North America." There's also a short film about the site and the restoration of the dredge. Nearby you can visit working gold mines or pan for gold yourself in Bonanza Creek, where the Klondike Visitors Association offers a free claim for visitors. Be sure to bring your own supplies. Exit the Klondike Highway at km Marker 74. ✉ *Mi 8, Bonanza Creek Rd. 867/993–7200* ⊕ *www.pc.gc.ca* ✉ *C$6* ⊗ *End May--mid-Sept., daily 10–4; restoration work continues on the dredge, so please confirm ahead.*

③ **Jack London's cabin** (✉ *8th Ave. and Firth St.* ☎ *867/993–5575* ✉ *C$2* ⊗ *Mid-May–mid-Sept., daily interpretation presentations*) is literally a stone's throw from Robert Service's cabin. This reproduction of London's home from 1897 to 1898 is constructed with some of the wood from his original wilderness home that was found south of Dawson in the 1930s. The small museum contains photos, documents, and letters from London's life and the gold-rush era. Half-hour talks are given twice daily during peak season.

4 Scholars still argue the precise details of the lives of writers Robert Service (1874–1958) and Jack London (1876–1916) in Dawson City, but no one disputes that between Service's poems and London's short stories, the two did more than anyone else to popularize and romanticize the Yukon. Service lived in his Dawson cabin from 1909 to 1912. **Robert Service's cabin** (✉8th Ave. and Hanson St. ☎867/993–7237 ✉C$6) is open for visitors June through mid-September and provides multiple daily readings, including an evening program.

SPORTS, THE OUTDOORS & GUIDED TOURS

BOATING The **Klondike River** offers a chance to relax on a Class 1 river. You can put in at the Dempster Highway Bridge or Rock Creek. The journey ends when the Klondike spits you into the Yukon River at Dawson. Plan for a four- to seven-hour trip, but don't forget to take advantage of fishing and photo ops along the way. **Gray Line** (☎867/993–5599 or 888/452–1737 ⊕www.graylinealaska.com/sightseeingtours.cfm) offers guided 3½-hour float trips twice a day at 12:30 and 4:30 for $75. Pickup is at Westmark Dawson City.

HIKING **Tombstone Territorial Park** (✉Box 600, Dawson City ☎867/993–6850 in Dawson City, 867/667–5648 in Whitehorse, 866/617–2757 toll free ⊕www.yukonparks.ca ⊗Interpretative center late May—mid.-Sept.), located an hour and a half north of Dawson City and bisected by the Dempster Highway, is a 2,200-sq-km (1,400-sq-mi) area, dubbed the "Patagonia of the northern hemisphere" and offering some of the best hiking and views of granite peaks in the Yukon. The unique geology and geography of this wilderness supports a vast array of wildlife and vegetation. The park maintains one trail at Kilometer 56, along with one campground and an interpretative center at Kilometer 71.4. Backcountry and mountaineering options are endless.

WHERE TO STAY

$-$$$ 🍴**Bombay Peggy's.** Named and fashioned after one of the last of Daw-
★ son's legal madams, Peggy's is done in elaborate Victorian gold-rush style, with heavy, plush draperies and rich color schemes. Bathrooms have claw-foot tubs and pedestal sinks, and the beds have elaborate headboards. In the evening, sherry, port, and sweets are served in the parlor, and in the morning, fresh croissants are delivered, while locally roasted coffee and tea coffee are available in the rooms. The adjoining pub serves appetizers along with a large selection of single-malt scotches. **Pros:** Little imagination is needed to step back in time thanks to elaborate refurbishing, nice touches like fresh croissants and the "Sherry Hour." **Cons:** No elevator, not all rooms have air-conditioning. ✉2nd Ave. and Princess St. 867/993–6969 ⊕www.bombaypeggys. com ➴3 rooms, 6 suites ⚒In-room: a/c (some), DVD (some), VCR, Wi-Fi. In-hotel: no elevator, public Wi-Fi, airport shuttle, no-smoking rooms ☰MC, V ⭐CP.

$$ **Downtown Hotel.** A large collection of local artwork, including mushing scenes and antiques, adds to the hotel's early-1900s decorations. The original structure was built in 1902, but was destroyed in 1980 by a fire. Rebuilt in 1981–82, the exterior preserves the look of the frontier. At the hotel's moderately expensive Jack London Grill, go for the

Dawson City

Canadian and American regional specialties, including daily appetizer, pasta, and prime-rib specials. The restaurant serves three meals a day and has an outside deck for summer dining. Suites have air-conditioning. **Pros:** Courtyard with a Jacuzzi, in the heart of downtown. **Cons:** Not all rooms have air-conditioning, no elevator. ✉*2nd Ave. and Queen St. 867/993–5346, 800/661–0514 reservations* ⊕*http://downtownhotel.ca* ⊷*59 rooms, 5 suites* ⌂*In-room: kitchen (some), refrigerator (some), Wi-Fi. In-hotel: restaurant, bar, no elevator, laundry facilities, airport shuttle, no-smoking rooms* ▭*AE, D, MC, V.*

$$ 🏨 **Eldorado Hotel.** The lobby of this hotel has gold rush–era decor. During the summer tourist season the staff dresses in 1898-era garb. However, the modern rooms, some with kitchenettes, are outfitted with decidedly non-1898 amenities such as cable TV and remote controls. The Bonanza Dining Room, open from breakfast to dinner, serves hearty Alaskan halibut, Yukon salmon, and flambéed steaks. **Pros:** In-hotel bar and restaurant, order a drink at the Sluice Box Lounge from a server in classic cancan garb. **Cons:** No elevator, basic rooms. ✉*3rd Ave. and Princess St. 867/993–5451, 800/764–3536 from Alaska* ⊕*www.eldoradohotel.ca* ⊷*46 rooms, 16 suites* ⌂*In-room: a/c (some), kitchen (some), Wi-Fi. In-hotel: restaurant, bar, no elevator, laundry service, airport shuttle* ▭*AE, D, DC, MC, V.*

$$ **Triple J Hotel.** Log cabins with kitchenettes, a central hotel, and a detached annex make up this clean, quiet compound next to Diamond Tooth Gertie's. All rooms have TVs, phones, and private baths. **Pros:** Coffeemakers and coffee in every room, coin-operated laundry facilities. **Cons:** Some rooms could use a face-lift, no DVD or VCR. ⊠*5th Ave. and Queen St. 867/993–5323 or 800/764–3555* ⊕*www.triplejhotel.com* ☏*29 rooms, 18 cabins* ♿*In-room: kitchen (some). In-hotel: restaurant, bar, laundry facilities, airport shuttle, no-smoking rooms* ☰*AE, DC, MC, V.*

$$ **Westmark Dawson City.** This downtown two-story hotel is built around a central courtyard and is convenient to the sights. With its flocked wallpaper and lace curtains, the lobby and rooms recall the days of the gold rush. Choose from Belinda's Full Service Dining Room or the famous Klondike Barbeque to fill your belly. **Pros:** Good location, laundry facilities, gold-rush ambience. **Cons:** No elevator, not all rooms have air-conditioning. ⊠*5th Ave. and Harper St. 867/993–5542, 800/544–0970 reservations* ⊕*www.westmarkhotels.com* ☏*177 rooms* ♿*In-room: no-ac (some) In-hotel: restaurant, bar, no elevator, laundry facilities, public Internet, some pets allowed, no-smoking rooms* ☰*AE, MC, V* ☉*Closed mid-Sept.–mid-May.*

WHITEHORSE

337 mi southeast of Dawson City, 600 mi southeast of Fairbanks.

Near the White Horse Rapids of the Yukon River, Whitehorse began as an encampment in the late 1890s. It was a logical layover for gold rushers heading north along the Chilkoot Trail toward Dawson. The next great population boom came during World War II with the building of the Alcan—the Alaska-Canada Highway. Today this city of more than 22,000 residents is Yukon's center of commerce, communication, and transportation and the seat of the territorial government.

Besides being a great starting point for explorations of other areas of the Yukon, the town has plenty of diversions and recreational opportunities. You can spend a day exploring its museums and cultural displays—research the Yukon's mining and development history, look into the backgrounds of the town's founders, learn about its indigenous First Nations people, and gain an appreciation of the Yukon Territory from prehistoric times up to the present.

GETTING HERE & AROUND

Air Canada (☎*888/247–2262* ⊕*www.aircanada.com*) flies in summer from Anchorage through Vancouver to Whitehorse. **Air North** (☎*800/661–0407* ⊕*www.flyairnorth.com*), based in Whitehorse, offers direct, seasonal air service between Alaska and Canada, flying regular runs from Fairbanks, Dawson City, and Whitehorse.

To take in all the scenery along the way, you can drive yourself up the Alcan Highway, or let someone else do the driving on a bus tour. Alaska Direct Bus travels to Anchorage and Fairbanks year-round. Trips to Dawson City are in summer only. Alaska/Yukon Trails provides transportation to Carcross, Jake's Corner, and Atlin. MGM Services offers service from Inuvik to Whitehorse year-round when weather permits; charter trips are available. There are multiple rental-car companies, buses, and taxis in Whitehorse; Whitehorse Transit has a city bus circuit that will get you where you need to go.

ESSENTIALS

Bus Contacts **Alaska Direct Bus** (✉ *501 Ogilvie St.* ☎ *800/770–6652 in Alaska, 867/668–4833 in Canada* ⊕ *www.alaskadirectbus.com*). **Alaska/Yukon Trails** (☎ *800/770–7275* ⊕ *www.alaskashuttle.com*)*ransportation to Alaska and Dawson City.* **Alaskon Express Operated by Gray Line** (☎ *907/451–6835 or 800/478– 6388* ⊕ *www.graylineofalaska.com*). **Atlin Express** (☎ *867/668–4444*). **MGM Services** (☎ *867/777–4295 or 867/678–0129* ⊕ *www.mgmbusservices.ca*).

City Bus **Whitehorse Transit** (✉ *139 Tlingit St.* ☎ *867/668–8394* ⊕ *www.city. whitehorse.yk.ca* ✑ *C$2*).

Currency Exchange **Bank of Montreal** (✉ *111 Main St.* ☎ *867/668–4200*). **Scotiabank** (✉ *212 Main St.* ☎ *867/667–6231*).

Emergency Assistance **Royal Canadian Mounted Police** (☎ *867/667–5555*).

Internet **Whitehorse Public Library** (✉ *2071 2nd Ave., Downtown* ☎ *867/667– 5239* ⊕ *www.pac.gov.yk.ca*) has free 30-minute Internet use.

Medical Assistance **Medicine Chest Pharmacy** (✉ *406 Lambert St.* ☎ *867/668– 7000*). **Second Avenue Walk-In Clinic** (✉ *102-2131 2nd Ave.* ☎ *867/667–6119*). **Whitehorse General Hospital** (✉ *5 Hospital Rd.* ☎ *867/393–8700*).

Post Office **Canada Post** (✉ *303 Olgivie St., Qwanlin Mall* ☎ *867/667–2858*).

Rental Cars **Budget Rent-A-Car** (☎ *867/667–6200 or 800/268–8900* ⊕ *www. budget.com*). **Hertz** (☎ *867/668–4224 or 800/654–3131* ⊕ *www.hertz.com*). **National Car Rental** (☎ *867/456–2277* ⊕ *www.nationalcar.com*). **Whitehorse Subaru** (☎ *867/393–6550* ⊕ *www.whitehorsesubaru.com*).

Taxis **5th Avenue Taxi, Yellow Cab, and Whitehorse Taxi** (☎ *867/667–4111*). **Yukon Taxi Service** (☎ *867/667–6677*)

Visitor & Tour Info **City Hall** (✉ *2121 2nd Ave., Yukon Territory, Canada* ☎ *867/668–8687* ⊕ *www.visitwhitehorse.com*). . **Whitehorse Visitor Reception Centre** (✉ *100 Hanson St., Yukon Territory, Canada* ☎ *867/667–3084 or 800/661–0494* ⊕ *www.travelyukon.com* ☺ *May–Sept., daily 8–8; Oct.–Apr., weekdays 8:30–5*).

WHAT TO SEE

The **Canyon City Archaeological Dig** provides a glimpse into the past of the local First Nations people. Long before the area was developed by Western civilizations, the First Nations people used the Miles Canyon area as a seasonal fish camp. The Yukon Conservation Society conducts free tours of the area twice a day in summer; it also leads walks and hikes from short, child-friendly tours to challenging five- to six-hour scrambles on the nearby mountains. All the hikes are free and provide a great way to see the surrounding countryside with local naturalists. The society office houses a bookstore on Yukon history and wilderness and sells souvenirs, maps, and posters. ⊠*302 Hawkins St.* ☎*867/668–5678* ⊕*www.yukonconservation.org* ⊒*Free* ⊙*Tours July–late Aug., weekdays at 10 and 2.*

The **MacBride Museum** is your best general introduction to the spirit and history of the Yukon. From gold-rush fever to the birth of Whitehorse, the museum offers a comprehensive view of the colorful characters and groundbreaking events that shaped the territory. The facility boasts a unique collection of wildlife, geology, historic artifacts, and photographs, alongside First Nation beadwork. Outdoor artifacts include the cabin of Sam McGee, who was immortalized in Robert Service's famous poem, "The Cremation of Sam McGee." MacBride also offers guided tours and a chance to try your hand at one of the Yukon's oldest professions—gold panning. ⊠*1124 1st Ave. and Wood St.* ☎*867/667–2709* ⊕*www.macbridemuseum.com* ⊒*C$7* ⊙*Mid-May–Aug., daily 9-6; Sept. –mid-May, Tues.–Sat. noon–4.*

Miles Canyon, a 10-minute drive south of Whitehorse, is both scenic and historic. Although the dam below it makes the canyon seem relatively tame, it was this perilous stretch of the Yukon River that determined the location of Whitehorse as the starting point for river travel north. In 1897 Jack London won the admiration—and cash—of fellow stampeders headed north to the Klondike goldfields because of his steady hand as pilot of hand-hewn wooden boats here. You can hike on trails along the canyon or take a two-hour cruise aboard the MV *Schwatka* and experience the canyon from the waters of Lake Schwatka. This lake was created by the dam built in 1959, putting an end to the infamous Whitehorse Rapids. ⊠*68 Miles Canyon Rd., 1 mi from Whitehorse city center 867/668–4716* ⊕ *www.yukonrivercruises.com* ⊙*Cruises depart daily early June–mid-Sept.*

★ The **SS *Klondike***, a national historic site, is dry-docked on the banks of the Yukon River in central Whitehorse's Rotary Park. The 210-foot stern-wheeler was built in 1929, sank in 1936, and was rebuilt in 1937. In the days when the Yukon River was the transportation link between Whitehorse and Dawson City, the *Klondike* was the largest boat plying the river. ⊠*Robert Service Way and 2nd Ave.* ☎*867/667–4511* mid-May–midSept., *867/667–3910* in winter ⊕ *www.pc.gc.ca/lhn-nhs/yt/ssklondike* ⊒*C$6* ⊙*Mid-May–mid-Sept., daily 9–6.*

At **Takhini Hot Springs**, off the Klondike Highway, there's swimming in the hot spring–warmed water (suits and towels are for rent), horseback riding, areas for camping with tent and RV sites, picnicking, an outdoor climbing wall, and a licensed (beer and wine) restaurant. ⊠*Km 10, Takhini Hot Springs Rd., 17 mi north of Whitehorse* ☎*867/633–2706* ⊕*www.takhinihotsprings.yk.ca* ⊒*C$9.50* ⊙*May–Sept., daily 8 AM–10 PM; call for winter hrs.*

The **Waterfront Walkway** along the Yukon River will take you past a few points of interest. Your walk starts on the path along the river just east of the MacBride Museum entrance on 1st Avenue. Traveling upstream (south), you'll go by the old White Pass & Yukon Route Building on Main Street.

7

If you're in Whitehorse in late summer, it's possible to see chinook (king) salmon. They hold one of nature's great endurance records: the longest fish migration in the world, which is more than 1,800 mi from the ocean to Whitehorse. The **Whitehorse Rapids Dam and Fish Ladder,** celebrating 50 years in operation in 2009, has interpretive exhibits, display tanks of freshwater fish, and a platform for viewing the fish ladder. The best time to visit is August, when between 150 and 2,100 salmon (average count is 800) use the ladder to bypass the dam. ⊠ *End of Nisutlin Dr.* ☎ *867/633–5965* ☉ *June–Labor Day, daily; hrs vary, so call ahead.*

Near the Whitehorse Airport is the **Yukon Beringia Interpretive Centre,** which presents the story of the Yukon during the last Ice Age. Beringia is the name given to the large subcontinental landmass of eastern Siberia and Interior Alaska and the Yukon, which were linked by the Bering Land Bridge during the latest Ice Age. Large dioramas depict the lives of animals in Ice Age Beringia and there are replicas of skeletons of the animals. The exhibits examine the area's prehistory up to the First Nations people and through to the mining era. ⊠ *Mi 914, Alaska Hwy.* ☎ *867/667–8855* ⊕ *www.beringia.com* ☎ *C$6* ☉ *Mid-May–late Sept., daily 9–6, and by appointment.*

The lobby of the Yukon Government Building displays the **Yukon Permanent Art Collection,** featuring traditional and contemporary works by Yukon artists. In addition to the collection on the premises, the brochure *Art Adventures on Yukon Time,* available at visitor reception centers throughout the Yukon, guides you to artists' studios with gallery and art-shop locations. ⊠ *2071 2nd Ave.* ☎ *867/667–5811* ☎ *Free* ☉ *Weekdays 8:30–5.*

The **Yukon Wildlife Preserve** provides a fail-safe way of photographing rarely spotted animals in a natural setting. Animals roaming freely here include elk, caribou, mountain goats, musk ox, bison, mule deer, and Dall and Stone sheep. Gray Line Yukon runs two-hour tours with an hour in the preserve. ⊠ *Gray Line Yukon, 2nd Ave. at Steele St.,* ☎ *867/668–3225* ⊕ *www.graylineyukon.com* ☎ *C$29* ☉ *Tours mid-May–mid-Sept., daily.*

OUTDOOR ACTIVITIES

HIKING   The **Kluane National Park and Reserve** (⊠ *Visitor Center, 119 Logan St., Haines Junction* ☎ *867/634–7207*), about 170 km (100 mi) west of Whitehorse, has millions of acres for hiking. The **Yukon Conservation Society** (☎ *867/668–5678*) leads hiking expeditions of varying lengths and difficulty.

SLED-DOG   Whitehorse and Fairbanks organize the **Yukon Quest International Sled-**
RACING   **Dog Race** (☎ *867/668–4711* ⊕ *www.yukonquest.org*) in February. The race's starting line alternates yearly between the two cities. This is one of the longest and toughest races in the north.

WHERE TO EAT

$$$–$$$$
CONTINENTAL

✕**The Cellar Steakhouse & Wine Bar.** In the Edgewater Hotel in downtown Whitehorse, this intimate two-room spot—down some stairs, as the name implies—is touted by the locals as the place to go for special occasions. The "front" room is less formal, with a bar and TV, while the back room, separated by an etched glass partition, is quieter. The menu offers seafood and meat dishes and a tapas selection, complemented by a decent wine list. ✉*101 Main St.* ☎*867/667–2572* ☰*AE, DC, MC, V.*

¢–$
CAFÉ
★

✕**Chocolate Claim.** Choose from fresh-baked breads and pastries, homemade soups and sandwiches, salads, and quiches at this charming café and deli. Artwork—ranging from paintings and pottery to rugs and quilts by local artists—is on display and for sale. On sunny days you can sit outside. Friday happy hour is from 5 to 7 PM, with live music. ✉*305 Strickland St.* ☎*867/667–2202* ☰*AE, MC, V* ☾*Closed Sun.*

$$$–$$$$
SOUTHERN

✕**Klondike Rib & Salmon BBQ.** If you're in the mood for something completely different, this is the place. It's one of the very few establishments where you can order arctic char, caribou, and musk ox, as well as the more common barbecue specialties: salmon, halibut, ribs, and chicken. It's open for lunch, but the game dishes are served only at dinner. It's very popular, so plan on a long wait on summer weekends. ✉*2nd Ave. and Steele St.* ☎*867/667–7554* ☰*MC, V* ☾*Closed mid-Sept.–mid-May.*

WHERE TO STAY

$$$

🏠**Edgewater Hotel.** Located on a quiet end of Main Street, this corner hotel, first built during the 1898 gold rush, is in its third incarnation (the first two burned down). Two great reasons to stay are the Cellar Steakhouse and Wine Bar, which is first-rate, if not classy, and the Edge Bar and Grill, which offers cheaper eats for breakfast through dinner. The small lobby is adorned with old photos of the hotel's predecessors, giving a feel for the gold-rush era. **Pros:** Rich history, good location across the street from the Yukon River. **Cons:** Small lobby and hallways to rooms, no continental breakfast. ✉*101 Main St.* ☎*867/667–2572 or 877/484–3334* ⊕*www.edgewaterhotelwhitehorse.com* ⤶*30 rooms, 3 suites* ♿*In-room: a/c (some), kitchen (some), Wi-Fi. In-hotel: restaurant, bar, no elevator, parking (no fee), no-smoking rooms* ☰*AE, DC, MC, V.*

$$–$$$$

🏠**High Country Inn.** At this downtown inn you'll find tastefully appointed modern rooms. Deluxe suites come with canopy beds, hot tubs, and kitchenettes. Public areas are cozy, complete with a fireplace, and the inn is near the SS *Klondike* and waterfront trails. In summer the hotel's Yukon Mining Company Saloon provides heated decks that draw in crowds to enjoy a late sunset. **Pros:** Stay connected with Wi-Fi, try locally brewed beers at the saloon. **Cons:** Not all rooms have air-conditioning, standard rooms are minimally decorated. ✉*4051 4th Ave.* ☎*867/667–4471 or 800/554–4471* ⊕*www.highcountryinn.yk.ca* ⤶*84 rooms, 18 suites* ♿*In-room: a/c (some), kitchen (some), refrigerator (some), Ethernet (some), Wi-Fi. In-hotel: restaurant, bar, gym, laundry facilities, public Internet, some pets allowed, no-smoking rooms* ☰*AE, D, MC, V.*

7

$$ **Westmark Whitehorse Hotel and Conference Center.** You can catch a nightly Klondike vaudeville show, the Frantic Follies, in summer at this full-service hotel in the heart of downtown, the largest hotel in the Yukon. The lobby has low tables and plush chairs, and a beautiful model of the *Klondike* riverboat. The restaurant serves nightly specials featuring local cuisine, filet mignon, salmon, and low-calorie selections. **Pros:** Laundry facilities, some pets allowed. **Cons:** Not the place to go to escape the action, not all rooms have air-conditioning. ✉ *2nd Ave. and Wood St.* ☎ *867/393–9700, 800/544–0970 reservations* ⊕ *www.westmarkhotels.com* ⇗ *180 rooms, 8 suites* ⚭ *In-room: no a/c (some), Wi-Fi. In-hotel: restaurant, bar, laundry facilities, parking (no fee), some pets allowed, no-smoking rooms* ▭ *AE, MC, V.*

The Bush

INCLUDING NOME, BARROW, PRUDHOE BAY & THE ALEUTIAN ISLANDS

WORD OF MOUTH

"There are places in Katmai with bears active in mid-August, but in places like Brooks Camp the bears are thick four weeks earlier and two weeks later...Make sure you book with a good outfitter who will fly to the right spots."

—Bill_H

WELCOME TO THE BUSH

Lunchtime for this Alaskan grizzly

TOP REASONS TO GO

★ **Spend time in the company of bears:** The Alaska Peninsula has the world's largest concentrations of brown bears, which congregate near salmon runs each year.

★ **Learn about native culture:** Native communities throughout Alaska are celebrating and supporting their cultural traditions. Come to the bush for everything from blanket tossing to arts-and-crafts exhibits.

★ **Go fishing:** You'll see 100-pound salmon, 8-pound trout, and you can be the only one on your block to know what sheefish tastes like.

★ **Experience the Land of the Midnight Sun:** Though all of Alaska has long hours of daylight in summer, only north of the Arctic Circle is the sun above the horizon 24 hours a day; in Barrow the sun doesn't set from mid-May to August.

★ **Get outside like never before:** Want the world to yourself? Bush Alaska includes millions of acres of remote parklands and wildlife refuges, including the least-visited national park in the United States.

1 **Southwest.** This broad area ranges from the northern shores of the Shelikof Strait to the Yukon-Kuskokwim Delta. It's Alaska's least-developed region; small native villages are scattered among an immense richness of wilderness, fish, and wildlife.

2 **Northwest & the Arctic.** This region runs from the Seward Peninsula to Alaska's northernmost mountain chain, the Brooks Range, and the vast plain of the North Slope. Also home to the Porcupine Caribou Herd and the Alaska National Wildlife Refuge, the Arctic is a balancing act of pristine wilderness, oil development, and villages where whale meat is still a vital part of the daily diet.

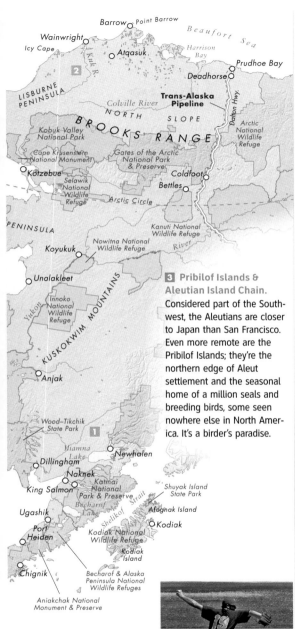

GETTING ORIENTED

As much a lifestyle as a place, "the bush" generally refers to all of mainland Alaska that lies beyond the road system, plus the western islands. And that really means about 90% of the state. Geographically, though, the bush encompasses all of western Alaska, from the North Pacific to the Beaufort Sea; that part of Alaska's mainland lying north of the Arctic Circle; and a good chunk of the Interior. Figure it this way: if your cell phone works, you're probably not in the bush.

8

3 Pribilof Islands & Aleutian Island Chain. Considered part of the Southwest, the Aleutians are closer to Japan than San Francisco. Even more remote are the Pribilof Islands; they're the northern edge of Aleut settlement and the seasonal home of a million seals and breeding birds, some seen nowhere else in North America. It's a birder's paradise.

Muskox in Brooks Range.

Baseball under the midnight sun.

THE BUSH
PLANNER

Timing

The best time to visit is from June through August, when the weather is mildest (though you should still anticipate cool, wet, and sometimes stormy weather), daylight hours are longest, and the wildlife is most abundant.. Because summer is so short, though, things happen fast, and seasonal activities may need to be crammed into just a couple of weeks.

Go birding in May and June, when migrants come through. The peak wildflower season is usually short, particularly in the Arctic, when most flowers may not blossom until mid-June and then go to seed by late July.

Salmon runs vary from region to region, so it's best to do your homework before choosing dates. For the most part, though, you're looking at July and August, which is also when the tundra starts turning from its summer hues to autumnal colors. Bear viewing coincides with salmon runs.

Getting Around

It's nearly impossible to travel to or around the bush without taking an air taxi. Still, a few areas are accessible by car or boat. The Dalton Highway (Haul Road) connects with the state's highway system and traverses the Arctic, but it only leads to the oil fields of Prudhoe Bay. In the Aleutians, the Alaska Marine Highway, the state's amazing ferry system, makes monthly trips April through October between Kodiak and Dutch Harbor/Unalaska.

Alaska Airlines flies within Alaska to most major communities, either via Alaska or its subsidiary, Horizon Air. Peninsula Airways serves the communities on the Alaskan Peninsula, the Aleutian and Pribilof islands, and parts of the Interior and northwest.

Anchorage and Fairbanks air taxis serve the bush, as do bush-based carriers such as Bering Air, which also offers flightseeing tours and, weather and politics permitting, specially arranged charter flights to Provid" eniya, on the Siberian coast across the Bering Strait. Frontier Flying Service serves the Interior and the Bering and Arctic coasts. Wright Air Service flies throughout the Interior and Arctic Alaska.

Information about certified air-taxi operations is available from the Federal Aviation Administration. Individual parks and Alaska Public Lands Information centers can also supply lists of reputable air-taxi services. Make your reservations in advance, and plan for the unexpected; weather can delay a scheduled pick-up for days.

Information **Alaska Airlines** (☏ 800/426–0333 ⊕ www. alaskaair.com). **Alaska Public Lands Information Center** (☏ 907/456–0527 or 866/869–6887 ⊕ www.nps.gov/ aplic). **Alaska State Ferry** (☏ 800/642–0066 ⊕ www. dot.state.ak.us/amhs). **Bering Air** (☏ 907/443–5464, 800/478–5422 in Alaska, 907/443–5620 Russian desk ⊕ www.beringair.com). **Federal Aviation Administration** (☏ 907/271–2000 ⊕ www.faa.gov). **Frontier Flying Service** (☏ 907/450–7250, 800/478–6779 for reservations ⊕ www.frontierflying.com). **Peninsula Airways** (☏ 907/243–2323 or 800/448–4226 ⊕ www.penair. com). **Wright Air Service** (☏ 907/474–0502, 800/478– 0502 in Alaska ⊕ www.wrightair.net).

Money Matters

Most small villages don't have bank offices, so visitors should bring money or, even better, traveler's checks and a major credit card; if possible, find out in advance what sort of payment tour companies, hotels, and restaurants accept. Certain hub communities that do have bank services are Nome, Bethel, Kotzebue, and Barrow.

About the Hotels & Restaurants

The dining options are few when traveling through Alaska's bush; smaller communities may have only one or two eateries, if any at all. On the bright side, you won't need to worry about reservations. If they're open, they'll get you in, and you'll likely be surprised at the variety available: not just Alaskan seafood, game, and locally grown vegetables, but Mexican and Asian fare are standard, even in the state's remotest corners. All food prices, including at grocery shops, will reflect large transportation charges, so be prepared to pay.

Lodging choices in the bush are also limited. Some communities have a single hotel; the smallest have none. Others have a mix of hotels and bed-and-breakfasts. As a rule, rooms are simply furnished. You may have to share bathroom or kitchen facilities. Rooms go fast during the summer season, so book as far ahead as possible. And it never hurts to carry a tent as backup—you'll never be without a place to stay.

WHAT IT COSTS

¢	$	$$	$$$	$$$$
RESTAURANTS				
under $10	$10–$15	$15–$20	$20–$25	over $25
HOTELS				
under $75	$75–$125	$125–$175	$175–$225	over $225

Restaurant prices are per person for a main course at dinner. Hotel prices are for two people in a standard double room in high season.

Getting Outside

The bush presents some of the world's best opportunities to participate in backcountry adventures, from sea kayaking to wildlife viewing. The following organizations can help you get in touch with your inner explorer.

Contacts

Alaska Department of Fish and Game ⬠ *Box 25526, Juneau 99802-5526* ☎ *907/465-4100 general information about fish and wildlife,* ☎ *907/465-4180 sportfishing seasons and regulations,* ☎ *907/465-2376 licenses* ⊕ *www.adfg.state. ak.us.*

Alaska State Parks Information ✉ *550 W. 7th Ave., Suite 1260, Anchorage* ☎ *907/269-8400* ⊕ *www.dnr. state.ak.us/parks.*

Anchorage Alaska Public Lands Information Center ✉ *605 W. 4th Ave., Suite 105, Anchorage* ☎ *907/271-2737 or 866/869-6887* ⊕ *www.nps. gov/aplic.*

Fairbanks Alaska Public Lands Information Center ✉ *250 Cushman St., Suite 1A, Fairbanks* ☎ *907/456-0527 or 866/869-6887* ⊕ *www.nps. gov/aplic.*

U.S. Fish and Wildlife Service ✉ *1011 E. Tudor Rd., Anchorage* ☎ *907/786-3309* ⊕ *www.r7.fws.gov.*

8

Updated by
E. Readicker-
Henderson

Alaskans call it the bush—those wild and lonely expanses of territory beyond cities, towns, highways, and railroad corridors, stretching from the Kodiak Archipelago, Alaska Peninsula, and Aleutian Islands in the south through the Yukon-Kuskokwim Delta and Seward Peninsula and into the northern High Arctic.

The bush extends over two-thirds of Alaska, where caribou outnumber people and where the summer sun really does shine at midnight; in fact, at the state's northern edge it remains in the sky for several weeks in June and July, disappearing altogether for weeks in winter. The bush is a land that knows the soft footsteps of the Eskimos and the Aleuts, the scratchings of those who searched (and still search) for oil and gold, and the ghosts of almost-forgotten battlefields of World War II.

If you visit the Arctic plains in summer, you'll see bright wildflowers growing from a sponge of rich green tundra dotted with pools of melting snow. Willow trees barely an inch tall might be a hundred years old, and sometimes berry bushes have berries bigger than the bush they grow on. In the long, dark Arctic winter, a painter's-blue kind of twilight rises from the ice and snowscapes at midday, but the moon can be bright enough to read by, and on a clear night you will have a new appreciation for the depth of the heavens. Spring and fall are fleeting moments when the tundra awakens from its winter slumber or turns briefly brilliant with autumn colors.

The Brooks Range, which stretches east–west across the state from nearly the sea to the Canadian border, separates the Arctic from the rest of the state. The Brooks are actually a superchain, including several mountain systems, from the pale, softly rounded limestone mountains in the east and west to the towering granite spires of the Arrigetch Peaks in the heart of the range. Large portions of the Brooks Range's middle and western sections are protected within Gates of the Arctic National Park and the neighboring Noatak National Preserve; its eastern reaches lie within the Arctic National Wildlife Refuge.

North of the Brooks Range, a great apron of land called the North Slope tilts gently towards the Beaufort Sea and the Arctic Ocean. The vast sweep of this frozen tundra brightens each summer with yellow Arctic poppies, bright red bearberry, and dozens of other wildflower species that pepper endless stretches of landscape. Beneath the surface, permanently frozen ground known as permafrost has shifted and shaped this land for centuries, fragmenting it into giant polygons that make a fascinating pattern when viewed from the sky. And at the very edge of all this wilderness, where land meets sea, America's largest oil field, Prudhoe Bay, was discovered in 1968. At its peak,

STOMPING GROUNDS

Great herds of caribou—some with more than a hundred thousand animals—move slowly across the tundra, feeding and fattening for the next winter and attempting to stay clear of wolves and grizzlies. In the Arctic Ocean's Beaufort Sea, polar bears, stained a light gold from the oil of seals they have killed, pose like monarchs on ice floes. One of Alaska's premier wildlands, the Arctic National Wildlife Refuge protects mountain and tundra landscape important to caribou, polar bears, grizzlies, wolves, and musk ox.

more than 2 million barrels a day of North Slope crude from Prudhoe and neighboring basins flowed southward via the 800-mi pipeline to the port of Valdez, on Prince William Sound in South Central Alaska. Now the flow has diminished to fewer than 900,000 barrels per day.

The rivers that drain the Brooks Range have names such as Kongakut, Kobuk, and Sheenjek, reflecting the native peoples who have lived here for thousands of years. The great Noatak River defies the Arctic's north–south drainage pattern and runs east–west, making a right-angle turn before emptying into Kotzebue (*kots*-eh-bew) Sound. Perched on this sound is the colorful Eskimo town of Kotzebue, the largest native settlement in the state and the jumping-off point to much of the surrounding area. Eskimo ceremonial dances are demonstrated at Kotzebue's Living Museum of the Arctic, as is the Eskimo blanket toss, a traditional activity dating to prehistoric times, when hunters were bounced high in the air so they could scan the horizon for seals.

Another coastal community, this one first settled by prospectors, is the former gold-rush boomtown of Nome, where you can still pan for riches. In early spring Nome shows off one of its more unique ways of celebrating when the sun finally comes out: a golf tournament where the "greens" are painted on the ice of the Bering Sea coast. Nome also serves as the end of the Iditarod Trail Sled Dog Race, which begins in Anchorage the first Saturday in March and finishes about 10 days later, when the fastest dog teams make their way up Front Street to the cheers of locals and visitors alike.

Southwest Alaska includes the biologically productive wetlands of the Yukon-Kuskokwim Delta, where the state's greatest river meets the wild ocean. Sloughs, ponds, marshes, mud, streams, and puddles in these flat regions near sea level can slow water travel to a standstill. The delta is one of the most important migratory flyways for birds in North

8

OVERWHELMED? TAKE A TOUR

Package tours are the most common way of traveling to bush communities, where making your flight connections and having a room to sleep in at the end of the line are no small feats. During peak season—late May through Labor Day—planes, state ferries, hotels, and sportfishing lodges are often crowded with travelers on organized tours; to create a trip on your own means making reservations a year in advance.

The type of tour you choose will determine how you get there. On air tours—the only way to get to most bush communities—you will fly to and from your destination, getting there relatively quickly and enjoying an aerial perspective of the Arctic en route. Most tours to Arctic towns and villages are short—one, two, or three days. These can often be combined with visits to other regions of the state.

On bus tours to Deadhorse and Prudhoe Bay, you will travel at least one way by bus, which gets you there at a more leisurely pace and gives you a ground-level view of sweeping tundra vistas. The route crosses the rugged Brooks Range, the Arctic Circle, and the Yukon River, and also brushes the edges of Gates of the Arctic National Park and the Arctic National Wildlife Refuge. Holland America Tours/Gray Line of Alaska operates package tours that travel the Dalton Highway to Deadhorse. Princess Tours also runs tours along the Dalton Highway.

The bush is home to many native Alaskan groups, many of which are active in tourism. Often, local native corporations act as your hosts—running the tours, hotels, and attractions. Nome Tour and Market-ing in Nome (book through Alaska Airlines Vacations) provides ground transportation, accommodations, and other services for visitors. The NANA Regional Corporation provides ground transportation and accommodations in Kotzebue as well as at Prudhoe Bay, in conjunction with bus tours. If you visit Barrow and stay at the Top of the World Hotel, Tundra Tours (book through Alaska Airlines Vacations), another native operation, will be your host.

The Northern Alaska Tour Company conducts highly regarded ecotours to the Arctic Circle, the Brooks Range, and Prudhoe Bay that emphasize natural and cultural history, wildlife, and geology. Groups are limited to 25 people on Arctic day tours and to 10 people on Prudhoe Bay overnight trips. Some tours are completely ground-based; others include a mix of ground and air travel.

Contacts Alaska Airlines Vacations (☎ 800/468–2248 ⊕ www.alaskaair.com). Holland American Tours/Gray Line of Alaska (☎ 907/451–6835, 800/887–7741 in Alaska, 800/544–2206 for reservations ⊕ www.graylineofalaska.com). NANA Regional Corporation (☎ 907/442–3301 ⊕ www.nana.com). Northern Alaska Tour Company (☎ 907/474–8600 or 800/474–1986 ⊕ www.northernalaska.com).Princess Tours (☎ 206/336–6000 in Seattle, 907/479–9660 in Fairbanks, 800/426–0442 reservations ⊕ www.princess.com).

America, and the waters teem with life. Farther south, Bristol Bay is the site of some of the largest salmon runs in the world. Nearby Wood-Tikchik State Park (the nation's largest, at more than 1.6 million acres) encompasses huge lake systems and vast stretches of untouched wilderness where moose with antlers the size of end tables browse their way through the glaciated landscape. And on the upper reaches of the Alaska Peninsula, the brown bears of Katmai rule a vast national park dominated by dramatic volcanic scenery, proof that Earth is not as unchanging as we like to pretend. Also in the Southwest, the lower Alaska Peninsula and the Aleutian (pronounced ah-*loo*-shun) Islands reach well into the Pacific Ocean toward Japan. This chain beckoned Russian explorers to Alaska in the 18th century, as they tried to turn the islands' sea otter population into furs to trade with China for tea. Along the islands, weathered onion-dome Russian Orthodox churches in Aleut villages brace against fierce Pacific winds.

TAKE TO THE SKIES

Roads in the bush are few, so airplanes—from jetliners to small bush planes—are the lifelines. Throughout Alaska you'll hear about the legendary pilots of the far north—Noel and Sig Wien, Bob Reeve, Ben Eielson, Harold Gillam, Joe Crosson, Jack Jefford, and others—who won their wings in the early years. They are Alaska's counterparts to the cowboy heroes of the Wild West. The bush is where America's favorite humorist, Will Rogers, died in a crash with famed aviator Wiley Post in 1935.

Dutch Harbor, the largest town in the Aleutians and a former U.S. Navy base pounded by Japanese bombs in 1942, is one of America's busiest commercial-fishing ports. Deep-sea trawlers and factory ships venture from here into the stormy North Pacific Ocean and the Bering Sea for harvests of bottom fish, crab, and other catches. Unalaska, an ancient Aleut village, is Dutch Harbor's neighbor and home to one of the oldest Russian Orthodox churches in Alaska. North of the Aleutian chain, in the Bering Sea, the remote volcanic islands of the Pribilofs support immense populations of birds and sea mammals as well as two small Aleut communities, St. George and St. Paul.

Alaskans who live in towns use the bush as an escape valve, a place to get away, the reason why they came to Alaska to begin with. And those who've made the bush their home are practically heroes to the rest of the state. Bush Alaskans have a deep affection for their often raw land, which is difficult to explain to strangers. They talk of living with complete independence, "close to nature." A cliché, perhaps, until you realize that these Alaskans reside in the bush all year long, adapting to brutal winter weather and isolation, preferring to live off the road system. They know a hamburger will never taste as good as moose meat, and whatever they're missing by not having a TV can't possibly be as interesting as the view out the cabin window. They have accepted the bush for what it is: dramatic, unforgiving, and glorious.

EXPLORING THE BUSH

Philosophically speaking, the bush is more of a lifestyle than a location. Technically, though, it's any place in mainland or western Alaska that can't be reached by road. A tour of the state's southwestern region can begin in Bethel, an important bush outpost on the Yukon-Kuskokwim Delta, surrounded by the Yukon Delta National Wildlife Refuge; off the mainland coast is the undeveloped wilderness of Nunivak Island. Next is the Alaska Peninsula, which juts out between the Pacific Ocean and the Bering Sea; here are Katmai National Park & Preserve, Aniakchak National Monument & Preserve, and the Becharof and Alaska Peninsula National Wildlife refuges. To the southeast of the Alaska Peninsula is the Kodiak Archipelago, where you'll find the Kodiak National Wildlife Refuge and Shuyak Island State Park. The Aleutian Islands start where the peninsula ends, and sweep southwest toward Japan.

The Pribilof Islands lie north of the Aleutians, 200 mi off Alaska's coast. Head north along the Bering Sea coast and you come to Nome, just below the Arctic Circle and the Bering Land Bridge National Preserve. Kotzebue, just above the circle, is a coastal Inupiaq town surrounded by sea and tundra and a jumping-off place for several parklands: Kobuk Valley, Noatak, Cape Krusenstern, and Gates of the Arctic (though the last is more easily reached from the inland village—well, really not much more than an airstrip and a couple of bars—of Bettles). Barrow, another Inupiaq community, sits at the very top of the state, and is the northernmost town in the United States. Follow the Arctic coastline eastward and you reach Deadhorse, on Prudhoe Bay, the custodian to the region's important oil and gas reserves. And east of Prudhoe Bay is the embattled Arctic National Wildlife Refuge, the nation's last great chance to truly show wilderness matters.

SOUTHWEST

The Southwest region encompasses some of Alaska's most remote, inaccessible, and rugged land- and seascapes. Reaching from the Alaska Peninsula down through the Aleutian chain, it also includes many islands within the Bering Sea, among them the Pribilof Islands, as well as the Bristol Bay watershed, the Kodiak Archipelago, and the Yukon-Kuskokwim Delta. A place of enormous biological richness, it harbors many of North America's largest breeding populations of seabirds and waterfowl and also supports the world's densest population of brown bears and the world's greatest salmon runs. Given all this richness, it's no surprise to learn that Southwest Alaska has some of Alaska's premier parklands and refuges, from Katmai National Park to Aniakchak National Monument and the Kodiak National Wildlife Refuge. Here, too, are dozens of rural communities, most of them small native villages whose residents continue to engage in a subsistence lifestyle, augmented by modern conveniences and, frequently, schools by satellite and computer terminal.

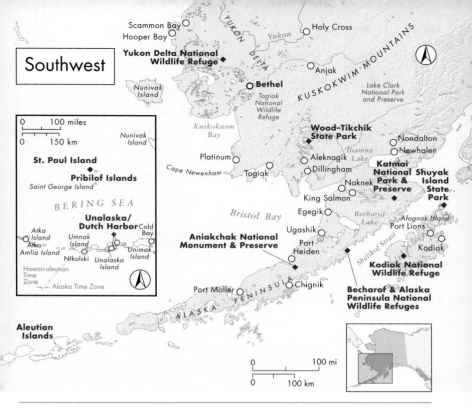

BETHEL

400 mi west of Anchorage.

Spread out on the tundra along the Kuskokwim River, Bethel is a frontier town of about 5,800 residents, originally established by Moravian missionaries in the late 1800s. One of rural Alaska's most important trading centers, it's a hub for more than 50 native villages in a region roughly the size of the state of Oregon. The surrounding lowland tundra is a rich green in summer and turns fiery shades of red, orange, and yellow in autumn, when plants burst with blueberries, cranberries, blackberries, and salmonberries. Salmon, arctic grayling, and Dolly Varden (a species of seagoing trout that biologists continually try to promote to salmon) fill the area's many lakes, ponds, and streams, providing excellent fishing just a few miles outside town. (How do you know you're in an Alaska grocery store? Never any fish for sale, because everybody already has all they need.) The wetlands are also important breeding grounds for more than 60 species of birds, from shrikes to warblers.

The town is also the northernmost freshwater port for oceangoing vessels. Among its businesses are radio and television stations, a theater, credit union, auto repair shop, car-rental agency, beauty/barber shop, DVD rental store, newspaper, two colleges (including a tribal college), and the largest Alaska Native Health Service field hospital in the state, which is contracted to the tribally owned Yukon-Kuskokwim Health Corporation.

Each year, on the last weekend in March, Bethel hosts a regional celebration called the Camai Dance Festival (in Yup'ik, *camai* means "hello"). Held in the local high school's gym, which is filled to capacity for the three-day event, this festival draws dance groups from dozens of outlying villages (⊕*www.bethelarts.com*).

GETTING HERE & AROUND

To get to Bethel, take a flight on Alaska Airlines, Frontier, or Era. Once you're there, the town itself is walkable.

> ### TOUR-SHY?
>
> So you've heard organized tours are the best way to go but still cringe at the thought of not doing it yourself. What's a traveler to do? Fear not: these resources can help you troubleshoot your own bush itinerary.
>
> **Alaska Travel Industry Association** (⊠*2600 Cordova St., Suite 201, Anchorage* ☎*907/929–2200, 800/862–5275 for vacation planner* 🖷*907/561–5727* ⊕*www. travelalaska.com*). **Southwest Alaska Municipal Conference** (⊠*3300 Arctic Blvd., Suite 203, Anchorage* ☎*907/562–7380* 🖷*907/562–0438* ⊕*www.swamc. org*).

ESSENTIALS

Banking Alaska USA Federal Credit Union (⊠ Bethel Native Corporation Bldg. ☎ 907/543-2619 ⊕*www.alaskausa.org*). **First National Bank Alaska** (⊠ 700 Front St. ☎ 907/543-7650 ⊕*www.fnbalaska.com*). **Wells Fargo** (⊠ 460 Ridgecrest Dr. ☎ 907/543-3875 b830 River St. ☎ 800/869-3557 ⊕*www. wellsfargo.com*)

Emergencies Police (☎ *907/543-3871 in Bethel*). **State troopers** (☎*907/543-2294*).

Mail USPS (⊠*1484 Chief Eddie Hoffman Hwy.* ☎*907/543-2525*).

WHAT TO SEE

★ The **Yupiit Piciryarait (the people's way of living) Museum** emphasizes cultural education through native elders, while also showcasing artifacts and artwork of three native cultures: Dene Athabascan, Cup'ik, and Yup'ik. In its galleries you'll find historic and prehistoric treasures: masks, statues, and carvings in ivory, baleen, and whalebone. The permanent collection features past and present clothing styles plus numerous implements and tools used in traditional subsistence lifestyles of the people inhabiting the Yukon-Kuskokwim region. A small gift shop has native artwork for sale, including water-grass baskets, wooden spirit masks, ivory-handle knives, grass and reindeer-beard dance fans, yo-yos, dolls, and seal-gut raincoats. ⊠*Museum, 420 Chief Eddie Hoffman Hwy.* ☎*907/543–1819 or 800/478–3521* ⊕*www.avcp.org/ services.html* 🖾*$1 (donations requested)* ☉*Tues.–Sat. noon–5.*

WHERE TO STAY & EAT

$$–$$$
CHINESE
✕**Shogun.** This rural café-style restaurant specializes in Chinese food and authentic Mexican cuisine, with daily lunch and dinner specials. It also serves Japanese and Italian dishes, plus American-style steaks and seafood. ⊠*320 Tundra St.* ☎*907/543–2272* ▭*MC, V.*

$–$$
⛫**Allanivik Hotel.** Three detached buildings make up this inn, which provides a quiet stay and bush-savvy owners who provide insightful tips. Alaska crafts and artwork adorn the modern rooms, some of which share a bath; others are full suites. The main building is wired for online access, complete with Internet café. Next door in a solarium, **VIP Restaurant** serves Alaskan salmon, halibut, steaks, and roasts, as well as vegetarian, Korean, and Mexican food. **Pros:** Great, knowledgeable staff. **Cons:** Many rooms share baths. ⊠*1220 Hoffman Hwy., Box 219,* ☎*907/543–4305* ⤶*30 rooms, 14 with bath* ♿*In-hotel: restaurant, public Wi-Fi, no-smoking rooms* ▭*AE, D, DC, MC, V.*

$$
⛫**Bentley's Porter House B&B.** Hospitality is never in short supply at this two-story B&B in downtown Bethel. Rooms are decorated according to theme, including African, southwestern United States, and English countryside. Several overlook the Kuskokwim River. Besides those in the main inn, rooms are available in a nearby smaller inn, made up of a duplex and two cottages. Rooms in the newer, smaller inn have their own baths; others share. **Pros:** River views. **Cons:** Not for those what want to stay up late making noise. ⊠*624 1st Ave., Box 529* ☎*907/543–3552* ⤶*35 rooms, 9 with bath* ♿*In-hotel: no elevator, public Internet, some pets allowed, no-smoking rooms* ▭ *MC, V* ⦿*BP*

SHOPPING

BOOKSTORE
The **Moravian Bookstore** (⊠*301 3rd Ave.* ☎*907/543–2474*) stocks arts and crafts as well as books about religion and Eskimo culture. It's open Tuesday through Saturday, noon–4.

OFF THE BEATEN PATH
Nunivak Island. Due west of Bethel, and separated from the Yukon-Kuskokwim Delta by the Etolin Strait, Nunivak Island is an important wildlife refuge. Part of the **Yukon Delta National Wildlife Refuge,** this site is noted for its large herd of reindeer, a transplanted herd of musk ox, and the Eskimo settlement of Mekoryuk.

For information on the island, contact the **U.S. Fish and Wildlife Service** (☎*907/543–3151* ⦿*yukondelta.fws.gov*) in Bethel. Visitors, lured by fine ivory carvings, masks, and items knit from qiviut (musk-ox wool), should check with **Bethel Chamber of Commerce** (☎*907/543–2911* ⦿*www.bethelchamber.org*) about transport and accommodations, which are limited and far from deluxe.

8

TAKE NOTE

Many of the bush communities have voted to be dry areas in order to fight alcohol-abuse problems affecting Alaska's native peoples. Sale and possession of alcohol is prohibited in dry communities. Enforcement is strict, and bootlegging is a felony. Nome remains wet, with numerous lively saloons.

YUKON DELTA NATIONAL WILDLIFE REFUGE

Surrounds Bethel.

At 20 million acres, Yukon Delta is the nation's largest wildlife refuge; nearly one-third of the area is water in the form of lakes, sloughs, bogs, creeks, and rivers—including the **Yukon** and **Kuskokwim** rivers, Alaska's largest. Both are huge and slow by the time they get this close to the sea, and they carry huge amounts of sediment; over the millennia, the sediments have formed an immense delta that serves as critical breeding and rearing grounds for an estimated 100 million shorebirds and waterfowl.

Of course, not all of the refuge is wetlands. North of the Yukon River are the Nulato Hills, site of the 1.3-million-acre **Andreafsky Wilderness area,** which includes both forks of the Andreafsky River, one of Alaska's specially designated Wild and Scenic Rivers. Rainbow trout, arctic char, and grayling flourish in upland rivers and creeks; pike, sheefish, and burbot thrive in lowland waters. These abundant waters are also spawning grounds to five species of Pacific salmon. Black and grizzly bears, moose, beavers, mink, and Arctic foxes also call this refuge home. Occasionally, wolves venture into the delta's flats from neighboring uplands.

> ### NESTING GROUNDS
>
> More than 100 species of birds nest here, traveling from nearly every state and province in North America and from every continent that borders the Pacific Ocean. Many of North America's cackling Canada geese and more than half the continent's population of black brant are born here. Other birds making the annual pilgrimage to the Yukon Delta refuge include emperor geese, huge tundra swans, gulls, jaegers, cranes, loons, snipe, sandpipers, and the rare bristle-thigh curlew.

Given the abundance of fish and wildlife, it's not surprising that the delta holds special importance to surrounding residents. The Yup'ik have lived here for thousands of years; despite modern encroachment, they continue to practice many features of their centuries-old subsistence lifestyle. Access is by boat or aircraft only, and, as in most of Alaska's other remote wildlands, visitor facilities are minimal. Refuge staff can provide tips on recreational opportunities and guides and outfitters who operate in the refuge. ✉ *Box 346, Bethel 99559* ☎ *907/543–3151* ⊕ *http://yukondelta.fws.gov.*

THE OUTDOORS & GUIDED TOURS

Opportunities for wildlife watching abound at the Yukon Delta refuge. With its abundance of lakes, ponds, streams, and wetlands, another big thing to do is get in a boat, or hang out on the shore and watch all the waterbirds. The refuge is also a great place for sportfishing, especially for rainbow trout, salmon char, pike, grayling, and sheefish. Flat-water paddlers will never run out of water to try, although camping can be a bit marshy and DEET-dependent. Or try hiking and river-floating in the uplands of the Andreafsky Wilderness area.

EXPERT LOCAL **Kuskokwim Wilderness Adventures** (☎907/543–3900 ⊕*www.kuskofish.*
GUIDES *com*) offers camping, fishing, birding, photo trips, and more, led by
local Jim McDonald.

WOOD-TICKCHIK STATE PARK

150 mi southeast of Bethel, 300 mi southwest of Anchorage.

In the Bristol Bay region, Wood-Tikchik State Park—the nation's largest state park—is a water-based wildland despite its inland setting. Two
separate groups of large, idyllic, interconnected lakes, some of which
are up to 45 mi long, dominate the park. Grizzlies, caribou, porcupines
(people who live in the bush will tell you they taste like squirrels),
eagles, and loons abound in the park's forests and tundra, but Wood-
Tikchik is best known for its fish. The park's lakes and streams are
critical spawning habitat for five species of Pacific salmon; they also
support healthy populations of rainbow trout, arctic char, arctic grayling, and northern pike. And where there are fish, there are fishermen:
Wood-Tikchik is kind of a holy grail locale for serious anglers; all that
water is perfect for canoes and kayaks, too.

Managed as a wild area, Wood-Tikchik has no maintained trails and
few other visitor amenities. ■TIP➔ Most of its campsites are primitive,
and those who plan to explore the park should be experienced in backcountry travel and camping. Access is by either boat or air. ⏲*Mid-May–Sept.,
Box 3022, Dillingham 99576* ☎907/842–2375 ⏲*Oct.–mid-May, 550
W. 7th Ave., Suite 1380, Anchorage 99501* ☎907/269–8698 ⊕*www.
alaskastateparks.org.*

Besides the many large lakes and streams that fill its 1.6 million acres,
the park's landscape includes rugged mountains, glaciers, and vast
expanses of tundra. Think of it as a kind of Cliff's Notes to the best of
Alaskan scenery.

You can also travel from Dillingham, a town close to Wood-Tikchik,
by boat or by air to view the walruses offshore on Round Island within
★ **Walrus Islands State Game Sanctuary.** So many of these giant sea mammals
come here in summer that you can barely see the islands' rock beneath
the heaving red blubber. The population has been fluctuating in recent
years; in 1998 more than 14,000 walrus stretched out in the island's
afternoon sun; the most recent count, though, was fewer than 2,000.
Walrus aren't the only thing there: the islands also support a large
population of Steller sea lions, and feeding in the offshore waters are
humpbacks, gray whales, and orcas. ⏲*Box 1030, Dillingham 99576-
1030* ☎907/842–2334 🖷907/842–5514 ⊕*www.wildlife.alaska.gov.*

THE OUTDOORS & GUIDED TOURS

Because it is largely a water-based region, it's easiest to explore Wood-
Tikchik by boat, whether that's canoe, kayak, or raft. The most popular fly-in float trip is the 90-mi journey from Lake Kulik to Aleknagik, a
Yup'ik Eskimo village. Most people doing this trip arrange for drop-off
and pick-up services with local guides in Dillingham. The lakes are large
enough to behave like small inland seas in stormy weather, so boaters

need to be cautious when winds are high; always be prepared for bad weather, know proper emergency procedures, and don't ever go out unless somebody knows where you're headed. The water systems also present some of the world's best sportfishing opportunities for salmon and rainbow trout; anglers come from around the world to stay at wilderness fishing lodges here. Hiking is difficult because of dense brush, except for the uppermost part of the park, where tundra makes on-land travel easier.

EMERGENCY CARE

Anchorage's Alaska Regional Hospital has been operating Alaska Regional Lifeflight (☎ 800/478– 9111 ⊕ www.alaskaregional. com)medevac services since 1985; it might seem far to go if you get hurt in, say, Kotzebue, but the crew begins emergency care as soon as a passenger is picked up, and planes can taxi right up to the hospital's entrance like regular ambulances.

FISHING LODGES **Tikchik Narrows Lodge** (☎ 907/243– 8450 ⊕ www.tikchiklodge.com) is owned and managed by Bud Hodson, who has been a guide in the region for more than 25 years. The lodge caters primarily to sportfishing enthusiasts who are also looking for comfortable housing and scrumptious gourmet-style meals at night—and who can afford $6,850 for a week's stay, which includes guided fishing trips throughout the region. The lodge rents kayaks and rafts and occasionally flies people into the park's most remote corners. If you're looking to reel one in, **Reel Wilderness Adventures** (☎ 800/726– 8323 ⊕ www.reelwild.com) offers an alternative to lodges, while emphasizing small groups, gourmet meals, and fly-fishing for rainbow trout and other species.

KATMAI NATIONAL PARK & PRESERVE

100 mi southeast of Wood-Tikchik, 290 mi southwest of Anchorage.

Katmai is the most famous of Alaska's remote parks for two simple reasons: bears and volcanoes. Although only a fraction of the number of Alaska visitors make it here as do to, say, Denali National Park, Katmai's name echoes with just as much mythical force. Remote and expensive (even by Alaskan travel standards) to get to, Katmai is true wilderness Alaska, with limited visitor facilities (except for a few nice wilderness lodges)—but that's reason enough to go and have Alaska to yourself. These 4 million acres offer up plenty of opportunities for wildlife viewing and an extraordinary perspective on the awesome power of volcanoes—still active throughout the park, echoes of the 1912 eruption sequence that was one of the most powerful ever recorded, covering more than 46,000 square mi with ash. Today, in this wild, remote area at the northern end of the Alaska Peninsula, moose and almost 30 other species of mammals, including foxes, lynx, and wolves, share the landscape with bears fishing for salmon from stream
★ banks, rivers, and along the coast. At the immensely popular **Brooks Falls and Camp,** you can see brown bears when the salmon are running in July and September. No special permits are required, though there is

Katmai National Park. "During summer, when the salmon is moving upstream in Katmai N.P.'s Brooks River, dozens of brown bears with their cubs gather to feast. This one ran up a nearby tree to escape with his catch." —Jose Vigano, Fodors.com photo contest winner

a $10 day-use fee at Brooks. Bears are common along the park's outer coast, where they graze on sedge flats, dig clams and sculpin on the beach at low tide (quite a sight!), and fish for salmon. But even on slow bear days, it's a beautiful place to be. Ducks fill the park's rivers, lakes, and outer coast, arguing over nesting space with huge whistling swans, loons, grebes, gulls, and shorebirds. Bald eagles perch on rocky pinnacles by the sea. More than 40 species of songbirds call the region home during the short spring and summer, and if you fall back into big mammal mood, Steller sea lions and a couple of species of seals hang out on rock outcroppings.

From Brooks Lodge, a daily tour bus with a naturalist aboard makes the 23-mi trip through the park to the **Valley Overlook.** Hikers can walk the 1.5-mi trail for a closer look at the pumice-covered valley floor. (Some consider the return climb strenuous.)

The Katmai area is one of Alaska's premier sportfishing regions. You can fish for rainbow trout and salmon at the **Brooks River,** though seasonal closures have been put in place to prevent conflicts with bears, and only fly-fishing is permitted; check locally for the latest information. For those who would like to venture farther into the park, seek out the two other backcountry lodges, **Grosvenor** and **Kulik,** or contact fishing-guide services based in King Salmon. A short walk up the Brooks River brings you to Brooks Falls, where viewing platforms overlook a

6-foot-high cascade where salmon leap to try and make it upstream, past the bears, to spawn. One platform is right at the falls; the other is a short way below it (an access trail and boardwalk are separated from the river to avoid confrontations with bears). ⌂ *National Park Service, Box 7, King Salmon 99613* ☎ *907/246–3305* ⊕ *www.nps.gov/katm.*

No roads lead to Katmai National Park. To get to it, at the base of the Alaska Peninsula, it's easiest to arrange a flight from Anchorage, which will take in the amazing scenery along Cook Inlet, rimmed by the lofty, snowy peaks of the Alaska Range (check out ⊕ *www.alaskaair.com* for fares and schedules). They land at **King Salmon,** near fish-famous Bristol Bay, where passengers transfer to smaller floatplanes for the 20-minute hop to **Naknek Lake** and Brooks Camp. Travel to Brooks from King Salmon is also possible by boat. You are required to check in at the park ranger station, next to Brooks Lodge (⇨ below), for a mandatory bear safety talk (for the safety of both you and the bears).

Fodor'sChoice
★ At the northern end of the Alaska Peninsula, 200 mi southwest of Anchorage, **McNeil River State Game Sanctuary** was established in 1967 to protect the world's largest gathering of brown bears. Since then, it has earned a reputation as the finest bear viewing locale in North America, and likely the world—the standard by which all others are measured. The main focus is **McNeil Falls,** where bears come to feed on chum salmon returning to spawn. All those *National Geographic* films you've seen of bears fishing? Odds are this is the spot. During the peak of the chum run (July to mid-August) dozens of brown bears congregate at the falls playing who can slap the most fish out of the water. When the salmon are running thickest, the bears only eat the fattiest parts of the fish—brains, roe, and skin—which means the leftovers are a smorgasbord for other animals; even the plant life depends on nutrients from bear leftovers. As many as 70 bears, including cubs, have been observed along the river in a single day, and more than 100 bears have been identified within a single season. Not just the sheer number of bears makes McNeil special; over the years several bears have become highly accustomed to human presence. They will play, eat, nap, and nurse cubs within 15 to 20 feet of the falls viewing pad, sometimes closer—which will let you learn firsthand that bears smell like very wet dogs. Do not think the bears are tame; they are still wild animals and the sanctuary staff makes sure that visitors behave in a nonthreatening, nonintrusive way.

To that end, no more than 10 people a day, always accompanied by one or two state biologists, are allowed to visit bear viewing sites from June 7 through August 25. Because demand is so high, an annual drawing is held in mid-March to determine permit winners. ■ TIP➜ **Applications must be received by March 1 to be eligible.** Nearly all visitors fly into McNeil Sanctuary on floatplanes. Most arrange for air-taxi flights out of Homer, on the Kenai Peninsula. Once you are in the sanctuary, all travel is on foot. ✉ *Alaska Department of Fish and Game, Division of Wildlife Conservation, 333 Raspberry Rd., Anchorage* ☎ *907/267–2182* ⊕ *www.adfg.state.ak.us.*

SPORTS, THE OUTDOORS & GUIDED TOURS

The Katmai region offers an abundance of recreational opportunities, including sportfishing, bear viewing, hiking through the Valley of Ten Thousand Smokes, running the wild and scenic Alagnak River and other clear-water streams, flightseeing, exploring the outer coast, and backpacking through remote and seldom-visited backcountry wilderness.

FLIGHTSEEING & WILDLIFE VIEWING

Emerald Air Service and Day Trips (☎907/235–6993 ⊕*www.emeraldairservice.com*), in Homer, leads guided bear viewing trips to remote reaches of Katmai National Park, including the seldom-visited outer coast. Though owners Chris and Ken Day specialize in day visits, they will also arrange overnight trips upon request. **Katmai Air Services** (☎907/246–3079 *in King Salmon, summer only; 800/544–0551 in Anchorage* ⊕*www.katmailand.com*) can arrange flightseeing tours of the park and also does charter flights to Brooks Camp. **Katmailand** (✉*4125 Aircraft Dr., Anchorage* ☎907/243–5448 *or 800/544–0551* ⊕*www.katmailand.com*) puts together bear viewing and fishing packages to Katmai National Park and also arranges trips to Katmai's Valley of Ten Thousand Smokes. **Lifetime Adventures** (☎800/952–8624 ⊕*www.lifetimeadventures.net*) organizes a variety of customized trips featuring small groups (eight people or fewer), from bear watching to river-kayaking, mountain-biking, and hiking in the Valley of Ten Thousand Smokes. **Northwind Aviation** (✆ *Box 646, Homer 99603* ☎907/235–7482), in Homer, offers charter flights to Katmai's outer coast and McNeil River.

RIVER RUNNING & SPORTFISHING

Ouzel Expeditions (☎ 907/783–2216 *or* 800/825–8196 ⊕*www.ouzel.com*) guides fishing and river-running trips down the Wild and Scenic Alagnak River, which flows through Katmai National Park and is widely known as a rainbow-trout heaven.

WHERE TO STAY

All of the four lodges below are on inholdings (publicly owned land inside a protected area) within Katmai National Park. Three are inland, and Katmai Wilderness Lodge is on the remote outer coast.

$$$$
Fodor's Choice
★

⌂ **Brooks Lodge.** All the attractions of Katmai National Park are at this lodge's doorstep: fly-fishing for rainbow trout, lake trout, arctic grayling, and salmon; brown bear–viewing; and tours to the Valley of Ten Thousand Smokes. Accommodations are in detached modern cabins adorned with Alaskan artwork; they accommodate two to four people. All cabins have heat, electricity, and private toilet facilities. The cabins surround the main lodge, which has a spectacular view of aquamarine Naknek Lake; it has a circular stone fireplace and a dining area where buffet-style meals are served three times daily. Price

WORD OF MOUTH

"I just returned from day trip with Emerald Air Service. It was wonderful. We saw over 20 bears digging clams and grazing. A very informative trip observing how bears live instead of just taking pictures of them. This is a great company to go with."

—Karenackermann

8

includes airfare from Anchorage; special trips to the valley are extra. **Pros:** Bear viewing at Brooks Falls. **Cons:** Fly-fishing only in Brooks River, unless you're a bear. ⊕*Katmailand, Inc.,4125 Aircraft Dr., Anchorage 99502* ☎*907/243–5448 or 800/544–0551* ⊕*www.katmailand.com/lodging/brooks.html* ➳*16 cabins* ⚲*In-room: no phone, no TV. In-hotel: restaurant, bar* ▤*MC, V* ☾*Closed mid-Sept.–May.*

$$$$ 🍴**Grosvenor Lodge.** Once you've arrived at this remote Katmai National Park lodge, reachable only by floatplane, you have access by motorboat to numerous rivers and streams filled with sport fish. The lodge can accommodate six people in three cabins; heated, with electricity, they share a separate bathhouse. The main lodge houses a kitchen, lounging area, and bar, and has an excellent view of Grosvenor Lake. Three-, four-, and seven-night packages include airfare from Anchorage, meals, lodging, and guiding. **Pros:** Great fishing. **Cons:** Absolute seclusion— but isn't that why you picked the place? ⊕*Katmailand, Inc., 4125 Aircraft Dr., Anchorage 99502* ☎*907/243–5448 or 800/544–0551* ⊕*www.katmailand.com/lodging/grosvenor.html* ➳*3 cabins with shared baths* ⚲*In-room: no phone, no TV. In-hotel: restaurant, bar* ▤*MC, V* ☾*Closed Oct.–May* ⎟⓿*FAP.*

$$$$ 🍴**Katmai Wilderness Lodge.** Built on land owned by the Russian Ortho-
★ dox Church, this rustic lodge straddles the rugged outer coast of Katmai National Park, along the shores of Kukak Bay. Mountains, coastal flats, and the waters of Shelikof Strait surround the modern log cabin–style lodge, where guests stay in private bedrooms with baths and gather to eat gourmet meals in the dining room or, if the weather is right, on outdoor decks. Recreational activities include bear viewing, sea kayaking, and fishing for halibut and salmon. You may stay from three nights to a week or more. Price includes a round-trip flight from Kodiak, meals, lodging, and guide services. **Pros:** Private rooms, hot showers, flush toilets. **Cons:** One room doesn't have a private bath—check at booking. ⊕*Box 4332, Kodiak 99615* ☎*800/488– 8767* ⊕*www.katmai-wilderness. com* ➳*6 rooms, 5 with bath* ⚲*In-room: no phone, no TV. In-hotel: restaurant* ▤*MC, V* ☾*Closed Oct.–mid-May* ⎟⓿*FAP.*

$$$$ 🍴**Kulik Lodge.** Positioned along the gin-clear Kulik River, between Nonvianuk and Kulik lakes, this remote wilderness lodge is reachable only by floatplane. It accommodates up to 28 anglers and is popular as a base for fly-out fishing to hot spots in the surrounding Katmai wilderness. Guests stay in two- or four-person cabins with

---

HALLO BAY

Bears also congregate in large numbers along the park's remote outer coast to fish for salmon. Located at the northern end of the bay, **Hallo Bay** is an eco-friendly camp with easy access to brown bear–viewing. Guests stay in rustic yet comfortable heated platform tents, and enjoy gourmet meals in an enclosed kitchen. This is true wild bear–viewing: no platforms, nothing but the scenery itself, where the bears are very much at home. The price tag, $2,400 for two nights, double occupancy, includes a round-trip flight from Homer, meals, lodging, and guide services. ☎*888/235– 2237* ⊕*www.hallobay.com.*

Continued on page 461

WELCOME TO BEAR COUNTRY

(top) Grizzly bears fishing in Katmai National Park (bottom) Polar bear

An 800–pound brown bear plows through the shallows of Pack Creek on Southeast Alaska's Admiralty Island, adroitly flipping a 20-pound salmon out of the current like an NFL lineman snapping a football. This bear, which stands over 8 feet tall when perched on his hind legs, can devour 50 pounds of food every day. And, when sprinting, he can reach speeds of 35 miles per hour. Governmentally speaking, Alaska is a democracy. But in the wilderness, the state is a monarchy—and the bear the undisputed king.

KING OF THE WILDERNESS

A GOOD HOME

Thanks to its vast stretches of wilderness, Alaska is the only state that is home to healthy populations of all three North American ursine species. Polar bears (*Ursus maritimus*) don't venture south of the state's chilly Arctic coastline, while black bears (*Ursus americanus*) and brown bears (*Ursus arctos*; also known as grizzlies) live throughout the state's many refuges and parks. Bear populations are plentiful here: the Alaska Department of Fish and Game estimates that Alaska is home to roughly 100,000 to 200,000 black bears and 25,000 to 38,000 brown bears.

Watching a bear gorge on salmon from a chilly creek or seeing a mother bear wandering the shoreline in the early morning, her two cubs trailing behind her is an unforgettable sight. Sure it's a matter of luck and timing. But sightings like this are a gift from the Alaskan landscape. However, as illustrated by *Grizzly Man*—a 2005 documentary by Werner Herzog about the troubled life and tragic death of Alaska bear activist Timothy Treadwell—Alaska's bears are wild, unpredictable creatures that should *never* be underestimated.

SAFE PLACES TO VIEW BEARS

Bear-viewing in Alaska has become an increasingly popular tourist activity—and one that is safely enjoyed by thousands of visitors using expert outdoor tour guides every year at such locations as Denali National Park & Preserve (⇨ Ch. 6), Kodiak Island (⇨ Ch. 7), Katmai National Park's McNeil River State Game Sanctuary (⇨ Ch. 7), Admiralty Island's Pack Creek (⇨ Ch. 3), Anan Creek Wildlife Observatory (⇨ Ch. 3), and Fish Creek Wildlife Observation Site (⇨ Ch. 3).

Keep in mind that your best bet is to hire an experienced guide and always to check in with rangers at the refuges or parks you plan to visit. It's never certain that you'll see a bear, though your chances increase dramatically if you're visiting one of the aforementioned premier viewing

Strolling black bear

BEAR OF THE NORTHERN REACHES

Along Alaska's icy northern coast roams the most majestic of all ursine species: the polar bear. Massive in stature (males can reach 1,700 pounds and 11 feet in height), polar bears are also cunning predators that prey chiefly on seals. With relatively short average life spans (15 to 20 years) and one of the slowest reproductive rates of any mammal on earth—females give birth to two cubs every two to five years—polar bear populations are especially vulnerable to human intrusion and, most recently, the continuing retreat of polar sea ice. These bears are worthy of the utmost respect: exercise special caution when traveling along the coastline, as they are known to be aggressive toward humans.

A Kodiak mama bear is followed by two young cubs.

areas during summer salmon runs on a guided tour or if you're traveling in Alaska's more remote backcountry regions. If it's the latter, the chances of an aggressive bear encounter are real but remote.

You should be very well prepared and well versed in safe travel and camping techniques, which include using bear-resistant food containers; never traveling alone; steering clear of forested areas, berry patches, and salmon runs; checking in with park rangers to find out about potential bear zones; and making noise to warn bears that humans are present.

BLACK VERSUS BROWN

Despite their given names, black and brown bears range in color from pure black to nearly blond. Size is the defining characteristic: male brown bears on Kodiak Island—home to the largest brown bear subspecies on Earth—can reach 1,700 pounds and stand 10 feet tall. Male black bears, by comparison, rarely exceed 500 pounds or stand taller than 6 feet. Brown bears have longer claws, longer faces, and a distinct shoulder hump. Brown bears are also more protective of their territory and less intimidated by human intrusion.

Black and brown bears feed on a diverse diet, the staples being salmon, berries, roots, carrion, and the occasional deer, moose, or caribou. Both species hibernate in winter, although bears in the southern coastal regions spend less time hibernating. In the wild, brown and black bears live for 20 to 30 years. Mature female brown and black bears produce a litter of one to four cubs every two years. And thanks to state and federal protections, Alaska's bear populations are holding steady.

THE SOFT SIDE OF TEDDY

Question: How did the bear—one of nature's largest, most fearsome creatures—become such a popular stuffed animal?

Answer: Because Theodore "Teddy" Roosevelt, former U.S. president, avid hunter, and all-around tough guy, refused to shoot a bear while hunting in Mississippi in 1902. Hence "Teddy's bear" was born. If Roosevelt were alive today, there's only one place he'd surely want to visit to see his beloved bears: Alaska.

A playful brown bear

THE BEAR FACTS: TIPS FOR STAYING SAFE

AVOID SURPRISE

Whenever possible, travel in open country, during daylight hours, and in groups. Make constant noise—talking or singing is preferable to carrying "bear bells"—and leave your dog at home. Most attacks occur when a bear is surprised at close quarters or feels threatened.

CAMP WITH CARE

Pitch your tent away from trails, streams with spawning salmon, berry patches, and other food sources. Avoid areas that have a rotten smell or where scavengers have gathered; these may indicate the presence of a nearby food cache, which a bear will aggressively defend.

BE BEAR AWARE

Keep your eyes open for signs of bears: fresh tracks, scat, matted vegetation, or partially consumed salmon.

ISOLATE YOUR FOOD SUPPLIES

Since bears are practically walking noses, it's imperative that you cook meals at least 100 yards from your tents and that you store food and other odorous items away from campsites (*never* in your tent). Hang food between trees or store it in bear-resistant food containers. Thoroughly clean your cooking area and utensils after each use. Store garbage in airtight containers—or burn it—and pack up the remains.

IF YOU ENCOUNTER A BEAR IN THE WILD

1 IDENTIFY YOURSELF. Talk to the bear in a steady, monotone voice. Don't yell. As for running: don't do it. Running has been known to trigger a bear's predatory instincts, and a bear can easily outrun you (remember, brown bears can run as fast as 35 mph). Back away slowly, and give the bear an escape route. Don't ever get between a mother and her cubs.

A grizzly bear strolls Katmai National Park's tidal flats.

2 BIGGER IS BETTER. To increase your apparent size, raise your arms above your head wave them slowly. With two or more people, it helps to stand side by side. In a forested area it may be appropriate to climb a tree, but remember that black bears and young grizzlies are agile tree climbers.

In 2005, fewer than 12 bear maulings occurred in Alaska; two were fatal.

3 AS A LAST RESORT, PLAY DEAD. If a bear charges and makes contact with you, fall to the ground, curl into a ball with your hands behind your neck, and remain passive. If you are wearing a pack, leave it on. Once a bear no longer feels threatened, it will usually end its attack. Wait for the bear to leave before you move. If such an attack persists for more than a few minutes—in other words, if the bear seems intent on actually harming you further—there's only one option: fight back with all of your might. Keep in mind that such worst-case scenarios are exceedingly rare.

electricity and private baths. In the evening, when fishing's done for the day, you gather in the spruce lodge, which has a large stone fireplace, dining area, and bar. Three-, four-, or seven-night packages include airfare from Anchorage, meals, lodging, and guiding. **Pros:** Great rainbow trout fishing. **Cons:** BYOT—bring your own tackle. ⌂ *Katmailand, Inc., 4125 Aircraft Dr., Anchorage 99502* ☎ *907/243–5448 or 800/544–0551* ⊕ *www.katmailand.com/lodging/kulik.html* ⟲ *12 cabins* ⚷ *In-room: no phone, no TV. In-hotel: restaurant, bar* ▤ *MC, V* ☉ *Closed mid-Oct.–May* ⦿ *FAP.*

¢ ⛰ **Brooks Campground.** This National Park Service campground is a short walk from Brooks Lodge, where campers can pay to eat and shower. Designated cooking and eating shelters, latrines, well water, and a storage cache to protect food from the ever-present brown bears are available. Reservations are required. ⚷ *Portable toilets, drinking water, bear boxes, picnic tables, ranger station* ⟲ *60 sites* ⌂ *Katmai National Park, Box 7, King Salmon 99613* ☎ *907/246–3305, 800/365–2267 reservations* ⊕ *www.nps.gov/katm* ▤ *D, MC, V* ☉ *Closed mid-Sept.–May.*

ANIAKCHAK NATIONAL MONUMENT & PRESERVE

100 mi southwest of Katmai National Park.

Aniakchak, an extraordinary living volcano, rises to the south of Katmai. Towering more than 4,400 feet above the landscape, it also has one of the largest calderas in the world, with a diameter averaging 6 mi across; **Surprise Lake** lies within it. Although Aniakchak last erupted in 1931, the explosion that formed the enormous crater occurred before history was written. Because the area is not glaciated, geologists place the blowup after the last Ice Age. It was literally a world-shaking event. To mark the volcano's significance, in 1980 Congress established the 586,000-acre Aniakchak National Monument & Preserve. The Park Service calls it "one of the least visited units of the National Park system"—maybe a handful of people a year make it out here.

Aniakchak is wild and forbidding country, with a climate that brews mist, clouds, and serious winds much of the year; the caldera is so big that it can entirely create its own local weather patterns, and it really seems to like the bad stuff. Although the **Aniakchak River** (which drains Surprise Lake) is floatable, it has stretches of Class III and IV white water navigable only by expert river runners, and you must travel through open ocean waters to reach the nearest community, Chignik Bay (or get picked up by plane, along the coast). In other words, not something for the unprepared to try, unless you're seriously into hypothermia and have an up-to-date will. An alternate way to enjoy Aniakchak is to wait for a clear day and fly to it in a small plane that will land you on the caldera floor or on Surprise Lake. But be aware that there are no trails, campgrounds, ranger stations, or other visitor facilities here; you must be prepared to be self-sufficient. Aniakchak is the world in the raw.

BELCHING GIANTS

Some evidence suggests that Alaskans inhabited Katmai's eastern edge for at least 6,000 years up to 1912. But on the morning of June 1 that year, everything changed. After five days of violent earthquakes, the 2,700-foot **Novarupta** blew its top, erupting steadily for the next 60 hours. Rivers of white-hot ash poured into the valley. A foot of ash fell on Kodiak Island, 100 mi away, and in all, more than 46,000 square mi of territory ended up under at least an inch of ash, winds carrying yet more ash to eastern Canada and as far as Texas. While Novarupta was belching away, another explosion occurred 6 mi east. The mountaintop peak of **Mt. Katmai** collapsed, creating a chasm almost 3 mi long and 2 mi wide. The molten andesite that held up Mt. Katmai rushed through newly created fissures to Novarupta and was spewed out. Over 2½ days, more than 7 cubic mi of volcanic material were ejected, and the green valley lay under 700 feet of ash. Miraculously, the people who called this remote region home made it out safely; no one was killed.

By 1916 things had cooled off sufficiently to allow scientists to explore the area. A National Geographic

expedition led by Dr. Robert F. Griggs reached the valley and found it full of steaming fumaroles (holes in the volcanic terrain that fume smoke), creating a decidedly moon-like landscape. The report on what Griggs dubbed the **Valley of Ten Thousand Smokes** inspired Congress in 1918 to declare the valley and the surrounding wilderness a national monument. Steam spouted in thousands of fountains from the smothered streams and springs beneath the ash and gave the valley its name. Although the steam has virtually stopped, an eerie sense of earth forces at work remains, and several nearby volcanoes still smolder, or even threaten to blow—every couple of years. Anchorage's airport will sometimes get shut down by smoke or ash from the peninsula's active volcanoes.

The native peoples never returned to their traditional village sites, though many now live in nearby communities. They are joined by sightseers, anglers, hikers, and other outdoors enthusiasts who migrate to the Katmai region each summer. Fish and wildlife are plentiful, and a few "smokes" still drift through the volcano-sculpted valley.

The park is also expensive to reach, even by remote Alaska standards. The only easy access is by air, usually from the town of King Salmon. Thus, few people visit this spectacular place—and those who do are likely to have the caldera all to themselves. Needless to say, come here and you get permanent bragging rights about what you did on your Alaska vacation. ⌖ *Aniakchak National Monument and Preserve, Box 7, King Salmon 99613* ☎*907/246–3305* ⊕*www.nps.gov/ania.*

SPORTS, THE OUTDOORS & GUIDED TOURS

FLIGHTSEEING **Branch River Air** (☎*907/246–3437 June–Sept., 907/248–3539 Oct.– May* ⊕*www.branchriverair.com*), in King Salmon, offers charter flights and flightseeing, and will also arrange fishing and bear viewing trips.

RIVER
RUNNING **Ouzel Expeditions** (☎ *907/783–2216* or *800/825–8196* ⊕*www.ouzel. com*) guides river-running trips down the Aniakchak River. Trips begin at Surprise Lake, within the caldera, and end at the coast, and feature white-water rafting and fishing for salmon, char, and rainbow trout.

BECHAROF & ALASKA PENINSULA NATIONAL WILDLIFE REFUGES

★ *Adjacent to Aniakchak National Monument & Preserve, 250 mi to 450 mi southwest of Anchorage.*

Stretching along the southern edge of the Alaska Peninsula, these two refuges encompass nearly 6 million acres of towering mountains, glacial lakes, broad tundra valleys, and coastal fjords. Volcanoes dominate the landscape; there are 14 in all, of which 9 are considered active. **Mt. Veniaminov**—named after Alaska's greatest Russian Orthodox bishop—last erupted in 1993. Other evidence of volcanic activity include **Gas Rocks**, where gases continually seep through cracks in granitic rocks, and **Ukrinek Marrs**, a crater that bears the marks of a violent eruption in 1977.

Aside from the rugged volcanic landscapes, which are reason enough to come, the two refuges are best known for Garden of Eden–quality wildlife. More than 220 species of resident and migratory wildlife use the refuges, including 30 land mammals, from moose to otter, and 11 marine mammals, including a couple of different kinds of whales, sharing the water with nearly three dozen species of fish—including the five main types of salmon. Look up for nearly 150 species of birds, from the bald eagle doing its perfect impersonation of life after taxidermy high in the tree, to Alaska's trickster, the raven, as well as enough waterbirds to keep a hard-core twitcher at the binoculars for a week. Just put the binocs down from time to time to keep an eye out for the brown bears that live in every corner of the refuges.

Becharof Lake, at 35 mi long and up to 15 mi wide, is the second-largest lake in Alaska (behind Lake Iliamna). Fed by two rivers and 14 major creeks, it serves as a nursery to the world's second-biggest run of sockeye salmon. **Ugashik Lakes** are known for their salmon and trophy grayling. The world-record grayling, nearly 5 pounds (most grayling weigh a pound or less), was caught at Ugashik Narrows in 1981.

Remote and rugged, with the peninsula's usual unpredictable weather, the Becharof and Alaska Peninsula refuges draw mostly anglers and hunters; however, backpackers, river runners, and mountain climbers also occasionally visit. No visitor facilities are available here, and access is only by boat or plane. Most visitors begin their trips in King Salmon and use guides or outfitters. ⌂*Box 277, King Salmon 99613* ☎*907/246–3339* ⊕*www.r7.fws.gov.*

8

KODIAK NATIONAL WILDLIFE REFUGE

50 mi south of Katmai National Park, 300 mi southwest of Anchorage.

The 1.9-million-acre Kodiak National Wildlife Refuge lies mostly on Kodiak Island and neighboring Afognak and Uganik islands, in the Gulf of Alaska. All are part of the Kodiak Archipelago, separated from Alaska's mainland by the stormy Shelikof Strait. Within the refuge are rugged mountains, tundra meadows and lowlands, thickly forested hills that are enough different shades of green to make a leprechaun cry, plus lakes, marshes, and hundreds of miles of pristine coastland. No place in the refuge is more than 15 mi from the ocean. The weather here is generally wet and cool, and storms born in the North Pacific often bring heavy rains.

Dozens of species of birds flock to the refuge each spring and summer, including Aleutian terns, horned puffins, black oystercatchers, ravens, ptarmigan, and chickadees. At least 600 pairs of bald eagles live on the islands, building the world's largest bird nests on shoreline cliffs and in tall trees. Seeing the Kodiak brown bears alone is worth the trip to this rugged country. When they emerge from their dens in spring, the bears chow down on some skunk cabbage to wake their stomachs up, have a few extra salads of sedges and grasses, and then feast on the endless supply of fish when salmon return. About the time they start thinking about hibernating again the berries are ripe (they may eat 2,000 or more berries a day). Kodiak brown bears, the biggest brown bears anywhere, sometimes topping out at more than 1,500 pounds, share the refuge with only a few other land mammals: red foxes, river otters, short-tailed weasels, and tundra voles.

Five species of Pacific salmon—chums, kings, pinks, silvers, and sockeyes—return to Kodiak's waters from May to October. Other resident species include rainbow trout, steelhead (long considered an anadromous—seagoing—trout, but recently promoted by biologists to full salmon status, so there are really six salmon species here), Dolly Varden (also an anadromous trout, but still waiting for promotion), and arctic char. The abundance of fish and bears makes the refuge popular with anglers, hunters, and wildlife watchers. Access is only by boat or plane. Refuge staff will provide lists of guides, outfitters, and air taxis. ✉ *1390 Buskin River Rd., Kodiak* ☎ *907/487–2600 or 888/408–3514* ⊕ *kodiak.fws.gov.*

SPORTS, THE OUTDOORS & GUIDED TOURS

BEAR
VIEWING &
SPORTFISHING
Rohrer Bear Camp (☎ *907/486–5835* ⊕ *www.sportfishingkodiak.com*) guides both bear viewers and visitors who come to Kodiak seeking the island's abundant sportfishing opportunities.

WHERE TO STAY

¢   ☒ **Kodiak Refuge Public-Use Cabins.** Some of the Park Service's lesser-known wonders are the fantastic cabins that they have scattered all over Alaska. If you have ever wanted to be off alone in the bush, but still with a roof over your head, this is the way to go. The Kodiak refuge has seven recreation cabins (accessible by floatplane or boat) available for up to seven days (longer in the off-season). Set along the coast and on inland lakes, the cabins are bare-bones, but do include bunks with mattresses (maybe), kerosene heaters (although you have to bring in your own kerosene), tables, and benches. Most cabins hold six or eight people. Reservations are awarded through quarterly lotteries, held on the first of January, April, July, and October. Although the most popular locations can be booked solid, if you get a sudden impulse, it's always worth checking to see if a lesser-known (although likely just as beautiful) cabin is available. The cabins on inland lakes are usually not accessible in winter, and it's important to remember that any time you fly into remote Alaska you should come prepared for delays getting back out. Pack extra food and supplies, just in case. **Pros:** The true Alaska wilderness, all to yourself. **Cons:** The chance of getting weathered in for a couple of days means a loose schedule is a necessity. ✉*1390 Buskin River Rd., Kodiak* ☎*907/487–2600* ⊕*www.r7.fws. gov* ⇨*7 cabins* ⚑*Reservations essential* ▬*No credit cards.*

SHUYAK ISLAND STATE PARK

50 mi north of Kodiak Island.

The 46,000-acre Shuyak Island State Park is one of the most remote and overlooked units in the state parks system. Located at the northern end of the Kodiak Archipelago, it is accessible only by plane or boat. Its rugged outer coastline is balanced by a more protected system of interconnected bays, channels, and passages that make the park a favorite with sea kayakers. It also has excellent wildlife viewing, especially for seabirds and sea mammals, and top-notch sportfishing for salmon. Wildlife ranges from Sitka black-tailed deer and brown bears to sea otters, sea lions, bald eagles, puffins, and whales. The park has four public-use cabins but no developed campgrounds; limited hiking trails pass through old-growth coastal rain forest. ✉*Alaska State Parks, Kodiak District Office, 1400 Abercrombie Dr., Kodiak* ☎*907/486– 6339* ⊕*www.alaskastateparks.org.*

SPORTS, THE OUTDOORS & GUIDED TOURS

For those new to the region or the sport of kayaking, companies based in Kodiak lead trips to local coastal areas, including Shuyak Island. Besides exploring the coastal land- and seascape, paddlers will have a chance to see a variety of birds and marine mammals, possibly including whales. The world holds few thrills quite as great as seeing a whale from kayak height, and hearing them exhale on a still morning.

SEA KAYAKING & WILDLIFE VIEWING **Mythos Expeditions** (☎*907/486–5536 or 907/486–1771* ⊕*www.thewildcoast.com*) organizes trips both in the Kodiak area and along the Katmai coast. **Orcas Unlimited Charters of Kodiak** (☎*907/654–1979* ⊕*www.orcasunlimited.com*) offers tours, wildlife viewing, and photography trips throughout the Kodiak Archipelago.

WHERE TO STAY

¢ Alaska State Parks Cabins. Alaska State Parks maintains four public-use cabins on Shuyak Island. All are accessible by boat or plane only. The cabins may be rented for up to seven days and hold up to eight people. Each has a woodstove, propane lights, hot plate, four bunks, outside shower and wash area, cooking utensils, and pit toilets. You can make reservations up to six months in advance. **Pros:** Scenery that can't be beat. **Cons:** Finding out that during the off-season, a considerable number of furry animals used the cabin for parties. ⊠*Alaska State Parks, Kodiak District Office, 1400 Abercrombie Dr., Kodiak* ☎*907/486–6339, 907/269–8400 DNR* 🖷*907/486–3320* ⚲*DNR Public Information Center, 550 W. 7th Ave., Suite 1260, Anchorage 99501* ⊕*www.alaskastateparks.org* ⛺*4 cabins* ⊟*MC, V.*

¢ Alaska State Parks Campgrounds. The state has three road-accessible campgrounds (Ft. Abercrombie, Buskin River, and Pasagshak) on Kodiak Island, with a total of 48 tent sites. All have toilets, drinking water, and fishing; two have nearby hiking trails. Camping at Pasagshak is free; the campgrounds at Ft. Abercrombie and Buskin River charge $10–$15 a night. Camping limits are 15 consecutive nights at Buskin River and Pasagshak, 7 nights at Ft. Abercrombie. Each site has its appeal, but Ft. Abercrombie, set in an old military base, complete with the ghosts of gun emplacements, has fantastic views; however, it's exposed enough that campers should be sure to stake their tents down tight if the wind starts to howl. ⚲*Portable toilets, drinking water, bear boxes, picnic tables* ⛺*48 tent sites* ⊠*Alaska State Parks, Kodiak District Office, 1400 Abercrombie Dr., Kodiak* ☎*907/486–6339* 🖷*907/486–3320* ⚲*Reservations not accepted* ⊟*No credit cards.*

ALEUTIAN ISLANDS

The Aleutians begin 540 mi southwest of Anchorage and stretch more than 1,400 mi.

Separating the North Pacific Ocean from the Bering Sea, the Aleutian Islands are not a single sequence of islands. Actually, they're a superchain, made of up eight smaller island groups—the Andreanof, Delarof, Fox, Four Mountain, Near, Rat, Shumagin, and Sanak islands. In all, this adds up to more than 275 islands, stretching from the Alaska Peninsula in a southwesterly arc toward Japan. The islands are volcanic in origin, treeless, and alternate between towering (and frequently smoking) volcanic cones, and high tablelands. Separating the islands is some of the wildest, deepest water anywhere: on the Pacific side of the chains the water can be more than 25,000 feet deep, and the north side's Bering Canyon is twice as long as the Grand Canyon, as well as twice as deep, bottoming out at 10,600 feet below the water's surface. The Aleutian Islands and surrounding coastal waters make up one of the most biologically rich areas in Alaska, harboring abundant seabird, marine mammal, and fish populations—and the fish feed the ships of one of the world's busiest fishing fleets.

Before the Russians arrived in the mid-1700s, the islands were dotted with Aleut villages, a total population of perhaps 3,000 people; within a hundred years, that number, through disease, war, and more, had dropped to maybe 200. Today's native communities include **Nikolski,** on Umnak Island; **Atka,** on Atka Island; and **Cold Bay,** at the peninsula's tip. Like everybody in the Aleutians, the descendants of the original inhabitants mostly work at commercial fishing or in canneries and as expert guides for those who hunt and fish. The settlements are quite small, and accommodations are scarce.

TAKE THE HIGHWAY

The Alaska Marine Highway System, that is. This much-loved form of Alaskan transport is best known for its routes along the Inside Passage. In summer these ferries also depart from Homer, in South Central, and pass by Kodiak on the three-plus-day trip to Dutch Harbor. It's an unforgettable way to see the Southwest's dramatic landscape (⊕ *www.dot.state.ak.us/ amhs.com).*

Visitors aren't allowed on Shemya Island, which has a remote U.S. Air Force base, without special permission. Because of downsizing, the military has closed its Adak operation, and the base's infrastructure provides the core infrastructure for what now is a small coastal community and commercial fishing port.

Unalaska/Dutch Harbor, twin towns midway out the chain, are by far the most populous destinations in the Aleutian Islands. Although they're sometimes called "the Crossroads of the Aleutians," even by Alaska standards people who live here are living remote. Usually referred to simply as Dutch (or, by people who spend winter there, "the gulag"), the towns are connected by a bridge that spans a narrow channel between Unalaska and Amaknak islands. (Locals playfully call the span the "Bridge to the Other Side.") Despite the often-harsh weather—this region is known as the "Cradle of Storms" for good reason—the Aleut people and their ancestors have occupied these islands and others in the Aleutians for thousands of years. Today Dutch is the region's tourism center, as well as one of the busiest fishing ports in the world. Scattered around both islands are reminders of history: the Japanese bombed Dutch Harbor during World War II (unexploded ordinance may still be out there, so don't handle any odd metal objects you see while hiking), and you can still explore concrete bunkers, gun batteries, and a partially sunken ship left over from the war.

It's worth the trip out to Dutch on the ferry just for the scenery along the way, but when travelers finally reach the islands, they discover a surprisingly gentle landscape of tawny, rolling hills sheltering a town that is built for work, not beauty. Which is not to say the town lacks pretty things. The most dramatic attraction in Dutch is the Holy Ascension Russian Orthodox Church, a perfect blue, onion-dome chapel right on the edge of the water, the best Russian church left in Alaska. The extant buildings date to the 1890s, although there has been a church on the site since 1808. Inside is a collection of Russian icons and artworks that is not to be missed, certainly the most impressive

8

in the Americas. These are not museum pieces; they have been used, regularly, and it shows.

Next to the church is the Bishop's House, which is undergoing continuing restoration. A walk in the graveyard between the two buildings shows the full history of the area: Aleuts, sailors, and, always oriented to face the church, the graves of the Orthodox parishioners.

Easy walking distance from the ferry terminal is the Aleutian World War II National Historic Area Visitor Center, on the edge of the airport. The Aleutians saw heavy fighting through much of the war—some of the outer islands were occupied by Japanese forces for years—and the museum does a nice job of presenting the history of the conflict. At the peak of the war, more than 60,000 servicemen were stationed out here.

The Aleut take on the islands is offered at the Museum of the Aleutians, behind the grocery store, about a 15-minute walk from the ferry. Small, but quite remarkable, displays include original drawings from Captain Cook's third voyage, a traditional gut parka, and more. A don't-miss stop.

Don't worry about opening hours: if the ferry is in, the town's attractions will be open.

For facilities, the towns have hotels and restaurants that rival those on Alaska's mainland, plus guided adventure tours, many geared towards birders. If you're feeling particularly planning oriented, contact the **Unalaska–Dutch Harbor Convention and Visitors Bureau** (*Box 545, Unalaska 99685* ☎*907/581–2612 or 877/581–2612* ☐*907/581–2613* ⊕*www.unalaska.info*) for a little extra guidance during your visit.

SPORTS, THE OUTDOORS & GUIDED TOURS

OUTDOOR
ADVENTURING

Grand Aleutian Hotel Tours (☎*800/891–1194* ⊕*www.grandaleutian. com*) offers outdoors activities, ranging from birding to wildlife photography, halibut and salmon fishing, and tours of cultural sites; make arrangements through the hotel.

WHERE TO STAY & EAT

$ **Grand Aleutian Hotel and Unisea Inn.** For travelers on a budget, this hotel on the water has clean, spartan rooms; try to book one with a view of the small-boat harbor. Pizza, burgers, and sandwiches are served in the Unisea Inn Sports Bar and Grill. Local bands play Top 40 or country music. **Pros:** What passes for budget prices in the Aleutians. **Cons:** Not as grand as the Grand Aleutian on Salmon Way. ⊠*185 Gilman Rd., Dutch Harbor* ☎*907/581–1325, 800/891–1194, 866/581–3844 reservations* ⊄*25 rooms* ⚇ *In-hotel: restaurant, bar, public Wi-Fi, airport shuttle, no-smoking rooms* ☐*AE, D, DC, MC, V.*

$$$ **Grand Aleutian Hotel.** An airy three-story atrium lobby with a large stone
★ fireplace conjures images of a Swiss chalet. Rooms have views of either Margaret Bay or Unalaska Bay. Each lushly carpeted, brightly lighted room is decorated with Alaskan artwork and is equipped with full bath, hair dryer, extra vanity and sink, and in-room coffeemaker. The

Chart Room Restaurant and Lounge specializes in Pacific Rim cuisine with locally caught seafood, and features a seafood buffet every Wednesday night and an elaborate Sunday brunch year-round. Barbecues are scheduled on Friday nights in summer, on the deck overlooking Margaret Bay. For more informal dining, there's the Margaret Bay Café. Guided activities include bird-watching, cultural tours, archaeological digs, marine wildlife tours, photography, and fishing. **Pros:** Bay-view rooms, massage. **Cons:** A bit generic; once you're inside, you could be almost anywhere. ⊠*498 Salmon Way, Dutch Harbor* ☎*907/581–3844 or 866/581–3844* ⊕*www.grandaleutian. com* ⤳*112 rooms, 2 suites* ⚭*In-hotel: 2 restaurants, bar, public Wi-Fi, airport shuttle, some pets allowed, no-smoking rooms* ⊟*AE, D, DC, MC, V.*

PRIBILOF ISLANDS

200 mi north of the Aleutian Islands, 800 mi southwest of Anchorage.

The Pribilof Islands are a misty, fog-bound breeding ground of seabirds and northern fur seals. Rising out of the surging waters of the Bering Sea, the Pribilofs consist of five islets, a tiny, green, treeless oasis with rippling belts of lush grass contrasting with red volcanic soil. In early summer seals come home from far Pacific waters to mate, and the larger islands, St. Paul and St. George, are overwhelmed with frenzied activity. The seals' barks and growls can roll out several miles to sea.

Although St. Paul and St. George are less than 50 mi apart, the island group itself is a 1,600-mi round-trip from Anchorage, over the massive snowy peaks of the Alaska Peninsula and past the rocky islands of the Aleutian chain. This was the supply route for U.S. forces during World War II, when Japan invaded Attu and Kiska islands toward the tip of the chain.

People come to the Pribilofs is to see wildlife. Together, St. Paul and St. George islands are seasonal homes to nearly 1 million fur seals (about 80% of them on St. Paul) and nearly 250 species of birds. Some birds migrate here from as far away as Argentina, whereas others are year-round residents. Most spectacular of all is the islands' seabird population: each summer more than 2 million seabirds gather at traditional Pribilof nesting grounds; about 90% of them breed on St. George.

For most travelers it is much easier and more efficient to sign up for package tours that arrange air travel from Anchorage, lodging, ground transportation on the islands, and guided activities. Guest accommodations in the Pribilofs are very limited.

DID YOU KNOW?

Of special interest to birders are the rare vagrant birds of native Asian species, such as the Siberian rubythroat and Eurasian skylark, sometimes blown here by strong winds.

WHAT TO SEE

At **St. Paul Island** nature lovers can watch members of the largest northern fur-seal herd in the world and more than 180 varieties of birds. In town you can visit with local residents; about 500 descendants of Aleut-Russians live here now, in the shadow of the old Russian Orthodox church and amid the vestiges of Aleut culture.

St. George Island is home to nearly 2 million nesting seabirds, but it is much less frequently visited, because no organized tours visit here and accommodations are limited.

SPORTS, THE OUTDOORS & GUIDED TOURS

The Pribilofs are considered a birders' paradise for good reason: species that are seldom, if ever, seen elsewhere in North America frequently show up here, including an array of "Asian vagrants" blown here by westerly winds. Birders can expect to find all manner of shorebirds, waterfowl, and seabirds, including puffins, murres, red- and black-legged kittiwakes, plovers—the list goes on and on. Tour guides will also show visitors the best places to view seals and whales.

BIRDING & SEAL WATCHING Contact **Tanadgusix Village Corporation of St. Paul Island** (⊠*4300 B St., Suite 402, Anchorage* ☎*907/278–2312 or 877/424–5637* ⊕*www. alaskabirding.com*) for St. Paul Island tour information. The owners of **Wilderness Birding Adventures** (☎*907/694–7442* ⊕*www.wilderness-birding.com*) combine birding, hiking, and river rafting in their wilderness adventures.

WHERE TO STAY & EAT

$$
SEAFOOD
✕**Trident Sea Foods.** This cafeteria-style eatery—the island's only restaurant—serves fish processors as well as visitors to St. Paul Island. Plan your day carefully, because meals are served according to a strict schedule: breakfast 5–6:30, lunch noon–1, and dinner 5–6. ⊠*Downtown St. Paul, 2 blocks from King Eider Hotel* ☎*907/546–2377* ▭*No credit cards.*

$$$$
🏨**King Eider Hotel.** More functional than luxurious, this rustic three-story clapboard hotel is filled in summer by tour groups. The original part of this historic landmark dates to the late 1800s; it's been expanded four times since. The hotel has simply furnished rooms, a TV room, reading lounge, and gift shop. If you are traveling on your own, make reservations months in advance, because most rooms are reserved for tours. **Pros:** Great birding. **Cons:** Pretty bare-bones rooms for the price. ⊠*523 Tolstoi St., Box 88, St. Paul* ☎*907/546–2477, 907/278–2312, 877/424–5637 to make tour reservations* ⊕*www.alaskabirding.com* ⚲*20 rooms, 2 shared baths* ☝*In-room: no phone, no TV. In-hotel: no-smoking rooms* ▭*AE, MC, V.*

$$$$
🏨**St. George Tanaq Hotel.** A national historic landmark, St. George Island's only hotel is a small, rustic building with a dark-wood interior and a mix of modern and vintage furniture. Originally built by the government to house visiting officials, the hotel can accommodate up to 18 guests and is within easy walking distance of fur-seal rookeries. Rooms are sparsely furnished with shared baths. The hotel's shared but renovated gourmet kitchen includes everything you'll need to make

your own meal—necessary, since the island has no restaurant. **Pros:** National Historic Landmark flavor. **Cons:** Come ready for every weather condition possible, all at once. ⊠*Downtown, Box 939, St. George* ☎*907/272–9886 or 907/859–2255* ⊕*www.stgeorgetanaq. com* ⤳*10 rooms share 5 baths* ♿*In-hotel: restaurant, no-smoking rooms* ⊟*MC, V.*

NORTHWEST & THE ARCTIC

This is a largely roadless region of long, dark, sunless winters and short, bright summers, when the sun provides nearly three months of perpetual daylight in places like Barrow. The round-the-clock sunshine lasts for only a few days farther south, but the extended twilight hours turn the midnights bright. It's the land of Eskimos and huge caribou herds and polar bears, a place where people still lead subsistence lifestyles and where native cultural traditions live on. It's also a place of gold rushes past and America's largest oil field, as well as a region with many of Alaska's most remote parklands—not to mention one of the country's grandest refuges, the Arctic National Wildlife Refuge.

NOME

540 mi northwest of Anchorage.

More than a century has passed since a great stampede for gold put a speck of wilderness now called Nome on the Alaska map, but gold mining and noisy saloons are still mainstays in this frontier community of 3,700 people on the icy Bering Sea. At first glance, the town may come off as a collection of ramshackle houses and low-slung commercial buildings—like a vintage gold-mining camp or the neglected set of a Western movie, rawboned, rugged, and somewhat shabby—but only a couple of streets back you'll find tidy, modern homes, and anywhere in town you'll find cheerful hospitality and colorful history.

Only 165 mi from the coast of Siberia, Nome is considerably closer to Russia than to either Anchorage or Fairbanks. And though you'll find a local road system well worth exploring, to get to Nome you must either fly or mush a team of sled dogs.

For centuries before Nome gained fame as a gold-rush town, Inupiat Eskimos seasonally inhabited the area in hunting and fishing camps. The Inupiat traditionally led a nomadic lifestyle, moving with the seasons, so although just outside town are the remnants of ancient ring houses (the Inupiat didn't like corners), no permanent settlement was established at the site until gold was found by Euro-American prospectors in the late 1890s.

Besides being known for its gold-mining origins, Nome's fame is closely tied to the historic **Iditarod Trail.** Some portions of that route were used for centuries by Eskimos and Athabascan Indians residing in Alaska's northwest region. But the Iditarod Trail's heyday was during the territory's gold-rush era, from the late 1800s through the mid-1920s.

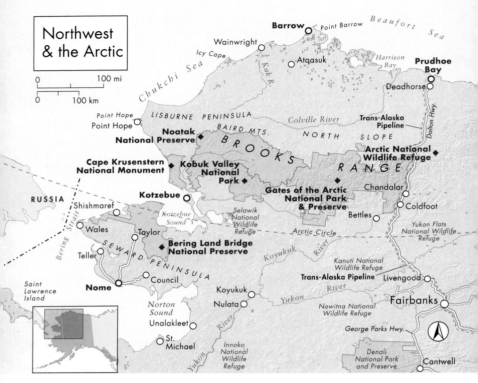

Primarily a winter pathway, the trail acted as a transportation and communication corridor that connected mining camps and villages. The Iditarod (derived from the Athabascan Indian word *haiditarod,* meaning "a far, distant place") began at the ice-free port of Seward and ended in Nome. Including all its branches, the entire system measured more than 2,000 mi. Through the 1920s, thousands of people traveled the Iditarod Trail; most drove dog teams, but some rode on horse-drawn sleds. Others walked, snowshoed, or even bicycled, usually because they couldn't afford to own or rent a dog team.

Though Nome today is most closely associated with the Iditarod Trail Sled Dog Race, in the early 1900s it was also the site of Alaska's first organized mushing event, the All-Alaska Sweepstakes. From 1908 through 1917, the Nome Kennel Club annually staged a 408-mi sled-dog race from Nome to Candle and back. The race established the reputations of several early-20th-century mushers, including three-time winners Scotty Allan and Leonhard Seppala. Seppala, a Norwegian, would race dogs over a career that spanned 45 years; he would also be a heroic figure in the 1925 "Great Race of Mercy," in which a relay of mushers and their dog teams transported diphtheria antitoxin serum to Nome to stop what could have been a disastrous outbreak of the disease, then commonly known as the "black death." The 1925 serum run is annually celebrated as part of the Iditarod race.

Besides its gold-discovering founders and famous mushers, Nome is also proud to be the hometown of General James H. Doolittle, the Tokyo raider of World War II. When Doolittle's bombers hit Japan in a daring raid in 1942, the headline in the *Nome Nugget* proudly announced: "NOME TOWN BOY MAKES GOOD!"

A network of 250 mi or so of gravel roads around the town leads to creeks and rivers for gold panning or fishing for trout, salmon, and arctic grayling. You can also see reindeer, bears, foxes, and moose in the wild on the back roads that once connected early mining camps and hamlets. Musk oxen are not uncommon around the high school, and in the hills beyond town. The roads are mostly good, packed gravel, suitable for almost any kind of car you can rent in town.

GETTING HERE & AROUND

Alaska Airlines Vacations packages air tours to Barrow and Nome. Local arrangements are taken care of by native ground operators. These trips are especially good for travelers who would otherwise move about independently. The Alaska Travel Industry Association can give tips on air travel and flightseeing opportunities throughout the bush.

If you're set on doing your own driving, head to Alaska Cab Garage or Stampede Ventures, which rent cars and vans of various types.

ESSENTIALS

Contacts **Alaska Airlines Vacations** (✈ *Box 68900, Seattle, WA 98168* ☎ *800/468-2248* ⊕ *www.alaskaair.com).* **Alaska Travel Industry Association** (✉ *2600 Cordova St., Suite 201, Anchorage 99503* ☎ *907/929-2200, 800/862-5275 for vacation planner* 🖷 *907/561-5727* ⊕ *www.travelalaska.com).* **Nome Convention and Visitors Bureau** (✈ *Box 240, Nome 99762* ☎ *907/443-6624, 800/478-1901 in Alaska* 🖷 *907/443-5832* ⊕ *www.nomealaska.org/vc).*

Banking **Credit Union 1** ✉ 110 Front St. ☎ *907/443-2737 or 800/478-2222* ⊕ *www.cu1.org.* **Wells Fargo** ✉ 109A Front St. ☎ *907/443-2223 or 800/869-3557* ⊕ *www.wellsfargo.com.*

Emergency **Police** (☎ *907/443-5262).* **State troopers** (☎ *907/443-5525)* . **Norton Sound Regional Hospital** (✉ *Nome* ☎ *907/443-3311* ⊕ *www.nortonsoundhealth.org).*

Internet **City Library** (✉ *220 Front St.* ☎ *907/443-6628* ⊕ *www.nomealaska. org/library/index.html).*

Mail **USPS** (✉ *113 E. Front St.* ☎ *907/443-2401).*

Vehicle Rental **Alaska Cab Garage** (☎ *907/443-2335 or 907/443-2939).* **Stampede Ventures** (☎ *907/443-3838 or 800/354-4606* ⊕ *www.aurorain-nome.com).*

8

WHAT TO SEE

Since the sun stays up late in the summer months, drive to the top of **Anvil Mountain,** near Nome, for a panoramic view of the old gold town and the Bering Sea. Be sure to carry mosquito repellent.

Nome's **Carrie M. McClain Memorial Museum** showcases the history of the Nome gold rush, from the "Lucky Swedes" discovery in 1898 to Wyatt Earp's arrival in 1899 and the stampede of thousands of people into Nome in 1900. The museum also has exhibits about the Bering Strait Inupiat Eskimos, plus displays on the Nome Kennel Club and its All-Alaska Sweepstakes. However, the highlight of the museum is the historical photo collection: thousands of pictures from the early days make it a perfect place to lose yourself on a rainy day. ⊠*223 Front St.* ☎*907/443–6630* 🖾*Free* ☉*June–early Sept., daily 10–5:30; early Sept.–May, Tues.–Fri. noon–5:30.*

For exploring downtown, stop at the **Nome Convention and Visitors Bureau** (⊠*301 Front St.* ☎*907/443–6624, 800/478–1901 in Alaska* 🖨*907/443–5832* ⊕*www.nomealaska.org/vc*) for a historic-walking-tour map, a city map, and information on local activities from flight-seeing to bird-watching.

SPORTS, THE OUTDOORS & GUIDED TOURS

LOCAL TOURS **Alaska Airlines Vacations** (☎*800/468–2248* ⊕*www.alaskaair.com*) arranges trips to Nome (such as the "Day in Nome" and "Adventure in Nome" packages), including air travel, hotels, and local tours. Visitors seeking to learn more about Nome and the surrounding region can join former Broadway showman Richard Beneville, flat-out one of Alaska's most entertaining guides, who emphasizes Nome's gold-rush and Inupiat history of the region in his **Nome Discovery Tours** (✇*Box 2024, Nome 99762* ☎*907/443–2814*). **Northern Alaska Tour Company** (✇ *Box 82991-W, Fairbanks 99708* ☎*800/474–1986 or 907/474–8600* ⊕*www.alaskasarctic.com*) arranges one-day cultural tours to Nome via Fairbanks or Anchorage.

SLED-DOG
RACING
The famed **Iditarod Trail Sled Dog Race**—the Olympics of sled-dog racing—reaches its culmination in Nome in mid-March. Racers start in Anchorage for a trip of nine days to two weeks. The arrival of the mushers heralds a winter carnival. For dates, starting times, and other information, contact the **Iditarod Trail Committee** (✇*Box 870800, Wasilla 99687* ☎*907/376–5155* ⊕*www.iditarod.com*).

WHERE TO EAT

$–$$$
STEAK
★
✕**Fat Freddie's.** This popular café-style eatery overlooking the Bering Sea serves New York steak and prime rib, plus notable burgers and seafood. During the Iditarod, many mushers hang out here after completing their grueling trips across Alaska. If you're staying at the Nome Nugget Inn, you can enter directly from the hotel. ⊠*50 Front St.* ☎*907/443–5899* ▭ *D, MC, V.*

$$–$$$$
PIZZA
✕**Milano's Pizzeria.** This Front Street restaurant has a casual atmosphere and offers dine-in service as well as takeout. Besides pizzas with a wide assortment of toppings, the pizzeria features Japanese and Italian food. ⊠*110 W. Front St.* ☎*907/443–2924* ▭*MC, V.*

RICHES OF THE PAST

Nome's golden years began in 1898, when three prospectors—known as the Lucky Swedes—struck rich deposits on Anvil Creek, about 4 mi from what became Nome. Their discovery was followed by the formation of the Cape Nome Mining District. The following summer, even more gold was found on the beaches of Nome. Word spread quickly to the south, and when the Bering Sea ice parted the next spring, ships from Puget Sound (in the Seattle area) arrived in Nome with eager stampeders. An estimated 15,000 people landed in Nome between June and October of 1900, bringing the area's population to more than 20,000. Dozens of gold dredges were hauled into the region to extract the metal from Seward Peninsula sands and gravels; more than 40 are still standing, though most are no longer operable (if you explore them, be sure to call out regularly, as warning to any bears that have taken shelter inside). Among the gold-rush luminaries were Wyatt Earp, the old gunfighter from the O.K. Corral, who

mined the gold of Nome by opening a posh saloon; Tex Rickard, the boxing promoter, who operated another Nome saloon (money made there later helped him run Madison Square Garden); and Rex Beach, the novelist.

The city of Nome was incorporated in 1901, making it Alaska's oldest first-class city, with the oldest continuously operating school district. But the community's heyday lasted less than a decade; by the early 1920s the bulk of the region's gold had been mined and only 820 or so people continued to live in Nome. The city's boom times ended long ago, but gold mining has continued to the present, though nowadays the existing operations are small ones. Visitors are welcome to try their own luck; they can pick up a gold pan at one of Nome's stores and sift through the beach sands along a 2-mi stretch of shoreline east of Nome. Visitors can also contact the Nome Convention and Visitors Bureau for information on tours that feature gold panning.

8

S–$$$ ✕**Polar Café.** Enjoy American diner food, from omelets to steaks. Locals
AMERICAN like to linger over coffee, making it a good place to eavesdrop on residents discussing area issues, or just to gaze out at the Bering Sea. With its sea views, good prices, and friendly service, it's a great place for early-morning breakfast. ⊠*Next to seawall, 205 W. Front St.* ☎*907/443–5191* ▤*AE, MC, V.*

WHERE TO STAY

$$$$ ⊡**John Elmore's Grayling on a Fly.** At the site of an early 1900s gold-mining camp, this high-end lodge (formerly known as Camp Bendeleben) sits along the clear-water Niukluk River, about 75 mi northeast of Nome. You can fish for arctic char, grayling, and four species of salmon; other outdoor activities include bird-watching and wildlife photography. The all-inclusive packages include transportation between the lodge and Nome. There is a three-night minimum and rates vary depending on the activities you choose to do. **Pros:** Great personal service. **Cons:** Limited personal space indoors. ⊡*In summer: Box 1045, Nome 99762* ⊠*In winter: 9351 Abbott Loop Rd., Anchorage 99507*

☎907/522–6663 ⊕*www.grayling-on-a-fly.com* ⇆*3 rooms* ♿*In-room: no phone, no TV. In-hotel: restaurant* ⊟*No credit cards* ⊘*Closed Oct.–May.*

$ 🏨**Nome Nugget Inn.** The architecture and decor of the Nugget Inn combine every cliché of the Victorian gold-rush era. Authentic it's not, but fun it is. Outside, a signpost marks the mileage to various points, serious and silly, around the globe. Inside, frontier memorabilia abounds in the lobby and lounge. Rooms are small and clean but not nearly as atmospheric. Arctic tour groups stay here. Fat Freddie's restaurant is conveniently attached to the hotel. **Pros:** Cool atmosphere in the public areas. **Cons:** A little less cool in the rooms. ⊠*Front St., Box 1470* ☎*907/443–4189 or 877/443–2323* ⇆*47 rooms* ♿*In-room:* Wi-Fi. *In-hotel: restaurant, public Internet, no-smoking rooms* ⊟*AE, MC, V.*

WORD OF MOUTH

"The more I think about it, the more I like Nome. I think the attraction is that it's so different. I love looking off in the distance and knowing there's nothing but wilderness for hundreds of miles. I've never been anywhere with such a sense of the vast and the remote. The town is funky and friendly. It seems to have a real sense of humor about itself. It is a bit of a rough town, with more than its share of local bars and saloons, but it's also a funky place with lots of character. The Iditarod ends here every March—it's quite an event."

—Julie304

¢ ⛺ **Bureau of Land Management Campground.** BLM manages a free campground at Mile 40 of the Nome-Taylor Highway. The campground, just off the highway, has six tent sites, and fishing is close by. The maximum length of stay is 14 days. There is a pit toilet and fire rings for cooking, but the only water is in nearby Salmon Lake and Pilgrim River; it must be boiled or otherwise treated. ♿*Portable toilets, fire pits, swimming (lake)* ⇆*6 tent sites* 🏛*Bureau of Land Management, Nome Field Office, Box 925, 99762* ☎*907/443–2177 in Nome, 907/474–2231 in Fairbanks, 907/267–1246 in Anchorage, 800/478–1263 Alaska only* ⊕*www.ak.blm.gov* ♿*Reservations not accepted* ⊟*No credit cards* ⊘*Closed Oct.–Apr.*

SHOPPING

Nome is one of the best places to buy ivory, because many of the Eskimo carvers from outlying villages come to Nome first to sell their wares to dealers. The **Arctic Trading Post** (⊠*Bering and Front Sts.* ☎*907/443–2686*) has an extensive stock of authentic Eskimo ivory carvings and other Alaskan artwork, jewelry, and books. **Chukotka–Alaska** (⊠*514 Lomen* ☎*907/443–4128*) sells both native Alaskan and Russian artwork and handicrafts as well as books, beads, and furs. The **Maruskiyas of Nome** (☎*907/443–2955*) on Front Street specializes in authentic native Alaskan artwork and handicrafts, including ivory, baleen, and jade sculptures, jewelry, dolls, and masks.

BERING LAND BRIDGE NATIONAL PRESERVE

100 mi north of Nome.

The frozen ash and lava of the 2.8-million-acre Bering Land Bridge National Preserve lie between Nome and Kotzebue, immediately south of the Arctic Circle, one of the most remote parks in the world. The Imuruk lava flow is the northernmost flow of major size in the United States, and the paired *maars* (clear volcanic lakes) are a geological rarity.

Of equal interest are the paleontological features of this preserve. Sealed into the permafrost are flora and fauna—bits of twigs and leaves, tiny insects, small mammals, even the fossilized remains of woolly mammoths—that flourished here when the Bering Land Bridge linked North America to what is now Russia. Early peoples wandered through this treeless landscape, perhaps following the musk ox, whose descendants still occupy this terrain. Flowering plants thrive in this seemingly barren region, about 250 species in all, and tens of thousands of migrating birds can be seen in season. More than 100 species, including ducks, geese, swans, sandhill cranes, and various shorebirds and songbirds, come here from around the world each spring.

The Bering Land Bridge National Preserve is pretty much exactly like it was when people first came to this continent from Asia: it has no trails, campgrounds, or other visitor facilities. Access is largely by air taxi, although there is a road north of Nome that passes within walking distance. 🖎 *National Park Service, Box 220, Nome 99762* ☎ *907/443–2522 or 907/442–3890* ⊕ *www.nps.gov/bela.*

8

KOTZEBUE

170 mi northeast of Nome.

Kotzebue is Alaska's largest Eskimo community, home to more than 3,000 people. Most of the residents of this coastal village are Inupiats, whose ancestors have had ties to the region for thousands of years. For most of that time, the Inupiat lived in seasonal camps, following caribou, moose, and other wildlife across the landscape. They also depended on whales, seals, fish, and the wide variety of berries and other plants the rich tundra landscape offers. Besides being talented hunters, the Inupiat were—and still are—skilled craftsmen and artists, known for their rugged gear, ceremonial parkas, Eskimo dolls, caribou-skin masks, birch-bark baskets, and whalebone and walrus-ivory carvings.

Built on a 3-mi-long spit of land that juts into Kotzebue Sound, this village lies 33 mi above the Arctic Circle, on Alaska's northwest coast. Before Europeans arrived in the region, the Inupiat name for this locale was Kikiktagruk; that was changed to Kotzebue after German explorer Otto von Kotezbue passed through in 1818 while sailing for Russia. Kotzebue is the region's economic and political hub and headquarters for both the Northwest Arctic Borough and the NANA

DID YOU KNOW?

The blanket toss is traditionally performed during Nalukataq, the spring Inupiaq whaling festival. Once a way for community leaders to distribute goods, the most commonly tossed item today is candy.

Regional Corporation, one of the 13 regional native corporations formed when Congress settled the Alaskan natives' aboriginal land claims in 1971. The region's other Eskimo villages have populations of 90 to 700.

Just as their ancestors did, modern Inupiats depend heavily on subsistence hunting and fishing. Some residents also fish commercially. This region of the state has few employment opportunities outside of the government and the native corporation. The biggest private employer is the Red Dog Mine.

WELCOME TO KOTZEBUE

Comprised of clusters of weather-bleached little houses and a few public buildings on the gravelly shore of Kotzebue Sound, this village provides you with a glimpse of the way Alaska's Eskimos live today. It was an ancient Eskimo trading center; now it is an example of the modern spirit nudging Alaska's native peoples into the state's mainstream culture without leaving their traditions behind.

Located on NANA land, Red Dog has the world's largest deposit of zinc, and is expected to produce ore for at least 50 years. Local government here, as in many bush villages, is a blend of tribal government and a more modern borough system. Other facilities and programs include the Maniilaq Health Center and the Northwest Arctic District Correspondence Program.

Kotzebue has long, cold winters and short, cool summers. The average low temperature in January is -12°F, and midsummer highs rarely reach the 70s. "We have four seasons—June, July, August, and winter," a tour guide jests. But don't worry about the sometimes chilly weather—the local sightseeing company has snug, bright loaner parkas for visitors on package tours. And there's plenty of light in which to take in the village and surrounding landscape: the sun doesn't set for 36 days, from June into July. One of summer's highlights is the annual Northwest Native Trade Fair; held each year after the July 4 celebration, it features traditional native games, seal-hook-throwing contests, and an Eskimo buggy race.

GETTING HERE & AROUND
Like pretty much everywhere else in the bush, your main mode of transportation into Kotzebue will be via airplane. The main air taxi services serve Kotzebue, and there's a daily flight from Anchorage. Cabs will take you anywhere in town for $5 flat, plus $5 per stop.

ESSENTIALS
Contacts **NANA Regional Corporation** (*Northwest Alaska Native Association* ☎ *907/442–3301 or 800/478–3301* ⊕ *www.nana.com*).. **Northwest Arctic Borough** (✉ *Box 1110, Kotzebue 99752* ☎ *907/442–2500 or 800/478–1110*).

Banking **Wells Fargo** (✉ 360 Lagoon St. ☎ 907/442–3258 or *800/869–3557* ⊕ *www.wellsfargo.com*).

Emergency **Maniilaq Health Center** (✉ *Kotzebue* ☎ *800/478–3321* ⊕ *www. maniilaq.org*).**Police** (☎ *907/442–3351* ⊕ *www.kotzebuepolice.com*). **State troopers** (☎ *907/442–3222 in Kotzebue*).

Internet Access **Chukchi Consortium Library** (✉ *604 3rd St.* ☎ *907/442–2410*).

Mail **USPS** (✉ *333 Shore Ave.* ☎ *907/442–3291*).

WHAT TO SEE

GETTING TO KOTZEBUE

Alaska Airlines offers regular flights between Anchorage and Kotzebue. Check out ⊕ *www.alaskaair.com* for more details.

If you're hiking the wildflower-carpeted tundra around Kotzebue, you are entering a living museum dedicated to **permafrost,** the permanently frozen ground that lies just a few inches below the spongy tundra. Even Kotzebue's 6,000-foot airport runway is built on permafrost—with a 6-inch insulating layer between the frozen ground and the airfield surface to ensure that landings are smooth.

Although most people come to Kotzebue as part of day trips or overnight package tours, for those with time to linger the town also serves as a gateway for three exceptional national **wilderness areas:** Cape Krusenstern National Monument, Kobuk Valley National Park, and Noatak National Preserve.

North and east of Kotzebue is the **Brooks Range,** one of Alaska's great mountain ranges. Stretching across the state, much of the range is protected by Gates of the Arctic National Park and Preserve and the Arctic National Wildlife Refuge.

WHERE TO STAY & EAT

$-$$$$
PIZZA

✕ **Bayside Café.** One of the few restaurants in Kotzebue, the Bayside is the best place in town for breakfast, and it features a selection of American, Italian, and Chinese food for lunch and dinner. ✉ *303 Shore Ave.* ☎ *907/442–3600* ▭ *MC, V.*

$$$

⛶ **Nullagvik Hotel.** This hotel overlooking Kotzebue Sound is built on pilings driven into the ground, because the heat of the building would melt the underlying permafrost and cause the hotel to sink. Images of Eskimo life adorn the spacious, modern rooms. Public areas on the second and third floors provide picture-window views of the bay. **Pros:** Great views. **Cons:** No in-house restaurant. ✉ *308 Shore Ave., Box 336* ☎ *907/442–3331* ⊕ *www.nullagvik.com* ⇆ *75 rooms* ⚭ *In-hotel: no elevator, some pets allowed, no-smoking rooms* ▭ *AE, D, DC, MC, V.*

CAPE KRUSENSTERN NATIONAL MONUMENT

10 mi north of Kotzebue.

Just north of Kotzebue, the 560,000-acre Cape Krusenstern National Monument has important cultural and archaeological value. This is a coastal parkland, with an extraordinary series of beach ridges built up by storms over a period of at least 5,000 years. Almost every ridge—more than 100 in all—contains artifacts of different human occupants, representing every known Arctic Eskimo culture in North America. The present Eskimo occupants, whose culture dates back some 1,400 years, use the fish, seals, caribou, and birds of this region for food and raw materials much as their ancestors did. They are also closely involved in the archaeological digs in the park that are unearthing part of their own history.

Cape Krusenstern is a starkly beautiful Arctic land shaped by ice, wind, and sea. Its low, rolling gray-white hills covered by light-green tundra attract hikers and backpackers, and kayakers sometimes paddle its coastline. The monument is a marvelous living museum. ■ TIP➔ It's possible to camp in the park, but be mindful, as are the native people when they pitch their white canvas tents for summer fishing, that the shoreline is subject to fierce winds. Both grizzlies and polar bears patrol the beaches in search of food, so clean camping is a must.

Check with the National Park Service in Kotzebue about hiring a local guide to the monument, which has no visitor facilities; it's accessible by air taxi and by boat from Kotzebue. *National Park Service, Box 1029, Kotzebue 99752* ☎*907/442–3890* ⊕*www.nps.gov/cakr.*

KOBUK VALLEY NATIONAL PARK

65 mi east of Kotzebue.

Kobuk Valley National Park lies entirely north of the Arctic Circle, along the southern edge of the Brooks Range. Its 1.14 million acres contain remarkable inland deserts and the **Great Kobuk Sand Dunes,** and are home to interesting relict (remnants of otherwise extinct) flora. The park is bisected by the west-flowing **Kobuk River,** a 347-mi-long stream born in the foothills of the western Brooks Range. The Kobuk, whose native name means "big river," has been a major transportation and trade route for centuries. Besides the Kobuk, this park contains two smaller streams that provide delightful river running, the Ambler and the Salmon. These brilliantly clear rivers are accessible by wheeled plane, and each provides a good week's worth of pleasure (if the weather cooperates).

Another place of special interest is the **Onion Portage.** Human occupation here dates back 12,500 years, and the region is rich in archaeological history; herds of caribou that fed the Woodland Eskimo centuries ago are still hunted at Onion Portage by present-day Eskimo residents of the region.

Kobuk Valley National Park is, like most other remote Alaska parks, undeveloped wilderness with no visitor facilities. If you come prepared, it can be a good place for backpacking and river trips. In nearby Kotzebue, the National Park Service has a visitor center where staff can provide tips for travel into the park. The villages of Kobuk and Kiana both provide immediate take-off points and have air service. *National Park Service, Box 1029, Kotzebue 99752* ☎*907/442–3890* ⊕*www. nps.gov/kova.*

8

NOATAK NATIONAL PRESERVE

20 mi northeast of Kotzebue.

Adjacent to Gates of the Arctic National Park and Preserve, the 6.5-million-acre Noatak National Preserve encompasses much of the basin of the **Noatak River.** This is the largest mountain-ringed river basin in the United States; part of it is designated by the National Park Service as a Wild and Scenic River. Along its 425-mi course, this river carves out the "Grand Canyon of the Noatak," and serves as a migration route between Arctic and subarctic ecosystems. Its importance to wildlife and plants has resulted in this parkland's designation as an International Biosphere Reserve.

The Noatak River also serves as a natural highway for humans, and offers particular pleasures to river runners, with inviting tundra to camp on and the Poktovik Mountains and the Igichuk Hills nearby for good hiking. Birding can be exceptional: horned grebes, gyrfalcons, golden eagles, parasitic jaegers, owls, terns, and loons are among the species you may see. You may also spot grizzly bears, Dall sheep, wolves, caribou, or lynx. The most frequently run part of the river, ending at Lake Machurak, is mostly an easy Class I–III paddle, worth the trip just for the chance to hunt freshwater snail shells as delicate as origami along the shores of the take-out lake (where the river trip ends). The mountains around the river make for excellent hiking, and along the way the geology goes wild a couple of times, including with a massive pingo—kind of a glacial bubble. As with other parks and preserves in this northwest corner of Alaska, no visitor facilities are available and you are expected to be self-sufficient. Do not neglect the bear precautions. ☝*National Park Service, Box 1029, Kotzebue 99752* ☎*907/442–3890* ⊕*www.nps.gov/noat.*

GATES OF THE ARCTIC NATIONAL PARK & PRESERVE

★ *180 mi east of Kotzebue.*

Gates of the Arctic National Park and Preserve is entirely north of the Arctic Circle, in the center of the Brooks Range; at 8.2 million acres, it's the size of four Yellowstones. This is parkland on a scale suitable to the country. It includes the **Endicott Mountains** to the east and the **Schwatka Mountains** to the southwest, with the staggeringly sharp and dramatic **Arrigetch Peaks** in between. To the north lies a sampling of the Arctic foothills, with their colorful tilted sediments and pale green tundra. Lovely lakes are cupped in the mountains and in the tundra.

This landscape, the ultimate wilderness, captured the heart of Arctic explorer and conservationist Robert Marshall in the 1930s. Accompanied by local residents, Marshall explored much of the region now included within Gates and named many of its features, including Frigid Crag and Boreal Mountain, two peaks on either side of the North Fork Koyukuk River. These were the original "gates" for which the park is named.

Wildlife known to inhabit the park includes barren-ground caribou, grizzlies, wolves, musk oxen, moose, Dall sheep, wolverines, and smaller mammals and birds. The communities of Bettles and Anaktuvuk Pass are access points for Gates of the Arctic, which has no developed trails, campgrounds, or other visitor facilities (though there is a wilderness lodge on private land within the park). You can fly into Bettles commercially and charter an air taxi into the park or hike directly out of Anaktuvuk Pass. The Park Service has rangers stationed in both Bettles and Anaktuvuk Pass; they can provide information for those entering the wilderness, including the mandatory orientation films and bear-proof canisters for food storage. ⊠ *National Park Service, 201 1st Ave., Fairbanks* ☎ *907/457–5752, 907/692–5494 in Bettles, 907/661– 3520 Anaktuvuk Pass* ⊕ *www.nps.gov/gaar.*

SPORTS, THE OUTDOORS & GUIDED TOURS

OUTDOOR
ADVENTURING

Arctic Treks (🖂 *Box 73452, Fairbanks 99707* ☎ *907/455–6502* ⊕ *www. arctictreksadventures.com*) guides wilderness hikes and backpacking expeditions, sometimes combined with river trips, in both Gates of the Arctic and the Arctic National Wildlife Refuge. **Spirit Lights Lodge** (🖂 *Box 90, Bettles 99726* ☎ *888/692–2857* ⊕ *www.spiritlightslodge. com*) guides wilderness hikes and backpacking expeditions, sometimes combined with river trips, in Gates of the Arctic.

DID YOU KNOW?

Arrigetch is an Eskimo word meaning "fingers of a hand outstretched," which aptly describes the immensely steep and smooth granite peaks here.

WHERE TO STAY

$$$$
★

🏨 **Peace of Selby Wilderness.** On Selby and Narvak Lakes within Gates of the Arctic National Park, Peace of Selby is perfectly situated for wilderness adventures. Crafted from white spruce, the main lodge includes a kitchen, small library, bathroom, and loft. Meals, included with some rates, are cooked with fresh vegetables, fruits, and meats. If you want to rough it, you can bring along your sleeping bags and cook your own meals in one of four remote rustic log cabins, which can accommodate up to four people each. The owners also organize custom guided expeditions. Activities include hiking, fishing, wildlife viewing and photographing, river floating, and flightseeing. **Pros:** Endless activity options. **Cons:** Small, so reservations and planning are a must. 🖂 *Box 86, Manley Hot Springs 99756* ☎ *907/672–3206* ⊕ *www.alaskawilderness.net* 🛏 *1 room in lodge, 4 cabins* 🛌 *In-room: no phone, no TV. In-hotel: restaurant* ▄ *No credit cards* ⊗ *Closed mid-Sept.–mid-June, except for specially arranged expeditions Mar. and Apr.*

BARROW

330 mi northeast of Kotzebue.

The northernmost community in the United States, Barrow sits 1,300 mi south of the North Pole. The village is 10 mi south of the Beaufort Sea and Point Barrow, from which it takes its name. Point Barrow, in turn, was named in 1825 by British captain Beechey, who'd been ordered by the British Navy to map the continent's northern coastline.

Beechey wished to honor Sir John Barrow, a member of the British Admiralty and a major force in arctic exploration. The region's Inupiat Eskimos knew the site as Ukpeagvik, or "place where owls are hunted." Even today, many snowy owls nest in the tundra outside Barrow each summer, though they're not hunted as they once were: they are now protected by federal law.

About 4,400 people inhabit Barrow today, making it easily the largest community on the North Slope. Nearly two-thirds of the residents are Inupiat Eskimos. Though they remain deeply rooted in their Inupiat heritage, Barrow's residents have adopted a modern lifestyle. Homes are heated by natural gas taken from nearby gas fields, and the community is served by most modern conveniences, including a public radio station and cable TV and Internet access. The community recreation center has a gymnasium, racquetball courts, weight room, and sauna and hosts a variety of social events, from dances to basketball tournaments. In Barrow, as in much of bush Alaska, basketball is the favored sport, played year-round by people of all ages.

Barrow is the economic and administrative center of the **North Slope Borough,** which encompasses more than 88,000 square mi, making it the world's largest municipal government (in terms of area). The village is also headquarters of the **Arctic Slope Regional Corporation,** formed in 1971 through the Alaska Native Claims Settlement Act (ANCSA), as well as the Ukpeagvik Inupiat Corporation, which economically and politically represents the community of Barrow. Several village councils are also headquartered in the town.

GETTING HERE & AROUND

Alaska Airlines Vacations packages air tours to Barrow and Nome. Local arrangements are taken care of by native ground operators. These trips are especially good for travelers who would otherwise move about independently. The Alaska Travel Industry Association can give tips on air travel and flightseeing opportunities throughout the bush.

ESSENTIALS

Contacts **Alaska Airlines Vacations** (*Box 68900, Seattle, WA 98168* ☎ *800/468-2248* ⊕ *www.alaskaair.com).* **Alaska Travel Industry Association** (✉ *2600 Cordova St., Suite 201, Anchorage 99503* ☎ *907/929-2200, 800/862-5275 for vacation planner* 🖷 *907/561-5727* ⊕ *www.travelalaska.com).* **Bethel Chamber of Commerce** (*Box 329, Bethel 99559* ☎ *907/543-2911* 🖷 *907/543-2255* ⊕ *www.bethelakchamber.org).* **City of Barrow** (*Box 629, Barrow 99723* ☎ *907/852-5211* 🖷 *907/852-5871).*

Banking **Wells Fargo** (✉ *1078 Kiogak St.* ☎ *907/852-6200 or 800/869-3557* ⊕ *www.wellsfargo.com).*

Emergency **Police** (☎ *907/852-0311* ⊕ *www.kotzebuepolice.com)..* **State troopers** (☎ *907/852-3783* ⊕ *www.dps.state.ak.us/ast).* **Samuel Simmonds Memorial Hospital** (✉ *Barrow* ☎ *907/852-4611).*

Internet **Tuzzy Library** (✉ *5421 N. Star St., Barrow* ☎ *907/852-4050* ⊕ *www. tuzzy.org).*

BARROW'S RICHNESS

Barrow is truly the land of the midnight sun. From mid-May until August the sun doesn't set for more than 80 days. (Conversely, the sun disappears during the dead of winter from November through January—this is called the polar winter.) Despite the season's unending daylight, summertime temperatures can be brisk—you should even be prepared for snow flurries. Nevertheless, midsummer temperatures can occasionally reach the 60s and low 70s. Despite the region's abundant wetlands, Barrow—and the North Slope in general—has a desert climate, with annual precipitation averaging less than 10 inches.

Archaeological evidence from more than a dozen nearby ancient "dwelling mounds" suggests that people have inhabited this area for at least the past 1,500 years. A highlight of those mounds is **Mound 44**, where the frozen body of a 500-year-old

Eskimo was discovered. Scientists have been studying her remains to learn more about Eskimo life and culture before encounters with outsiders. Described as members of the **Birnirk culture**, these early residents depended heavily on marine mammals, a tradition that continues to this day. Combining modern technology with traditional knowledge, Barrow's whaling crews annually hunt for the bowhead whales that migrate through Arctic waters each spring and fall. If the whalers are successful in their springtime hunts, they share muktuk—whale meat (to the uninitiated, it tastes kind of like really greasy tuna mixed with steak)—with other members of the village and celebrate their good fortune with a festival called **Nalukataq**. Besides whales, residents depend on harvests of seals, walrus, caribou, waterfowl, grayling, and whitefish.

8

Mail **USPS** (✉ *Post Office Bldg.* ☎ *907/852–6800*).

Nonnatives established a presence at Barrow in the early 1880s, when the U.S. Army built a research station here. Drawn to the area by the Beaufort Sea's abundant whales, commercial whalers established the **Cape Smythe Whaling and Trading Station** in 1893; a cabin from that operation still stands, and is the oldest frame building in Alaska's Arctic. The station is now listed on the National Register of Historic Places (as are the Birnirk dwelling mounds).

By the early 1900s, both a Presbyterian church and U.S. post office had been established. Recalling those days, an Inupiat elder named Alfred Hopson once recounted that the famed Norwegian explorer Vilhjalmur Stefansson used the church as a base for studies of local residents, including measurements of their head sizes. From then on, Stefansson was known locally as the "head measurer." Oil and gas exploration later brought more whites from the Lower 48 to the area; even more came as schools and other government agencies took root in the region. Hopson, too, played a role in the area's development, as he funneled millions of dollars in tax revenues into road building, sanitation and water services, and heath-care services.

Barrow has opened its annual springtime whale festival to outsiders, and there are several historic sites, including a military installation, points of native cultural importance, and a famous crash site. The Barrow airport is where you'll find the **Will Rogers and Wiley Post Monument,** marking the 1935 crash of the American humorist and his pilot 15 mi south of town.

Drawn by both cultural and natural attractions, visitors to Barrow usually arrive on a one- or two-day tour with Alaska Airlines, the only national carrier serving the area. Packages include a bus tour of the town's dusty roads and major sights. ■TIP➜ Though Barrow's residents invite visitors to attend their annual whale festival in spring, summer is the ideal time to survey the town and its historic sites.

SPORTS, THE OUTDOORS & GUIDED TOURS

CULTURAL
TOURS

From mid-May through September you can take an **Alaska Airlines Vacations** (☎800/468–2248   ⊕*vacations.alaskaair.com*) package from Anchorage or Fairbanks to "the top of the world" and get a chance to learn about the natural and cultural history of the area. Year-round tours are organized through **Tundra Tours** (☎*907/852–3900*). Offered from mid-September through mid-May, the winter tours feature visits to a traditional hunting camp, the whaling station, the DEWS site, and opportunities to visit Point Barrow and watch northern lights. The summer program is highlighted by visits to local historic sites and opportunities to witness traditional cultural activities such as Eskimo dances, sewing demonstrations, and the blanket toss. In both winter and summer, visitors can purchase locally made Inupiat arts and crafts.

WHERE TO STAY & EAT

$$–$$$$
MEXICAN
★

✕**Pepe's North of the Border.** The warmth of Pepe's will make you forget that you're in the middle of the Arctic tundra in the most famous restaurant north of Fairbanks. Murals depicting Mexican village scenes highlight the Mission-style decor, and an extensive selection of Mexican dishes, from soft tacos to burritos and flautas, makes this restaurant a favorite of locals and visitors alike. The restaurant's menu is also spiced up with dishes that feature Alaskan seafood and, at the high end of things, steak and lobster. Dinner at Pepe's is surprisingly refined for being on the very fringe of civilization. ⊠*1204 Agvik St., next to Top of the World Hotel* ☎*907/852–8200* ▤*MC, V.*

$

☷**Barrow Airport Inn.** As the name suggests, this modern and well-appointed property is convenient to the airport (it's only two blocks away). **Pros:** Convenient, clean. **Cons:** Must like the odd bit of airplane noise. ⊠*1815 Momegana St., Box 933* ☎*907/852–2525, 800/375–2527 in Alaska only* ⇱*15 rooms* ⚬*In-room: kitchen (some), refrigerator. In-hotel: no elevator, public Wi-Fi, no-smoking rooms* ▤*AE, DC, MC, V* ⦿*CP.*

$$$
★

☷**Top of the World Hotel.** Built in 1974, this refurbished hotel on the shore of the Arctic Ocean has just about every imaginable modern convenience, including cable TV and Internet access. Still, it retains a frontier atmosphere; the lobby, for example, has one complete stuffed polar bear and the mounted head of another. You can mingle in the

Visiting in Winter

Although many people think visiting Alaska in winter is insane, there are plenty of good reasons for doing so. It takes a bit of attitude adjustment, an adventurous spirit, and proper clothing.

The northern lights (aurora borealis) are active all year long, but it has to get dark before you can enjoy them. On a clear night, these shimmering curtains of color in the sky are absolutely breathtaking: rippling reds and greens and blues that seem to make the entire sky come alive. Weather and solar activity have to cooperate in order to make the aurora performances happen, but when they do, the results are astounding.

There are fewer bugs in the winter months; if you've visited in summer and been subjected to the mosquitoes, no-see-ums, and white socks, this alone might entice you.

For a real Alaska winter experience, dog mushing is the ultimate. Spectators can watch sprint and long-distance races all over the state, capped off by the Yukon Quest and Iditarod races in February and March. There are numerous outfits in the Interior and South Central that will train you to mush your own team. Fodor's discusses dog mushing and surrounding competitions with the expectation and hope that all the animals are treated with care and respect. And if you hang out with serious mushers, you'll see that their animals are more pampered than the average Park Avenue poodle.

For both downhill and cross-country skiing adventures, you can charter a helicopter to go backcountry skiing in the Valdez area or visit one of the downhill areas near Anchorage, Fairbanks, or Juneau. You can also ski year-round winter or summer by chartering a plane to a glacier in Denali National Park.

At Juneau, Eaglecrest is across from the city on the slopes of Douglas Island. Skiing is also done on the glaciers of the Juneau Ice Field, reached by helicopter. Turnagain Pass, 59 mi from Anchorage on the Seward Highway, is often trafficked with backcountry skiers and snowmachiners. Hilltop Ski Area and Alpenglow are small alpine ski areas within 10 mi of downtown Anchorage.

The World Extreme Skiing Championships are held at Valdez every April. Cross-country skiers will find many miles of groomed trails in Anchorage. Additional cross-country ski trails can be found around Fairbanks, Homer, and Palmer. Snowboarding has more than caught on in South Central Alaska, and boarders are welcome at all three Anchorage ski areas. Rentals are available at the various ski areas and outdoor equipment shops.

lobby or in front of the community television. Modern, spacious rooms have sitting areas; ask for a room with an ocean view. **Pros:** Every modern convenience. **Cons:** Except elevators, which means you're taking the stairs to the top of the world. ✉*1200 Agviq St., Box 189* ☎*907/852–3900, 800/882–8478, 800/478–8520 in Alaska* ⇆*44 rooms* ⚲*In-room: refrigerator. In-hotel: no elevator, public Wi-Fi, nosmoking rooms* ⊟*AE, D, DC, MC, V.*

SHOPPING

The AC Value Center, or, as it's known locally, **Stuaqpak** (*"Big Store"* ✉*4725 Ahkovak St.* ☎*907/852–6711* ⊕*www.alaskacommercial. com*), is the largest store in town. Though it mainly sells groceries, the store also stocks Eskimo crafts made by locals, including furs, parkas, mukluks, and ceremonial masks.

PRUDHOE BAY

250 mi southeast of Barrow.

Most towns have museums that chronicle local history and achievements. Deadhorse is the town anchoring life along Prudhoe Bay, but it could also serve as a museum dedicated to humankind's hunt for energy and its ability to adapt to harsh conditions.

The costly, much-publicized Arctic oil and gas project is complex and varied. One-day tours with the Arctic Caribou Inn explore the tundra terrain from oil pipes to sandpipers. Along with chances to spot caribou, wildflowers, and an unusual stand of willow trees at the edge of the Arctic Ocean, the field tour surveys oil wells, stations, and oil-company residential complexes—small cities themselves. Your guide will discuss the multimillion-dollar research programs aimed at preserving the region's ecology and point out special tundra vehicles known as Rolligons, whose great weight is distributed to diminish their impact on delicate terrain.

GETTING HERE & AROUND

In the past, individual travelers rarely turned up in Deadhorse and Prudhoe Bay. But now that the Dalton Highway has been opened as far north as Deadhorse, adventurous independent travelers are finding their way north. Still, most people traveling to Deadhorse either work here or come on a tour with one of Alaska's airlines or bus-tour operators. And even those who travel here on their own must join a guided tour (arranged through the Arctic Caribou Inn) if they wish to cross the oil fields to get to the Arctic Ocean. You'll find no restaurants here, though meals can sometimes be arranged through the Prudhoe Bay Hotel.

ESSENTIALS

Contacts **Arctic Caribou Inn** (☎*800/468–2248* ⊕*www.alaskaair.com*).

WHERE TO STAY

$ ⌧ **Arctic Caribou Inn.** Located near the end of the Haul Road, this simple hotel is open only from May through September. It is the center of visitor activity at Deadhorse during the summer months, with a cafeteria-style restaurant, gift shop, and visitor center, plus the only tours offered to nearby Prudhoe Bay. **Pros:** They run good tours. **Cons:** Basic accommodation. ⌂*Pouch 340111, Prudhoe Bay 99734* ☎*877/659–2368* ⊕ *www.arcticcaribouinn.com* ⇝*50 rooms* ♿*In-hotel: restaurant* ⊟*AE, MC, V.*

Arctic National Wildlife Refuge. A hiker stands atop a rocky summit.

$$$ 🏨 **Prudhoe Bay Hotel.** Located near the end of the road at Deadhorse, this hotel is primarily intended for the workers employed in the Prudhoe Bay oil-field complex, but tourists are also welcome. Some of the rooms are bare-bones dormitory-style rooms, whereas others are slightly more upscale, with TVs and phones. All rooms share baths. The hotel includes a cafeteria/dining hall with specific hours for breakfast, lunch, and dinner; meals are buffet style. Food and drinks can be purchased from vending machines around the clock. The hotel is also just a short hop from Deadhorse's airport. **Pros:** Convenient. **Cons:** Sharing a bathroom with someone who just got off a 24-hour oil-rig shift. ✉ *Pouch 340004, Prudhoe Bay 99734* 📞*907/659–2449* 🌐*www.prudhoebayhotel.com* 🛏*170 rooms, shared bath* ♿*In-room: no phone (some), no TV (some). In-hotel: restaurant, no elevator* ▬*AE, MC, V.*

ARCTIC NATIONAL WILDLIFE REFUGE

70 mi southeast of Prudhoe Bay.

The 18-million-acre Arctic National Wildlife Refuge, lying wholly above the Arctic Circle, is administered by the U.S. Fish and Wildlife Service and contains the only protected Arctic coastal lands in the United States (and some of the very few protected in the world), as well as millions of acres of mountains and alpine tundra, in the easternmost portion of the Brooks Range.

★   This is the home of one of the greatest remaining groups of caribou in the world, the **Porcupine Caribou Herd.** The herd, its numbers fluctuating around 100,000, is unmindful of international boundaries and migrates back and forth across Arctic lands into Canada, flowing like a wide river across the expansive coastal plain, through U-shape valleys and alpine meadows, and over high mountain passes. The refuge's coastal areas also serve as critical denning grounds for polar bears, which spend most of their year on the Arctic Ocean's pack ice. Other residents here are grizzly bears, Dall sheep, wolves, musk ox, and dozens of varieties of birds, from snowy owls to geese and tiny songbirds. The refuge's northern areas host legions of breeding waterfowl and shorebirds each summer. As in many of Alaska's more remote parks and refuges, there are no roads here, and no developed trails, campgrounds, or other visitor facilities. This is a place to experience true wilderness—and to walk with care, for the plants are fragile and the ground can be soft and wet in summer. Footprints in tundra can last a hundred years. You can expect snow to sift over the land in almost any season, and should anticipate subfreezing temperatures even in summer, particularly in the mountains. Many of the refuge's clear-flowing rivers are runnable, and tundra lakes are suitable for base camps (a Kaktovik or Fort Yukon air taxi can drop you off and pick you up). The hiking is worth it; upon scrambling up a ridge, you'll look out on wilderness that seems to stretch forever. ✉ *Refuge Manager, Arctic National Wildlife Refuge, 101 12th Ave., Room 236, Box 20, Fairbanks* ☎ *907/456–0250 or 800/362–4546* ⊕ *arctic.fws.gov.*

SPORTS, THE OUTDOORS & GUIDED TOURS

EXPERT **Arctic Treks** (☎ *907/455–6522* ⊕ *www.arctictreksadventures.com*)
GUIDES guides wilderness hikes and backpacking expeditions in both Gates of the Arctic and the Arctic National Wildlife Refuge. The owners of **Wilderness Birding Adventures** (☎ *907/694–7442* ⊕ *www.wildernessbirding. com*) are both experienced river runners and expert birders.

THE ULTIMATE WILDERNESS

For those who love vast wilderness landscapes, few places can match the Brooks Range; Alaska's most northerly mountain chain, it stretches east–west across the state above the Arctic Circle. Fortunately, most of this "ultimate wilderness" is protected by national parklands and the Arctic National Wildlife Refuge. Here you can go days, and even weeks, without seeing another person. The Brooks are the homeland of grizzlies, wolves, Dall sheep, caribou, moose, musk oxen, and golden eagles. They are also the homeland of Athabascan Indians and Inupiat and Nunamiut Eskimos, who have lived here for centuries, traveling the mountain pathways and paddling the great rivers like the Noatak.

Arctic Treks (✉ *Box 73452, Fairbanks 99707* ☎ *907/455–6522* ⊕ *www. arctictreksadventures.com*) guides wilderness hikes and backpacking expeditions, sometimes combined with river trips, in both Gates of the Arctic and the Arctic National Wildlife Refuge.

Understanding
Alaska

WORD OF MOUTH

"I had been lucky enough to get close to several bald eagles over the summer. Most of the time I didn't have my camera ready, but on this day I did. I was able to get a nice series of the bird taking flight."

—Brian Embacher, Photo Contest Winner

FISHING THE LAST FRONTIER: IN SEARCH OF HOLY WATER

After the floatplane roared off and the silence settled in, I found myself standing on a remote Southeast Alaska beach, feeling vaguely lost and wondering aloud if we'd come too early for good fishing. Seated on a log surrounded by yellow beach rye, my friend Tony Route fiddled with his fly rod. Without looking up, he shrugged and replied, "Maybe."

But who knew? We had come here to discover—to explore a coastal stream that was little known and rarely fished. It was one more Alaska enigma, and the steelhead we hoped to find there—big, bright, sea-run rainbow trout that come and go with the tides—were the most mysterious game fish of all.

From that lonely Southeast stream to the Arctic's coastal plain, Alaska remains a startling composition of mass and isolation. From an angler's point of view, this is our continent's Amazon. The state's 375 million acres span several distinct climate zones, each with its own mélange of weather and geography through which 3,000 rivers and uncounted smaller streams collectively flow. Little-explored places and unfished waters can still be found here.

Not many years ago, a commercial fisherman friend who worked Alaska's gulf coast shared stories of steelhead turning up in nets off the mouth of a particular stream. I later found the place on a map, but my efforts to learn more about it and its fish turned up little. Like many other remote waters here, the stream had not been thoroughly surveyed.

Weeks later, in mid-April, I paid a bush pilot to drop me off on a windswept beach near the stream. Once I started fishing, only a few casts were needed to answer the riddle for good: the waters, as untouched and unspoiled as when time began, were a steelhead fisherman's dream. I spent two long, lovely days catching and releasing hard-fighting, sea-run trout as long as my arm. When the time came to leave, I hiked back out to the beach, met my pilot, and simply flew away.

To this day the stream's name and location remain my secret. I've never told a soul. And I've never been back.

Fish species here are hardly limited to coastal steelhead. There are five species of Pacific salmon that return each summer by the millions to natal rivers and rills. In the Kenai River alone, the state's most readily accessed and popular sportfishing river, more than 5 million sockeye salmon (locally called reds) returned to spawn in the summer of 2005.

The Kenai is also known for enormous king salmon: the official state sportfishing record, a 97-pound, 4-ounce monster, was pulled, lunging and flopping, from its glacial-tinted waters in 1985. Even so, more than a few hard-core anglers believe bigger kings remain, if not in the Kenai then somewhere else in Alaska. Indeed, a whopping 126-pounder was taken in 1949 from a commercial fish trap near Petersburg in the Southeast.

Beyond sockeyes and kings, Alaska's streams and oceans are periodically darkened by silver (coho) salmon, pinks, and chums. Meanwhile, insect-sipping arctic grayling, set apart by their sail-like dorsal fins, dimple the surfaces of ponds and creeks from the Copper River delta to the high Arctic. The planet's finest rainbow trout fishing is found here as well; in the Southwest's Bristol Bay region, trout sometimes grow to a yard in length and weigh up to 20 pounds.

Dolly Varden, pink-spotted char related to eastern brook trout and named for a character in Dickens' *Barnaby Rudge*, are found throughout the state in such large numbers that prior to statehood in 1959 a jealous commercial salmon fishing industry had a bounty placed on their tails. In an effort to keep the ubiquitous Dollys from gobbling up too many young salmon, the program paid 2½ cents per tail and ended only after authorities realized that more trout, grayling, and salmon tails were being turned in than Dollys.

Northern pike weighing up to nearly 40 pounds are stalked in weedy muskeg ponds and river sloughs of the Interior, and sheefish (which bear a passing resemblance to the tropical tarpon) heavier than 50 pounds run in the rivers like the Kobuk and the Pah in the northwestern part of the state. Beyond all of these species, there are lake trout, whitefish, cutthroat trout, and a curious but tasty freshwater lingcod called burbot.

Those are the main freshwater fish and anadromous transients. The ocean along Alaska's 6,640 mi of coastline—a bouillabaisse of halibut, snapper, cod, mollusk, crab, and salmon sharks weighing 500 pounds or more—is quite another kettle of fish indeed.

Back on the beach in the far-flung Southeast, Tony Route and I hauled our gear into a USDA Forest Service cabin set in a bench of hemlocks over a remote salt chuck (a sort of brackish lake, connected to the sea by a channel that floods and drains with the tides). Reserved months in advance for 25 bucks a night, the place came with a skiff, four bunks, and a woodstove. The cabin would be our steelhead fishing base camp for the days ahead.

That night, beneath the angular forms of Orion and the Big Dipper, our backs cold against the April darkness, faces warm and orange by the fire, we sipped peaty single-malt Scotch from our camp cups and absorbed the solitude that defines wilderness in Alaska. We kicked around our chances of finding steelhead, believing the odds for the next day were in our favor. And as it turned out, we were right. Tony would catch the first one, a

respectable 8-pound fish. There would be others, and silver-sided Dolly Varden and cutthroat trout, too, all hoodwinked by our flies in that tannic stream which flowed amber in the sunshine and black in the shade.

One afternoon something shocking happened. Tony had wandered alone to the salt chuck's outlet to catch and release some sea-run cutthroat trout. "Just little ones," he'd said. "Eight or 10 inches." He was wading navel-deep, casting in the tidal current, when a 10-ounce trout struck and struggled with all of its heart. The little cutthroat was splashing near Tony's rod tip, a skipping silver flash, when a shark struck. "Ripped the fish right off my hook," he said, his expression still faintly startled. Tony later surmised that he likely wasn't in any danger; the shark was a dogfish, a toothy fish-eater virtually harmless to humans. But the sight of it was enough for him to hastily rush out of the water and quit fishing for the day. "I'm sure it was four feet long," he said that night in the glow of the campfire, "Forty pounds, easy."

That's the way it is in Alaska. Sharks come with the territory, along with 800-pound grizzly bears and unpredictable weather. For anglers, the danger and mystery form a beguiling edge—this is extreme fishing, and exploring Southeast Alaska's temperate rain-forest streams for wild steelhead trout is on par with probing Amazon backwaters for peacock bass or casting Australia's coastal fringes for barramundi. Caribou still outnumber people here, and unsurveyed streams remain to be fished. To cast here on a wild river is to be, as the late Charles Kuralt once wrote, "alone in the universe."

—By Ken Marsh

AT A GLANCE

FAST FACTS

Nicknames: Great Land, Land of the Midnight Sun, Last Frontier

Capital: Juneau

Motto: North to the Future

State song: "Alaska's Flag," by Marie Drake

State bird: Willow ptarmigan

State flower: Forget-me-not (*Myosotis alpestris*)

State tree: Sitka spruce (*Picea sitchensis*)

Administrative divisions: 27 counties

Entered the Union: January 3, 1959, as the 49th state

Population: 683,476

Population density: 1.1 person per square mi

Median age: 33.5

Ethnic groups: White 69%; American Indian or Alaska native 13%; other 5%; Asian 4%; Latino 6%; black 3%

Religion: Unaffiliated 66%; Protestant 18%; Catholic 9%; other 4%; Mormon 3%

The really heroic people are not the ones who travel 10,000 miles by dog sled, but those who stay 10,000 days in one place.
—William Gordon, Episcopal Bishop of Alaska

GEOGRAPHY & ENVIRONMENT

Land area: 586,412 square mi, the largest state

Coastline: 6,640 mi (33,904 mi of shoreline, including all islands) along North Pacific Ocean, Bering Sea, Chukchi Sea, Arctic Ocean

Terrain: Rough, tundra-dominated coast, with grass-covered, treeless islands along the western edge; barren, mountainous inland, carved by more than 3,000 rivers and dotted by more than 3 million lakes; icebound and permanently frozen North Slope; highest point: Mt. McKinley, 20,320 feet (the tallest mountain in North America)

Islands: 1,800 named islands, largest is Kodiak (3,588 square mi)

Natural resources: Arable land, cod, crab, forests, halibut, herring, natural gas, petroleum, salmon, seals, shrimp

Natural hazards: Earthquakes, extreme cold, flooding, tsunamis

Environmental issues: Climate change is affecting polar bear habitat along the state's northern coast, as seasonal sea ice continues to recede. The effects of the 1989 *Exxon Valdez* spill are still being felt in the ecosystem; oil accidents continue to be a problem. Fish are monitored for mercury, heavy metals, dioxins, and pesticides from runoff. Cruise ships are tightly regulated for wastewater and air pollution.

There is much to be said against the climate on the coast of British Columbia and Alaska; yet, I believe that the scenery of one good day will compensate the tourists who will go there in increasing numbers.
—Franklin D. Roosevelt

ECONOMY

GSP: 29.3 billion

Per capita income: $38,138

Unemployment: 6.7%

Workforce: 296,300; government 27%; trade, transportation, and utilities 21%; educational and health services 10%; leisure and hospitality 10%; professional and business services 8%; construction 5%; financial 4%; natural resource and mining 4%; other 5%; manufacturing 4%; information 2%

Major industries: Fishing, mining, oil, timber, tourism

Agricultural products: Crab, cod, dairy products, halibut, herring, potatoes, salmon, shrimp

Exports: $4 billion

Major export products: Seafood (50%), minerals (27%), energy (7%), fertilizer (4%), forest products (3%), precious metals (2%)

DID YOU KNOW?

■ **Alaska is home to Mt. McKinley** (20,320 feet), the highest peak in North America, as well as 17 of the 20 highest mountains in the United States.

■ **Dog mushing, once the only way to get around in many areas, is now the state sport.**

■ **With an estimated 100,000 glaciers, Alaska has more than anywhere else in the inhabited world.** Five percent of the state, or 29,000 square mi, is covered by them.

■ **North America's strongest earthquake was recorded in Alaska's Prince William Sound on March 27, 1964, with a magnitude of 9.2.** Alaska has approximately 5,000 earthquakes each year.

■ **The trans-Alaska pipeline moves oil from the North Slope of Alaska to Valdez, the northernmost ice-free port.** The pipeline is 48 inches in diameter and moves oil at about 5½ mph, requiring just under six days to travel from Prudhoe Bay to the sea.

■ **Alaska is home to both the easternmost and westernmost points in the United States, due to the 180th meridian, which is the global dividing line between all eastern and western longitudes on the globe.** Amatignak Island, at 179° west, is only 70 mi away from Semisopochnoi Island at 179° east.

NATIVE ALASKANS

The history of Alaska's native peoples—Eskimos, Indians, and Aleuts—is not unlike that of aboriginal people throughout Central and North America. After they had held domain over their land for thousands of years, their elaborate societies were besieged by a rapid onslaught of white settlers. Unable to stem the tide, the native peoples were forced into retreat.

Eskimo Kotzebue

The first European to visit Alaska—in 1728—was Vitus Bering, a Dane serving in the Russian navy. Bering died on his journey home, but survivors from that voyage returned to Russia with a rich booty of sea-otter furs, sparking a stampede that would crush the traditional lifestyles of Alaska's native peoples. The way was open for eager Russian fur traders who plundered Aleut territory along the Aleutian Islands.

Records indicate that the native population of the Aleutian chain dropped from perhaps 20,000 to about 2,500 in the first 50 years of Russian rule. Diseases took a heavy toll, but the more ruthless among the Russian frontiersmen were also responsible—killing Aleut leaders to discourage uprisings. Stories of brutality are common. One trader, Feodor Solovief, reportedly tied together 12 Aleuts and fired a musket ball through them to see how far it would penetrate. It stopped in the body of the ninth man.

In 1867, when the United States purchased Alaska, the native peoples were classified in the Treaty of Cession as "uncivilized tribes." To early tourists, they were little more than "those charming folk you take pictures of in their quaint villages."

Early missionaries and government teachers in Southeast Alaska ordered Indian totem poles destroyed, mistakenly believing them to be pagan symbols. Important works of art were lost. The totem poles of the Tlingit and Haida Indians were—and still are—simply the decorative record of outstanding events in the life of a family or clan.

The plight of the natives improved little as Alaska grew more prosperous by exploiting its great natural resources. A painful split between traditional and modern living developed—public health experts call it "a syndrome of grief." Under increasing pressure from this clash of cultures, alcoholism grew to epidemic levels, and the suicide rate of Alaskan natives climbed to twice that of Native Americans living on reservations in the continental United States. Still, by the 1960s, native groups were making major strides toward claiming overdue political clout. In 1966 native leaders from across the state gathered and organized the present Alaska Foundation of Natives. It was a fragile coalition of differing cultures, but the meeting was a significant move. With 16% of the state's population, a unified native voice was suddenly a political force to be reckoned with.

At the same time, Eskimo leaders founded the *Tundra Times* and selected Howard Rock, a quiet but persistent man from Point Hope village, as its editor. Rock, whose background was in art rather than journalism, quickly prodded natives to press their aboriginal land claims.

"The natives are reticent by nature, and time was passing them by," the Eskimo editor said. "At first, it was kind of discouraging. Nothing happened. And then, one by one, the native leaders started speaking up."

The *Tundra Times* helped file the first suit for native land claims. More lawsuits followed, and soon the whole state was tied up in litigation. Oil companies, hungry to build a pipeline from the newly discovered giant oil field at Prudhoe Bay to Valdez, on Alaska's southern coast, soon realized they could not get federal construction permits until the native land claims were settled.

In 1971 the natives won a spectacular settlement in Congress: 40 million acres of land and almost $1 billion in cash. The settlement has not been a cure-all for the many problems of Alaska's natives. Poverty is still widespread, as little of the land-claims money (allocated mostly to 13 regional, for-profit native corporations by Congress) has trickled down to the village level. But the settlement has given many a sense of dignity and purpose. Several villages in the Arctic have voted themselves dry (prohibiting alcohol) to combat drinking problems.

Today the fundamental issue is whether the natives will be allowed by the larger Alaskan society to pursue their own future, says Byron Mallott, former chief operating officer of Sealaska Corp., the regional native corporation for Southeast Alaska.

"In one way, Alaska is truly the last frontier," Mallott says. "Will the final chapter of the total and unremitting decimation of our nation's Native American people be written in Alaska—or will, with the benefit of the lesson of history, Alaska be the place where native peoples finally are able to become a part of the overall society with their pride, strength, and ethnicity intact?" There are, he adds, few guideposts to suggest the answer.

Most of Alaska's natives still reside in widely scattered communities spread across the 0.5-million square mi of Alaska. Unlike the Native Americans of the Lower 48 states, the Alaskan natives have never been restricted to reservations. Many villages remain isolated, the preference of traditional villagers; others have plunged into modern life with mixed results. Recently, Alaska's native peoples have become more enterprising in the tourist business. No longer content to let out-of-state tour operators have all the business, they are now starting to take charge of tours in their communities.

The various native peoples tend to group in well-defined regions. Here is a brief look at the different native cultures and their locations.

Eskimos. Most of Alaska's more than 40,000 Eskimos are found in scattered settlements along the Bering Sea and Arctic Ocean coasts, the deltas of the lower Yukon and Kuskokwim rivers in western Alaska, and on remote islands in the Bering Sea such as St. Lawrence, Nunivak, and Little Diomede. The principal Arctic and sub-Arctic Eskimo communities include Barrow, Kotzebue, Nome, Gambell, Savoonga, Point Hope, Wainwright, and Shishmaref.

The Eskimos are divided into two linguistic groups: the Inupiat of the Far North and the Yup'ik, who reside mostly along the coastal regions of the west. The Yup'ik share the same dialect as the Eskimos of Siberia. Both groups are famed for their hunting and fishing skills. They are also noted craftspeople, carving animals and creating jewelry from native materials.

Indians. Alaska has four major Indian cultures: Tlingit, Haida, Athabascan, and Tsimshian.

Once among North America's most powerful tribes, the **Tlingits** (pronounced *klink*-its) are found mostly throughout coastal Southeast Alaska. They number about 13,000 and live in cities such as Juneau, Ketchikan, and Sitka and in villages from Hoonah, near Juneau, to Klukwan, near Haines.

The Tlingits developed a highly sophisticated culture and fought hard against Russian incursions. Social status among early Tlingits depended on elaborate feasts called potlatches. Heads of families and clans vied in giving away vast quantities of valuable goods, their generosity so extravagant at times that the hosts fell into a form of ancient bankruptcy. There are still potlatches for important occasions, such as funerals, but they are greatly scaled down from earlier times.

Haidas are also found mainly in Southeast Alaska, as well as in British Columbia. They number only about 1,000 in Alaska. Their principal community is Hydaburg on Prince of Wales Island, near Ketchikan. The Queen Charlotte Islands of British Columbia are another Haida center. Historically, the Haidas were far-ranging voyagers and traders. Some historians credit the artistic Haidas with originating totem carving among Alaska's natives.

Most of Alaska's 7,000 or so **Athabascan** Indians are found in the villages of Alaska's vast Interior, including Fort Yukon, Stevens Village, Beaver, Chalkyitsik, and Minto, near Fairbanks. Other Athabascans are scattered from the Kenai Peninsula–Cook Inlet area, near Anchorage, to the Copper River area near Cordova. Linguistically, the Athabascans are related to the Navajo and Apache of the American Southwest. They were driven out of Canada by Cree tribes more than 700 years ago.

The ancestral home of the **Tsimshian** (pronounced *sim*-shee-ann) Indians was British Columbia, but Tsimshian historians say their forebears roamed through much of southeastern Alaska fishing, hunting, and trading long before the arrival of the white man. The 1,000 or so Tsimshians of Alaska settled in 1887 on Annette Island, near Ketchikan, when a dissident Church of England lay missionary, William Duncan, led them out of British Columbia to escape religious persecution. The town of Metlakatla on Annette Island is their principal community. Their artwork includes wood carvings, from totem poles to ceremonial masks.

Aleuts. With their villages on the Aleutian Islands, curving between Siberia and Alaska like broken beads, the Aleuts (pronounced al-ee-*oots*) were first in the path of early explorers and ruthless fur traders. There are about 7,000 Aleuts in Alaska today, their principal communities being Dutch Harbor/Unalaska, Akutan, Nikolski, and Atka in the Aleutians and St. Paul and St. George in the Pribilof Islands. Grass basketry, classed by museums as some of the best in the world, is the principal art of the Aleuts. Finely woven baskets from Attu, at the tip of the Aleutian chain—where villages were destroyed in American–Japanese combat during World War II and never rebuilt—are difficult-to-obtain treasures.

—Stanton H. Patty

ALASKA: A GEOLOGIC STORY

Most people know about Alaska's oil and gold. But did you know that the state has a desert? That camels once roamed here? That there's a fault line nearly twice as long as the San Andreas Fault? That the largest earthquake ever to hit North America struck Alaska in 1964 and affected the entire planet? That the state has 80 potentially active volcanoes and approximately 100,000 glaciers?

All these physical wonders are geological in origin and are in addition to a North Slope oil supply that accounts for 5% of U.S. production and more than 2% of U.S. consumption, as well as caches of gold that fueled more than 20 rushes.

Glaciers

Nearly all visitors to Alaska will have at least one encounter with a glacier, since 29,000 square mi of the state's land are covered by these icy monoliths. Thanks to the Pleistocene Ice Age, a high-latitude location, and abundant moisture from the North Pacific, Alaska has approximately 100,000 glaciers of varying sizes. The vast majority can be found in the southern and southeastern parts of the state, where precipitation is most abundant. (How abundant, exactly? Very. Portions of the Chugach Mountains can gather 600 inches of snow each year, an amount that is comparable, in rain, to the annual precipitation in Seattle.) And in north-central Alaska, the Brooks Range contains a glacial ice field of approximately 280 square mi. Although small by Alaskan standards, it is larger than all the glacial fields in the rest of the United States combined, which comprise approximately 230 square mi.

There are three primary types of glaciers that can be found in Alaska: alpine, piedmont, and tidewater. Alpine glaciers—also known as valley glaciers—typically form high in mountain valleys and travel to lower elevations. Alaska harbors several of the great alpine glaciers in the

world, which originate in the high country of the Alaska Range, the Talkeetna, Wrangell, Chugach, St. Elias, and Coast mountains. Some, such as the Bering Glacier, come tantalizingly close to the water. At more than 100 mi in length—and with an area of more than 2,250 square mi—the Bering is the longest and largest Alaskan glacier, its seclusion guarded by Cape St. Elias and the stormy waters of the Gulf of Alaska. Also impressive are the Hubbard, with its imposing terminus dominating the head of isolated Yakutat Bay; and the Columbia, foreboding and threatening, calving icebergs that tack in line like Nelson's fleet across the mouth of Valdez Arm.

Piedmont glaciers are characterized by their fan-shape fields of ice that usually spread across large, relatively flat plains. The Malaspina Glacier, an Alaskan icon, is one of the state's signature piedmont glaciers. Formed by the coalescence of several glaciers, this 850-square-mi mass occupies a benchland on the northwest side of Yakutat Bay. So much of the Alaska Range, Wrangell, Chugach, St. Elias, and Coast mountains is covered by glacial ice that it is often more appropriate to talk about ice fields than individual glaciers.

The third type of glacier in Alaska—and perhaps the most sought-after—is the tidewater glacier. These stunning seaside ice floes are found throughout the state's coastal areas, but Prince William Sound and Glacier Bay are the best areas to view them. Tidewater glaciers are essentially alpine glaciers that come right to the water's edge. They creak, moan, thunder, and calve off great bergs and little "bergeys." The world's longest tidewater glacier is the previously mentioned Hubbard Glacier, which stretches more than 70 mi from its head in Canada to its terminus in Yakutat Bay. Sixteen tidewater glaciers can be found in Glacier Bay National Park, and 20 in Prince William

Sound. Alaska's tidewater glaciers have been known to behave somewhat erratically; in 1986, for example, a surge by the Hubbard Glacier blocked the Russell Fjord at the upper end of Yakutat Bay, turning it into Russell Lake and raising its surface to over 80 feet above sea level. Later that year, the portion of the glacier acting as a dam in front of Russell Lake gave way, violently releasing the backed-up water in a flood of epic proportions. Although exceedingly uncommon in modern times, surging glaciers can move downhill hundreds of feet per day. The Hubbard's greatest surge was in September 1899, when it advanced 0.5 mi into the bay in just five minutes, courtesy of an earthquake.

Of utmost importance to Alaska's many glaciologists is the phenomenon of global warming and its effects on the state's glaciers. While the causes of Earth's recent warming trend continue to be debated, there is one fact that is indisputable: almost all of Alaska's glaciers—like the vast majority of glaciers across the globe—are retreating, and most at an alarming rate. The Columbia Glacier, which covers more than 400 square mi and reaches its terminus in Prince William Sound, has retreated more than 9 mi in the last 25 years. It is also only 8 mi from the shipping lanes traveled by oil tankers leaving the Alaska pipeline terminal at Valdez. Since the Columbia began receding in the early 1980s, it has sent berg after berg into Prince William Sound and into the shipping lanes to Valdez. Although a shallow sill, or shoal, of underwater glacial deposits keeps icebergs more than 100 feet thick from entering Prince William Sound, some big bergs still make it to the shipping lanes. Columbia's calving took its toll just after midnight on March 29, 1989, when Captain Hazlewood of the *Exxon Valdez* steered too far east while trying to avoid bergs in Valdez Arm and ran aground on Bligh Reef.

Despite their continuing retreat, travelers can still view glaciers across the state. For glacier fans, the Alaska Marine Highway is one of the best routes to travel. The tidewater glaciers of Glacier Bay and the Malaspina and Hubbard glaciers in Yakutat Bay are best seen by boat or ship. Sailing into Valdez Arm, you may see more of the Columbia Glacier than you want—in fact, it's often coming to see you in the form of scores of bergs and bergeys, forcing you east toward Bligh Reef. Once you are safely ashore in Valdez it's time to look at valley glaciers. You can access either the Valdez or Worthington Glacier by road. If you're in the Matanuska Valley, go see the Matanuska Glacier. If you're on the Kenai Peninsula, try either the Exit or Portage Glacier. If you are visiting Juneau, the Mendenhall Glacier is on the outskirts of town.

Volcanoes

More than 80 volcanoes in Alaska are potentially active. Novarupta, Pavlof, Augustine, Redoubt, and Spurr are Alaskan volcanoes that are part of the "Ring of Fire," the volcanic rim of the Pacific. From Mt. Wrangell at 144° west longitude in Southeast Alaska to Cape Wrangell at 173° east longitude at the tip of the Aleutian archipelago, southern Alaska exists, to paraphrase historian Will Durant, by volcanic decree . . . subject to change.

Anchorage (and the greater Cook Inlet area) is a great place to watch volcanoes erupt. Augustine, Redoubt, and Spurr volcanoes have put on shows up and down the Cook Inlet; the Mt. Spurr eruption of August 1992 temporarily stopped air travel into and out of Anchorage. The most violent Alaskan eruption? The 2½-day eruption of Novarupta in 1912 in what is now Katmai National Park. The 2.5 cubic mi of ash deposited there has left an Alaskan legacy: the surreal Valley of Ten Thousand Smokes.

Earthquake Country

The length of a fault system and whether or not the fault is straight over great distances are of interest to geologists. Fault length is related to earthquake magnitude. Generally speaking, the longer a fault, the greater the potential magnitude. If you're impressed by the 600-mi length of California's San Andreas, take this into consideration: the onshore portion of the Denali Fault System is more than 1,000 mi long. Numerous long faults around the world move horizontally. This produces some interesting results if the fault trace is not straight. A fault system such as the Denali has a large component of horizontal movement (called strike-slip motion): crustal blocks on either side move past each other, rather than up or down. If a strike-slip fault bends, one of two situations results: a gap or hole in the crust (usually filled by volcanic outbreaks and/or sediments sloughing into the hole) or a compression of the bend, resulting in vertical uplift (mountains). Which condition occurs is a function of fault motion, whether into or out of the bend. South of Fairbanks, the Denali Fault System changes trend, from northwest to southeast to northeast to southwest. The sense of horizontal motion is into the bend, resulting in vertical uplift. What mountain just happens to be in the vicinity? Mt. McKinley, which, at 20,320 feet, is the tallest mountain in North America. Moreover, its relief (difference in elevation between the base and top of the mountain), at 18,000 feet, is unsurpassed. Mt. Everest is more than 29,000 feet, but "only" 11,000 feet above the Tibetan Plateau, which forms its base.

With such big faults, it's no wonder geologists look at Alaska as big earthquake country. Seward, Valdez, Whittier, and Anchorage are just some of the more-prominent names associated with the Good Friday Earthquake of 1964. Registering a catastrophic 9.2 on the Richter scale, the Good Friday quake is the largest on record for North America. Fif-

teen to thirty seconds is not unusual for ground motion in a big, destructive earthquake; Alaskans shook for three to four minutes during the Good Friday quake. The epicenter was about 6 mi east of College Fjord in Prince William Sound, some 70 mi east of Anchorage. Vertical deformation (uplift or down-dropping of the land) affected an area of 100,000 square mi. By the time the shaking had stopped, the area of Latouche Island had moved 60 feet to the southeast and portions of the Montague Island area were uplifted by as much as 30 feet. The area of Portage was down-dropped by approximately 10 feet. The largest tsunami (often misnamed a tidal wave) that hit Hilo, Hawaii, checked in at 12.5 feet; the largest at Crescent City, California, was 13 feet; and in Chenega, Alaska, native residents were never sure what rose from the sea to smite them . . . just that it was 90 feet tall. The entire planet was affected: the area in which the quake was felt by people is estimated at 500,000 square mi—South Africa checked in to report that groundwater was sloshing around in wells.

Geologists generally describe tsunamis with respect to displacement on a fault underwater. They use the more general term "seismic sea wave" when other things, such as submarine landslides, cause enormous waves. The 90-foot seismic sea wave that hit Chenega was topped by the 220-foot wave reported from the Valdez Arm area. But a few years earlier in southeastern Alaska, on the evening of July 9, 1958, an earthquake in the Yakutat area dumped an enormous landslide into the head of Lituya Bay. The result was a seiche, or splash wave, that traveled 1,740 feet up the opposite mountainside.

Impressed yet? In the last century the average recurrence interval for Alaskan earthquakes in excess of 8.0 on the Richter scale was 10 years. The recurrence interval for earthquakes over 7.0

is just over a year. Never mind California—Alaska is the most seismically active state in the Union. Volcanic hazard? Well, Pavlof has averaged an eruption every 6 years over the last 240.

Desert

And now about that desert. The North Slope of Alaska is 80,000 square mi of frozen, windswept desert where Inupiat Eskimos live. It's a desert from the climatological perspective in that the North Slope receives less than 10 inches of precipitation each year. If you go around the west end of the Brooks Range, you can even find sand dunes—Great Kobuk, Little Kobuk, and Hunt River sand-dune fields. Temperatures during the short, cool summers are usually between 30°F and 40°F. Temperatures in winter can average –20°F. In winter, the Arctic Ocean moderates temperatures on the North Slope, but there is nothing to moderate the wind.

Rocks & Minerals

The first people to come into the country came across the Bering Land Bridge from Asia, between 10,000 and 40,000 years ago. The Bering Land Bridge was a product of the Pleistocene epoch—the Great Ice Age—which lowered the sea level enough for the bridge to form. At the start of the Mesozoic era (beginning about 245 million years before the present), sandstones and conglomerates deposited in a warm, shallow sea marked the beginning of Prudhoe Bay. That abundant organic matter is now abundant oil under the North Slope. Also during the Mesozoic era, oil-bearing shales were deposited in the Cook Inlet, home of Alaska's first oil boom; copper and silver deposits were formed in what is now the Copper River country; Cretaceous swamps in South Central Alaska became the Matanuska coalfield; and gold was emplaced around present-day Fairbanks and near Nome on the Seward Peninsula.

The oldest rocks in Alaska are of Precambrian age (the "Time Before Life") and are in Southwest Alaska. They have been dated at 2 billion years of age, nearly half the age of Earth. Rocks 1 billion years old have been identified in the area of the Brooks Range south to the Yukon River. Interestingly, the 1-billion-year-old rocks are native; the 2-billion-year-old rocks are expatriates. In fact, southern and southeastern Alaska are composed of a mosaic or quilt of microplates, all much smaller than continent size. Some terranes (blocks or fragments of Earth's crust that may vary in age, geologic character, or site of origin) arrived in Alaska from as far south as the equator.

Certain Alaskan rocks tell a tale of warm climates and seas. Evidence? Hike the Holitna River basin in Southwest Alaska and look for fossil remains of the many trilobites (those now-extinct three-lobe marine arthropods that scavenged the bottoms of warm, shallow, Cambrian seas—parents, if you don't know what they look like, ask your children). The central interior of Alaska evidently was never covered by ice but was instead a cool steppe land roamed by mammoths, bison, horses, saber-toothed cats, and camels. Yes, camels.

A Geological Wonder

Alaska's stunning expanse incorporates fire and ice, wind and rain, volcano, glacier, windswept tundra, towering rain forest, and mist-shrouded island. Its geologic story covers a great deal of time and distance. In the north, the rocks tell a story of relative stability—geological homebodies born and raised. In the south, the patchwork terrains tell a tale of far-traveled immigrants coming into the country. Geological processes still produce both homebodies and expatriates that create a land in constant flux. But the majesty of the land is the unchanging legacy of Alaska.

—Dr. Charles Lane

BOOKS & MOVIES

Books

Alaska has long been a setting for tales of heroes, great journeys, and people's epic struggle with nature. Novels with rich descriptions of the state's people, wildlife, and landscapes include Ivan Doig's *The Sea Runners* (Penguin), an adventure set in 1853, when Alaska still belonged to Russia; *Athabasca* (out of print), an Alistair MacLean thriller set around the trans-Alaska pipeline; and *Sitka* (Signet), by the popular chronicler of the American frontier, Louis L'Amour. *Alaska* (Random House), by James Michener, is a weighty historical novel about the state from prehistoric to modern times.

Alaskan authors have written a number of mystery novels about their state. Among the best are Sue Henry's *Murder on the Iditarod Trail* (Avon); John Straley's *The Woman Who Married a Bear* (Signet), about the adventures of private eye Cecil Younger; and Dana Stabenow's *A Cold-Blooded Business* (Berkley Books), whose hero is Aleut private investigator Kate Shugak.

Alaska has produced an even more significant collection of high-quality nonfiction literature. John McPhee's *Coming into the Country* (Noonday Press) is considered by some to be the most insightful book ever written about Alaska. Joe McGinniss, in *Going to Extremes* (Plume), presents a provocative outsider's portrait of Alaska's varied communities, people, and landscapes. Velma Wallis's best-selling *Two Old Women: An Alaska Legend of Betrayal, Courage and Survival* (Epicenter Press) recounts a traditional native Alaskan story. And Peter Jenkins's *Looking for Alaska* (St. Martin's Griffin) describes one family's 18-month immersion in the society of the Kenai Peninsula with gusto and aplomb. For lovers of adventure, Art Davidson's *Minus 148 Degrees: The First Winter Ascent of Mt. McKinley* (The Mountaineers Books) describes the harrowing survival story of mountaineers caught in a ferocious storm on North America's highest peak. Jon Krakauer's *Into the Wild* (Anchor) wonderfully constructs the life and death of a young man who died in the Alaskan wilderness while on a personal vision quest. *Fish Camp: Life on an Alaskan Shore* (Counterpoint Press), by Nancy Lord, describes the natural and cultural history of the place where she and her partner have fished for salmon for the past two decades. Hunters, fishermen, and roughnecks of all stripes will appreciate the man-size servings of machismo in Rocky McElveen's *Wild Men, Wild Alaska: Finding What Lies Beyond the Limits* (Thomas Nelson Press), a collection of stories from McElveen's 20-plus years of guiding. Former Alaska poet laureate John Haines has written several books of poetry and essays. Among his best is the essay collection *The Stars, the Snow, the Fire* (Graywolf Press), which recounts 25 years in Alaska's wilderness. Another compelling collection of essays with natural-history themes is Sherry Simpson's *The Way Winter Comes: Alaska Stories* (Sasquatch Books). One anthology of special note is Wayne Mergler's *The Last New Land: Stories of Alaska Past and Present* (Alaska Northwest Books), a wide-ranging collection of poems, short stories, and essays about Alaska; another is Bill Sherwonit's *Denali: A Literary Anthology* (The Mountaineers Books), which presents a century's worth of published stories about Mt. McKinley, North America's highest mountain, and the surrounding wilderness.

Movies

The Last Frontier has also inspired a number of filmmakers. *White Fang* (1991), based on the Jack London novel, is a Walt Disney production about the life of a wild wolf dog and the hardships prospectors faced during the Klondike Gold Rush. The movie set is now a tourist destination in Haines. The animated family film *Balto* (1995) tells the story of one of the canine heroes in Alaska's 1925 Great Race of Mercy, in which mushers and dog teams carry diphtheria serum to Nome to stop an outbreak of the deadly disease. More pooches star in the family comedy *Snow Dogs* (2002), in which Cuba Gooding Jr. plays a Miami dentist who inherits a team of huskies. Another popular family flick is *Alaska* (1996), in which two teens set out to rescue their bush pilot dad from the wilderness.

A number of action-adventure pictures have also taken place in Alaska. *Runaway Train* (1985), a thriller starring Jon Voight, was filmed south of Anchorage; the scenery and ending are equally dramatic. The terrible *On Deadly Ground* (1994) stars Steven Seagal as an oil-company troubleshooter who rebels after discovering his employers are exploiting the land and its native peoples. *Limbo* (1999), set in Southeast Alaska, is an excellent frontier drama about a commercial fisherman who has become afraid

of the sea. In *The Edge* (1997) Anthony Hopkins and Alec Baldwin have a great deal to be afraid of while lost in the Alaskan wilderness. *Insomnia* (2002), starring Al Pacino and Robin Williams, sees two Los Angeles detectives sent to Alaska to investigate a murder.

Werner Herzog's documentary *Grizzly Man* (2005) tells the fascinating and ultimately sordid story of Timothy Treadwell, a zany nature lover and actor who lived among Alaska's grizzly bears (and who was found, along with his girlfriend, mauled to death in 2003). Herzog uses Treadwell's original footage of bears as well as dozens of interviews with family members and friends.

Adapted by Sean Penn from Jon Krakauer's book of the same name, *Into the Wild* (2007) depicts Christopher McCandless's ultimately fatal journey into the Alaskan Bush. Based on a true story, the movie was nominated for several Academy and Golden Globe awards.

Travel Smart
Alaska

WORD OF MOUTH

The trouble with just "showing up" in summer is that Alaska is very busy with cruise ship people and other tourists. You might get shut out of some of the best opportunities.... There are lots of adventurous and unique experiences to be found. But you need to do research and figure them out. Some things will need advance booking. You could set up one or two of those activities (along with appropriate lodging), and then fill in the blanks...when you get there.

—enzian

GETTING HERE & AROUND

▌ BY AIR

Alaska Airlines is the state's flagship carrier, with year-round service from its Seattle hub to Anchorage, Fairbanks, Juneau, Ketchikan, and Sitka. The airline and its subsidiary, Horizon Air, also fly to many other North American cities from Seattle. In addition, Hawaiian Vacations, which is owned by Alaska Airlines, offers year-round flights between Anchorage and Honolulu.

Other airlines that fly to and from the Lower 48 states include American, Continental, Delta, Frontier, Northwest, and United. Note, however, that few offer nonstop flights and many of those that do offer such flights do so only seasonally.

The average travel time (nonstop flights only) from Seattle to Anchorage is 3½ hours. Travel times from other destinations depend on your connection, since you'll probably need to route through other cities. Many of the low-fare flights out of Anchorage depart around 1 AM, so be sure you're at the airport on the correct day when flying just after midnight.

Major Airlines Alaska Airlines (☎800/252–7522 or 206/433–3100 ⊕www.alaskaair. com). **American Airlines** (☎800/433–7300 ⊕www.aa.com). **Continental Airlines** (☎800/523–3273 ⊕www.continental.com). **Delta Airlines** (☎800/221–1212 ⊕www. delta.com). **Frontier Airlines** (☎800/432–1359 for U.S. reservations ⊕www.fron-tierairlines.com). **Northwest Airlines** (☎800/225–2525 ⊕www.nwa.com). **United Airlines** (☎800/864–8331 for U.S. reservations, 800/538–2929 for international reservations ⊕www.united.com).

AIRPORTS

Anchorage's Ted Stevens International Airport is Alaska's main hub. There are also major airports ("major" meaning that they serve more than just bush planes) in Fairbanks, Juneau, and Ketchikan. The Fairbanks airport is the largest of the three; Juneau and Ketchikan have few facilities and gates.

Unless you're flying from the West Coast or manage to get a nonstop flight, chances are you'll spend some time in Seattle's international airport (known locally as Sea-Tac), waiting for a connection. And Vancouver, Canada, is often the starting point for Alaskan cruises that make their first stop in Ketchikan, Alaska's southern-most town.

You won't find much in terms of entertainment in Ted Stevens, Sea-Tac, or Vancouver's airport, so if you have really long layovers at any of the three, consider taking a taxi into the city. Ted Stevens is only 6 mi from downtown Anchorage; Seattle's downtown area is 14 mi from the airport, and if you don't get stuck in the city's notorious rush-hour traffic you can get there in 20 minutes. It can take 30 to 45 minutes to get to downtown Vancouver from the airport.

There are no departure taxes for travel within the United States. Vancouver's airport does have a departure tax of C$5 for flights within British Columbia and the Yukon or C$10 to U.S. destinations, payable before you board at automatic ticket machines or staffed booths.

Airlines & Airports Airline and Airport Links.com (⊕www.airlineandairportlinks.com).

Airline Security Issues Transportation Security Administration (⊕www.tsa.gov).

Airport Information Fairbanks International Airport (FAI ⊕www.dot.state.ak.us/faiiap). **Juneau International Airport** (JNU ⊕www.juneau.org/airport). **Ketchikan Airport** (KTN ⊕www.borough.ketchikan.ak.us/airport/airport.htm). **Seattle-Tacoma International Airport** (SEA ⊕www.portseattle.org/seatac). **Ted Stevens Anchorage International Airport** (ANC ⊕www.dot.state.ak.us/anc). **Vancouver International Airport** (YVR ⊕www.yvr.ca).

WITHIN ALASKA

Air travel within Alaska is quite expensive, particularly to bush destinations where flying is the only option. A round-trip flight between Anchorage and Dutch Harbor typically costs more than $900. Flights from Anchorage to Fairbanks or Juneau run $300 and up one way.

AIR TAXIS

The workhorse planes of the north are the Beavers, most of which were built in the 1950s and are still flying. The cost of an air-taxi flight between towns or backcountry locations depends upon distance and the type of plane used, whether or not the plane is on floats, the number of people in your group, the length of the flight in each direction (including the time the pilot flies back after dropping you off), and the destination. Typical hourly rates are approximately $600–$800 for a Beaver, with room for up to six people and gear; or $400–$600 for a Cessna 185, with room for three people and gear. Expect to pay more the farther you are from Anchorage.

SMALL PLANES

Many scheduled flights to bush communities are on small planes that seat 6 to 15 passengers. These planes have played a legendary part in the state's history: bush pilots helped explore Alaska and have been responsible for many dramatic rescue missions. That said, small craft have their inconveniences. They can only transport a limited amount of gear, so plan to leave your large, hard-sided suitcases behind. Small, soft duffels make more sense, and are easier for the pilot to stash in cramped cargo spaces.

Small planes also can't fly in poor weather, which could mean delays counted in days, not hours. And even on good days, turbulence might leave you white-knuckled and green in the face. Fortunately, most flights are uneventful, with the scenery below—rather than a rough ride—making them memorable.

Contact Bering Air for flights from Nome or Kotzebue to smaller communities of the Far North; Era Aviation for flights from Anchorage to Cordova, Homer, Iliamna, Kenai, Kodiak, Valdez, and 17 western Alaska villages; and Frontier Flying Service for flights from Anchorage to Fairbanks, Bethel, and many bush villages.

Try Warbelow's Air Ventures and Larry's Flying Service for flights out of Fairbanks to Interior destinations. Peninsula Airways (PenAir), based in Anchorage, covers southwestern Alaska, including Aniak, Dillingham, Dutch Harbor, McGrath, King Salmon, Sand Point, St. George, and St. Paul. Wings of Alaska serves several Southeast Alaska towns, including Gustavus, Haines, Juneau, and Skagway. Grant Aviation flies from Anchorage to Homer and Kenai as well as Bethel, Dillingham, Emmonak, and St. Mary's.

Carriers Bering Air (☎907/443–5464, 800/478–5422 Nome reservations; 907/442–3943, 800/478–3943 Kotzebue reservations; 907/443–5464, 800/390–7970 Unalakleet reservations ⊕www.beringair.com). **Era Aviation** (☎907/266–8394 or 800/866–8394 ⊕www.flyera.com). **Frontier Flying Service** (☎907/450–7200 or 800/478–6779 ⊕www.frontierflying.com). **Grant Aviation** (☎888/359–4726 ⊕www.flygrant.com). **Larry's Flying Service** (☎907/474–9169 ⊕www.larrysflying.com). **PenAir** (☎907/243–2323 or 800/448–4226 ⊕www.penair.com). **Warbelow's Air Ventures** (☎907/474–0518 or 800/478–0812 ⊕www.warbelows.com). **Wings of Alaska** (☎907/789–0790 ⊕www.wingsofalaska.com).

▌ BY BOAT

If you're looking for a casual alternative to a luxury cruise, travel as Alaskans do, aboard the ferries of the Alaska Marine Highway System. These vessels may not have the same facilities as the big cruise ships, but they do meander through some beautiful regions. In summer you won't be completely without entertainment.

Forest Service naturalists ride larger ferries, providing a running commentary on sights, and select routes also have an Arts-on-Board Program, which presents educators and entertainers.

Most long-haul ferries have cabins with private bathrooms. You'll need to reserve these accommodations in advance or settle for a reclining seat on the aft deck. Most ships also have cheap or free showers as well as spaces where you can roll out sleeping bags or even pitch tents. All long-haul ferries have cafeterias with hot meal service (not included in the fare), along with concession stands and vending machines. Some larger boats even have cocktail lounges.

ROUTES

The Inside Passage route, which stretches from Bellingham, Washington (or Prince Rupert, British Columbia) all the way up to Skagway and Haines, is the most popular route, mimicking that of most major cruise lines. The Bellingham-to-Ketchikan trip, the longest leg, takes roughly 37 hours. (The trip from Prince Rupert to Ketchikan takes six hours; BC Ferries provide service from Vancouver to Prince Rupert.) Other trips along the Inside Passage take from three to eight hours.

Sporadic summer service across the Gulf of Alaska from either Prince Rupert, Ketchikan, or Juneau links the Southeast with South Central Alaska destinations (trips usually end in Whittier, about 60 mi south of Anchorage). There's further service to limited ports in South Central Alaska as well as connecting service to the Southwest from Whittier and Homer to Kodiak and Port Lions, respectively. Southwest ferries can take you all the way to Dutch Harbor.

Two high-speed catamarans can cut travel time in half. The *MV Fairweather* is based in Juneau and serves Haines, Skagway, and Sitka. In summer, the *MV Chenega,* based in Cordova, serves Prince William Sound, with stops in Valdez and Whittier. In fall and winter its route

changes, serving either the same route as the *Fairweather* or Ketchikan to Juneau via Wrangell and Petersburg.

The Inter-Island Ferry Authority connects Southeast Alaska's Prince of Wales Island with the towns of Ketchikan, Wrangell, and Petersburg.

Note that although major ports like Juneau and Ketchikan will likely have daily departures, service to smaller towns is much more sporadic—one departure per week in some cases.

RESERVATIONS & FARES

You can make reservations by phone or online and have tickets mailed to you or arrange to pick them up from the ferry office at your starting point. Book as far in advance as possible for summertime travel, especially if you have a vehicle. You should also book ahead for the Bellingham–Ketchikan journey.

You can pay for ferry travel with cash, credit card (American Express, Discover, MasterCard, or Visa), cashier's check, money order, certified check, or personal check from an Alaskan bank.

The Bellingham-to-Ketchikan route costs roughly $230 one way in summer. Shorter trips cost anywhere from $30 to $140 one way. Note that there are surcharges for vehicles (including motorcycles), bicycles, and kayaks. Renting cabins will also increase the fare significantly.

ALASKAPASS

The AlaskaPass offers rental-car usage and unlimited travel on ferry and rail lines in Alaska, along with rental-car usage and ferry travel in British Columbia and the Yukon. Passes are available for 15 consecutive days of travel ($929), as well as for 8 days of travel in a 12-day period ($799) or 12 days of travel in a 21-day period ($979). There's an $85 booking fee. Most travelers book their entire itinerary in advance; if you don't have a car, there's usually room on ferries for those without prebookings.

From Anchorage

TO	TIME BY AIR	ROAD MILES	TIME BY ROAD
Denali	N/A	264 mi	5–6 hrs
Fairbanks	50 mins	364 mi	7-9 hrs
Homer	50 mins	223 mi	5–6 hrs
Talkeetna	20 mins	113 mi	2–3 hrs
Valdez	40 mins	302 mi	6–8 hrs

Information **Alaska Marine Highway** (☎907/465–3941 or 800/642–0066 ⊕www. ferryalaska.com). **AlaskaPass** (☎206/463–6550 or 800/248–7598 ⊕www.alaskapass. com). **B.C. Ferries** (☎250/386–3431 or 888/223–3779 ⊕www.bcferries.bc.ca). **Inter-Island Ferry Authority** (☎907/826–4848 or 866/308–4848 ⊕www.interislandferry.com).

▌BY BUS

Traveling by bus in Alaska can be more economical than traveling by train or by air, but don't count on it being your main mode of travel. Always confirm your trip via phone, as schedules often change at the last minute.

Greyhound Lines of Canada serves Vancouver, with service as far north as Whitehorse in the Canadian Yukon. Two companies provide onward bus service into South Central and Interior Alaska from Whitehorse. Alaska Direct Bus Lines operates year-round van service connecting Anchorage and Fairbanks with Glennallen, Delta Junction, Skagway, and Tok in Alaska, along with Whitehorse in the Yukon. Alaska/Yukon Trails provides year-round bus service between Anchorage and Fairbanks, plus seasonal service connecting Fairbanks with Dawson City in the Yukon.

Denali Overland Transportation has frequent van service in summer between Anchorage, Talkeetna, and Denali National Park & Preserve. The Alaska Park Connection has summertime bus service between Seward and Anchorage,

continuing north to Denali. Homer Stage Line provides year-round service between Anchorage and Homer, plus summertime service connecting Seward with Anchorage and Homer.

Quick Shuttle buses run between Vancouver and Seattle. Green Tortoise provides a casual alternative way to travel north, with funky classic buses that are popular with backpackers.

Many bus lines—particularly those heading to Denali—either require or strongly recommend reservations. Accepted forms of payment vary among bus companies, but all accept MasterCard, Visa, and traveler's checks. The AlaskaPass allows unlimited travel on ferry, rail lines, and Holland America buses (Whitehorse to Fairbanks only) in Alaska and the Yukon. *(For more information, see By Boat, above).*

Bus Information **Alaska Direct Bus Lines** (☎907/277–6652 or 800/770–6652 ⊕ www. alaskadirectbusline.com). **Alaska Park Connection** (☎907/245–0200 or 800/266–8625 ⊕www.alaskacoach.com). **Alaska/Yukon Trails** (☎907/457–2034 or 800/770–7275 ⊕www.alaskashuttle.com). **Denali Overland Transportation** (☎907/733–2384 or 800/651–5221 ⊕www.denalioverland. com). **Green Tortoise** (☎415/956–7500 or 800/867–8647 ⊕www.greentortoise.com). **Greyhound Lines of Canada** (☎604/482–8747 or 800/661–8747 ⊕www.greyhound.ca). **Homer Stage Line** (☎907/235–7090 or 907/399–1847 ⊕www.homerstageline.com). **Quick Shuttle** (☎604/940–4428 or 800/665–2122 ⊕www.quickcoach.com).

▌ BY CAR

Though journeying through Canada on the Alaska Highway can be exciting, the trek from the Lower 48 states is long. It's a seven-day trip from Seattle to Anchorage or Fairbanks, covering close to 2,500 mi. From Bellingham, Washington, and the Canadian ports of Prince Rupert and Stewart, you can link up with ferry service along the Marine Highway to reach Southeast Alaska.

The Alaska Highway begins at Dawson Creek, British Columbia, and stretches 1,442 mi through Canada's Yukon to Delta Junction; it enters Alaska east of Tok. The two-lane highway is paved for its entire length and is open year-round. Highway services are available about every 50 to 100 mi (sometimes at shorter intervals).

The rest of the state's roads are found almost exclusively in the South Central and Interior regions. They lie mainly between Anchorage, Fairbanks, and the Canadian border. Only one highway extends north of Fairbanks, and one runs south of Anchorage to the Kenai Peninsula. These roads vary from four-lane freeways (rare) to nameless two-lane gravel roads.

If you plan extensive driving in Alaska, join an automobile club such as AAA that offers towing and other benefits. Because of the long distances involved, you should seriously consider a plan (such as AAA Plus) that extends towing benefits to 100 mi in any direction. *The Milepost,* available in bookstores or from Morris Communications, is a mile-by-mile guide to sights and services along Alaska's highways. It's indispensable.

The Alaska Department of Transportation is a great resource for road reports, animal alerts, and other advisories.

Contacts **Alaska Department of Transportation**(☏511 in Alaska, 907/282–7577 outside Alaska ⊕511.alaska.gov).

American Automobile Association (AAA ☏315/797–5000 ⊕www.aaa.com).**The Milepost** (☏907/272–6070 or 800/726–4707 ⊕www.themilepost.com). **National Automobile Club** (☏650/294–7000 ⊕www.thenac.com); membership is open to California residents only.

GASOLINE

Gas prices in the Anchorage area are comparable with those in the Lower 48, but expect to pay more elsewhere, for example Juneau or Ketchikan, and far more in remote areas, particularly small villages off the road network, where fuel must be flown in. Fuel prices in Canada along the Alaska Highway are also very high. Most stations are self-serve and take Visa and MasterCard; many also accept other credit cards and debit cards.

Many stations remain open until 10 PM, and in the larger towns and cities some stay open 24 hours a day. Most are also open on weekends, particularly along the main highways. In the smallest villages gas may be available only on weekdays, but these settlements typically have only a few miles of roads.

ROAD CONDITIONS

Driving in Alaska is much less rigorous than it used to be, although it still presents some unusual obstacles. Road construction sometimes creates long delays on the Canadian side of the border, so come armed with patience and a flexible schedule. Also, frost damage creates dips in the road that require slower driving.

Moose often wander onto roads and highways. If you encounter one, pull off to the side and wait for the moose to cross. Be especially vigilant when driving at dusk or at night, and keep your eyes open for other moose in the area, since a mother will often cross followed by one or two calves.

Flying gravel is a hazard along the Alaska and Dalton highways, especially in summer. A bug screen will help keep gravel and kamikaze insects off the windshield, but few travelers use them. Some travelers use clear, hard plastic guards to cover their headlights. (These are inexpensive and are available from garage or service stations along the major access routes.) Don't cover headlights with cardboard or plywood, because you'll need your lights often, even in daytime, as dust is thrown up by traffic in both directions.

Unless you plan to undertake remote highways (especially the Dalton Highway to Prudhoe Bay), you won't need any special equipment. But be sure that the equipment you do have is in working condition, from tires and spare to brakes and engine. Carrying spare fuses, spark plugs, jumper cables, a flashlight with extra batteries, a tool kit, and an extra fan belt is recommended.

If you get stuck on any kind of road, be careful about pulling off; the shoulder can be soft. In summer it stays light late, and though traffic is also light, one of Alaska's many good Samaritans is likely to stop to help and send for aid (which may be many miles away). In winter, pack emergency equipment—a shovel, tire chains, high-energy food, and extra clothing and blankets. Never head out onto unplowed roads unless you're prepared to walk back.

Cell phones are an excellent idea for travel in Alaska, particularly on the main roads. There's no ban on using cell phones in cars in Alaska, and you aren't required to use a hands-free set while driving. Check with your provider about service, though, as gaps in service, even on the road system, are the rule rather than the exception.

RULES OF THE ROAD
Alaska honors valid driver's licenses from any state or country. The speed limit on most highways is 55 mph, but much of the Parks Highway (between Wasilla and Fairbanks) and the Seward Highway (between Anchorage and Seward) is 65 mph. State troopers rigorously enforce these limits.

Unless otherwise posted, you may make a right turn on a red light after coming to a complete stop. Seat belts are required on all passengers, and children under age five must be in child safety seats.

State law requires that slow-moving vehicles pull off the road at the first opportunity if leading more than five cars. This is particularly true on the highway between Anchorage and Seward, where RV drivers have a bad reputation for not pulling over. Alaskans don't take kindly to being held up en route to their favorite Kenai River fishing spot.

RVS
The secret to a successful RV trip to Alaska is preparation. Expect to drive on more gravel and rougher roads than you're accustomed to. Batten down everything; tighten every nut and bolt in and out of sight, and don't leave anything to bounce around inside. Travel light, and your tires and suspension system will take less of a beating. Protect your headlights and the grille area in front of the radiator. Make sure you carry adequate insurance to cover the replacement of your windshield.

Most of Alaska's public campgrounds accommodate trailers, but hookups are available only in private RV parks. Water can be found at most stopping points, but it may be limited for trailer use. Think twice before deciding to drive an RV or pull a trailer during the spring thaw. The rough roadbed can be a trial.

RV Rentals & Tours ABC Motorhome Rentals (☎907/279-2000 or 800/421-7456 ⊕www.abcmotorhome.com). **Alaska Motorhome Rentals** (☎907/258-7109 or 800/254-9929 ⊕www.alaskarv.com). **Clippership Motorhome Rentals** (☎907/562-7051 or 800/421-3456 ⊕www.clippershiprv.com). **Fantasy RV Tours** (☎970/642-4562 or 800/952-8496 ⊕www.fantasyrvtours.com). **GoNorth RV Camper Rental** (☎907/479-7272 or 866/236-7272 ⊕www.paratours.net). **Great Alaskan Holidays** (☎907/248-7777 or 888/225-2752 ⊕www.greatalaskanholidays.com).

RENTAL CARS

Rental cars are available in most Alaska towns. In Anchorage and other major destinations, expect to pay at least $55–$75 a day or $300 (and up) a week for an economy or compact car with automatic transmission and unlimited mileage. Some locally owned companies offer lower rates for older cars. Also, be sure to ask in advance about discounts if you have an AAA or Costco card, or are over age 50.

Rates can be substantially higher for larger vehicles, four-wheel drives, SUVs, and vans. (Although the extra space for gear and luggage might be nice, note that you don't need four-wheel drive or an SUV to navigate Alaska highways.) Rates are also higher in small towns, particularly those off the road system in Southeast Alaska or the bush. In addition, vehicles in these remote towns are typically several years old, and some would rate as "beaters."

You must be 21 to rent a car, and rates may be higher if you're under 25. When picking up a car, non-U.S. residents will need a reservation voucher, a passport, a driver's license (written in English), and a travel policy that covers each driver. Reserve well ahead for the summer season, particularly for the popular minivans, SUVs, and motor homes. A 10% state tax is tacked on to all car rentals, and there are also local taxes.

Be advised that most rental outfits don't allow you to drive on some of the unpaved roads such as the Denali Highway, the Haul Road to Prudhoe Bay, and the McCarthy Road. If your plans include any sketchy routes, make sure your rental agreement covers those areas.

Local Agencies **Arctic Rent-A-Car** (☎800/478–8696, 907/561–2990 in Anchorage, 907/479–8044 in Fairbanks ⊕www.arcticrentacar.com). **Denali Car Rental** (☎907/276–1230, 800/757–1230 in Anchorage ⊕ www.denalicarrentalak.com). **U-Save Auto Rental** (☎907/272–8728, 800/254–8728 in Anchorage, 907/479–7060, 877/979–7060 in Fairbanks ⊕www.usave.com).

Major Agencies **Alamo** (☎800/462–5266 ⊕www.alamo.com). **Avis** (☎800/230–4898 ⊕www.avis.com). **Budget** (☎800/527–0700 ⊕www.budget.com). **Hertz** (☎800/654–3131 ⊕www.hertz.com). **National Car Rental** (☎800/227–7368 ⊕www.nationalcar.com).

CAR-RENTAL INSURANCE

If you own a car and carry comprehensive car insurance for both collision and liability, your personal auto insurance will probably cover a rental, but read your policy's fine print to be sure. If you don't have auto insurance, then you should probably buy the collision- or loss-damage waiver (CDW or LDW) from the rental company. This eliminates your liability for damage to the car.

Some credit cards offer CDW coverage, but it's usually supplemental to your own insurance and rarely covers SUVs, minivans, luxury models, and the like. If your coverage is secondary, you may still be liable for loss-of-use costs from the car-rental company (again, read the fine print). But no credit-card insurance is valid unless you use that card for *all* transactions, from reserving to paying the final bill.

You may also be offered supplemental liability coverage; the car-rental company is required to carry a minimal level of liability coverage insuring all renters, but it's rarely enough to cover claims in a really serious accident if you're at fault.

U.S. rental companies sell CDWs and LDWs for about $15 to $25 a day; supplemental liability is usually more than $10 a day. The car-rental company may offer you all sorts of other policies, but they're rarely worth the cost. Personal accident insurance, which is basic hospitalization coverage, is an especially egregious rip-off if you already have health insurance.

▮ BY CRUISE SHIP

Flip to Chapter 3: Cruising in Alaska for information about cruises and our favorite voyages.

▮ BY TRAIN

The state-owned Alaska Railroad has service connecting Seward, Anchorage, Denali National Park, and Fairbanks, as well as additional service connecting Anchorage and Whittier. The Alaska Railroad also offers a variety of package tours that range from 1-day Denali excursions to 10-day tours, which include many excursions along the way between Anchorage and Fairbanks.

Traveling by train isn't as economical as traveling by bus, but it is a wonderful way to go; the scenery along the way is spectacular. Some cars have narration, and food is available on board in the dining car and at the café. Certain private tour companies that offer glitzy trips between Anchorage and Fairbanks hook their luxury railcars to the train.

ROUTES

Travel aboard the Alaska Railroad is leisurely: Anchorage to Seward ($69 one way) takes 4 hours, Anchorage to Denali ($108–$135) takes a little over 7 hours, and Anchorage to Fairbanks ($265–$304) takes about 12 hours. The trip to Whittier takes a little over 2 hours and costs $60 one way (but only $74 round-trip).

For a less-expensive alternative, ride one of the public dome cars, owned and operated by the railroad. Seating in the public cars is unassigned, and passengers take turns under the observation dome. The railroad's public cars are a great place to meet residents.

Except for the Seward–Anchorage leg, all service operates year-round. Trains run daily in summer; service is reduced from September to late May. Dining cars are available on all trains.

Gray Line of Alaska offers three-day packages that include luxury train travel from Anchorage to Fairbanks or vice versa. You can opt for one-way or round-trip travel. All packages include at least a day of exploring in Denali National Park.

For a scenic and historic five-hour trip between Skagway and Fraser, British Columbia, take the White Pass & Yukon Route, which follows the treacherous path taken by prospectors during the Klondike gold rush of 1897–98. (As this trip is popular with cruise-passenger excursions, advance reservations are strongly recommended.)

RESERVATIONS

Reservations are highly recommended for midsummer train travel. You can buy tickets over the phone using a credit card. If your reservation is a month or more ahead of time, the company will mail you the tickets; otherwise you can pick them up at the departure station.

Trains usually leave on time, so be sure to arrive at the station at least 15 minutes prior to departure to ensure that you make it aboard.

The AlaskaPass allows unlimited travel on ferry and rail lines in Alaska; *see By Boat, above.*

Information Alaska Railroad (☎907/265–2494 in Anchorage, 907/458–6025 in Fairbanks, 800/544–0552 ⊕www.alaskarailroad.com). **Gray Line Alaska** (☎907/277–5581 in Anchorage, 907/451–6835 in Fairbanks, 888/452–1737 ⊕www.graylinealaska.com). **White Pass & Yukon Route** (☎907/983–2217 or 800/343–7373 ⊕www.whitepassrailroad.com).

ESSENTIALS

■ ACCOMMODATIONS

Off-season hotel rates are often much lower, but most travelers prefer to visit Alaska in summer, when days are long and temperatures are mild. Shoulder-season (May and September) travelers may find slightly lower rates, but some businesses and attractions may be closed. Camping is always an option, and, if you're willing to sleep in bunks, you can check out the state's many hostels, some of which have family rooms.

■TIP➔ Assume that hotels operate on the European Plan (**EP**, no meals) unless we specify that they use the Breakfast Plan (**BP**, with full breakfast), Continental Plan (**CP**, continental breakfast), Full American Plan (**FAP**, all meals), or Modified American Plan (**MAP**, breakfast and dinner), or are **all-inclusive (AI**, all meals and most activities).

BED-AND-BREAKFASTS

Nearly every Alaskan town (with the exception of most bush villages) has at least one B&B, and dozens of choices are available in the larger cities. At last count, Anchorage had more than 175 B&Bs, including modest suburban apartments, elaborate showcase homes with dramatic vistas, and everything in between.

Reservation Services **Alaska Private Lodgings/Stay with a Friend** (☎907/235–2148 ⊕www.alaskabandb.com). **Alaska's Mat-Su Bed & Breakfast Association** (⊕www.alaskabnbhosts.com). **Anchorage Alaska Bed & Breakfast Association** (☎907/272–5909 or 888/584–5147 ⊕www.anchorage-bnb.com). **Bed & Breakfast Association of Alaska** (⊕www.alaskabba.com). **Bed & Breakfast Association of Alaska, INNside Passage Chapter** (⊕www.accommodations-alaska.com). **Fairbanks Association of Bed & Breakfasts** (⊕www.ptialaska.net/~fabb). **Kenai Peninsula Bed & Breakfast Association** (☎907/776–8883 or 866/436–2266 ⊕www.kenaipeninsulabba.com).

HOSTELS

Hostels offer bare-bones lodging at low, low prices—often in shared dorm rooms with shared baths—to people of all ages, though the primary market is young travelers, especially students. Most hostels serve breakfast; dinner and/or shared cooking facilities may also be available. In some hostels you aren't allowed to be in your room during the day, and there may be a curfew at night. Nevertheless, hostels provide a sense of community, with public rooms where travelers often gather to share stories. Many hostels are affiliated with Hostelling International (HI), an umbrella group of hostel associations with some 4,500 member properties in more than 70 countries. Other hostels are completely independent and may be nothing more than a really cheap hotel.

Membership in any HI association, open to travelers of all ages, allows you to stay in HI-affiliated hostels at member rates. One-year membership is about $28 for adults; hostels charge about $10–$30 per night. Members have priority if the hostel is full; they're also eligible for discounts around the world, even on rail and bus travel in some countries.

There are HI hostels in Ketchikan and Sitka. Many other Alaskan hostels are not affiliated with HI, including ones in Anchorage, Denali, Fairbanks, Girdwood, Haines, Homer, Juneau, McCarthy, Petersburg, Seward, Skagway, Slana, Sterling, Talkeetna, Tok, and Wrangell. Most of these are only open seasonally, but hostels in Anchorage, Fairbanks, Girdwood, Homer, Juneau, Skagway, and Talkeetna provide year-round lodging. Hostels.com has contact information for all Alaskan hostels.

Information Hostels.com (⊕www.hostels.com). **Hostelling International—USA** (☏301/495–1240 ⊕www.hiusa.org).

HOTELS

Alaskan motels and hotels are similar in quality to those in the Lower 48 states. Most motels are independent, but you'll find the familiar chains (Best Western, Comfort Inn, Days Inn, Hampton Inn, Hilton, Holiday Inn, Marriott, Motel 6, Super 8, and Sheraton among others) in Anchorage.

Westmark Hotels is a regional chain, owned by cruise-tour operator Holland America Westours, with hotels in Anchorage, Fairbanks, Juneau, Sitka, Skagway, Tok, and Valdez in Alaska, plus Beaver Creek, Dawson City, and Whitehorse in Canada's Yukon Territory.

Princess Tours owns a luxury hotel in Fairbanks and lodges outside Denali National Park, near Denali State Park, near Wrangell–St. Elias National Park, and on the Kenai Peninsula. All hotels listed have private bath unless otherwise noted.

WILDERNESS LODGES

To get away from it all, book a lodge with rustic accommodations in the middle of breathtaking Alaskan wilderness. Some of the most popular are in the river drainages of Bristol Bay, throughout the rugged islands of Southeast Alaska, and along the Susitna River north of Anchorage.

Some lodge stays include daily guided fishing trips as well as all meals. They can be astronomically expensive (daily rates of $250–$1,000 per person and up, plus airfare), so if you're not interested in fishing, avoid these.

Lodges in and near Denali National Park emphasize the great outdoors, and some even include wintertime dogsledding. Activities focus on hiking, rafting, flightseeing, horseback riding, and natural-history walks. For getting deep into the wilderness, these lodges are an excellent alternative to the hotels and cabins outside the park entrance. *For some of our favorite lodges, see Chapter 2.*

▌ EATING OUT

Alaska is best known for its seafood, particularly king salmon, halibut, king crab, and shrimp, and you'll find fine seafood on the menu in virtually any coastal Alaskan town. At the open-air, often all-you-can-eat salmon bakes in Juneau, Tok, Denali National Park & Preserve, and Fairbanks expect excellent grilled salmon and halibut.

Anchorage has the greatest diversity of restaurants, including classy steak houses, noisy brewpubs, authentic Thai and Mexican eateries, and a wide variety of other ethnic places.

PAYING

Credit cards are widely accepted in resort restaurants and in many restaurants in major towns like Anchorage. Many small towns only have one or two eateries; some establishments may not take credit cards. *For guidelines on tipping see Tipping below.*

RESERVATIONS & DRESS

During summer high season, make reservations as soon as and wherever possible, especially in the Southeast. We only mention specifically when reservations are essential or when they are not accepted. For popular restaurants, book as far ahead as you can (often 30 days), and reconfirm as soon as you arrive.

Alaska is a casual place. Cruise ships are probably the only places you'll encounter formal wear, though some of the pricier lodges may have dress codes for dinner. We mention dress only when men are required to wear a jacket or a jacket and tie.

WINES, BEER & SPIRITS

Alcohol is sold at liquor stores in most towns and cities along the road system, as well as in settlements along the Inside Passage. Alcoholism is a devastating problem in native villages, and because of this many of these bush communities are "dry" (no alcohol allowed) or "damp" (limited amounts allowed for personal use, but alcohol cannot be sold). Check the rules before flying into a bush community with alcohol, or you might find yourself charged with illegally importing it.

Alaska's many excellent microbrews include Glacier BrewHouse, Silver Gulch, Sleeping Lady, Kodiak Brewery, and Moose's Tooth. The state's best-known beer, Alaskan Amber, is made by Alaskan Brewing Company in Juneau.

Anchorage is home to several popular brewpubs, and their beers are sold in local liquor stores. Homer Brewing Company in the town of Homer sells its beers in local bars or in take-away bottles. You'll also find brewpubs in Fairbanks, Haines, Skagway, and Wasilla.

∎ HOLIDAYS

In addition to the standard nationwide holidays, Alaska also celebrates two statewide holidays: Alaska Day (October 18), celebrating the transfer of the state's ownership from Russia to the United States; and Seward's Day (last Monday in March), which marks the signing of the treaty that authorized the transfer. Although these are not major holidays, some businesses may be closed, particularly in Sitka.

∎ MONEY

Because of its off-the-beaten-path location, Alaska has always been an expensive travel destination. Major roads link Anchorage with Fairbanks and other cities and towns in South Central and Interior Alaska, but most other parts of the state are accessible only by air or water. This is even true of Alaska's state capital, Juneau. Costs in Anchorage and Fairbanks are only slightly higher than for Lower 48 cities, and you will find discount chain stores, but as you head to more remote parts of the state, prices escalate. In bush communities food, lodging, and transportation costs can be far higher than in Anchorage, since nearly everything must be brought in by air.

∎TIP→ Throughout this guide, the following abbreviations are used: AE, American Express; D, Discover; DC, Diners Club; MC, MasterCard; and V, Visa.

∎ PACKING

Befitting the frontier image, dress is mostly casual day and night. Unless you're on a cruise, pack just one outfit that's appropriate for "dress-up," though even this one set of nice togs probably won't be necessary.

FOR INTERNATIONAL TRAVELERS

CURRENCY
The dollar is the basic unit of U.S. currency. It has 100 cents. Coins are the penny (1¢), nickel (5¢), dime (10¢), quarter (25¢), half-dollar (50¢), and the very rare golden $1 coin and even rarer silver $1. Bills are denominated $1, $5, $10, $20, $50, and $100, all mostly green and identical in size; designs and background tints vary. You may come across a $2 bill, but the chances are slim.

CUSTOMS INFORMATION
Contact **US Customs and Border Protection** (⊕ *www.cbp.gov*).

ELECTRICITY
The U.S. standard is AC, 110 volts/60 cycles. Plugs have two flat pins set parallel to each other.

EMBASSIES
Contacts **Australia** (☎ *202/797–3000* ⊕ *www.usa.embassy.gov.au*). **Canada** (☎ *202/682–1740* ⊕ *www.canadianembassy. org*). **United Kingdom** (☎ *202/588–6500* ⊕ *www.britainusa.com*).

EMERGENCIES
For police, fire, or ambulance, dial 911 (0 in rural areas).

MAIL
You can buy stamps and aerograms and send letters and parcels in post offices. Stamp-dispensing machines can occasionally be found in airports, bus and train stations, office buildings, drugstores, and convenience stores. U.S. mailboxes are stout, dark-blue steel bins; pickup schedules are posted inside the bin (pull down the handle to see them). Parcels weighing more than a pound must be mailed at a post office or at a private mailing center.

Within the United States a first-class letter weighing 1 ounce or less costs 42¢; each additional ounce costs 17¢. Postcards cost 27¢. An airmail postcard or 1-ounce letter to most countries costs 94¢.

To receive mail on the road, have it sent c/o General Delivery at your destination's main post office (use the correct five-digit zip code). You must pick up mail in person within 30 days, with a driver's license or passport for identification.

Contacts **DHL** (☎ *800/225–5345* ⊕ *www.dhl. com*). **Federal Express** (☎ *800/463–3339* ⊕ *www.fedex.com*). **Mail Boxes, Etc./The UPS Store** (☎ *800/789–4623* ⊕ *www. mbe.com*). **United States Postal Service** (⊕ *www.usps.com*).

PASSPORTS & VISAS
All foreigners need a passport to enter the United States. Visitor visas aren't necessary for citizens of Australia, Canada, the United Kingdom, or most citizens of European Union countries coming for tourism and staying for fewer than 90 days. If you require a visa, the application fee is $131 (citizens of some countries may also be required to pay visa issuance fees, which vary based on the type of visa and the country), and waiting time can be substantial. Apply for a visa at the U.S. consulate in your place of residence; check the U.S. State Department's special Visa Web site for further information.

Passport & Visa Information **Destination USA** (⊕ *www.unitedstatesvisas.gov*). **U.S. Department of State** (⊕ *http://travel.state.gov*).

PHONES
Numbers consist of a three-digit area code and a seven-digit local number. (Believe it or not, one area code, 907, covers the entirety of Alaska.) Within many local calling areas you dial only the 7 digits; in others you dial "1" first and then all 10 digits—just as you would for calls between area-code regions. The same is true for calls to numbers prefixed by "800," "888," "866," and "877"—all toll free. For calls to numbers prefixed by "900" you must pay—usually dearly.

For international calls, dial "011" followed by the country code and the local number.

FOR WINTER

Not all of Alaska has the fierce winters usually associated with the state. Winter in the Southeast and South Central coastal regions is relatively mild—Chicago and Minneapolis experience harsher weather than Juneau. But it's a different story in the Interior, where temperatures in the subzero range and biting winds keep most visitors indoors.

The best way to keep warm is to wear layers of clothing, starting with thermal underwear and socks. The outermost layer should be lightweight, windproof, rainproof, and hooded. Down jackets (and sleeping bags) and cotton clothing have the disadvantage of becoming soggy when wet; the newer synthetics (particularly wind-blocking fabrics) are the materials of choice. Footgear needs to be sturdy, and if you're going into the backcountry, be sure it's waterproof. Rubber boots are often a necessity in coastal areas, where rain is a year-round reality. When wearing snow boots, be certain they are not too tight. Restricting your circulation will only make you colder.

FOR SUMMER

Summer travelers should pack plenty of layers, too. Although Alaskan summers are mild, temperatures can vary greatly through the course of a day.

The summer months are infamous for the sometimes dense clouds of mosquitoes and other biting insects. These pests are generally the worst in Interior Alaska but can be an annoyance throughout the state. Bring mosquito repellent with DEET! Also occasionally used (but less effective) is the Avon product Skin So Soft. Mosquito coils may be of some help if you are camping or staying in remote cabins. Head nets are sold in local sporting-goods stores and are a wise purchase if you plan to spend extended time outdoors, particularly in the Interior or on Kodiak Island.

OTHER CONSIDERATIONS

Wherever you go in Alaska (and especially in the Southeast), be prepared for rain. To keep yourself dry, pack a collapsible umbrella or bring a rain slicker, as sudden storms are common.

Always bring good UVA/UVB sunscreen with you on outings, even if the temperature is cool. Sunglasses are also essential, especially for visits to glaciers. A pair of binoculars will help you track any wildlife you encounter.

▌ PASSPORTS

U.S. citizens of all ages traveling between the United States and other countries by air need to present a valid U.S. passport.

If you're traveling by land or sea prior to June 1, 2009, you need a passport; a passport card; or a government-issued photo ID, such as a driver's license, along with proof of citizenship, such as a birth certificate, upon returning to the States. Also accepted are Western Hemisphere Travel Initiative–compliant documents, including trusted traveler cards and U.S. Military IDs with military travel orders.

After June 1, 2009, all American citizens will need either a passport (for all modes of travel and for anywhere in the world) or a passport card (for land or sea travel only between the United States and Canada, Mexico, Bermuda, and the Caribbean).

Note that parents traveling with small children should bring photocopies of their children's birth certificates to avoid any problems.

U.S. Passport Information U.S. Department of State (☎877/487–2778 ⊕http://travel.state.gov/passport).

PHONING HOME

For help, dial "0" and ask for an overseas operator. Most phone books list country codes and U.S. area codes. The country code for Australia is 61, for New Zealand 64, for the United Kingdom 44. Calling Canada is the same as calling within the United States, whose country code, by the way, is 1.

For operator assistance, dial "0." For directory assistance, call 555-1212 or occasionally 411 (free at many public phones). You can reverse long-distance charges by calling "collect"; dial "0" instead of "1" before the 10-digit number.

Instructions are generally posted on pay phones. Usually you insert coins in a slot (usually 25¢–50¢ for local calls) and wait for a steady tone before dialing. On long-distance calls the operator tells you how much to insert; prepaid phone cards, widely available in various denominations, can be used from any phone. Follow the directions to activate the card (there's usually an access number, then an activation code), then dial your number.

CELL PHONES

The United States has several GSM (Global System for Mobile Communications) networks, so multiband mobiles from most countries (except for Japan) work here. Unfortunately, it's almost impossible to buy a pay-as-you-go mobile SIM card in the United States—which allows you to avoid roaming charges—without also buying a phone. That said, cell phones with pay-as-you-go plans are available for well under $100. The cheapest ones with decent national coverage are the GoPhone from Cingular and Virgin Mobile, which only offers pay-as-you-go service.

Contacts **Cingular** (☎ *888/333-6651* ⊕ *www.cingular.com*). **Virgin Mobile** (☎ *No phone* ⊕ *www.virginmobileusa.com*).

▌ SAFETY

Alaska does have a high crime rate, but that doesn't mean it's unsafe for tourists.

Women are generally safe in Alaska, but sexual assaults do occur at an alarming rate, so a little extra caution is in order when traveling alone. Common sense is enough of a safeguard in most cases: don't hike in secluded areas alone, be sure to keep your hotel room door locked, don't accept drinks from strangers, and take cabs if you're returning to your hotel late at night. Some of the out-in-the-middle-of-nowhere work towns can resemble frontier towns a little *too* much, and women may experience unwanted attention (catcalls and the like).

In addition to following the bear-safety rules listed below, women who are camping during their menstrual cycle should take extra care in how they dispose of feminine hygiene products—seal them tightly in plastic bags and store them in bear-proof containers.

OUTDOOR SAFETY

Alaska is big, wild, and not particularly forgiving, so travelers lacking outdoor experience need to take precautions when venturing away from the beaten path. If you lack backcountry skills or feel uncomfortable handling yourself if a bear should approach, hire a guide, go on guided group tours, or join a class at the National Outdoor Leadership School, which is based in Palmer (one hour north of Anchorage).

Education National Outdoor Leadership School (☎ 907/745-4047 or 800/710-6657 ⊕ www.nols.edu).

BEARS

The sight of one of these magnificent creatures in the wild can be a highlight of your visit. By respecting bears and exercising care in bear country, neither you nor the bear will suffer from the experience. Remember that bears don't like surprises. Make your presence known by talking, singing, clapping, rattling a can full of gravel, or tying a bell to your pack, especially when terrain or vegetation obscures views. Travel with a group, which is noisier and easier for bears to detect. If possible, walk with the wind at your back so your scent will warn bears of your presence. And avoid bushy, low-visibility areas whenever possible.

Give bears the right-of-way—lots of it—especially sows with cubs. Don't camp on animal trails; they're likely to be used by bears. If you come across a carcass of an animal or detect its odor, avoid the area entirely; it's likely a bear's food cache. Store all food and garbage away from your campsite in airtight or specially designed bear-proof containers. The Park Service supplies these for hikers in Denali and Glacier Bay national parks and requires that backcountry travelers use them. If a bear approaches you while you are fishing, stop. If you have a fish on your line, cut your line.

If you do encounter a bear at close range, don't panic, and, above all, don't run. You can't outrun a bear, and by fleeing you could trigger a chase response from the bear. Talk in a normal voice to help identify yourself as a human. If traveling with others, stand close together to "increase your size." If the bear charges, it could be a bluff; as terrifying as this may sound, the experts advise standing your ground. If a brown bear actually touches you, then drop to the ground and play dead, flat on your stomach with your legs spread and your hands clasped behind your head. If you don't move, a brown bear will typically break off its attack once it feels the threat is gone. If you are attacked by a black bear, you are better off fighting back with rocks, sticks, or anything else you find, since black bears are more likely to attack a person as prey. Polar bears can be found in remote parts of the Arctic, but tourists are highly unlikely to encounter them in summer.

For more information on bears, ask for the brochure "Bear Facts: The Essentials for Traveling in Bear Country" from any of the Alaska Public Lands offices. Bear-safety information is also available on the Internet at ⊕ *www.state.ak.us/adfg*.

▮ TAXES

Alaska does not impose a state sales tax, but individual cities and boroughs have their own taxes. (Anchorage has no sales tax.)

In addition to local taxes, a hotel tax is often applied to your hotel bill. Rates are variable, generally ranging from 2% to 6%.

You won't have to pay any departure taxes if you're flying within the United States. Vancouver's airport has a departure tax of C$5 for flights within British Columbia and the Yukon or C$10 to U.S. destinations, payable at automatic ticket machines or staffed booths before you board your flight.

▮ TIME

Nearly all of Alaska lies within the Alaska time zone, 20 hours behind Sydney, 9 hours behind London, 4 hours behind New York City, 3 hours behind Chicago, and 1 hour behind Los Angeles and western Canada. The nearly unpopulated Aleutian Islands are in the same time zone as Hawaii, 5 hours behind the East Coast.

▮ TIPPING

In addition to tipping waiters and waitresses, taxi drivers, and baggage handlers, tipping others who provide personalized services is common in Alaska. Tour-bus drivers who offer a particularly informative trip generally receive a tip from passengers at the end of the tour. Fishing guides are commonly tipped around 10% by their clients, particularly if the guide helped them land a big one. In addition, gratuities may also be given to pilots following a particularly good flightseeing or bear-viewing trip; use your discretion.

TIPPING GUIDELINES FOR ALASKA	
Bartender	$1–$5 per round of drinks, depending on the number of drinks
Bellhop	$1–$5 per bag, depending on the level of the hotel
Coat Check	$1–$2 per item checked unless there is a fee, then nothing
Hotel Concierge	$5 or more, if he or she performs a service for you
Hotel Doorman	$1–$2 if he helps you get a cab
Hotel Maid	$1–$3 a day (either daily or at the end of your stay, in cash)
Hotel Room-Service Waiter	$1–$2 per delivery, even if a service charge has been added
Porter at Airport or Train Station	$1 per bag
Restroom Attendants	Small change or $1 in more-expensive restaurants
Skycap at Airport	$1–$3 per bag checked
Taxi Driver	15%–20%, but round up the fare to the next dollar amount
Tour Guide	10% of the cost of the tour
Valet Parking Attendant	$1–$2, but only when you get your car
Waiter	15%–20%, with 20% being the norm at high-end restaurants; nothing additional if a service charge is added to the bill

▌ TOURS

For certain types of travelers, package tours in Alaska can eliminate some of the guesswork and logistics-induced headaches that often accompany a self-planned tour. For others, the grandeur of the 49th state begs to be explored without such a fixed itinerary. The choice, dear Alaska traveler, is yours.

Several cruise lines—including Holland America and Princess Cruises and Tours—offer "cruisetours" that combine the comforts of cruise-ship travel with inland forays to luxury lodges. A host of smaller tour companies offer package tours as well. Standouts include **Alaska Tours**, which offers tours in almost every corner of the state; and **Alaska Railroad Scenic Rail Tours**, which operates a variety of train-based tours between the state's iconic destinations, including Seward, Denali, and Kenai Fjords. In addition, chances are good that there's a tour operation with itineraries to match your needs and interests—whatever those may be.

For information on outdoor-activities tours, see Chapter 2, Sports & Wilderness Adventures.

Organization United States Tour Operators Association (*USTOA* ☎212/599–6599 ⊕*www.ustoa.com*).

Recommended Companies Alaska Airlines Vacations (☎800/468–2248 ⊕www.alaskaair.com). **Alaska Bound** (☎231/439–3000 or 888/252–7527 ⊕www.alaskabound.com). **Alaska Railroad Scenic Rail Tours** (☎907/265–2494 or 800/544–0552 ⊕www.alaskarailroad.com). **Alaska Tour & Travel** (☎907/245–0200 or 800/208–0200 ⊕www.alaskatravel.com). **Alaska Tours** (☎907/277–3000 or 866/317–3325 ⊕www.alaskatours.com). **Alaska Wildland Adventures** (☎907/783–2928 or 800/334–8730 ⊕www.alaskawildland.com). **Gray Line of Alaska** (☎206/281–3535 or 888/452–1737 ⊕www.graylinealaska.com). **Holland America Line** (☎206/281–3535 or 877/932–4259 ⊕www.hollandamerica.com). **Homer Travel & Tours** (☎907/235–7751 or 800/478–7751 ⊕www.alaskahomertravel.com). **Knightly Tours** (☎206/938–8567 or 800/426–2123 ⊕www.knightlytours.com). **Princess Cruises**

(☎661/753-0000 or 800/774-6237 ⊕ www. princess.com). See Alaska Tours (☎907/278-5704 ⊕ www.alaskatours.net). **Viking Travel** (☎907/772-3818 or 800/327-2571 ⊕ www. alaskaferry.com).

SPECIAL-INTEREST TOURS

ECO TOURS

Contact **Alaska Wildland Adventures** (☎907/783-2928 or 800/334-8730 ⊕ www. alaskawildland.com).

LEARNING VACATIONS

Contacts **Earthwatch Institute** (☎978/461-0081 or 800/776-0188 ⊕ www.earthwatch. org). **National Audubon Society** (☎212/979-3000 or 800/967-7425 ⊕ www.audubon.org). **Natural Habitat Adventures** (☎303/449-3711 or 800/543-8917 ⊕ www.nathab. com). **Nature Expeditions International** (☎954/693-8852 or 800/869-0639 ⊕ www. naturexp.com). **Naturequest** (☎949/499-9561 or 800/369-3033 ⊕ www.naturequest-tours.com). **Oceanic Society Expeditions** (☎415/441-1106 or 800/326-7491 ⊕ www. oceanic-society.org). **Sierra Club** (☎415/977-5522 ⊕ www.sierraclub.org). **Smithsonian Journeys** (☎202/357-4700 or 877/338-8687 ⊕ www.smithsonianjourneys.org).

NATIVE TOURS

Contacts **Alexander's River Adventure** (☎907/474-3924 ⊕ fairbanks-alaska.com/ alexander.htm). **Cape Fox Tours** (☎907/225-4846 ⊕ www.capefoxtours.com). **Goldbelt Tours** (☎907/586-8687 or 800/820-2628 ⊕ www.goldbelttours.com). **Northern Alaska Tour Company** (☎907/474-8600 or 800/474-1986 ⊕ www.northernalaska.com). **Sitka Tours** (☎907/747-7290 or 888/270-8687 ⊕ www.sitkatribe.org).

NATURAL HISTORY TOURS

Contacts **Camp Denali** (☎907/683-2290 ⊕ www.campdenali.com). **Great Alaska Adventure Lodge** (☎907/262-4515 or 800/544-2261 ⊕ www.greatalaska.com). **Hallo Bay Wilderness Camp** (☎907/235-2237 or 888/535-2237 ⊕ www.hallobay.com). **Walrus Islands Expeditions** (☎907/235-9349 ⊕ www.alaskawalrusisland.com).

PHOTOGRAPHY TOURS

Contacts **Alaska Photography Tours** (☎907/781-2208 or 888/440-2281 ⊕ www. alaskaphotographytours.com). **Joseph Van Os Photo Safaris** (☎206/463-5383 ⊕ www. photosafaris.com). **Naturally Wild Photo Adventures** (☎740/774-6243 ⊕ www.naturallywild.net).

■ TRIP INSURANCE

Comprehensive trip insurance is valuable if you're booking a very expensive or complicated trip (particularly to an isolated region) or if you're booking far in advance. Comprehensive policies typically cover trip-cancellation and interruption, letting you cancel or cut your trip short because of a personal emergency, illness, or, in some cases, acts of terrorism in your destination. Such policies also cover evacuation and medical care. Some also cover you for trip delays because of bad weather or mechanical problems as well as for lost or delayed baggage.

Another type of coverage to look for is financial default—that is, when your trip is disrupted because a tour operator, airline, or cruise line goes out of business. Generally you must buy this when you book your trip or shortly thereafter, and it's only available to you if your operator isn't on a list of excluded companies.

Always read the fine print of your policy to make sure that you are covered for the risks that are of most concern to you. Compare several policies to make sure you're getting the best price and range of coverage available.

Insurance Comparison Sites **Insure My Trip. com** (☎800/487-4722 ⊕ www.insuremytrip. com). **Square Mouth.com** (☎800/240-0369 or 727/490-5803 ⊕ www.squaremouth.com).

Comprehensive Travel Insurers **Access America** (☎866/729-6021 ⊕ www. accessamerica.com). **AIG Travel Guard** (☎800/826-4919 ⊕ www.travelguard.com). **CSA Travel Protection** (☎800/873-9855 www.csatravelprotection.com). **HTH World-wide** (☎610/254-8700 ⊕www.hthworldwide.com). **Travelex Insurance** (☎888/228-9792 ⊕www.travelex-insurance.com). **Travel Insured International** (☎800/243-3174 ⊕www.travelinsured.com).

MEDICAL INSURANCE & ASSISTANCE

Consider buying trip insurance with medical-only coverage. Neither Medicare nor some private insurers cover medical expenses anywhere outside the United States. Medical-only policies typically reimburse you for medical care (excluding that related to preexisting conditions) and hospitalization abroad, and provide for evacuation. You still have to pay the bills and await reimbursement from the insurer, though.

Another option is to sign up with a medical-evacuation assistance company. Membership gets you doctor referrals, emergency evacuation or repatriation, 24-hour hotlines for medical consultation, and other assistance. International SOS Assistance Emergency and AirMed International provide evacuation services and medical referrals. MedjetAssist offers medical evacuation.

Medical Assistance Companies **AirMed International** (⊕www.airmed.com). **International SOS** (⊕www.internationalsos.com) **MedjetAssist** (⊕www.medjetassist.com).

Medical-Only Insurers **International Medical Group** (☎800/628-4664 ⊕www.imglobal.com). **International SOS** (⊕www.internationalsos.com). **Wallach & Company** (☎800/237-6615 or 540/687-3166 ⊕www.wallach.com).

∎ VISITOR INFORMATION

The Alaska Travel Industry Association (a partnership between the state and private businesses) publishes the *Alaska Vacation Planner,* a free, comprehensive information source for statewide travel year-round. Alaska's regional tourism

councils distribute vacation planners highlighting their local attractions.

Get details on Alaska's vast public lands from Alaska Public Lands Information centers in Ketchikan, Tok, Anchorage, and Fairbanks.

Statewide Information **Alaska Department of Fish and Game** (☎907/465-4112, 907/465-4180 sportfishing seasons and regulations, 907/465-2376 license information ⊕www.state.ak.us/adfg). **Alaska Division of Parks** (☎907/269-8400 Anchorage, 907/451-2705 Fairbanks ⊕www.alaskastateparks.org). **Alaska Public Lands Information Center** (☎866/869-6887, 907/271-2737 in Anchorage, 907/456-0527 in Fairbanks, 907/228-6234 in Ketchikan, 907/883-5667 in Tok ⊕www.nps.gov/aplic). **Alaska Travel Industry Association** (☎907/929-2200, 800/862-5275 to order Alaska Vacation Planner ⊕www.travelalaska.com).

Regional Information **Kenai Convention & Visitors Bureau** (☎907/283-1991 ⊕www.visitkenai.com). **Kenai Peninsula Tourism Marketing Council** (☎907/262-5229 or 800/535-3624 ⊕www.kenaipeninsula.org). **Southeast Alaska Discovery Center** (☎907/228-6220 ⊕www.fs.fed.us/r10/tongass/districts/discoverycenter). **Southwest Alaska Municipal Conference** (☎907/562-7380 ⊕www.southwestalaska.com).

British Columbia & Yukon **Tourism British Columbia** (☎604/435-5622 or 800/435-5622 ⊕www.hellobc.com). **Tourism Yukon** (☎800/661-0494 ⊕www.touryukon.com).

ONLINE TRAVEL TOOLS

ALL ABOUT ALASKA

Alaska.com (⊕*www.alaska.com*) is a subsidiary of the *Anchorage Daily News* and has travel features, photo galleries, and a service that allows you to order a variety of brochures and e-newsletters. **Alaska Department of Fish and Game** (⊕*www.adfg.state.ak.us*) has tips on wildlife viewing, news on conservation issues, and information about fishing and hunting licenses and regulations. **Alaska Geographic** (⊕*www.alaskageographic.org*)

has links to sites with information on the state's public lands, national parks, forests, and wildlife refuges, as well as an online bookstore where you can find maps and books about the Alaskan experience. **Alaska Magazine** (⊕*www.alaska-magazine.com*) posts some of its feature stories online, and maintains an extensive statewide events calendar. **Alaska Native Heritage Center** (⊕*www.alaskanative.net*) has information on Alaska's native tribes, as well as links to other cultural and tourism Web sites.

WORD OF MOUTH

After your trip, be sure to rate the places you visited and share your experiences and travel tips with us and other Fodorites in Travel Ratings and Talk on www.fodors.com.

INDEX